OUR TOWN

OUR TOWN

A Heartland Lynching, a Haunted Town,
and the Hidden History of White America

CYNTHIA CARR

CROWN PUBLISHERS   NEW YORK

Grateful acknowledgment is made to the following for use of the
photographs printed herein:
On the frontispiece, "Without Sanctuary," plate 31, courtesy of the
Allen-Littlefield Collection.
On the half title and part title pages, courtesy of Hulton Archive.

Published in the United States by Crown Publishers, an imprint of the
Crown Publishing Group, a division of Random House, Inc., New York.
www.crownpublishing.com

Crown is a trademark and the Crown colophon is a registered trademark of
Random House, Inc.

Parts of chapters one and two first appeared in *The Village Voice* in
somewhat different form. Copyright © 1994 Village Voice Media, Inc.
Reprinted with permission of *The Village Voice*.

Library of Congress Cataloging-in-Publication Data
Carr, Cynthia.
Our town : a heartland lynching, a haunted town, and the hidden history
of white America / Cynthia Carr.—1st ed.
Includes bibliographical references and index.
1. Marion (Ind.)—Race relations.   2. African Americans—Indiana—Marion—
Social conditions—20th century.   3. Lynching—Indiana—Marion—History—
20th century.   4. Cameron, James, 1914- .   5. Racism—Indiana—Marion—
History—20th century.   6. Carr, Cynthia.   I. Title.
F534.M34L96   2005
305.896'073077269—dc22   2005011697

ISBN 13: 978-0-517-70506-3
ISBN 10: 0-517-70506-0

Printed in the United States of America

DESIGN BY BARBARA STURMAN

10 9 8 7 6 5 4 3 2 1

First Edition

For my nieces and nephews—
Ben, Marissa,
Isabelle, and Jeremy

. . . "We can only go" "down" "farther down—"
"Down" "is now the only way" "to rise" . . .

—ALICE NOTLEY, *The Descent of Alette*

CONTENTS

PART I

"A Veil Hangs Over This Town"

ONE

MY MARION

I was an adult before I ever saw the picture. But even as a girl, I knew there'd been a lynching in Marion, Indiana. That was my father's hometown. And on one of many trips to visit my grandparents, I heard the family story: the night it happened back in 1930, someone called the house and spoke to my grandfather, whose shift at the post office began at three in the morning. "Don't walk through the courthouse square tonight on your way to work," the caller said. "You might see something you don't want to see." Apparently that was the punchline—which puzzled me. *Something you don't want to see.* Then laughter.

I now know that, in the 1920s, Indiana had more Ku Klux Klan members than any other state in the union—from a quarter to a half million members—and my grandfather was one of them. Learning this after he died, I couldn't assimilate it into the frail Grandpa I'd known. Couldn't assimilate it at all and, for a long time, didn't try. He was an intensely secretive man, and certainly there had been other obfuscations. He always said, for example, that he was an orphan, that his parents had died when he was three. I accepted this, but the grown-ups knew better. After Grandpa's funeral, my father discovered a safe deposit box and hoped at last to find a clue to the family tree. Instead he unearthed this other secret: a Klan membership card. All my father said later was "I never saw a hooded sheet. He'd go out. We never knew where he was going."

Much of this story is about shame. My grandfather was illegitimate, a fact that someone born in small-town Indiana in 1886 would rather die than discuss. And so he did. But if that particular humiliation seems foreign today, what about the other secret? A lot of us who are white come from something we would rather not discuss. "That's in the past," we like to say, as if that did anything but give us another hood to wear.

I was in my late twenties when I first came upon the lynching photo in a book: two black men in bloody tattered clothing hang from a tree, and below them stand the grinning, gloating, proud, and pleased white folks. I couldn't believe that this was my Marion, the lynching referred to in my family, a tree I'd walked past as a child. I looked anxiously for my grandfather's face in that photo. Didn't find it. That was some relief. But he too had gone to the square that night. There'd been *something you don't want to see.* Then laughter. And as I began to tell people this story, that was one detail I left out, because it shamed me: there was laughter.

MY MARION. AS A CHILD, I loved the town. And one thing I loved most was the fact that it had a past, unlike the various midwestern suburbs where I grew up. Directly in front of my grandparents' house—tall, dark green clapboard with a black stone porch—stood an iron hitching post, a black horse's head with a ring through its nose. It was no decoration. They'd just never taken it down. They lived with history. And every visit gave me a chance to ask Grandma for the family stories, to page with her through the family album. Somehow I never noticed that all the stories and pictures were my grandmother's. My grandfather had none.

During one summer vacation when I was nine or ten, I found a brittle yellow newspaper clipping in a desk drawer at my grandparents' house. The headline said JOSIE CARR, and parts of certain lines had been cut out with a razor blade. I walked it into the living room asking, "Who's Josie Carr?" No one said anything, but Grandpa took the clipping from my hand and left the room. Someone explained then that Josie was his mother. I had just found her obituary. We'd been told that she had died about 1890 "from tuberculosis." Or perhaps she had died "from grief," said Aunt Ruth, my father's sister, who liked brooding on the mystery. For all those years my grandfather kept the obituary, certain facts trimmed out with a razor blade. Then that day he took it from my hand, and no one ever saw it again.

We didn't know who Grandpa's father was or why he abandoned Josie. Nor did we know when she died, what killed her, where she was buried—nothing. My grandmother knew everything, of course. But she said, "We don't talk about it. It makes your grandpa feel very bad." So we waited till my grandparents were out of earshot before discussing our slender clues.

Aunt Ruth would take the tintypes from the old beige Nabisco box. Many of those pictured were strangers to us. Uncle Rad? Aunt Pet? We couldn't ask Grandpa. We relied on Aunt Ruth to find the images of Grandpa's mother: "This is Josie before the tragedy. This is Josie after the tragedy." Aunt Ruth showed us in the later picture where clumps of Josie's hair had fallen out. "Maybe someone poisoned her," my aunt mused. "Maybe someone was trying to get rid of her."

Aunt Ruth held both possessions of Josie's that came down to us. One was a locket with a handsome young man's picture, a date—February 11, 1883—and the words "All twisted up. N" Or was it W? Or H? The other was a letter in different handwriting addressed to "Josie kind Josie" from a P.W.H., Bluffton, Indiana—October 28, 1885. A letter full of nonsense about a dog and "I have no time to write you." Why had this one letter been saved? She must have received it around the time she became pregnant. My grandpa was born in July 1886.

My aunt was both guardian of these artifacts and the one who most needed to know what they meant. She had a recurring dream about the family mystery—that she and Grandpa were in a mausoleum, watching someone pull out a casket. In real life, of course, Grandpa did his grieving alone. My father and my aunt recalled from childhood that on every Memorial Day he rode the interurban to Gas City, just south of Marion, taking three geraniums to the cemetery. We guessed that Josie must be buried there. He, of course, never said.

Aunt Ruth would tell us the story about applying for a job in a Marion furniture store, how Grandma had warned her, "They'll only want to talk to you about your family." And sure enough, the man interviewing her said, "Young lady, do you know who your grandfather is?"

Then Aunt Ruth would recount the words of her long-dead auntie Mame: "Could you ever forgive us for what we did?" But Aunt Ruth never knew who "us" referred to or why they needed her forgiveness. "I guess I was brought up not to ask questions," she said.

We had a drawing my grandfather did as a child—a palatial sort of Victorian mansion. At the bottom he had signed his initials: E.R. His name was Earl Carr. He'd taken his mother's last name. But clearly he'd known from boyhood who his father was, and he'd imagined taking that identity. Young Mister R.

Finally on his deathbed Grandpa told us, "They cheated me. I could have had ten thousand dollars." That was all he ever said about his secret: *They cheated me.*

This is Josie before the tragedy. This is Josie after the tragedy. My grandpa was the tragedy. In the first picture we have of him, he is paying for this sin in sad eyes three years old. He was raised by Josie's mother, his grandma Carr, who ran a boardinghouse in Marion at 18th and Adams. As a boy, my grandfather sat on the lap of the star boarder, Eugene Debs, the great American socialist who organized on behalf of railroad workers. Grandpa loved Debs enough to name my father after him. But he said very little about his childhood. I picked up hints that the grandmother who had raised him was less than kind.

He was always so quiet, so remote. It was part of the family lore: he had never smiled in one photograph in all of his life. He hated cars and never learned to drive. I don't think he liked what the world had turned into. He took long walks for recreation, one time all the way to Jonesboro and back. Twenty miles. He never let my grandmother have any money and did all the grocery shopping himself: tongue, mush, hominy, green tomatoes to fry, the fatty cuts of meat. He would get up at two A.M. to be at work by three. He worked at the Marion Post Office from 1908 to 1956. There he accumulated a record one thousand days of sick time and gave it back to the government. "To act tough," said Aunt Ruth.

For a hobby he studied railroad timetables and knew which trains rode on what tracks, every track in America. A little rack of timetables sat next to his favorite chair. I used to see him study, then refold them. He was always walking to the tracks to see a train. I often wondered why he hadn't worked for the railroad, why he hadn't simply hopped one of those trains and left Marion. I think he felt obligated to the family that hadn't abandoned him. And what I finally understood was that he would not take a risk.

Grandpa wore a necktie and long-sleeve dress shirt with cufflinks every day of his life, even in the hottest weather. He owned a single necktie and would wear it till it wore out before he bought another. Such peculiarities made him a figure of intense interest to me as a girl. The way the pleasures had been carefully measured out. Every year he took the family on the same vacation: one day in either Cleveland or Chicago to window-shop and ride the elevated. If we offered him an iced tea or juice, he would specify just how much. "Two fingers," he'd say. Maybe three. He was a teetotaler who did not allow liquor in the house. Every now and then he made us kids some little milk shakes, served in jelly jars.

He had one living relative, his cousin. We called her Great Aunt Catherine, and I remember how very old she was, how very old her dog, how steep the stair leading up to the ancient house. She had been to Josie's funeral when she was maybe three—so Aunt Ruth said—but Catherine recalled nothing except being at a church in the country.

Great Aunt Catherine had been like a sister to Grandpa. He dropped out of school after eighth grade to work for Catherine's father, his Uncle On. That's how I heard the name, though really his name was Alonzo or Lon. I liked having someone in the family named On. He was Josie's brother and ran a grocery store in downtown Marion. He's the one who said of Josie: "When all the other girls were riding sidesaddle, she rode astride and her hair blew in the wind." It's the only thing anyone remembers that anyone said of her.

Aunt Ruth didn't even know her grandmother's name till she went to see a fortune-teller during World War II, and the fortune-teller said, "I get a Jo or a Josie." So Aunt Ruth reported this to one of the relatives, who snorted, "Oh, she mentioned *that* one, did she?" *That one.* Still unmentionable as the world changed, as Grandpa became a grandpa, as he stooped ever lower with Parkinson's disease till he was bent nearly double. He shook uncontrollably, and his spine curved. All twisted up. *This is Josie before the tragedy. This is Josie after the tragedy.* Soon there would be no one who remembered the tragedy.

When Grandpa died, I was seventeen, old enough to see how not-knowing had hurt my father and my aunt. What if my grandfather had realized that, decades after his death, his silence would still reverberate in all of us? I'm not sure even that would have moved him. As he lay dying, I remembered how I'd found that obituary, thus ensuring the loss of our only real clue. I hoped that my grandpa would speak, but all he ever told us was, *They cheated me.* Lying there in the hospital, he was no different than he'd ever been. Born old in the other century, already a tiny shaking grandpa, he would die still fatherless.

So I had that life for proof, that you could die and still not fix it. And as I grew older, I saw that this, in fact, was the usual story: A life of things un-fixed. A whole history of things unfixed.

MY FATHER FELT FREE to look for the truth after my grandpa died. It was 1967. For a while he drove to Grant County every weekend, searching for Josie. He never found her. Cemeteries didn't always keep records in the old days, he'd tell us. Hardly anyone bothered with death certificates. No one knew when she died—or for that matter, when she'd been born. My father found no evidence that she'd ever existed. But it had been there in that clip-ping, the one cut with a razor blade. My father went to all the little newspa-pers to look at back issues, but there was no obituary for Josie Carr. In a Gas City graveyard, he found the brother and sister who'd preceded her in death, their names on two sides of the obelisk that marked the plot. We spec-ulated that Josie was there too but unmarked. My father checked all the cemeteries. He talked about getting caretakers to stick long steel rods in the ground. He explained that if they hit an air pocket, a body had been there once, in a pine box—both turned to nothing now. "Might have been her," my dad would say. I didn't ask him how he'd know the right air. He wasn't really looking for the dust she'd become. He wanted her story. And if he got just the very last page—the scene with the preacher's incantation and the coffin lifted slowly from the back of a wagon—that would have been some-thing. He could have said, *Here's where they stood once: my family, my great-greats, the people who knew all the things that were kept from me.*

It was Great Aunt Catherine who finally told us something. My father and my aunt had assumed that she wouldn't. They'd known her all their lives, after all, and she'd never said a word. But when Aunt Ruth finally blurted out "Who is our grandfather?" the old woman replied, "Don't you know that?"

So one day after returning from one of his trips to Marion, my father came up to my room and said he had to tell me who he really was. He pulled out a picture of a man named Odos Roush, and I saw my grandpa's nose, my father's ears. This Odos, my grandfather's father, had been the youngest son of a well-to-do farmer. Six hundred acres east of Gas City. What Odos had done with his life, we didn't know—except that he'd lived till the 1940s. He'd lived to be old, and for much of his life he was right there in Marion, just blocks from where my father spent his boyhood. "I might have passed him on the street," my father said, amazed. "I might have passed his house." He remembered one time when he was a boy, an old man had followed him up the alley. He was certain now: that was Odos. "Living three blocks away from us like that, he probably wondered how we were." Yet as far as anyone knew, Odos never even said hello to my grandpa, his son. And his was not the face in Josie's locket.

Aunt Ruth believed that he'd tried to make contact. "We were living in that house on Gallatin. I swear it was my second birthday, maybe third, and just inside those double doors stood a golden thing. I think maybe . . . a doll house. And Mama was saying to Daddy, 'We can't let her keep it, can we?'" Aunt Ruth believed the golden thing was a gift from Odos Roush. Now this became the story that haunted her. She said she'd stopped dreaming about the trip to the mausoleum.

Apparently Josie and Odos had been quite the talk of the town, a real scandal. Everyone knew the story except my father and my aunt, or so they believed. They'd been ridiculed as children and never knew why. Whatever had happened was over eighty years gone, and for some reason people still were not talking. But after Aunt Catherine's revelation, my dad and aunt went looking for the Roush family. They found a cousin. This man drove them around, showed them the old homestead, gave them pictures of Odos. But Aunt Ruth said later, "He knew more than he was saying." She was sure of it. She'd been acquainted with this man for years. She'd bought shoes from him at a store on the square, and he had certainly never mentioned that they were cousins, though he'd known. Now he had furniture made by Odos's father, but he wouldn't let my aunt or my father even see it, implying that they would want some and weren't about to get it. So they hadn't exactly come home.

Now my dad had a theory about why his grandparents hadn't married: the families prevented them. The Roushes had money and social standing. They would have wanted Odos to marry someone else. So it was tragic, a Romeo-Juliet situation. Sort of. And Josie was a fine young woman who died of grief. I asked my father how he knew these things. Well, he said, Odos didn't marry until he was sixty-five. Probably never got over it.

One weekend my father took us all back to Indiana to show us this history. I must have been eighteen. We drove into the country east of Marion to see the house where Grandpa was born. Great Aunt Catherine had given us directions. We parked at the end of a rutted road from which we could see a church with its graves. We walked through a field of knee-deep grass, me behind my father, my aunt, mother, sisters, and brother. There was the little house, now a shelter for horses. And here where horses stood browsing through the grass—here Josie had been, with my baby grandpa. Her eyes might have seen these same trees. But what could I learn about her just by walking where she'd walked, unmarried and pregnant in 1886? I had no context in which to understand "ruin."

We got back in the car and drove to Gas City, where Dad showed us the Roush graves: substantial even in death, all buried together, anchored by a central monument inscribed with the family name. That would have been *our* name. Someone had told my father that after Josie became pregnant, her brothers—Alonzo and Evrad—rode into Gas City with their guns to have it out with the Roushes. But Old Man Roush kept his boys at home.

Maybe something had created bad blood between the families, my father said. Maybe they'd been on opposite sides in the Civil War. Of course, he was wildly guessing. Really, we didn't know anything. We hadn't answered the most basic questions: Why hadn't Josie married? What killed her? When? And who was the man in the locket?

HAD MY GRANDMOTHER outlived him, she would have told us everything about Grandpa. So we speculated. She was as open as he was secretive.

I had always felt deeply connected to my grandmother. Sometimes I think my love for Marion was just my love for anything close to her. I gave her my kid gifts, once decorating the evergreen in our front yard in her honor—full dandelion regalia. On each visit to Marion I would ask her to sing to me, though she could barely carry a tune. I didn't even mind doing chores, if I could be in the same room with her.

In her family there had been a mystery, not a secret. Her own grand-mother, she told me, was an Indian. More than that she didn't know. "She died before I was born," Grandma explained. I didn't even think to ask this woman's name, much less her tribe. Nor did I realize how unusual my grandmother was in her day, since she clearly felt no shame about "Indian blood."

My grandmother liked knowing where she came from. She liked all of it, and through her I felt connected to all of American history. She was proud to belong to the Daughters of the American Revolution, able to trace her ances-try back to one Thomas Greene, cousin and aide-de-camp to General Nathanael Greene. She had been born in a one-room log cabin with a dirt floor in a now-vanished town called America. The log cabin impressed me, too; that was just like Abe Lincoln.

For a while her family lived in a mill on the Mississinewa, the river that runs through Grant County. One day she opened a trap door near the water wheel and saw hundreds of black snakes in their glistening home. That's all I recall hearing about her years at Barley Mill. Then the family moved to a farm across the river. She had an old photo of everyone posing with cabbage heads.

I relished even the details of her family's poverty. "One year for Christmas I got a shoebox with a string attached—my pull toy. Another year I got an orange." For a while she had to sleep in the same bed with a tubercular aunt, and that's how she got TB the first time. She had to move in with the high school principal's family in Marion, serving as nanny and maid, just so she could go to high school. She'd gone on to become a teacher in a one-room schoolhouse. And then she became a writer, working mostly for her beloved church publications, for pin money.

Whenever I asked, she would tell my favorite of the family stories—the one about her great-uncle in the Civil War. It seemed that his parents had not heard from him for a while, and they were very worried. Then one night an angel appeared to them, standing at the foot of the bed. The angel said, "Don't be afraid. Your son has been killed and is now with the Lord." The angel gave them the date of death and disappeared. Of the two parents, only the mother believed it. But later they got word that their son had been killed on the day the angel said, at the Battle of Shiloh.

In this world turned by God, my grandmother loved her church and often said so. She taught Sunday school, directed Bible school, and quietly became a leader in religious education, known to ministers all over the state. I remember her talking through one whole Sunday dinner about a missionary.

My grandparents' house in Marion was the only one of my relatives' homes where I ever saw black people. They were women my grandmother knew, somehow involved with her in church work. Grandma always seemed to be walking to the church, wincing audibly, feet tender with arthritis and corns. On Sunday afternoons she would lie down exhausted. Besides, it was sinful to work on the Sabbath.

Out on the sun porch I leafed through my grandma's books, the Writing-Made-Easys, the inevitable devotions, the bound editions of *Harper's* from the time of the Civil War. I opened zippered bags of clothing to hold the cool dresses against my face. Grandpa never gave her money. She still dressed like the 1940s. She took her old hats apart and remade them to have something new for church.

And then Grandma died a year before Grandpa did. During my last visit with her in the hospital, I asked her to tell me that story again—the one with the angel. She couldn't remember it, so I told it to her. "Oh yes," she said, but in her eyes I saw puzzlement. She didn't remember the story at all, and she didn't remember me. She'd gone back in time to when my father was a boy. She reminded him to carry a pie to the church. She had already left me. In shock, I looked out the window to where life was going on. Grandpa came in. That is, he jerked along. He hopped. He was all quivery and bent by then, refusing to consider a cane. "Are you warm enough?" he asked her. He tried to tuck her in better.

Back in Marion with my grandmother dead, I looked around the house to find something with her handwriting on it. The house felt so strange, I wanted proof that she'd been there. Finally I found her list: what to take to the hospital. I had decided that if I found such a thing—this evidence of her hand, her reality—then everything I knew of that place would be true.

TWO

THE SURVIVOR'S STORY

After my grandparents died, I began writing things down. My memories. The stories told by my aunt or my father. I've been writing about Marion my whole adult life, though there was always an element of taboo. Looking through my earliest version of the Josie material, I find the line: "Now I'm telling it—the story no one's supposed to tell." Of course, the real story I wasn't supposed to tell, I didn't write at all.

By the time I saw the picture of the Marion lynching, my grandparents were long dead. Through all of my childhood I had heard this event discussed twice, three times at most. Grandpa would have walked by on his way to work that night. The courthouse square lay directly in his path. There he played no part in the violence. It had already happened. He just had a look. So big deal. Him and ten thousand other people—or was it fifteen? That was the figure given out by Jack Edwards, the man who was mayor of Marion in 1930. He estimated that fifteen thousand people saw this thing. I'd been worried enough to look for Grandpa's face in the photo, and I learned later that my sister had done the same. But there had to be thousands like us. Really, thousands and thousands of people had grandparents, uncles, aunts who witnessed the lynching.

When I first learned that my grandfather had been a Klansman, I didn't want to know more and I didn't talk about it. The news wasn't just shameful, it was frightening. It suggested that someone I loved wasn't who I thought he was, that maybe I'd never really known him. Still, I felt that my sense of my grandfather couldn't be all wrong. I didn't just visit periodically for seventeen years; he lived the last year of his life at our house. He'd always been quiet, a homebody, never given to racial slurs. At least I never heard any, though I'm sure he shared the received ideas of other white men of his generation. So what did it really mean to be a Klansman in his day, in that place? Would looking closer illuminate anything? Or merely cause pain for my family? And why *my* family? There were millions like us.

Historians don't agree on how many joined the Indiana Klan, but the numbers vary from roughly a quarter to a half million. According to the most detailed scholarly analysis I could find, Leonard J. Moore's *Citizen Klansmen: The Ku Klux Klan in Indiana, 1921–1928,* the organization enrolled between one-quarter and one-third of all native-born white men in the state. The lowest membership estimate I found was in Kenneth T. Jackson's *The Ku Klux Klan in the City, 1915–1930,* and if this one is true, the KKK signed up just under 18 percent of all white men. (At the same time Alabama, for example, initiated about 7.6 percent.) The point remains: clearly, millions and millions of white Americans have had a grandfather or great-grandfather in the Ku Klux Klan.

For years I just made notes and kept my silence. One of the first people I talked to about my grandfather happened to be a friend named Robbie Mc-Cauley, an African American theater artist whose performances about racism often emphasize the importance of black-white dialogue. As she and I sat in her living room one day agreeing that white people tend to have trouble speaking personally on this painful topic, I was all too aware of my own untold story. Suddenly, not telling Robbie about my grandfather felt hypocritical. So I did.

I thought I'd just taken a big risk, that I'd tainted myself in her eyes, that she might be disdainful or even angry. But Robbie's response surprised me. "Hearing that is a relief," she said. "It makes me feel like I'm not crazy, like I'm not making up something. The 'nice white people' I know all come from something." It hadn't occurred to me that discussing it could actually do some good.

Robbie's point was that old stories continue to shape black-white relationships because the past has never been dealt with, and racism won't change till white people enter the dialogue. Then I told her about searching the Marion lynching photo for my grandfather's face and learning that my sister had done the same thing. Robbie said, "Those are the stories we need to hear, that white people aren't telling." But at that time, 1991, I wasn't ready to go further. Too scary, too close to home. What would it even mean to "go further"?

Two years passed before I discussed the possibility of writing about this with my brother. Inconclusively, I thought. But not long afterward, he sent me a newspaper article he happened to see while visiting our sister in Detroit. This was how I learned that there had been a third man lynched that night in Marion—and he'd survived. He was living in Milwaukee. My birthplace. I seized upon these coincidences, made them a sign.

The clipping my brother sent said that this man, James Cameron, had opened a museum devoted to the history of lynching and that he'd written a book called *A Time of Terror*. I reread the piece many times, then lost it at some point along the swing shift of my ambivalence. Even so, I felt I would have to meet this man or forever regret it. Here was a living connection to the lynching I had heard about as a child. More than that, here was a first thread into a larger story about race that began with the paradox in my own family—Grandpa in the Klan, Grandma apparently in some tribe.

Cameron came so close to dying on Marion's courthouse square that he had rope burns around his neck from the noose. He'd been dragged from the jail and beaten bloody and carried to the tree where the other two men were already hanging. In his account of those last moments—when he was certain he was about to die—he had a vision. Then, miraculously, the mob let him go, just let him walk away. He believed he was saved by divine intervention, sent back to us with news—our Ishmael. *And I only am escaped alone to tell thee.*

Yet who would hear what he'd come back to tell? For over forty-five years Cameron tried to find a publisher for his story, a rare written record by a lynching survivor. Finally in 1982 he mortgaged his house for $7,500 and published *A Time of Terror* himself. By 1993 he was struggling to renovate his museum building, an old boxing school and fitness center that the city of Milwaukee had sold him for a dollar. The museum, even more than the book, was the true work for which God had saved him, he thought. His near-death had become his life. He was then nearly eighty years old.

IN THE YEAR MY QUEST BEGAN, 1993, Black Classic Press was about to reissue the book Cameron had once self-published and sold from the trunk of his car. Eager to find out what had happened in Marion, I secured an early galley.

This is Cameron's story of the lynching as reported in *A Time of Terror:*

It began on the evening of August 6, 1930. Cameron had been pitching horseshoes with a school friend, Tommy Shipp, and an acquaintance, Abe Smith—both nineteen. Cameron was sixteen. The three decided to go for a joyride in Shipp's car. As they drove past city limits into the countryside, Smith announced that he wanted to rob someone to get money for a new car of his own. Cameron wavered inside; he wanted to get out but didn't. The three young men drove to the River Road—Lover's Lane—to look for a victim. Spotting one parked car, Smith pulled out a .38-caliber pistol, handed it to Cameron, and ordered him to tell the white man and woman inside to "stick 'em up." Cameron didn't even know Smith very well, and later he would tell the sheriff that he didn't know why he'd followed Smith's orders. Actually he did know. While something inside him said "go back go back" even as he approached the car, he felt propelled forward by someone with a stronger will.

There he stood, pistol in hand, ordering the driver and the woman to get out. When they did, Cameron realized that he knew the man, Claude Deeter, a regular customer at his shoeshine stand, someone who'd always tipped him, who'd always been decent to him. Now he knew he couldn't go through with it. He handed the gun back to Smith and ran. A few minutes later he heard shots, but he never stopped running. As it turned out, Deeter had been mortally wounded.

Cameron arrived home with new eyes, because he saw that a gulf had opened between past and present. He looked at his mother differently, feeling sorry for her for the first time in his life, though he lied when she asked him why he was so agitated. He couldn't sleep. He kept telling himself he hadn't really done anything wrong; he'd just been foolish. "The trouble was," he writes in his memoir, "this was Marion, Indiana, where there was little room for foolish Black boys." Cameron hadn't been in bed long when the police arrived—guns drawn, surrounding the house, raking it with searchlights. He could hear his mother getting up from the sofabed to answer the pounding at the door.

Shipp and Smith were already locked in separate cells in the Grant County jail by the time Cameron got there. In his book he describes three hours of interrogation, the kicks and punches delivered when it was over, the confession he then signed without even reading it. The officers locked him into an upstairs cell block with thirty black men arrested for riding a freight train.

By next morning—August 7, 1930—rumors were circulating through Marion that the white woman in the car, Mary Ball, had been raped. The spark was lit. Cameron writes that there was no particular "race problem" in the town, just the strictly enforced segregation common to so many towns at that time, just an everyday sense of limits, if you were black. "And once the boundary was crossed, anything might happen to the trespasser. . . . The realization dawned on me that I had crossed the boundary into the most sacred area of all, the world where white women lived."

He noticed a crowd of white people gathering outside the jail right after breakfast, some pointing to the windows of the cell, some shaking their fists. He could feel the tension among his older cellmates, who'd abandoned their usual card games to pace. Small groups of white people kept coming upstairs to peer into the cell block. A white prisoner assured Cameron that "people in this part of the country wouldn't lynch anybody." A black prisoner countered that the white guy was "nuts." Hadn't Cameron been charged with the rape of a white woman?

The mob outside the jail grew steadily larger. Then around midday Deeter died. His bloody shirt went on display outside the police station like a red flag. White people began to stream in from the surrounding countryside, while entire black families fled Marion. Around five-thirty a reporter from the *Marion Chronicle* came by to interview Cameron. He told the journalist his story, but he could see that he wasn't being heard, that the truth didn't matter. "Ask the girl," Cameron finally implored him. But the reporter just smirked: "You'll never get out of this."

In his book, recalling how he felt as that day built toward its violent climax, Cameron couldn't quite fit the dimensions of his fear into words. "At times, even now," he wrote, "I awaken in the middle of the night, reliving that whole day—and night. . . . I can never return to sleep. I suffer headaches all through the night. I just lie there, thinking, praying, saying my rosary, hoping, reassuring myself that it all happened a long, long time ago. I am not the same man. I am somebody else now."

At dusk Cameron peered out from his second-floor cell block and saw white faces for as far as he could look in any direction. He heard people demanding "those three niggers." The crowd began to throw rocks at the windows of the jail. Some carried shotguns. Some carried pistols. Some carried bats, clubs, crowbars, or stones. And among them Cameron recognized people he knew: customers from his shoeshine stand, boys and girls he'd gone to school with, people whose lawns he'd mowed. He saw Klan members in robes, faces unmasked, who seemed to be monitoring the crowd. He sensed a carnival air. And there, laughing and talking with them all, were the scores of policemen ostensibly protecting the jail.

The assault began at nightfall. Some men ran into the alley with gasoline cans and doused the brick wall, but they couldn't get it to burn. Then, for the next hour, men took turns pounding with a sledgehammer on the door of the jail and the stone casement around it, while the mob chanted itself into a frenzy, and people pulled stones out with their bare hands. Cameron could hear Sheriff Jacob Campbell ordering, "Don't shoot! There are women and children out there!"

The ringleaders burst in and pulled Shipp out first. As Cameron wrote: "I could see the bloodthirsty crowd come to life the moment Tommy's body was dragged into view. It seemed to me as if all of those 10 to 15 thousand people were trying to hit him at once." Clubbed and stoned, then hung from the bars of a jailhouse window, Shipp was dead long before the hysterical mob ever got him to the tree. Smith fared no better. Both were killed several times over. Someone rammed a crowbar through Smith's chest, while souvenir hunters cut off Shipp's pants and distributed the pieces. Cameron couldn't stop watching: the delirium, the sadism, and finally a weird ecstasy. Over at the tree, "people howled and milled around the lifeless bodies, their voices a mumbo jumbo of insane screams and giggles." They began posing for pictures with the bodies.

And then he could hear the men coming up the steps to get him. Cameron remembers what they carried—ropes, swords, rifles, and, he thinks, a submachine gun. He remembers the chanting outside: "We want Cameron!" But when the ringleaders pushed into his cell block, they couldn't pick him out. At first none of the other prisoners would identify him either, but the white mobsters threatened to "hang every goddamn one of you niggers," and Cameron watched in horror as about half of his black cellmates dropped to their knees groveling. Finally one old black man pointed him out.

He remembers the white men gripping him viselike, and the chorus of voices yelling "Nigger! Nigger! Nigger!" as they got him outside. He remembers the bricks and rocks and spittle that hit him as they carried him toward the courthouse, and the crowbar glancing across his chest, and the pickax handle hitting his head, and children biting his legs. "Once or twice, I thought I saw a kind face in the press around me. To each of them I called out for some kind of help. . . . But nothing happened." Police began clearing a path to the tree where the other two bodies were hanging, and someone called out for the rope. Cameron felt numb, encased in ice, and as someone put the noose around his neck and snaked the other end up over a branch, he remembered what his mother had told him about sinners facing death, about the thief on the cross, and he prayed, "Lord, forgive me my sins. Have mercy on me." In his mind and body and soul he was dead at that moment, and he stopped thinking.

Suddenly a woman's voice called out, sharply and clearly, "Take this boy back! He had nothing to do with any raping or killing!"

A silence fell over the mob, as Cameron remembers it. Or perhaps it was part of what I call his vision—because he recalls that the people around him were struck dumb, and that he suddenly felt himself surrounded by what seemed to be a film negative and on it were the images of the people in the crowd, and he couldn't tell anymore if they were black or white.

Then the spell broke. "And hands that had already committed murder became soft and tender, kind and helpful," he writes—and believes to this day. "I could feel the hands that had unmercifully beaten me remove the rope from around my neck. Now, they were caressing hands!"

Then the crowd drew back. He says that many bowed their heads, that they couldn't look at him as he staggered back to the jail.

In the years after the lynching, Cameron spoke to many white people who were present in the square that night. No one had heard any voice. No one but him. "You were just lucky," people told him. But something had stopped the rampage cold, and Cameron knew he hadn't imagined the voice. Sometimes he could still hear it.

FOR THE FIRST HOURS, days, months after his near-death, however, Cameron felt sick with rage and wanted to kill a white man. Any white man.

The four white detectives who drove him out of Marion that night—to a jail in nearby Huntington—ordered him to lie on the floor of the backseat the whole way, for safety, while they cracked jokes like "this nigger back here is as white as a sheet." Then as soon as he got to the Huntington jail, the old white man in the facing cell began apologizing to him. The old man had had a fight with his son because the son wanted in on the lynching. The old man said that, for all he knew, his son had put the rope around Cameron's neck. "I am sorry, son," he told Cameron. "Sorry to my heart."

Early the next morning, the detectives drove Cameron back to Marion. He lay down on the floor beneath a mat while they cruised the courthouse, where part of the lynch mob remained on guard. Cameron remembers the cops crowing gleefully that "those niggers are still hanging on the tree" and "look how their necks have stretched." One detective called out to a newsboy, bought the day's paper, and pulled the mat back to show Cameron the front page. There he saw for the first time the infamous photograph of his dead companions surrounded by festive white people.

Later that morning the detectives delivered Cameron to the state reformatory at Pendleton, where, he says, certain white guards gathered to laugh at him—his shredded clothing, his ashen complexion—while others stood watching in the distance with tears running down their cheeks. As incredible as this sounds, Cameron insists on it, writing that he never forgot the white people who shed tears for him: "They are etched in my memory, stamped upon my heart."

What ultimately defused young Cameron's rage was his friendship with one particular and unlikely benefactor, Sheriff Bernard Bradley of Anderson, Indiana. Cameron had been charged with both murder and rape. Granted a change of venue for his trial, he moved to the jail at Anderson, a town about thirty miles south of Marion. As he arrived there, word spread that Marion mobsters planned to storm the Anderson jail, lynch Cameron, and "break in" Sheriff Bradley, who had just taken office. But Bradley promised his young prisoner that if any mob showed up, he and his deputies would shoot to kill. Bradley had patrols in the streets every night for weeks. Rumor had it that he had even armed the town's black residents. Cameron writes in *A Time of Terror* that that clinched it for the mob leaders, who decided not to try anything.

Once the tension eased, Sheriff Bradley called Cameron to his office and announced that he was going to make him a turnkey trusty, which would allow him to leave jail during the day. The sheriff said he didn't believe Cameron was guilty of rape or murder. "I want you to treat me like a father," Bradley told him, "and I'll treat you like a loving son." Utterly shocked, Cameron studied the sheriff's eyes and body language, "because no white man had ever spoken to me like that before." But he decided that "my concentration, my scrutiny, could detect no deceit or falsity." He came to love this sheriff, this anomaly who'd grown up in the all-white town of Elwood—a town about halfway between Marion and Anderson, a town still notorious today for its association with the Ku Klux Klan. Cameron could only conclude in retrospect that Sheriff Bradley must have been "a weird sort of person, because he was mysterious and apparently outside natural law. By his nature, he seemed to have belonged to another world." And indeed he did. Sheriff Bradley was a Catholic, a group both feared and hated by the 1920s Klan.

Meanwhile, back in Marion, a grand jury concluded that the authorities had acted "in a prudent manner" on the night of August 7, 1930.

To LEARN THAT SOMEONE had lived through it and never let it go—that was the catalyst for me. In August 1993 I went to Milwaukee to meet James Cameron. I went not as a journalist on assignment but on my own time. That way I would have no obligation to write about it. Really, I felt anxious just calling him up, making the appointment. I told him nothing of my own connection to Marion on the phone; nor did I know what I would say to him when we met. I told myself that I was merely going to find what had been hidden from me. I didn't analyze my intentions beyond that. Certainly there was nothing I could do about a lynching that happened decades before I was born, though somehow I felt I was living with it. I didn't see a way to set that right. But I could go to Milwaukee.

As it happens, that was where I'd first learned something about racism. I was born in Milwaukee and lived there until I was seven, then moved to an all-white county just north of the city. I know that I didn't learn hatred from my parents. They never used what we now call the n-word, for example, and I can't imagine them tolerating that word in our house. But I did learn a certain caution, a certain fear. My parents had told me about black people. That my aging great-aunts, still living in inner-city Milwaukee, were afraid of them when they walked to the German church service on Sunday. That if some moved to your neighborhood, you should stay away. And if you drove through their neighborhood, you had to roll up the windows.

When I was eight or nine my parents sent me to an art class in Milwaukee on Saturdays, where I met some black children for the first time in my life—one boy and one girl—and I paid particular attention to them. The boy was very serious and spoke to no one, and I realized after a session or two that he was the best artist there. The girl was lively and friendly, and I decided to get to know her. She and I took adjoining desks. After class we would wait together outside for our parents to pick us up.

One day when my mother came for me, I told her about my new friend, who at that time I probably called "Negro." I thought my parents had been misinformed, that they'd be happy to hear the good news: "She's really nice." My mother didn't reply. "Could I invite her to our house?" My mother kept driving, acting like she hadn't heard me, and soon enough I realized that she wasn't going to answer.

I had presented my mother with a real dilemma. We didn't just live in an all-white county, we lived in a county where our new minister greeted us with the words: "Carr." Pause. "You're not German, are you?" We lived in a town where the neighborhood children ran over to greet us on day one, calling out as they entered our yard, "Are you Catholic or Lutheran?" This was the hidebound little town that I was proposing to integrate.

So I lost my new friend when the art class ended, but even at that age I knew that something was wrong with this setup. So I moved to the next stage of racism—relating to black people as "those we have wronged." That guilt would build another barrier.

Now I was going to meet Cameron, and I would have to acknowledge my connection to that defining moment in his life under the lynching tree. I considered this with some apprehension. As I drove into the neighborhood near his museum, I realized I must also be near the parochial school where I attended kindergarten and first grade. Back then the area was undergoing "white flight."

America's Black Holocaust Museum sat on a quiet street between a public school and a soul food restaurant. Greeting me at the museum's locked steel door, Cameron was more robust than I expected. At seventy-nine, he had a lot of presence. A full head of gray hair, a kind face, soft-spoken, a down-home midwesterner, he had in many ways lived an ordinary life. He put in six days a week at the museum, all alone. It was not yet open to the public. As we sat down in a small makeshift office crammed with books, I asked him to talk about his life between the lynching and the present.

First came four years in prison as an accessory to voluntary manslaughter in the death of Claude Deeter. Ordered to serve his parole outside the state, he went to Detroit, eventually returning to Anderson to live. There Cameron organized a chapter of the NAACP. One day early in the 1950s a local movie theater refused his son a seat on the ground floor, directing him to the balcony, and Cameron called on the state attorney general to enforce the equal accommodations law. "We began to get threatening letters, and my wife became frightened," he said. They moved to Milwaukee in 1953. It was a homecoming of sorts. Cameron had been born in La Crosse, Wisconsin.

All along Cameron worked a series of blue-collar jobs—at a shoeshine parlor, the Delcro factory, a cardboard-box factory. He attended night school to learn air conditioning and steam combustion, then worked at a shopping mall. After retirement he went into business for himself as a rug and upholstery cleaner. He converted to Catholicism in 1953, attributing his faith to the example of Sheriff Bernard Bradley and his belief that the Virgin Mary had been the "voice from heaven" who saved his life. He attended mass daily. By the time we met, he'd been married for fifty-five years and raised five children.

But mostly what he'd done for more than six decades was struggle obsessively to bear witness. He'd begun writing *A Time of Terror* in prison, but authorities confiscated the manuscript when they paroled him. By early the next year he'd written it out again. Once he moved to Anderson, he began going back to Marion to interview white people who'd witnessed the lynching. Cameron estimates that he then rewrote the book about a hundred more times as he accumulated nearly three hundred rejections before self-publishing.

He also became a self-taught historian, filling the basement of his home with books. As I sat in his office, he pulled out pamphlets he'd produced over the years—on the Klan, the Confederate flag, the Thirteenth Amendment, slavery, Reconstruction, the first civil rights bill, the second civil rights bill. He'd written hundreds. His latest bore the title: "Definite and Positive Proof That Free Black Men Did Vote Right Along with Free White Men in the Formation of the Constitution of the United States of America." Cameron self-published as much as he could afford at $20 per copyright.

He hadn't even begun to renovate the ex–boxing school. He gave me a tour of the disassembled premises. Here where I saw old weightlifting machines, lockers, and a pool table, he would someday have his bookstore, his contemplation room, and his lecture and screening room. Cameron pointed into the gymnasium with its basketball hoops and piles of chairs. "That'll be my Chamber of Horrors." That would be the room with, for example, the photo taken in Marion's courthouse square. Cameron intended to exhibit large pictures in the style of the Jewish Holocaust museum Yad Vashem in Israel. He recalled how that institution had inspired him when he and his wife, Virginia, visited in 1979. "It shook me up something awful. I said to my wife, 'Honey, we need a museum like that in America to show what happened to us black folks and the freedom-loving white people who've been trying to help us.'" He figured he would need $150,000 to $200,000 to renovate. He was paying utilities and phone out of his Social Security.

The building was his third location. With $5,000 of his own money he opened the museum in 1988 on the second floor of Milwaukee's Black Muslim headquarters, then moved to a storefront around the corner, but he never had room to exhibit more than ten photos or to store many of his ten thousand books on race relations. And to his utter frustration, he would sometimes go for days without a single person coming in. *And I only am escaped alone to tell thee.*

His exhibits had been packed away for over a year already, while the approach of his eightieth birthday kindled a sense of urgency. "I got one foot in the grave and the other one got no business being out," he chuckled, then looked somber. Black Classic Press had delayed the reprinting of his book again. "I wish that book would hurry up and come out so I can get some speaking engagements under my belt and then I can get my money to put the boiler in."

Clearly Cameron was part of that tradition of African Americans who would hold this country to her ideals. He said he wanted to replace the word *racism* with *un-American.* He pulled out a copy of Ralph Ginzburg's *100 Years of Lynchings:* "This should be in every home, just like the Bible." When I asked him if he'd ever studied history—meaning formally—he replied, "Yes. I live in history."

"My grandparents were from Marion," I announced.

"They probably remember it," said Cameron.

This benign assessment of what I felt to be shameful slowed me down. "My father remembers it, too, even though he was only six when it happened."

"Yeah, that made an impression on him. Sure."

He began to tell me his story, even though he had said he didn't like to do that one on one. It was still too emotional for him. Showing me a postcard of the Marion jail, he pointed out where Tommy was, where Abe was, where he was. Almost compulsively, he described how they were beaten, how he'd been told later that the Marion sheriff, Jake Campbell, was a Klansman, and how, when the mob was about to hang him, he prayed. "And then this voice spoke from heaven. It was from heaven. No human voice could have quelled the fury of that mob." Then a great silence fell over the crowd, and he entered what seemed like a room made of film negatives, where everyone stood "petrified," and he couldn't tell anymore if they were black or white.

I told him my family's story, leaving out the cruel part—the laughter. "Then, after he died, we found out that my grandfather was in the Klan."

"That happens," he replied.

"All my father said was that he never saw a hooded sheet."

"You know what?" Cameron told me. "During the Roaring Twenties

Indiana had over a half million Klansmen, and Marion had the first chapter. They were called the mother den of all the Klans in Indiana. It was an upgoing thing. If you weren't in the Klan, you were nobody, and that's what gave them the liberty to lynch black people with impunity. Sure."

"My grandfather may well have approved of it."

"Sure." He got up, saying that he had something special to show me, a new artifact for the museum. Someone in Marion had sent him one of the infamous "souvenirs" that were always part of a classic lynching. The ropes used to hang Tommy Shipp and Abe Smith had been cut into pieces and distributed among the spectators. From a letter-sized envelope Cameron pulled a piece of fraying rope, like a thick clothesline, maybe an inch and a half long. "I'm going to put that in a glass case with all kinds of padlocks on it," he said, placing the little plug of rope in my palm. "You're the first one to have seen this."

In my conversations with Cameron I found myself constantly astonished at some of his reported interactions with white people—not the brutal ones, the "nice" ones. The actual lynch mob probably numbered between twenty-five and fifty, he said, while thousands watched. Cameron eventually interviewed more than two hundred of these spectators, and all were happy to see that he'd survived (rumor had it he'd died of the beating), but none had lifted a finger to help him, and no one apologized.

I was reminded of one more thing I'd heard as a child. That the lynching was "necessary." That "those guys would have gotten off." I did not share this with Cameron, but I thought about the infamous photograph. The white people posing with those bodies look so pleased with themselves, so confident that they've done the right thing.

Before I left, Cameron gave me a manila envelope labeled "The Pardon." This was important to him. In 1991 he had decided that he would ask to be forgiven. He wrote a letter to Indiana governor Evan Bayh, requesting a pardon "for the foolish role I played in the commission of a crime that resulted in the loss of three precious lives." Cameron said the idea to request a pardon just came to him. He wanted to clear his name before he died. He wanted to "wipe this whole thing clean." Bayh signed the pardon in February 1993, and Cameron went back to Marion. The mayor gave him a key to the city in a ceremony at a Marion hotel, and Cameron wiped away tears as the inscription on his pardon was read.

"Now that the state of Indiana has forgiven me for my indiscretion," he told the overflow crowd, "I, in turn, forgive Indiana for their transgressors of the law in Marion on the night of August 7, 1930. I forgive those who have harmed me and Abe and Tom, realizing I can never forget the traumatic events that took place that night."

His hope now was that Marion would show the rest of Indiana how people of all races could "be welded into one single and sacred nationality." The newspaper printed the text of Cameron's speech, using one of his phrases as a headline: LET MARION SET A BEACON LIGHT.

I LEFT THE ENCOUNTER with Cameron knowing that I had to write about it. Not that my reluctance just melted away.

This was still a hard story to own. As Robbie had put it, most white people "come from something"—slaveowners, Klansmen, dissemblers, dehumanizers, averters of eyes. And we do not have stories that make us proud.

I knew I was merely one among the many reluctant. Years ago I met with a large group of women—white, black, Asian, Latino—to discuss whether we could work together on a special issue of a women's journal that would address racism. Many of those who were not white spoke eloquently about their struggles, while we white women sympathized. Then one of the black women challenged us to speak personally. Basically, she was saying, "Why do you really think racism should end? What's it to you?" And she made it clear that "It's wrong" would not suffice. There was a painfully long silence. Finally I got up and talked about the little girl in my art class. The story ended very dramatically when one of the black women got to her feet and declared, "I was that little girl." Not literally, of course, though I stopped breathing for a moment. This was the point Robbie always harped on—the "dialogue." We had become characters in the same story.

And this, for one thing, is what it will take to end racism. When it is no longer a black story but a white story, too. Or as Robbie put it, "It won't be over until you have to live with it the way we have to live with it."

So I had these encouragements. I had my own belief that the silence of white people was a lie of omission, distorting history, straining relationships with black people and keeping them unequal, even permitting terrible things to happen. (Why shouldn't they happen, if they can just be erased?) Yet speaking was painful, too. It's easy to make all the right noises about racism in general ("terrible" "wrong"), but make it specific, and we're talking about ourselves and the people we know and love.

I could barely stand to think about it. I knew that my grandfather hadn't participated in the lynching, but I felt he was implicated. Beyond the mob of twenty-five to fifty killers were thousands of witnesses like those in the infamous photograph, and beyond them were the white people at home who condoned it. Because no one was guilty, everyone was guilty. All participated in the code of silence.

I couldn't follow my grandfather's lead. I had to break the code. Thoughts of Marion always brought me back to the biggest lesson I had learned there as a child: how my grandfather erased his own mother from history, as if that would erase his shame. *Parts of certain lines cut out with a razor blade.* Then the last record of her existence, that obituary, taken and— what?—burned? It's just a family story, but I saw it as a model for the larger American family, with its repressed history of racial traumas: not just slavery but something as recent and as shared as Jim Crow. Who learns the details in school? I didn't. Someone razored them out, so Jim Crow becomes "a time when people were ignorant." But the details can send you reeling, and if you're white, they're shameful.

James Baldwin once said that you have to accept the history that created you, that if you don't accept it, you cannot atone. So even as I asked myself, Why me? Why my family? I knew that I was being handed an opportunity to find that history and to begin the process of atoning. I could go to Marion as a journalist and gather the facts. Soon finding the details of what happened became an obsession with me. It was personal. I felt that I had to know whether the Klan—my grandfather's Klan—was behind it. I dreaded what I might find. His choices distressed me, yet I felt terrible for him. And I could only hope my family would see that I had done this with love.

I would make my grandfather a partner in this work. That is, I would use "my grandfather in the Klan" to open doors with white people who were even more reluctant than me to speak. It would let them know that I wasn't there to be self-righteous or superior. Because that was the other part of my story. I wasn't just a journalist—I was in it and of it.

THREE

"WE NEVER RECOVERED"

I had not been back to Marion in more than twenty-five years. Driving north from Indianapolis through the winter stubble, I crossed the Grant County line into a landscape suffused, for me, with drama and pathos. Here I had learned early on how the past weighs on people. Even so, I did not expect to find the large shadow still cast in Marion by the events of August 7, 1930. In those first days back a few people volunteered the opinion that the lynching had poisoned the town. "We never recovered," said one. These were white people, and I wondered if this was guilt talking, though I was startled myself at how the town had deteriorated.

My Marion had been the ideal American small town, with rambling Victorian homes, brick streets, and church bells chiming out hymns, a place where even shabbiness had a certain gentility. Perhaps my child eyes just had never noticed the poverty there, but now the Marion I saw was downright needy, a grim godforsaken shell of a place. Half the buildings around the courthouse square looked empty. Since my childhood, the population had dropped by one-fourth (to about thirty thousand), and the new nerve center seemed to be a depressing strip of road along the western edge of town—the bypass—home to neon fast food, used car lots, and cheap motels. Of course, during the years I remember as so idyllic, the lynching was already decades in the past. Logically, rationally, Marion's problems had to be simply economic. This was a factory town struggling into the postindustrial age. But that isn't what people there told me during those first couple of days. They thought the lynching did it.

By the time I arrived in Marion, I had inadvertently altered its psychic terrain. Early in 1994 I published an article in *The Village Voice* about James Cameron, the lynching, and the fact of my grandfather's Klan membership. About a dozen film and television producers contacted me, and even more called Cameron. I said no to everyone, but Cameron said yes. So Marion endured a media blitz. A modest one, but still—the town cringed.

I had not anticipated this reaction to the article. What I had hoped was that Cameron might somehow benefit—might get, say, enough money to open his museum. In fact, his whole life changed. Suddenly at age eighty he had an audience. *A Time of Terror*, his newly reissued book, sold out its first printing of five thousand copies in a week. The publicist hired by Black Classic Press described media interest around the book as a "feeding frenzy." Cameron began making trips back to Marion with network news and magazine shows, a Dutch film crew, and the BBC, so that they could interview him in or near the old jail. Small contributions to the museum began to pour in through the mail; then came the one large one that finally bought him his new boiler. He opened America's Black Holocaust Museum in November 1994.

Cameron's new fame seemed long overdue, given that he was one of the very few ever to survive a lynching. I wondered why the national media hadn't picked up on him sooner. But the attention directed at me seemed misplaced or at best premature. I'd only begun to discover my story and couldn't just turn it over to other journalists. Much to my chagrin, my decision didn't stop some of them from going to Marion anyway to poke around. "We're going to get the name of every person in that photograph," one producer announced. I don't think I heard from him again. Marion wouldn't give up its secrets so easily, but I worried about the anger and alienation these crusading reporters would leave in their wake.

I hated their attitudes myself. Most were white, and in most I sensed an eagerness to play the role of the noble Caucasian who shows the rednecks a thing or two. That's how some white people atone: by going after worse white people. And in Marion the media folks thought they'd found a whole town's worth of worse.

Really my article had failed, because people were missing the point. I had written about Marion not because it was the worst place but because it was *my* place. I had tried to suggest that there can never be a real dialogue in this country between white people and black people until those of us who are white begin to tell our terrible stories. I had tried to suggest a different atonement pattern, one that starts with just admitting to the truth.

But I know full well why the millions like me aren't all exposing their grandfathers' Klan memberships. Because there's a price to be paid for breaking a silence, just as there's a price for keeping one. Publishing the article caused my parents, especially my father, tremendous pain. I had dishonored the grandfather who loved me. I had dishonored the family name. And if I didn't see it that way, I couldn't trot out some political rhetoric to address the hurt my parents felt. I backed off. So while the rest of the media charged into Marion because it meant nothing to them, I waited nearly a year because it meant so much. And then I arrived feeling that I was not supposed to be there.

I won't forget that first night back in Grant County, sitting in one of those bypass motels with the wind whipping through the cracks around the door. It was the end of November 1994, sixty-four years after the lynching. How many people were even alive who could tell me anything? And if I found them, would they tell it? I also had to look at the KKK—and look hard—since James Cameron said the mobsters were Klansmen, the crowd outside "monitored" by Klansmen, that he could see hoods from the jail window. Few organizations were more secretive. And what if I found something to implicate my own grandfather? Did it make sense for me to try to solve this mystery? That's what I was there to determine, but already I felt doubtful and daunted.

TOM WISE FIGURED THAT nearly every white person in town saw the lynching. He was certain that anyone who'd lived in Marion for a year could tell me what had happened the night of August 7, 1930, and that even today "when whites get in their own circles, they talk about it. They brag about it." Wise was the cousin of James Cameron and a detective with the Marion police force, a big man in his late fifties who leavened a gregarious nature with a certain diffidence. He seemed to be acquainted with half the people in town. Obsessed with uncovering the truth about the lynching, he'd been helping all the researchers and camera crews who came to Marion. And now he would help me.

I arranged to meet him at a restaurant on the bypass my first night there.

Wise had lived his whole life in Marion, hearing about the lynching as a kid—probably from friends. It was not discussed in his family, and he grew up with no idea that he was related to one of the victims. But because his mother and James Cameron's mother were sisters, he began meeting Cameron at family funerals. The first time was probably when James's mother passed in the 1960s. Tom didn't know even then that this cousin from Milwaukee had survived the lynching. He can't recall exactly when he did learn this or who told him. His mother? Maybe he discussed it with his cousin when Cameron returned for his sister's funeral in the 1970s. What Wise remembers for certain is a conversation in which Cameron said that he'd written a book but could not find a publisher. By the late 1970s Wise was doing research for Cameron to try to corroborate his story.

Tom interviewed witnesses, all of whom had since died except for the old mayor, Jack Edwards. He had also searched the Grant County courthouse. Wise was a Marion policeman, after all, and he knew where to look and who to ask, yet he found nothing at the courthouse but a list of names: some of the people indicted for lynching Shipp and Smith. Those names had never been secret. Two men had actually gone to trial early in 1931, earning quick acquittals and moving the prosecutor to drop charges against everyone else. The two trial transcripts, however, had disappeared.

"A veil hangs over this town," Wise told me. I would come to understand that his efforts to lift that veil put him somewhat at odds with both black and white Marion. Different communities might be silent for different reasons, but almost everybody in town wished that August 7, 1930, would recede into oblivion. Recently James Cameron had proposed moving his Black Holocaust Museum to Marion—installing it right in the old jail from which he'd been carried by the lynch mob. Wise just shook his head at Cameron's prospects, certain the move would not happen. Ever.

The infamous photo was bad enough. Wouldn't let the thing vanish. Wise told me that the photographer, Lawrence Beitler, still had a daughter in town, but she wouldn't talk. She proved impossible to track down, but Betty Beitler had given an interview to the *Marion Chronicle-Tribune* in 1988. As she recalled then: "[My father] was sitting on the front porch when someone came by and told him about the lynching and urged him to go down to the square. He didn't even want to do it, but taking pictures was his business." Beitler was a professional photographer with a studio downtown. According to his daughter, he carried his eight-by-ten-inch view camera to the square, took the one picture, and left.

Wise wasn't sure he believed this story of one photo. He knew other pictures had been taken that night, because he'd met people who'd seen them. And witnesses had described seeing flashes around the square. Searching for these photographs had become another of his quests. Wise had been at it for fifteen years, though, and hadn't turned up a single one.

I think in my first days back in Marion the details about the photograph were the most shocking and disturbing things that I heard—because of what they said about mass complicity and the pride white Marion took in this public execution. "The orders for the picture started coming the next day," Betty Beitler had said of the demands placed on her father. "He stayed up ten days and nights making prints. He sold thousands of them. I don't know how many thousands he sold. They were fifty cents apiece. It wasn't unusual for one person to order a thousand at a time." Betty Beitler also asserted that her mother destroyed the negative sometime during the 1940s.

In Marion the photo was everywhere and nowhere. Ed Breen, then managing editor of the *Marion Chronicle-Tribune* and author of the Beitler story, explained to me: "We're still a ways away from being able to publish that picture in this newspaper." Indeed, the photo never appeared in a Marion newspaper. I flashed on Cameron's story—the detective buying a paper the next morning as they drove around the Grant County courthouse, pulling the mat back to show him the photo on the front page. It's possible that out-of-town newspapers were for sale. In Hartford City, just fifteen miles away, the photo ran on page one, as it did in Muncie and Anderson. Within four days of the lynching a New York picture agency called Acme News Service also had a copy of Beitler's powerful photograph. Eventually Acme's collection became part of the Bettmann Archive. Beitler's picture is now an iconic image of racial injustice in America.

I first saw it in *Alistair Cooke's America*. The caption in the hardcover edition reads: "No one knows who took this picture or exactly when. But lynch law ruled the South in the years after World War I." My family owned the paperback edition, where place and date are identified.

Every year, Breen continued, people called the *Chronicle-Tribune* because they found a copy of the picture in their attics, and they wondered if it was valuable.

The photograph still had a real totemic value in Marion, though it had officially "disappeared" from the town's history. One man, George Sharp, told me that when he went to work at Marion's Fisher Body plant back in the 1970s, he was required to buy a copy of the photo from his foreman, a Klan member—to prove that he was "okay." He described a certain Marion pizza parlor where, he assured me, I could buy a copy of the photograph today.

I DON'T REMEMBER EVEN noticing the Grant County jail as a child, though I could have walked there from my grandparents' house. Just a block from the square, this massive brick edifice has a feudal air not completely explained by its corner turrets. I found it hard to imagine, but the county actually held prisoners in this dank and crumbling eyesore until 1981. The jail with its attached sheriff's residence then stood empty for close to ten years.

A retired farmer and carpenter named Rex Fansler bought the place in 1990 for $500 and moved into the old sheriff's house with his wife. He had never had enough money for more than minimal repairs, and the house, formerly regarded as a showcase, was falling apart from the inside out. Once there had been chandeliers and leaded glass windows and seven working fireplaces. Now there were holes in the roof; vandals had ripped out the brass and copper pipes; and someone had taken an ax to the banister, reducing it to a set of variegated wooden stumps. In every big vaulted room, plaster had fallen and paint had peeled, revealing older layers of color or wallpaper or bare wooden slats. The Fanslers had arranged their own belongings tidily amid the wreckage.

"Perfect for a bed and breakfast," Fansler suggested. He was desperate to sell the place.

Tall, bald, paunchy, and flannel-shirted, the seventy-year-old Fansler addressed me with a constant enigmatic smile. We sat down in a living room overdecorated with fake Christmas greenery, stuffed animals in Santa suits, and lit candles. He directed me to take a chair next to a roaring fire.

Right outside the window to my right was a porch shared by the main door of the jail and the side entrance to the sheriff's house. Every prisoner who ever entered or left the jail passed within inches of the sheriff's living room. So had the mob when it came at the jail door with sledgehammer and telephone pole. So had the helpless bodies of Shipp, Smith, and Cameron.

By coincidence, Fansler had practically been a witness to the crime on Lover's Lane that started it all. Claude Deeter and Mary Ball had been parked at the edge of the Fansler property when they were accosted by Cameron and his buddies. In a farmhouse just up the hill, six-year-old Rex Fansler stood at the window listening as his father ran out with a shotgun and fired at Shipp's fleeing car. Then Fansler's mother and older brother went out to give Deeter first aid. According to the Fansler family story, Deeter had been hit in the head with a hickory pole, shot, and thrown into the nearby Mississinewa River, though no "official" account has ever mentioned the pole or the river.

The brother who'd helped Deeter was still living in Gas City. But Rex had already taken another journalist to see him, and brother Walter had been rude. He'd refused to talk on camera, and now he refused to talk, period. Apparently Walter thought publicity about the lynching would help Rex sell the jail for big money—and he was determined not to help Rex, for reasons I never pursued.

"The rope they used for the lynching came from my father's barn," Fansler declared, with an odd glint of pride. He was proud, I decided, of his connection to this "historic" event, terrible though it was. The horror of it seemed to be unreal to him. He told me that his father had relayed a message to Sheriff Jake Campbell from "a group that congregated at Eighteenth and Adams."

The lynch mob? Getting a message to the sheriff? What was at 18th and Adams? About a mile south of the square, this happened to be exactly where my grandfather had lived as a boy. Sitting on the lap of Eugene Debs. In my great-great-grandmother's boardinghouse.

Fansler didn't have any answers. His own theory was that people "out in the county"—from Gas City and Jonesboro—instigated the lynching. The Fanslers had owned a copy of the infamous photo, but Rex didn't know anything more about why his father was relaying messages or how he had come to provide the rope or whether he had belonged to the Klan. The old man had never been one for talking. The old man wouldn't even tell Rex who his grandparents were: "He'd say to me, 'You have clothes on your back and food in your belly. Isn't that enough?' " Fansler didn't seem defensive, didn't seem to be hiding anything. He had simply never penetrated a certain generational wall of silence.

He took me out to see the jail. Fansler assured me that yes, this was the same front door that had stood there in 1930. It was wood, nearly two inches thick, with hinges about a foot high. I noted the scraped paintless area where I could still see indentations left by the sledgehammers. Apparently evidence of the violence was not considered noteworthy. I was astonished at this, yet it fit the general pattern: act like nothing happened.

Fansler, too, was blasé about the scars on the wood. What he thought more interesting was that as soon as we passed the wooden door, another door stood immediately to our right, this one made of steel with a center handle, like a New York City police lock. That opened into what had once been the turnkey's office. Across it was another steel door leading into a corridor. There stood a door with bars, and down that hallway another steel door. Past that we stood in a hallway between the two cell blocks on the ground floor. Here two more sets of bars stood in front of each cell block, according to Fansler. Those were gone, but I found them discussed in the depositions taken after the lynching. The depositions also mention the first two steel doors. I couldn't know if all the other doors were there in 1930, but they could well have been. How did they fly open? Could the story be true—that Sheriff Campbell had thrown the keys out to the mob? I'd heard this from two different people within my first two days in town. Of course, they hadn't seen it themselves and didn't know anyone who had. That was just the story in the air, the folklore.

What I could determine with my own eyes was that access to the prisoners should not have been easy. And there had been an escape route from the jail. Fansler showed me a "secret passage" connecting the third floor of the lockup to an upstairs bedroom in the sheriff's house.

The old jail was a shambles, fetid and creepy. In each of the remaining cell blocks, six cells faced six others, with a walkway down the center and a bullpen surrounding them. Most of the six-by-eight pens had been stripped of their beds and toilets, and peeling blue paint flaked from the bars and walls.

Fansler offered to drive me out to the site of the old family farm—the site of the shooting. Soon we were heading east in his car to Stone Road, formerly River Road, which used to be Lover's Lane and home to a few bootlegging joints. We pulled over right where Deeter had. In 1930 the Fansler farmhouse sat right up the hill, where I could now see Stonecrest Manor Trailer Park.

Fansler drove on to show me the route Cameron would have taken on his run home. What struck me was the length of that journey. Stone Road lies just east of the Mississinewa, and Cameron would have had to run about a mile to get to the bridge at 38th Street, where he turned west into Marion, crossing the width of the town to 30th and Poplar, near what is now the bypass. All together he would have run two, even three miles.

Meanwhile Fansler was telling me the rumors he'd heard about the woman in Deeter's car, Mary Ball. That she made a practice of taking guys out to Lover's Lane to get them rolled. That she had been the lover of either Shipp or Smith. And in his opinion, she hadn't been raped—"There wasn't time." Because I had never questioned Mary Ball's claim to be a victim, whether or not she'd been raped, I found what he was telling me incredible. "How did you hear this?" I asked Fansler. From Mark Van Vector, a recently deceased friend who had picked it up from "everyday talk." Indeed, I would soon hear this from others as well. Mary Ball would become one more mystery to solve.

Fansler added that Van Vector's mother was in the lynching photo—the woman standing closest to the camera. He spoke easily about the events of 1930, but at one point he asked me to turn off the tape recorder. Then he announced that he'd called the mayor of Marion to tell him I was in town. The mayor "wanted to be informed of everything going on." Like—every media visit to the jail. Fansler also implied that the mayor would have a say in who bought the place. And the buyer could be James Cameron, who, according to Rex, might just get a rich black person like Bill Cosby to give him the money. Fansler seemed to really believe this, and he'd set the price at $160,000. But, he said he'd already been warned by Ruth Cartwright, the eighty-five-year-old editor and publisher of a local right-wing paper: "Don't go selling to that nigger."

IN 1929 JACK EDWARDS became the youngest mayor the city of Marion had ever had. He was then twenty-eight. Jack Edwards left town for a meeting in Indianapolis on the afternoon of August 7, 1930. Tom Wise was convinced that the mayor knew a lynching was in the works and that that was why he really left. Wise had been trying to get Edwards to admit this for years. The old mayor was now ninety-three.

"Jack may be ready to come clean," Wise told me when he took me out to the nursing home to meet him. "His wife died a few months ago, and he's going to the chapel every day."

Jack Edwards had lived with a flair unusual in small midwestern towns. He'd been a jazz musician, a grocer, a stockbroker, a nightclub owner, mayor in 1930 and again in 1960, a Democrat popular in a largely Republican town. Older people still talked about how he'd hunted for John Dillinger in an armored car, how he once fell over drunk during a campaign speech, how—during the Depression—he made people pay their fines in potatoes, which he then distributed to the poor. Ol' Jack. The Potato Man. The Boy Mayor. Just the mention of his name made people smile. Even my aunt Ruth, who loathed Democrats, admitted, "He was a fun and joy boy." Jack's very foibles were beloved, the stuff of legend. One old man, laughing so hard the tears ran, recalled for me the time Jack got drunk and drove the city's big armored car straight into a pond, and they had had one heck of a time trying to pull the thing out. Jack denied this when I asked about it, though, telling me gravely, "That was my own car."

He was a thin frail man with a thick shock of white hair, and he still wore his trademark bow tie and dress shirt every day. He sat in a wheelchair. The flamboyant former life had shrunk into half a nondescript room at the old folks' home, where he'd surrounded himself with political mementos: a framed telegram from Jack Kennedy, a portrait of JFK and Jackie, a photo of himself with Harry Truman. He announced proudly that he had had the best-equipped police department of any city in America and that he used to fly a plane that was sister ship to the *Spirit of St. Louis*. I could see in the framed photo of it on the wall that this plane had the words MAYOR JACK EDWARDS painted in giant letters along the sides.

On learning why I was there, he became a bit defensive, telling me several times that he had had nothing to do with the lynching, that he'd left for Indianapolis that day at one P.M., that he was a Democrat while every other official was a Republican, that "the colored people were our friends." While I think it likely that Edwards knew a lynching was in the works and left town to avoid entanglement, I have no proof of this. I do know that he could have at least called the statehouse for help, but he left that to Flossie Bailey, state president of the National Association for the Advancement of Colored People and a local resident. When Edwards returned to Marion the morning of August 8, 1930, he apologized to her.

I hadn't come to get a confession from him, however. I wanted information. Both hearing and speaking had become difficult for the old mayor. He could not always get enough breath to push the words out. But mentally he was sharp and alive. I asked him about Klan involvement in the lynching. He said the Klan was dead by 1930. But back in 1923 and 1924, it must have had more than five thousand members in Grant County. "For a while they did good," Edwards insisted. "They made big donations to churches and poor people. They had nothing to do with the lynching." He said fifteen thousand people came to see that event. "There was no foreign element. Everybody was a Hoosier." He said that Marion had a black population of 1,081 at the time, "all good people. We never had no trouble."

Spontaneously he then began to tell me who some of the people in the lynching photo were, though I hadn't asked about the picture and never even showed it to him. He seemed to know the photograph by heart. The guy in the straw hat—that was Ed Stephenson, who ran the Flyer streetcar between Marion and Indianapolis. The old lady's name was Ancil. The grinning man who's holding a woman's hand—that was Phil Boyd. The man whose face is blurred—William Lennon, a preacher, "a good man." He told me with no equivocation that Phil Boyd and Charlie Lennon (no relation to William Lennon) were the ringleaders. But the son of a former Grant County sheriff had already assured me that everyone indicted for the lynching—like Boyd and Lennon—were merely scapegoats.

"I heard that a message was relayed to Sheriff Campbell from someone at Eighteenth and Adams," I said.

"Eighteenth and Meridian," Jack corrected me. Meridian was four blocks east of Adams. "That was the hotbed."

"Of what?"

"Of that group."

"The Bucktown group?" I asked.

"Yeah."

I couldn't get him to say more. My father had always told me that the lynch mob came from Bucktown, a Marion neighborhood where the Kentucky "hillbillies" lived. Edwards seemed to be agreeing with that assessment. "Mary Ball lived in Bucktown," he pointed out. The neighborhood around 18th and Meridian was nowhere near Bucktown, but back in 1930 it had enough so-called hillbillies in residence to be known as Little Kentucky.

I felt sure that the old mayor knew more than he was saying. He confirmed the story about the chief of police hanging Deeter's bloody shirt out a window at the police station—a fact many in Marion had denied over the years. Not only had it happened, said Edwards, but he suspended the police chief for doing it. (I could not corroborate this. If Edwards did suspend him, the local papers did not cover it.) As for his own story, the former Boy Mayor could not be moved. He told me what he had always told everyone: he left town the afternoon of August 7, 1930, with no knowledge that a lynching had already been planned.

So he was holding back. I still left feeling encouraged, even elated. I'd seen both Fansler and Edwards my first day. Now I had a new impression of what might be doable in Marion, and this only solidified over the rest of my week there. Puzzle pieces were scattered on the ground, and no one had ever bothered to pick them up, much less put them together. This I could do.

TOM WISE HAD ALWAYS tried to work through the system. But as a black man on the police force, and as an active member of the Democratic Party in a basically Republican town, he faced an uphill battle. He'd actually been assistant police chief from 1988 to 1991, certainly one of the highlights of his career. Democratic mayor Robert Mitchell had also appointed a black chief—Marion's first—a man named Amos Randle. But Wise remembered this era of "the two chiefs," as he called it, with more than a little bitterness.

He would come to work some mornings and find what he called "Klan literature" pushed under his office door. He showed me these papers. He'd saved them all. One, for example, was a crude cartoon of a bus following an arrow from Marion to Africa. The bus had been labeled "Niggerville, Ind." Three figures in the windows were identified as Tom Wise, Amos Randle, and "Massa Mitchell." An inscription read: "With any luck at all, the accelerator will stick, the brakes will fail. We're taking the niggers back; the African trail; back where they belong: Feed the animals a diet of watermelon, carp, and rice. Back where they belong, wouldn't it be nice."

I pointed out that nothing identified this as "Klan."

"Same mentality," Wise explained. This ugliness had originated within the police department, and if Wise suspected who'd done it, he wasn't naming names.

As he saw it, the whole 1991 election was about getting rid of "the black chiefs." Republican Ron Mowery won in November of that year, but Randle and Wise retained their titles till January. One night in December, a friend of Wise's heard an officer on the police radio singing, "I'm Dreaming of a White Police Chief." Standard procedure within the department was to tape everything going out over police radio, but the tape for that night went missing. "They just couldn't wait till the first of the year."

For Wise, the police work had always been political. He'd joined the force in 1970, at the height of civil rights unrest in Marion, taking a big pay cut to do so.

Before that he had worked at the RCA plant, beginning in 1956 when he was still a senior in high school. His building trades teacher had tried to get him an apprenticeship as a steamfitter or electrician, but RCA didn't give apprenticeships in skilled trades to blacks. "Growing up, I guess you learn to live with it," said Wise. He took a production job instead, working full time on the night shift, getting off at seven A.M. and going to school at eight. (A tornado had torn up the high school that year so everyone was going to class half a day at the junior high.) Over the next fourteen years at RCA, he did get promoted, finally rising "about as high as a black could go there at the time." Machine attendant. Semiskilled. Wise remembered that he tested for that job and scored well, but management still wanted to put a white kid in the position. His white coworkers finally "raised sand" with personnel, and Wise was hired. Along with the white kid.

I guess you learn to live with it. He remembered being bused the thirty miles to Anderson to swim. Until 1954 blacks were not allowed in the pool at Marion's Matter Park. The time allotted to kids from Marion at Anderson's Carver Center was Monday morning. A black policeman from Marion, Don Hawkins, would ride down with two busloads of black kids and give swimming lessons. Wise also mentioned that during junior high he joined a basketball league at the Marion Y, and after the game the white kids would go swimming there, but the blacks weren't allowed.

"You didn't let it bother you," said Wise, who sounded like it was still eating at him after forty years.

When racial unrest prompted the city to hire fifteen new policemen in 1970, Wise was one of the two African Americans. He still had vivid memories of the night his fellow cops shot up a pool hall in South Marion, after someone reported that black militants were in there making Molotov cocktails. A neighbor who'd been through firefights in Korea told him it sounded just like the war. Wise had been ordered to the rear, to guard against any approach. "Then they shot off the lock, and I was expecting to see the bodies of friends." But the pool hall was empty. He remembered this as one of the longest nights of his life.

In 1975 or 1976 he made detective. On one case involving the Klan, he worked with an agent from Alcohol, Tobacco and Firearms. There'd been an explosion during a factory strike in Upland, a small town east of Gas City. Wise had information on a certain Klansman with dynamite and automatic weapons. "He lived in a trailer. I remember he said he didn't belong to the Klan anymore. He'd gone south and brought back the dynamite but got rid of it." The man's weapons turned out to be legal. They asked if he still had his robe. He got it out and showed it to them.

Once an ex-Kluxer took Wise to a little cement block building the klavern owned, near one of Grant County's all-white towns. The ex-member had a key, and they intended to have a look inside, only to find that the lock had been changed. Wise couldn't remember where the building was when I asked for directions. He hadn't been there in decades.

But he was rather fascinated by the Klan. He said he wished he could get a robe. For a souvenir.

Wise was a collector, as was his wife. They enjoyed antique shows and auctions. (One of the flyers slipped under his door had mocked him for going to rummage sales.) Among other things, he collected old oil lamps, cut glass, toby cups, and furniture he'd strip and refinish.

His house was very orderly but packed with these items. He pointed to a beautiful old leaded lampshade under a cabinet. That was how he started. His mother had been a domestic, and the people she worked for would give her things they no longer wanted. When she died in 1968, Wise and his sister had a rummage sale, everything priced at the nickel, dime, and dollar level. "This one white guy picked out all the good stuff and offered us thirty-five dollars." Wise thought it a good deal, until someone else came along and pointed out that the leaded lampshade alone was probably worth over a hundred dollars. "That's when I started reading up and going to antique shows."

Another thing he collected was racist kitsch—fat mammies, bug-eyed watermelon eaters, vases painted with slavery scenes, black dolls whose caricatured features were clear signs of the maker's racial pathology. This particular collection seemed akin to Wise's detective work, as if he'd set out to assemble the evidence.

ONE NIGHT I WENT OUT to a certain pizza parlor to see if I could really buy one of the infamous lynching photos. My quest ended anticlimactically as I entered the pizza joint to find an Asian couple behind the counter. Startled, I said something like "Are you new here?" They'd taken over five years ago—yesterday in Marion years. Later, when I told Tom Wise about this, he laughed, "Oh, that place." He'd heard it was once run by Klan people.

But how much of a Klan still existed in Grant County? Tom said he'd let me Xerox the KKK file he kept in his desk at the police station, then discovered that the file was missing, apparently stolen. Given what he had been through in the early 1990s, Tom took this apparent inside job in stride. I found it chilling. But I had arrived in Marion thinking there might be lots of Kluxer activity thereabouts, so I wasn't surprised. It would take me years to assess the truth of this, to realize that Grant County was *not* a Klan hotbed anymore.

What Tom did loan me was an out-of-print book on the notorious Indiana Grand Dragon of the 1920s Klan, D. C. Stephenson, and included in this book was a list of Indiana Ku Klux Klan officials for 1924–25. According-ing to this list, the Exalted Cyclops for Grant County (and Great Titan for its seven-county "province") was Alfred Hogston of Marion. Lesser officers were also listed, while in its assessment of local officials, the list classified both the judge of superior court and the local sheriff as "O.K."

I went back to the nursing home to see Jack Edwards. He was up in his wheelchair looking perky in a striped bow tie, striped shirt, and letter sweater. He'd been watching the O.J. Simpson trial every day and told me he thought O.J. was innocent. "I'm for him, but they're making a three-ring circus out of it."

I asked him if Alfred Hogston had run the Marion Klan back in the 1920s. "Yes," said the old mayor, "and everyone knew it." Hogston had been Jack's lawyer. He'd also been a state senator, a state fire marshal, a Mason, a Lion, and an Elk. Edwards added that Ruth Cartwright, editor and publisher of the local right-wing weekly, now had all of Hogston's papers. She and the late Cyclops/Titan had once been political cronies.

The old mayor did not recognize the other names I read him from the list of old Klan officials, but he gave me the name of another prominent lawyer involved—Dave Bell. He said the KKK used to meet downtown on Washington Street in their 1920s heyday. Then he began describing Marion's Klan parades, held once a month on Saturday nights from 1922 till 1925. He'd witnessed many of these marches. They'd start with a bugle call, kicking off from Third and Adams—which, I realized, was the corner where the lynching occurred. Jack described the exact route they would take around the courthouse and named the bugler, Bill McDonald from Gas City. Some of the robed Kluxers rode horses. Maybe a thousand would parade, and many more came to watch. D. C. Stephenson himself sometimes came to march. Then once a week Klan members assembled somewhere outside the city limits, always at a different location, and they'd burn a cross made from a telephone pole. Edwards said that because he was in the musicians' union, he happened to know that their theme song was "Onward Christian Soldiers."

Back at the hotel, I called Ruth Cartwright. She was eighty-five years old and not exactly a native, having arrived from Alabama in 1950. But, she said, the lynching was the first thing she was told about when she got here. "They gave me papers and the court transcript."

"Who gave them to you?" I asked.

"None of your business!" she snapped, suddenly hostile. I remembered Tom Wise telling me that if I called Ruth Cartwright, I would find out what kind of person tried to wield influence in Marion.

"Why in the hell don't you go back to New York?" she screeched at me. "Stop stirring up trouble! Get out of town!"

I learned later that she had called Rex Fansler to ask him if I was black.

I WASN'T EXACTLY SOLVING mysteries at this point. But if nothing else, maybe I could find my great-grandmother Josie's obituary. The library had indexed every nineteenth-century death notice ever published in Grant County, yet there was no trace of the one lost to my childhood curiosity. I did find evidence of Odos Roush, my deadbeat great-grandfather—listed everywhere as "Ode." I traced the peripatetic Ode through city directories, finding him on rural routes, at Marion addresses, and in Jonesboro, ten miles south. What was that life about? It seemed unrecoverable.

I also tried to check my aunt Ruth's latest theory—that Josie had been engaged to the so-called town catch, who supposedly lived in a big house around 18th and Washington. Aunt Ruth had this thirdhand from her cousin, the daughter of Great Aunt Catherine, but she'd added her own twist: the town catch was our real progenitor, not Ode. He was, perhaps, the man in the locket. According to Aunt Ruth, his home had a yard stretching a city block, and it was still there in the early 1940s. But old maps and directories didn't seem to bear that out.

I drove to my grandparents' house and parked across the street. I had grown up in five different houses in four different towns in three different states—but Grandma and Grandpa's had forever been the same. The new owners had painted it white, yet I could still see it vividly as the dark green house with black stone porch where I sat on the swing with my grandmother. The trees I'd climbed in the backyard were gone, as was my grandmother's grape arbor.

Many times I'd imagined returning here. But now I realized I couldn't knock on the door. For me, it had to remain my grandparents' house. I could still walk through it in my head remembering furniture and textures, the pictures of my father in his World War II uniform, every letter he'd written them saved amid the heat and the bees in the attic, and all of us kids asleep in one room, me in the tilted bed with a lump in its middle. Above me, a drawing: "Carr coat of arms."

My aunt Ruth usually took the bus up from Indianapolis when we visited. Like my grandparents, she never learned to drive. And now it seemed odd, but the memory of that house that came to me was Aunt Ruth, in her room upstairs. The room was just big enough for a bed and a dresser, but she spent a lot of time up there, thinking about how to redecorate. The perfect wallpaper. The right antique. She considered that year's colors and the pictures in *Town and Country*. Sometimes she would walk to the square, wearing a *Vogue* suit. That's what my mother said. A *Vogue* suit. Those were the only patterns Aunt Ruth would buy. She worked in Indianapolis as a private secretary. Grandma could have gotten her into a church college, my parents told me, but Aunt Ruth wanted Sarah Lawrence, "where the rich girls ride their horses." So it was explained. That she never went to college because nothing was good enough for her. She sighed through every dinner and looked mad and smoked cigarettes. She took a cup of coffee back up to her room. Couldn't eat the ham loaf. Couldn't eat dessert. She had it down to two choices up there, where she spent occasional weekends. A muted striped salmon and silver would be tasteful. Or maybe a delicate flower. She would look out her window for hours, cigarette pluming. She could see the grape arbor or the roof of the corner laundry. Then my dad would drive her back to the bus station. "This town with its rednecks and crackers and trash," she fumed. She hated Marion.

NEAR THE END OF my week in Marion I got a Klansman on the phone. Cordial if guarded, Jim Ferguson acted as a sort of media spokesman for the local klavern and had no problem with his name being public. He assured me that the Klan was just a "political support group" and not about hate. Why had he joined? "Family tradition's a lot of it." He had ancestors involved from the beginning, in the 1860s. He held "conservative views." When I asked about August 7, 1930, Ferguson told me that the lynching "wasn't backed by the Klan, wasn't organized by the Klan, wasn't condoned by the Klan."

I despaired of ever getting past the general tone of disingenuousness and evasion, and the fact that—bottom line—the group was about secrecy. Throughout this initial visit I'd been looking for other members with the help of a local playwright named Don Newton, a black man—not the interceder I had expected to have with the Ku Klux Klan. But Newton seemed to know quite a few white people who were related to Klan members. He thought the nearby towns of Elwood, Fairmount, and Greentown were "the major Klan contributors," not Marion. He'd been in Marion "only twenty years," he said, "but there's never been a racial disturbance." Newton made calls for me but couldn't find anyone willing to talk. Not one single Klansman. Not one friend related to a Klansman. Not even off the record. "Some-body stirred something up," he reported. Another researcher had been around a couple of months earlier and spread Klansmen's names. Newton couldn't believe how touchy they were. "No way they'll ever get involved again. There's a complete blanket. Everybody's scared."

Newton had given me one of his screenplays to read. Obsessed like Tom Wise with getting more information about the lynching, Newton had written a script based partly on Cameron's book and partly on the testimony of an old white man he refused to name. One of his Klan-connected white friends put Newton in touch with this old man, who had witnessed the lynching and wanted to talk about it before he died.

Newton had gone all the way to the backwoods of Kentucky to visit him, an old man who was dying of stomach cancer and was still afraid. He would not let Newton tape the conversation. Nor would he take money. Newton had been startled at the old man's poverty. This was a white man who didn't have plumbing.

He told Newton that back in 1930 his father had been a high official in the Klan, living in Greentown, about twenty miles from Marion. The old man thought the lynching had been planned at the highest levels of govern-ment and that the Klan was deeply involved. Someone high up in the state KKK had arrived in Marion before Deeter was even dead. There was a white reporter on one of the Marion papers who had actually tried to stop the lynching. The reporter had gone to Mrs. Flossie Bailey of the NAACP and warned her that the lynching was imminent. Later the KKK burned a cross on the reporter's lawn. I've never been able to confirm any of this.

The dying man had been eighteen in 1930, and he'd been standing forty or fifty feet from Cameron when they brought him to the hanging tree. In Cameron's story, of course, a woman's voice called out from heaven com-manding the mob to stop and everything froze. As the old white man re-membered it, a mighty wind began to blow, and the mob that had been so frenzied suddenly fell back to form a tunnel so that Cameron could walk away. I didn't know what to make of this deathbed confession with its parting-of-the-Red-Sea imagery.

Newton described it to me one afternoon in an unadorned and down-scale fast-food stand. He was voicing the frustration, as Wise had, that some-where out there people knew the solutions to these mysteries. "The truth is what they're afraid of," Newton concluded. He also felt that there was a limit to what he could ever uncover himself, since he was black. Or as he put it, "Someone from the white race will have to tell you."

▲ ▲ ▲

INTRIGUED BY THE STORY of the hero reporter, I made one last stop before leaving town. Sarah Weaver Pate, known to most people as Sadie, had been working, in 1930, for Marion's black physician, Dr. W. T. Bailey, husband of NAACP president Flossie Bailey, and an activist in his own right.

Now Sadie was ninety years old, and as I walked through the door of her little white frame house, she announced, "I'm one of the Weaver girls."

Weaver, an all-black farming community just south of Marion, had been named for Sadie's father, John Henry Weaver, near the end of the nineteenth century. The settlement had actually been there since before the Civil War, and the Weavers were one of the oldest black families in Grant County. Sadie wanted me to look at her family album. She didn't want to talk about the lynching, though she kept saying, "August seventh, 1930. I'll never forget that day." Most of the black people in town had stayed awake the whole night, she said. They all thought they were going to die. Sadie had seen the bodies hanging. She and Dr. Bailey went down to his office the next morning with a police escort, and they were still there on the tree. She said they were hanging there for days. I'm sure it must have seemed that way.

August seventh, 1930. I'll never forget that day. Sadie Pate remembered how Mrs. Bailey had appealed to the sheriff, and he swore a mob would have to get 'em over his dead body. I asked Sadie how Mrs. Bailey had known there'd be a lynching. Had she been told by . . . a white reporter?

"Oh, there were flyers," Sadie said. *Flyers.*

She remembered Jack Edwards coming by to tell Mrs. Bailey how sorry he was. Then they'd buried Shipp and Smith out at Weaver. To this day the graves have not been marked.

I asked her if she had ever heard of Alfred Hogston. "Yes," she brightened. "He was a friend."

This so startled me that I decided not to tell her that her "friend" had run Grant County's Ku Klux Klan back in the 1920s. Eventually I would learn that, of course, she knew this. But she liked discussing the Klan even less than the lynching. She and Hogston had met in local Republican circles. (Many of the old Weaver families joined the party of Lincoln and just never changed.) The complexities and contradictions of Jim Crow time are hard to parse today, but I was getting a taste here—the most vicious racism interlarded with presumptions of "friendship." Behind the civility lay a coercion that was utterly brutal: *Stay in your place. Or else.* And occasionally the mask came off: the lynching. Sadie asked me, at one point, did I think a lynching could happen today?

During much of this interview I was so mesmerized I forgot to take notes. I realized that hers was the first emotional account of the lynching I'd heard from anyone in Marion. I told this woman, who thought the head of the Ku Klux Klan was her friend, that my grandfather had been in the Klan, too, and I nearly burst into tears for the first time since coming into town. My impromptu confession seemed to startle her, but she didn't address it. She took pains to emphasize that she had many white friends, and she had raised many white children, and they were devoted to her. She laid their pictures out on the table for me to see. She wished I had time to go to Weaver with her. I left her house feeling devastated. What could ever set this right? My little confessions—what did they matter? How could they change the fact that, more than sixty years after the lynching, this old woman was still afraid of the Ku Klux Klan?

On the way out of town I drove to the cemetery where my grandparents were buried. I didn't have much time, but I still remembered the curve in the gravel road where we buried them, and I parked where I thought it was. They weren't there. I was lost. The day was drizzly and the ground squishy, covered with slick leaves. I walked over strangers' graves, worried I might sink in where the ground had settled, crying the tears that had started to come at Sadie Pate's house. More than anything I wished I could speak to my grandparents, so I said the words "I'm here. I'm looking for you." Then I got back into the car.

FOUR

THINGS I DIDN'T LEARN
IN SCHOOL

The Marion lynching had a context and a history of which I was only dimly aware. Why didn't I know more? One of the few term papers I even remember writing was my eighth-grade analysis of the Battle of Gettysburg. But once the Civil War concludes, the American history in my head goes blank for several decades. The era of Reconstruction and its demise: a blank.

I had to learn the unspeakable on my own.

First, I began researching the Hooded Order and its various incarnations. The Klan filled every role needed to promote white supremacy—sometimes its cheerleader, sometimes its terrorist. The group morphed with the times. In both the 1860s and the 1960s the KKK declared war on African American progress as represented by Reconstruction and the civil rights movement. The 1920s Klan was more of a fraternal organization, since white supremacy needed less enforcement at that point. Between these three periods of major Ku Klux activity, the group lay dormant like a virus. It does not seem to really die.

The first Klan lasted just six bloody years, 1866 to 1872. Founded in Pulaski, Tennessee, by six Confederate veterans, it was purely a southern beast, spreading terror among newly freed slaves and their white allies in the former Confederacy. Klan atrocities were so numerous as to be hard even to catalog, but the message was always unmistakable: African Americans were to be kept down by any means necessary. Favorite targets included those newly freed people who sought political power, wanted an education, or had somehow managed to prosper. Add to that whites who'd opposed the Confederacy or anyone who voted Republican (the party of abolition; many Democrats had supported slavery). This first Klan included legislators, newspaper editors, sheriffs, and other prominent citizens. Its first national leader, or Grand Wizard, was Nathan Bedford Forrest, a former Confederate general who had once been a wealthy slave trader. State leaders, or Grand Dragons, included other rebel generals.

In the Hooded Order the Confederacy fought on. Paging through *White Terror,* the first scholarly study of the Reconstruction Klan (published in 1971), I found fresh outrage on nearly every page: blacks shot as they worked in their fields, blacks mutilated or lynched, freedmen driven from their homes and crops so white farmers could reap the harvests, Republican newspaper offices sacked and destroyed, teachers at black schools beaten or killed, black schools and churches burned, black homes burned, a black man whipped two hundred lashes for voting Republican, and so on and on. Whipping with switches was a favorite Klan punishment, since it harked back to slavery. As for how many the Kluxers killed, no one can give a precise measure of the carnage, but estimates of the dead go as high as twenty thousand.

The mayhem reached such a pitch that the federal government finally had to step in. The so-called Ku Klux Klan Act of 1871 empowered Washington to declare martial law if necessary. President Ulysses S. Grant went so far as to suspend habeas corpus in a particularly hard-hit section of South Carolina, where hundreds of Klansmen were arrested. Some even went to prison. By 1872 the Klan had disintegrated, but as Philip Dray points out in his history of lynching, *At the Hands of Persons Unknown,* the organization had accomplished many of its goals by then: "It had initiated the process of making full black participation in politics and in the mainstream of Southern life unattainable," Dray writes, "and had established that intimidation and terror could be used to accomplish this end."

The U.S. Supreme Court then snuffed out what remained of "full black participation," gutting the Fourteenth and Fifteenth Amendments passed during Reconstruction. Here things get a little complicated, since the Court's reasoning constantly defies all logic. For example, the Fourteenth Amendment prohibits any state law from infringing on such rights as due process and equal protection. So the Court decided in 1873 that civil rights came from state citizenship while the Fourteenth Amendment applied only to one's federal citizenship—whatever that meant. Next the Court went after the 1875 civil rights law that prohibited segregation, declaring it unconstitutional because, said the justices, the Fourteenth Amendment prohibited states but not citizens from discriminating against blacks. Then in 1896 their *Plessy v. Ferguson* decision turned "equal protection" into "separate but equal," thus legalizing segregation. Next the Court began picking at the language of the Fifteenth Amendment, which promised men the right to vote, regardless of "race, color, or previous condition of servitude." According to the Court, this prohibited disenfranchisement on racial grounds but did not confer a right to vote. By the 1890s southern states had figured out how to work with that loophole, imposing suffrage qualifications like literacy tests or the ability to interpret a legal document. White southerners did not have to take these tests, since a "grandfather clause" gave the ballot to any man whose ancestors had voted before 1866.

Summarizing the victory for southern whites, the notorious demagogue Ben Tillman, Democratic governor of South Carolina in the 1890s and later a U.S. senator, bragged (in the *Congressional Record*): "We took the government away. We stuffed ballot boxes. We shot them. We are not ashamed of it."

So the first Klan faded away, but plenty of white people were willing to carry on its work without benefit of hood. During this era, as a first generation of African Americans reached adulthood outside the institution of slavery, lynching became an epidemic across the South.

During the eighteenth century lynching wasn't necessarily lethal; nor had it been directed at blacks. (Slaves were worth money, after all.) The namesake was one Charles Lynch, a Virginia justice of the peace who found himself some two hundred miles from the nearest trial court during the Revolutionary War. Lynch passed judgment on local horse thieves and Tories, sentencing the guilty to a whipping or incarceration. When the Tories sued after the war, the Virginia legislature decided that "Lynch's Law" had been acceptable given the circumstances.

A hundred years later, "lynching" had come to mean a summary execution carried out by a mob. The Tuskegee Institute began to keep records of these deaths in 1882, the same year the *Chicago Tribune* added lynching to its yearly summary of crimes. The numbers from both sources are problematic, almost certainly underreported. For the year 1892, for example, the

Tuskegee archive cites 162 lynchings of blacks, while the *Chicago Tribune* put the number at 241. What Tuskegee collected was news coverage, which tended to focus on "spectacle lynchings"—those hangings or burnings carried out publicly in a carnival atmosphere before throngs of men, women, and children.

"Frontier justice" is an American tradition, and white lynching victims outnumbered blacks until 1886. But spectacle lynchings went beyond any real interest in revenge, much less justice, and they happened only to African Americans. These were symbolic killings, rituals meant to drive home the point that black bodies still belonged to white people. That's why these executions were done so publicly. That's why the victims were often killed many times over, their bodies reduced to pulp or cut up for souvenirs. That's why crowds of gloating whites posed for pictures with the corpses, never bothering to conceal their identities. Indeed, the "best citizens" were at it again. "I led the mob which lynched Nelse Patton, and I am proud of it," declared former U.S. senator from Mississippi William Van Amberg Sullivan in 1908. (And he was no anomaly.) Spectacle lynchings did not end until the mid-1930s. Marion's can be numbered among the few to occur outside the South.

One of the most notorious was the gruesome public burning in 1899 of Sam Hose, a twenty-one-year-old black man charged with killing the Georgia planter who employed him and raping the planter's wife. Hose was on the run for a few days, but as a headline in the *Atlanta Constitution* promised, DETERMINED MOB AFTER HOSE; HE WILL BE LYNCHED IF CAUGHT. Word of his capture reached Atlanta on a Sunday morning, setting off a stampede from the city's white churches to the railroad station, where a special excursion train waited. People quickly filled six cars, and police had to pry them from the sides. Another train of ten cars took the overflow, and they raced south to the town of Newnan. There hundreds were already watching as mobsters tortured Hose for nearly half an hour, cutting off each finger, his ears, and his genitals, then skinning his face. They doused him in oil and began to burn him alive. Despite his injuries, Hose pulled so hard at the chain binding him to a tree that he burst a blood vessel in his neck. By the time the four thousand Atlantans on the trains arrived, however, he was dead, and they began clamoring for souvenirs. So before the body cooled, trophy hunters removed Hose's heart and liver and cut them into small pieces. The tree where he died was chopped up, along with the chain that had held him. Even his ashes were carried off in handkerchiefs. An investigator determined later that Hose and his employer had argued, that the white man had drawn a gun, and that Hose had thrown an ax, killing him. Arguably it was self-defense, and Hose probably did not assault the wife.

W.E.B. DuBois remarked that the entire direction of his life changed the day he set out to carry a letter to the *Atlanta Constitution* office, protesting the lynching promised in the headline, and learned that Sam Hose's knuckles were already on display in a nearby store window. He returned home immediately and, as he put it, "began to turn aside from my work." DuBois was then a highly regarded social scientist, teaching at Atlanta University. He had always assumed that most white people would oppose racial injustice if they were just better informed. But in Hose's death he saw the pathology. The truth would not set them free. DuBois left academia to become director of publicity and research for the newly formed NAACP in 1910, editor of its magazine, *The Crisis,* and in the words of his biographer, David Levering Lewis, "civil rights role model to an entire race."

According to the Tuskegee archives, 3,417 blacks and 1,291 whites were lynched during the sixty-two years beginning in 1882. But, when the NAACP released its report *Thirty Years of Lynching in the United States, 1889–1918,* it had found 2,522 black and 702 white victims for less than half that time. The peak year for mob violence was 1892, with 155 black and 71 white victims, according to the NAACP list. Some of these people had been charged with serious crimes, but blacks could be lynched simply for not showing enough humility around white people. The crusading African American journalist Ida B. Wells-Barnett included case studies in one of her antilynching pamphlets, *A Red Record* (1895), like "Lynched Because They Were Saucy," "Burned Alive for Adultery," and "Hanged for Stealing Hogs."

Of course, the justification used most often by white people, made even by southern lawmakers on the floor of Congress, was that lynching was necessary to protect white women from black men. "The anxiety over interracial sex was so great," writes Dray, "it fostered the related notion that sex with white women was the real objective behind all black aspiration, that money, education, accomplishment of any kind were for black men mere stepping-stones en route to the bedroom and the ultimate nirvana of intimacy with white women. This, of course, was an expression of the whites' deeper concern about losing control of the status quo and of seeing their own position in society diminish if blacks were allowed to join the middle class; lynch mobs that sought to punish such strivers were often spurred into action by the idea that successful blacks represented just as keen a threat to Southern life as the black rapist."

Wells-Barnett raised the first lone voice of protest from her small Memphis newspaper, the *Free Speech,* after three such strivers of her acquaintance were lynched in March 1892. Owners of the successful People's Grocery, they got embroiled in a dispute with some white grocers. It escalated into a shooting match when whites tried to raid the store one night and three of them were injured. (All recovered.) The blacks went to jail. A couple of nights later a white mob broke into the lockup, took the three grocers outside the city limits, and shot them at point-blank range. Wells-Barnett would spend the rest of her life challenging the conventional wisdom that lynching was all about protecting white womanhood. She even dared to assert that many sexual liaisons between black men and white women were consensual. She had seen, after all, the real reason the three grocers were lynched: "to get rid of Negroes who were acquiring wealth and property and thus keep the race terrorized."

The NAACP's antilynching campaign began with the organization's inception in 1910. For decades the group pressured Congress for federal legislation against this crime, without success, though it was able to provoke a national debate on the subject. In 1929 Walter White, an NAACP officer who would eventually investigate some forty-one lynchings including the one in Marion, worried in his book, *Rope and Faggot,* that people had simply grown inured to the horror: "an uncomfortably large percentage of American citizens can read in their newspapers of the slow roasting alive of a human being in Mississippi and turn, promptly and with little thought, to the comic strip or sporting page. Thus has lynching become an almost integral part of our national folkways."

An appendix to White's book provides a state-by-state breakdown of lynching victims. For Indiana, he lists forty-one whites and eleven blacks between 1882 and 1903. From then until 1929, when his book was published, there were none.

The Hoosier State had a long history of vigilantism, however, that seemed to intensify after the Civil War. In the last six months of 1868, for example, mobs strung up thirteen men, all of them white. But the number of black victims in the state was proportionately greater, since they constituted a mere two percent of the population at the end of the nineteenth century. According to *The Negro in Indiana Before 1900,* at least twenty African Americans were lynched between 1865 and 1903.

Examples cited in *The Negro in Indiana* are every bit as sadistic, preventable, and racially motivated as the events of August 7, 1930. But the book also notes one town in Indiana where the lynching of a black man was foiled by the local sheriff in 1885. That town was Marion.

Some of the details of this case read like an eerie foreshadowing of the 1930 tragedy. A black man named Frank Wallace, the accused, had already done time in prison for rape, and according to the *Marion Chronicle,* "he was feared by every white woman in town." On a Saturday night in July 1885 he allegedly followed three white women home from the square. They said he'd chased them and thrown a stone. One of them "fell unconscious" at the gate of her house, apparently from fright, and didn't wake up until the next afternoon. Wallace was arrested on Sunday, charged with "assault and battery with intent to commit rape." He denied approaching the women.

By Monday a lynching was in the works. "Whispered conversations were in progress all through the evening by knots of men gathered in dozens of places around the public square." At eleven-thirty P.M. the mob marched on the jail led by two men carrying sledgehammers. This was an older jail, and they broke the door down with ease, but then someone in the mob began shooting. A ricocheting bullet hit a mobster in the head and killed him, which "broke up the lynching party for the evening."

But just for the evening. On Tuesday "the town about the public square wore a holiday appearance" as people began flocking in from the surrounding towns and countryside. By nightfall several thousand men and boys had gathered around the jail. The *Chronicle* reporter waited with the lynch mob organizing itself in a grove east of Branson Street. The reporter watched someone take a plaited rope from a flour sack and give directions on how to adjust it around a neck. "It was settled that the hanging should take place at the north portico of the courthouse, and with hearts throbbing with a patriotic devotion to duty, the vigilance committee marched forward." By the time the mob reached the jail, however, their leader had vanished. Grant County sheriff Orange Holman then came outside and told them he intended to protect the prisoners, and they'd better go home. They did. Two months later the accused Frank Wallace was found "guilty of a trivial assault" and fined ten dollars.

A year and a half after the foiled lynching, in January 1887, Grant County formed a chapter of Horse Thief Detectives. These were citizen cops—vigilantes, basically, but legal—authorized by the Indiana legislature back in 1852 to help local sheriffs. They could even make arrests. Grant County's founding members included John Ratliff, a Quaker legislator and former abolitionist, and other men distinguished enough to now have streets and towns named after them.

By the late nineteenth century, with mob justice increasingly in the news all over the country, Indiana spawned yet another group of regulators, the White Caps. These self-appointed moral arbiters wore masks and took it upon themselves to flog drunks, wife beaters, and other sinners. I found news stories that mentioned them, but no evidence that there was a single ongoing group in Grant County.

Headlines like LYNCH HIM! CRIED A FRENZIED MOTHER were usually about mobs that formed around some individual outrage. That article, from 1903, concerned a music teacher in a small town just west of Marion who allegedly raped a thirteen-year-old girl. Other stories I discovered at random: a mob hunts a man who got a fifteen-year-old pregnant (1889); a gang whips two women for gossiping (1889); a mob in Gas City tries to lynch "a wretched tramp" after he rapes a farm woman (1890); a mob in Van Buren threatens to lynch a lawyer who's defrauded a "half-wit" out of seventy-six dollars (1902); a young man is nearly hanged after a neighborhood brawl. None of these incidents ended with an actual hanging, and only the last one involved black people. All the rest of it was white-on-white violence.

IT SEEMS AMAZING THAT the Klan could reemerge less than fifty years after Reconstruction, stronger than ever and with its biggest support in the North. Of course, by then the history of Reconstruction had been rewritten as melodrama, the terrible denouement to the story of the "Lost Cause," the Confederacy. This process began even as Congress debated the Ku Klux Klan Act in 1871. Southern Democrats downplayed Klan violence, insisting that it had all been exaggerated. They came up with their own minority report blaming evil carpetbaggers and "the insolence of the negroes" for forcing southerners to turn to the Klan in "hopeless despair." This minority report, says historian Wyn Craig Wade, "became the key document upon which histories of the Klan would be based for the next sixty years."

As the twentieth century began, the image of the Klan as savior of white civilization was popularized by Thomas Dixon in best-selling novels like *The Clansman: An Historical Romance of the Ku Klux Klan,* published in 1905. *The Clansman* was so successful that Dixon adapted it for the stage, toured it around the country, and longed to make it into a film. That dream came true when he met D. W. Griffith, the son of a Confederate officer, and a director who wanted to make something both epic and innovative. Griffith's version of *The Clansman* pioneered all sorts of technical novelties that would soon become standard, from close-ups to chase scenes. He also changed the name of Dixon's tale to what he thought better suited its scope and grandeur: *The Birth of a Nation.*

"More people saw *The Birth of a Nation* than had seen any previous movie in history," wrote film critic J. Hoberman in 1993, "and it's possible that the record still holds. It grossed more than $60 million during its first run—a figure . . . roughly equivalent to a billion 1993 dollars." In compari- son, *Titanic* made a bit less than $601 million domestically in its 1997 run.

Released in 1915, *The Birth of a Nation* is not just blatantly racist; it is propaganda for everything the South did to keep black people down, in- cluding lynching. It tells of a white northern family (the Stonemans) and a white southern family (the Camerons), friends before the Civil War, who come together afterward to protect their white women from black men. Here all evil flows from the radical idea that blacks should be equal with whites. The drama really begins to roll when a Reconstruction legislature, taken over by crude freedmen (dressed like a minstrel troupe), gleefully passes a law allowing interracial marriage. Young Cameron, an ex–Confederate colonel, sulks down at the river, "in agony of soul over the degradation and ruin of his people." Then, observing how some black children run from white children hidden under a sheet, he is inspired to found the Ku Klux Klan. Meanwhile a black Union soldier, Gus, is stalking the Cameron daugh- ter—to propose marriage. She runs, and he chases her, foaming at the mouth. When she can't escape him—"having learned the stern lesson of honor"—she throws herself off a cliff. Soon a heroic KKK captures Gus and lynches him. Meanwhile, an evil mulatto prepares to force marriage on the daughter from the northern family. She faints. The Klan saves her, then rides to the rescue at a cabin where the remaining members of both northern and southern white families face off a horde of marauding black men. As one of the caption cards puts it: "The former enemies of North and South are united again in common defence of their Aryan birthright."

With the film a huge hit, "Ku Klux fever" gripped the nation. People bought Ku Klux hats and aprons and attended Ku Klux parties. This was not just a southern phenomenon. Gallant Klansmen on horseback appeared on a huge Times Square billboard advertising the film. Dray reports that "where no movie theater existed, special excursion trains were arranged to bring country people en masse into urban areas to take part in this national rite of passage." The film's version of Reconstruction corroborated what was then available in American history books. President Woodrow Wilson screened it in the White House and told Griffith: "It is like writing history with lightning, and my only regret is that it is all so terribly true."

THAT YEAR, 1915, A DEFROCKED Methodist circuit rider named William Joseph Simmons revived the KKK in Atlanta, greatly aided by the *Birth of a Nation* craze and by the atmosphere of excited approval that followed the lynching of "filthy perverted Jew" Leo Frank.

Frank had received a life sentence for the rape and murder of fourteen-year-old Mary Phagan, after her body was discovered in the basement of the Atlanta pencil factory he managed. (Frank's innocence was finally established in 1982.) The lynchers, the self-described Knights of Mary Phagan, abducted Frank from a prison farm in August 1915 and drove him to Marietta, planning to kill him on Phagan's grave. With daybreak fast approaching, however, they stopped at the edge of town and hanged him. Two months later they commemorated the moment by burning a cross on Stone Mountain, near Atlanta. It inspired Simmons to initiate his KKK charter members on Stone Mountain a month later, with the first Klan cross-burning. When *The Birth of a Nation* finally premiered in Atlanta the following week, real Klansmen were parading in front of the theater in full regalia.

Although that first klavern included a few of the Knights of Mary Phagan and a couple of Reconstruction Klansmen, the Invisible Empire of the 1920s was not the terrorist organization it had been after the Civil War. Thanks to Jim Crow, black disenfranchisement, and lynchings carried out by the finest citizens, it didn't have to be. White supremacy was in fine shape. Simmons didn't seem to have much of an idea about what "The World's Greatest Secret, Social, Patriotic, Fraternal, Beneficiary Order" actually *would* do. He was obsessed with ritual and hierarchy as the Reconstruction Klan had never been, inventing, for example, preposterous officer names that began with *kl*, like *klokard, kleagle,* and *klexter.* But Simmons didn't have the skill to capitalize on the Klan's potential, enrolling just a few thousand members.

Simmons's Klan remained a regional force until 1920, when he hired two promoters who worked for 80 percent of the membership fees. They decided they would have to broaden the appeal beyond white supremacy, which was just too ordinary. In the wake of the Great War, economic insecurity, and waves of new immigrants, they settled on the catchphrase "one hundred percent Americanism." Now the Invisible Empire spread into northern states, selling itself as a morality crusade. Disguised as a defender of traditional values, the Klan claimed that Jews, blacks, and Catholics were purveyors of vice and social decay.

In Indiana the KKK allied itself with the Anti-Saloon League and made a concerted effort to recruit Protestant ministers. Calling cards distributed by Indiana's Klan recruiters read: "Remember, every criminal, every gambler, every thug, every libertine, every girl ruiner, every home wrecker, every wife beater, every dope peddler, every moonshiner, every crooked politician, every pagan papist, every shyster lawyer, every K of C [Knights of Columbus], every white slaver, every brothel madame, every Rome-controlled newspaper, every blackspider—is fighting the KKK. Think it over. Which side are you on?"

THERE WAS ONE OTHER THING I began to search for after meeting James Cameron: books by white people about the emotional impact of racism on their lives. I was looking for a guide.

The one I gravitated to was Lillian Smith, a white southerner who died in 1966. She said she wrote her classic, *Killers of the Dream,* "to find out what life in a segregated culture had done to me, one person." Published in 1949, it remains fresh, unfortunately, as a study of racism. After all, when segregation ended, white people did not exactly gather in front of their newly integrated facilities to say, "Welcome." There were always white renegades and radicals who supported equality. Some even died for it. But in general, white people never met black people halfway.

Smith always said it was the apathy of white people that most disturbed her. Acting as if racism had no impact on our lives. Doing no wrong, but also doing no right. As she saw it, racism created pain for everyone, but white people learned to numb themselves to it. She concluded that in a racist society, a white person cannot feel whole.

Killers of the Dream illustrated what it would mean for me to truly witness, to truly own the history of my family and my Marion, and to take in the impact racism had had. If I encountered something uncomfortable, I would have to stay with the discomfort. No guilt-tripping. No distancing. No escape. I was reminded of something my friend Robbie once said to me: "If I can go through the pain, you can go through the pain."

One other thing I had to remember. As Lillian Smith put it, begin your search for answers with sympathy for those who have not found them.

FIVE

MARION'S HOODED ORDER

From the notebook where I wrote the family stories down decades ago: "Klan. Local chapter. You could not be weak."

I suppose it's something my father said. Some reference to that enigma, my grandfather, I so wished to understand.

For years I ran an image of him through my mind, a little tape loop, a fiction: My grandpa is walking through a hot field, insects on his white Sunday shirt. He is looking for the little house where he was born. Already he's bent and shuffling. Long grasses sway for him. Birds hover and dicker. And I'm there, a girl again. I'm helping him.

It wasn't hard for me to see my grandpa as a tragic figure, but I didn't understand the nature of his tragedy. There was a fury in him he never showed the grandkids. I heard the stories with some astonishment: When the alarm clock didn't work, he stomped it in the backyard; he smashed it into a telephone pole. When my dad got pericarditis as a boy, Grandpa flew into a rage; it was going to cost money. When Aunt Ruth brought friends home from high school to listen to the radio, Grandpa declared, "No more of that music!"—then snapped off the dial. When I heard that one, I ran right upstairs to where my aunt stood smoking at her window. "Aunt Ruth, what music did you listen to in high school?" As if I really learned something when she told me: "The big bands. Glenn Miller. He was really smooth."

In a photo of my grandfather in the prime of this life, he wears a straw boater and double-breasted suit, but he looks grim and stiff-necked. There aren't many pictures of him. In the two from his boyhood, he looks no more cheerful, as if something had already hardened in him. Something hardened around a wound. Even as a child, I could sense this about him. Still, I couldn't excuse him for so disheartening my father.

My young dad used to build large delicate planes from balsa wood and paper and fly them with little motors on the outskirts of Marion, while my grandfather ridiculed him. "Makes more sense to stay on the ground," Grandpa said of my father's interest in airplanes. When he wanted to study aeronautics in college, Grandpa warned him off. "A new field. Might dry up." So my father designed earth-moving equipment his whole working life, though he did learn to fly and got a pilot's license. After my grandfather died, Dad began to build an airplane in our basement. When he finished, he decided he was too old to fly it.

My father used to drive us by the Marion house where he was born, making jokes: "See, kids? Someday they'll search this out. Turn it into a national shrine." Often on our vacations we toured the boyhood homes of great men. But long ago, when my father thought that he too could be great, my grandfather had said to him, "You won't be great. You'll be like me."

Now my Dad shrugs at anything Klan. *He went out. We never knew where he was going.*

In INDIANA THE KLAN HAD its brief golden age, from about 1922 to 1925. The Hoosier State initiated more members than any other. (Ohio ranked second.) Only in Indiana did the Kluxers charter a klavern in every single county. By 1924 Klansmen were literally running the state. They had taken over the Republican Party and elected the governor, a majority of the state legislature, the mayor of Indianapolis, and numerous other mayors, sheriffs, prosecutors, and school boards. At the time most Hoosiers were native-born (95 percent) and white (97 percent), while Jews numbered fewer than 25,000 in a state population of nearly three million.

Many a scholar has tried to explain kluxdom's curious hold on Indiana. They mention the large number of southerners who settled there, the popularity of fraternal organizations, and early in the state's history at least, a belligerent philistinism. It was a "don't-tread-on-me" state, reluctant even to set up a system of tax-supported public schools until after the Civil War. *Hoosier* originally meant an uneducated rube, but the put-down was proudly embraced. "By 1920, the word *Hoosier* implied a practical simplicity that quickly got to the heart of things," writes historian Wyn Craig Wade. "At its worst it implied a narrow-minded arrogance that neither saw nor heard. It was the weakness that the Ku Klux Klan would exploit to the hilt."

In *Citizen Klansmen: The Ku Klux Klan in Indiana, 1921–1928,* the most thorough study to date (published in 1991), historian Leonard J. Moore asserts that Kluxers of that era were most concerned with law-and-order issues like Prohibition enforcement and political corruption. In 1923, probably the peak year for KKK recruitment, Indiana's governor went to federal prison for embezzlement and mail fraud. In 1924 a Klansman replaced him. The organization focused on acquiring that kind of political power, not on vigilantism. There was little violence. Moore's thesis is that the Indiana Klan of the 1920s was a populist movement "that concerned itself primarily not with persecuting ethnic minorities but with promoting the ability of average citizens to influence the workings of society and government." Moore's assessment is more benign than others.

Indiana historian James H. Madison puts it this way: "The Ku Klux Klan was like the League of Women Voters or the Indiana Farm Bureau. It offered a community of membership, a program of action, and a potential to engage in politics outside the structure of the two major parties." But, adds Madison, the KKK's core beliefs were "a narrow and anxious patriotism and religion, often defined by reference to the ideas and peoples meant to be excluded, opposed, and hated."

In *Citizen Klansmen* Moore works with available membership lists to analyze who joined. Average citizens, he concludes. In the town of Terre Haute, for example, where 31 percent of all native white men belonged to the Klan, the officers included two grocers, a physician, a bank teller, an insurance agent, a tinner, a carpenter, a truck driver, a blacksmith, a minister, the owner of a clothing store, a coal miner, and the manager of an auto repair shop. Moore finds these occupations to be "typical of those held by Indiana Klansmen." The organization did not seem to attract either the wealthy or the poor.

Marion showed less enthusiasm for the organization than nearby cities of its size, with 15 percent of native white men signing up. Muncie, Kokomo, and Anderson enrolled 27, 31, and 33 percent respectively. It was hard to imagine a populace so in thrall to the Klan, and I had to keep reminding my-self that this did not happen too long ago—some eighty years, the span of a single life.

The 1920s Klan operated so openly and unabashedly, at least for a few years, that it was relatively easy to get names of members or supporters. Back issues of the Klan's Indianapolis-based newspaper, the *Fiery Cross,* carried many Marion advertisers: downtown restaurants like the Interurban Café and the Washington Café, contractors and service stations, and quite a few grocery stores. None of the names were familiar to me except the man listed as manager at W. L. Farthing Groceries: one M. J. Edwards. Merrill Jack Edwards. The Boy Mayor. It certainly didn't make him a Kluxer, but he must have known many, including, possibly, his boss. He would have been twenty-one at the time of the ad.

There was something so naïve about the Klan culture presented in the *Fiery Cross.* It was almost pathetic—from a distance. The most popular Klux social appeared to be the rabbit supper, and the most commonly run photos were those taken at Klan funerals, the robed and hooded posing around a grave. Display ads offered everything from Klan pocket knives to record albums like "The Jolly Old Klansman" and "Wake Up America and Kluck-Kluck-Kluck."

I don't want to imply that the Klan wasn't secretive at all in the 1920s, that no one wore a hood. The Chicago-based anti-Klan newspaper *Tolerance* so delighted in publishing members' names that in May 1923 the Hooded Order went to federal court seeking an injunction to stop it. Subse-quently *Tolerance* named even more (though only twenty all together from Grant County), often referring to members as "face coverers," "dunce caps," or "Koo Koos."

But joining certainly conferred no stigma. Some local newspapers, in-cluding Marion's, publicized impending Klan rallies and parades as if they were sponsored by the Rotary Club, while city directories often listed KKK chapters under "lodges and churches." Marion's directory for 1923 simply lists it in the alphabetical roster with every other name in town: "Ku Klux Klan, 423½ S. Washington." (That was a block and a half south of the square, above Woolworth's.) One historian notes, "In the Indiana of the 1920s, respectability lay in being a Klan member."

Learning all this was a great relief to me. I could understand my grandfa-ther's need to be part of "an upgoing thing" like the Klan. That was James Cameron's description for it: "an upgoing thing." I believe my grandfather's illegitimate birth remained the bitter core of his identity. And I imagined him joining the Klan for the most painfully human reasons.

But, of course, there was more. For all its "respectability" in the 1920s, the Klan was built on enmity, and it was a place for him to take his rage. My grandfather had a particular hatred for Catholics, though no one in the family knew why. As far as I know, Catholics had no impact on his life. But the 1920s Klan in Indiana identified "Romanists" as their most serious problem.

"Escaped nuns" and former "priests" worked the rallies as Klan recruiters, regaling their audiences with lurid tales of Romanist sadomasochism, kidnapped white Protestant girls turned sexual slaves, and nuns forced to have abortions by the priests who fathered their babies. Many Klan members anticipated the imminent invasion of the pope, who, it was believed, already had a papal palace under construction in Washington, D.C. Catholics were simply not good Americans; the "mackerel snappers" owed their loyalty to "the dago on the Tiber." A couple of Klan researchers cite the story of a KKK leader in Wabash County, just north of Grant County, who announced one day that the pope was coming through on the next train, prompting a thousand people to rush to the station. The mob stopped the train, which had one passenger car, and forced its single passenger to disembark. Eventually he convinced the crowd that he wasn't the pope, just a salesman.

I still recall the worried dinner conversations at my grandparents' house over the possible election of John F. Kennedy—who would most likely be turning the country over to the pope. And I knew that when my father was growing up, my grandfather had warned him never to marry a Catholic. I believe the exact admonition went: "I'd rather you married a nigger than a Catholic."

I also remember the family story about "two New York Jews" who conned both my grandfather and Uncle On into buying worthless stock in a gold refinery in 1915. Here my grandfather's parsimony paid off, because the loss didn't ruin him. Uncle On, however, had mortgaged everything he had and borrowed more. He lost his wholesale grocery business and never recovered financially. That would have embittered my grandfather permanently. Uncle On was as much of a father as he ever had.

Trying to find a logic to my grandfather's Klan membership, I can spell out his bigotries and confess to his narrowness. I can reveal that he was part of the intolerance in the town. But I did not go back to Marion to uncover a monster; nor did I find one. To my relief and dismay, I discovered that my grandfather was the norm, a regular American, respected in his community.

Certain facts about him will never add up. The man my grandfather so revered, Eugene V. Debs, went to prison for sedition in 1918. Debs had opposed both American involvement in World War I and the Espionage Act that put conscientious objectors in jail. He had a message opposite to the Klan's. During his trial Debs made the famous statement: "Your Honor, years ago I recognized my kinship with all living things and I made up my mind that I was not one bit better than the meanest of the earth. . . . I said then, I say now, that while there is a lower class, I am in it; while there is a criminal element, I am of it; while there is a soul in prison, I am not free."

The day before Christmas 1921 President Warren Harding ordered Debs's release from the penitentiary but did not pardon him, and Debs's citizenship was never restored. I wish I could have asked my grandfather how he felt about all of this, but I know he didn't repudiate the man who had been kind to him when he was a boy. As I said, he named my father for Debs—my father born in 1924. By then, my grandfather was already a Klansman.

IN AUGUST 1995, NINE MONTHS after the journey that introduced me to Tom Wise, Jack Edwards, and Sadie Pate, I returned to Marion and rented a furnished studio near Bucktown, thinking I'd be there for six months. I ended up staying a year.

I had set myself the goal of uncovering the truth about August 7, 1930. Who planned it? Who covered it up? How did it unfold? And how could this deed ever be undone? Might as well be ambitious, I thought. Then I wanted to look at the racial conundrum embodied in my own family—my grandfather in the Klan, my grandmother's apparent connection to some tribe. With Grant County as the American microcosm, I would look for all the hidden histories connected to race. I wanted to see the big picture, the context that had allowed the lynching to happen. Certainly that was the mystery behind the mystery.

As a journalist, I now had the luxury of turning this inquiry into my job, but I felt overwhelmed by my task and my sense of transgression. I began with great guilt. I didn't immediately tell my parents what I was doing, and though they seldom visited the town anymore, I kept imagining that I saw them—driving by on the square or walking out the front door of my building.

During one of those first days, on impulse, I drove one county south to Elwood. I just wanted to see the town where at one time, according to local legend, every single resident had been a member of the Ku Klux Klan. I'd also heard that when Elwood native Wendell Willkie ran for president in 1940, locals hid the sign posted at the city limits and commonplace in small Indiana towns at the time: NIGGER DON'T LET THE SUN GO DOWN ON YOU HERE. After Willkie lost, the sign went back up. Or so the story goes.

Now Elwood was just another dead little all-white town, but a town with that shadow self, a town at least partly hooded, so everything looked sinister to me. For a while I thought I was being followed. And the grandmotherly type who'd pulled over to idle her car right behind mine—what was she up to? Just making me feel the fool. But over time I would begin to recognize unwarranted paranoia as one of the Klan's biggest weapons. Often the Kluxers didn't have to do a thing. They were a rumor and a threat. They might all be sitting drunk in some bar, but the mystique of their violent history and continued invisibility never stopped working for them.

At the library I looked up the lynching coverage in the *Elwood Call Leader.* The headline on August 8, 1930: MARION RELAXES AFTER LYNCHING. *Relaxes?* I got directions to Willkie's house, which hadn't been marked in any way. But then he too had been at odds with the homeplace. For one thing, he had rather famously denounced the Klan. He was liberal, a "one-worlder," and—by the time he ran for president—a Wall Street lawyer.

I decided to visit an antique store and ask for Klan memorabilia, wondering if the proprietor would be offended at the query. It didn't faze her a bit. She used to have Klan things, she said, but they'd sold.

"I hear the Klan was big around here in the twenties."

She replied: "Even since."

JACK EDWARDS HAD TOLD ME that Elwood was headquarters for whatever was left of the area KKK. He'd been the first person I visited on my return.

More frail than ever, the Boy Mayor—now ninety-four—lay asleep under an afghan that was pulled up to his trademark bow tie. Rock music pumped out of a boombox next to the bed. I was reluctant to wake him until one of the nurses advised me, "They hate to miss a visitor."

Nine months after our first brief encounter, Edwards remembered me, "the granddaughter of the mailman." He was still sharp, but now he couldn't get more than a few words out at a time. I sat in his wheelchair, facing the bed. He never even tried to sit up, but each time I suggested that perhaps I should return another day to ask my questions, he'd say, "Ask me now."

I got right to the point. I wanted to know which of the authorities in power at the time of the lynching were Klansmen. Sheriff Jake Campbell?

Yes, the old mayor told me. But he wasn't sure about Lew Lindenmuth, the police chief who'd hung out the bloody shirt.

"You knew for a fact that Campbell was in the Klan?" I pressed.

"Common knowledge," he replied.

And what about the prosecutor, Harley Hardin, who failed to convict anyone indicted for the lynching? A Klansman?

"Yeah," said Edwards. "And the judge was, too. They were all Republicans."

Would most voters have known that Campbell and Hardin were Klansmen?

"Yeah. There were no secrets. If you were a Ku Kluxer, you were all right."

I asked Edwards if Grant County had more Klan members than other places.

"No. No. Just the usual."

None of this information surprised me. I had speculated that Klan involvement in the lynching came after the fact; that they wouldn't have done the dirty work themselves, just made sure no one was punished. But since so many of the "right people" (including most Indiana politicians elected in the 1920s) were Klansmen, the fact that key players like the judge were Klan members could actually be coincidence, not conspiracy. Also, Klan membership had dropped off after 1925, and there was no way to know if these men were still enrolled in 1930.

Besides, Edwards insisted that the Klan had *no* involvement, and I couldn't imagine why he would cover for them. All that seemed to matter to the old mayor was that he himself be exonerated. He'd known these men personally. Used to watch them go upstairs to their meetings. Once a month, seven-thirty P.M. Just by telling me they were Klansmen, he was breaking a Klan rule.

When I told the old mayor I'd called Ruth Cartwright, the eighty-five-year-old who'd told me to "stop stirring up trouble," he advised me not to do that again. "She don't need no honorary mention." He remembered how Cartwright and Al Hogston used to "cry on each other's shoulders" over politics. Hogston had run the Grant County klavern during the Ku Klux heyday. I wondered if Edwards had ever talked to Hogston about the Hooded Order. Yes, Edwards said. Hogston had told him that the Klan "just tried to do good."

That day I thought I was learning so much, yet exchanges like this one with the old mayor left me baffled:

"I've heard that there's a transcript of the grand jury proceedings about the lynching and that nobody knows where it is."

"Could be."

"What do you think would have happened to that?"

"Destroyed."

"Who would have destroyed it?"

"Somebody didn't want their name mentioned. Al Hogston could have been one of them."

"Think his name would have come up in the grand jury?"

"Yeah. By being the Great Titan. By being an officer."

"So his name was in the grand jury proceedings?"

"Yeah."

"Did they talk about the Klan?"

"Yeah."

"What did they say about it?"

"Just the usual. What happened. Everybody wants Charlie Lennon and Phil Boyd."

"So they decided the Klan had nothing to do with it."

"They didn't."

"But the grand jury talked about them anyway."

"Yeah."

He reminded me that the anniversary was coming up in a few days. August 7. I asked him if he thought about the lynching every August 7. "No," he replied. "You said you'd be in town. If you're here, call on me."

So on August 7, late afternoon—exactly sixty-five years from the late afternoon when a mob began gathering outside the Grant County jail— the former Boy Mayor was up in his wheelchair, feeling better and telling me less.

I asked Edwards if he thought the Klan would have tried to help Boyd and Lennon and the others indicted for the lynching. "Well," he replied, "they had feelings for them." I couldn't get him to elaborate, but I'd learned that Boyd's lawyer was Dave Bell, whom Edwards had already named as a prominent Klansman. The old mayor started telling me that he himself had always gotten along with Phil Boyd, that Boyd was "a pretty good guy" whose brother-in-law became a prosecutor after the lynching.

Between my two visits with the mayor, I had spent a couple of days going through Attorney General James Ogden's papers down in Indianapolis. On August 8, 1930, Ogden sent an investigator to Marion and then a couple of his deputy attorneys. Just mentioning Odgen's name sent the old mayor into a fit of defensiveness. "He tried to indict me!" sputtered Edwards with all the force he could muster.

"What for?" I asked.

"Conditions!" Indeed. Looking through all of Ogden's correspondence, I found next to nothing about the lynching. Instead, I turned up letter after letter from citizens of Marion begging Ogden to clean up the town, complaining about whiskey rings, speakeasies, and gambling joints running wide open. But Edwards denied to me that anybody had been corrupt—including Sheriff Jake Campbell and Prosecutor Harley Hardin, the two officials accused most often in the letters. The old mayor claimed, in fact, that Ogden never had any real interest in resolving the lynching case, that Ogden only wanted to get *him*.

Dressed in a green-check bow tie, striped shirt, and black and white sweater, Edwards prepared to wheel himself away to supper, stopping first to kiss the red and green rosary hanging over a portrait of himself and his wife. I left feeling dissatisfied, though I knew that, in his own way, ol' Jack *was* "coming clean." He'd named the supposed ringleaders and told me who the Klansmen in city government were. But he certainly had his limits, and I thought I might have reached them. He would never admit to anything that might make him look bad.

BOTH THE PRECIPITOUS RISE and the sudden collapse of the Indiana KKK have been linked with the fate of one man: the talented, charismatic, and possibly psychopathic Grand Dragon, D. C. Stephenson. "Steve" his cronies called him. A master politician, Stephenson got control of Klan operations in twenty-three northern states after helping a Texas dentist named Hiram Evans move into the office of Imperial Wizard, unseating William Joseph Simmons in November 1922.

Stephenson's induction as Grand Dragon during the Kokomo "Klonvocation" on July 4, 1923, became the stuff of legend. Many otherwise reliable texts still repeat the tale, probably apocryphal, that Stephenson swooped down from the sky in a gilded airplane, emerged in purple robe and hood, and swept majestically to the stage where the crowd roared and sobbed its adulation, surging forward to throw flowers, coins, and jewelry at his feet. A less-than-dazzled journalist from the anti-Klan *Indianapolis Times,* however, reported that Steve wore a business suit, no one threw money, and attendance was closer to ten thousand than to Steve's own estimate of two hundred thousand. Still, without a doubt the Kokomo Klonvocation was the largest, most spectacular gathering in the history of Indiana's Invisible Empire. The parade that night through the streets of Kokomo stretched for two miles and included nine Klan bands and a dozen floats. Stephenson seems to have completely overshadowed Imperial Wizard Evans, the highest officer in the nation, who had come all the way from Atlanta to induct him as Grand Dragon, highest officer in the state.

Grandiosity was Steve's style. Just thirty-two at the height of his power and thirty-four when he lost it all, he often signed himself "The Old Man" on missives to the politicians he controlled. On his desk in Indianapolis sat a telephone he claimed was a hotline to the White House, and he became famous for his boast "I am the law in Indiana."

In fact, Stephenson was a brilliant organizer and recruiter. It had been his idea to appeal to fundamentalist clergymen. Those who gave pro-Klan sermons were rewarded with donations, usually delivered in dramatic fashion by robed and hooded Klansmen during Sunday services. Stephenson instructed local klaverns to do a good deed every week, and he created a women's KKK, the Queens of the Golden Mask. He also revived the moribund Horse Thief Detective Association. Back in 1852 when the Indiana legislature authorized the Detectives, local sheriffs in sparsely populated parts of the state may have needed the help. But by the 1920s the Horse Thief Detectives were a posse without much purpose. After Stephenson made them the enforcement arm of the Klan, they zeroed in on bootleggers and "petting parties," bolstering the group's image as a champion of law and order.

Then, long before the practice was common, Stephenson broke each county down, precinct by precinct—for polling, distributing Klan-approved voter guides, and turning out the vote on election day. Politicians knew he could deliver, and some sold their souls.

In 1922 Stephenson helped defeat Indiana's anti-Klan senator Albert Beveridge and was already dictating to Secretary of State (and Klansman) Ed Jackson about who should chair the Republican Party. (While the KKK usually supported Republicans, they did back the occasional Democrat who proved to be "one hundred percent American.") Steve selected Jackson to run for governor in 1924, the election in which the Klan triumphed all over Indiana.

The organization might have steamrolled its policies into place if it hadn't been mired in internal conflict. Friction between Stephenson and Wizard Evans actually predated the Kokomo Klonvocation. They distrusted each other but had real philosophical differences as well. For Stephenson, the KKK was more a moneymaker and a political machine than an ideological commitment. He actually regretted the Hoosier Klan's strong anti-Catholicism, according to one historian: "He disliked narrowly defined scapegoats. He much preferred broad categories—like un-Americanism—in which anyone could fit when you needed to ruin him."

Kluxing Indiana had made Steve a millionaire. He got $2.50 out of every ten-dollar membership fee and probably doubled that on the sale of robes and hoods. Five dollars was supposed to go to Atlanta (and the other $2.50 to the kleagle, or recruiter). Evans suspected that Stephenson was short-changing him and sent auditors to Indianapolis to go through the books, while Stephenson complained that Indiana, with the most members, sent the most money to Atlanta and got nothing in return. He wanted the Klan to purchase what is now Valparaiso University and turn it into a Klan college, but Evans would not back the idea.

Whatever caused the final rift between Dragon and Wizard—and no one seems to know exactly—Steve resigned just months after taking office in Kokomo. The Klan newspaper, the *Fiery Cross,* announced on October 26, 1923, that the Old Man had surrendered his leadership, "broken in health" because of his tremendous exertions for the Hooded Order. The average member would have known nothing then of his feud with the Wizard, who soon appointed a new Grand Dragon, Walter Bossert.

Steve now intended to create his own KKK. In May 1924, after the Kluxer victory in the primaries, he summoned seven to eight hundred of the state's Klan leaders to Indianapolis, went public with his criticisms of Evans, and urged other Kluxers to join him in breaking with Atlanta. He then had himself elected Grand Dragon of this new Klan.

The next issue of the Evans-controlled *Fiery Cross* called Stephenson a mouthpiece of Rome: "Well does he know that should he secure enough followers to this campaign of hate, the Klan organization, founded on love, would be disrupted. . . . Klansmen, stick by your guns. Do not let Rome, in this new disguise, secure so much as a toehold within your Klavern."

In June 1924 a Klan tribunal convened in Evansville (Steve's home klavern) to hear six charges against him. He himself did not deign to attend. The judgment: "banishment forever" from the KKK. No one in politics seemed to notice, since no one outside the Invisible Empire knew that a tribunal had occurred. And within the Klan the Old Man still had a following.

As Governor Jackson took office early in 1925, the majority of state legislators were either Klansmen or Klan-friendly. So were most of the new mayors taking office around the state. And so were all five of the men going to the House of Representatives—including Albert Hall of Marion, Grant County's superintendent of schools and an officer in the local klavern. Governor Jackson was soon appointing Klansmen to state jobs, among them Great Titan Al Hogston of Marion, who became state fire marshal. Within a year Indiana's Senator Sam Ralston had died, and Jackson appointed Klan legal adviser Arthur Robinson to finish out his term in Washington.

Steve remained the most powerful man in the state. He controlled the executive branch, the state senate, and the Republican Party. But Bossert, the other Dragon, controlled the house, and they had completely different legislative agendas. Bossert, for example, was pushing a bill to ban "religious garb" from classrooms (which would have effectively banned nuns from teaching) and another to require Bible reading in schools. Stephenson's legislative agenda was designed to further line his pockets. For example, his stream pollution bill would have banned manufacturers from dumping waste into waterways, but Steve planned to extort money from the industries affected and then kill the bill. The Old Man never had a chance to cash in, however.

Unknown to rank-and-file Klansmen, Steve had a long history of sexual misconduct: harassment of women, attempted rapes, deserted wives, and late-night orgies. One of the charges against him at the Evansville tribunal had been "disrespect for virtuous womanhood."

In March 1925 Stephenson forced a twenty-eight-year-old woman named Madge Oberholzer onto a train to Chicago and sexually assaulted her en route, savagely biting her tongue, breasts, back, legs, and ankles. After they disembarked in Hammond, Indiana, Oberholzer tried to poison herself. Stephenson, who'd brought one of his bodyguards along, refused to let her get medical help for either her injuries or the poison until they returned to Indianapolis. She died a few weeks later.

In November 1925 the Old Man went on trial in Noblesville, just north of Indianapolis, where a jury convicted him of second-degree murder, mostly on the strength of Oberholzer's account of the trip, her "dying declaration."

Stephenson assumed that the Klansman in the governor's mansion would pardon him. He was wrong. He eventually served twenty-five years in prison and maintained for the rest of his life that Wizard Evans had framed him. So much about the case remains unexplained, even puzzling, that this is a remote possibility. But if so, what an irony.

The scandal broke the back of the Klan in Indiana, although the Evans-Bossert faction tried desperately to distance itself from the disgraced ex-Dragon. KKK influence and power did not die overnight, however. Not in Grant County. Not in most counties.

I'D GONE TO THE MARION LIBRARY to see how the local papers covered the Kokomo Klonvocation and quickly realized that a partial history of the local klavern was right there for the assembling—for anyone who cared to look through several years' worth of the two different newspapers published in the 1920s.

I could trace the initial recruiting drive through the autumn of 1922, or so I imagined. The first mention of KKK activity in Marion appeared on September 6 of that year, when the *Leader-Tribune* reported that a Klan organizer from Muncie had been working in town for several weeks. This would have been part of D. C. Stephenson's effort to "ku-klux" the entire state of Indiana. On September 8 an initiation of several hundred new Kluxers made the front page of the *Leader-Tribune,* though the story of the secret ceremony is based merely on "reports in circulation." As the anonymous reporter admits, "It was impossible to get any facts on the subject." Interest in the group must have been keen if it justified printing raw hearsay on page one. But the membership drive had only begun.

Days later both papers ran the first of many reports on masked robed men appearing suddenly at public functions to bestow their money and approval. I sensed fascination, if not awe, in the reportage. Three Kluxers in full regalia had driven up to an outdoor band concert in Jonesboro on Saturday night, September 9, where they handed the bandleader an envelope. Apparently he then read the text out loud, since it was faithfully reported in both Marion papers: "Read this to your people. You will find enclosed $5 which the Ku Klux Klan has chosen to give to members of your band. The Klan never forgets the tenets of the Christian religion, of upholding the constitution of America, our glorious country, the United States of America. We want you to play the hymn of our country, 'The Star Spangled Banner.' May God give us Grace never to let another take its place—Knights of the Ku Klux Klan." Two of the Klansmen then stepped onto the bandstand and asked if there was a minister present. An elderly local pastor mounted the platform, and as he began to pray, the Klansmen dropped to their knees. After the band played the requested "Star Spangled Banner," the Kluxers drove off in the direction of Marion.

My grandparents would have taken the evening paper, the Republican paper—the *Chronicle,* which ran a story September 18 on thirteen Klansmen interrupting a revival meeting, giving the minister $28.50, and "commending him on his high moral character." (That sum was about a week's salary for a male factory worker or a high school teacher at the time.) The night of September 26 two Klansmen appeared on a country road between Marion and Gas City to break up a "spooning party." The *Chronicle* says the masked Kluxers stopped the car and then stood at either fender, where "one of the outlandish shapes found his voice—an impressively hollow and sepulchral one—and said: 'Go to your homes.' " In the *Leader-Tribune*'s account, the two couples in the car had just gotten out when the Klansmen appeared, pointed at the vehicle, then pointed down the road, saying nothing. Early reports revel in these quaint attempts at portent and mystery, and I couldn't help but wonder who was keeping the papers informed—or misinformed— about encounters on country roads. But maybe most noteworthy: none of these stories have anything to do with race.

The Klan had been recruiting for about a month, and they must have been the talk of the town. On Sunday, October 1, Reverend E. F. Rippey, the minister at my grandparents' church, First Presbyterian, denounced the Invisible Empire to a filled sanctuary in a sermon discussed at length in the *Leader-Tribune* (the morning paper, the Democratic paper, which generally carried more Klan news). Four men had warned him not to talk, said the Reverend; many Klan newspapers had been left on his porch, "and this is one reason why I shall speak tonight." According to my father, who heard it from my grandfather, nearly every minister in Marion was a Klansman or Klan sympathizer in the 1920s, so Reverend Rippey would have been quite an aberration—therefore newsworthy. And he *did* talk about race. One thing that made the KKK "a peril to America," he announced, was "the plan to keep the negro in his place." He also condemned the intolerance shown Jews, Catholics, and immigrants. "Men, we are taking chances with our nation," Rippey warned the congregation.

Many Klansmen, including Al Hogston, belonged to First Presbyterian, one of the oldest congregations in town and one of its most genteel. "A long wheel-base church," my father called it. They had genuine Tiffany stained glass in the sanctuary. At some point my grandfather served as an elder there. But my grandmother had joined first, when she lived with the high school principal's family, as their nanny, and began attending with them. Among her many services to this congregation, my grandmother wrote a history of First Presbyterian in 1943 when it celebrated its centennial. The book was not an exposé, but I looked through it for some clue to Rippey's fate and found this: he left town for a pastorate in Iowa in June 1923, a time when the Klan was still on the rise.

In early October 1922, however, a debate over the Klan seemed to be raging through Marion with Rippey in the thick of it. He lectured again on "real Americanism," both at church and at the Lions Club. If anyone else was making a public stand against the KKK, that person was not making the papers. On October 16 a Klan recruiter ("Dr. Newton of Oklahoma City") spoke from the steps of the courthouse to what the *Leader-Tribune* described as "a large crowd." Meanwhile, half-inch ads began appearing on nearly every page of both Marion newspapers, warning: "Look Out for the Mysterious Eyes of the Ku Klux Klan." In mid-October "an authorized photoplay sensation" on the KKK opened at a local vaudeville theater, where it purportedly spilled "inside dope on the inner workings of this great question of the hour." No doubt it was straight propaganda.

I wondered what had become of it. What had happened to all those robes and hoods worn so proudly in 1922? Once people knew enough to find them embarrassing, they probably destroyed the evidence. Yesterday's common knowledge becomes today's terrible secret. Just so with the little newspaper items I'd found. No doubt others just like them were there for the harvesting in every Indiana town of any size: riches of embarrassment.

Yet the stories told me so frustratingly little. They were merely a vapor trail, hinting at larger dramas. Three women in neighboring Blackford County go to a Halloween party dressed as ghosts. Someone mistakes them for Kluxers and turns a hose on them. It rated three short paragraphs on October 25. No one was named.

Much Klan news was church-related. In early November a Reverend W. R. Howard found a piece of black crepe at his church door with a note warning him to leave the city, but he told the *Leader-Tribune* that he didn't think it came from the Klan. On November 14 the paper reported that a Fairmount minister's pro-Klan speech on "Americanism" was interrupted by four masked Kluxers, who marched down the aisle, knelt in prayer, presented the minister with an envelope, and marched out. Reverend J. P. Williams read aloud from the letter in which the Klan promised to back his efforts with money and "spoke in the highest terms of his efforts to spread Americanism." The very next day sixteen touring cars loaded with Kluxers and led by a bugler cruised through Fairmount. Robed and hooded men threw "a large amount of literature" from the caravan, mostly small circulars bearing the words: "The eyes of the Ku Klux Klan are upon you. Law breakers beware." I found several more reports of either church donations or ministers defending the Klan in the weeks leading up to Thanksgiving 1922.

Then came the kicker to these giddy months of breathless enthusiasm. On Saturday, November 25, a spectacular Klan parade around the courthouse culminated in the public initiation of seventeen hundred men at Goldthwait Park just east of Marion. Seven masked trumpeters on horseback led this procession past "one of the largest crowds of the year." I wondered how it had been advertised. Posters? There was nothing in the papers till after it happened. They describe a large electrically lighted cross in an automobile, one (according to the *Chronicle*) or two *(Leader-Tribune)* flaming crosses—carried they say not how—followed by the Muncie Klan band, the Grant County Klan band, huge American flags, five hundred marching masked Klansmen, and others wearing their everyday clothing. Thousands of spectators accompanied them the half-mile to Goldthwait to watch the usually secret initiation—here performed openly since there was "nothing to conceal," as both newspapers put it.

The initiates gathered on an old baseball field, lit by the electric cross and a flaming one. After the playing of "Onward Christian Soldiers," an official known as the Masked Knight rode up before them on a black horse and gave a short speech, "stating that the Klan was not anti-Jew, anti-Negro and anti-Catholic, as had been charged." After listening to this declaration that they weren't bigoted, the new members swore that they were by taking the Klan oath. "Several questions were asked of the candidates . . . if they believed in the tenets of the Christian religion, white supremacy and others which are supposed to be the tenets of the Klan. . . . The scene of the 1700 candidates, surrounded by many hundred Klan, under the glare of the burning cross, was one of the most odd scenes witnessed in the county and hundreds of people braved the cold to watch every detail until the close, which was eleven-thirty."

Less than a year later Daisy Douglas Barr, a Grant County native who became a prominent national player in the Klan, appeared at Goldthwait to address a state KKK rally. Here she made her famous declaration: "I believe that if Jesus was on earth today, He would belong to the Ku Klux Klan."

Goldthwait today is Grant County's 4-H Fairgrounds, but in the 1920s it had amusement park rides, boating in a man-made lake, and maybe more than its share of KKK events. A march of the robed and the hooded from the Grant County courthouse to Goldthwait would have passed directly through Johnstown, a neighborhood that was one hundred percent black.

Goldthwait Park also had a nickname, no doubt borrowed from the much larger fairground in Chicago at the World's Columbian Exposition of 1893, but all too appropriate here: the White City.

> *I am the Spirit of Righteousness.*
> *They call me the Ku Klux Klan.*
> *I am more than the uncouth robe and hood*
>   *With which I am clothed.*
> *YEA, I AM THE SOUL OF AMERICA.*
>
> —From a poem by Daisy Douglas Barr,
> read by her at a national meeting of Grand Dragons in 1923

HISTORIANS OLD AND NEW say that all this activity was dead by 1930, killed off by the Stephenson scandal. But I didn't buy it. In November 1925—right in the middle of Stephenson's murder trial—Marion elected a new mayor, James H. McConnell, with what both of the town's newspapers described as "the open support of the Klan." The Stephenson scandal had not broken the back of the local klavern. During the tribunal that banished Steve, one Marion Kluxer testified that the Grant County organization had "absolutely" turned against him. Apparently they'd lined up with the Evans/Bossert faction. A 1924–25 list of Klan officers and members indicates that they did indeed lose half their membership in Grant County. But they didn't disband.

In one of the Marion papers, I found proof that the Grant County klavern still existed in 1930. Klan news, ubiquitous from late 1922 through 1925, appeared rarely after those years, but I had assigned myself the task of looking at every page published during the year of the lynching. An inch-long item published in the *Leader-Tribune* on May 29, 1930, reads: "The Men and Women's Organizations of the Knights of the Ku Klux Klan of Grant County will hold an open meeting in their hall on the north side of the square Tuesday night, June 3. There will be a speaker. Lunch will be served, 8 P.M."

I went to the old mayor and read this to him. Jack gave me a funny look. He didn't know about any "hall" on the north side of the square. "They had a meeting on the courthouse steps," he finally said. I couldn't get any more out of him. He would just shut down when he didn't want to talk. But he had also once told me that in 1929, when he beat Mayor James McConnell in the Democratic primary, he thought he did so because of Marion's disenchantment with the KKK.

SIX

THE THREE P's

James Cameron once told me that there were still Klansmen in Grant County and that they were there "to keep the stink going." I also knew this: No one could get away with a spectacle lynching today, but in the contemporary Klan the impulse to do such a thing still had a refuge.

I wanted to hear from these Klansmen on their own terms. I wanted to see what I could learn about that impulse, about racism, from people who embraced it without apology. Like—what were they getting out of it? Were they driven by hatred? By fear? What exactly were they trying to preserve?

Jim Ferguson was the spokesman for the local klavern, the man who'd told me on the phone that his Klan membership was "a family tradition." He suggested that we meet at the Moose Lodge. He liked to eat lunch there before starting his three P.M. shift at General Motors, where he worked as a die-maker. I noted the sign at the end of the Lodge driveway: THE FAMILY FRATERNITY. When I arrived in the dark wood-paneled dining room, six or eight Moose were eating and chatting, ignoring *The Young and the Restless* at play on a big-screen television. Ferguson had taken a table in the center of the room. Apparently he wasn't too concerned about keeping our conversation private, though at first he seemed a bit ill at ease.

Ferguson proved to be a personable guy, forty-eight years old with thinning gray hair, sturdily built, wearing a blue plaid shirt. He told me as I sat down that he had had a great-grandfather named Carr in Kentucky. So we could be related.

"It's possible," I said, though I don't think my family even passed through Kentucky. I just didn't want to appear to be distancing myself.

I had decided that I could not demonize the Kluxers I interviewed. How could I, when my own grandfather had been one? And I had rejected the idea of becoming a superior white person by finding worse white people to look down on. But here, with the first Klansman I met, my quest for understanding led directly and immediately to the irrational.

Someone had told me that Ferguson was part Indian, so I thought I'd just clarify that before we started. To my surprise, he proudly admitted it. "There's Cherokee on my mother's side, and then my dad's grandmother was part Apache," he said. "I've got an old picture of her father at the White Mountain Indian Reservation. The funny part is, my brother's daughter looks like she walked off the reservation. And my granddaughter does, too." He hastened to add that the Cherokee were said to be descendants of Leif Eriksson and other "early day explorers," and "a lot of 'em were fair-skinned, blue-eyed and blonde-haired."

It was all news to me. In fact, I was dumbfounded and managed only the obvious: "I thought the Klan was for white people."

Ferguson assured me that this was a misconception advanced by liberals. "The Klan is an organization of native Americans and that includes the Indians," he declared. "The Klan has never had any prejudice against Indians and has never had—" He stopped and began again: "People take 'prejudice' to mean a lot of different things. The Klan has never been for the annihilation of any race, whether it be black or Indian. But they're for the separation of the races." As for the notion that he himself would seem to be of mixed race—he was having none of it. "I think of myself as being American."

Born in Louisiana, Ferguson had grown up in Wabash County, just north of Grant. He now lived on a farm in Blackford County, just east of Grant, where the KKK didn't have a "unit." He'd joined the Grant County klavern back in 1968, when he was twenty-one. The membership had empowered him to speak to the press, he said, "as long as I don't divulge names or dates." Making the organization sound reasonable and harmless was a job Ferguson did well. Temperate, careful never to speak ill of black folks or anyone else, he was the aw-shucks face of the Ku Klux Klan. I couldn't help but like him as he sat there hedging and dissembling.

The "lodge," as he liked to call it, was so misunderstood and maligned and never got credit for all its good works. He allowed that "Klansmen have a wild reputation a lot of times, and they deserve part of it." But really, the Klan was "family oriented." The Klan revolved around "the three P's: parades, picnics, and politics."

The three P's: more startling news. And what, I wondered, were the "good works" done by the Klan? Ferguson said charitable organizations would come to them asking for donations of groceries or money several times a year. And the klavern had also helped sandbag the river during floods. But, he added, "we don't much anymore. We got so harassed back in the seventies and early eighties, that the Klan for the most part went underground. We're going back to the old ways of what they called the Invisible Empire."

The waitress approached with menus as Ferguson described how the klavern had divided itself into seven-man units, because then if the FBI put the screws to someone, they wouldn't get more than seven names. "Being in it as long as I have, though, I know a lot of the other guys in different units. They still meet at the klavern." He hadn't censored his Klan talk in front of the waitress, and she apparently found it unremarkable. He ordered the pork tenderloin with macaroni and cheese.

"Things are coming true today that we predicted twenty and thirty years ago. That the country would bankrupt itself with all the giveaway programs." Back in the 1960s he'd written critiques of welfare, affirmative action, and integration. He had felt great discouragement but was heartened now by the country's growing conservatism. "A year ago the whole lodge got together for a meeting, the first we'd had in about five years, and they're planning on another one this winter. With people being a little more receptive to right-wing ideals, the Klan may become visible again. That's just something being discussed."

AT THE TIME OF THIS CONVERSATION, I had read only the history of my grandfather's Klan in 1920s Indiana and still thought of the KKK as a robed monolith. In fact, the modern incarnation has been splintered since the 1940s, when the Internal Revenue Service filed suit against the Invisible Empire for taxes unpaid during the 1920s. The national organization disbanded to avoid liability. But the Klan always shatters like mercury, reconstituting itself in smaller and smaller entities. It does not go away. In 1949 *Newsweek* reported that at least a dozen different Klans were operating independently in the South.

Ferguson's klavern had been affiliated with United Klans of America, created in 1961 to unite splinter Klans in their fight against the civil rights movement. UKA left a bloody trail through the South, its members convicted of some of the most notorious crimes of that era—the Birmingham church bombing that killed four little girls in 1963; the assassination of Lemuel Penn, a black National Guardsman shot while driving down a Georgia highway in 1964; and the murder of civil rights worker Viola Liuzzo during the Selma-to-Montgomery voting rights march in 1965.

According to Ferguson, UKA was the true descendant of the original Klan founded by six ex–Confederate soldiers in Pulaski, Tennessee, and then led by former Confederate general Nathan Bedford Forrest. Ferguson seemed proud of this connection, but what really tied UKA to the first Klan was its unapologetic violence. This was not a group worried about the pope invading Indiana. This was not some "new" David Duke–ish group talking about oppressed white people. This was the old-line Klan delivering the original three P's: pain, prejudice, pathology.

Ferguson, however, maintained that the Klan was nonviolent. "Now they've been involved in some skirmishes and a few cross-lightings over the years," he allowed. "No denying that. But as far as being out-and-out brutal, the Klan has never advocated brutality."

He admitted to a certain kind of nightriding. The Klan would deliver thirteen switches to someone's porch, and in the stories he told me the porch always belonged to a white man who was beating his wife and kids, or a white man who was constantly "laying out drunk." If the switches didn't persuade this man to change, then maybe he'd get a cross burned in his yard. Or maybe the Klan would get right to the part where they beat him with the switches, thus curing him of his bad behavior and saving a family. "Some people may call it brutal to tie a man up to a fence and whup his backside real good with thirteen switches," said Ferguson, "but if it straightens out the problem at home, I think it's worth the effort." Clearly Ferguson had gotten a kick out of these "efforts." He was proud of them. They were part of the Klan's good works.

But the more deadly form of nightriding finished UKA in the end. In 1981 two UKA Klansmen in Mobile, Alabama, killed a nineteen-year-old African American named Michael Donald. The Kluxers wanted revenge after a local jury failed to convict a black man of murdering a white police officer. It was a mistrial, not an acquittal. Still, the Klansmen were moved to go out cruising for a random black victim. They happened upon Donald, abducted him, beat him, and strangled him. The picture of his lifeless body dangling from a tree limb, where the Klansmen put it on display, looks like an image from Reconstruction—but Donald's white sneakers say otherwise. So did the sentences for the two Kluxers. One got death; one got ten years to life.

Then in 1987 the Southern Poverty Law Center and Morris Dees, its cofounder and chief trial counsel, brought a civil suit against the United Klans, alleging that the whole group was liable in the Donald case because the killers had been carrying out UKA policy. In the end a jury awarded Beulah Mae Donald, the victim's mother, $7 million in damages, and UKA lost everything, including its national headquarters building in Alabama. Since that didn't come close to netting $7 million, the UKA, like the old Invisible Empire, had to disband to avoid liability.

The first time I'd spoken to Ferguson on the phone, he'd talked about the local Klan being "strong as ever," but in several conversations over the next couple of years, he kept qualifying that. "We're just as strong in our beliefs. Conservative ways and family values." He kept paring it all back, emphasizing how very inactive they were. "As far as I know, in Grant County there's not been a cross lit or a bundle of switches delivered since 1980," he declared. "That's the last one I know of. By the UKA."

The units met only to stay prepared, he said, "in the event that something does come up and we have to regroup."

"What do you mean?" I asked. "What would come up?"

"Oh, in the event of, say, a nuclear attack," Ferguson explained, "from a foreign source. People in this country have gotten so dependent on somebody else producing their food, producing their transportation and so forth, that they'll die faster than you could bury 'em. I'm convinced it will happen someday. So we're getting prepared to take care of ourselves and our own and be ready to bring in neighbors, friends, people that would be sympathetic to the cause, to our way of thinking, to how we think things should run after it happens. It might not necessarily be an outside attack. It could be a natural disaster. People are either gonna starve or gonna steal. And that's what we're trying to avoid. We're keeping ourselves prepared with food and enough arms to protect what we've got so that we can survive."

Here was a working scenario of Klan triumph in the twenty-first century: they survive the apocalypse, since they're the only ones with guns, then set things up "to our way of thinking." This scenario also fit Ferguson's general nostalgia for how things used to be. Survivalism was everyday life in pioneer days. And this was a man who still liked riding a horse and buggy. He also owned a carriage and a sleigh and used a horse-drawn hitch wagon in his farm fields. He enjoyed the past. He had a television, he said, but hadn't hooked it up. He'd heard there wasn't much on it worth watching.

I REMEMBERED JAMES CAMERON telling me that the Grant County klavern was "the mother den" of all the Klans in Indiana. Could it be? Cameron said he'd heard this years ago from a Marion newspaper man, who had since died. But none of my Klan histories confirmed it. They named Evansville, at the southern tip of the state, where a first klavern convened late in 1920. Jim Ferguson told me Grant County had the tenth unit chartered in the state, but it was the second oldest "continuous unit," after Indianapolis—and he seemed quite proud of this. His klavern had never shut down.

Ferguson had all the old charters, records, and membership lists from the early Grant County Klan—or had access to them. At the Moose Lodge he told me the first charter was dated 1903. I wondered how that could be. I explained what the history books said: that the first Klan had disbanded in 1872, that it was dead for sure by the end of Reconstruction in 1877, that William Joseph Simmons brought it back to life in Atlanta in 1915.

"A lot of local chapters went on independently [after Reconstruction]," Ferguson informed me. He maintained that the Klan had never really died, just lost its centralized leadership for a while. Grant County's 1903 charter had been signed by someone affiliated with a Kentucky Klan, part of "the original that came from Nathan Bedford Forrest."

Twice, but about nine months apart, I asked Ferguson how many members they had currently in Grant County. I didn't expect an answer, but once he told me there were about thirteen cells of seven men each, and another time he said, "It's over seventy-five and less than five hundred."

Sometime after our second meeting, Ferguson consented to look at the membership ledgers to see when my grandfather and his uncle On had joined. There was a certain etiquette involved with such a query. One could ask about family but that was all.

Ferguson then informed me over the phone that yes, Grandpa and Uncle On were at one time "in the lodge." Grandpa had joined in 1923 and quit in 1936. Uncle On had joined in 1917, but he too quit in 1936.

I kept hoping that Ferguson would put me in touch with other Klansmen. I assured him that I could guarantee anonymity, that I only wanted to "understand." One of these pleas drew this reply from Ferguson: "The Aryan race has always been a proud people. No matter what difficulties they've run into, whether it be war or famine or disease, they've always managed to come through it and get back on their feet. They haven't waited for somebody else to pick 'em up. This is one of the things that kind of sets the Aryan race apart from other races. They'll take care of themselves. They'll always be there. They'll be the leaders. They always have been throughout history, and I don't see any reason for it to change." Ferguson never did direct me to a single other Klansman.

Yet somehow I wasn't worried about finding the Klan. I knew I would find them.

BY THE SUMMER OF 1995 Tom Wise was back in a blue uniform, driving a patrol car. This after twenty-five years on the Marion police force, including sixteen as a detective and four as assistant chief. "That's politics," he said. Wise thought the mayor was behind it. First they'd made him a traffic investigator, in uniform, with Tuesdays and Wednesdays off. "They know I do antique shows on weekends." Then when he still didn't quit, they put him on second shift, working four-thirty P.M. to three A.M. So he went back to patrolman, "as low as you can go," to hold his day shift. He still didn't have weekends off.

So it was that on a Sunday afternoon of August steam heat, a mere two days after meeting Ferguson at the Moose Lodge, I happened to be walking out of a flea market with some pulp fiction I'd purchased there, *The Klansman*—"a powder-keg drama of agonizing personal decisions and violently released passions"—just as Tom Wise passed by in his patrol car. He pulled over.

Wise told me he'd just been out on a call. Two brothers. One of them chasing the other around the backyard with an ax, the brother with the ax screaming that he belonged to the Klan and was going to move in with the Grand Dragon. "So maybe you'd like to go over and interview these guys," Tom suggested in his jaded cop drawl.

"Sounds a little . . . volatile," I said.

Tom assured me that the guy with the ax wasn't even there at the moment. He'd probably gone to the hospital.

I hesitated. I was wilting. I was tired. And I could think of several other reasons not to meet a Klansman with an ax. Wise shrugged. He'd just show me where it was then, he said. I followed him up Nebraska Street in my car and watched as Tom got out and knocked on the door of a small gray two-story house with a tiny yard full of broken toys. That was a little more than just showing me. Now I would have to get out, too. And how was this alleged Klansman going to react to a journalist who came calling with a black policeman?

Tom was right about the Kluxer, though. Not home. Instead, the brother came outside. The chasee. Bobby. He was a mountain, one of the heaviest people I've ever met, covered with prickly-heat rash and wearing a T-shirt that said "Nuthin' But the Dog in Me." He said his brother, the Klansman, had gone to the Grand Dragon's house out in Bucktown. Bobby didn't know the address but began describing a particular trailer in a particular trailer park. I was too unfamiliar with the territory for his description to make sense. Tom didn't seem to know it, either. Bucktown was full of trailer parks.

Apparently the two brothers had been arguing over the Klan. Bobby didn't like the organization; he had black friends. But he said he'd just spoken to his brother on the phone, and they'd made up. The Kluxer, Larry, would be home soon.

Tom took off, and soon a car pulled up down the block. A tall man I judged to be pushing thirty emerged carrying a small suitcase and a black plastic file box. I would soon discover that Larry had left home with all his Klan material—and nothing else. The suitcase contained his robe and hood and a couple of KKK flags, while the file box was filled with folders, many stamped in red: CONFIDENTIAL. He was brown-haired, dressed in purple shorts, a gray sleeveless shirt, a baseball hat, and a utility belt.

As he walked into the yard, I told him I was writing a book and wondered if I could interview him. Larry said I would first have to answer some questions.

"Are you a fed?" he demanded.

"No."

"Are you a Jewbaby?" He said this word so quickly, I only heard two syllables that sounded like . . . *joober*. What was a joober?

"Am I what?" I asked.

He repeated the word in the same rush.

I was still puzzled. "A joober?"

"A JEW!!!!"

"Oh! No." I felt shame rise up in me but pressed on.

I told him that, in fact, my grandfather had been a Klansman. And before I could even get my tape recorder turned on, he announced that *his* grandfather had been an Imperial Wizard. And involved in the lynching. Larry whipped a framed color photo of this grandfather out of his suitcase. But the man was too young and the picture too recent for that claim to make any sense. What was going on? The man was wearing a blue and turquoise robe and hood, 1970s to 1980s vintage, and he looked middle-aged. I noticed that he'd also autographed the photo: "Larry Hitler from John Howard, Emperor."

"You're Larry Hitler?" I asked.

"Larry Allen Hitler," the Klansman announced, adding: "That's an alias."

As I got the tape on, he was talking fast: "My grandfather died at one hundred and thirteen years old. Died in 1975. He was a Ku Klux Klan member from 1865. He started up the KKK in 1865 under the command of General Nathan Bedford Forrest. Nathan Bedford Forrest, which is my great-great-great-great-cousin." He pulled out a picture of the ex–Confederate general, then suggested: "Let's walk on inside cuz I don't want no nigger passing by here catching a glance of this stuff." Peering up and down Nebraska Street with a John Wayne squint, he dropped his voice into a more menacing register: "Cuz I'll end up killing a nigger."

I didn't quite know what to make of that threat. And had he really just told me that his grandfather founded the Klan at age three? My head was already spinning as we entered the living room, where a teenage boy who looked Mexican sat watching a big television. "Would you disappear for me?" Larry said to the kid. "Run down to the store, buy myself a pop, and buy you a pop." The kid shrugged dismissively but otherwise didn't respond or even look at Larry. "C'mon, you wetback!!!" Larry shouted.

A middle-aged woman entered the room. Larry asked her to go "buy myself a pop and buy you a pop. And to hell with this lousy no-good taco-bending tomato-picker!" She left to buy sodas, and Larry took me into the next room, which was nearly filled by a smaller television and a hospital bed. In it sat a huge woman, Larry's mother, wearing a blue shift and an oxygen tube. She invited us to talk in this room, where it was slightly cooler. On the walls were pictures of Jesus and the Virgin Mary and silver hearts labeled HAPPY MOTHER'S DAY.

"You were telling me about the lynching that happened here," I prompted Larry.

"Yes," he said. Hands behind his back, eyes in the distance, Larry stood at parade rest, declaiming as if he were reciting before a class: "On August sixth, 1930, there at the Marion courthouse due to the fact that they raped a white girl. And they went into the old jail, they took over the old jail, brought three niggers out. They spared one guy's life who is the guy that presently holds the key to Marion, Indiana. My grandfather was a very respected man. He was a commanding Imperial Wizard for the Knights of the Ku Klux

Klan, started in 1915, but he was with the kuklos, another Greek word for Ku Klux, in 1865." And so on. Larry made even less sense as he elaborated, and most of the history he expounded on was wrong. But I didn't stop him to argue. It's impossible to have a dialogue with someone who's doing a monologue.

As Larry concluded with the news that his grandfather had been a sort of partner to "Robert" Simmons, who revived the Klan in 1915, he asked his mother, "What was Grandpa's middle name?"

"William Walter Tidwell," said the mother. "That was my daddy."

"He was the Grand Dragon," Larry announced.

Of course, just a minute ago, he'd been a Wizard. And Tidwell was not the man in the photograph. I'd just have to untangle this.

"He came all the way from Birmingham, Alabama," Larry went on, "just to hang those two stupid big-lipped rughead wide-eyed bigmouth niggers."

I listened in despair. This was not just racism at its crudest. It was phony. Larry was showing off. And for some reason his mother was supporting him. They both tried to tell me that the grandfather had driven all the way from Birmingham, Alabama, to orchestrate the Marion lynching. It wasn't remotely plausible. But maybe the real question was: why did Larry want his grandfather to get credit for this shameful event?

He was a textbook example of someone who thought the Klan was going to bring him prestige and respect, and I was very aware of his need to impress me. I thought of Mark Fuhrman, the detective at the heart of the O. J. Simpson trial. For both, being racist was part of a tortured macho pose, a pathetic attempt to assert some authority.

But Larry also seemed to be some kind of mental case. Or was he just a liar? Would everything he said be untrue? Or just some? I didn't know what to think when he informed me next that he too was a Wizard, the founder of his own organization in Marion, the Patriotic Knights of the Ku Klux Klan. He admitted he'd only been a Klansman for a little over a year, but he'd mastered all the secrets of Klancraft in that time and achieved the rank of KQuad—roughly the equivalent of a thirty-third-degree Mason. Few Klansmen ever get to that level, but Larry pulled out his membership card to prove that he had. I saw no evidence of his mastery there but read the words: "The Most Sublime Lineage in All History Commemorating and Perpetuating as It Does the Most Dauntless Organization Known to Man."

"Here I thought things like this were secret," I said, as I wrote down the words.

"It's not a secret," Larry declared.

"It's supposed to be," the mother piped in.

"It's supposed to be secret," the KQuad then concurred, putting the card away.

I asked him if he'd joined because it was family tradition. "While I was incarcerated in the Indiana Department of Correction," he replied, "I was jumped by niggers who burned me up in my cell. Almost tried to kill me as well. I was just setting back, relaxing and seeing how these dingo jungle-bunnies was jumping around from tree to tree wishing to get to the banana, and I just got sick and tired of it. So after the second incident that occurred by niggers, I became fully completely prejudiced. I am racist, and I believe that there is only one good nigger in this world, and that's a dead one. I do not play no games with no one. I can get along with everyone under the stipulations that they can respect me for my viewpoints and my racism. So," he concluded, with a typical leap in logic, "it's a family tradition. My mother, she was a member."

The mother confirmed this but said her second husband—Bobby's father—had forced her to resign. Then her third husband—Larry's father—had been a Grand Dragon with the Southern Knights out of Georgia.

"How'd you get my address?" Larry asked suddenly.

"The police were here and heard you talking about the Klan," I replied, because I couldn't think what else to say, moving quickly to: "So there's another klavern here in Marion?"

"Yes," said Larry, and he began what I already recognized as the standard Klan rap: "We are a nonviolent organization." But in Larry's case it concluded with: "You upset us or anybody upset us, you'll know because we'll be the person's nightmares. The only way we will interfere with a case is if we find out that a person has either murdered somebody else's family, molested somebody else's child, or raped somebody else's child. If we find out about it, and the justice system did not give 'em any time, we do not care if you're white, black, pink, polka-dot, yellow, green, or whatever the heck color you are. So help you God, they will bend over and they will kiss their ass good-bye."

"Can you tell me how many members you have in Grant County?" I asked.

"I cannot divulge that," Larry declared. "I refuse. The only thing I can say is, throughout Grant County, we'll probably give an estimate of anywhere between fifty and sixty thousand."

"Oh yeah?" I said, suspecting that this nondivulged membership figure might come close to the county's total population. I looked it up later. Grant County had about 74,000 residents in 1990.

"Did you tell her about the other organization?" the mother asked Larry, as he sat down on the edge of her bed.

"I'm not gonna send her over there," Larry puffed, "because they'll kick off in her fucking ass. You come up and say, 'I'm writing a book.' They'll go, 'I don't give a fuck, you fuckin' Jewbaby. You better get the fuck out of my face.' That's how rude they are. Those guys there—Mom, they are the original Klan. The original. The Knights of the Kamelia!"

The mother protested, "No, it's not the Knights of the Kamelia over there."

"Yes, they are," Larry argued.

"No, it's not. It's the Knights of—of—"

"Knights of Columbus," Larry decided, naming the well-known Catholic benevolent organization.

"Knights of Columbus for Supremacists!" the mother concluded in triumph. I choked back a laugh.

"That's right," Larry agreed. "The Knights of Columbus for the Supremacists. Which is the Knights of the Kamelia. They are the ones that people needs to watch out for."

I assumed he was talking about Jim Ferguson's klavern, and I hoped he'd say more. Obviously he knew something, and maybe I could find a kernel of fact amid the fantasies, craziness, and outright lies. "So you have a brother organization over there," I prompted.

"We wear our robes together," he said, pointing at the suitcase. "I've got my robe in there. I'm not sure if you've seen it."

"I got a glimpse."

He went to the suitcase to get his robe out, as the mother suggested: "Larry, do you have any kinds of literature you might can give her? She wants to see your flags, too."

"Miguel!" Larry called to the kid in the front room. "Get my flags out of there." Then as if suddenly remembering that he was trying to impress me with his racism, he shouted, "Hey, don't stick your dingo paws on my flags!"

"Well, you tell him to do it!" the mother laughed. "He's liable to hit 'em in the floor. You don't put 'em in the floor."

A young woman, Larry's sister, entered the room with a blond toddler. She looked at me and announced, "I don't believe in that kind of stuff."

"Who gives a care?" Larry retorted as he retrieved his flags.

"We're talking about 'em hittin' in the floor," said the mother. "They're not supposed to hit the floor."

The first one Larry unfolded was half green, half white, with red griffin rampant. "This is called a dragon flag."

"Don't let it hit the floor!" the mother called out again, as he turned it around and lost hold of a corner.

"Thank God you caught it," Larry said to the mother. Then he unfurled a blue one with a white star in the center, identifying this as "a Bonnie Blue, the first actual Confederate flag of the United States of America."

The toddler was screaming for a cookie, as Larry donned his robe and hood—white with green trim, face showing. "That's a KQuad," he said, turning around to model the ensemble. "KQuad stands for the Knights of Security Armor. You never cover your face for anything."

"So when do you wear these robes?" I asked.

"When we're in the klav—Hey!" he screamed as his sister got up from her seat on the mother's bed. "Get off my robe!"

"She didn't know she stood there," the mother asserted. "Don't holler."

"She's stickin' her goddang old nigger shoes on my robe!" Larry complained.

"Behave," the mother ordered.

" 'Nigger' shoes?" the sister mocked.

"So. You wear these robes," I interrupted.

"During our meetings. During our naturalization ceremonies," Larry continued, referring to the Klan initiation. Eyes focused in the distance, he proclaimed: "I would personally advise all police officials, all law enforcement officials, and every official there is—to stay away while there is a naturalization ceremony. Because they will get shot. We are armed out there. We either have AKs, SKSs, Uzis, M-16s, M-203 grenade launchers, shotguns, pistols, the whole fucking nine yards. Nobody will be ordered to shoot unless the order is given. Like if I'm in a naturalization ceremony, and I'm contacted on the radio—because I've got a radio on underneath my hood—and once you're inside the klavern, the door is shut, locked. Nobody will be allowed through the outer den or the inner den."

"Gimme kisses," the young woman was saying to the child, "gimme kisses."

"If I am called on the radio," said Larry, still robed as he acted out the fantasy: " 'Hey, Hitler. We're having a problem out here. We got a police officer out here.' I'll say, 'Okay, I'll be out. Do not fire.' I'll go out, and I'll say, 'Is there a problem?' If he asks, 'What are you doing?' Then we're going to ask the question back, 'What the fuck are you doing? So I advise you to get off private property.' "

"So you have a klavern somewhere around here?" I asked.

"I have not gotten my klavern yet," Larry admitted. "Because I'm trying to find a building that's out into the country. Where I can have the cross-lighting and all that type of stuff. Because after you have taken the fellow soldier Klansman through the first step of naturalization, he is asked ten important questions. And then we take him to the outer den, and I cannot tell you what we do to 'em then." He chuckled. "That's top secret."

"You said you had some literature," I reminded him. I was actually drawing a blank on further questions. I felt thoroughly depleted and wanted nothing more than to leave. What was getting me down? The playacting? The glib hatred?

"Some of the things is going to have to be removed," Larry said as he began digging through his file case full of top-secret folders. "I'm gonna give you a different packet, because it's got the State of Indiana nigger-hunting license in there."

"Okay," I said. "Whatever."

"Possibly it's got the federal nigger-hunting license as well."

The young woman announced, "I got the federal honky license!"

"Fuck you," Larry snarled. "You goddamn niggerlover."

"Oh Larry, stop it!" said the mother.

"Better get your fuckin' ass away from me," Larry told his sister.

"She's just playin' with you," the mother advised.

"I don't give a fuck!" he declared. "I'm not in no fuckin' mood!" He stood up with a paper he'd found in the case. He read it to me: " 'At times, life becomes nothing more than making the best of a bad situation. But it is true—where there is good, there must be bad. Therefore where there is worse there must be better. In which case, prepare yourself for what we are about to experience: the best White Pride worldwide. Participate.' "

He mentioned almost as an aside that his group had a rally coming up at the Marion courthouse. September 30. Now this was real news. "So you're more than welcome to come there," he declared, "and you're more than welcome to talk to the fellow Klansmen afterward. If there's some things that you may disagree on, that was said during the protest rally, speak your mind while it's still hot."

He pulled another paper from his case. "This right here is something for when we warn a person . . . 'Knights of the Ku Klux Klan are watching you.'

If that don't work, then a cross goes in his fuckin' yard. And if that don't work, so help his fuckin' house."

And what, he wondered, was my grandfather's name? Maybe his mother had known him. He declared confidently to the mother that my grandfather "died in 1973. Something like that."

My grandfather had died in the 1960s, I informed him.

"I knew it was somewhere in that area, because we've done some full complete research," Larry said. "They got researches on Carr over there."

"Where?" I asked.

"They have things over at the public library."

"A list of members?"

"Yes. Oh, yes. He was—I think he was a Grand Dragon."

Sure. Yeah. Right up there with D. C. Stephenson. And I knew that the library had no membership roll. It was no small thing to have such a list. Old Klan records from the 1920s had just turned up down in Noblesville, found in an old trunk out in a barn. The discovery had sent a tremor through the town that didn't settle until the county historical society voted to keep the names secret.

Larry had now found his membership applications but said he couldn't give me one.

"That's okay," I laughed.

"Now if your grandfather comes out of his grave and says, 'Hitler, give her one!' I'm just a nut anyways. I just gotta have some fun sometimes. Especially since I've had a bad day today. Getting into a fight with my brother."

I hated that Larry kept dragging my grandfather into this. Why had I even mentioned him? I changed the subject, telling Larry about an account of a Klan funeral I'd just found on the front page of a Marion newspaper from 1923. This too was a mistake, since Larry thought he knew everything there was to know about Klan funerals and felt compelled to describe the whole ritual, the sabers, the hymns, the similarity to Klan weddings. Then he moved on to the central Klan ceremony, the cross-lighting: "We do not burn the cross. Quote. We light the cross. The cross symbolized Christianity. It does not symbolize terrorism. It does not represent hatred. They say the guys that wears these white robes, white hoods—they are hatred, racism. They don't understand the concept on the Ku Klux Klan. Because if it wasn't for us, niggers would be running this dingo country. Because these days you gotta be a nigger to get a welfare check. You gotta be a nigger to get food stamps. You gotta be a nigger to get a job. If you ain't got big lips, rug head, wide eyes, and big mouth—and jump from tree to tree getting the fuckin' bananas—you ain't getting nothing. We light the cross. It represents Christian-anity."

Everything Larry was telling me just left me incredulous. On the television the mother's show had ended—a Chinese show, I suddenly realized. I watched the pictogram credits scrolling by.

"This is a charter," Larry announced, pulling out the document that, as he put it, "each and every klavern must have." He didn't let me look for long, but I had a chance to note the date: "the desolate day of the wailing month of October" 1994. It was signed by someone affiliated with the National Knights. He packed his robe away and again took out the photo of the alleged grandfather.

"Have you ever talked to any other Klansmen?" he asked.

"Just the other day."

He wanted to know who it was, and I decided to tell him since Jim Ferguson was so public about his membership. Larry hooted with laughter: "Oh, James! James! Fergy! Jimmy!"

"You know him?"

"Yeah. He's a fuckin' nut, man. He's a fuckin' lunatic."

I flipped through the seven or eight pages of propaganda he'd handed me: the drawing of a robed Klansman in classic Uncle Sam pose ("I Want You"), some screed about "our constitutional rights," a couple of pages of coarse racist cartoons. I felt that I'd reached my limit on how much garbage I could absorb. My reaction was physical; my throat was closing.

Larry pulled another paper out of his file box. "This is my certificate, when I was Titan," he said, claiming yet another Klan office. I was feeling completely disoriented.

"The Klan is a strictly nonviolent organization," Larry repeated. "I'm sure Jimmy told you that, did he?"

"Yeah."

"Cuz if he don't, I'm going to his fuckin' house right now and I'll put a size fourteen up his ass."

He asked if we could go outside. He needed a cigarette. Fine. Once there I could make my exit, so I said good-bye to the mother.

"That's my father," she said, pointing to the photo of John Howard, Emperor.

"Great," I told her. "Thank you." Eventually I would learn that John Howard was in fact the man who opened the controversial Ku Klux Klan Museum and Redneck Shop in Laurens, South Carolina. And he was several years younger than the mother. But at that moment his picture was just one more part of what wasn't adding up in the Hitler household.

Outside I told Larry that I was leaving town the next morning but would return in a month. He promised he would introduce me then to the Wizard, the Dragon, and the Exalted Cyclops. "High-up officers. I'll let you talk to them. And if you're wishing to have a picture of me in my robe and hood, I will have one for you. That robe in there was my Titan robe." He began describing the Klan patch, a symbol called a myoak, missing from that robe.

Just then Tom Wise pulled up in front of the house, now in street clothes and his own car. He was checking up on me. Larry wheeled and shot him a look of horror. I walked over to Tom's car and poked my head in the window. "It's okay," I told him. "I'll call you later." Tom drove away.

"You know him?" Larry asked.

"That's the policeman who was here before."

"Is he the one who told you?"

"He's the one."

Larry didn't react to this news at all but began pointing out the cuts he'd gotten in the fight with his brother. "That. That. That. That. He was throwing me around like a rag doll."

"You were telling me about the myoak," I reminded him.

As if I really cared. The description of a myoak—blood drop and four hidden K's—I could get from a book. I really wanted to leave.

"If you're ever traveling the city limits of racist towns," Larry was advising me, "and you see a sign that says 'KIGY,' that means 'Klansman I Greet You.' That means there's a rally going on, so that would be very interesting there. Even though you're not a cardholder, you can possibly talk to them. Did Jimmy ask you were you a federal agent?"

Somehow he hadn't, but Larry suddenly didn't care. He was explaining more "Klancraft" to me. That "thirty-three-five stands for Ku Klux Klan." And so on. I asked him if there were any militias in the area.

Yes, he said. It was a biker club. Once he found out its name, he was going to do research, and "if I find out that they're like the Black Panthers, I'm gonna run 'em out. There's also some Black Panthers here. I'm not for sure if you've heard of the Black Panthers."

I had, I assured him. But I thought they'd been active in the 1960s.

"Yeah, back in the sixties we ran 'em out," he said. "We banished them. And that was when that racial war took place. Back in 1963. After they passed the civil rights, stating coonheads were allowed to date the whites. That pisses me off there. That turns my—that turns my skin. And that turns my stomach, and just makes me want to just do something to 'em. And then half-breed babies running around, which I call zebras. That pisses me off bad. There's a lot of things that goes on in this town. I've already been shot at twice. By some coonheads. Also I have been threatened by a Black Panther militia organization, saying that they're gonna kill me. I tell 'em, bring it on. Anybody kills a Klansman," he spit, "they better bend over, kiss their ass good-bye, because the Klan comes in this town, this town is gonna be fuckin' leveled. From that end to that end. It will be leveled. Especially a high-ranking and respected officer like myself."

Suddenly he decided he had to show me his Kloran, the official book of Kluxer rituals. "Bobby!" he shouted to the fat brother in the house. "Can you bring my black thing?" His file box. "It's there on Mom's Porta Potti!

"I'll let you get a brief glance of it," he told me as Bobby brought the box outside. "Where you at, Kloran?" He pawed through the box. "I know I put you in here. Okay. Evidently I don't have it in here. I'll have a Kloran for you next time you come. It'll be for you. And I'll have other various information and a picture of myself in my robe and hood. Also a picture of a cross-lighting with other Klansmen standing around. I'm sure that'll stand out real good in the book."

I thanked him and said I'd be back in town before the September 30 rally.

"It will be a KKK protest rally concerning a lot of problems going on. We totally disagree. We're not taking it anymore. We've had it up to our fuckin' heads, okay? And I'm gonna be straightforward and honest with you. Presently at this time, underneath my command as Imperial Wizard, I have four hundred eighty-one members for the Patriotic Knights of the Ku Klux Klan. Four hundred eighty-one members. That's just within Marion, Gas City, Fairmount, Sweetser, and then just moving into Huntington. What we do is, we get on our robes and hoods or sometimes we get on our shirts that say 'Boys in the Hood.' Or some other shirts that say 'If you don't like my rebel flag, you can kiss my rebel ass.' I like that one the best." He grinned. "We've got some other shirts that say, 'If I'd have known that this was gonna happen, I'd have picked my own damn cotton.' And we have other ones that say, 'It's a white thing—you wouldn't understand.' All kinds of T-shirts." He kept watching my face as if he expected me to break into hearty laughter.

Just being cordial had worn me to a nubbin. But it seemed like Larry didn't want me to leave. He began describing a recruiting drive. They'd worn the T-shirts. Two days ago in Wabash. Thirty-six hundred packets gone in just five hours, while guys drove by yelling "White Power!"

And had I heard the story about Randy Weaver, "a White Aryan Recep-tionist"? Larry talked on and on. The Weavers. The wife. The feds. And David Koresh. "They tried to say David Koresh was part of the Klan as well. We totally disowned him."

Meanwhile a black kid of about fourteen was walking in and out of the front door as if he belonged there. I watched him gently lead one of the dirty little blond kids inside. Larry ignored him.

I didn't have the strength to question it. Next time. I asked Larry for his phone number.

"Well, the phone's due to be shut off," he said a bit sheepishly.

"Then I'll just come by," I told him, taking a step toward my car. He reached into the file case and pulled out a stapled packet of a dozen pages or so—Uncle Sam Klansman on the cover, and Larry's card attached, identify-ing him as part of the American Knights of the Ku Klux Klan. "This is the organization I broke away from. I was Grand Dragon for them," he informed me. "That's a full complete packet. Has the application on the back. Also, you have a nigger-hunting license."

"Okay," I said, not even glancing at the new stuff. I took another step back.

"So that's everything. Next time when you come back . . ."

"Okay."

". . . I'll have some information for you."

"Okay."

"Full complete history on the Ku Klux Klan."

"Great."

"Also I'll have you some newspapers."

"Okay."

"I'll have you some newspapers from *The Truth at Last*. It's from the Southern Knights of the Ku Klux Klan from Marietta, Georgia."

"Okay."

"Which my grandfather was the Grand Dragon of the organization."

"Right."

"I mean my dad. My dad's the Grand Dragon."

"Okay."

"I'll have you a picture of myself in my robe and hood."

"Okay."

"And I'll have you a picture . . ."

"Okay."

". . . of a cross-lighting . . ."

"Okay."

". . . and Klansmen standing around."

"Great."

"A cross-lighting."

"Okay."

"And it will be the triple cross-lighting."

"Okay."

A car zoomed past honking, and Larry raised his arm in the white power salute.

"A friend?" I asked.

"Some more of the fellow brothers."

"Right."

"Did you hear when they yelled 'Hitler'?" he beamed.

"Ah. Uh-huh. Okay."

I got into the car, ready to drop with emotional exhaustion. I had not asked Larry how he made a living, why he'd been in prison, or even how old he was. I felt like I'd been slogging through deep water. Later, listening to the tape, I realized I was panting as I drove away.

SEVEN

"THEY WERE STRANGERS
TO ME"

One detail about the crimes of August 6 and August 7, 1930, spoke volumes to me. Someone from the Fansler family—the people who gave first aid to the mortally wounded Claude Deeter—found a hickory branch covered with blood at the crime scene the next day. The police never came to get it. In fact, they apparently never went back to search the Lover's Lane site for any kind of evidence. I realize that police methodology has changed over the years. Still, I couldn't help but wonder: did certain people know as early as the morning of August 7 that Thomas Shipp and Abe Smith were never going to have a trial?

Whatever happened to Claude Deeter and Mary Ball was as underinvestigated as the lynching itself. From the beginning Marion authorities behaved as if they just wanted the whole thing to go away. On August 8 the *Wabash Plain-Dealer* was already noting the Grant County prosecutor's ambivalence about going after those responsible for the hanging: "[Harley] Hardin declared that any conviction of any leaders of the mob depended entirely on public sentiment and that if the public sentiment condoned the ghastly affair, no successful prosecution of the ring leaders was possible."

On the state level, meanwhile, there was at least a need to save face. The infamous photograph had appeared in newspapers all over the country, and

as the *Indianapolis Star* editorialized on August 9: "All Indiana is humili-
ated and is ashamed of the tragedy enacted at Marion Thursday night. . . .
every Hoosier has a right to expect that those in authority will see that law
and order are vindicated." On August 8 Attorney General James Ogden sent
two of his deputies, Earl Stroup and Merl Wall, to Marion to help Hardin
put a case together. It was Attorney General Ogden who eventually indicted
eight Marion men, leading to two brief, pointless trials and no convictions.
He stepped in after a Grant County grand jury failed to indict anyone at all.

In Indianapolis, among Ogden's papers, I found over three hundred
pages of depositions taken by prosecutors Wall, Stroup, and Hardin about a
week after the lynching, mostly from law enforcement officers. Beyond that
any records had disappeared. At the Grant County courthouse, they didn't
even have the indictments of alleged lynchers that Tom Wise found there in
the 1970s, much less the transcripts from the two trials. But then I wondered how much the documents mattered. They wouldn't have told me
who committed the crime. In 1930 most white residents of Grant County
saw the lynching as an act of moral rectitude. That meant that two men were
murdered in front of thousands of witnesses, but—on the record—nobody
saw a thing.

Off the record, of course, everybody had a story.

I SET OUT TO FIND eyewitnesses who'd been at least ten when they saw
the lynching—though obviously the older the better. People in Marion gave
me names, and one sometimes led to another. ("Ask *me,*" one old man demanded, as I sat interviewing his roommate in one of the local nursing
homes.) I discarded whole interviews if the testimony was spotty or confused. For most people, however, the lynching had been the worst thing they
ever saw, and certain images had been burned into their brains. I heard striking and very credible accounts from a couple of people who'd been just
seven when they saw it. But most who'd witnessed the lynching were already
dead. This was a race against time. Even so, working more than sixty-five
years after it happened, I got information I hadn't seen in any published
source.

Part of the folklore around the tragedy was that it hadn't been planned,
that it just happened spontaneously. I suspected otherwise, but didn't
have proof till I found Ed Shelley, who had been nineteen at the time of the
hanging.

Ed had not actually been present when it happened, though he walked by the next morning on the way to work and watched them cut down the bodies. He seemed a little embarrassed by that, even more so by the fact that his brother had accepted a piece of the rope as a souvenir. (Ed didn't realize this until they got home that night, and his brother said, "Looka here.") He remembered that when the bodies came down, it was after sun-up. There was a big crowd, and he couldn't see who actually took them down. Or who cut the rope into pieces.

But Ed held a major puzzle piece. He told me that on August 7, during his lunch hour at the Midwest Paper and Envelope Company, some men came by to recruit lynchers.

"They wanted it very secretive, you know. They didn't talk to me. They talked to people I worked with." These coworkers told Ed what the men wanted.

I asked if any of them had participated in the lynching. Ed didn't know.

The two or three recruiters hadn't actually come inside the plant, which was seven blocks south of the courthouse. Ed saw them outside, as he sat on the curb with the other workers, eating lunch. I asked him if he could describe the men in any way. "They were just regular working fellas," he said. He had never seen them before.

His lunch hour was between twelve and one. Claude Deeter died at one-thirty.

ON THE MORNING OF August 7, 1930, Marion woke up to the banner headline SHOOT MAN, ASSAULT SWEETHEART emblazoned across the front page of the *Marion Leader-Tribune*. In retrospect, the luridly written story seems almost calculated to provoke a groundswell of outrage. "Shot down in a valorous effort to save the honor of his sweetheart," it begins, "Claude Deeter, 23, of R.F.D. 2 Fairmount, is in the Grant County hospital probably fatally wounded by four shots from a large caliber revolver, in the hands of one of three colored hold-up men. The girl, Mary Ball, 19, of 2111 West Eleventh Street, was torn from Deeter's arms, carried to the brush, and assaulted, she reported to police."

According to the *Leader-Tribune,* Abe Smith had already confessed to the rape but blamed Tom Shipp for the shooting, while Shipp had named "the third member of the gang" as the triggerman. Apparently James Cameron had not been apprehended before deadline.

The *Leader-Tribune* told the story this way: The robbers tried to take a watch and high school ring from Mary Ball, but Deeter intervened and suffered a blow "across the eyes" from a blackjack. The girl screamed, and Deeter struck out at the man nearest him. Then according to the newspaper, one of the thieves grabbed the girl while the other two took Deeter to the bank of the Mississinewa. There they shot him four times. Soon afterward a car approached, scaring the assailants into flight. Farmer Dave Fansler, who lived up the hill, fired at the fleeing robbers, then rushed with his wife and son to the wounded Deeter. Meanwhile, Mary Ball tried to stop the passing motorists, screaming, "They've killed him! They've killed my sweetheart!" The driver refused to stop but drove the mile or two into Marion and reported it at a fire station. Firemen called police.

Smith already had a police record. Auto theft. Stealing chickens. He'd done six months at the state farm. By August 6, 1930, he and Shipp were under investigation for several filling station robberies, so the description of Shipp's car sent police directly to his home. They found the engine still warm and weeds like those near the River Road stuck under the chassis. Later that night police also picked up a man named Robert Sullivan, allegedly an accomplice in the filling station robberies.

The evening paper, the *Chronicle,* printed a double-banner headline the afternoon of the seventh: SEEKS DEATH CHAIR FOR TRIO IN MURDER. Deeter had died.

And the story had changed. The *Chronicle* reported that one assailant walked Deeter to the river immediately, while the other two robbed Mary Ball and one then raped her as the other held her down. Shipp and Smith were blaming each other for the fatal shooting.

"Miss Ball was unable to identify any of the suspects due to her nervous condition," said the *Chronicle.* "Police officers declared that the case against the suspects was so strong that they did not plan further attempts to have her identify the youths as her assailants."

Everyone involved was quite young. Both Shipp and Smith were nineteen. Cameron was sixteen. The ages of Deeter and Ball, misreported in the paper, were twenty-four and seventeen.

SOME GROUP SOMEWHERE came up with a master plan. I felt sure of it after hearing Ruth Thomas's story. She was living in New York City with her son when we spoke on the phone. Though ill with spinal meningitis, she was still mentally sharp.

Ruth had been twelve years old in 1930. Her older sister had a dress shop in a building on the north side of the square, on the second floor. On

August 7, Ruth said, Sis stayed past her usual five P.M. closing time to finish beading a wedding dress. She began to hear noises, but looking outside, she noticed that the streets were empty.

Meanwhile their father had come home from his job at a local lumber company, where he'd heard lynching talk all day. "There was a *feeling* in the community," Ruth recalled. "There wasn't anybody on the streets. Nobody outside of their houses. It was August. Nobody on their porches. It was a dead city. And Mother and Dad got concerned. Mother called Sis and told her regardless of what she was doing, put her things away and come home. And come immediately."

Sis closed the shop and went downstairs to find the street deserted except for small groups of white men clustered on the sidewalks. One of these men approached her and demanded to know what she was doing on the street.

Going home, she said.

The man told her: You can't go home. You have to get off the street.

I'm just going to catch the streetcar, Sis told him.

They're not running, he said.

She tried to call for a taxi, but was told that there were none available. When Sis couldn't get home, the whole family drove downtown to get her. Ruth's father was afraid to leave anyone home. Their car was stopped at Ninth and Washington, five blocks south of the square.

"There was a line of men with their arms hooked completely across the street," Ruth remembered. As she got out of the car, she saw a number of trolley cars sitting there, disconnected from their overhead wires, or "pulled off the lines" as Ruth put it. "There were people around 'em, wouldn't let you put them back." Somehow the disabling of Marion's public transit system did not merit comment in a single newspaper story; nor was it discussed at the court of inquiry.

Ruth and her parents walked the rest of the way to Sis's place on the square. It was about six-thirty P.M., and people were gathering down at the jail. "My folks made me go into the back room of the shop, where I couldn't see and where I couldn't hear, and my mother came back there with me and put my head down in her lap and covered it up and wanted me to have no part of it. But I could still hear the mob," Ruth said. "I'll tell you. Once you hear a mob like that, you never forget it. It was like wild animals."

The family was in the shop only long enough to plan an escape. Coming down the front stairway, they ducked into the nearest alley and ran, circling north and then west to avoid the downtown area entirely.

Ruth had been hesitant to talk to me about the lynching, worried about "stirring it up." So we had talked first about the Marion Easter Pageant, which she cofounded in 1937, and in this way I learned that she had known my grandparents. They'd been sponsors of the interdenominational group— young adult, all Protestant—that started the pageant and "closed some awful gaps" in the community, as Ruth put it. Awful gaps? I wondered if the pageant was some symbolic attempt to address the lynching. "Partly," said Ruth, who had served as its drama director for thirty-five years. "We wanted to do something for the community that would show our unity and our to-getherness."

What stayed with her most after the lynching was the new uneasiness between white and black Marion. She had had black friends, but the lynch-ing severed those connections. It took her years to get them back. She also remembered her feelings about a new custom she observed—new to Mar-ion, but common in the Jim Crow South: "If you walked down the sidewalk and a black person was coming towards you, I can remember they stepped off the walk. I didn't like that. I didn't like that at all.

"I've tried to put a lot of it out of my mind, because it was such a weight to carry when I worked at the newspaper," she said. Ruth had been the paper's librarian for twenty years and remembered, "There was hardly a day went by that somebody didn't come in and want to read about that."

THE NIGHT OF AUGUST 6—the night of the robbery, murder, and alleged rape on the River Road—five thousand people poured into downtown Mar-ion to watch a Human Fly scale a building diagonally across the square from where the lynching would take place the next night. Also making news was an oppressive three-week-long heat wave. The day of the lynching, tempera-tures hit one hundred degrees, with high humidity.

"It was a hot day. Just a tense smothery day, because you didn't know what was going to happen next," Charlotte Vickery told me in her room at a local nursing home. "We had had all kind of reports about the happening out along the river and about the girl getting help."

Charlotte was about to turn ninety-six when we spoke and had been thirty at the time of the lynching. She remembered that her husband was out of town that day. "I was concerned because every highway was full of cars," she said. "Mostly cars from—not our local area. And town was full of people. In groups. The street corners. What they should do. I had a couple of girls rooming at my house who worked at the creamery, and I think a couple girls that worked at the shoe factory. So we got supper over, and everybody got home that was supposed to be, and of course that's all the conversation you heard, was something pertaining to the incident and the crowd of people coming here from all directions. And we wondered what would happen to our town."

Then after dark, as Charlotte put it, "Everybody in the neighborhood took a drive."

She just "followed the line of traffic" and drove right past the jail. "We saw them bringing one of the men out of the jail, and he was hanging on to anything he could hold on to, like the railing. Of course his hands were hit, and he just dropped down. I think this was the third one, but that's immaterial. They brought them up there, and I remember traffic, of course, was just car after car. You just barely moved because traffic was so tight, and as we came along they were bringing this third one up, and when they had the rope around one of their necks—they had all three of them there, and when they went to pull the one up, he put his hands up to hold on to the rope, so it wouldn't tighten around his neck, and they let him down enough that they could reach with clubs and hit his hands and break his arms. And then they pulled him back up."

Charlotte had probably seen the second man hanged, and she expressed no particular feeling about what she'd witnessed. She seemed to think that the prisoners had already had a trial.

But she'd been deeply upset about the rape of Mary Ball. That too had been the talk of the dinner table. "The girl's family. That such a thing could happen."

When I was a girl, I never even knew about the murder of Claude Deeter, only about the rape. Clearly that's what galvanized the town.

ALMOST IMMEDIATELY I NOTICED a difference between the way white people and black people named what had happened that night. Few used the L-word. Whites usually called it "the hanging," while blacks referred to it as "August seventh, 1930." Behind those two labels were two very different interpretations: a justifiable punishment versus a day that would live in infamy.

Barbara Stevenson, president of the Grant County Black History Council, told me that on the night of the lynching, black residents of Marion armed themselves and congregated together in one another's homes or left the city altogether. Some went out to Weaver. Many stayed up all night.

"There was talk that the Klan was going to do some burning," said Stevenson. She told me no black person would have been downtown that night, unless they were there by mistake.

I did speak to a black woman who'd walked around the courthouse late that afternoon, though I sought her out originally because she'd reportedly been acquainted with Shipp and Smith. Lucille McGwin was twenty-four at the time of the lynching. When we met, she too lived in a nursing home, in a room nearly devoid of personal effects except for a radio blaring out country music and a stuffed animal on the chair with her. She sat bent nearly double, wearing an orange housecoat, bracelets on each arm, and three rings on her wedding finger.

Lucille was ninety years old, and she was an angry woman. Fiercely she repeated my questions as if she couldn't believe how stupid they were. Abram Smith was "kind of a no-good," she said, but Tommy Shipp was a good boy and "helped his mother." Mary Ball was also a "no-good"—and involved with Abram Smith.

"What did you hear about her?"

"What did I hear about her?"

"What makes you think Mary Ball was no good?"

"Everybody knew her!"

I asked if it was common knowledge that Mary Ball and Abram Smith had been lovers. She snapped, "Nobody talked about it 'cause everybody knew it!" Lucille gave a mirthless little chuckle to my question about Mary Ball being raped, declaring, "Nobody would rape her. They wouldn't have to."

Sheriff Jake Campbell was also a "no-good, a Negro-hater," a Klansman. She said accusingly that I probably didn't realize that a lot of Negroes were Republicans. And those black Republicans couldn't believe that Jake was no good. They wouldn't believe there'd be a lynching.

I knew that Flossie Bailey of the NAACP had called the governor and the sheriff on August 7, trying to get Shipp, Smith, and Cameron moved to safety.

"The NAACP tried to do something," I said. Lucille responded with her hollow laugh.

Had the Klan been involved? "Was the Klan involved?!? Anybody with a brain in their head would know they were!"

She was hunched so far over I could barely see her face. Hunched, and spitting tacks. I had no doubt that her cynicism was well earned.

Sure, she used to see the Klan around. "They didn't make no bones about it." The talk had been that the lynching was all Klan, Lucille reported, but she wasn't sure if it was them or white trash. And she felt sure that the Republican Party was somehow involved as well.

Lucille had worked for twenty years in the laundry at the Spencer Hotel, right off the square. On August 7, 1930, she left work in the afternoon and walked around the courthouse and saw white people standing around in little groups. "Everybody knew what they were talking about. They'd talked about it all day long. Everybody knew what was going to happen."

On her way home Lucille stopped to see another black woman, to warn her. She recalled going up on the woman's porch and advising her: "You got any ammunition, you better get it. Because you're gonna need it."

This woman's husband owned the pool hall frequented by blacks and had been to see the sheriff about the lynching rumors. And so the woman told Lucille: "Jake said there wasn't nothin' to it."

Lucille replied: "Jake told a lie. It's gonna happen. I seen the way they're gathered up."

She then went home and got her gun out and loaded it and stayed up all night. "I thought, anybody want to come, let 'em come. Don't make me any difference. I meant to fill somebody full of lead." The next morning when she went to work, the bodies were still hanging on the tree. Lucille could see them from the hotel. "One fella came down to the department where I worked and he had a picture and he handed it to my boss and he said, 'Where were you last night?' and my boss said, 'Home where I oughta be.'"

Lucille kept railing against the black Republicans. "They said Jake wouldn't let it happen. Jake was in it with 'em!"

She had not known James Cameron. "He was almost the third one hanged," I told her, "but they let him go at the last minute."

"That was *his* story," she said. "I don't believe it." It was May 1996. I had come to understand by then that many black people of Lucille's generation did not believe James Cameron. They just couldn't believe that any lynch mob would get a black man as far as a hanging tree, then let him go.

JAKE SAID THERE WASN'T NOTHIN' TO IT. Six days after the lynching Sheriff Jake Campbell told the court of inquiry that he hadn't had a clue to what would happen on August 7 until maybe seven or seven-fifteen P.M. That's when Flossie Bailey called to tell him that she had information about a mob forming. The sheriff still did nothing till her husband, Dr. Bailey, called about ten minutes later to reiterate the threats they'd heard. "I thought after I had the second call it might be advisable, if that was the rumor, to get [the prisoners] out," the sheriff told Earl Stroup, one of the deputy attorney generals who'd come from Indianapolis.

Campbell said he then went to the garage "to see how the gasoline was in my car" and found that the tires on both his vehicles had been slashed, the gas drained, and the distributor cap removed. In the alley behind the jail he noted "possibly a dozen fellows lined up against the wall." Four more men were sitting in a car across from the jail. "That was the first intimation I had," he testified. He did not approach these men, much less question them. He could not describe them beyond "young fellows . . . medium built fellows." He had not tried to secure another car.

What Campbell told investigators was that he thought he could handle an assault on the jail. Yet he took no precautions. He made no effort to break up the crowds that kept gathering nearby, did not put extra deputies on duty, did not make any contingency plan with Marion's police. And the Baileys' warnings certainly weren't the first he heard. *Wasn't nothin' to it.*

The city police had also been hearing rumors. They also did nothing. Their headquarters were about four blocks from the county jail. Officer Garl Peterson said that when he reported for duty at five forty-five, Captain Charles Truex told him "it looked pretty bad from what he had been hearing." One patrolman, Chester Marley, testified that a lynching was "talked on the street" early in the day; and he'd reported it to his superiors around noon.

Asked whom he told, Marley replied, "I think the chief was there and the assistant chief, probably others."

"Did you hear any order given by the chief or other officers in command, looking toward clearing the street or anticipating any trouble that evening?"

"No sir."

Marion police chief Lewis Lindenmuth, who had hung Deeter's bloody shirt out the window at the stationhouse—"to dry," he said—told the court of inquiry that he didn't hear anything until seven-thirty P.M. He was in an ice cream parlor when a man came in to say that there was "a big mob on the road to hang the colored fellows." Lindenmuth went directly to the jail, where he found the sheriff and deputies sitting outside. "I told them what this fellow said. They didn't seem to think there was anything much to it." But it wasn't long before a crowd "sprung right up," in the words of Chief Lindenmuth.

The chief was either mistaken or lying about his estimate of the time. Billy Connors, manager of a downtown movie theater and a friend of Campbell's, said that he'd come by the jail around six-thirty. The sheriff was sitting in a chair on the sidewalk leading to the jail and twenty-five to thirty people were hanging around. Connors and Campbell spoke about a trip they planned to make out of town, and within twenty minutes, Connors estimated, the crowd had multiplied to more than three hundred, forcing the sheriff to move back to the porch. It was then that Campbell got the phone calls from the Baileys and found his cars sabotaged.

A *Chronicle* reporter named Drysdale Brannon had stopped by around six, he said, and "a large chap, who I afterwards learned was Charles Lennon, was whispering to Sheriff Campbell. . . . He was leaning over the chair, whispering to Sheriff Campbell." Brannon returned at about eight to find a mob clustered around the porch, spilling from the jail yard into the street and across the street. He stayed to witness the carnage. Again he saw Lennon, a large man dressed in a blue work shirt, "rather roughly shaven" with a heavy beard. "He was on the jail steps; because of his unusual size I observed him for several minutes; later I saw him striking the jail door with a bar or a sledge." Charles Lennon would remain one of the few people identified in 1930 as an active participant.

As THE COURT OF INQUIRY began on August 13, Grant County prosecutor Harley Hardin told the *Marion Chronicle* "that public opinion was opposed to the prosecution of any members of the mob," yet he would do his duty. As I went through the depositions, however, I noticed that he rarely elicited any information I could use. Earl Stroup and Merl Wall, the two prosecutors sent from Indianapolis by the attorney general, did most of the questioning and all of the goading. They must have been unwelcome guests in Marion. Wall also met secretly with the NAACP's Mrs. Bailey, advising her as early as August 9 that getting indictments would not be easy.

Still, even Wall and Stroup may have been surprised by the evasions and obvious lies they heard at the inquiry from law enforcement officers. Their very first witness, assistant police chief Roy Collins, said he'd arrived at the jail before eight, when the confrontation was still at the talking stage. In theory he'd been in a position to see everything. But asked whom he recognized in the mob that night, the assistant chief replied, "I wasn't just exactly trying to recognize anyone. I was thinking of something else." The depositions, though filled with ridiculous statements like this one, are still the best account available of police activity—and more important, inactivity—during the lynching. No one could claim total amnesia. Certain facts leak through.

From roughly eight to nine P.M. Jake Campbell stood on the covered square porch with its east door leading into the sheriff's residence and its north door leading into the jail, and he pleaded with the steadily growing crowd to go home. Or so he would later claim, and he may well have done it, at least going through the motions. He couldn't know who exactly was in that throng to bear witness. And Campbell must have been aware of Indiana's 1905 lynching law, which stated that any sheriff who allowed a prisoner to be taken from his custody and lynched was "guilty of failure of official duty" and subject to removal from office.

Fourteen other law enforcement officers would eventually join Campbell at the jail that night—five from the sheriff's own squad and nine from the police department. The police all came of their own volition; they had not been summoned. Even when the sheriff finally did call police headquarters, he told them only that he "might need some help and to get their men available in case we did need anybody."

So, for example, when Patrolman Charles Bellville reported for duty at the police station at eight P.M., he was told only to "watch the lights"—police signal lights at each corner of the square indicating that there was trouble somewhere. Since his beat was the east side of the square, Bellville immediately saw the crowd at the jail a half block away and walked over. He entered the sheriff's residence and came out the side door onto the porch where several officers, including the police chief, had already joined the sheriff.

In another creative excuse offered to the court of inquiry, Bellville would explain that he had not noticed anyone in the mob, because the porch put him three steps higher than the crowd, and "I was listening to the sheriff, what he had to say, more so than looking down."

"You didn't notice any of the men up against you?" Stroup asked.

"Not to recognize who they were."

"None of them had on masks."

"I didn't notice that they had; they possibly had caps on, kinda pulled down; I noticed some that way."

"Were the general run of them young or old men?"

"I couldn't say whether old or young."

"Did you know any man in that crowd that you paid enough attention to, that you could pick him out again if you saw him?"

"No sir."

"You couldn't identify any one if they all paraded in front of you again?"

"They looked like strangers to me."

A special deputy named John Fryer left a Spanish War veterans meeting around nine and saw the police signals on, so he walked to city hall. The desk sergeant there was calling the fire department, ordering a truck to the jail, so Fryer rode along. Upon his arrival, Fryer testified, the sheriff "requested me to tell the firemen not to throw any water . . . that [the mob] had dynamite there and was going to use it."

Asked if he could identify anyone in the crowd, Fryer replied, "I never saw so many strange people around here in my life." But he would recognize one man if he saw him again: "an old gentleman, gray headed, rather heavy set; he made the remark, that was the way they did in Kentucky; he said you couldn't get law enforcement here. They let the niggers in the school with the white children here and march in the band."

Apparently all the talk came to a head when Hoot Ball, "father of the girl," came forward and demanded, "Give us the keys and let us get the niggers." Campbell testified later that he told Hoot the case should go through the system, and Hoot replied, "The court will give them about two years."

At some point Prosecutor Hardin joined the sheriff in trying to dissuade the mob. According to the *Wabash Plain-Dealer,* Hardin shouted, "Don't make this mistake. I'll give 'em the limit." And the shouted reply went, "We want them now!"

Billy Connors, the theater manager, was also on the porch during this confrontation. The code of silence did not apply to Connors, and he freely described the three men he'd picked out as leaders of the mob. The first one he noticed after the sheriff's parley with Hoot Ball. Once Ball had been quieted, said Connors, "that cry was taken up by some big fellow. I imagine he was about six feet tall, very broad shoulders, he had a blue shirt on and a couple days' growth of beard . . . he started to lead the yelling of the crime." The description matches that of Charles Lennon. Connors identified another leader as the brother-in-law of the Ball family. And the third, he said, was "some little thin wiry kid that couldn't be over fifteen or sixteen years of age, wild as a hawk." Phil Boyd? Named by Jack Edwards as the other ringleader, Boyd had been all of seventeen.

According to Connors, the sheriff continued to plead with the mob until "at last there was a giant shove and they crashed right through up on the porch. I was pinned back to the wall of the jail . . . and somebody holloed [sic] 'get the sledgehammer and crowbar.' "

Campbell called Connors inside the jail and told him, "I am going up and give those fellows some tear gas." One policeman joined Campbell and Connors in throwing several tear gas bombs. Apparently the pins were never pulled on some, and these were thrown back inside. Connors noted that

Hoot Ball was in the jail, too. Ball had been jostled out in the crowd (hit in the stomach with an elbow, Connors thought), and he'd collapsed. "[Hoot] was sitting there very much subdued from his warlike spirit," said Connors. "He didn't want anything done to the colored boys then. He was in a very lenient mood, very sorry he started it. . . . I heard him tell the sheriff he was sorry. The sheriff said this was a hell of a time to be sorry."

The tear gas, reported Connors, "had some effect, not much . . . they came right back. . . . I went upstairs and called Anderson, Muncie, and Kokomo on the telephone and asked them to send help. While I was telephoning, they got through the other door. I imagine it took me somewhere near twenty minutes to get the calls through to the different towns. By that time they were dragging out one of the men."

And where were the other police officers and the sheriff's deputies while the theater manager dispensed tear gas and called for reinforcements? According to their testimonies, seven of the fifteen officers who were present spent the entire time inside the sheriff's house. One of them, Deputy Sheriff Charles Love, reported for duty at nine-thirty as the assault on the jail door was under way.

"How many men did you recognize in that mob?" Wall asked Love.

"I didn't try to recognize any; I was in a hurry to get over there."

"Sure; but how many did you recognize?"

"I don't know I recognized any."

"You are positive you didn't know a single man in that mob?"

"I didn't know any one; there were people down around there, but I didn't pay no attention to them; I didn't know what was going on till I got there."

"Why didn't you pay attention to that seething mob around the jail?"

"They were strangers to me."

Most of the officers testified that they received no orders that night. But Love had orders—to escort the sheriff's family to the Spencer Hotel. Then, upon returning to his spot inside the sheriff's residence, he did nothing. Or as he put it, "There were four or five of us that stood there watching the door."

Wall and Stroup questioned most of the men who stayed in the sheriff's house rather sarcastically. How did they expect to protect the prisoners from there?

Chief of Police Lindenmuth explained that he had to stay there because he had tear gas in his eyes. Of course, the tear gas, as Wall observed, "didn't seem to be affecting the rioters." These officers could have easily entered the jail without going outside, through the passageway connecting the second story of the residence with the third-floor cell blocks. Campbell himself went back and forth several times that night between his house and the jail.

So eight officers were actually in the jail while it was under siege. Two of the eight stayed in the basement the entire time, guarding the windows. They admitted, however, that rioters would have had to crawl through one at a time, so no one tried to crawl through at all. One of the officers down there was Chester Marley. Asked if he'd been given any orders by any superior officer, Marley said, "Well, I don't remember them giving any orders; only they said, somebody go to the basement." The mob had broken the windows down there, and Marley could see them outside.

"What kind of looking fellows were they?" asked Stroup

"They were strangers to me."

"Can you give a description of them?"

"I couldn't."

"Is that your usual custom, when you see a crime being committed, you don't take note of their characteristics so you might describe the persons, identify them?"

"They might have been recognized if somebody would see them; in this case, everybody was in an uproar, doing all they could do, you know." But nine of those officers were doing all they could do in places the mob didn't want to go.

That left six men to defend the prisoners. Briefly, they took out guns. Almost immediately, they put them back. On account of the women and children, they would later explain.

On account of the alleged dynamite.

Marion police captain Charles Truex made this extraordinary statement to the court of inquiry: "Understand me, I am not arguing for the mob. That was a terrible thing, a black eye on the county. I am sorry it happened. But if it hadn't been a fair mob, they would never have brought this fellow Cameron down there with the doubt in their minds as to whether he was or was not guilty. . . . They were only asking for two lives, and both of them confessed to two of the worst crimes in the history of the county. And they were only asking for two lives. If we had went to shooting, we would have filled the morgues in Marion before it was through with."

Unable to budge the front door, the mob hammered at the large stones framing the door, concentrating on the one where the lock was set. (A photo published in the Wabash newspaper on August 9 shows a gap where that stone used to be, with a sledgehammer and crowbar still leaning against the wall.) By most estimates, the mob broke through around ten. The sheriff thought he was on the third floor at that point, or maybe the second floor of the residence.

"What were you doing there?"

"It is hard to tell you."

Tobe Miller, the turnkey, testified that when the mob got to the front door, the officers told them they would be stopped.

"Outside of telling them that, you didn't?" Stroup noted.

"We done all we could do."

"That is not the question; what did you do outside of telling them?"

"I got out of their way, mostly."

Once the mob got past the outside door, the steel door to their right posed no problem. It was open. They would have walked through the turnkey's office to the next door, which led into the main section of the jail. It too was open. The turnkey insisted later that he had never had a key to either door. As the lynchers moved down the corridor to the cells, Campbell and Captain Charles Truex were nowhere to be seen, and three officers were at the northernmost end of the corridor on the stairway leading to the second floor. That left exactly one officer—Deputy Sheriff Bert White—between the mob and the first lynching victim.

White stood alone behind the locked grating in front of the west bullpen. (There were two sets of bars between the hallway and the cell block; White was in between them.) He watched as a man came forward with a sledgehammer and began pounding at the lock. Then someone jammed a gun into White's ribs.

"You may describe the man you saw do that sledging," Stroup prompted.

"I couldn't do that," said White. "I couldn't describe them."

"You mean to say you didn't see them?"

"I stood right there and saw them: I couldn't describe them, there was too many there."

"You are not attempting to say here, that people stood up close to the man who was slinging that sledge and you couldn't see him?"

"Why certainly I saw him."

"That is what we want, we want you to describe the man that did the sledging."

"I couldn't give you any description, only that he was a young looking man; all the way from 20 to 30 years old."

"You say that there were three or four different men that did the sledging."

"I expect two or three different men."

"On that particular lock?"

"Yes sir, on that lock."

"Can you describe the size of any of them?"

"No sir, I couldn't."

"Would you be able to identify one of them if you saw them?"

"I don't think so."

"Can you give an explanation of why that is?"

"Of what?"

"Why it is you are not able to give any particular description of these men who you saw some ten minutes?"

"Very near all of those men when they came in there had wet towels and handkerchiefs tied over their face, I imagine from tear gas."

But asked again later whether the man who started the sledging had covered his face, White replied, "I couldn't say whether he did or not."

According to White, the prisoner in the bullpen behind him was Abe Smith, while Tommy Shipp had been isolated in a cage on the third floor—usually the women's floor. Campbell corroborated this, explaining that he'd had Shipp downstairs earlier, trying to get a confession out of him, and then he'd sent him to the third floor. "I thought I would lock him in the cage, along about nine o'clock I would let him sweat a little bit and go up and get him."

Somehow the mob knew to go to the women's floor to find him. Blocking the stairway were Miller, the turnkey; Officer Garl Peterson; and Fryer, the Spanish War vet. First the three watched Bert White outside the bullpen, arguing with the mob, and as Fryer put it, "We were making a bluff we were going to shoot." But they'd been ordered not to shoot and bluffed no one.

Wall asked why they couldn't have used billy clubs to help White. Fryer replied that the mob pushed them all the way to the third floor, "clear back in the corner."

Once on the third floor, Fryer heard a yell from downstairs: "We got the son of a bitch down here!" As the crowd rushed back down, Fryer went along and saw the first prisoner taken out. "They held him up above the crowd."

The prosecutors asked very little about what happened to the third-floor prisoner, but there's a bit more about Cameron, who was on the second floor. Captain Truex declared that he and the sheriff "storied just a little to save his hide . . . we said he hadn't confessed to it." But they "storied" at a point when just two men were asking for Cameron. Truex then went to the basement where people had begun throwing things in the windows. So Campbell was the only one there when the actual mob came up and took Cameron away.

"How did they get him?" Stroup asked.

"They just went in and got him," replied the sheriff.

One startling fact slowly becomes clear from reading the police testimony: none of these law enforcement officers ever left the jail. Or perhaps I should say, none of them *admitted* to leaving the jail—either to intervene in the killing outside or to see who was doing it. The sheriff apparently didn't go outside until he cut the bodies down in the morning.

So they had nothing to offer about whatever voices or miracles spared Cameron's life, though Patrolman Frank Neeley admitted to witnessing his return.

"Who brought him back?" asked Stroup.

"I couldn't say," Neeley replied. "I didn't know the men."

"How many brought him back?"

"I don't know. They were all around him there."

"Did you see anybody there that you recognized their face?"

"I did not."

"Can you describe any of them?"

"No sir, I couldn't."

"When you were out on the porch and this crowd was surging trying to get on the porch, did you recognize anybody?"

"Not a soul. They were all strangers to me."

Neeley's beat included the square, so he went back to patrolling it that night as the mob stood guard around the bodies and, at one point, tried to light a fire under them.

"What was the crowd doing?" Stroup asked him.

"I didn't pay no attention," said Neeley. "I never looked at them."

Around two in the morning Grant County coroner Orlando Stout walked down to the courthouse, intending to cut the bodies down. But he was unwilling to defy the wishes of the mob. He left the bodies hanging. The coroner testified: "One fellow said, 'By god, they ought to stay here until nine o'clock tomorrow morning.'"

"Who said that?" the prosecutor asked.

"I don't know," Stout answered. "He was a stranger to me."

TOM WISE PLAYED ME the taped interviews he'd done with eyewitnesses back in 1979 and 1980. By the time I heard them, everyone on the two cassettes was dead, except for Jack Edwards. Tom had not told any of these people that he was related to James Cameron.

Certain images from their accounts stuck in my mind: signs posted along county roads that read NECKTIE PARTY AT MARION; hundred of horse-driven farm wagons on the road filled with white people, all headed to the courthouse; the mob using a telephone pole as a battering ram; the mob pressed against the fire truck that arrived in front of the jail, not allowing the firemen to get down.

Tom had found a white woman named Kate Barnett who'd been at a Kokomo dance hall when news of the imminent lynching at Marion came over the public address system. Somebody made the announcement there'd been a rape of a twelve-year-old girl. "Fourteen of us jumped in this old Ford," Barnett said in her flat nasal drawl. By the time they arrived at the courthouse, the two bodies were hanging; Cameron had come and gone. Barnett said she recognized the couple at the front of the famous photo and the pregnant girl right behind them: "They were at the dance." Of the victim hanging closest to the tree, Barnett said, "This one with the shirt hanging around him—they'd cut him. His privates. They was getting ready to build a fire under them guys. It made me sick. I couldn't stand it." She told Tom she saw Kluxers there. "They had some white uniforms. I remember that, because they were ornery about setting fires around colored people. They was there. As we was coming, we seen 'em. They was around that jail, but I didn't see 'em do anything."

Tom had also tracked down the last living member of the 1930 police force, Roy Cox, who said he'd spent the night of the lynching playing miniature golf but got a call at five-thirty the next morning to come downtown and direct traffic. There he arrested a drunken black man who tried to get through the crowd still milling around the courthouse: "I grabbed him to save his bacon." Thus did a black man become the only person arrested that day as a consequence of the lynching. "It was told that there was a bloody shirt hung up at the police department . . . at the window," Cox declared. "I feel certain that's a false statement. Nobody on the Marion police department would have stood for that."

Cox remembered that the day before the lynching, he'd arrested a black man named Spuds "for the rape of some colored girl," and he heard that the mob got Spuds all the way to the corner of Third and Adams before they realized they had the wrong guy. Both Marion papers mention the mob getting someone to Third and Adams, then letting him go. I wondered if they meant Cameron. It could not have been the man nicknamed Spuds, William Bronough.

In 1980 Tom found him. Spuds told Tom that he'd been in the bullpen with Abe Smith, that he and Smith had talked, but that Abe said nothing about his crime. Somehow Spuds had been oblivious to the dramas going on outside the jail that night. He said that he and a few other men were playing cards when they heard a noise. Three to five minutes later the mob broke in. "They wanted to know if there was any colored guys in there," Spuds told Tom. "Abe had went back to climb up in the racket of the jail where they lock the door." He was referring to a narrow compartment housing the locking devices for the cells. (Deputy Sheriff Bert White mentioned in his deposition that Smith had hidden in "a vent.")

Bronough continued: "Someone in front asked me, 'What is your name?' And someone that was in the bunch knowed me. He said, 'No, Spuds ain't the fella you lookin' for. You lookin' for another fella.' Of course, they didn't have to break that door. All they had to do was pull the latch. They come in and got him [Abe] and brought him on out. About five minutes after that the jailer—he come in and said, 'You know that boy they took outta here? They hung him over on the east side of the jail.' "

Spuds's story answered one question I had. There were two sets of bars and two doors between the corridor and the bullpen; the police talk only about the mob sledging the first door. What about the second? *All they had to do was pull the latch.* It was one more door left unlocked.

But his story also confused me. Cameron and most newspaper accounts all reported that the first prisoner out was hanged from a window on the east side of the jail. Spuds says that that was Smith, when almost everyone else, including Cameron, said it was Shipp.

I was also perplexed by Kate Barnett's testimony. She'd identified the couple at the front of the famous picture as people she'd seen at the dance, while Jack Edwards maintained that the young man was Phil Boyd. Tom Wise said so, too. He'd worked with Boyd for a couple of years in the early 1960s. Maybe Barnett was mistaken. In 2004 I learned the identity of the young woman whose thumb he's holding. She was Bernadine Whitlock, daughter of an Upland minister, one month past her sixteenth birthday at the time of the lynching, and an unlikely attendee at a Kokomo dance, according to her daughter Barbara Andrews. Andrews knew no details of how her mother came to be at the lynching, only that her presence there was "an accident." Nor had Andrews ever heard anything about the identity of the man holding her mother's thumb.

Such details mattered to me, perhaps too much, since I had set myself the unrealistic goal of uncovering the whole truth about August 7, 1930.

▲ ▲ ▲

AMONG ALL THE CONFOUNDING stories I heard about that night, this one was the most unexpected:

Sometime after dark a black girl of thirteen came walking toward the jail. A Klansman approached her and said, You shouldn't be here. Then he put her in his car and drove her home.

That much I heard secondhand, and I was wild to confirm it. The image of a Klansman driving a black girl home from the lynching would be hard to top in the annals of American paradox. But now she was a woman in her eighties and very reluctant to talk.

"I don't need to be targeted," she told me on the phone.

I wondered who would target her. The Klan?

"Yeah!" she said. "They're thick and heavy around here."

I finally set up a meeting through a third party she trusted, her lawyer, with a promise of anonymity. I'll call her Violet. We talked informally at the lawyer's office for an hour before she agreed to let me tape. But this was not a timid person. She told me, in fact, about how she fought back the first time she was ordered off the sidewalk after the lynching. "Walk in the gutter where you niggers are supposed to be" was what the pregnant white woman told her. Violet hit and kicked the woman, inducing premature labor and earning six months' probation.

As for the Klansman story—Violet told me first about a house at 17th and Nebraska where there had been monthly Klan meetings back in the 1920s. She'd lived right down the street, "and of course us snoopy kids" would go spy on them. Behind the house, barren then but for the railroad tracks and Boots Creek, the Kluxers engaged in what Violet described as "skeet shooting," some with pistols, some with shotguns. In those days, she added, "They didn't arrest you all the time for shooting a firearm in town."

Sometimes she saw them at that house in robes, though not when they were shooting. If she didn't know their names, she knew their faces. "They didn't hide themselves," she said, "and they never bothered us. We were taught, this is ours, that's theirs. You let their stuff alone, they let yours alone."

On August 7, 1930, Violet went to the all-black neighborhood of Johnstown to visit a friend. As evening came on, people there heard what was happening downtown and told her to go home. It was after dark by the time she walked down Third Street and encountered "a person," as she emphatically put it—one of the Klansmen she recognized from the house on Nebraska Street. She was not going to name him but said he knew both her parents.

The Klansman ran up to her and asked her what she was doing there. She was still a block east of the jail. He told her to turn her back to the street, face the building at the corner, and wait for him to blink his headlights three times.

"He told me they were bringing people out of the jail and was going to lynch them. And he says, you got no business down here. Now you get over here out of the street lights, out of the car lights, and when I hit my headlights that third time, you'll know it's me, and you run and get in the car, and I'm gonna take your butt home. Now that was his exact words."

I wondered if he was there with other Kluxers.

"Didn't see him break loose from no crowd," said Violet.

He wore no hood, and she was unclear about whether the "light type of thing" he had on was actually a robe. It was open down the front but cream-colored. "It could have been a real light tan coat."

I asked her if she'd seen *anyone* in robes.

"He did say the Klans were there, but I did not see them in the robes."

I had had another reason for wanting Violet's testimony. Apart from Tom Wise's interview with Kate from Kokomo, hers was the only story I heard putting a Klansman at the scene. Of course, there was Cameron's book. He defined the whole lynching as a Klan event to the point of describing the yell from the crowd—"We want Cameron!"—as "that chant of the Ku Klux Klan."

But as I gathered eyewitness testimony in Marion, I began to realize that no one was talking about the Klan. At some point I began asking every eyewitness I interviewed whether they'd seen any robed Klansmen. No one had, and I didn't think they were lying. Violet's story was inconclusive as well. *The Klans were there.* But had they come as individuals or as a klavern? Were they among the mobsters? Or among the spectators?

"It wasn't a Klan-sanctioned activity, but there were a lot of Klan people there," according to David Bish, the grandson of Al Hogston—the man running the Grant County Klan back in 1930. Bish remembered that the lynching came up for family discussion once, maybe over a story that ran in the newspaper. "My grandfather went off on it while we were all there," Bish recalled. "My grandfather used quite colorful language. He could swear and make it sound like poetry almost. 'I told that son-of-a-bitchin' sheriff to get them niggers out of there. They were coming for 'em. Get 'em down to Indianapolis right now.' And [the sheriff] wouldn't do it."

Bish claimed that Hogston quit the Klan over this, upset because Kluxers participated. "I don't know how much longer he was in the Klan, but I knew that made him sick and he got out of it."

WALTER GUNYON WITNESSED the lynching when he was seven years old. I found him at the same home where the old mayor lived, seated near the back of a dining room/recreation area.

Walter told me that his father had taken the whole family to the hanging. Not only that, but Gunyon Senior was obviously privy to certain information. He drove them to the courthouse at four or five P.M. and parked directly in front of the hanging tree. The mob would not have its first victim there till about ten-thirty that night.

Walter remembered watching through the car window as the mob dragged one victim down the street by his heels, his head bouncing up and down on the bricks. "I didn't like it," Walter said. He couldn't remember two men being hung, only one. He couldn't recall seeing a third one brought out, just the one. "As they was pulling him up, he was grabbing the rope, and they let him back down and tied his hands behind his back. Pulled him up again. Somebody grabbed a pinch bar from the railroad. A railroad pinch bar. Threw it. Went in the guy's stomach and came out his back.

"While he was hanging there?" I asked.

"While he was hanging there."

I asked Walter if he'd ever seen the lynching photo. "My dad had a copy of it. He took it with him to California when he moved, and I never saw it again. He had a piece of the rope."

I tried to imagine the sort of person who would force a seven-year-old to witness this gruesome event. Gunyon Senior was a grocer, and Walter speculated that he may have been a Klansman, "but I don't know for sure."

"Did your father ever get out of the car that night?" I asked him.

"No."

"Did your father ever talk to you about the lynching later?"

"No. What surprised me," Walter declared, "was the cruelty of the women. They tore the clothes off the guys hanging there. They really did." He wouldn't say anything more.

Walter didn't like talking about any of this. It never should have happened, he said. The lynching disgraced the town.

"I'm an artist," he suddenly volunteered.

Dimly, I inquired whether that had been his occupation. He looked startled at the very idea. No, he'd joined the Air Corps during World War II, and he wished he'd made that a career. Instead, he came back to Marion and sold insurance, painting in his spare time. His sales territory included Elwood, where a guy named Charlie Fowler kept trying to get him to join the Klan. Charlie would always have his robe flung over a chair. From his wallet Walter then extracted photos of his wedding, his son, and a pen pal, and he showed them to me—as if he were working to erase certain memories from his mind. He had never once looked me in the eye.

THERE IN THE SAME nursing home was a man who'd probably been standing right near the Gunyon car that night. What Blaine Scott remembered most was the ornamental post in front of the courthouse entrance, where one end of the hanging rope had been secured. He saw a woman there pulling on the rope, swinging one of the bodies, holding a baby in her other arm.

Blaine Scott was twenty-seven when he saw this. When I met him, he was ninety-one and lying flat in a hospital bed. He had been a fireman in 1930, working at the very firehouse where the motorists came from Lover's Lane to report the shooting of Claude Deeter. (The real reason they did not stop when Mary Ball tried to flag them down—so the gossip went—was that they were having an affair. They were both married to other people.) Blaine recalled that the woman had "come in hollering" to report it, and someone on his crew called the sheriff.

Shipp and Smith, he said, "they ran around together. And this girl they was with that night, she didn't amount to too much. Her name was Ball, and she didn't pick her company very good. She was with the coons. Uh, the coloreds."

Blaine could tell "by the police activities" that there was going to be trouble. "The police department—they was in a house by the Number One Fire Station, and that's where I witnessed all of their doings. They hung [Deeter's] clothes on the porch of the house. So I knew it was kind of a sure thing. After they hung 'em out there, they had a crowd they couldn't handle, and I think that started a lot of it right there for the Marion people."

Blaine believed that the organizers of the lynching came from Fairmount. They had driven past his house yelling from a car, "Seven o'clock tonight!" Blaine admitted to a fear of the lynching that was puzzling to me.

He'd been desperate to get out of town before it started, so he went fishing with a friend at Deer Creek, just south of town. Then they began hearing the sirens advancing up Highway 9, and the friend finally talked Blaine into going back to have a look.

"When I got there, I could tell that it was nothing but mob fever," he said, "and one guy that I knew said, 'Let's go get the other one.' And that's when they went after Cameron. They got him back up to Adams and Third, and this Charlie Truex—he talked them out of it. Said they had the wrong guy."

Blaine's testimony was a curious mix of confession and denial. He mentioned a couple of times that he was afraid he'd be hanged himself and said he didn't stick around very long at the lynching scene. Then he claimed to know nothing about the Klan. He'd seen their parades but asserted that those weren't Marion people. Those Klansmen were all "from the county." They'd come into town on the interurban, wearing their robes. I was startled by this transparent lie, but knew I couldn't budge him. I saw fear in his eyes. What could that possibly be about?

I ALSO WONDERED ABOUT Blaine Scott's account of seeing Charlie Truex save Cameron. It made sense only after I spoke to William Henry, the man elected mayor of Marion in 2000. Back in 1930 it was William Henry, Sr., who drove the fire truck to the jail with orders to turn the hose on the mob.

Henry Junior first told me that story: his father was starting to hook up the hose to the hydrant, when a man Henry Senior identified as "a hillbilly" came up, pointing a knife with a blade a foot long. The hillbilly told Henry Senior that if he touched even one piece of equipment on the truck, he and the truck would end up in the river. "My dad—he just reached around and pulled the hydrant wrench out of its slot and said, 'I won't be the only thing going in the river.' And just then the fire chief, who was Burr Hamilton, came running up Third Street and said, get this truck back to the station. Dad said, 'What could I do?' So he said, 'I took the truck back and put it in the station.'"

Henry Senior had worked closely with Jake Campbell on Republican politics and knew the other law officers involved. The other story he'd passed on to Henry Junior explained to me for the first time how Cameron had survived. "Cameron, when they got ready to hang him, somebody said, 'No, no, that's not him. He's not the kid. This young man was caught coming off a freight out here at the railroad yard.'" So they went and got police captain Charlie Truex. "And Truex told them, 'Yes. This is a guy I caught getting off the freight.' Lied through his teeth. And that's why they didn't hang Cameron."

The story fit with others I'd heard like a puzzle piece. Not just Blaine Scott's. The NAACP's Walter White also named Truex as Cameron's savior. It even helped account for Truex's extraordinary comment to the court of inquiry about the "fair mob." Of course, nowhere in his deposition did the police captain admit to even leaving the jail. Nowhere did he mention that he had saved a life.

SOMETIMES I SENSED THE regret felt by certain whites, the fear or the rage felt by certain blacks, the horror felt by everyone not caught up in "mob spirit." But no one in the generation that experienced the lynching had figured out how to talk about it.

George Sharp was a white man who'd been seven in 1930. "My great-grandfather told me he went down there and put a pitchfork through one of the guys hanging there. I don't know if that was true or not, but he told me that. And his attitude was, there's no good niggers but dead ones." Sharp's great-grandfather, Herman Pontzious, appears in the infamous photo—the old man on the right side wearing the painter's cap. "Of course," Sharp continued, "he was from Florida."

Sharp made it clear that he did not share the old man's feelings. Sharp had black friends, and it seemed to amaze him that his great-grandfather would have bragged about such a thing to a seven-year-old. (Pontzious, a night watchman at Marion Machine, testified at one of the lynching trials that six young men came to the factory the night of August 7 to get a sledge-hammer and crowbars.) Sharp seemed eager to get off the phone. He hadn't even been in Marion that night, he explained. His parents knew it was going to happen, so they'd taken him and his sister to his uncle's farm. What he remembered most vividly was that, after the lynching, the National Guard came in, and black people had to get a pass to cross Nebraska Street just to buy groceries.

He told me that if I wanted someone who *really* knew things, I should go see his friend Don McFarland.

McFarland was a black man who had witnessed the lynching by accident. I drove out to the VA Hospital, where he worked as a full-time volunteer. We sat in his office, and he told me he remembered the Klan parading every Friday around the courthouse. McFarland had lived just a few blocks east, in Johnstown, and he'd witnessed many of these marches. Once he hollered out the name of a masked Klansman walking by, and the Kluxer stopped and asked, "How did you know it was me?" McFarland told him: "Those two-toned shoes."

On the night of August 7, 1930, he'd gone downtown to get his mother some ice cream, and he'd walked right past the jail, right through the crowd. He was thirteen at the time, and no one paid any attention to him. "I thought it was a football rally," he said, because everyone was cheering "like when the team runs out on the playing field." Then on his way home he noticed that some men had broken into Marion Machine and were walking out with sledgehammers and crowbars, and there were fire trucks in front of the jail. Later he saw a movement around the square where, he suspects, the victims were being dragged. After he got home, he could still hear them "cheer and cheer and cheer."

McFarland exuded sweetness of character and seemed determined to think the best of white people. Even the lynch mob—they'd just been caught up in the excitement. "I think they wasn't people that was bad people." In fact, he'd heard about one man involved who killed himself over it. "Said every time he went in his room, he could see those boys." McFarland spoke calmly of the rumors that circulated after the lynching, that white people would drive all the blacks from Marion. "We slept under the bushes," he recalled. "Some of us had shotguns and everything, laying under the bushes for several days. We didn't know if somebody would try to burn our house down or run everyone out."

McFarland then pulled out his high school yearbook and showed me pictures of himself—the only black on the football team, the only black on the basketball team, the only black on the track team. (Marion High had always been integrated.) He insisted that he never knew of the Klan really bothering anybody. As an example, he told me that when the Marion team played Elwood—the Klan stronghold—nothing ever happened to him. State police would escort him onto the field, and then they'd escort him back to the locker room. No problem.

THEN WITHOUT EVEN TRYING, I found another story about the origin of the rope.

I encountered Lucky Miller in the smoking lounge at one of the nursing homes, sitting in his wheelchair. Lucky was an amiable wreck, with a missing right leg and a hearing aid in each ear. Lucky was white and had been to the square the night of August 7, 1930, to visit a doctor.

He hadn't seen a thing but volunteered: "My foster brother drove a moving van, and they took the rope out of his truck to hang them colored fellas." According to his family's story, the mob demanded the rope his brother used for tying down furniture, and the brother said, "Well, I'm not gonna argue with you."

This was the second rope story I'd heard. The old guy who owned the jail, Rex Fansler, said they'd come from his father's barn. Or one had. Was it about wanting some kind of weird credit? Of course, both stories could be true. Maybe the mob never thought they'd get three prisoners out, so they weren't prepared with three ropes? Maybe they weren't so organized after all?

The brother had been parked right in front of the jail, at the corner of Third and Branson, and had always said that the men who demanded the rope were from Fairmount.

"He recognized them?"

"Yes, ma'am."

"Did he know any names?"

"No."

Lucky had been nine years old in 1930, and he suggested that I talk to his older roommate. He wheeled himself down to his room to introduce me to the Reverend Raymond Street. The reverend hadn't been to the square that night, but I was interested to hear that he'd preached against the lynching the Sunday after it happened. He'd been twenty at the time, declaring to a congregation in the little town of Roseburg, near Weaver: "If you agree with this mob hanging, when you come to the judgment you're gonna answer just like the guy that pulled the rope."

"Maybe I was pretty radical," the reverend concluded, "but I was agi'n it."

MOST OF THE EYEWITNESSES had at least one indelible image they could not erase from their minds, even if the edges of the mental picture had dimmed over the years. Still, I had to wonder how time and trauma had warped each of these stories.

Clearly the depositions were riddled with lies, so the problem with the law officers was to determine whether every single thing coming out of their mouths was false. All that amnesia about what members of the lynch mob looked like is certainly fabricated, but calculated liars usually tell whatever truth they can, to help the important lies stand up. Therefore I figured the officers were probably telling the truth at the inquiry about where they were in the jail, for example.

Then there were professional observers like newspaper reporters. But what had they really seen in all the frenzy? Had any of them, apart from the Marion reporters, even been there when it happened? (The two nearest towns with daily papers were Wabash and Hartford City.) And did some of them also have hidden agendas?

Outside the jail, where the police mostly didn't venture until it didn't matter, accounts of what happened become even harder to sort out. None of the press reports even agree on how many were in the lynch mob. Only twenty-five, according to the *Marion Leader-Tribune,* while the *Marion Chronicle* cited "150 to 200 enraged youths." The *Wabash Plain-Dealer* imputed responsibility to six hundred men from Fairmount, "many under the effects of liquor and heavily armed." Were there even six hundred able-bodied men *in* Fairmount? Whatever the case, most of the out-of-town papers claimed that the mob had formed there, and most of them later printed retractions. The Anderson paper cited a source for the original information that blamed Fairmount: Marion police chief Lew Lindenmuth.

The *Indianapolis News* reported that a group of twenty-five men had met in a billiard room on the north side of the square and debated whether to storm the jail. "In this debate much stress was said to have been laid on the possibilities that Smith and Shipp would escape the electric chair even though convicted," said the *News,* "and when it was finally argued that under the statute the two might obtain paroles in a few years, the determination to storm the jail was unanimous. A leader, tall, light-haired and youthful, was selected. The men went to the Marion Machine Foundry, near the jail, where they demanded sledges and crowbars."

A number of officers who testified at the court of inquiry remarked on the youthfulness of the mobsters. Theater manager Billy Connors told the court of inquiry there weren't more than ten grown men in the mob. The rest were "about sixteen to twenty years of age; I figured them regular hoodlums." Connors also said that he had come outside while they were dragging a body down the street and saw "five or six boys on the end of the rope."

Chronicle reporter Drysdale Brannon was the only other witness at the court of inquiry who admitted to seeing some of the savagery outside. Most observers agreed that the first prisoner taken was hanged on the east side of the jail, but Brannon said he had been hauled first to a truck parked at the corner. "He was lying face down. It appeared like he was trying to shield his face with his arms; several of the mob that were on the truck were kicking him. One girl had her shoe off and was beating him with the heel of her shoe. Almost immediately he was pulled off the truck and taken down to the side of the jail. He was lying there in the street; a young boy came through the crowd, not over sixteen or seventeen years old, yelling, 'Make way for the rope.' They put the rope around him and pulled him to the jail." He was hanged from the bars in a window.

Another Marion reporter who witnessed the carnage, Harry Young, had been interviewed by Tom Wise. Young said that as the first prisoner emerged from the jail, someone hit him in the face with a brick. "A woman put her spike heel into his cheek and turned it."

None of this grisly detail ever made the pages of either Marion newspaper. Both the *Leader-Tribune* and the *Chronicle* played down the brutality as best they could. Both omitted the scene at the truck Brannon describes. But the *Wabash Plain-Dealer* described a seventeen-year-old girl standing on a truck with the first prisoner: "She flew at the prostrate and unconscious negro and kicked him and spit at him while the crowd thundered all around. The girl worked herself up to such a fury that she fainted."

Once this prisoner had been hanged from a jail window's bars, said the *Hartford City News,* "a man mounted the side of the building and was said to have kicked the dying negro in the face, breaking his front teeth and crushing his face. He was hit with bricks, cut down and taken to the courthouse lawn. As [the second prisoner] was being raised to the tree with the hemp rope about his neck, he held to the rope above his head. Shouts filled the air and he was said to have been pummeled with fists, boards and stones. As he was lowered, a report was that he was stabbed with a knife in the breast. Another report was that an angered member of the mob struck him with a crowbar, plunging it into his body." Clearly the reporter did not witness this vicious scene firsthand, but unfortunately much of it can be corroborated.

There is some anecdotal evidence that the dead bodies were then dragged around the square behind an automobile, but none of the newspaper accounts mention this. A United Press correspondent wrote in the *Indianapolis Times* that he saw the man "who knotted ropes around the Negroes' necks" go with his wife into a restaurant after the lynchings and remain there for half an hour eating. Then, according to the Wabash paper, "a group of youths piled up rubbish and packing boxes to cremate the bodies of the Negroes. The flames did no more than scorch the corpses which were hanging 15 feet above the lawn."

"A sign was posted nearby by members of the mob," said the *Hartford City News,* "warning that the bodies were not to be cut down until 9 o'clock Friday morning. Later as dawn began to break, the scene became so ghastly that the mob permitted the officers to cut down the bodies at 5:10. There was talk in the milling crowd of cutting down the bodies earlier, tying them to the back end of cars and dragging the bodies through Marion's colored belt. Officers were able to subdue the crowd and prevent this act, however, fearing that the Negro element might attempt reprisals and [a] general race riot start."

That was what Marion law enforcement focused on for the next couple of days—their worry that the town's 1,087 blacks would rise up and attack the more than 23,000 whites. Police broke up an "indignation meeting" held late the night of August 7 in Johnstown. "Officers found between 400 and 500 Negroes meeting in the open, listening to speeches in which the sheriff was criticized for ordering his men not to shoot when the mob attacked the jail," according to the *Hartford City News.* Somehow Marion law enforcement managed to disperse this crowd, when they hadn't been able to handle a lynch mob that, at least initially, was of significantly smaller size. That's what police chose to do, instead of going to the courthouse to see just who was guarding those bodies.

A Wabash police officer told the *Plain-Dealer* that the bodies had been cut down around five-thirty but then lay for a while on the courthouse lawn. "Even then, someone went up and kicked one of the dead bodies. They were mutilated beyond recognition and even this morning there was a spirit of sullenness about as if the mob feeling was still present."

No undertaker in Marion would accept the bodies, for fear that the funeral home would be stormed. An African American mortician had to come from Muncie to collect them.

Spectators kept streaming into town throughout the day, and many sought souvenirs. After the pieces of rope and clothing were gone, the bark of the elm was stripped off to a height of about seven feet. A few people took whole branches.

EIGHT

"NO LIKELIHOOD OF CONVICTION"

The day after the lynching the following story ran in the *Hartford City News* and the *Indianapolis News* but not in the Marion newspapers:

(United Press Leased Wire)

FAIRMOUNT, IND., Aug 8 — Deep regret that the negro slayers of their son Claude, were lynched in Marion last night by a mob, was expressed today by Mr. and Mrs. William Deeter, members of the Apostolic faith, a sect similar to the Quakers.

"God should have been the judge," said the elderly Deeter. "They had no right to do it," his wife assented.

Both are opposed to capital punishment and did not want to see the negroes put to death for their crime.

THE *MARION CHRONICLE* DID GIVE the Deeters a paragraph, downplaying it with placement on page six, buried in the larger story of the lynching. It mentioned their regrets. And "God is the only judge." But the *Leader-Tribune* said nothing about them. And neither paper quoted Mary Ball, who appeared in the *Hartford City News* declaring: "They got what they deserved."

128

No doubt the reactions from the Deeters and the Balls mirrored the spectrum of opinion among white people, and it was reflected in the very different attitudes of the two Marion newspapers. The first to weigh in editorially was the *Chronicle,* the evening paper, on August 8: "Today we wake up to a sense of the great shame and humiliation the lynching has brought upon us. Never have we had a feeling of so great sadness as we felt last night as we looked helplessly on that seething mass of humanity milling around the jail, knowing all the while that a great humiliation and sorrow were coming upon our fair city in this unfortunate and distressing affair."

But while the *Chronicle* anguished, the *Leader-Tribune* smirked. "The Main Street Reporter," a daily *Leader-Tribune* column of "breezy gossip" written by editor-in-chief Carl Houston, always invited one to read between the lines, but never more so than on August 9: "Friday [August 8] was one of the prettiest days we have seen for a good long time. Things seemed so calm. The world has never seemed so peaceful. . . . A fellow can say 'the weather is ideal, and how do you like it? Fine day, isn't it?' And you can respond to him, 'isn't it glorious?' He can say, 'it surely is. Here no damage is done. No feelings hurt, Best of harmony, love and admiration.' "

On that day's editorial page, of course, the *Leader-Tribune* adopted a more sober tone: "We cannot recall the past. Regretful as was the very unfortunate occurrence of Thursday night, it cannot be recalled. That event constitutes a sorrowful chapter in the history of this city. The discussion of it, much less the rehashing of the events that led up to it, can get us nowhere. Marion will have to live down the odium that attaches to its memory by its future achievements. This splendid city is composed of as public spirited citizens and as fine a lot of men and women as any in America."

Still, the barely repressed glee kept resurfacing. "The Main Street Reporter" opined on August 12, for example: "You can talk about this or that misfortune. You may talk of this or that tragedy. But the worst news we have heard in a long time is the fact that some of the Golden Bantam corn is not its true self. Think it over. Isn't that about the saddest news you have heard in a long time?"

On August 13, the day the court of inquiry began, the *Chronicle* editorialized: "The lynchers went into the matter with their eyes open. They must now face the consequences of their acts." But in that day's *Leader-Tribune* "The Main Street Reporter" declared: "We believe if the average community could declare a closed season on gab, and padlock every mouth in town for a period of time, that when it was over happiness, peace, prosperity, and contentment would prevail."

I read every page of every paper published for the rest of 1930 and most of 1931, and it seemed to me that eventually the disparate views of the two papers converged into an attitude that more closely resembled the *Leader-Tribune*'s and has carried through to present-day Marion: "Let's forget it and move on."

THE DAY AFTER the lynching Mrs. Flossie Bailey of the NAACP wrote to Walter White, the organization's acting secretary in New York, asking that a representative from the national office come to help investigate the crime. White himself arrived in Marion on August 15, the day the court of inquiry ended, the day Stroup and Wall told the local press "that their future plans were uncertain and that they did not know when they would return to Marion."

Sometime on August 7 Mrs. Bailey had called L. O. Chasey, secretary to the governor and a Marion native, to ask that the state militia be sent to prevent the lynchings. Chasey had hung up on her. In an article Walter White eventually wrote for the *New York World*, he said that Chasey was "reputed to be one of the leaders of the Ku Klux Klan."

On August 8 Mrs. Bailey wrote in a second letter to White, "The mob is still congregating and uttering threats to get the other two boys tonight." (She meant Cameron and Robert Sullivan, the alleged accomplice of Shipp and Smith in earlier robberies.) Even so the NAACP was the group being watched by the police. "I am sending this message in a special letter," she wrote, "as every telegram is passed on to the authorities. Even the one Mr. Bailey sent for me last night was repeated all day on the street today."

An NAACP delegation met with Jack Edwards at some point on August 8. The mayor had arrived back in town early that morning, shortly after the bodies were cut down. At the delegation's urging, Edwards also called the governor's office and asked Chasey to send troops. Edwards too was rebuffed. But later that day Sheriff Campbell called Chasey and told him there was imminent danger that the black population would rise up to retaliate. Chasey mobilized the National Guard immediately. Two companies from Camp Knox, Kentucky, arrived in Marion early on August 9 and left after the funerals for Shipp and Smith on August 11.

The mayor also cooperated fully with Walter White, who called Edwards "the only bright spot in official Marion." But much more could have been done immediately—and wasn't—to defuse racial tensions. It almost looks like another conspiracy: first the plot to do the lynching, then a plot to revel in it.

The Marion authorities were barely going through the motions. During the inquiry Stroup and Wall asked a number of law officers just what they were doing to gather evidence. They replied that they had no orders to gather any.

Ogden's investigator Arthur Bruner wrote a report in which he described going to the lynching site on August 8 at around two in the afternoon. Bruner found about sixty people standing around a young man who was holding up a lynching photo, pointing at stab wounds on one of the bodies, describing how he'd seen those made by a crowbar. Bruner walked over to the jail and found Campbell sitting on the porch. He told the sheriff about the man lecturing near the hanging tree, and the sheriff said he'd look into it. At four-thirty Bruner went back to the courthouse square and saw the same young man. Again he walked to the jail, just as Sheriff Campbell was entering the residence with some groceries. Campbell again said he'd look into it. But he didn't. The next day Bruner and Merl Wall were at the jail taking testimony from prisoners. As Bruner came down the jail steps, he saw the young man in front of the jail and pointed him out to the sheriff, but "Campbell made no effort to get him."

In her August 9 letter to White, Mrs. Bailey said she had "reliable information" that Claude Deeter "made a dying statement to his aunt that [Mary Ball] was not attacked by either of the boys, but that he [Deeter] recognized the Smith boy and called him by name, which was the reason he thought he was shot." According to Mrs. Bailey, the Deeters had tried—and failed—to get the local newspapers to publish the aunt's statement.

If most of white Marion wanted to be defiant about the rightness of the lynching, the rape of Mary Ball had to remain part of the story.

Walter White was only in Marion for about forty-eight hours (arriving the fifteenth and leaving the seventeenth), but he gathered information "without great difficulty," as he put it in a letter to Attorney General Ogden. I imagine he was helped by the Baileys. I think it's even possible that white people who were horrified by the lynching and knew the identities of mobsters called the Baileys with their information. (They certainly couldn't call the police.) But that is speculation. By the time he got to Marion, White had investigated dozens of lynchings. Not only was he experienced, his physical appearance had probably helped him every time. Just five thirty-seconds black, he had blond hair and blue eyes and regularly passed for white, though he identified as black. In her August 12 letter to him, Mrs. Bailey suggested that he stay at the Spencer Hotel and keep his racial identity secret, "as the hotels do not keep colored people."

On August 22 White sent Ogden a list of "persons reputed to have participated" in the lynching. The first name on the list was a barber named Bailey, who had a shop at the corner of 18th and Meridian.

THAT ADDRESS AGAIN. Within my first two days in Marion I'd heard two anecdotes about 18th Street. First Rex Fansler's story that his father relayed a message to the sheriff from "a group that congregated at Eighteenth and Adams." Then Jack Edwards's statement that no, it was the barbershop at 18th and Meridian that was "the hotbed of that group." Meridian and Adams were just a few blocks apart, and right between them lay Superior Body, the factory where Claude Deeter had worked.

Herman Bailey, the barber in question, was a white man and no relation to the NAACP Baileys. According to Walter White, this Bailey had been "bitten on the right arm by Smith as Bailey and others were tying Smith's hands." The second name on White's list of "persons reputed to have participated" was Waller, someone who'd reportedly struck Smith in the face with a crowbar to loosen his teeth from Bailey's arm. An Arnold Waller would be among those eventually indicted.

During the inquiry eight different witnesses were queried about a barber named Bailey "from 18th and Meridian" who'd been bitten on the arm. Only Police Chief Lindenmuth admitted, "I heard he was there. That is hearsay." The hearsay had been passed to him by Clark Seybold, the police commissioner.

Eventually I spoke to one of Bailey's daughters, who told me the lynching "was never mentioned in our house. It never came up." She had no idea that her father had been named in the depositions. "We weren't racial," she said. I also tracked down one of the barber's sons, who told me he couldn't recall a thing. But a grandson (born after the barber died) admitted to having "suspicion." He'd heard the "legend" of his grandfather's involvement. He just couldn't remember who told him, and he knew nothing else.

Walter White would eventually supply Ogden with seventeen names, including one more who was indicted, Everett Clark. Also on his list was "Thin" Beard or Bird, "reputed to be a bootlegger" who lived on Florence (one block from Meridian) between 18th and 19th. An old woman, who asked for anonymity, had mentioned this man to me without, of course, knowing anything about White's list. That is, she told me that a man named Finn Byrd was definitely involved. She also pointed him out to me in the middle of the famous photograph. His head is partially visible at the back, just to the left of the victim in the center of the photo. He's wearing a hat that's tipped back, light in color. According to White, "Bird" had boasted that he "put the rope around one of the black sons of bitches."

I FOUND A SLEDGEHAMMER used the night of the lynching. One of them, anyway. I already had stories about hammers coming from Marion Machine, but then I also had more than one story about the origin of the ropes. It seemed possible in both cases that they didn't all come from one source. Or maybe a hammer just made for a nice souvenir and somebody took it home.

Told that a certain farmer out in the county owned such a thing, I decided to show up without calling ahead. I found him at one of his outbuildings. The farmer froze for a moment, taken aback, when I asked about the hammer, then led me into the shed and pulled it out. "That's supposed to be it." A sixteen-pounder. The handle had been replaced since 1930, he added.

As we talked, he relaxed a little. I had promised that no names would be used, and he recovered from the shock of being asked.

He'd heard the story from his uncle, his father's brother: "He said that was the hammer that was used to beat the bricks and the blocks out, trying to get the door of the jail open." On his mother's side there was "mystery," the farmer said. "Nobody will elaborate. Nobody ever did admit how much anybody had to do with it. Honest to God, that's all I know. And they're all passed away now."

His father and uncle had been very good friends with the Deeters, he said, but he thought the hammer actually came from his mother's side of the family. He named her family, from a nearby farm. He'd seen pictures of the lynching years ago. Maybe at his great-grandmother's—on his mother's side.

"My father would never talk about it," the farmer said. "But when I got older I worked with my uncle, and I was working with him through the sixties and seventies, when there was a lot of civil unrest. I'm sure that's how we got to talking about it. He just told me he had it, and then when he passed away, I bought it off my cousin. Conversation piece," he laughed.

WHEN I WENT TO VISIT Harley Burden, Jr., I was looking for anything he might have learned from his father, one of two black officers on the 1930 police force. Cameron mentions him in his book. Burden Senior was one of the policemen who arrested him.

Burden Junior told me that his dad worked a six A.M. to six P.M. shift, patrolling the square, but he remembered that the night of August 6, the captain came to the house and asked his dad to go on a call. They were about to arrest Shipp, Smith, and Cameron, and Burden Senior was to act as "a buffer between the parents and the police."

Burden Senior wore a Number One badge. "He'd been on [the force] longer than anyone else," his son told me. But no one who was black could ever advance to detective back then. Marion had two black policemen and two black firemen. Quotas, it seems.

On the night of the lynching Burden Senior had apparently done nothing: "It was after six o'clock. I think he was off."

It was Burden Junior who got close. He happened to be best friends with Dr. and Flossie Bailey's son, Walter Charles, and was at their house on August 7, intending to stay overnight. Dr. Bailey had planned to take them fishing early the next morning. Burden heard Mrs. Bailey on the phone calling Lieutenant Governor Cliff Townsend, calling the sheriff, trying to get someone to take the prisoners to another jail. He remembered that she couldn't get the governor and couldn't find Jack Edwards. Later she would be the one who called the black undertaker in Muncie.

That night Dr. Bailey actually drove down to the square to have a look, taking his son and Burden Junior with him. The bodies were hanging by the time they arrived.

Harley Burden didn't seem to have any feelings about this. He was ten at the time, and he hadn't been scared. He did not recall seeing Klansmen, policemen, or anybody he recognized. They circled the square once and went back to the Bailey home.

The lynching hadn't been "the worst part," as he put it. No, the worst part was what he called "the belling" a couple of nights later. A huge belling. White people drove their cars down into South Marion, dragging cans from their bumpers and shooting guns in the air. "I bet you every car in town was in that belling," said Burden. "They said they were gonna run all the blacks out of town. Well, a lot of them did leave. Went to Weaver."

Home alone with his mother that night, Burden had been terrified. They had a shotgun, but "I was so scared I would have shook a bullet out of the gun." All the cars were headed for the Baileys' house.

Burden's description of his fear during the belling was all the more striking because he refused to admit otherwise that the active racism he grew up with had had an impact—even insisting that "the lynching didn't seem so bad." He recalled going downtown to watch the Klan parades, an activity he clearly regarded as nonthreatening. The KKK just didn't have an element of danger then, and most people knew who the Klansmen were. "It wasn't any big thing."

I spoke to Burden at his home in northern Indiana, where he'd moved after retiring. He'd worked in Marion for forty years as an accountant and served as president of the school board from 1982 to 1987. He still seemed to love his hometown. He insisted that after the lynching "by and large, people were really in a state of shock that they had fallen so low," and this, he speculated, was what prevented them from coming forward as witnesses.

"It hurt Marion," Burden said. "At one time Muncie and Kokomo and Marion were all the same size. They grew and Marion never did. No one wants to come where the relationships among people are bad."

He thought the jail should be torn down and forgotten. "Why would you want to keep that in remembrance? Cameron should thank his lucky stars he wasn't lynched, and let it go at that."

Before I left, Burden got out his purple and gold Marion Giants jacket and put it on, turning so I could see the years of their state basketball championships emblazoned across the back.

ANOTHER WHO REMEMBERED the postlynching trauma was Don Stewart, who'd grown up near the Shipp family. First, though, Stewart recalled the last conversation he ever had with Tommy Shipp.

Stewart was dead by the time I started my research, but he'd been interviewed back in the 1970s. He was Shipp's age. One day, the two were in Stewart's backyard, when Shipp began to tell him about the robberies. He tried to talk Stewart into going along, then tried to talk another friend into going along. "My mama would have had a fit," said Stewart. He advised Shipp, instead, to quit the holdups. Tommy, after all, had a good foundry job at the Malleable. He even had a car. What if he got caught?

"You're just a 'fraidy cat," Shipp replied. Besides, he felt justified in committing these crimes. White people in the South had killed his uncle, he told Stewart. So he was gonna show 'em.

Stewart argued that if he was mad at white people, he should go get his revenge down South: "Don't bring it up in this part of the country because we don't live like that." The conversation became heated, ending when Shipp declared that he was going to go get his gun. "A little old pistol," as Stewart described it.

The night of the robbery and shooting on the River Road, Stewart heard the police come to the neighborhood. He knew they were taking Tommy. Next day rumors about a lynching "began to sweat," Stewart recalled, but everyone thought the sheriff would stop it. "Both colored and white had the confidence in that."

That night, Stewart first knew his confidence to be ill-founded when Mrs. Shipp began to scream—"the horriblest scream you ever heard in your life." Like other residents in the area, he never forgot it.

And afterward he sensed that something in the town had changed, though the white and black people in his neighborhood acted the same as always. "When you'd go through town, you could just sense . . ." He couldn't articulate the "*it*" he felt, but "*it* kept beginning to get worse. They was not going to let us lay down in our homes. They were gonna burn the city."

Like other black residents, Stewart spent days on guard duty at his house, hardly sleeping. "We'd hear the bells a-ringing" as cars loaded with white people approached. "Most homeowners are like I am now. I'm not going nowhere. They can start anything they want. I'm gonna die here. I got a [cemetery] plot paid for." But once he'd become exhausted, his mother did send him the eight miles out to Weaver to stay with his uncles. Carloads of white people showed up there too, as Stewart remembered, "hollering 'Hey you niggers, we know you're in there.' "

So Stewart told his family, "I'm going back to town to die."

As I gathered information on the lynching, I often felt tremendous frustration. Nailing down the simplest facts about this event was never simple. Still, I had come up with what I thought of as a likely scenario—at least a partial one—based on my eyewitnesses, the sometimes conflicting press coverage, those problematic depositions, the handwritten notes made by Ogden's chief investigator, the NAACP correspondence, and the findings of Walter White.

Of course, I also had Cameron's book, but I was beginning to understand just how much of it was based on hearsay, and this really dismayed me. There were now some big differences between my "scenario" and his account. Most had to do with things he had not witnessed himself. For example, according to Cameron, Deeter's bloody shirt was run up a flagpole at the police station, while I had heard from eyewitnesses that it was hung out a window. Cameron could not have seen the shirt; he was locked up four blocks away. He describes a scene in the first-floor corridor where ringleaders fussed with the keys. Cameron was incarcerated on the second floor, and while stories about the mob getting the keys had become folklore in Marion, I didn't regard them as fact. Then among other discrepancies, he stated that the bodies hung on the tree till the afternoon of Friday, August 8, and that Attorney General Ogden himself cut them down, while I had a lot of testimony about their removal that morning between five and six A.M.

I had accepted Cameron's book at face value. In fact, his book had been the catalyst for my own. I'd been moved by him. I never doubted his sincerity. I still don't. So at first it didn't occur to me to question how he could have witnessed these things, and I felt guilty about questioning them later. He'd been there. I hadn't. He was the victim. I wasn't.

Finally I called Cameron and asked him, "How did you hear about the ringleaders having keys?"

"Oh, some of the white people in nursing homes told me about that," he said. "I don't exactly know who it was."

Cameron told me he'd been standing at a window near the alley during the break-in. Second floor, west cell block. I went to that spot several times to check the sightlines. He would have had a clear view of about half the front lawn, but only part of the porch leading into the jail. (The porch had a roof but was open on the west side.) He could not have seen the front door; nor could he have witnessed what happened on the first or third floors or on the east side of the jail. A building blocked his view of the hanging tree a half block away.

So like a good reporter, Cameron had tried to fill in the rest of the story by talking to eyewitnesses. He'd done it decades before I had, so he had many more witnesses to hear from, and I felt sure that he had reported accurately what was told him. Still, talking to the people who almost let him die might not have been the best way to get information. And few white people apart from the mob actually ventured into the jail that night. So where had these stories originated?

For me, that was an important question. But his job and mine weren't really the same. As I tried to piece this chaotic evening into a narrative, I'd become obsessed with accuracy. Facts would be the antidote to the cover-up, and I would gather them, following journalistic rules. Get things corroborated. Consider the source. And so on. But the cover-up had been so total and immediate, I now had to face the reality that I would never get closure on the details. And accuracy is an issue separate from getting people to face repressed material. Cameron's mission was to make denial impossible. He was "the voice crying in the wilderness."

I asked Cameron more about what he'd seen from the second floor, hoping to straighten out the puzzle over which victim had emerged from the jail first. "You saw them take the first prisoner out," I began.

"I just saw from my window when they took Tommy out."

"Did you actually see his face or recognize his clothing?"

"I knew they had a black fella in line," said Cameron. "I found out later it was Tommy that they'd hung on the jail windows around the side." He'd learned this from white people who'd been there.

The bodies hanging till noon? He'd heard it in prison, while serving time for his part in what happened on the River Road.

Then there was everyone's favorite thing to doubt: the voice from heaven. Some of the newspaper stories said that Cameron himself talked the mob out of it. Others reported that Mary Ball's uncle declared himself "satisfied" with two victims. Walter White attributed the escape to pleas not just from Cameron himself but from two white boys Cameron knew (ages thirteen and sixteen) and from Captain Charles Truex. Since I had two other stories naming Truex as the savior, this was the scenario I believed.

Cameron's own belief in the voice from heaven remained unshakable. He had heard it clearly, and he believed that it was the voice of the Virgin Mary. This was another reason he'd felt compelled to convert to Catholicism. In 1990 he even made a pilgrimage to Medjugorje, in what was then Yugoslavia, where certain locals had seen apparitions of the Virgin.

He had put together a personal narrative that made sense to him, that matched the way he experienced the night. He had been sixteen and about to die violently after watching two friends subjected to unspeakable butchery. What level of trauma would that take him to? What out-of-body experience? He wasn't fully present to be his own witness. He insisted, for example, that he had walked back to the jail completely alone. That never made sense to me. And during the inquiry Officer Frank Neeley went ducking and weaving through questions about the men who *did* bring him back, when it would have been easier just to say that Cameron was alone. But he hadn't been.

So many had a stake in denying his credibility. People in Marion didn't want to believe Cameron and seized upon any variation as a way to dismiss his entire story. I'd heard people criticize him for writing that Anderson is twenty-nine miles from Marion. *Hah! It's forty! He lies!* (According to city-data.com, however, the distance is 31.1 miles.) Cameron has no guile or deceitfulness about him, however. And on a symbolic level, everything he said was true: His escape—voice or no voice—*had* been a miracle. Figuratively speaking, the bloody shirt *had* been run up a flagpole. In effect, the mob *had* been given the keys. And he *had* been completely alone. These things did not happen yet were true. It was like the story I heard from Sadie Weaver Pate. She told me that the bodies had hung on the tree for days. Sadie Weaver Pate was no liar, either. The bodies have been hanging there for years.

TWO PEOPLE I SPOKE TO saw James Cameron in the custody of the mob that night near the hanging tree. One was Don Millspaugh, who was a year older than Cameron and still working full time at his Shoe City store in North Marion when I met him. A well-known local character who always wore a white cowboy hat and black eyepatch, Millspaugh had been Democratic county chairman for sixteen years and was a good friend of Jack Edwards.

On August 7, 1930, he'd gone swimming in a gravel pit near Gas City, his hometown. Out there, in the middle of the afternoon, a man came by to inform everyone that there was going to be a lynching that night. "Of course, we all knew about the episode out on the River Road," said Millspaugh. It was dark by the time he and his friends got to Marion. Shipp and Smith were "already lifeless."

Millspaugh was standing right on the courthouse lawn, between the corner and the hanging tree, when he saw the mob drag Cameron through the middle of the intersection: "I always imagined I seen sparks emanating from his heels. He was dragging his feet so hard that I could—I either seen 'em or imagined seeing sparks. He tried to hold back. I've still got a memory of seeing sparks. In those days they wore heelplates on their shoes, and that was brick then. A brick street."

He lost sight of Cameron by the time he was even with the tree. There were too many in the way: "A sea of people." Nor did he recall seeing a rope: "All I can remember is the look on his face—a man facing death. He had a look of terror on his face." Millspaugh never heard a voice call out in all the "noise and commotion and hullabaloo." And he had no idea why the mob let Cameron go. He did not recall seeing him walk back to the jail.

"Maybe we'd become sickened by that time and left," he said. "Those boys hanging there lifeless was a pretty sobering thing. Wasn't something I wanted to stand around and look upon. What took us there in the beginning was just youthful curiosity, you know. I didn't have any idea what we was gonna see when we got there." He paused. "How is James's health?" Mills-paugh wanted to know.

The second witness I found had been closer to the tree. Betty Bandy was eight years old on August 7, 1930. She and a brother and sister had already gone to bed when their dad came home, got them all up, and took them down to the square in their pajamas. There they saw the bodies of Shipp and Smith being dragged around the square behind a car. "It was gruesome," said Bandy. "My little sister—she was only six, and she had nightmares."

"Did the third victim go back to the jail by himself?" I asked.

"No, somebody was leading him back."

"Did you see the rope around his neck?"

"That's right."

"Do you know why they didn't hang him?"

"He swore he was innocent of this crime, and somebody believed him."

"He always said that a voice called out from heaven, saying to let him go."

"I didn't hear that," said Bandy. "All I heard was 'Hang him, hang him.' "

Cameron once told me that people were always phoning him to say they knew who called out to save him. He was derisive about such claims. He'd never even written down their names. "I tell 'em I don't believe it—but thank you if you did. I realize God picks out people to be messengers and healers and prophets and teachers. It could have been somebody in that crowd, but I'm the one that has to believe it."

People had told him other stories he dismissed—the guilt stories, as I thought of them. In one, the ghost of one of the dead lynching victims appeared suddenly in some mobster's automobile, grabbed the steering wheel, and sent the driver off the road to his death. Cameron told me that one, and he'd heard more. But he wouldn't relate them to me. Such stories were nonsense, he scoffed.

IN 1930 MY GRANDPARENTS were living just a couple of blocks from the square. I imagined my grandfather walking past the bodies on the way to his three A.M. shift at the post office. At least he hadn't taken my six-year-old father with him. But how *did* my family explain the lynching to themselves? I remember hearing as a girl that it had been organized in Bucktown, among "the hillbillies." And I remember hearing that it had to be done, that the law in Marion was incompetent and "those guys would have gotten off." In other words, my family was part of the mass rationalization that allowed the whole thing to go uninvestigated and unpunished. This is the unbearable part— facing the fact that my grandparents went along with it.

Those guys would have gotten off. The attitude was widespread. After the lynching the *Indianapolis Star* even did a series of investigative pieces citing the leniency and ineptitude of Marion law enforcement as an aid to "mob spirit." The *Star* reporter put together some startling statistics on things like convictions and appeals, noting that while the state as a whole did not have good numbers, those in the Grant County courts were far worse. In 1929, for example, Indiana's average for dismissals was 30.8 percent while in Grant County it was 60.2 percent. Statistics like this, declared the *Star,* "would explain that cold, dogged, after-the-event satisfaction [with the lynching] said by competent observers to prevail with startling generalness among the people of the county."

Marion had seen an unusual level of carnage for a town its size in the year leading up to the hangings. Between October 3, 1929, and February 26, 1930, five men had died in a rash of bombing murders, all of them members of the local Mould Makers Union. The first bomb destroyed Marion's Labor Temple. The last blew to bits a Model T and its driver when the unfortunate mould-maker pressed the ignition. At the time the car was parked diagonally across the street from the Grant County jail, as if the bomber wanted to thumb his nose at the local Keystone cops. No one was ever indicted for these crimes. "The public is seldom called upon to witness a sadder case of official incompetence," the *Marion Chronicle* editorialized on May 17, 1930, after a grand jury dismissed charges against five suspects who'd been ar- rested with great fanfare in April, though no one had any evidence against them. The bombings remain unsolved to this day.

In June 1930 the trial of a bank robber who'd stolen $27,000 from the Gas City bank was making news. It ended in a hung jury, and there was never a second trial. That same month a man named Jack Kingery confessed to being an accessory in the robbery and murder of a Jonesboro man. Kingery got just two to twenty-one years. The *Indianapolis Star* also cited, among many other Grant County cases gone awry, that of a married man who had killed a woman "as the result of a love affair." He received a light sentence and appealed; the case never even had a hearing. He went free. By the way, none of these cases involved black people.

The town's inept law enforcement allowed white Marion to tell itself that the lynching was not about race. The *Chronicle* went so far as to declare in its August 8 editorial, "The lynching was done not by men of violent and lawless dispositions. These men were ordinary good citizens, but they were stung to the quick by an atrocious crime and spurred on to their violent act by a want of confidence in the processes of the courts."

But there can be no doubt that if Shipp and Smith had been white, they would have gone through the system. The night of the lynching a white man named Edward Blotz was also a prisoner in the Grant County jail. The mob ignored him, though Blotz had been arrested for a murder that was perhaps the grisliest crime ever committed in the county. He had dismembered his victim, buried him in his garage, then dug him back up when the corpse began to smell. Blotz apparently forced his own son, at gunpoint, to help move the body parts. Two women found the torso in a creek three miles north of town. While the victim's head was never recovered, a couple of limbs turned up in a nearby pond and a couple more in neighboring farm fields. The younger Blotz confessed, and his statement was corroborated by Blotz's wife. Even so the first trial ended with a hung jury. (And this after the lynching.) At the second trial prosecutor Harley Hardin could not get more than a manslaughter conviction and a sentence of two to twenty-one years.

Hardin told the *Star* that the problem lay with local juries.

NEVERTHELESS IT'S TELLING that Walter White found Grant County's prosecutor to be "the least friendly and courteous" of all the officials he interviewed during his stay in Marion. In his piece for the *New York World* White described Harley Hardin as "a timid, blustering official who has failed miserably, according to general opinion, to convict criminals after they were apprehended." White cited another recent case that had been the talk of Grant County. A Fairmount couple adopted a four-year-old, whose life they insured; then they poisoned the child. "Evidence of their guilt seemed unmistakable," wrote White, "but so poorly was the case handled by the prosecutor that the man and woman received sentences of two to 14 years, and the woman has already been released. . . . One prominent citizen remarked bitterly that under the present regime, he was absolutely confident that he could murder in cold blood anybody in Marion and with only a fairly good lawyer could escape punishment because of the ineffectiveness of the prosecutor."

Hardin himself had been at the jail when the mob broke in, yet the experience had added little to his usefulness at the court of inquiry. When interviewed by Walter White, Hardin said that he worked late that night and didn't have a clue that anything was going to happen until he left his office at nine-thirty. Then, upon seeing the crowd at the jail, Hardin "mingled in it, trying to find leaders whom he could dissuade from going through with the murders," White wrote. "Upon being questioned as to how many of these persons he identified, he hastily declared that 'the ones I talked with I did not know,' which seems somewhat strange in view of the fact that the mob, according to other eyewitnesses, was made up in large part of citizens of Marion and Grant County in which Prosecutor Hardin had lived for some forty years." White noted that Hardin was up for reelection in November and "seems most apprehensive of antagonizing whites by causing the arrest and punishment of any of the lynchers and at the same time he is solicitous of not offending Negro voters by appearing to be negligent in doing his duty."

If Hardin was reluctant to go after the mob, he wasn't alone. On August 18, the day after White left town, Judge O. D. Clawson refused to sign indictments for the arrest of six men allegedly involved. This news was not even reported in either of the Marion newspapers. Apparently the official excuse given to Mrs. Flossie Bailey was fear that the lynch mob would rise again. As she wrote that day in a letter to White, "Sheriff Campbell says the Grant County jail will not hold the men if they are locked up." According to the *Indianapolis Star*, tension in Grant County eased with the judge's refusal to sign the indictments: "The early investigation of the lynching had aroused opposition in many sections and had resulted in threats of violence against Prosecutor Hardin unless he abandoned the probe."

On the twentieth, an NAACP delegation that included Mrs. Bailey met with Governor Harry Leslie in Indianapolis, demanding Jake Campbell's removal from office, punishment for the lynchers, and protection for witnesses who could identify them. Mrs. Bailey later reported to White that Governor Leslie "was reserved almost to the point of indifference" during this meeting. According to press reports, the governor had urged caution. Moving too quickly could cause "a race war," he said. He thought the investigation should remain where it was, in the hands of a grand jury convening in September. Besides, he said, he had heard reports that if anyone was arrested for the lynching, "Negroes planned to use dynamite to demolish the jail." The NAACP delegation assured him, apparently to no avail, that this was a myth.

On August 22 Walter White sent a summary of his findings to Attorney General Ogden. He charged the Grant County authorities with "gross if not criminal negligence," singling out Campbell and Hardin for special criticism.

On October 9 the Grant County grand jury singled out Campbell for special praise. In their report to Judge Clawson, they declared that the sheriff "conducted himself and directed others acting with him in a prudent manner and, had he acted differently, it is more than probable that a race riot would have ensued. . . . He is entitled to be exonerated by us of blame and criticisms, and we accordingly exonerate him." The same jury indicted James Cameron for murder in the first degree while perpetrating a robbery, for rape in the first degree, and as an accessory before the fact in both the murder of Claude Deeter and the rape of Mary Ball.

They indicted no one for the lynching. As Hardin explained to the local press: "Although several witnesses testified they saw particular persons active in the mob when they were breaking in the jail, all suffered lapses of memory when asked who actually hanged the two colored youths."

A week later, when it was clear that Grant County authorities were not going to act, Attorney General Ogden drove up from Indianapolis with Merl Wall and personally filed charges against Jake Campbell and seven alleged members of the lynch mob: Bob Beshire, 45, pool room owner; Phil Boyd, 17, mechanic; Everett Clark, 22, laborer; Arnold Waller, 22, truck driver; Chester Pease, 32, taxi driver; Charles Lennon, 30, taxi driver; and a man named Praim, whose first name was never known, nor was he ever apprehended, though rumors circulated that he was working in a Marion garage. In December, Wall indicted an eighth suspect, Asa Davis, musician.

So Grant County was forced to take action after all, and the *Leader-Tribune* urged quick arrests. Always a cheerleader for Marion's position as "one of the best cities in America," the *Leader-Tribune* deplored the injury done to the community's good name on August 7. It certainly didn't share the *Chronicle*'s assessment that the lynchers were "ordinary good citizens." An unnamed out-of-town paper had asserted editorially that Grant County wasn't doing anything about this crime because "leading men of the county were involved"—a charge that outraged the boosters at the *Leader-Tribune.* As one of their editorials put it: "The city was in the control of a small gang of boys and hoodlums and the better citizens stood as if helpless and let them get away with it. That is the truth and the truth is eternal."

JURY SELECTION IN the trial of Robert Beshire began December 29, 1930, and the acquittal came in on January 2. Beshire, a Turkish immigrant sometimes referred to in newspaper pieces as "the Assyrian," asserted that on the night of August 7 he himself had been attacked by the lynchers, "who believed that he was a negro." Police Chief Lindenmuth and Officer Garl Peterson, however, both testified that Beshire had been an active member of the mob storming the jail.

The jury deliberated over his acquittal for just thirty minutes. But a couple of intriguing facts emerge from the trial coverage. A reporter who'd been a witness for the state identified both Phil Boyd and Asa Davis as active members of the mob. The journalist also said that Beshire had been injured that night—not by mobsters but by a policeman, while rushing the jail door. A housewife named Clara Newhart also testified at this trial that she'd seen another of the indicted men, Everett Clark, carrying a rope, shortly after Shipp and Smith were hanged. This made Clara Newhart the only private citizen I knew of to come forward publicly with information. I wondered if I could find her family, but there weren't any Newharts in the 1930 city directory. Maybe she was from out of town. Maybe that explained her willingness to talk.

On January 14, 1931, Charles Lennon was finally arrested. He had eluded the police for three months, explaining that he'd gone to Illinois because his mother was sick. Lennon was incarcerated at Huntington, some thirty miles north, "because open threats had been made that if he were jailed here, his friends would form a mob, break into the jail a second time and release him," according to the *Leader-Tribune*. As soon as that information hit the papers, the nervous Huntington sheriff made it known that he had moved Lennon again—to parts unknown.

Wall and Stroup, who prosecuted the lynching trials without Hardin, decided to try Lennon next. He was the one against whom they had the most evidence. Certainly he had been the man most mentioned during the court of inquiry by officers willing to remember anyone at all. Officer Garl Peterson, who recognized Lennon among the men who'd forced their way to the third floor, described him as a taxi driver and a pimp. "We have had a lot of trouble with him," Peterson said. Apparently Lennon was expendable.

But then how did a man like Lennon come to have an attorney like Roy Dempsey? Dempsey had a distinguished career in Grant County. He was elected county prosecutor in 1934, then president of the Indiana Prosecutors Association.

Jury selection in the Lennon case took three days, while the trial took just two—February 26 and 27, 1931. Lawyers had to question 139 people before selecting their panel. Like the Beshire jury, it was all white and male and mostly farmers. William Pickens, field secretary for the NAACP, attended part of the Lennon trial, though he'd been warned not to. Pickens had been told that if Lennon was convicted, the mob would "get" him and Dr. Bailey—that they were both marked. "It was astonishing to see and feel the mob atmosphere that still prevailed nearly seven months after the murder," Pickens wrote in a piece for *The Nation*. The hostility extended to Stroup and Wall, for Pickens observed that they "were looked upon as enemies of the community, not only by the mob, but also by most of the court officials." Seven witnesses, including Jake Campbell, Police Chief Lindenmuth, and reporters from both newspapers, testified to seeing Lennon swing the sledgehammer at the jail door. Defense witnesses who swore that Lennon was merely a spectator included his wife and his in-laws.

After the jury deliberated for ten and a half hours, they sent word to Judge Clawson that they were hopelessly deadlocked. Clawson refused to accept a hung jury, instructing them to work until they agreed. Someone on this jury held out for a full twenty-one hours, then caved in and voted to acquit with the others. Lennon was even cleared of the lesser charge of aiding and abetting.

In a letter to Pickens, Mrs. Bailey reported that there had been a big celebration "all over town" Saturday night, after the verdict came in. During both nights of the Lennon trial, white men had come to the alley behind the Bailey home, backfiring their engines to simulate gunfire, and a white woman had called to warn them to be careful; the taxi drivers were going to try to get them. Pickens noted in his *Nation* piece that Dr. Bailey now carried a gun at all times. "One night, after the firing of many shots near his residence, four automobiles filled with men drew up and parked directly in front of his house on the opposite side of the street," Pickens wrote. "The doctor opened his front door so that the flare of his brightly lighted house fell right across the porch and down the front walk. The mob decided not to accept his invitation and silently withdrew."

In March 1931 charges against all the other suspects were dropped. As the motion to dismiss put it: "There is no likelihood of conviction."

WHEN I MET THE EX-DEPUTY, I got my first real taste of white rage, and it started when I called to request the interview. The Ex was so heated on the phone, so vociferous, swearing he wouldn't talk if I planned to "stir things up." I was baffled.

The Ex hadn't become a deputy sheriff until the 1950s, long after the Campbell era. I'd called him because he'd known both the Deeters and the Balls. But once I got to his house, the Ex had two main points to make to me: that Mary Ball was "a sweet thing" and that James Cameron (whom the Ex called Connors, Conlon, Connon, or Cannon) was "a dead outright liar."

How had the Ex known Mary? He'd owned a 1925 roadster: "I'd drive around in that little car, and I could just about get any little girlfriend I wanted, and Mary Ball was in the class." What did that mean? They hadn't gone to school together. I finally concluded that she was just one of the kids he ran around with. "She didn't have a low name!" he declared, though I hadn't said anything about her reputation.

He too had been downtown the night of the lynching, but he wouldn't say what he'd seen until I promised him anonymity. "Everybody's afraid to say anything," he explained. "Because they'll drive by and burn your house or wreck you or anything else." At first I thought "they" might be the Klan. Then I realized "they" were black people.

The Ex told me that on the night of the lynching "a Fairmount gang" placed a can of blasting powder under a car to chase away some out-of-town law enforcement. I didn't know what to think, since he'd heard this second-hand, but he had an interesting source: the late Ralph Deeter, Claude's brother. Then the Ex admitted that he himself had seen the powder under the car, parked "right where the 222 Pool Room used to be." I remembered the *Indianapolis News* item about a group of twenty-five men meeting in a billiard room on the north side of the square, debating whether to storm the jail. It was just another tantalizing loose end. Suggestive. Circumstantial.

The Ex didn't have details. He'd just walked through the scene really fast. There was a roar in the downtown streets, and it scared him. He tried to imitate it for me—this hum. "Hhmmmmhmm hmhmhmmmhm. It was people actually talking that was doing that. It was a wicked-sounding thing." He'd walked quickly by the bodies. One had his teeth broken out, "hanging on the side. Drug his clothes off. And knocked one eye out of one guy. Out on his cheek."

"Just made a loop around and got out of there," said the Ex. "Too wicked sounding. But I do know this, and you better be sure of it!" His voice rose. "That Connors lied all the way through! Ask him one time. What did you go with them for?" The Ex was practically hyperventilating. "To see the moon go up or hear the birds a-whistling at night? On old Lover's Lane? Three of you guys went together. Why? Did you know that he had a gun on him? What did you plan to do with a gun? Shoot at the moon?!?" He took a breath. "And then he comes here and tells what a horrible thing that was!"

The Ex couldn't leave it alone. "Connon's a liar! Why do you go out on that Lover's Lane? To shoot birds? It don't make any sense! Says he just happened to be with 'em. So President So-and-so pardoned him. It ain't so at all! Stay out of this town! You'll be better off!"

I left the Ex-Deputy feeling completely puzzled about his anger, still so visceral after all these years. It took me quite a long time to realize the obvious: in 1930, at least, white Marion didn't merely regard the lynchings as justified—they were totally self-righteous about it. When I first met Cameron, I was shocked that white people in Marion had never apologized to him. Then I began to realize that of course they hadn't apologized. They thought *he* should apologize.

IMAGES THAT ARE PROBABLY pure mythology stick in my mind, like the sheriff throwing the keys out to the mob. But that's what happens when the facts are not determined. Mythology takes over.

And the power of the mythic material here made the truth harder to get at. What of that central enigma, Mary Ball, for example? Was she really a paragon of white innocence, a young woman raped by a black man? Or was she a paragon of white guilt, colluding with a black man to rob white men and then letting him take the fatal blame for a rape that never happened? I thought it quite possible that neither story was true—that she wasn't in cahoots with Abe Smith *and* wasn't raped. But I could never know for sure.

Nor was there enough evidence to pin the lynching on any particular group, though somewhere—I was sure of it—there had to be someone who knew more. Suspicion fell in four different directions. First the story I had heard as a child—that the lynching was organized in Bucktown, Mary Ball's neighborhood. Certainly the Ball family was present that night and right in the thick of things. I also had anecdotal evidence pointing to men from the neighborhood along 18th Street. Other stories suggested Fairmount and Deeter's friends. Or had it all been put together by the Klan? Though much diminished by 1930, it still existed and had the organization to mobilize a lot of people quickly. And wouldn't a large group have been necessary if the plan included guarding disabled streetcars and posting signs about a "necktie party" on country roads? I'd been told that Klansmen participated, though the hanging wasn't "Klan-sanctioned." Were they among the people streaming into town from all over? Or had the Klan mostly participated later, when certain men in authority made sure no one was punished?

Ironically enough, the only person who ever suggested that any lyncher came from anywhere but Marion was James Cameron himself. His lawyers, Robert L. Brokenburr and Robert L. Bailey, secured a change of venue for his trial, from Marion to Anderson, where he was locked up only at night after becoming a trusty at the jail. So one day while Cameron was out in the town of Anderson, he saw a man on a bicycle, riding with a little blond girl perched on the handlebars, both of them laughing. Suddenly Cameron realized that this was one of the raging men who had grabbed him in the Marion jail and pulled him out into the street. In his book he describes feeling a flicker of intense rage, but mostly he felt confounded by the purely human mystery of it. How could it be that this "happy-go-lucky man with that equally happy child had been capable of doing the things I knew he had done?"

What about Charles Lennon, who had certainly aided and abetted, even if "no one," including the police, saw him put a rope around anyone's neck, since "no one" including the police saw anyone do that? Lennon did not live in Bucktown or Little Kentucky or Fairmount, and no pimp would have been allowed to join the moralistic Klan of the 1920s. So had the lynching been organized by taxi drivers (Lennon) and mechanics (Boyd)? Were these the men who allegedly met in a downtown pool hall? Had the sheriff been privy to the plan from the start? Did Jack Edwards leave town because he knew he couldn't stop it? Did kids swimming in gravel pits really know more than the sheriff did? Than the mayor did? Just who was out there alerting people at swimming holes, anyway? Had the law officers met afterward and agreed to certain memory lapses? Who was dictating to the sheriff if he *was* involved? And if many in the mob were really sixteen or seventeen—Cameron's age—couldn't they still be alive?

Such unknowns. Such knowns.

During the year I lived in Marion, when I collected most of this testimony about the lynching, I drove past the courthouse countless times without ever losing consciousness that *this* was the site. *That* bush replaced the tree. And there had to be some answers just a little further on. And a little further on.

PART II

Good History/Bad History

NINE

THE IRONIES

What about this place had given rise to such an infamy? I traced the lineage of racial attitudes in Grant County back to the beginning of (literally) recorded time, thinking maybe I'd find more bigotry here than elsewhere. Instead, I saw why a lynching had seemed implausible. Instead, I saw what senior citizens in the black community meant when they said to me, "Marion wasn't that way." Actually, there hadn't been *enough* bigotry to suit certain white people. As one mobster outside the jail complained, "They let the niggers in the school with the white children here and march in the band." What did that have to do with Shipp and Smith?

Racism will always manifest in violent ways to preserve itself. I began to see the lynching as a grisly form of backlash.

I began to see, in the history, the deep sadness of my story. The men who told about the "belling," for example—Burden and Stewart—came from a couple of the oldest families in Grant County, black or white, and suddenly they were supposed to be intimidated into leaving. That illustrated to me how all forward progress in the town reversed that night. Because there had been forward progress, early on. African Americans had been among the pioneers here. This was no small thing. Certain other counties in the state still had a black population in single digits at the end of the twentieth century.

153

Terrible things happened elsewhere. So I discovered as I read the unhappy history of race relations in Indiana. This was a state where slavery had been banned mostly to keep black people off Hoosier soil. Even so the 1820 census found 190 slaves still living in a couple of southern counties. Indiana had been settled from south to north, and most of those first white Hoosiers in the southern part of the state came from the South, from the nonslaveholding class, and they manifested the predictable bigotries all too well. One prominent historian even suggested that there may have been more racism in Indiana than in other northern states, and described the pre-vailing white attitude before the Civil War as neither proslavery nor antislav-ery, just "anti-Negro." The African American presence loomed large in the white imagination and in politics, though it never amounted in fact to more than one percent before the War Between the States. By 1831 the Indiana legislature had passed a law requiring black settlers not only to register with county authorities but to post a $500 bond (big money in those days) "as guarantee of good behavior." Then in 1851 lawmakers passed a new state constitution that banned African Americans from moving into the state at all. So what if these laws were never systematically enforced? It's the thought that counts.

Meanwhile in Grant County a white Quaker named Aaron Betts brought the first black settlers to what later became the village of Weaver in a town-ship called Liberty and helped them to enter their land claims sometime in the 1840s. The histories don't agree on the year, but the county was still carving itself out of the forest at that point, its only roads marked by blazed trees. A spot of cleared ground called Marion didn't exist until 1831, when two of the original settlers, Martin Boots and David Branson, donated thirty acres apiece from their adjoining farms. At the heart of that acreage they built the courthouse. According to local folklore, Boots made it a condition for giving his land that if anyone ever received the death penalty in Grant County, the property would revert to his heirs. No such stipulation actually appears in the deed. But how interesting, I thought, that such a thing had be-come legend.

Quakers, or the Society of Friends, established the county's first church, and they were in the vanguard of the white antislavery movement. Nearby Jonesboro was founded by an ardent abolitionist, Obadiah Jones, in 1837, and the second newspaper started in the county (1844) was his abolitionist *Herald of Freedom.* In 1843 Frederick Douglass visited Jonesboro, which was enough of an abolitionist center by then to host the annual meeting of the Indiana Anti-Slavery Society. By 1850 Grant County had one of the

largest Quaker populations in the state. When the constitutional convention
wrote the exclusion of blacks and mulattoes into state law that year, petitions
arrived from just three counties to urge delegates *not* to bar African Americans—and one of those was Grant County. In 1877, when the state finally
opened public schools to black children, the measure was due to the work of
John Ratliff, a state legislator from Grant County and former "conductor"
on the underground railroad. He'd been able to get money to open a school
in Weaver in 1869.

Some counties drove every black resident out, but not Grant County.
Some communities were so hostile that no African American dared spend
the night in them, but not Marion. If the place looked downright progressive
next to others, it was never a paragon of tolerance, either. Like the rest of the
state—like the rest of the nation—early Grant County could be more accurately described as a battleground where white people fought each other
over the fate and the future of black people.

I THOUGHT OF IT as the county's founding irony: a courthouse built on a
graveyard. All over east-central Indiana the first eager settlers found earthworks now known to be a couple of millennia old—and they were in the way.
On one of the largest burial mounds in Grant County—sixty feet in diame-
ter, ten feet tall—pioneers raised the first courthouse in 1833. Five years
later they turned the clay from this mound into brick to build the second
courthouse. Some of the skeletons uncovered were reportedly seven feet tall,
though none survived, having crumbled "on the slightest touch." The third
and current courthouse opened on the site in 1881.

No one has ever found a connection between the mound builders and
the Miami, who once claimed the entire state of Indiana (and more). In most
of the Midwest, of course, all traces of the original population are long gone.
But in Grant County, Native Americans fought one of the last Indiana battles
against white soldiers, in 1812 on the banks of the Mississinewa—an event
now commemorated yearly with a "living history" weekend. Here too, just
northwest of Marion and extending north into Wabash County, lay the last
Miami Indian reservation in the state.

I wanted to look at the racial paradox in my own family (the Klan, the
tribe). So I immediately began searching for my alleged Indian ancestor, who
I assumed was Miami. The two central traumas in the tribe's history can
complicate a genealogical quest, however. First, in 1846, half the tribe was
shipped off to Kansas. The chiefs who agreed to this deal got to stay behind

in Indiana with their families. Most Miami leaders after the War of 1812 were of mixed blood, sons of French traders and Miami women, with names like Lafontaine. They'd acculturated fast. But those who got to stay in Grant County were the least acculturated, the least French, and the poorest. They had a chief named Meshingomesia who lived near the tiny Grant County town of Jalapa.

The other big blow to the tribe came in 1897, when the Indiana Miami were suddenly declared American citizens—not Indians. To this day the Western Miami remain a federally recognized tribe, while the Indiana Miami are not.

As I learned what I could about them, I decided that the Miami Indians of Indiana embodied every paradox and ambiguity of the race question, beginning with the most basic: what *is* race?

The most famous member of the tribe was a white woman, at least by blood. Frances Slocum *became* Miami after she was captured at age five in eastern Pennsylvania during the Revolutionary War. Perhaps this "becoming Indian" angle, her rejection of whiteness, is what so fascinated people about Slocum, "The Little Lost Sister," "The White Rose of the Miami."

Though she grew up among the Delaware people who took her captive, she eventually married a Miami named Deaf Man and wound up living on the banks of the Mississinewa east of Peru. In 1835 an Indian trader learned of her true identity when he stopped at Deaf Man's village for the night. The woman, now called Ma-con-a-quah (Little Bear Woman), told the trader that her white name had been Slocum, but she'd forgotten her first name. She didn't know the year of her capture, but it was "before the two last wars." She provided a detailed description of her Quaker father and said that, as she was now probably near eighty, her immediate family must be dead. She could no longer speak English.

Ma-con-a-quah apparently asked the Indian trader not to share this story until after she died. But he wrote it up anyway and sent it to the post office at Lancaster, Pennsylvania, hoping that someone would get it published in local newspapers, where surviving family members might see it. "She is old and feeble and thinks she will not live long," the trader wrote. "These considerations induced her to give the present history of herself which she never would before, fearing her kindred would come and force her away. She has lived long and happy as an Indian."

Indeed, the Slocums had spent years looking for their lost sister, and as it turned out, Frances still had two brothers and a sister living in Pennsylvania. She was not eighty years old but closer to sixty-two. Before the siblings could reunite, however, there was one last delay. The trader's letter did not see print for two years—not until 1837, when a new postmaster took over at Lancaster. His predecessor had tossed the missive aside.

The rest of the Frances Slocum story is about her awkward reconnection with her white family. When the brothers showed up at Deaf Man's Village, she greeted them with what one chronicler called "civil indifference." She could not believe they were really her relatives until Isaac Slocum told her how she'd gotten the scar on her finger. Even then Ma-con-a-quah maintained her reserve, her suspicion. Finally the interpreter convinced her that the Slocums would not kidnap her and carry her back east. She then consented to travel into Peru to see her sister. One account describes Ma-con-a-quah, her two Miami daughters, and their husbands riding into town on their ponies and presenting the white siblings with a haunch of venison, "in accordance with formal Indian etiquette." For the rest of her life Ma-con-a-quah would refuse all invitations to visit Pennsylvania. Nor did she have to spend the last year of her life in Kansas. As a sentimental gesture approved by Congress, she and her heirs received permission to stay behind. She died at home on the Mississinewa in 1847.

For Frances Slocum, Miami was not a race but an identity. And "blood" meant nothing.

GRANT COUNTY IS A BOX with Marion near its center. Back in the volatile times before the Civil War, proslavery folks prevailed in the northeast corner of the county, which was all white, while most of the antislavery partisans had settled just south and southwest of Marion, around Jonesboro, Fairmount, and Weaver. Jonesboro supported an antislavery store where nothing produced by slave labor was ever sold, and the underground railroad had a stop just north of Fairmount as early as 1833.

At its inception the African American settlement of Weaver lay nestled among the farms west of Jonesboro belonging to Anti-Slavery Friends. A sign posted at the one structure that remains, Hills Chapel A.M.E. (African Methodist Episcopal), says the congregation was established in 1842. But Mrs. Asenath Peters Artis, writing the first definitive history of the county's African Americans in 1909, put the arrival of the founding families at 1847. Those first families were the Weavers and the Pettifords.

I won't forget ninety-year-old Sarah Weaver Pate greeting me at her front door with *I'm one of the Weaver girls,* when I went to talk to her about the lynching. While I knew that many other descendants of the pioneering families lived in Marion, I thought of Sarah Pate as the heart of that community. Weaver had been named for her father, John Henry Weaver, after a post office opened at his general store in December 1880. Before that the little farming community was known simply as "the crossroads," since that's what it was: an intersection of two county roads. It was never a town with streets; most everyone lived on a farm. John Henry Weaver's homestead stood near the intersection. So did his store, and next to it sat the Pettiford blacksmith shop. At its zenith in the 1880s, Weaver had two schools and four churches, and a number of other homes were clustered around the crossroads. Sarah Weaver Pate painted an idyllic picture of her girlhood there in the early 1900s: church socials, spelling bees, taffy pulls—all of small-town America's pleasures.

From a distance, at least, this part of Grant County looked like a place where there had always been racial harmony. Quentin Pettiford, born in Weaver in 1929, told me, "The Quakers were real friendly. It was just like a family out there. I didn't know there was black and white." Pettiford "never knew prejudice" until he moved into Marion in the fifth grade. John Henry Weaver's store had functioned as a community center for all the local farmers, regardless of race. The annual camp meeting in Weaver woods, a combination revival service and carnival that raised money for Hills Chapel, drew both black and white people from miles around and "was looked forward to with great anticipation," according to *The Centennial History of Grant County*. In the 1920s a racetrack opened near the crossroads, enjoyed by everyone. On a day of harness racing that drew five thousand people to the track, an article in the *Leader-Tribune* declared that the scene resembled an "old time county fair." That was in September 1922, the same month the Klan began recruiting in Marion, apparently worlds away.

Weaver began losing young people to factory jobs in the late 1880s and disintegrated further during the Depression. By about 1950 most of the buildings had disappeared, yet the community never really died because so many still felt such a strong connection to the home place. In the early 1990s John Taylor, a grandson of John Henry Weaver, commissioned an artist to paint a large picture of the long-gone country store and neighboring blacksmith shop. This he mounted on the store's site, a quarter acre he'd purchased at the crossroads. I realized that for many black people in Grant County, Weaver was the Good History. Peaceful and safe.

In my first visit to Hills Chapel, where a tiny congregation still worshiped every Sunday, I immediately noticed that the names of the founding families had been mounted on nameplates at the end of each pew: Weaver and Pettiford, Wallace and Smith, Burden and Casey, Gulliford and Beck, Stewart and so on—a total of sixteen. These were among the families who had arrived before the Civil War, some freeborn, some slave. What all the town's families shared was an obvious pride in their roots.

Opha Beck Betts, raised on a farm south of Weaver, had just retired from a nursing career when I met her, and she was looking forward to writing a history of the community. She'd been researching the project for years. Her great-grandfather, the extremely enterprising Matthew Becks (at some point, the family dropped the *s*), had arrived in Grant County sometime in the 1850s after living for forty-six years as a slave in Virginia. His obituary relates how Becks set out, after gaining his own freedom, to raise $1,500 so he could buy his wife and children from another plantation. According to the Beck family story, it was actually $1,000 in gold and had to be raised within a year. Either way, this was a princely sum in the 1850s. Becks decided "to visit the strongholds of abolitionism" and appeal for help. After telling his story at churches and public gatherings all over New England, Becks ended up with pledges from Horace Greeley, William Lloyd Garrison, Wendell Phillips, Henry Ward Beecher, Harriet Beecher Stowe, and hundreds more. Thus did Matthew Becks succeed in freeing his family. He then worked for the rest of his life as a blacksmith at Weaver.

Matthew Becks's youngest son, Silas, taught at the Weaver school. Opha Betts got out a text she'd copied from one of her great-uncle Silas's textbooks, *Political Economy*. Sitting in her Marion living room, she read to me: "Now there are three desires in men which contend for mastery. Desire of ease. This tends to repress labor. Desire of present gratification. This tends to consume the fruits of labor at once. Desire of means for future gratification. This tends to stimulate labor and to save its fruits. A man or a nation grows rich only as the third of these desires overrules the other two." This, she told me, was the philosophy of Weaver.

A soft-spoken, meticulous woman, Mrs. Betts had begun studying the genealogies of the Weaver, Pettiford, Beck, and Smith families. "Our roots take a diverse route simply because there are 'fair' members in each generation all the way back up the line, and their origins are very diverse," she said. "I'm not sure where it's going to lead. I have to assume that some of them were so-called white."

One historian who researched Indiana's black rural settlements concluded that those established by 1860 "were composed to a large degree of people of racially mixed heritage. Many had white and Indian ancestors, and often it was the white ancestry that had resulted in their freedom and migration." The Pettifords were a case in point. Like the Weavers, they had never been in slavery. The founding legend in the Pettiford family "concerns an English woman whose attraction for a black male servant led her to transgress the boundaries of race and class," as the family's genealogical study delicately explains. Shipped off to the colonies, this woman gave birth to a son she named Beverly in memory of her home in Beverley, England. As the study puts it, the children of such unions were "usually accorded the free status of their mother." Quentin Pettiford told me later that, the way he heard it, the English woman then gave her baby to the Cherokee Indians to raise. He figured he was part Cherokee.

Over the years all the old families in the Weaver community had intermarried. Opha Betts was a Pettiford on her mother's side. She speculated that one of the reasons such a connection to the home place had developed among the descendants was the yearly reunions. These began when Martha Weaver Pettiford, John Henry's sister, insisted that her eighteen children return home every year at the same time. The Weaver-Pettiford reunion had been held the third Sunday in August every year since 1919 and was a major event, often covered in the Marion newspaper. Some of the other founding families also held reunions on other Sundays, always on the land next to Hills Chapel, land still owned by Prince Hall, the black Masonic lodge.

I had my own theory on why the community's descendants still felt such a connection. There were still a few older black people living in farmhouses near the crossroads. There were still services at Hills Chapel, on the site of the original church built by black pioneers in the 1840s. There was still the Prince Hall land, where black Masons had built an old folks' home in the 1920s (since torn down). There was the Weaver cemetery, donated by a black resident named Lewis Wallace in 1866. No wonder this all felt like hallowed ground. This was land that had never been owned by white people.

SINCE SO MUCH IN history that related to race was unknowable or undiscussable, I relished the irony in the name of the county's other early black settlement: Telltale. This small community just north of Jonesboro was founded in 1847 by five settlers, three escaped slaves and two freedmen. It's unknown how long the settlement lasted, how big it got, or what became of its people, since Telltale disappeared without leaving a legacy.

I found another irony in Dark Secret, a community situated, like Telltale, somewhere between Jonesboro and Marion. I only heard of it by chance while interviewing a man who'd seen the lynching. Neither he nor his roommate at the nursing home could remember, though, if the Secret in question had to do with the bodies reportedly dumped there by criminals—or with the interracial couples who lived there. Interracial marriage was illegal in Indiana until 1965.

In the autumn of 1995 I went to see Leslie Neher, then the Grant County historian, with high hopes that he would know something more about Telltale, Dark Secret, the underground railroad, and a legendary pro-Confederacy group known as the Knights of the Golden Circle. Neher had some limited information on all of them, though he seemed surprised by my interest in Dark Secret. "Not really a neighborhood," he said, but he promised to drive me past it. Neher had devoted a room of his Gas City home to his research on the county and pulled some things from his files for me. But he refused to tell me anything about the Klan or the lynching. The county historian felt that the lynching should be written out of county history. (Neher, who was then eighty-nine, would soon retire as county historian. His successor, Richard Simons, did not share this attitude.)

Neher, a retired soldier, told me of his own tangential connection to the event. On August 7, 1930, he had been a second lieutenant with the field artillery stationed at Camp Knox, Kentucky. He'd tried—unsuccessfully—to accompany the National Guardsmen sent to Marion on August 9. Now, as he put it, "I'm suspicious of anyone who comes to Grant County to know about the lynching."

We drove off toward Marion, Neher's frail wisp of a wife in the backseat. Dark Secret turned out to be an unremarkable patch of land north of the VA Hospital. Neher was embarrassed to put it so bluntly, but he managed to indicate that here was where soldiers used to come on payday to spend time with prostitutes. Articles I found later in old newspapers suggested that it was probably also racially mixed. I began to think of Dark Secret as Grant County's old demimonde.

We drove to the approximate site of Telltale along a county road near Jonesboro. Neher wasn't sure which house it was behind, only that the settlement had been on the bank of a stream south of the Frog College. That was the one-room schoolhouse built there in the woods near many ponds (and their many frogs) but now long gone. Neher thought Telltale had actually been a mixed settlement, black and white. Two members of the Jonesboro Historical Society had seen the foundations of the Telltale cabins as children.

I returned on my own a couple of weeks later to search for Telltale. No one in the area, which is now all white, had ever heard of it or seen a trace of an old settlement, but the first man I spoke to knew people who'd been to the Frog College as children. Everyone was happy to talk about it, happy to talk about the Good History. Their eyes lit up. One old man said he was seventy-seven and he'd lived in Jonesboro his whole life, the Jonesboro that had become another all-white town, and he wanted "to pass something on." He gave me his phone number and suggested with a palpable yearning that maybe I would join him and his cronies at the Gas City McDonald's some morning and discuss the old days. I didn't have the heart to pop a question about the lynching or the Klan.

AS A CHILD, I THOUGHT OF Marion as "southern." This certainly had nothing to do with race or the lynching but with vague sensory impressions. Humidity. June bugs. The bulge in the screen door. Maybe I'd heard some southern accents, too. They were there.

The town went through a midlife change. In 1886, the year my grandfather was born, Marion was just a quiet farming community of about 3,300 people. This unindustrialized village disappeared suddenly a year later.

One night in February 1887 someone struck natural gas at the corner of 14th and Boots. Three years later twenty-five new factories moved into Marion while the population more than doubled to about 8,800. Marion entrepreneurs had tapped into a five-thousand-square-mile Gas Belt spread over parts of nineteen Indiana counties with Muncie at its hub. Gas fever swept the area. The supply was thought to be inexhaustible. Wells went uncapped. Gas lights ran at intersections twenty-four hours a day. Special excursion trains took citizens to the gas fields where towering flames burned over the wells. The little village of Harrisburg, just across the river from Jonesboro, decided in a fit of enthusiasm to claim the unfortunate name of Gas City, while Marion promised free fuel to any factory willing to relocate. Marion was to become "a metropolis of dreams." That was the plan, and by 1900 the city's population had doubled again to 17,337.

Five years later the gas was depleted, but now Marion was a factory town, and it still is. Many of the new residents, both black and white, came from the South—many of those from Kentucky. As Ed Breen, former managing editor of the *Marion Chronicle-Tribune*, told me, "That Kentucky subculture never gets absorbed. They never intended to stay, and they never assimilated." I encountered many Marion natives with southern accents. And in both the black and white communities, feelings of pride, even entitlement, went hand in hand with being the descendant of an *old* family, a pre–Gas Boom family.

My grandfather liked to tell the story about one of the new "hillbillies" coming into the post office and proudly announcing that his family now had "a board floor." The Kentuckians were looked down upon by other white people, and I wondered if that was part of the unproven accusation I heard so often about the lynching: the Kentuckians did it.

BY THE TIME KLAN RECRUITERS arrived in the 1920s, Marion was one more town in the grip of Jim Crow. African Americans could not stay in hotels or eat at most restaurants. At movie theaters they were confined to the balcony or, if there was no balcony, to the back rows. When the town finally built a pool at Matter Park in 1924, blacks could not swim there. Nor could they bowl, skate at the roller rink, or join the Y. Even the reportage on black social life was segregated in the two Marion papers, appearing in "Colored News" or "Colored Notes." At local factories blacks worked mostly as unskilled labor with little hope of rising into a skilled trade, no matter their aptitude.

Bad as this was, other towns were worse. Marion is about forty miles northwest of Muncie, the subject of *Middletown,* Robert and Helen Lynd's classic sociological study of a city "as representative as possible of contemporary American life." The Lynds, who conducted their research in 1924–25, observed that Muncie blacks were allowed to attend local schools only "under protest" and could not patronize movie theaters at all, while "Negro children must play in their own restricted corner of the Park." In a follow-up study done ten years later, *Middletown in Transition,* the Lynds added that the whole of Muncie's black population lived in just two sections of the city, and that "Middletown shuddered and felt confirmed in its views when two Negro boys were lynched in a nearby city [Marion]."

The African American community in Marion was actually better off— up until that lynching, at least. Though North Marion was all white and East Marion (also known as Johnstown) was all black, the rest of the town was never strictly segregated. It's also fair to say that a majority of African Americans lived on the south side. That's where the major Baptist and A.M.E. churches were. In the 1920s Marion had one all-black grade school in South Marion, D.A. Payne, but African Americans were not required to go there; they could choose it. Most other schools had always been integrated—and never "under protest." After state law opened high schools to blacks in 1877, Marion was one of the first two towns outside Indianapolis to have a black high school graduate (in 1888). Two African American contractors laid down most of Marion's brick streets early in the twentieth century. On the first day of free mail delivery in 1890, one of the four carriers was black. The town also had a black police officer as early as 1894. Then, from sometime early in the 1900s up until the 1960s, Marion always had two black cops and two black firemen, a quota strictly observed. The two firemen had to work separate shifts so they could use the same bed, so I'm not exactly describing an enlightened approach here. Blacks did not have equal opportunity in Marion, just *some* opportunity compared with so many other midwestern towns where, for example, no blacks were allowed in the police and fire departments until the civil rights era.

In 1904 a black man ran for Marion City Council for the first time, after finishing second (among five in his ward) in the Republican primary. Candidate John Robinson then endured crudely racist front-page cartoons in the Democratic paper, the *Daily Leader,* up until election time. He was defended, though a bit tepidly, in the Republican *Chronicle.* Robinson lost this election, though he finished third among five in a race where the top two were winners. The *Leader*'s rubbery Sambo caricatures were vile but not exactly unusual for their day, while a Robinson win would have been remarkable.

Blacks still seemed to regard the town as progressive, early in the twentieth century. In 1913 a national African American weekly based in Indianapolis, the *Freeman,* published a long hosanna to Marion. "Colored People are Home Owners!" read a subhead. In fact, the article reported that in Marion blacks owned more property "in proportion to their numbers" than in any other town in Indiana. "The white and colored people of this city sustain the best of relations," declared the *Freeman.* "They are respectful to each other and they show a spirit of fair play." That quote comes from an introduction to twenty-four thumbnail sketches of prominent citizens—contractors, business owners, and other members of the black middle class.

At this time Marion had black professionals: lawyers, doctors—even an architect, Samuel Plato. There was a black physician in town by 1897. In fact, during most years from then until the 1920s, Marion had two black doctors. All these men had white clients. Plato's nineteen years in Marion illustrate the contradictions. When he arrived near the end of the Gas Boom, in 1902, he couldn't find any work except carpentry finishing. But he went on to design a couple of Baptist churches, the Weaver school, two factory buildings, an apartment complex, and a number of dwellings for prosperous white people. A few of these places still stand. The Neoclassical home Plato built for a prominent citizen in 1912, now a public space known as the Hostess House, remains one of Marion's finest structures and was added to the National Register of Historic Places in 1988.

The NAACP chartered a Grant County branch in January 1919, but by the years of peak Klan activity (1922–25) the group had become inactive. It was Flossie Bailey who revived it in 1929. She was a dynamo, still a vivid memory to every senior citizen in town who'd once known her. Even so the Marion branch had only thirty-four dues-paying members by March 1930. This in a town with close to eleven hundred African Americans. But, by October 1930, two months after the lynching, the Marion chapter of the NAACP had more than quadrupled to 155 members.

By the late 1930s the only black professional still in Marion was Flossie Bailey's husband, Dr. W. T. Bailey.

I BOUGHT A 1930 Marion High School yearbook at a local "antique" store, and occasionally I'd page through it thinking, Were *you* there? Were *you* there?

But this was the unexpected thing. The 1930 annual had been dedicated to the Frances Slocum Trail, once the scenic route between Marion and Peru. Nearly every page had been decorated with "Indian" patterns and arrows, while short texts related, sympathetically and sentimentally, the various tragedies of Miami history. The battle. The removal. And so on.

It's easy to romanticize people after you obliterate them, and that's been the Native American experience everywhere. Grant County has no corner on it. Still, I wondered how I would feel about attending Mississinewa 1812, the living history event observed every October since 1988.

I had found many an article in old Marion newspapers about the so-called Battle of the Mississinewa and couldn't help but notice that it was always presented as *the* victory in Indiana "Which Vanquished the Supremacy of the Red Man," as the *Leader-Tribune* put it in 1924. It struck me as an odd thing to celebrate. One of the villages destroyed by federal troops belonged to a chief named Metocina, who still had descendants in the area. Only after I met some Miami people did I understand the big irony about Mississinewa 1812. While it marked the defeat of their tribe, this was one of the few options they now had for connecting with their heritage. The Miami had a longhouse on the grounds, and some would camp near it every year, in costume.

People come from all over North America and Europe to spend a few days in Grant County living in 1812. Wearing the old clothes. Doing the old crafts. Inhabiting the past without the context of the past. I didn't understand this need, yet I became a convert to the event and found myself urging people in Marion to attend. All the neat white tents looked so picturesque among the trees—pointy ones for soldiers, round ones for Indians. Organizers did not re-create the local battle but choreographed a bit of Napoleonic war. There were storytellers, old-timey musicians, and refreshments authentic to the period. Mostly I just enjoyed strolling out among the trappers, Hussars, and oddballs of 1812.

I happened to discuss the experience with Linda Mui, a white woman who'd done a great deal of work in Marion on racial reconciliation. "The event is really neat and in all of this we have to face our history," said Linda. She'd recently joined the Black History Council, and they'd discussed an article in the paper about African American participation in the War of 1812.

Local blacks seemed alienated from the proceedings: "it's not about us." I told Linda I'd noticed how few were present out there, even among the vendors. The *Chronicle-Tribune* ran a picture of a reenacter from the Regiment of Colored Men (Canadian), but I hadn't seen any of them in person. Now Linda's children wanted to participate, but since they were half Chinese, she wasn't sure what part they could play. It was a reminder of tough realities—like what was actually going on in this country in 1812 for anyone who wasn't white.

The Mississinewa event presented a utopian past, a wonderful illusion of harmony. It showed the very different and distinct cultures of the period coexisting with ease, sharing resources. Sometimes I imagined it as mythology especially created for a county still best known for a racial crime. But it was also appropriate in a county that began with more "diversity" than was common in Indiana. Sometimes I saw the 1877 *Combination Atlas of Grant County* as a book of possibilities. On the plat maps showing who owned each and every piece of property in the county, Weaver is an actual town: small lots, two churches, and a school. All around it, inscribed on their acreage, are the names of the original African American settlers. Weaver and Pettiford, Burden and Casey, and so on. At the northern end of the county are plats belonging to Meshingomesia, Chapendoceah, Aw-taw-waw-taw, and others of the Miami tribe. Elsewhere I found the names of my own great-great-grandparents.

SOMETHING SHIFTED THE night of August 7, 1930. The place that began with at least some potential for racial harmony became the place where certain white people felt they'd been granted permission to express their racism. They got away with something big, and from that night on the county's bad history would cast a shadow over the good.

That's what I saw in Marion's failure to capitalize on the legacy of its most famous son, actor and cult figure James Dean. The archetype of white America's misunderstood youth was born in Marion, in a house just two blocks from the Grant County jail on February 8, 1931—six months after the lynching.

Dean lived in that location for only a year before his parents began to move around, renting on South Adams Street and in Fairmount and Jonesboro, while Dean got his boyhood introduction to performance downtown at the Marion College of Dance and Theatre Arts. Dean's father worked as a dental technician for the Veterans Administration, and they transferred him to Los Angeles in 1936. The family moved. But after the death of his mother in 1940, Dean returned to Grant County to live with Ortense and Marcus Winslow, his aunt and uncle, on their farm just north of Fairmount. Here, ten miles south of Marion, Dean lived for more than a third of his short life.

Fairmount celebrates Dean every September with a three-day event that draws tens of thousands of visitors. The town is charming, barely changed since 1955 when Dennis Stock photographed the young actor during his last visit home, pacing the downtown streets and playing bongos in the barn-yard. Old men who were once his high school buddies like to assure visiting fans that the beloved actor was just Jim. No loner. No rebel. No different from anyone else in town.

Dean would have probably disagreed—much as he enjoyed projecting the farmboy image for Stock's camera. After he moved to New York, he scrawled a poem about Fairmount inside his copy of Edwin Honig's *García Lorca*. "My town thrives on dangerous bigotry" went one of the lines. While he also called the place "sweet," he concluded: "My town is not what I am, I am here."

Marion has only recently seemed interested in claiming this icon. When Grant County marked the fiftieth anniversary of the actor's death with a summer festival in 2005, it was the first Dean event centered in Marion rather than Fairmount.

I regarded this as one of the more mind-boggling facts I ever learned about Marion: that the city tore down the Dean birthplace in 1975 and replaced it with a parking lot. By then, Dean had been a cult figure for twenty years. In 2001, a civic group trying to revitalize the downtown hit on the idea of making miniature ceramic replicas of the Dean birthplace. But they soon discovered that they could see only two sides of the house in old photographs. No one had even bothered to document the place before they demolished it. The city simply marked the spot with a small Walk-of-Fame star embedded in the sidewalk about a foot from a fire hydrant. Every autumn, when fans from around the world flock to Grant County for the Dean festivities in Fairmount, they can't visit the farm where he grew up. Dean's cousin still lives there. Obviously, Marion could have had a huge tourist draw if it had restored the birthplace. Preservationists might have even learned how the apartment was furnished by consulting with Dean's father, who died in a Marion nursing home in 1995. (The aunt and uncle who raised Dean, Marcus and Ortense Winslow, died in 1976 and 1991, respectively. Presumably they would have also visited the birthplace.) I speculated that this appalling lost opportunity had to do with Marion's inability to look at its own past, where there was, in the words of my family's lynching story, *something you don't want to see.*

History's layers are not always easy to separate. Claude Deeter was another Fairmount farmboy. Anyone standing at Dean's grave in Park Cemetery—almost always decorated with lipsticked kisses, flowers, and cigarettes left by fans—can look north and see Deeter's modest headstone. Then about thirty feet east of Dean lies Daisy Douglas Barr, once the national head of the women's Ku Klux Klan. All three were buried from the same Fairmount Church.

LARRY HITLER HAD DISAPPEARED. I'd met him in August 1995, then spent several weeks in New York organizing my move. By the time I got back to Marion in September, the Hitler residence was empty. The house had been condemned. Tom Wise reported sighting the giant brother at a cheap motel on the bypass. I called that place, then every motel on the strip. Nothing. Wise also informed me that Larry would not be getting a permit to do his Klan rally at the courthouse. So I'd really lost him, along with all those promised connections to Ku Klux bigshots.

Then, less than a week later, an Indianapolis television station reported that a Marion Klan rally was on again. This news did not make the local paper. When I called the city clerk's office, they claimed to know nothing. I was back to no leads, no access, the news that's never fit to print.

Mayor Ron Mowery would not announce until October 30 that the Ku Klux Klan planned to rally at the Grant County courthouse on Thanksgiving weekend.

Somehow, whenever an issue touched on race, the authorities first had to lay out their eggshells to walk on. They would equate keeping secrets with keeping the peace. Back in the 1970s the Klan marched on the Grant County courthouse, and the Marion newspaper did not cover it at all. I only learned of this 1970s march by chance, from a retired white minister who attended an interracial prayer breakfast every Sunday. He'd heard it discussed there when it happened. He said that all the blacks at the breakfast knew about it, and none of the whites did.

Maybe those newspaper editors back in the 1970s thought they could render the Klan impotent by ignoring it. But the Kluxers still hit their mark—the black community—while the refusal to even acknowledge their presence let white people off the hook. I thought about those men at the prayer breakfast—the targeted blacks, the oblivious whites. I couldn't think of a better description of the status quo.

TEN

THE ANCESTORS

In the journal where I made notes on family history decades ago, I had written: "Great-grandmother Newell was a full-blooded Indian." That would have been Sarah Scarlett Newell, my grandmother's great-grandmother.

Aunt Ruth had a tintype of this ancestor, somewhere. My aunt had the curdled temperament I associate with artists who never manage to make art, who steam and stew instead. Still, she and I always got along, and whenever I visited my parents, I would drive over to see her. I hoped during each visit to get access to the family pictures. Aunt Ruth had everything that had once belonged to my grandparents, but she always told me she didn't know where to look among her boxes. She'd spent years in the town where my parents lived, hundreds of miles from Marion, and never really unpacked. Boxes lined many a wall. This had always been one of her idiosyncrasies. When I was a girl and Ruth lived in Indianapolis, much of what she owned stayed in boxes there, too. She always said she was decorating.

On one visit she told me that she also had pen and ink drawings, or maybe they were watercolors, of Sarah Scarlett Newell's daughter and son-in-law—my great-great-grandparents, George and Emily Nixon. Aunt Ruth

170

knew where they were but still wouldn't get them out. She was busy finding the right shade of pale yellow for the living room, constantly starting over when the color didn't look quite right because of the tint in the window glass. No one but her, the five cats, the feeble dog, and occasionally my parents were ever in that house.

She did tell me the family legend about the origin of the Scarlett name, however. Some ancestor had been a foundling left on a doorstep, wrapped in a scarlet shawl. She didn't know how far back that went on the family tree, but all I could think was—great, an ancestor on a doorstep. The genealogy stops there. And I just didn't see any Native American connection.

Aunt Ruth seemed more interested in talking about my grandfather's side of the family. Grandpa, with his mother Josie dead, had been raised by a hellcat. That's how Aunt Ruth described Josie's mother, Margaret Jane Fankboner Carr, the one with the boardinghouse at 18th and Adams. Aunt Ruth wanted me to go back to Marion and look again for the home of the "town catch," a home that took up a whole city block—home to the man in Josie's locket, she was now convinced. I'd already failed to find such a residence in the whole history of Marion, but told her I'd try again.

In 1853 my grandfather's forebears settled in Jonesboro, where my great-great-grandfather Abram Carr worked as a wagon-maker. He had married Margaret Jane Fankboner in Ohio in 1851, then moved to Grant County with swarms of in-laws. There were Fankboners all over Fairmount and Jonesboro in the early days. Margaret Jane's brother, Morris Fankboner, even became Grant County sheriff in 1877. But I know nothing of the family's politics then. Nothing of the Jonesboro years had come down to us but a single line, a memory from Uncle On's boyhood: *He saw Colonel Stretch march in to put down the copperheads.* (Copperheads were southern sympathizers.) By the time my great-grandmother Josie was born in 1865, the Carr family had moved to the farm east of Gas City.

One day at the Marion library I suddenly solved the family mystery, at least the part about Josie's fate. In an obituary for her father, Abram the wagon-maker, I found Josie's date of death. She had predeceased him. There she was in the Marion paper for September 16, 1887—dead of typhoid fever at five that morning, with burial at Jonesboro cemetery (in Gas City). She was a few weeks short of her twenty-second birthday, while her son, my grandfather, was fourteen months old. Her passing had earned a full two sentences in one of those local news columns devoted to less permanent comings and goings, on the order of "so-and-so went to the fair."

I still hadn't found the obituary my grandfather had, in which parts of certain lines had been cut out with a razor blade. But just to learn how she died—at last—brought a feeling of relief, then anticlimax. The truth was so ordinary.

What I remembered hearing as a girl was that Grandpa's parents had died in a wreck when he was three. I remember picturing a conflagration in my mind. I saw them sitting in an open car on some tracks where they were hit by a train. It couldn't be further from the truth, but that was the story in my head. Could I have proposed this scenario to some adult family member who said yes? More likely I imagined it with such fervor that it became real. As a girl, I hadn't quite figured out that there were no cars when my Grandpa was three; nor had I thought about the fact that he carried his mother's name. At first I wondered why a death from typhoid had been kept so hush-hush. Then I realized that, of course, both parents had to be killed off somehow in the family story. I had always appreciated the Aunt Ruth theories—that Josie was poisoned by someone. *They wanted to get rid of her.* Or more recently, that Josie had killed herself. Then there was my father's theory—that she died of a broken heart.

Secrecy breeds mythology. We had all invented deaths for her.

My grandfather's father, Odos Roush, lived in Jonesboro at the end of his life on a street facing the Mississinewa, directly across the river from the Gas City cemetery where Josie was supposedly buried. I thought there was a sort of romance to that, until I drove to the site of Ode's house and realized he couldn't have seen a thing through the trees.

On a whim, I went to the Grant County courthouse to look for his will. I discovered that he never made one, but the estate went through probate anyway. His administrator, Guy Roush, had made a list of "sole and only heirs . . . as far as is known." All of them were nieces and nephews. And great-grand-nephews. And "grand-grand" nieces. The only claim against the estate came not from my grandfather but from some Roush relatives who wanted $2,045 for buying the old guy groceries and driving him around. I found long lists of Ode's property, beginning with the most valuable, "1 Emerson Cabinet Piano," down to "1 Schick Electric Razor." He had also owned land. And clearly my grandfather had known something about this. So at the end of his life he told us, *They cheated me. I could have had ten thousand dollars.* The money handed out to nieces and nephews actually came to fifteen.

▲ ▲ ▲

AS FOR GRANDMA'S SIDE of the family—one of the first things I did as I began my research in Marion was to check the Miami tribal rolls assembled in the nineteenth century. I didn't see a single name I recognized. I knew that both my grandmother and her mother had been born in Wabash County in the now-vanished town of America, not far from the Miami Reservation. Then when they moved to Grant County, my grandmother went to grade school in the little town of Jalapa, where many of the Miami kids went to school. And one of my Aunt Ruth's mantras about Grandma went: "She was friends with the daughter of the last Miami chief."

All I had to go on was family stories. I remembered clearly that we were in the living room on Fifth Street when my grandmother told me that her own grandmother had been an Indian. And she did mean Sarah Scarlett Newell, whom she'd called "Grandma." But that was one of the fine points—well, even the large points—I didn't go into. I couldn't have been more than ten or eleven at the time and didn't know how to ask the right questions. But I did calculate my Indian blood. Grandma's grandma made me one-sixteenth.

What I remember even more vividly is going immediately to the back-yard to tell my father how "neat" I thought it was that we had an Indian ances-tor. He responded: "They were a Stone Age people." End of conversation.

Then there was my grandmother's story about her mother, Elizabeth Nixon. Elizabeth's father, George Nixon, never really recovered from his Civil War wounds and died when Elizabeth was still young. Elizabeth's mother, Emily—the alleged part Indian—remarried but died soon after. The rest of the family Emily had married into then began to treat Elizabeth like a servant and would lock her in an upstairs bedroom whenever they went out. Racism? Or just meanness?

At the Marion Public Library I found the George Nixon family in the 1860 census for Wabash County. In the category "Color [Black, White, Mu-latto]" there was a checkmark after Emily's name but not after George's name—or any of the children's names. Looking at how other families had been categorized under "Color," I saw more checkmarks. I speculated that it meant "okay"—that is, "white." Of course, "Native American" wasn't ex-actly one of the options. "Mulatto" applied to those who were somewhere between black and white, while Indians weren't even officially included in the census until 1890. Emily would have definitely wanted to pass for white. Or maybe she *was* white.

Maybe I was just one of those "wannabes" the real Native Americans were always complaining about. Yet I felt certain that my grandmother had talked about this, so I asked my father again. And again, he assured me, that if someone was part Indian, they wouldn't talk about it. My aunt Ruth also denied knowledge of any native ancestry, declaring that her great-grandmother "sort of looked like an Indian but she wasn't an Indian."

Finding a Native American somewhere on the family tree was not going to make me an Indian. It would not erase the fact that I have lived with every privilege accorded to someone white. But somehow I still wanted to know.

Had I made it all up? I asked my sister, who's a year and a half younger than I am, if she remembered Grandma talking about the fact that she was part Indian. Yes. My sister remembered it clearly, because after Grandma told her, my sister went off to the woods to see if she could walk without breaking a twig.

I THOUGHT I MIGHT be able to learn something from the Miami still in Grant County. But when I found them, I realized that they were searching, too.

Like other Native Americans, the Miami went through a forced assimilation, but theirs had an extra edge. Those who'd stayed in Indiana were no longer part of a federally recognized tribe. They were, apparently, no longer Indians. For one or two generations most of them did everything they could to deny their Miami identity. They stopped speaking the language. They didn't transmit the heritage to their children. And since this was a culture with an oral tradition, the tradition died. So at the end of the twentieth century, when the moment came for pride in a Native American identity, the years of repression had done their damage. The younger generation of Miamis I began to meet were all engaged in trying to recover their obliterated culture.

I heard many poignant stories about the pain caused by this loss. One that stayed with me came from a man I met at a pow-wow—Eugene Brown, born in 1926. He thought his mother might have even been a full-blood Miami, but she wouldn't tell him anything. Confined to a nursing home at the end of her life, her mind gone, she was taken one day to a family gathering and suddenly began to chant what could only have been an Indian chant. Suffering from Alzheimer's or dementia and back to the core of herself, she had forgotten to hide her Miami identity. "So," concluded Eugene, "that was the only real heritage I ever heard."

For the most part the Miami I met had no physical characteristics that would identify them as Indian rather than white. They could easily "pass." Asserting that identity is a radical act when you're "the vanishing race." One woman still remembered reading in her fourth-grade textbook on Indiana history that all the Miami were dead, while she sat there thinking, "How can that be? I'm a Miami."

Indeed, *The History of Wabash County,* published in 1914, states: "As a race, they are now almost a thing of the past and live only in the songs of their exterminators." Was it some kind of wishful thinking? During the course of my research, I'd come upon so many articles about "the last Miami" that I began collecting them. The last full blood. The last to speak the language. And of course, the last chief—though there seemed to be quite a few of those, beginning with Meshingomesia.

Native Americans suffer the ignominy of being the only ethnic group whose identity is determined by the federal government, but that's because of the government money involved. First annuities. Then various land claims. Left to themselves, the tribe had always incorporated outsiders, but that practice ended during the treaty years. Too many outsiders were just there for the cash. In 1838 the tribal council decided that only Miami Indians would have a right to future annuities or land. From then on, they enforced the "border" around their identity.

If "blood" meant nothing to the likes of Frances Slocum, it now meant everything. No one could be part of the tribe without an ancestor on a federal treaty roll—the lists drawn up in the nineteenth century to determine who would get annuity payments. So one of the most important positions in the contemporary Miami tribe is that of historian and genealogist. Tribal secretary Lora Siders filled that role when I met her in 1996 at Miami headquarters, the former Peru High School.

Siders was then seventy-seven and had been part of the tribal council for nearly fifty-five years. Her hair was still dark but white at the crown. With her broad face and stout body, Siders had some of those physical characteristics associated with Native Americans. But I was also looking for my grandmother's face and thought I could see it. The mouth. Exactly the same. Or was this *my* wishful thinking?

It did make me uncomfortable. Who knows what a Native American looks like anymore? It didn't matter that I was looking for something identifiably "Indian" about my own family. I was still part of the authenticity game, and there was almost no way not to play it. Even the Miami played it. The whole setup was about, Who's the "real Indian"? And what might "real" mean? Do you look like it? Dress like it? Have family stories about it? Have federal recognition? Have an ancestor on a tribal roll?

For a while we discussed this question of Indian blood. "I used to just get furious when somebody would come up and say, 'How much Indian are you?'" Siders declared.

I told her that I had figured out a percentage for myself when my grandmother said she was part Indian. And Siders continued: "What other nationality, *any* nationality, do people walk up and say, how much Irish are you? How much Italian?"

She also found it very offensive when people claimed to be Miami and weren't, but she added, "People who really don't know and are trying to find out—I can cope with that. I can feel for them." She knew that people used to hide their Indian identity to get work, and maybe some of their descendants were trying to reclaim it for real. "But some of these people—you have a feeling. They just want to *be* somebody. And I don't feel that it's our place to make them Miami."

"Isn't it strange that for such a long time people didn't want to be Indians and now they all want to join up?" I asked.

Siders laughed. "Yeah, there's a big tribe of wannabes now. A *big* tribe." There had to be many reasons for that kind of yearning, but a simple reason was greed. In the 1950s the government began to settle claims, paying additional compensation for land originally purchased at pennies per acre. The Miami had to create a new tribal roll, fending off the many wannabes who wanted a cut. Then, over a period of twelve years, Miami descendants got three checks of $1,200 to $1,300 each.

One complicating factor: at the time of the 1846 removal to Kansas, some people managed to stay behind. "Some of 'em hid and were not found," Siders confirmed. Their names would never have made a tribal roll since they weren't supposed to be in Indiana. That would have ended their claim to Miami identity right there. Siders directed me to Thelma Hart, someone all the elders accepted as Miami, though Hart did not have the papers to prove it and was, therefore, not a member of the tribe.

I had several conversations with the elderly Hart, who seemed to know more about the tribe than anyone else. Yes, her great-grandmother was supposed to go to Kansas, she said, "but the Indians took her to the woods and hid her." That particular ancestor was Potawatomi, but Hart was also descended from Meshingomesia's brother, which should have been easy to prove.

A couple of generations of denial got in the way. "Grandma, she smoked a clay pipe, and in the summer she went around barefoot and her hair braided down the back. But it made her mad to tell her that she was an Indian."

Hart's real problem with her "papers," though, could be traced to her mother, who had changed her name at least four different times in order to lose her identity—and she'd succeeded. Hart had never been able to untangle it and claim her place in the tribe.

Naturally I wondered about my own ancestors. Did someone hide in the woods?

ONE DAY WHEN I PASSED Estates of Serenity, the town's oldest cemetery, I saw cars at the office and stopped to finally get the location of my grandparents. My searches hadn't been too far off. They were on a corner just as I remembered, with a single headstone. They'd been dead for thirty years, yet I stood there weeping, imagining their faces. I felt a lot of sadness I didn't understand. I noticed for the first time that they were one grave away from Alonzo Carr. Uncle On. I sat in the car then for a while, writing in my notebook: "Because I miss them. Because they are still so present for me. Because I don't want them to be gone, though they'd both be over one hundred. Because I want to know everything they knew and saw and felt."

Then I wrote down my two feelings about writing this book: *You are meant to do this. You are not supposed to.*

When I finally told my parents that I was writing about Marion, they were surprised, maybe even astonished, but accepting. This was a relief. I hadn't known what to expect, but I had not set out to distance myself from either my family or my history. Just the opposite, really. I was there to claim ownership of it all.

ELEVEN

UNDERGROUND

The underground railroad running through the county—that should have set a certain tone. I thought. Instead it was just another part of the larger history puzzle.

I began researching local "conductors" and other abolitionists, expecting to have an easy time gathering information. This, after all, was the Good History. But it proved to be almost impossible to get concrete details. One of the few stories related in the county histories concerned the very first underground railroad station, set up near Fairmount. Here a Quaker farmer named Charles Baldwin built a second log cabin in a thicket a quarter-mile east of his own, expressly for the purpose of hiding runaway slaves. At one point he kept nine men concealed there for a week. Then, on the day that Baldwin brought them to his home for the trip farther north, three slaveowners and two law officers suddenly showed up at the end of his lane. One of the fugitives crept up close enough to confirm that these were the three Kentucky slave masters from whom he and his companions had escaped. Back in Baldwin's living room, the nine runaways formed a circle, joined hands, and swore to die right there rather than be taken back into slavery. Meanwhile the men at the end of the lane conferred among themselves, never realizing how close they were to their prey. After some thirty minutes the slaveowners remounted and headed south.

No slave was ever recaptured in Grant County. That much I could ascertain, but I found only two more stories in the old histories: the two conductors who led three fugitives through the swamps and backwoods in broad daylight with the owners right behind them; and the conductor who covered seven people with hay in the back of his wagon and drove them through downtown Marion under bright moonlight, breaking into a gallop as soon as he crossed the bridge out of town. There had to be more. I'd compiled a list, no doubt incomplete, of twenty-eight conductors in the county, all of them white. But I also noticed that their obituaries, and the biographical memoirs that appeared in stately tomes once the county had a sense of itself as a historical entity, often failed to mention their antislavery activity.

It's impossible to comprehend now just how far out of the mainstream the underground railroad conductors were. For one thing, they were breaking the law. Anyone caught helping runaway slaves faced jail and a heavy fine. Not even all Quakers agreed that it was the right thing to do. When two abolitionists, one black and one white, visited Marion in 1839, they could not get permission to speak at any church, including the Friends meetinghouses. Local antislavery men went to get the key to the courthouse so the two could speak there. As related in 1899 by prominent lawyer James Brownlee, who witnessed the encounter, the man with the key refused to turn it over at first, saying that, on the contrary, he would purchase eggs to throw "at the nigger and the old Abolitionist." But in the end the man did relinquish the key, and the event came off without incident. Brownlee noted that "if a man was charged with being an abolitionist, that was enough— 'away with him,' 'crucify him,' 'egg him.'" Most white Americans, including most northerners, did not want blacks to be free. As Brownlee put it, "Slowly did public opinion change on the great wrong of slavery."

A schism developed among Indiana Quakers over how far to go for the abolition cause. Some conservative Friends supported the back-to-Africa movement or refused to get involved at all. In 1842 the radicals led by Levi Coffin of Wayne County, "president" of the underground railroad, withdrew from the Yearly Meeting to form the Anti-Slavery Friends. Historians estimate that of 25,000 Quakers in the state, only two thousand were committed enough to make the break. In Grant County radicals pulled out of the two Quaker churches early in 1843 to create the Deer Creek Monthly Meeting of Anti-Slavery Friends. All these seceders were then disowned by the mother church. By the late 1850s, however, the rift had healed, at least in Grant County, where "there was more unity among the members of the two divisions than they had imagined."

I FOUND MY FIRST underground railroad site when I met Bill and Marita Fields, two retired teachers who lived just south of Marion in a house built in 1844 by a Quaker named George Shugart. When the Fieldses bought the place in 1967, it was a dilapidated shell occupied by raccoons. Despite the broken windows and the holes in the ceilings, they could tell that the place had once been something special. Yet while both were Marion natives, the Fieldses were unaware that the house had been a stop on the underground railroad—further proof of how thoroughly this legacy had disappeared.

Once the Fieldses found out, however, they did a great deal of research into the same questions that intrigued me: How many fugitives had been helped here? Where did they hide? What stories had the family passed on? Marita Fields told me that there had once been seventeen Shugart homes between Marion and Fairmount. The renegade congregation of Deer Creek Anti-Slavery Friends built a school and cemetery on acreage donated by George's father, John Shugart. The whole extended family had moved over en masse from Wayne County, the epicenter of the underground railroad in Indiana, about eighty miles southeast. Apparently they had come to Grant County, at least in part, just to be the next way station on the road to Canada.

As Bill and Marita restored their house, they realized that it had been designed with hiding places and escape routes in mind. The last man to own it told them that upstairs behind a bedroom wall he'd found a ladder leading all the way to the basement. Apparently there'd once been a tunnel from the basement to the creek that had since collapsed. And in another upstairs bedroom they found space behind two walls. *Big enough to hold a choir,* I thought when Marita showed it to me, though neither hiding place would have been obvious to anyone entering the room. Each still had traces of hay on the floor when the Fieldses took over the house.

The Shugarts were originally from North Carolina. They'd owned slaves themselves, back when patriarch John was a boy, before concluding that it was unconscionable. Of course, once they freed all the people they'd owned, they could no longer compete with the other plantation owners. They moved to Indiana. Marita knew only one complete story about what the Shugarts had actually done to help runaway slaves—this gleaned from Shugart descendants who'd come from out of town to visit the house.

One day some bounty hunters stopped at the farm, and George Shugart went outside to talk to them. (Bounty hunters generally knew who the "conductors" were.) By chance, there were two slave girls in the house at the time. Mrs. Shugart gave each a wide-brimmed Quaker bonnet and told them to walk out to the buggy in front, keeping their backs to the bounty hunters, who were in the side yard. Mrs. Shugart then walked over to her husband and told him that she was going down the road with their two "daughters," because a neighbor lady was having a baby. And so the two girls escaped with her.

I found another story of pursuit and escape in a newspaper article about the nearby farm of Henry Shugart, George's brother. Henry had five slaves hidden in the haymow one day when some bounty hunters rode up. One of them said he wanted hay for his horse and headed into the barn. Henry intercepted him, saying, "I'll get it," and climbed up to the loft, where he tossed some hay down onto the barn floor, then turned and dropped another pile of hay onto the fugitives. That night Henry sent a family member out to the barn to tell the runaway slaves to hide in the woods.

Henry Shugart still had a great-granddaughter living in Marion, and she was a local legend—Adeline Nall. She'd been James Dean's high school drama teacher, the one who "took the time to see the proficiency behind the eccentricity," as one of his biographers put it. She had coached the shy, petulant teenager to a state championship in forensics and encouraged him to become an actor. I'd noticed that at the yearly Dean festivities in Fairmount, all the fan attention centered on her rather than on the actor's family. The self-appointed leader of the procession to the cemetery, a leather-clad biker named Nicki Bazooka, always presented the frail old lady in the wheelchair with a scarf—each year a different color—wrapping it gently around her neck.

Adeline Nall lived at a Marion nursing home in a room filled with pictures of the movie icon who had once been her student. I wasn't quite prepared for how far gone she was. She spoke in a low gravelly voice, barely audible at times, slipping back and forth between confusion and clarity. She told me there had been a hiding place in her grandfather's house under the stairway for runaway slaves. "Very cramped. And no light. I don't know how they ever managed, but they did." A little bit later she declared that there was no hiding place in the house at all, that people always hid in the barn.

But she too told me the story of the haymow, how her great-grandfather Henry Shugart stood up there tossing hay, "covering the citizens." *The citizens.* She would not use the word *slave.* She told me that the men chasing the fugitives knew they were there in the barn, and "it was a very awkward situation for a while. My great-granddad stood at the edge of the haymow and proceeded to give a sermon." She told me this story twice, but each time she came to "the famous words" that drove off the bounty hunters, the punchline came out differently. Once it was "You better watch out. You're playing with fire. You don't know the fiery works of the pilgrims." Another time it was "A Puritan would not attack anybody, but he knows that they're safe with us as far as being protected. You're safe with us."

That must have been what he said to the slaves, I speculated.

"Slaves? Slaves? I wouldn't call them slaves," said the old lady. "Poor people. And they lived life like anyone else, and they had no roots anchored anyplace, and someone around Michigan had said, 'Come up here, there's land up here you can use.' "

The haymow story had frayed and corroded over time, and it was the only one she knew. Long ago she had tried without success to learn more from her grandfather, Con Shugart, who had been just a boy when these things happened. "I'd go in his room and talk at night and try to get him to tell these stories, and he didn't care to, I guess. He didn't say much."

She began sidetracking into other subjects, always managing to circle back to James Dean. Asked when she started teaching, she replied, "The year James Dean came to Fairmount." (That would be 1940, when Dean was nine.) She had a poster of him labeled "Always and Forever" on her wall, along with stills from *East of Eden,* her favorite of his films, additional Dean pictures pasted to a piece of cardboard, and an oval portrait of the actor on top of the television. She also pointed out to me that she had some of the more obscure Dean offerings, his TV work, on videotape. I noticed a small framed sampler that read, "What is Essential is Invisible to the Eye," with a pair of eyeglasses (like the ones Dean wore) embroidered above the words. I asked her the significance of this line from Saint-Exupéry's *Little Prince,* and she said, "That's the philosophy Jim Dean took with him. He and the black boy from Chicago—it was their philosophy together." This was another puzzle. Though I'd read several Dean biographies, I had no idea who "the black boy from Chicago" might be.

"Do you remember the lynching?" I asked.

"Oh, that was terrible." She'd been in Chicago when it happened, she said. "I never talked to people about it. Not very much, and I never let them talk much in class about it."

As I got ready to leave, she announced that she was about to turn one hundred. That surprised me. On my way out I asked at the desk, and the receptionist told me that Adeline Nall had recently turned eighty-nine. She'd been born in 1906.

I felt disappointed with this encounter, wishing I'd met her years ago. Then I reconsidered, because at least I had heard that one word reverberating with the convictions of another age: *citizens*.

ONE DAY I HAPPENED UPON Moses Bradford's memoirs while looking through old microfilm. This abolitionist and underground railroad conductor had taken the unusual step of serializing his life story for a Marion newspaper in 1885. Apparently he'd always been voluble about his politics. Shortly after moving to Grant County in 1849, he took it upon himself "to talk on the abolition subject" one day on the east side of the courthouse square. Several men tried to shut him up, warning him that they'd driven another abolitionist out of the county, but he declared that he would never give in. He particularly relished tales of his encounters with the Knights of the Golden Circle, the notorious band of southern sympathizers. Bradford had the sort of pride I'd expected to find—but seldom did—among white people who'd been on the righteous side of the slavery question. No doubt it helped that he was a Methodist unconstrained by Quaker modesty.

Since nearly all of Marion's newspapers from the Civil War era and earlier are gone, Bradford's stories shed a rare light on how volatile the racial politics were in this relatively progressive county. He and two brothers who also worked for the cause, Joseph and William, all had farms north of Marion, far from the abolitionist strongholds around Jonesboro and Fairmount. Bradford seemed to enjoy taunting his proslavery neighbors. One day while he had seven runaways hidden in his house, two of these neighbors came to the door and demanded to know if he was harboring any fugitives. Bradford took them right to the little room where they were hidden and asked one old man to stand and show his lacerated back "received from his kind master." Then Bradford told his neighbors it was the custom to give the runaways a dollar, which they did. Bradford then informed them that they had just aided fugitive slaves and would be subject to prosecution if they dared to turn him in.

In 1858 the black abolitionist Frances Ellen Watkins came to Grant County to lecture. Bradford and other local abolitionists decided that Watkins, "who was almost white and fair," might make one appearance in Van Buren township northeast of Marion, stronghold of the county's proslavery movement. Bradford, who drove Watkins to this meeting at the township's one church, wrote that a crowd of some five hundred people met them there, where the trustee informed Bradford that "the door was closed against all negroes." Nor could Watkins speak outside the church. Nor in the woods just north of it. The man who owned that land, Esquire Malcolm, the township's chief justice, told Bradford to take his "damned negro" back where he came from. (Bradford was also unusual in naming names.) Finally a man named Shipley volunteered his log cabin some two miles farther east. Everyone followed. And here Frances Ellen Watkins finally spoke, after "the landlady" rolled Watkins's bonnet out of the cabin, saying she "didn't want negro lice on her bed." Watkins had the nerve to use sarcasm, praising the intelligence and bravery of the township "and the religious qualities that wouldn't allow a colored woman to pray for them." Then dozens of men, lined up on either side of the road she would leave by, tried to stop the carriage and grab "the yaller gal," as they called her, but Bradford had brought antislavery supporters who fought them off.

Bradford reported that, once the Civil War started, men in the northeastern part of the county mustered and drilled "every moonshining night" to resist the Union draft. It's a fact that the most serious draft riot in the state occurred just east of Grant County in Hartford City, where a mob destroyed enrollment lists and trampled the draft box to bits in 1862. But I don't think anyone ever identified these rioters as part of a specific political group. Some historians have asserted that the proslavery Knights of the Golden Circle never actually existed in Indiana. If not, they certainly generated strong folklore. I had heard about their clandestine drills east of Marion as a little girl a hundred years later. What's indisputable is that there was plenty of opposition to the Lincoln administration in Indiana.

The ruffians Bradford kept encountering could have been fanatical Democrats, the party of unabashed white supremacy at the time, but maybe they were more. Bradford was certainly not the only old-timer to talk about the Knights of the Golden Circle. Perhaps this mystical and unforgettable name was just loosely applied to the secret political societies that *did* exist and did embrace copperhead sentiments: the Order of American Knights and the Sons of Liberty. The leaders of the Sons of Liberty actually plotted an armed uprising in Indianapolis in league with Confederate agents. The group's Grand Commander had arms and ammunition shipped to his office labeled "Sunday School books," but that's as far as it got. Enrollment records reveal that Grant County had 201 members in the Sons of Liberty.

Bradford relates how the local copperheads beat the Wesleyan minister outside the Marion post office in 1861 for supposedly impugning the character of George Washington. It was usually either that or "preserving the

Constitution" that gave them their excuse to attack. At Bradford's farm they sometimes knocked over fences or fired their revolvers as they passed.

Shortly after the attack on the minister these same hotheads decided that everyone had to hang out a flag "to indicate whether they loved the Constitution and Washington or not." Bradford purchased nine yards of red, white, and blue calico and had his children make a large flag, which they stuck in the yard. Some six weeks later a mob marched out to Bradford's to take the flag down. "It did not have enough stars on it," they charged. And because it had hung in the weather and the cheap calico had darkened, his flag now had black stripes—"and that was a sign of negro equality." Bradford emerged from the house with two rifles and a revolver and announced that he would kill the man who tried to take his flag down. The mob departed. "Their politics: 27 Democratic and 4 Republicans," wrote Bradford, "and pretty near every one of them forgot to join the army to fight the rebels. Most of them proved true to the Knights of the Golden Circle."

Bradford also mentions making a trip to "the settlement." It had not yet been named Weaver. According to Bradford, thirty-eight black men had enlisted in the Union army but wanted to "consult" with him after hearing rumors "that if they went to the Army they would be shot by our own boys in blue." Bradford reports that John Ratliff, the future Quaker legislator, was also there to assure them that they would be protected "by God Almighty." When Bradford returned home that night, he went into his corn crib to get some feed for his horse when he saw four men ride up and say, "Let's give old Moses a round." They fired at his house, where his wife and daughter dropped to the floor, "which most certainly saved their lives." Bradford recognized the men as residents of Van Buren township. "True, Van Buren township produced some great men," he wrote, oozing contempt. "I could hear their lovely voices very near every Saturday night giving the war whoop and firing off some of their Sunday school books."

What's striking is that the local copperheads, or whatever they were, enjoyed picking on an isolated abolitionist like Bradford but never made any violent gesture in the direction of the black settlement at Weaver. It was a pattern I would find again with the Klan. There could be spectacular and deadly moments of force aimed at blacks, but everyday business involved policing other whites.

MOSES BRADFORD'S FARM lay along what is now the Bradford Pike in North Marion, a street six or seven blocks north of the Mississinewa and downtown. Before the Civil War everything north of the river was farmland, but no doubt his proximity to town helped make him a tempting target. His brothers, William and Joseph, lived farther north. They make one appearance in Moses's memoirs. Four days after the confrontation over the flag with "black stripes," a much larger mob made ready to attack, and these brothers came to Moses's house to help fight them off. The mob assembled at the bridge but dispersed when they heard that the Bradfords had assembled "a large force."

One afternoon I drove out to what was once the Joseph Bradford farm with Bill and Marita Fields, the ex-teachers who owned the old Shugart home. They happened to have friends living on the Bradford place. I couldn't help but notice that the white people who owned these old underground railroad houses were terribly proud of them, but Allen and Connie Newby had found less information about the Bradfords than the Fieldses had about the Shugarts. Their abstract indicated that Joseph and William Bradford purchased the land in 1856. Connie Newby showed me what she assumed had been the hiding place for fugitives, upstairs in their teenager's bedroom: a door about four feet high and a foot and a half wide led into a space behind the spiral staircase. She figured the door had been hidden behind a piece of furniture in the old days. Then, down in the basement, she pointed out that part of the wall was made of different stone, indicating that it had once been a door. The Newbys had heard a story about a long tunnel connecting their house with another Bradford home nearby, probably William's, but they didn't seem to believe it. They hadn't heard any stories at all about the fugitives who'd passed through.

But they did know a grandson of Joseph Bradford, an old man living in Hartford City. A grandson. That was close. Moses Bradford would have been his great-uncle. I went to see him the very next day, thinking I'd gotten lucky at last. Instead, as with so many of my interviews, I went looking for one thing and found another.

Bernard Cox was out cutting his grass when I drove up. Before we'd even gotten inside, he began telling me about his wife, who'd died two months earlier. He had married her right out of high school in 1928, "the only girl I ever went with," and now he was ninety-three years old, obviously heartsick and desperately lonely. He had never known his grandfather, the conductor Joseph Bradford. His mother had been the conductor's youngest child. But he'd grown up in the house where the Newbys now lived, and the first thing he demythologized was its status as an underground railroad house. He assured me that the house hadn't been built until

1871 and had never housed a single fugitive slave. What stood there during underground railroad days was a log cabin. "There was only a few logs left when I saw it. It laid about a hundred feet north of the house and probably ten feet east. There was logs on the ground and Mom said, 'That was the underground railroad.' I imagine that was the original house. She told me 'those logs there.' Probably it was 1915, 1918—the last time I remember seeing the logs."

He had never asked his mother for more information. The only other thing he'd heard about the underground railroad came from his father's side of the family, from his grandpa Cox, who'd grown up near the Bradford place: "He said when a load of hay come down the road, black heads would be sticking out of it." Bernard had never been much interested in these stories. And he'd never even heard of his great-uncle Moses Bradford, that incredibly vivid figure. I was surprised, but then some people are indifferent to history and their own family trees.

Bernard had worked for Woolworth's in Marion during the 1920s, so I asked him if he'd been aware of the Klan meetings that went on upstairs. "I didn't know anything about that."

"Did you ever see their parades around the square?"

"Oh, I saw the circus parades," he declared. "But the time they had that lynching in Marion, we lived in LaPorte. I didn't live in Marion at that time or I might have been there and watched."

He had brought up the lynching on his own. In 1930, he continued, he'd been an assistant manager at the Woolworth's in LaPorte, Indiana, and he had "a colored fella" working for him. This black man made a pass at one of the white girls working there, and, said Bernard, "I got a hold of him as he come in the door. I said to him, 'Does the name Marion, Indiana, mean anything to you?' He said, 'Yes sir, it does.' I said, 'Now just remember one thing. I am from Marion. And it could happen to you.'"

Bernard told this story with a touch of pride and nary a hint of self-consciousness or shame. Soon he had hauled out the pictures of the eight grandchildren and fifteen great-grandchildren. He talked and talked, eventually giving me the name of a Bradford cousin he had no contact with. "I didn't go to college," Bernard explained. "He did. I'm not in the society class with him."

I'd dutifully taken my notes and kept the tape running, but I'd stopped taking things in after those chilling words *It could happen to you.* This was someone whose grandfather and great-uncle had both been underground railroad conductors, radical abolitionists, and here was the legacy: nothing but the usual malicious bigotry. Bernard was not a hard-core racist, just un-conscious and narrow, like so many white folks. He was all too typical.

Maybe coming from abolitionist ancestors didn't mean any more than coming from Klan ancestors. Maybe antislavery convictions didn't translate into antiracism. Since most conductors never wrote their memoirs as Brad-ford did, their deeds would have to be passed on through family stories. Most of what I'd learned about the Shugarts came down that way. But what if the descendants had no wish to remember? Racism too could feed that si-lence, and in this way the Good History could be erased.

I went home and called Bernard's "society class" cousin. He didn't know a thing about his ancestors' work on the underground railroad.

TWELVE

WEAVER

I originally went to see Sarah Weaver Pate because she'd worked for Dr. W. T. and Flossie Bailey, and I'd been disappointed when she couldn't tell me much about their efforts, first to stop the lynching and then to get it prosecuted. Really, it took quite a while before I figured out what I was learning from Sarah Pate.

A second interview with her, to talk about the Weaver community, took months to arrange. She was much in demand as the oldest living descendant and the last child of John Henry Weaver who was actually available. (One sister was alive but very ill.) So she put me off for a while, saying that she was "tired of giving out history," that she was "worried about August seventh, 1930." And she just didn't understand why she had to keep talking about these things.

But Sadie, as most people called her, tried to oblige me when we finally did talk. She got out all her Grant County history books, along with probably every old picture and duplicate snapshot in the house. Then she sat there in her blue polka-dotted dress and pink shawl with this pile of pictures, narrating them for me: her ninetieth birthday party; last Thanksgiving at her nephew's house; the wedding of a white woman she'd raised. As for the Weaver pictures, it seemed she could name every person in them. It wasn't really what I'd come for, but for her these were the good memories.

I think she found the past painful to contemplate, except for the Weaver days, which she remembered as an idyllic period of racial harmony. "It was wonderful to see the association and friendliness." She had known the old Quakers, the Shugarts. "Oh, they were very best friends." And the Ratliffs. "Those white people there—we were just one big family."

She didn't seem to know any family stories about how the Weavers happened to come to this place from North Carolina or how it was that they had never been in slavery. She talked about her brother, Howard Weaver, the schoolteacher for the Weaver community. What Sadie wanted me to know about him was that after the one-room Weaver school closed in the late 1940s, Howard could not get a teaching job in Marion: "They said it wasn't time for blacks." Howard Weaver left Grant County for a distinguished career in Indianapolis, where he became principal of the city's largest elementary school, president of the Indianapolis Elementary Principals Association, director of religious education for the Indiana Conference of the A.M.E. Church, and a grand master of the Masonic lodge, Prince Hall affiliate.

Sadie had moved from Weaver to Marion around 1923—she couldn't quite remember, but that's when the Baileys' daughter died. The Baileys had hired her when the entire family came down with the flu. After they and son Walter recovered, Sadie stayed on, working at the house and attending high school.

So she would have been eighteen when she found out that in Marion she could not go to the movies unless she sat in what she called "Pigeon Heaven," couldn't go to restaurants or beauty shops, then couldn't go to the new swimming pool. She said she hoped I would never have to go to a place where a door shut in my face because of the way God made me: "They must think there's a heaven for us and a heaven for them." After high school she wanted to get her R.N., but Dr. Bailey said he would train her since he needed her help right away. So she never got that certificate and couldn't work as a nurse once Dr. Bailey stopped practicing. Instead she became an elevator operator and then spent years taking care of white people's children. She had worked until she was eighty-nine years old.

She wore a large gold angel pin on her collar—because a guardian angel watched over her, she said. Spontaneously she began to talk about the lynching. It still unnerved her. One of the white policemen who escorted her and Dr. Bailey to and from work every day after the hanging had been so frightened that the doctor had to give him a sedative. He'd been afraid for his own safety, this white man. And that had frightened Sadie more than anything. She couldn't really articulate what the lynching had done to Marion except that it hurt the churches and it hurt the community. "Someone's gonna have to pay for this," she concluded.

But just as she had the first time we met, she emphasized the white friends in her life. I thought she was being polite, working hard not to make me uncomfortable. But the impact of a lifetime of white treachery leaked out inadvertently when she described a neighbor who was always checking up on her, always asking if she needed anything. Sadie said of this woman who'd been so caring: "She was white, but you'd never know it."

My conviction that she was holding back prompted me to borrow tapes of Barbara Stevenson's two interviews with Sadie Pate, done for the Black History Council's oral history project in 1994. And there it was, emerging from a story about how she'd once inadvertently gotten a ground-floor ticket—a white person's ticket—to a Marion movie theater back in the 1920s. "I could write a book on Marion," she suddenly announced to Barbara Stevenson. "Marion is the most prejudiced place in the state of Indiana. We can't keep any doctors here [in the black community]. Can't keep any dentists here. Can't keep our undertaker here. No lawyers. Nothing. It is pathetic. And this lynching shouldn't have happened. I know all about that, Barb. I was right in it. You wouldn't think it would happen in the North, but it did. And Marion hasn't changed one bit. One bit."

She described for Stevenson how she and her aunt had moved in to the Baileys' house the night of the lynching: "Everybody was just shaking. But we had guns and ammunition up there at Baileys'. A lot of the people from Marion went out to Weaver and Michaelsville. They went out there and laid on floors. They laid on floors!"

Most intriguing to me, she told Barbara Stevenson that she had seen Klansmen around the courthouse when she and Dr. Bailey went to work the next morning: "They had these light hoods and it looked like they had white coats or something on. I remember these hoods and it really scares you. It looks like a ghost milling around. . . . It's just like I can see them now, and I said, 'Oh that's the Ku Klux Klan.' I remember they said one of 'em was Al Hogston."

"Al Hogston?" asked Stevenson.

"He was a lawyer here in Marion. I knew him."

"Somebody said that was him or you knew it was him?"

"Well, I knew it was him."

The Klansmen were just "browsing around," Sadie reported. "More or less milling around watching. Trying to see what next was going to break out or what they were going to do because they had said they were going to kill all the black people."

Her description seemed to contradict what Hogston's grandson had told me—that Hogston disapproved of the lynching, did not like the fact that certain Klansmen had participated, and eventually quit the Hooded Order over this. I had a family story versus a ninety-year-old eyewitness and couldn't corroborate either one. I went to see Sadie again, hoping for more details. To me, she denied seeing Al Hogston near the lynching site. In fact, she denied seeing any Klansmen there at all. She even denied going near the courthouse that morning.

As Barbara Stevenson explained to me: "She's afraid of the Klan. When I talked to her, she cried."

JOHN TAYLOR AGREED to drive me around the area that had once been Weaver. We met at Hills Chapel, second oldest African Methodist Episcopal church in the state and the oldest to still have services every Sunday, according to Taylor. He was the one who'd attached the names of the old families to the ends of the pews and hired an artist to paint the sign that now stood at the crossroads. A grandson of John Henry Weaver and Sadie Pate's nephew, he'd come to Weaver for his grandfather's funeral when he was a year old in 1929 and stayed on to live with his grandmother. So he grew up in the disappearing town, then farmed eighty acres at the home place until 1965. Someday he would move back here, he said.

As we stood in front of the church, he pointed northeast across the field to where there'd once been a Quaker farmhouse. He'd seen where they hid the slaves, underneath the stairwell in the kitchen. But now, like so much else in the area, the house was obliterated. I had hoped he'd have a story about the underground railroad. He didn't. "I would have loved to have talked to some of those people who actually knew the stories," he said.

Weaver had been one of many little communities depleted by the Gas Boom as people left the farming life for factory work. We drove slowly up and back over county roads. He seemed to know the history of each plat within a mile of the crossroads. He'd point at some bare field and say, That's where the so-and-so house used to be. At the cemetery he said, "I helped dig some graves in there." He pointed to a grove of trees now in the middle of someone's crop, where there had once been a Baptist church and a few more graves. He showed me where the school for whites once stood and then, a half mile down the road, the school for blacks. He had loved that beautiful school, designed by the African American architect Samuel Plato. He tried to buy it some years ago but was outbid by people (white people, though Taylor didn't mention this) who then used it to store corn and broke the floor out. Then they tore it down. "They just had no interest," he said. "That's what gets me." The fact that nearly every trace of the old community was gone really disturbed him. His latest obsession was the racetrack. By the time he'd been old enough to have memory, the track was gone, so he didn't even know what it looked like. He'd been looking everywhere for a photo. He wanted to hire an artist to make a painting of that, too.

We pulled into a farmyard a mile or two from the crossroads where Taylor wanted to say hello to some old friends, Raymond and Lavonne. They would remember the racetrack, he said.

"How are ya!" called Raymond from back of the house, delighted to see Taylor.

They had all known one another most of their lives. Raymond and Lavonne had been born in 1916 right down the road. After inviting us in, they pointed out to me that they could see both their birthplaces from the kitchen window. They began to reminisce about the track, the Weaver schools, and John Henry Weaver sitting outside his store. Raymond and Lavonne were white.

Raymond began talking about a black friend, Vaughn Casey. How he'd been born right on this farm back when this was "all colored." How Raymond had promised Vaughn he'd keep a certain fence in place for as long as he lived—and Raymond had kept that promise. How Vaughn would ride by on his John Deere, standing up waving. "They only made one Vaughn," said Raymond.

"I miss him, too," said John Taylor. He'd met Raymond back in the 1930s, when Raymond's dad bought and sold cattle for John Henry Weaver's widow. They indulged in a little farm talk about crops and weather.

Then Lavonne mentioned in passing that many years ago her father had opened a park on their property, Clearwater. With a start I realized that this was the park someone had told me about. Where black people from Weaver were not allowed to swim.

We sat around Raymond and Lavonne's kitchen table, and as the three of them chatted about who owned Clearwater now, I tried to decide how much painful stuff I could go into. Though these three had grown up together, I had a feeling that certain things were taboo. And I wondered if the amiable relationship had been kept intact by the silence about those painful topics.

I decided that I had to plunge in, and I asked all of them if they remembered the hanging. They did. But they didn't seem eager to talk about it—none of them—and I suddenly felt a sort of tension among these three old friends. I could see a pall descending on Raymond especially. I suspected that he and Lavonne just didn't want to talk in front of John.

Raymond remembered that, right after the lynching, the sheriff had blocked off the state road where it turned off into Weaver, and "we were up there that morning."

"In Marion?" I asked, but he went back to describing the roadblock and my instinct was not to press him.

"I know exactly where they're buried in there," Raymond volunteered. He meant, of course, Tommy Shipp and Abe Smith, whose graves had never been marked for fear that another mob of white lunatics would dig them up. Some people even disputed the notion that they'd been buried at Weaver.

"Did you go to the funeral?" I asked, astonished.

"I remember when it happened," Raymond continued, describing for me precisely where the graves were. How quickly mysteries end when they aren't really mysteries at all but secrets.

"Well, folks, thanks so much for your time," John Taylor suddenly declared. A few minutes later we were back out in his car.

I thought about this encounter for days. About Lavonne's pride in her father's segregated park. She'd even hauled out her photo album to show me pictures of it along with flyers she'd saved. Then Raymond's reticence and the shadow of guilt that passed over his face when I asked about the lynching. The fact that talking about it had spoiled the party. I would have to talk to Raymond and Lavonne again—just us white folks, and I wasn't looking forward to it.

I WENT BACK TO WEAVER on my own to draw a map based on what John Taylor had told me. I walked through the Weaver cemetery, where most of the graves are now unmarked. Barbara Stevenson of the Grant County Black History Council had complained to me that the county workers who cut the grass were never careful about the headstones. This was the resting place for black people born as early as 1804, black men who'd fought in the Civil War, and it had been completely full for fifty years. The ground was spongey. Few had been able to afford a vault.

When I pulled in at Raymond and Lavonne's place, I nearly pulled right back out, but Lavonne spotted me from the kitchen window and waved. I took a deep breath and went to the door.

Once Raymond came inside—he'd been working—we resumed the conversation of a few days ago without a bit of tension. They started talking about the two schools. The blacks had such a good schoolhouse, Raymond mentioned: "That was the one that had a basement." He and Lavonne struggled to remember the name of the teacher there. Howard Weaver. That was it. The very same who had had to leave Grant County and carve out a distinguished career for himself in the Indianapolis school system because the Marion schools told him "it wasn't time for blacks." But none of that would be mentioned today. Lavonne remembered him because her own father had taught at one of the local white schools, and he and Howard Weaver had been friends. She recalled how they always set up ciphering and spelling matches between their students. I thought it odd that this island of racial harmony had had segregated schools when it wasn't mandated by law. The question of whether to "mix" had been left up to local authorities since 1877. But it seemed that everyone at Weaver had accepted this segregation as the way of things.

I asked them if black and white had always gotten along here. Always, they said, "even after the lynching."

They brought up their friend Vaughn Casey again. They seemed to think he was the greatest guy you could ever hope to meet. Vaughn had had a "This Is Your Life" party, and they'd been one of four white couples invited.

"I felt it was an honor really," said Raymond. "He was high up in the Masons."

"That was quite an honor to us," Lavonne confirmed. They were still thinking about that party after fifteen years.

"You're the only person I've talked to who described what happened out here after the lynching," I told Raymond. "Could you describe what you saw? Did you go to the funeral?"

"My dad thought my brother and I should see it," Raymond answered. "You know what I mean."

"Thought you should see it?"

"My dad said, I think this is something you boys ought to remember. And they were still hanging there." Finally it dawned on me that he'd actually seen the bodies hanging at the courthouse.

Raymond had been fourteen. His whole family went to Marion the morning after. He said his dad's point was, Never get into a mob. He hadn't known Tommy Shipp or Abe Smith, though the latter came from one of the old Weaver families. Abe's grandfather, Alfred Smith, ran the racetrack, but Abe lived in Marion. So Raymond hadn't gone to the funerals, just "saw where the dirt was put back from the graves." He remembered deputy sheriffs guarding Weaver Cemetery for close to a week.

He and Lavonne both knew the Deeters, though. They'd gone to school with them. "I think what instigated it," Lavonne suggested, "was that everybody around knew the white family. And first thing you knew, it turned into a mob."

I asked if they'd ever heard talk about who did the organizing. Lavonne said she wouldn't know names. Raymond said you wouldn't *want* to know names. "But I'm sure it was somebody around Fairmount," he added.

"Sympathetic to the family," Lavonne agreed.

I told them *my* family always said it was people from Bucktown.

"I'd say Bucktown had nothing to do with it," Raymond countered, although he thought those would be "the kind of people" who'd enjoy such a thing. Lavonne then objected to him labeling a whole group of people so broadly.

If their theory was right, the county's worst racial tragedy had been fomented from what was once the antislavery stronghold. I'd come back to see Raymond and Lavonne for a closer look at such awful paradoxes. In a way, they were exemplary white people—who had always lived around black people, who had black friends they loved. But yes, Lavonne freely admitted, "colored were not allowed" at Clearwater Park. "Not that we had anything against the colored." Her father, after all, was good friends with the black teacher, Howard Weaver, and probably with many others. But, Raymond pointed out, admitting them to the park would have ruined his business. He kept blacks out by selling memberships, which were nontransferable and had to be purchased in person. "There weren't more than two or three instances where blacks tried to come in," said Lavonne. "They knew."

"Very few blacks wanted to come in," Raymond declared, "because they respected you for it."

Lavonne added that black people would have felt out of place anyway, surrounded by hundreds of white people.

"Just like we did when we went up there where all the colored were," Raymond said, referring to the party of fifteen years ago. "I felt out of place, but I still felt like I was honored if they asked you."

And Lavonne reiterated that she too had been so honored.

The conversation kept taking this strange seesaw course between explaining how wonderful "the colored" could be and assuming that you didn't associate with them—some fantasyland of separate-but-equal. Neither had ever set foot inside John Henry Weaver's store, perhaps in Raymond's case because his family had moved away in the 1920s and the store closed soon after his return to Weaver in 1929. But Lavonne, who'd always lived within a couple miles of it, thought the store was for blacks only. Raymond recalled white people hanging around outside but couldn't say if they went in.

I came to understand that they believed in this thing they called "respect," which was a sort of euphemism for segregation. So black people didn't want to come to Clearwater, because they had respect, while Raymond and Lavonne didn't enter the store, out of respect. "There's a different attitude in life now and I don't understand it," said Raymond.

I found this encounter very painful—this illustration of the racial divide, these nice white people who apparently didn't discuss things like "respect" with black friends. Could it be that Weaver had experienced "tolerance" because not too much was said?

BARBARA STEVENSON OF the Grant County Black History Council presented her oral history project at the library about a month later. She'd done a great deal of work on Weaver but said she also wanted to challenge the idea that "everything went bad" when "all those people from the South came up here." (Her own family had come from the South.) Someone in the audience asked her if she could do a family tree of Weaver. Impossible, she said, with so much intermarriage: "We're all connected in some way and that doesn't exclude whites or Hispanics. If we look at history and understand we're connected, maybe we'll be more tolerant."

We all went upstairs to look at a photo exhibit the Black History Council had put together. I noticed Sadie Weaver Pate going through picture after picture, naming everyone in every photo. As we were leaving, I knew I now had to get confirmation on one of the central legends of Weaver.

So I asked Sadie Weaver Pate if it was true that her father's store in Weaver was only for blacks. "No," she said, looking distressed by the question. "I believe there was more white than black who traded there." She began to tell me again about all her white friends.

The white friends. I felt sad. How much real connection had there ever been, if some of the white people who'd lived near Weaver their entire lives thought they couldn't enter the store at the heart of the community? This was segregation in the passive, almost classical mode. They had created an invisible line, then decided not to cross it.

THIRTEEN

A RIOT GOIN' ON

Marion's passage through the 1960s was downright ugly. I mark it as the beginning of the town's decline, as the place already infamous for the last classic lynching north of the Mason-Dixon Line only added to its reputation for intolerance.

No doubt a number of 1930's mobsters and many witnesses were still alive during the civil rights era, but this was really their children's time, and the younger generation made no attempt at redemption. Instead, they allowed the lynching to fuel their paranoia, while the extremists among them invoked it as a threat, right from the start.

At the end of the preliminary battle in the 1950s—desegregating the Matter Park pool—an anonymous letter came to one of Marion's more outspoken black activists, Henry Mills. Punctuation and grammar here are the writer's own:

> "What do you Negroes want some more of you Black
> rats strung up again. You Negroes just keep on we will
> string you up out there to some of them trees at the
> park some nice ones out there,
>   & if that don't work we will blow up the pool."

199

▲ ▲ ▲

THE MATTER PARK POOL BATTLE gave everyone a taste of more incendiary times to come. By the summer of 1954 segregation was doomed, technically. The Supreme Court's ruling in *Brown v. Board of Education* in May had thrown out the "separate but equal" doctrine. *Brown* applied to schools, but in effect, segregation in public facilities didn't have a legal crutch to stand on anymore. Of course, for the next couple of decades all over America, white people would try to maintain the status quo by any means necessary.

In Marion, one Chester Shawley announced that "Negroes will never set foot in Matter Swimming Pool as long as I have anything to do with the park board." He was its president. On June 20, 1954, the local NAACP sent seven carefully selected upright citizens to purchase tickets at the pool. They included activist Roger Smith and Meredith "Don" Ward, then the state high school record-holder in the 440-yard dash. Shawley had warned the sheriff that "colored people were coming out to Matter Park to tear up jack," that "they were going to destroy property and the swimming pool." Standing nearby while the seven black citizens failed to gain entrance were the police, a paddy wagon, and forty to fifty "special deputies"—private citizens who brought their own guns.

A photo of one vigilante-deputy packing a sidearm ran in the *Indianapolis Recorder,* a weekly paper by and for African Americans. The Marion papers didn't even mention the incident. Forty-plus armed enforcers at the pool and not one dot of coverage. Maybe as a journalist I'm hyperaware of what's deemed unfit for print, but this wasn't really censorship. This was just the usual response to racial perfidy: *Act like nothing happened.*

I have a family story about the pool. The source was—let's just call him a family friend, someone who knew those guys on the park board. On his deathbed he told my father that members of the park board went to the poolhouse one night and smashed the valves. According to the family friend, they did this to protect people, especially blacks. Because if the pool was desegregated, "that element" in Bucktown would cause trouble again. "That element" meant the Kentuckians who, according to our family lore, had carried out the lynching.

On July 6 NAACP members showed up at a city council meeting to demand desegregation. This fact made the papers. The park board proposed that Marion build a second pool. The council proposed that they open the Matter Park facility to blacks three days a week as an "educational program" for whites. "We think that on this basis the white people will break the segregation barrier of their own accord," one councilman concluded. Unacceptable, said the NAACP. They had filed a lawsuit in federal court. Meanwhile, according to the *Recorder,* the pool itself had been closed because of "a giant leak." (And that's the only corroboration I can offer for my family story.) Then the two Republicans on the park board resigned, leaving the four-man body without a quorum.

On July 23, realizing that the court would rule against it, the city council opened the pool to everyone. They'd predicted that integration would lead to violence. Instead, attendance dropped radically—seventy people, six of them black, on the first day. Normal attendance was seven hundred. One white woman told me that when this happened, her parents declared, "You will never be in that swimming pool again."

I'D NEVER EVEN KNOWN about the struggle to desegregate the Marion swimming pool. It's not like I thought I could have done something. (I was born in 1950.) But I began to see my ignorance as part of a bigger problem.

Here was the follow-up to Things I Didn't Learn in School: things that happened during my lifetime that I hadn't much noticed.

This came home to me when I went to visit Roger Smith, a former NAACP president and an activist into the 1990s, when he was instrumental in turning Marion's Justice Middle School into Justice Thurgood Marshall Middle School. Before we even got to those stories, however, he mentioned a minor incident involving his daughter. One day, probably in the early 1960s, she'd gone to roller-skate with her Brownie troop. The rink was known to be whites-only so, said Smith, "I told my wife, 'They won't let her skate out there.' And my wife said, 'Well, she's with the Brownies, so they'll probably let her.'" So the daughter went with her troop, and sure enough someone soon called from the rink. Smith had to go pick her up and try to answer the question, *Daddy, why can't I skate?*

"It's hard to explain to children," Smith concluded, as I sat there absorbing the fact that his daughter was younger than me. By five years! I had never even known that I could do things a black child couldn't do. I don't remember the issue ever coming up, but if it had, I didn't pay attention.

And wasn't that part of the trouble? One lesson I would soon learn from the Kluxers I met is that white racists are always paying attention and the rest of us are not. We were blind. We let things happen.

So Smith went on to tell me about the Matter Park pool, all the meetings and protests leading up to the NAACP's triumph in 1954. But this other story hit me harder, all the little pieces of it: the Scouts choosing that rink in the first place, the parents discussing whether they dared let their daughter go, then Smith having to explain it to her. Suddenly I was no longer dealing with the benighted days of slavery, or 1930, but with the benighted years of my own lifetime. Suddenly I could no longer feel that nothing implicated me. I knew that if the daughter had been in my own troop, I would have been disturbed and confused to see her turned away, but what would I have done? What *could* I have done? It isn't easy for children to defy adults on issues this taboo.

Really, the lynching was easier to deal with—not just safely in the past but a moment when racism had gone too far, become too visible, and most white people knew it. At least most knew enough to feel some shame after the hysteria died down. But plenty of white people who would never lynch anyone went right along with segregation, the acceptable face of racism. It didn't kill. It just hurt in ways we white folks never had to think about.

How ironic, I thought, that Smith would turn out to be the first person I met in Marion who had actually known my grandfather. They had both worked at the post office when Smith began there as a mail carrier in the 1950s, and Grandpa was his supervisor. "Mr. Carr's granddaughter!" he said, amazed. I told him that my grandfather had been a member of the Ku Klux Klan, and Smith looked a bit surprised. Immediately I regretted telling him and wondered why I'd done it. I didn't want him to think ill of Grandpa.

"Want me to give you a secret?" he said. He confessed with a little smile that his uncle, Thaddeus Smith, had poisoned the lynching tree. He'd gone to Tuskegee, studied with Dr. Carver, and become a tree surgeon. Back in Marion, Thaddeus Smith then worked for a few wealthy families and finally for the county. "He put something in the tree, and later it died. I remember him telling Daddy, 'Well, that tree won't be there very much longer.'" Smith laughed.

As I was leaving his house, he showed me a bullet hole in the front siding. "From the sixties," he explained. That was his bedroom inside. The bullet had lodged in a dresser.

NEVADA PATE HAD BEEN the last teacher in Grant County's last one-room schoolhouse, the all-black D.A. Payne School. When those students were absorbed into the rest of the system in 1953, Pate lost her job. Marion was not ready for a black teacher with white students.

The first irony hit me at her front door. Nevada Pate was so light-skinned, I thought I had come to the wrong house.

She was eighty-eight years old when we met, the last child of a father born in 1861 and a mother born right after the Civil War—two lives fed by slavery. One grandmother had been sold at age two and never known her parents. Both grandfathers had escaped their plantations to fight for the Union. Nevada knew of two great-grandfathers and one great-great who had been slaveowners. "That's why." She gestured at her own light arm. "And people talk about biracial like it's something new."

She gave me another tiny piece of the lynching puzzle. On August 7, 1930, she was out at Matter Park with Flossie Bailey and the rest of the NAACP junior auxiliary. A black man came out to tell Mrs. Bailey that trouble was brewing downtown, so they all left for home. A few days after the hanging, when a rumor circulated that white people intended to burn down the black sections of town, her brothers and other family came to stay at her parents' house, where Nevada now lived. With white neighbors on both sides, the Pates felt that their house was safe.

When we got to the events of 1953, Nevada laid out the facts quickly and succinctly, without drama. The school superintendent had given her an option: resign or be fired. "I told them they'd have to fire me," she said calmly, but she began to shred a Kleenex in her lap. "Sometimes if you don't know what to do, you don't know exactly where to go." The NAACP had not been able to help her.

"I love teaching. See, they tried to put a stigma on the fact that they took my students. I didn't really think they would do a thing like that. I know the parents had asked me, 'Miss Pate, don't you think we ought to have a meeting?' And I said no. I didn't think there'd be any problem. I figured if they were taking my students, surely they'd hire the teacher. But they hired other teachers."

The school superintendent who fired her was none other than Fred Ratliff, a grandson of underground railroad conductor John Ratliff, the man who had been so instrumental in passing the legislation that allowed black children into public schools in the first place.

Nevada Pate had wanted to be a teacher since the second grade. For eight years after her dismissal, she tutored out of her home. In 1961, with a new superintendent in charge, she reapplied and was offered special education. They said it was all they had—the brain-damaged, the retarded, and the "slow." So it seemed to me that the school system assigned the students they didn't want to the teacher they didn't want.

Nevada Pate and the "trainables," as she called them, were given a portable classroom behind the Marion Coliseum. But she loved this work. The parents were cooperative and grateful. And the children: "They couldn't walk, or couldn't talk. But lovely little faces. Little smiles." And every once in a while she found those who shouldn't have been placed in special ed, and she was able to raise their skills enough to get them into regular school.

I asked her if she'd ever seen any Klan activity, like those parades in the 1920s. She laughed and said that just a couple of years ago she'd been walking downtown and a young white woman had handed her a flyer. A Klan recruiting flyer. It said to Nevada Pate, the woman who came from slavery and lynchings and being too black to teach in the school: "Whitey, have you had enough?"

She got up to find the flyer for me. She'd kept it, because she thought it was hilarious.

At some point I came across a story about Pate in the Marion newspaper, written to honor her the year of her retirement, 1973. The piece said that her career had had "a variety of interruptions," as if the twelve years (1931–43) she had spent as an elevator operator had been a choice. "An extended break from teaching," the article called it. More euphemism to keep white people from feeling guilty. Certainly everyone in the black community knew the real story. Before the 1960s, no African American could have taught anywhere in Marion except at D.A. Payne—which employed one teacher—so Pate rode that elevator for twelve years, waiting for the one job to open up.

My visit with Nevada Pate left me feeling very sad. I wasn't just there to gather facts, after all, but to try to take responsibility as a descendant of that place. To do that, I had to hear such stories. I found this one quite painful to take in, and there was nothing I could do to fix it.

It did not feel good to acknowledge that we white people had thwarted and stunted so many lives. The alternative, the refusal to acknowledge black people's reality (thus our role in it), was a special kind of crazy-making, and Nevada Pate knew it well. When the school system fired her in 1953, they simply told her, "It won't work." They never said they were dismissing her because of her race and thus implied that something else about her was the problem. That seemed especially cruel.

I asked her again: "No one ever said, 'We don't want black teachers?' "

"No," she said. "Uh-uh. They came out with 'It isn't going to work.' "

▲ ▲ ▲

THE SCHOOL SYSTEM REPRESENTED turf that the avowed white supremacists couldn't touch. This was where certain other white people made their
stand—those who were not Klan, not racist (they would insist), and in a
phrase heard wherever racial barriers were breaking, "not ready." For example, when Oatess Archey returned to his hometown in 1959 with a degree
from Grambling, the school system made him a janitor. The official word on
his teaching possibilities: "Marion isn't ready." In 1960, however, they let
him teach gym and health. In 1961 Archey began coaching, but he saw that
he wouldn't exactly get a chance to blossom in the Marion schools. So the
town's first black teacher left in 1969, recruited away by Ball State. There he
coached and got his master's. Archey was then recruited by the Federal Bureau of Investigation and eventually taught at the FBI Academy. By the time I
got to Marion, he'd become something of a legend. The undervalued man.
One who got away.

Another black woman hired to teach in 1961 told me she nearly left
town as well. Katherine Bobson, like Archey, belonged to that generation of
African Americans who were so often "the first" or "the only." By the time I
met her in 1996, Bobson was principal at a grade school in Bucktown,
where the majority of both students and staff were white. But she still had
bitter memories of trying to begin her career. Back in the 1950s she even
dropped out of college for five years, because "I wasn't sure there'd be a future in teaching, especially in Marion, Indiana." She switched to business
school and began a career she didn't want, believing all along that teaching
was what she was meant to do with her life. Finally, she decided she *would*
teach—"wherever"—and returned to college.

Hired the same year Nevada Pate went to work with the "trainables,"
Bobson too was assigned to a "special" class. In her case, it was "special
reading" and music. She had no particular training in either. In fact, she
could barely play the piano and wondered if blacks were simply supposed to
be "musical." Worst of all, this kept her from getting a regular class. She put
up with it for a couple of years, then began sending her résumé around. She
was all but hired in Gary—she had only to sign the contract—when the Marion schools finally relented and gave her a fourth-grade class. It was 1963,
the year of Dr. Martin Luther King, Jr.'s, "I Have a Dream" speech, the year
white supremacists assassinated Medgar Evers in Mississippi and killed four
little girls in the Birmingham church bombing. Now, the irony to Bobson's

story: she began to notice astonished looks from many parents during their first visits, along with blunt questions like "You're the teacher?" The children, she realized, had failed to mention at home that their teacher was black. Either they had not noticed or they were more "ready" than the administration cared to imagine.

The school system was also where the long estrangement between black and white Marion finally erupted in violence.

In November 1968 fighting broke out between black and white students in the high school cafeteria, an incident known forever after as "the riot." It was Marion's first and only. This was not a town of radicals on any side of the color line, and the Black Power movement attracted few followers here, but 1968 was a year of maximum racial tension across America. The assassination of Martin Luther King, Jr., in April led to race riots in hundreds of cities. It was also the year when students seized buildings on half a dozen campuses, demanding more black representation in every aspect of student life. And at the Olympics in October two African American athletes stood defiantly on the victory stand holding one gloved hand aloft while the national anthem was played—a Black Power demonstration seen by millions.

On November 15, 1968, at least twenty African American students arrived at Marion High School wearing one black glove. What then ensued during the lunchroom "riot" was minor and avoidable, though the facts didn't come to light for a week, not until the Indiana Civil Rights Commission visited Marion to investigate. Harold Hatcher, director of the commission, said it had all started the day before with a fight between one black student and one white student. A story circulated—and it was untrue—that two black students and no white students had been punished. So a group of African American teens met that night to plan to wear the gloves. The next day, when twenty to thirty students with black gloves came into the cafeteria with an estimated five hundred white students, "the whites thought this was it," according to Hatcher. "The whites took it upon themselves to attack." He said a white truant officer was right in the middle of it, swinging away. Several students ended up at the hospital, but no one was seriously hurt. Later fourteen (from both races) were suspended.

Marion High School had one black faculty member at the time—Oatess Archey, track coach. The gloved ones had drafted a list of demands: black teachers, a black history course, a black truant officer, an Afro-American Club. The day after, Marion's school board agreed to hire a black truant officer and promised that the selection of new and more "multi-ethnic" textbooks was already under way. Of course, at the next school board meeting, fifty white people showed up with petitions demanding more discipline at the high school and assurances that "no policies be adopted in response to overt or threatened acts of violence."

What seems most striking now about "the riot" was the overreaction of the white power structure. Administrators had immediately shut the school down, and the city put the entire police force on duty that night. But then perhaps white Marion had been dreading and anticipating some kind of payback ever since a certain night when the authorities did *not* think it necessary to put the whole force on duty—August 7, 1930.

AT THE TIME OF THE so-called riot, the school board had one African American member, Dr. Joseph Casey. For fifty-two years Casey practiced podiatry in Marion, the town's only black professional apart from the teachers. His election to the school board in 1965 made him the first African American to win a citywide office.

He'd since moved to northern Indiana, near one of the small lakes where many older Hoosiers retired. "My Golden Pond," he called it. But he missed Marion. He loved the town.

Casey remembered his community service there with pride: ten years on the school board, one of them as president: "We worked, we built, we accomplished things." He saw Marion's expanded refurbished school system as his legacy: "Today they're using everything to its fullest [and it's there] by our sweat. Just go to the auditorium. That was on my watch." He also recalled visiting the site of what is now Justice Thurgood Marshall Middle School, walking the cornfield where it would stand, and I could easily imagine him there, reveling in the school-to-be. It seemed to eat at Casey a little that he'd been ridiculed "for ultra conservatism, for spending money, for making bonds." He admitted to being a moderate and "partial to the Republicans."

He had wanted to run for city council, but that seemed out of the question for a black man at the time, and he didn't dwell on the disappointment. (Marion would not have an African American on the city council until 1982.) Always an active citizen nonetheless, Casey had been president of the Urban League, vice-president of the Chamber of Commerce, and in 1968 one of the founders of Breaking Barriers, the town's first attempt to create black-white dialogue in small discussion groups.

Our conversation was filled with contradictions. But he'd lived them. He waited twenty-five years to buy a house in Hickory Hills, one of Marion's more bucolic neighborhoods, with a middle management demographic. It had a racial covenant, and Casey became the first black ever to live there. He'd been denied a membership at the country club, and he too had been sent to the balcony at the movie theater. Yet he insisted that racism had never been a problem for him in Grant County. He was light-skinned, and some assumed he was white. "My skin tones were available to me," as he put it, "not to deny who I was, but I didn't go around with a sign on my back saying that I was a black citizen." He laughed as he recalled how new patients occasionally came in and said, "I was expecting a colored doctor," and he'd reply, "You're looking at him."

Yet an undercurrent of pain ran through our interview. The lynching.

Discussing that hadn't been high on my agenda. But he brought it up himself about five minutes into our talk, when I pressed him on this contradiction—that racism didn't affect him, yet he saw it. "Oh, yes," he said. "When you go back to the legacy or the stigma of August seventh, 1930. I was seventeen years old. That impacted my mental attitude greatly. Greatly. I grew with that in the back of my mind. That was one of the reasons I was reluctant to come [back] to Marion." But he never thought his practice suffered because he was black. He had white patients. And most people knew his racial identity. Everybody knew the Casey family.

They were among the earliest settlers in Weaver, where Joe Casey was born in 1914. His grandfather, Washington Casey, set up the first school there at a time when blacks were not allowed in public classrooms, bringing a tutor up from Indianapolis to teach his ten children. When I met the white couple who lived near Weaver, Raymond and Lavonne, and they waxed on about their neighbor, Vaughn Casey, they were talking about Joe Casey's cousin. "I wanted to have something that my father worked awfully hard for. The legacy of Weaver," the doctor remarked. "But I couldn't raise a sou to get any acreage out there to say it was mine."

He strongly disapproved of lynching survivor James Cameron, who "publicizes what I hate and despise." Like many other African Americans of his generation, Casey believed that Cameron was only in it for the money. Yet while he was on the school board, Casey himself suggested that the lynching be taught in the local schools. So went the seesaw: the lynching should be laid to rest, yet he himself could not lay it to rest. "To think that nobody would cut them down," he declared with some anguish. He brought this up twice during our talk: "That it had to be a man from out of town!"

With the lynching, he thought, "came all the progression of hatred and prejudice and everything." He figured the mob to be southerners. And the stigma wasn't fair to Marion, "the town that gave me a chance." He hoped that I would not emphasize it. Marion deserved better.

"I don't think anybody's dealt with racism more than I when I went into the service in 1943." He'd set up his podiatry practice in Marion in 1939. Then during the war he joined the navy—where he was immediately sent for psychiatric evaluation because they did not believe he was black. Once they determined that he was, they issued him orders that he had to carry at all times, bearing the three-inch-tall letters N-E-G-R-O. "So they wouldn't make that mistake again," Casey explained. His unit was all black. His whole basic training camp was black—except for the officers, who were all white. And everyone in his unit "who had something to offer as far as the medical side were given the job as"—he paused to enunciate—"*litter bearer.* Trained to survive and bring the guy in." Casey described his navy years as the most painfully racist experience of his life: "I carry it around with me like I do about the lynching."

I kept circling back to that distasteful subject to get his story. He finally told me he'd been out at Matter Park that day, in the same group with Nevada Pate, though he insisted they were on a church picnic, not with the NAACP junior auxiliary. He too remembered someone coming to tell them that things were heating up downtown. He too remembered that they all went quickly home. "My folks became concerned so we drove out to Weaver." His family remained there all night. They sat in their car.

"You feel the lynching should stay in the past, but you also feel a certain pain about it," I said.

"I feel pain for Emmett Till," he replied. "I feel pain for James Meredith. For all the people who had to go through things. But to try to make a buck off it! That's the thing about Cameron."

For years Casey tried to recruit other black doctors to come to Marion. Two came, then left. Casey said the black community wouldn't patronize them. The black community wanted white doctors. Though I'd heard many African Americans speak highly of Casey, he clearly felt that Marion's black community had not appreciated his efforts with the school board and the Urban League, either. As he put it: "It's rare that I get an accolade from the colored community." When he, as a school board member, came to the high school the day of the so-called riot, the black students called him an Oreo. He hadn't even known what it meant.

"I'd seen the Klan march when I was a boy," he told me. "And I learned that a lot of the people who were Klans were the head of our city." The particular melancholy of Dr. Joe Casey was that of the good citizen let down by the city he loved.

IN THE END, CIVIL RIGHTS activists didn't derail racism any more than the abolitionists had a hundred years earlier, but they managed to collapse the rigid structures still housing Jim Crow. Marion's black community was simply not going to take it anymore, and for the first time in the town's history, a few of them resorted to political violence. I was fascinated to see that 18th and Meridian, the location of Bailey's barbershop in 1930 (*"the hotbed of that group"* in the old mayor's words) became the "geographic and political center of black unrest" in the 1960s. White people avoided it at all costs.

A rash of firebombings hit Marion at the end of June 1969. The trouble started forty miles away in Kokomo, where the Klan lit the spark. Apparently. Though the instigators were never identified as Kluxers, it's hard to imagine another group of eleven white people going to a black neighborhood to burn a cross. Police arrested the eleven, but by then Kokomo's war of symbols was under way. Black youth came to the intersection where the cross had burned and began smashing watermelons taken from a fruit stand. Then came the real violence: two to three hundred people throwing bricks and bottles at cars; six stores looted; thirteen policemen injured by snipers. Kokomo's NAACP president said there'd been no particular tension before the cross-burning.

One day later a more covert uprising hit Marion. The town never went through a classic rampaging riot, never a "kill-the-pigs" face-down in the street, never a looted store. But late at night parties unknown were throwing Molotov cocktails into lumber yards, factories, and grocery stores. The newspaper coverage, my only source of information on the firebombings, focused on downplaying the bad news. Fires that broke out Friday the twenty-seventh didn't even make the paper till Sunday the twenty-ninth. The headline reported: "Custer Lumber Company fire ends hours of calm in city." Three lumber company buildings burned down, but not till halfway through the piece does it reveal that there were six other firebombings late Friday and early Saturday, along with thirty-nine arrests. Another lumber company had burned, too, while at the five other sites Molotov cocktails failed to ignite. With Monday's paper came the news that the town's one country club had been hit Saturday night as well, causing $150,000 worth of damage. While most targets seemed chosen for their flammability and accessibility,

Meshingomesia Country Club was rather famously all white. (It was hard to imagine its namesake, the old Miami chief, as a welcome guest.)

On Sunday night Grant County Lumber Yard burned to the ground out in Swayzee, a town about fifteen miles west of Marion. The sheriff's department reported a black man running from the scene, getting into a car carrying other black men. In Marion that night fires were set at a paper box company and at a vacant house, facts buried in a story titled THREE MEN FACE WEAPONS CHARGE. Marion's mayor, Gene Moore, puzzled over the violence, declaring, "We have neither heard nor received any requests or protests."

It was classic, really: the years of bottled-up rage suddenly exploding. In Monday's paper the executive director of the Marion Urban League, Henry Curry, attributed the disturbances to a " 'Negro frustration problem' brought on by many things." But he estimated that less than one percent of the black community was involved. That night another terrible arson fire swept through a laboratory that bred pigs for medical research, killing 196 animals. Killing pigs!

Tuesday afternoon, July 1, a fire hit the Marion Poultry Company, knocking it permanently out of business. Town residents were deputized in Fairmount, Gas City, and Jonesboro. Roadblocks went up in Swayzee. Extra patrols covered Sweetser. That same day NAACP national president Roger Wilkins sent a telegram to Indiana's governor decrying the "breakdown of law and order" in Marion, meaning that he had had reports "of continued police brutality, abuse, harassment and refusal to protect young black people."

That night Marion's all-white city council addressed the racial tensions by voting unanimously to buy police dogs, though various black activists tried their best to dissuade them. Roger Smith, the man I'd spoken to about the swimming pool and the skating rink, for example, pointed out what sort of message the council would be sending: "I think you know what [the dogs] have been used for in the past in other cities." Arguing in favor, however, was local UAW president James Dutton, identified to me by several people as a Klansman. If the city did not purchase the dogs, Dutton warned, many citizens, including his union members, would have to arm themselves.

Then the firebombings stopped as mysteriously as they'd started. On July 7, 1969, the first-ever formal discussion of the town's race relations took place among leaders from the police department, the NAACP, the Chamber of Commerce, the Urban League, and the Human Relations Commission. Carlyle Gulliford, president of Marion's NAACP, called it "a step that should have been taken twenty years ago." The only concrete idea that emerged was to set up a telephone hotline that citizens could call to check out rumors.

The Human Relations Commission met with African American leaders the next day. Though the commissioners were there to hear complaints about civil rights violations, they admitted during this meeting that no one in Marion had ever filed one. This indicated a certain lack of confidence. Or as one commissioner suggested, maybe no one knew they existed. The NAACP reps wanted to know why the commission hadn't opposed the police dogs. Roger Smith complained about the circulation of Ku Klux Klan material at Fisher Body, the city's largest employer and, at that time, a Klan stronghold. A young activist named Marcus Cannon declared, "The situation at Fisher Body is what the community lets it be. You support the Klan by the way you motivate your community, and it's not motivated at all."

A little over a week later petitions praising the police and defending them against "the overworked police brutality charge" found their way to the mayor with 3,626 signatures. The police chief called it "a shot of adrenaline to the morale" of the force. The same day the NAACP announced plans for a March on Marion to protest racial injustice.

And so on July 20, 1969, while the first white men landed on the moon, six hundred protesters marched from Marion High School to the courthouse, where the notorious white radical priest from Milwaukee, Father James Groppi, urged the black community to further activism—because "the man" would give them nothing unless they demanded it. Executive secretary of the local NAACP Henry Mills then read a manifesto asking that more blacks be employed in city hall and in the police and fire departments, that the phone and power companies promote their black employees, that unions give blacks a chance at apprenticeships, and that businesses hire them in positions "other than janitor." The manifesto also demanded a halt to "right-wing activities" at Fisher Body and the immediate suspension of union leader Dutton, fair housing, an end to redlining, an NAACP-appointed member of the school board, a food stamp program, and access to all public accommodations including Idyl Wyld roller-skating rink. It took an NAACP district field representative to remind the crowd that they were standing near the site of the 1930 lynching, and "I want to serve notice right here and now that they aren't about to ever do that again in Marion, Indiana."

A couple of days later Mayor Gene Moore responded: "Most of the things in this 'manifesto' are just something somebody dreamed up to say. There's really no basis for them."

▲ ▲ ▲

MARCUS CANNON FOUNDED Marion's chapter of the Black Panther Party sometime after the high school riot. We sat at a table in his dining room, while New Age music played softly in the background. Cannon spent the civil rights era in a rage but finally had to give up his hatred of white people. "I was getting like Nat Turner. Gonna kill 'em all, you know?" He laughed. "It was destroying me."

Cannon was not exactly a militant turned mellow. He was still deeply cynical, but what really informed everything about him was his refusal to be passive. Now he was the man most likely to confront the drug dealers in his neighborhood. As he put it, "If I was in the Klan today, I'd be dropping off drugs and guns in the black community." And if he knew who'd done the firebombings of old, he was not going to say.

He was one of the few people I met in Marion who thought the lynching should be dealt with openly. "When you hide something—it's like that wound is not healing. It's not going to heal until air gets to it." But he did not believe James Cameron, either. Based on what he'd heard from older people in the black community, he figured Cameron was never involved with Shipp and Smith. "That's why he got away. Because he wasn't one of them. But he made a big long story about what happened, just loving every minute of it."

Marcus Cannon was born in 1937. He remembered just accepting the life he knew as a boy in 1940s Marion, where he had to go to the balcony at the movie theater, could not sit down in a restaurant, and went to Matter Park to "watch them white kids in the swimming pool. I thought, man I wish *we* had a swimming pool. I never knew anything was wrong with it."

Then he joined the army. "My attitude started changing when I was in Korea. They called them Chinese prisoners 'niggers,' too. So I wanted to let them out of the cage. See what I'm saying? I made up my mind, when I come home, I'm not taking this no more. I'm not going to ask you, 'Do you want me here? Can I eat here?' I'm going to go on in." He had been such an innocent. He recalled his first trip to California: "It was just shocking to me. I had never seen real black and white friends before. Associating together. I could just sit there and watch that all day."

His real radicalization, though, came with the high school riot, when he was pegged as one of the instigators. He was in his thirties by then, working at Klan-infested Fisher Body. But one day he picked up some hitchhikers, black teenagers, and drove them to the home of a Baptist preacher. Cannon asked them if they wanted to hear *The Grassroots,* a Malcolm X record he was carrying in his car. "They were making plans to do something at the high school," said Cannon, "but I wasn't involved in it." Nevertheless he was arrested for riotous conspiracy. As he tells it, he was arrested for playing a Malcolm X record.

He didn't take the charge too seriously until he was arraigned, and the judge started talking about a possible prison term, and he had to get a lawyer, and "it just came to a time where I wasn't going to let them run over me."

That's when he decided to join the Panthers, even making a pilgrimage to party headquarters in Oakland to get a firmer grip on the politics. Back in Marion he enrolled seventy-two members, though he figured there were only six who were hard-core, who would "go to jail with you." Cannon was nothing if not hard-core. He denied membership to a few of his own relatives whom he judged to be "too light-complected."

In Cannon's stories of the late sixties and early seventies, South Marion sounds like a war zone. As one of the few outright militants in town, he became a target for assorted Kluxers and kooks, and he wanted other Panthers around for security. "I had people stealing their parents' guns, shotguns, real kind of raggedy rifles and stuff. We started walking the streets. Just steady building up. See what I'm saying? Pretty soon it's out of control." He remembers cops driving through the neighborhood four to a patrol car with shotguns sticking out the windows. And he wasn't about to call on them if he had trouble with the Klan. "The police department's worse than the Klan to me."

For one summer—he can't remember which—he lived under siege. He says the police kept him under constant surveillance, sitting in a car a block from his house and following him wherever he went. If he went to Indianapolis, the state police followed. If he had to go to the store, he would wear his undershorts, so they could see that he wasn't armed. "I was even scared to carry a bottle of pop because any reason they had to shoot me, they would have done it at the time. And I was blamed for it all."

I kept running across Cannon's name in news stories from that era. He was arrested four or five times but never convicted. "I had so much hate in me, I went almost crazy. I saw the effect it was having on me where I couldn't sleep and—at one time, any white person that looked at me I'd think that was one of 'em. 'I bet that's the one that did this, that's the one that called, that's the one that's threatening my family,' and I just had to change. Get myself together. Then of course a lot of black people thought I was starting problems and that Satan had me. I almost had a nervous breakdown. But you know, when I got to my maximum hate, a white friend would come by who I hadn't seen for a while or offer help and just mess up my whole pattern. And that bothered me. I didn't *want* them to like me. See what I'm saying? Hate is a trip."

The turning point came when a white police officer called to tell Cannon that the Nazi Party was coming from Elkhart to attack him, and he better get his family out of the house. Instead of leaving, Cannon decided he was ready for war, having as he put it "a lot of good weapons." He would set the example. "Actually changed me right there. I just wanted to kill up some people so bad at that time. I was walking back and forth with this machine gun, I got four babies in bed, and it just clicked. It just clicked. That's when I found myself thinking, 'What am I doing?' " Cannon was lucky. The police called back to say they'd stopped the Nazis at Four Mile Bridge and turned them around.

But he was also dealing with the Klan daily at Fisher Body, where bright orange stickers scattered here and there through the plant warned, THE KLAN IS WATCHING YOU. One of the men he worked with was Jim Ferguson, the Klansman I'd interviewed at the Moose Lodge. In fact, the Panther trained the Kluxer for his job on the overhead crane. "All the blacks thought I was crazy," Cannon recalled. "Asking 'Why do you talk to him?' and stuff like that. I said, 'Man, you can learn from your enemy.' Know what I'm saying?" Cannon told Ferguson he didn't care about his politics, "as long as you don't bother me." And he read the KKK material Ferguson passed out around the factory.

"Ferguson—he was the big wheel," said Cannon. "They would burn the cross on his farm. That's where they used to hold the rallies. He invited me out one time. He said they would not kill me because I was good recruiting material. That's what he said: 'Man, we can't kill *you*.' " And Cannon took him up on the invitation. Or tried to. "On my way out," he complained, "the state police cut me off. 'Either go home or go to jail.' They don't care if you're invited or what."

Cannon certainly seemed to relish confronting the Kluxers. He told me that one day a black coworker came to him and said he'd just been beaten by Klansmen right there in the plant. They'd kicked and punched him and stuck a KLAN IS WATCHING YOU sticker on him. Cannon's response was "Where they at? I'm gonna walk back there and see if it happens to me." He soon found his fight, and "it was my lucky day. I got the upper hand." Cannon dragged one Kluxer by the neck up to "the guy in labor relations" and told him, "You gonna do something with this so-and-so, or am I gonna do it? You're not letting him go." Then Cannon called friends to "watch his back" when he left work. He was on second shift, three to eleven P.M. "So when I got out of work, I had all these brothers out there in cars. They got guns and everything. But I don't see where anything's gonna happen, so I tell 'em all to go home. So they all left. I go get in my car. *Pow. Pow.* As soon as everybody left, they start shooting at me." He laughed, for with time the story of Klansmen shooting at him in the Fisher Body parking lot had become funny. None of the five shots hit him.

He named the man who fired, along with one of his two accomplices. The shooter was still alive, "but he's in bad shape now. I feel sorry for him. I don't hate him no more. He can't look me in the eye." One of the accomplices was the man who'd owned the Klan bar in Elwood, where, according to local legend, they kept the shrunken head of a black man.

"Everybody claimed to be Klansmen then," said Cannon. "I'm gonna tell you like it is. Lot of them guys in the Klan—they was threatening me and stuff—the same guys, after this was over a few years later, I'd party with 'em, get high with 'em. One of the most radical [ex-Klan] guys from Fairmount, I could call him up right now, he'd watch my back."

As time went on, I began to notice the symbiosis that sometimes developed between white supremacists and black nationalists, a symbiosis of mutual fascination and revulsion, an obsession. So even if it applied to just a few of them, I liked the image—both sides of the Hate Club smoking dope together, mellowing out.

I also thought that the stories of fights and guns, posturing and one-upmanship were more about macho than race. On both sides. And that's why it ended with male bonding. Cannon insisted, however, that he was no tough guy, that he lived with constant fear after the Klan shot at him. "Almost every evening after that, when I come out [of work], I was waiting for a bullet to rip me through the back." The point for Cannon was to stand up anyway. He was disappointed, even disgusted, when certain friends were so afraid they wouldn't walk out with him. "If it had been the other way around, if a man was right, I would have stuck by his side regardless. That's what I feel."

A couple of weeks after the parking lot incident, the Klansman from Elwood did shoot at him again—inside the plant. Cannon and a friend were waiting at the coffee machine when the Kluxers ordered them to leave. The friend took off, but Cannon just stood there. "So what they did, they shot right down between my feet." Cannon reported the incident, even though that was "a waste of time, because the people up front didn't like me, either."

To Cannon, the March on Marion was kind of a joke, though he described himself as one of its leaders. He thought most of the six hundred marchers were from out of town. "Marion was standing on the side of the street like it was a parade. You know, watching," he laughed. "Oh, it was sick."

Meanwhile his focus on guns and ammo did not endear him to the local NAACP. They finally told him he was no longer welcome at meetings. But Cannon justified his militancy, explaining, "Used to be that the cops come and beat you, and you just took it. I was educating them. 'Protect yourself. It's your right to survive. A man hits you—hit him back.' "

This refusal to be intimidated had evolved over the years into "I do whatever I want, within the law." On the wall of his living room I noticed a photograph of Cannon water-skiing. He loved strenuous physical activity and was in better shape than most men decades younger. After retiring early from GM (formerly Fisher Body), he took up Rollerblading. He went to the gym daily, enjoyed scuba diving, and sometimes rode his bicycle to Elwood some twenty-five miles away. Cycling through the former all-Klan town was just what he wanted to do within the law. Sure, people would come out and call him names, but, said Cannon, "I don't pay no attention to 'em. I look at 'em like I do at dogs barking."

SOMETIMES THE EVENTS of the 1960s seemed as remote as those of the 1860s. I was just collecting random vignettes from an undocumented war. I couldn't even assemble a proper chronology. At some point during the 1960s, for example, restaurants on the bypass began, one by one, opening to African Americans—but only after NAACP activists showed up at each, got turned away, and the restaurant was then fined for violating the Civil Rights Act, one hundred dollars for each person who wasn't seated. Usually a sign saying EVERYBODY WELCOME would be posted the next day. Such turning points did not make the newspapers, and I noticed, when I talked to the activists from that era, that none of them could remember any dates. After meeting with Roger Smith, I spoke to two others who'd been NAACP president during the civil rights years, Pearl Bassett and Joyce Dixon. Neither they nor Smith could even remember the dates of their presidencies. It was as if they'd blanked it all out.

"Been a long time since I've thought about this stuff," sighed Joyce Dixon, born in 1939 and the youngest of the three. She recalled one night during her tenure, God-knows-when, but the police came to get her because, they said, there was a sniper in a house in South Marion. They wanted her to go to this house and walk up to the door.

Her husband insisted on coming along. Once the police got them down there, Dixon saw that it was the house where she'd grown up. She remembered how the police had it surrounded, not just uniformed police but off-duty cops and maybe militia—"all these guns." She had an aunt still living there. And now there was a sniper inside. Supposedly. The police told her to go to the front door and knock.

"I can remember two things," Dixon said. "My husband wanting to go with me, and me telling him, 'No. Somebody has to stay here and raise these kids.' And then not being afraid of any sniper, but being afraid of what was behind me. 'I'm gonna get shot in the back.' I think that probably stands out in my mind more than anything about that time."

The tension broke when her uncle answered the door wearing "these horrible boxer shorts." And he didn't know a thing about any sniper. But the police took Dixon along as they searched more houses. Meanwhile she and her husband had left their nine- or ten-year-old son at home with a shotgun, and they had told him, "If anybody tries to come in, shoot."

She'd been getting telephone threats from the Klan. "Being that afraid," Dixon said. "I don't ever want to live like that again."

Pearl Bassett had also been threatened. "The grand dame," Dixon called her. Still a force to be reckoned with in her eighties, Bassett was born in 1911, knew the lynching victims when they were all kids together, often wore African-print clothing and headgear, and worked with the NAACP and the Urban League for decades. Back in the 1960s she'd gone from business to business downtown with other activists, reading the Civil Rights Act. She'd also participated in that demeaning trek down the bypass, getting the cold shoulder at restaurants so the fines would kick in. Marcus Cannon, the Black Panther, was her nephew.

The KKK used to call her when she was NAACP president, she told me. They would threaten to burn a cross in front of her house. They threatened to come in and rape her. "All that kind of talk at two, three o'clock in the morning," Bassett recalled.

She was another one who began her activism under Mrs. Flossie Bailey, but she'd been living in Ohio at the time of the lynching. "They say a town's never right when they have a lynching," said Bassett, "and I don't think Marion has ever been the same."

CERTAINLY THE TOWN has failed to thrive. Population peaked in 1970 at 39,607, then began to decline. By 2000 inhabitants numbered 31,320. But a shrinking population wasn't the big problem. In the mid- to late 1990s, during the biggest economic expansion in American history, the county lost 2,100 jobs. Then the *Chronicle-Tribune* ushered in the millennium with a devastating ten-month series on the city's troubles, called "Moment of Truth." The first headline said it all: TIME'S RUNNING OUT FOR MARION.

The statistics quoted in this series were shocking: The town had a poverty rate that was almost double the state average. Twenty-two percent of Grant County residents couldn't read well enough to fill out a job application. Nearly a third of Marion's adults had not graduated from high school. The county was among the state leaders in per capita aid recipients, and over 40 percent of all children were born to single mothers, nearly 25 percent of them to teenagers. As one interviewee told the newspaper, "Something has gone awry, and we don't know what."

I kept hearing the words of one of the lynching witnesses, the old woman who watched the hysteria build throughout the infamous day, saw the people streaming in, the gatherings on street corners. And she said to me, *"We wondered what would happen to our town."*

Well, it became the town that never repudiated, investigated, or fully acknowledged the events of August 7, 1930. So the lynching never took its place in history, never receded into the past. It remained alive in the Marion psyche. And then it became the town that could not embrace civil rights, because that would have opened up the past, and most white people couldn't face it.

The civil rights era was a turning point, and Marion had turned the wrong way. "Race trouble" doesn't exactly attract new business. Worst of all, Marion began to suffer a brain drain. When Oatess Archey, the town's first African American teacher, left in 1969 for a position at Ball State and then a career in the FBI, there must have been others, including some whites, who decided they didn't want to stay and fight. Archey's older brother Thomas, for example, had also returned after college and applied for a teaching job at Marion High School. "They had positions and would not hire me," Thomas Archey told me by phone from his home in Louisiana. "They didn't know how the white community would accept an African American teacher." So he moved to the South, got a doctorate, and never came back.

More and more I saw Marion as a town with self-inflicted wounds, some attributable to racism, and I wasn't even sure that the lynching was the worst of it. After living there for a year, I did not regard Marion as more racist than other Indiana towns. I thought it about average on that score. Nor was it inhabited solely by narrow minds. Yet at two crucial points in its history, racism and narrow minds had triumphed.

At the library I found more newspaper coverage of the periodic guerrilla warfare that flared during the civil rights struggle. This time it was seven days in September 1970, seven days of firebombing, sniping, police brutality charges, and a shoot-out at the pool hall where the Black Panthers met. Right in the middle of it all was Joyce Dixon. I'd found her term as NAACP president.

The pool hall was the big story, a conflagration I'd already heard about from both Marcus Cannon, who was arrested that night (September 20, 1970), and Tom Wise, who was then a rookie cop. Wise told me the police had gotten word that night that the Panthers were at the pool hall making Molotov cocktails and were also planning to rob a nearby gun shop. He and his white partner had been among those assigned to guard the guns. They were then called to the pool hall scene after someone nearby (and never identified) shot at a police car.

Cannon admitted, "We had plans to rip off the gun shop." But when he and his comrades got there, they saw that the police had it surrounded. According to Cannon, he then headed for home, directly north of the pool hall. He never admitted to making firebombs ever. Indeed, the pool hall would prove to be empty—a very lucky thing.

Though Wise and Cannon were on opposite sides of the law that night, both talked about the excessive firepower used by the police. I was actually surprised by the brazenness of the statements I found in the *Chronicle-Tribune,* where stories focused on a policeman wounded in the hand by a sniper. The authorities were denying that any cop had even used a weapon. Photos printed in the paper show bullet holes in a police car attributed to a shotgun, and pellet holes around a pool hall window that "did not come from a police weapon." They quoted Quentin Pettiford, the first African American to make chief of detectives, saying, "No fire was ever returned by our officers." Ron Mowery, assistant police chief in 1970 and mayor of Marion during much of the 1990s, told the *Chronicle-Tribune,* "We checked the weapons on all officers this morning and none of them had been fired. There were no expended cartridges." Jim Perkins, another African American on the police force in 1970, did not return my phone calls, but he'd been interviewed for the Community History Project, and there in his transcript at the Marion library was his recollection of that night: "The police shot that place up. There must have been 100 rounds that went through there."

I still couldn't tell what had triggered all this violence in the autumn of 1970, and no one I spoke to could remember. Two nights before the pool hall shoot-out Joyce Dixon was arrested at a high school football game for disorderly conduct, resisting arrest, and interfering with a police officer. Newspaper accounts of this incident don't even hint at what happened, so I called her. Dixon told me that the authorities simply needed a scapegoat. She'd received a call at home from her aunt about a fracas at the football game between cops and some black teenagers. So, arriving at Memorial Field, she asked a police officer what was going on. He just put her in a police car and drove her downtown. Dixon did not know why she was being arrested, and when they got to the jail, she told the officer, "I want to see the chief." He was someone she'd dealt with as NAACP president. But the cop refused, and Dixon said, "I pay your salary." The arresting officer then pulled a coin out of his pocket and said, "Do you want your quarter back?" Dixon still remembers that moment clearly: "To me, that says, 'You ain't worth shit.' "

She said, "My hands shake now as I share that with you."

She felt that she was currently doing more for race relations in her job as a substance abuse counselor than she ever had as a political leader. Working one on one to change people's attitudes—"that's what it's going to take."

Six days after her arrest at the football game she was walking up to the house where the alleged sniper lurked. Details in the newspaper version don't jibe with her memory of the event, but I thought her more credible than the *Chronicle-Tribune* of 1970, clearly a house organ for the local authorities.

Some of the printed quotes from Dixon and other black leaders during that week now struck me as prescient. After the city declined to act on recommendations from black leaders, for example, Dixon commented: "For the mayor and police chief to take the attitude they have makes me feel they don't care about their town, so why should I?" In the same article Reverend J. D. Williams of Greater Second Baptist declared, "When I've been lied to all day by a mayor and a police chief, I'm ready to tear this town up myself." Within a day or two of these comments a delegation of black militants—so I assume, though the paper doesn't identify them—warned the police chief that "the town would burn" unless charges were dropped against activists arrested that week.

I thought it noteworthy that in both 1930 and 1970 certain citizens (white the first time, black the second) intimated that they would burn all or parts of the city to the ground. Both times to express something unspeakable about race.

"*. . . they don't care about their town, so why should I?*" Dixon couldn't remember making such a comment, but she did remark that none of her children lived in Marion, and that was fine with her. She wasn't sure the town had a future.

"I feel more racism today than I did back then," said Dixon. "Back when I was in my twenties, I knew where the lines were drawn, and it was my choice to step over them. Today I don't know the lines. I feel even more that I have to be better at everything I do, and I don't like feeling that way. We're talking about Marion, all aspects of my life in Marion. I have never been so aware of being black."

THE ERA OF OVERT racial warfare ended with an event so ugly it reverberated all the way back to 1930. On the night of May 14, 1973, a fourteen-year-old black boy named Robert Johnson was shot dead as he walked home from the roller-skating rink with three friends. The shooter had fired from a speeding vehicle near the corner of 18th and Nebraska.

Many people in Marion, both black and white, know who killed Robert Johnson. Many say that the killer was one of "four juvenile drunked-up cops," as one of my informants put it. Unfortunately there's no forensic evidence anymore to support that allegation. But getting the names of the men involved wasn't even difficult. I thought of Walter White visiting Marion for just a couple of days in August 1930 and leaving town with a list of the people involved in the lynching. Not that the list was wholly accurate, but I believe some of it was. Hundreds of people must have known who was in that mob.

Given the disdain for a young black life, given the fact that someone did this for "fun," given that what happened later had every appearance of a cover-up and nothing could be done about it, I saw the Johnson killing as another lynching. "Not so. That would be incorrect," said one of the white folks who knew the names of all the men in the car. "They were just drunks, shooting at things randomly." But I didn't think those drunks would have fired at four white boys. Another white person who knew the whole story told me it was probably an accident. But if so, it was a malicious accident. This same person recalled a joke that white people sometimes told back in those days when they drove past black people: "Hit the little one. You get more points for that."

Was that any different from what white people said in other towns? Maybe not. But here the lynching still festered, and the inability to ever confront it sent a message to blacks and to racist whites. Here you could get away with certain things. Here there was a culture of permission. The Johnson killing and apparent cover-up were proof positive that forty-three years after the lynching, the town was still racially sick.

Certainly the black community understood the murder to be racially motivated. The night after the shooting, all the old hot spots flared again. Firebombings hit a couple of lumber yards and a warehouse. In another unharmonic convergence at 18th and Meridian, an arson fire destroyed a garage and the car inside, while a large crowd threw rocks at the firemen. Earlier that day unrest also returned to Marion High School when 150 black students surrounded a police officer on duty there, resulting in one arrest and thirteen suspensions.

Incidents continued the next day and night: fights on the street, windows broken out, "three instances of wooden crosses burning." Police said then that the killing wasn't racial but random. Someone had just been driving around, shooting. They dug a bullet fired from the same gun out of a bakery. The *Chronicle-Tribune* offered a reward of $500. The Klan canceled a two-day rally scheduled for Jim Ferguson's farm the coming weekend. At Johnson's funeral Reverend J. D. Williams prayed, "We commit the remainder of this investigation into your hands, oh Lord." And there it would stay. The reward rose to a pinnacle of $1,905 on May 30, and that was the last mention in the paper of the Johnson case.

In 1995 I spoke to the detective who'd been in charge of the investigation, Quentin Pettiford. (It would take years before I found the pool hall story, and by then Pettiford was dead.) Born in Weaver, he was the first black sergeant on the Marion police force, and then the first black chief of detectives. After leaving the force, he worked for a downtown bank, retiring as a vice-president. A lifelong Republican, he was about to be elected to his fourth term on the Grant County Council when we met.

"I had that case solved," he told me. "I know the kid was shot with a twenty-five. I know the car that was used. And I know the people who were involved. That was 1973 or 1974, wasn't it? I put it all together." But the evidence he sent to the laboratory never got there. Fingerprints. Bullets. Somehow it all vanished. Poof.

"I got a call from a real prominent person, and I'm not gonna call that name because he's still alive," said Pettiford. "He gave me a warning [about pursuing the case], and I said, 'Hey, you guys don't have to worry about me anymore. My twenty years are up.' I just went on and retired. Left it alone. Because the guy told me, he said, 'You've got a family.' And I can't protect my wife and kids. I wasn't worried about me, but I can't protect *them* all the time. So I said, 'Forget it.' It's the hardest thing I ever did in my life."

I had the clear impression that many others in Marion law enforcement, past and present, knew the facts and were disgusted by them. Four cops out joyriding, none in uniform. A fifth loaned them the car but was not present himself. Then, what ultimately befell most of these guys brought to mind a song by another Robert Johnson, the blues singer: "Hellhound on My Trail." Nearly everyone who spoke to me about the case said of those cops: "Something bad happened to all of them." Things that might make them too clearly identifiable here.

Pettiford wouldn't even say their names, though I'd already heard them. I named the one who was supposedly the triggerman, and he replied, "That's what I heard."

"I had one that I was going to crack. With him and the evidence I had— but I never got to crack him," said Pettiford. "I think that's where that pressure came to me from the other end. And I know what they can do to you, and I can't be with my wife and my kids all the time. So I just took the easy way out."

Later I went to see the Johnson family and regretted it immediately when I saw that they didn't know anything. Our interview was uncomfortable and short. The police "made a lot of promises," but then they disappeared, Mrs. Johnson told me. She had such an air of resignation about her. Her son had been shot through the heart, which didn't sound all that "random" to me. Mrs. Johnson didn't have much to say. Finally she told me she'd tried to convince Robert not to go to the skating rink that night. It was in a neighborhood with too many white people.

THIS IS THE UNFORTUNATE story arc for the civil rights movement in Marion—from the girl who couldn't skate to the boy who could.

FOURTEEN

THE AUXILIARY

While the leader of the 1920s Klan could brag, "I am the law in Indiana," the 1960s Klan served more as a lawless adjunct to the authorities. At least, that's what I gleaned from the stories I collected—that during the civil rights era the KKK operated from the shadows, but the threat it represented was always clear enough.

An old white man who lived downtown across from the railroad tracks back then told me that one night around one A.M. he saw flatcars and boxcars pull in to the sidings, loaded with white men. "Maybe three hundred guys, armed to the teeth. This was Klan. Must have been." He watched as the men climbed onto lumber company flatbed trucks and were driven away into the night.

Jim Ferguson readily admitted that the Klan had been out patrolling then. Businesses would contact them—and just how remained mysterious—but according to Ferguson, they'd say something like " 'We've heard that somebody's planning on firebombing us. Is there a chance we can get some guys to drive by periodically tonight?' " Ferguson estimated that the Klan performed this volunteer work mostly on weekends for a period of two years. "We'd do what we could," he declared. "Worked out pretty good."

The only near confrontation happened one night in Van Buren, in northeastern Grant County, where Ferguson and other Kluxers had stationed themselves around a couple of grain elevators. They were sitting on their tailgates, armed but not holding their rifles, when three carloads of Black Panthers showed up. "As soon as they turned in the driveway and the lights hit us, they knew we was there," said Ferguson. "They just did a U-turn, throwed a little gravel, and back out they went. They was gone. All it took was just a presence. Somebody being there. It was a deterrent."

What intrigued me most was the implied connection between the Klan and the cops. How, for example, did Ferguson know that those cars carried Panthers? "We got the license numbers and had them all checked the next day."

ANYONE WHO THOUGHT the 1960s Klan benign had only to speak to Margy Carter, who was run out of Indiana by the Hooded Order back in 1968.

When I first met her in 1996, she'd been back in Marion for a year, drawn by her ties to those family members still willing to speak to her. The rest of the family, starting with her parents, had disowned her. The problem? Margy Carter was a white woman who had married a black man. We sat down in her living room below photographs of two young black women, her daughters, and Carter related what was still a painful story.

By nature outgoing, even bubbly, the red-headed Carter had grown up unhappy in North Marion. Her mother worked as a nanny to the wealthy Matter family—the people who'd given the town its largest park—and it seemed to Margy that those children soaked up all her mother's affection. "My mother was very cruel to me. She was a beater. She never once held me and said 'I love you.' There was none of that. And my stepdad was very detached, very self-centered and extremely prejudiced."

Her parents kept a suitcase filled with family photos, she recalled, and at the bottom was a manila envelope she was warned never to open. One day when she was nine or ten, her stepdad pulled it out and said, "Wanna see this?" Out came the lynching picture. Margy recalled him saying something like "This is what we do with niggers when they mess with white women" and how upset and angry this made her. When she said, "Daddy, that's not right. Why did they kill them?" he came back with "Goddamn nigger raped a white woman." Margy knew he'd gone down to watch the lynching, along with his father, his sister, and his brother-in-law, but apart from this instructional moment with the famous photo, discussing what had happened on August 7, 1930, was taboo.

Growing up in North Marion, one of the most segregated neighborhoods in town, Carter was never around people of color till high school. There during senior year she got acquainted with one African American girl who was in several of her classes. But that was all. "It was frightening for me," said Carter, "because I had all these programmed beliefs in my head."

She began to confront this misinformation about race in the most elemental way. Working after high school as an OR tech at Wabash County Hospital, she saw a black woman come in for surgery one day. "They opened her up and inside was the same blood, the same [everything]—I can remember thinking these things: 'Well, I'll be damned. Not a bit of difference, is there.' If you don't have somebody there to tell you, this is what it's like, you have to make these decisions and discoveries on your own."

Her husband-to-be was in the air force, stationed near Peru at Grissom Air Base. "Oh Lord, it was a blind date," Carter recalled of their first meeting, "and I had no idea that the person I was going to see would be black. Al Carter. Six foot seven and a little bit. Big guy and dark as he could be, and it freaked me out. All I could think in my head was 'Oh my God, what's my dad going to say? What's my dad going to say? He'll kill me.' And to be honest, I didn't want to see Al again. It scared me." But she kept running into him and decided "he was just such a super person." Soon they started dating.

The day she told her mother that she'd fallen in love and was going to get married, she had "really the first conversation with my mom that was positive, and I didn't want to spoil it, so I didn't tell her he was black. I just didn't want to ruin the moment and I knew it would. So a couple of days later I got a call from them—'Please don't do this.' Somebody had called my mother from Wabash and told her that he was black, and she told me at that point that my sisters and my brother were all in agreement that if I didn't drop this man, I'd be disowned. She said, 'If you stop seeing him, we'll get over this. People will forget.' And I said, 'Mom, I love him. I love him and I'm going to marry him.' "

Margy prepared to cut her ties, returning some things to her sisters' houses and going to her brother's place to say good-bye. There she discovered that her brother, a Marion police officer, didn't even know about the impending marriage. He asked to meet her fiancé. When Margy returned with Al Carter, she found her parents waiting. The brother was trying to set up a reconciliation. Her mother asked Margy if she could at least wait till Al was back from Vietnam before marrying him. "I said, 'Mom, if I wait to marry him till he's back, will you give me your blessing?' and she started to say yes and my dad shoved her aside and said, 'No daughter of mine is going to marry a goddamn nigger,' and my mom started crying, and I said, 'Well, what's the use then, Mom?' "

Tears welled up in Margy's eyes as she told me this. She said her father then warned her brother that he too would be disowned if he had anything more to do with Margy. But her brother did stay in touch with her secretly, and he was a major reason she had decided to move back to Marion.

None of her family or friends came to the wedding, however, except for her roommate who acted as bridesmaid. The doctor for whom she worked gave her away. His nurse was there, and Al's friends. Thirteen people all together. In 1968 interracial marriage had been legal in Indiana for just three years.

Margy and Al moved into a little house outside Wabash, just north of Grant County. "We were married less than a week when Al said, 'I think someone's following us,' and of course [my thought] was that it was my dad. So then one night I was standing at the kitchen window, and it had snowed out there, and I looked down, and there was a man standing down there looking at me. And I called Al, and Al came running. The guy ran across the field, and Al and I ran out of the house, and we found footprints around the windows, and it was real apparent from [tracks in the] snow that he had been watching us over a period of time. Not just that time.

"So about three days later—I guess it was like five-thirty in the evening—my aunt Lillian called me from Marion. She was crying, and I said, 'What's wrong?' "

"She said, 'Get out of there as fast as you can. And if you love your husband, take him with you.'

"I said, 'What are you talking about?'

"She said, 'Margaret, get out of there now. The Klan's on their way.' "

Margy and her husband threw some clothes in a bag and drove to the air base. Though Al explained their predicament, his commander told him there was no place for Margy. "They turned me out. I had nobody to call." She and Al had been married for two weeks.

Later they found out from neighbors that six cars filled with six men each had driven up to their house, broken down the door, and burned a cross in the yard.

Margy never went back to that house. For three weeks she hid at the home of the nurse who'd come to her wedding. Then Al took her to his family in Philadelphia.

Al then went off to Vietnam, and suddenly Margy was living in a black community, not always comfortably. "I met a lot of black women who hated my guts. I used to try to be understanding, go the extra mile, and I don't do that anymore. Now I come back like they do. I think I was being a naïve white girl trying to prove I wasn't racist." Worse, Al Carter came back from Vietnam a different man, and he walked out on her when their daughters were two and a half and three and a half. "He pretty much left me stranded, took the car, and was gone. I was hitchhiking to work, doing diapers in the bathtub. It was a real shock." She didn't hear from Al again for ten years.

Desperate, she moved to Cincinnati, where she had a cousin, and within six months she was diagnosed with uterine cancer. But Margy recovered and gradually put a life together there that she loved. For one thing, she started housing exchange students, and her own daughters went abroad when they were twelve and thirteen. "I got to appreciate a whole world that, if I had closed my eyes to Al Carter, I never ever could have experienced."

She thought Marion was about forty years behind the rest of the country in terms of race relations. Her daughters and grandkids had come to visit her and endured three racial incidents in four days. Like a car pulling up alongside them on the bypass full of white men, screaming "Nigger get out of town." The daughters had declared that they would never come back.

I thought the incident atypical, but maybe I just didn't know.

Margy never saw her mother again after the failed reconciliation at her brother's house. But once, while visiting her brother when her girls were eight and nine years old, she ran into her father on the street. That is, Margy and her daughters—his granddaughters—saw him.

And he saw them. He turned around and ran.

As Jim Ferguson presented it, of course, the 1960s Klan was mostly out reforming drunks and wife-beaters, and in his stories these were always other white men. But even this distorted picture reveals something about how the Klan functioned as frightener, self-appointed cop, and sometimes police auxiliary.

Ferguson told me first about two guys, hard drinkers, who got the classic KKK warnings: thirteen switches tied with a black ribbon; then, when their behavior didn't change, a cross burned in the yard. "And then I think Child Protection Services in Grant County took a look to see what was going on there, so they kind of put the fear into 'em, too. So all things considered, it worked out," said Ferguson. "Over the years the Klan has done their share of good."

But he admitted that switches and crosses didn't always work. Some guys were hardheads. "We had one guy here a while back . . . was always getting picked up for DUI [driving under the influence], wouldn't support his family, lay out drunk and knocked around his kids. And the Klan took him out to the river one night and took all his clothes away from him, and it was cold—it was in November—and made him take a good cold swim and he finally saw the light. To this day, I don't think he's ever took another drink." By his estimate, this unscheduled swim occurred in 1990.

Then he told me about a couple of other riverside interventions from the 1970s. A deputy contacted the klavern about dealing with a young man who'd been in and out of jail "for petty larceny, car theft, any number of things, and he knowed better, but no amount of talking seemed to be hittin' home. He'd been in front of the judge a couple times. So the deputy got ahold of me and wanted to know if there was anything we could do to convince him to straighten up, because his family was a good family. I said, 'Yeah, we can talk to him.' So a couple of us got together one night, and for all intents and purposes we kidnapped him.

"We took him out here to the river. He'd been drinking a little bit, so we stripped him off naked. It was cold, and we throwed him in the river and sobered him up, and he come out a-fightin' and a-cussin'. He was gonna whip all of us, so a couple of [Klansmen] got ahold of him, and we just happened to have a buggy whip with us, and while he was naked, we bent him over the front of the car and we laced his rear end real good with that buggy whip and told him what it was all about. That he was gonna straighten up whether he wanted to or not. Well, after that—I don't think he was ever in trouble another day after that," Ferguson concluded proudly. "Your local police force—they just can't do things like that."

He laughed as he recalled one other guy, a habitual drunk with grown kids and a nice wife. Dressed in their hoods, the Kluxers kidnapped him outside a tavern one night and drove him to an area of the Mississinewa near Jalapa, about ten miles north of Marion. They threw him into the water in his shorts, and after he crawled back onto the bank, he took off running. He didn't even pick up his clothes.

"We thought maybe he got in the river and drowned," said Ferguson. "We was scared to death that night. Next morning about eight o'clock or so, another guy we knew went by his house—he lived in Bucktown—and sure enough, the guy was home. He was still scared. But he'd run home in his shorts all the way from Jalapa." Ferguson laughed. "He never drank another drop after that till the day he died."

"So was that another case where you got his name from the police?"
I asked.

"Yeah. They just kept pulling him over for drunk driving."

"Seems like the police here always knew who was in your group."

"Oh, yeah," said Ferguson. "At that time [the 1970s] we weren't invisible. We always had somebody that they could contact and so forth. And it worked out good. We maintained good relations with the police department here in Marion."

"Did you have members on the police force?"

"Yeah, there was a couple."

"Are there still?"

"I'll put it this way," said Ferguson. "I'm sure there are, but I don't know who." He laughed. "I know they're not in my cell." The only thing I felt sure of, though, was that Klansmen like giving the impression that their members are both numerous and influential.

I WANTED TO UNDERSTAND the Klan mentality, and to that end I had to find more of them. Clearly there was quite a difference between the only two I'd met, Ferguson and Larry Hitler.

Ferguson told me a story about young Hitler, whom he'd met once. Larry had called, wanting to talk about the Klan. Ferguson agreed to meet him in a bar. "He's just plain weird," Ferguson concluded. "He had all these grand ideas about how to destroy the whole black population all over the world. As far as I was concerned, he could stay as far away from me as possible."

Ferguson was still the only Klansman from the old days who would talk to me, and he wouldn't name his comrades. But I had other leads on former Kluxers, all of them supposedly active with Ferguson in United Klans of America back in the 1960s and 1970s.

I decided I would have to go right to their front doors. If I called them, they could just hang up, but if they slammed their doors on me, at least I'd see the looks on their faces. I hated doing this. But with information so hard to come by, the names were like stones I could not leave unturned.

One of these names came from Larry Hitler. I stood at this alleged Kluxer's door and told him that I was working on a book, that I'd heard he once belonged to the Klan.

The man came outside to talk so his family wouldn't hear, a grizzled paunchy guy with a bad eye and missing teeth. He was meek, sheepish. He admitted he "used to run around with some Klans" back in the 1960s when they were all working on the George Wallace campaign. One of these Kluxer friends was dead, and the other was back in Kentucky. He couldn't give me any names. He insisted that he hated the Klan but did not hate blacks since they had feelings, too, and they were Americans.

He said the white people across the street had spread the story that he was Klan. They were trying to get back at him—it was a long story—and most of the other neighbors were black. No, he said, he wouldn't live in this neighborhood if he was Klan.

It was his word against Larry's, so he was an easy winner.

I was more hopeful about another man who'd been described to me as "remorseful" about his Klan membership. Down at his shabby little house there was a yellow sign in the front yard: NOTICE OF PUBLIC HEARING REGARDING THIS PROPERTY. I went to the front door, where a panel was broken out of the storm door and a sticker announced: NEVER MIND THE DOG; BEWARE OF OWNER. After I knocked, a dog inside began barking furiously. No one was home.

It took me a couple of days to work up the nerve to go back. This time a daughter (I'm assuming) answered the door. Mr. Remorseful came outside to see what I wanted, inadvertently allowing his dog to escape. I told him I was working on a book and wanted to know about the Klan.

"What about 'em? Who told you I had anything to do with the Klan?"

With a nervous laugh, I told him I couldn't say. I didn't want to spread names around.

"Well, I'm not gonna talk about it."

Mr. Remorseful was a husky bearded guy in a sweatsuit, who smiled as he refused me. He actually had kind eyes. "Them days are gone. Water under the bridge."

I kept talking—about my grandfather, about my hope to understand.

"It's not the hate organization everybody thinks it is," he said, then immediately contradicted himself by saying that he was half Indian "and I found out they even hate Indians. So I left."

Of course, Jim Ferguson was also part Indian, and he'd told me that UKA accepted that.

"They still look down on it," countered the ex-Klansman, "so I didn't need anything else to do with it." He admitted he'd even been an officer in the local klavern, but he'd only joined "to protect the white heritage, and that was not what it became." Then he told me again that he didn't want to talk about it and walked back into his little house, forgetting about the dog.

At the third alleged Kluxer house, I never even made it to the door. The place was heavily shuttered, and there were three cars out front. As I drove by, I made note of the bumper stickers. WHERE'S LEE HARVEY OSWALD WHEN WE REALLY NEED HIM? HAPPINESS IS CLINTON'S FACE ON A MILK CARTON and 1000 CONFIRMED KILLS with a red line through something I couldn't see from the car. My note on this man said "still sympathetic."

I drove off berating myself for my cowardice, and decided to check out the one flea market in town I'd missed. There in a glass case right inside the door, I found Klan material: old-time applications and membership cards going for $35 each. I'd been to probably every "antique mall" and junk shop in north-central Indiana looking for this sort of thing.

"It's not supposed to be for sale to the general public," dealer Virgil Purvis explained. He was bearded, in his mid-forties, wearing a Texas baseball cap, and he collected Klan-abilia himself, describing it as an offshoot to his Civil War collection.

Purvis had purchased the things in the case from an old man in Richmond, Indiana, who also had a ledger, a membership list. The old man wouldn't part with that, though Purvis promised he would never divulge the names. Soon afterward the old man died. Purvis then called the widow, but she couldn't find the ledger, and Purvis assumed that the old guy burned it. He thought that was probably the right thing to do.

Purvis described a few other items in his collection at home, like a chalk Klansman about four inches tall, a 1926 Klan statue with removable arm (in "White Power" position), and a postcard from 1905 showing an old guy in a garden wearing one of the old-style Klan robes—short, "like the originals." Then he showed me a picture of a Nathan Bedford Forrest medal he'd bought. "You could only get that medal by killing a black," he informed me.

Purvis mentioned that he had a friend who joined the Klan after he got back from Vietnam, but he'd quit soon after. This was the friend's story as Purvis recalled it, interesting because of its obvious parallels to stories I'd heard from Ferguson:

"There was a black guy messing around with a white girl out at RCA. Kept harassing her and stuff. So some of the Klansmen working there took it into their own hands, and my friend happened to belong to their group. One night after work they grabbed the black guy, threw him in the car, took him out here to Four Mile Bridge, stripped him down naked, chained him to a fencepost, and horsewhipped him. Then they drove off and just left him chained naked to the post. There was snow on the ground. I guess he got loose after a while, and he never messed with the girl anymore. But my friend got out of the Klan after that. It got to be too big a power trip for some of them guys." The ex-Klansman hadn't exactly achieved enlightenment. He was now a big Nazi collector and, according to Purvis, "Hitler's his idol."

I asked Purvis to call this friend for me to ask for an interview— anonymity guaranteed and so on. Purvis obliged immediately, but the friend said no. As Purvis explained his friend's response, "You just don't talk about it."

A FORMER EXALTED CYCLOPS was the man who still sold the lynching photo locally. Harvey, however, was in full denial about his Klan membership by the time I met him and his wife Hazel at their little shop.

Harvey and Hazel used to own the pizza parlor where I'd been directed to buy a photo my first week in town. But now they lived in the country and opened their flea market irregularly, so I'd called to make an appointment, telling them on the phone that I wanted a picture. Harvey didn't sound too friendly, so I told him my grandfather had been a Klansman, and he asked for the name. When I tried to steer the conversation Klanward again, though, he said, "Well, I wouldn't know about that." His membership was still a rumor then, so I dropped it. Only after our meeting did I find his name and title in an old newspaper article about a 1970s Klan rally.

Our encounter at their shop opened on a bizarre note when Harvey and Hazel told me that their son had just bought the deed to Manhattan, the actual twenty-four-dollars-worth-of-beads deal between the Dutch and the Indians. Harvey thought it might not be authentic but wondered how he could check. On a piece of paper I wrote down, "Museum of the City of New York, 212 area code." I figured the people there could tell him he'd been had.

Harvey then pulled a manila envelope from the bottom shelf of a glass case filled with jewelry and other small items. In the envelope I saw a short stack of maybe fifteen to twenty lynching pictures. He gave me the top one, apologizing because they'd had to cut off the edges. The original was so old and worn. Whoever printed it had added a label with the wrong date: August 6, 1930. Hazel explained that they didn't tell people they had the picture. You just had to know.

I paid them six dollars, asking, "Do you sell a lot of these?"

"On and off, yeah," Harvey replied.

I said I wanted to ask a few questions.

"Well, a lot of people try to bring up old wounds and stuff like that," said Harvey.

"We don't really know anything," Hazel added. "Nobody who knows will say anything about it."

Harvey was polite but very nervous, and it was soon clear to me that he was just not going to spill anything. He told me he owned "the original"— meaning, I suppose, one of the thousands of photos sold for ten days or so after the lynching. When I asked if it had come down to him through his family, he said, "Well, yeah," and quickly changed the subject. He said he had a man who ran off prints on the condition that his identity never be revealed, but this man's brother-in-law was in the photo. Harvey and Hazel had been selling the prints for ten years.

"Why do you think people still want to buy it?" I asked.

"They just want to know part of the history," said Harvey.

"Curiosity," said Hazel.

"Curiosity," Harvey repeated, going on to tell me his own lynching story—a good safe one. He hadn't seen a thing. He'd been nine years old. He came back from swimming in the Mississinewa that day, and no one was home. The neighbors weren't home. In fact, the whole neighborhood was deserted. So he headed downtown and ran into his father a block from the square. The father told him to get home fast right now, so he did. "Your father stayed?" I asked. "Yeah," said Harvey, changing the subject again: "Would you like a receipt?"

I managed to shake out one more little detail. Harvey finally admitted that, well, he did know someone whose dad had been involved. This particular dad had torched the bars off. A welder. I didn't know what to make of this tidbit. In all my research I'd turned up only one other reference to a welder cutting through bars. And that from someone who had not been there. Harvey wouldn't give me the name of the alleged welder's son. "Yeah, he's dead—his dad. But like I said, I don't know anything about it." He wouldn't look me in the eye.

He sidestepped my question on what he'd learned about the lynching growing up, and my question on whether he'd sold the photo at his pizza parlor, and every question I had about the Klan. They clearly couldn't wait to get rid of me.

I SPENT MONTHS CRUISING by the house of a man described to me as the last living member of the "old" Klan, meaning the 1920s. He'd been a member at the time of the lynching. I had high hopes for this encounter. He was just never home.

But suddenly one day he was. His wife came to the door and let me in. When I told her I was writing a book related to Grant County history, she said, "Oh, he couldn't." Fred was seated in an easy chair in the corner, white-haired and fit looking, though there was a walker in front of him. He paid no particular attention to me. He was ninety-one, suffering from Alzheimer's.

The odd thing about the encounter was that the wife clearly knew I was there to discuss "the hanging."

Before I even brought it up, she volunteered: "He walked down and looked with his first wife, but that's about all he could tell you." She said she didn't understand how people could go look at such a thing.

She was agitated, upset over Fred, because he'd taken off in the truck that morning. Now she would have to sell it, because he was apt to take off again and she couldn't figure out where he hid the keys. I had a hard time getting away. She just kept talking. Her brother-in-law was an anti-Semite, she announced, and she thought it was terrible. And look what we did to the Indians. Terrible. Black people would probably run the country someday. "You can't judge people by the color of their skin." She said she was German and couldn't stand it when people said Germans were Nazis.

While his wife stood there talking to me, the last living member of the 1920s Ku Klux Klan put his glasses on, picked up that day's *Chronicle-Tribune,* and sat there staring at it. Loud 1950s lounge music played on the hi-fi.

PART III

"This Assemblage of Pseudo-Americans"

FIFTEEN

IN HIS BULLETPROOF VEST

When Marion's mayor, Ron Mowery, announced that the Klan would rally at the Grant County courthouse on the Saturday after Thanksgiving 1995, he asked that everyone in town boycott the event. This is the strategy now advocated by veteran Klanwatchers at, for example, the Southern Poverty Law Center. Deny the Kluxers the publicity they crave. Ignore them.

James Cameron disagreed vigorously. On November 21 Cameron faxed Mowery an eleven-page letter from his office at America's Black Holocaust Museum in Milwaukee.

"This same mentality once engulfed the people of Germany," the lynching survivor declared on page one, "when Adolf Hitler, an upstart local hoodlum, started his REVIVAL speeches against the Jewish people and word was, don't worry about demonstrating against him and his policies, they will soon fade away. History records what happened because the people did not band together to run his behind out of the country. That is a lesson for Marion and all other cities, towns, and villages who are urged to not demonstrate against the klanism seeking to spread its venom all over our country—again. They will not fade away as long as permits are granted to them to hold and demonstrate their un-American activities in the midst of a populace that should know better."

Cameron saw the rally not as a First Amendment issue but as an outrage: that the police would protect the Kluxers during their "efforts to enlist more ignoramuses into their ranks." He made an impassioned case for putting them "out of business" instead—and why not in Marion?—outlining the group's history, the origins of lynching, its incorporation into Klan practice as Kluxers repeatedly operated above the law, and the ways in which the KKK still represented "a direct continuance" of the Confederate rebellion.

While Mayor Mowery never did consent to speak to me, I suspect the attention-getter for him appeared on page ten: "I will be in Marion, Indiana, on November 25, 1995, to protest the rally of the Ku Klux Klan in your town. If there is no one but me, alone, to protest this assemblage of pseudo-Americans, it shall be done."

Cameron added that he hoped the mayor didn't now think him ungrateful for the key to the city he'd received in 1993. In a postscript he inquired as to "the time and scheduled rallying point of the Klan that wishes to disgrace the people of Marion."

He complained, when I spoke to him a few days later, that Mowery had called him within half an hour of receiving this fax and had begged him not to come.

ON THE SAME DAY Cameron sent his fax to the mayor, the Marion Redevelopment Commission convened a public meeting to discuss the old jail. Rex Fansler still owned the dilapidated eyesore, and still lived in it, but he owed $17,000 in back taxes on the property. Now the city clearly wanted the building back, and I couldn't help but wonder if James Cameron was part of the reason. The lynching survivor thought it would be the perfect place in which to open a branch of America's Black Holocaust Museum.

I stopped by to see Fansler. The old sheriff's residence was now even shabbier than I remembered it, and Fansler's circumstances had changed rather dramatically. His wife had left him, and he was on the outs with the mayor. This time there were no requests to turn off the tape recorder every time we got to something sensitive. Rex was in a jam. We sat in the living room, one of the three he now kept heated—and that with a gas fire in the fireplace behind some artificial logs. Fansler was seventy-one, on the verge of a divorce, living on Social Security and a tiny pension. He hadn't even known about the public meeting to discuss the future of his living space till he read that morning's paper.

Fansler told me that on October 25 he'd gone to see Mowery, and the mayor had told him to sign the jail over to the city or he'd have it condemned. Fansler was thoroughly intimidated. He had already squeaked through two tax sales and could not get any bank to loan him $17,000. So on October 25 he'd signed an Option to Purchase saying the city would pay him $25,000. Yet the article in the newspaper said the city would seek federal funds to get the jail, as if its acquisition were in question.

The mayor did not return phone calls, but his signature was on the Option to Purchase. According to Fansler, they had discussed Cameron, whom Fansler regarded as his "best prospect" to buy the jail. According to Fansler, the mayor then said, "You're not going to sell to James Cameron. I'll screw that up. I'll see to it that that don't happen." As if Cameron could have afforded it. Fansler still wanted to charge the lynching survivor $160,000, while one bank had appraised the property's value at $10,000. I didn't think Cameron could raise even that.

But he'd never made a secret of his dream to open a branch of America's Black Holocaust Museum in the old jail. After my article on Cameron appeared in 1994 and he began showing up at the jail with various camera crews, so many rumors circulated about his supposed purchase of the place that Cameron wrote a clarifying letter to the *Chronicle-Tribune,* which they printed. "The people of Marion would have to voice their approval of such a museum in their midst," Cameron assured them. And the jail would have to be designated a historic landmark to get federal funds for the rehab work.

"I live from day to day on my Social Security," Cameron wrote. As for the talk that he would bring his museum in whether people wanted it or not—"I can well imagine manufactured propaganda from the grist mills of the Ku Klux Klan spreading such false rumors."

As MARION BRACED for the Klan rally, community leaders decided against a counterdemonstration. So the Reverend T. A. Hunter of Rising Star Baptist announced that the Saturday before the rally he would lead a prayer vigil at the courthouse. Nine people attended.

I'll admit it: I wanted to see Marion take a stand against the Klan. So I hoped for better results at the Community Unity Service, set up to combine the Thanksgiving Eve worship of thirty area churches, both black and white. Eight ministers participated, two of them black, while the worshipers were about 70 percent white. Approximately 250 attended, and this was declared "a good start." But I was disappointed when most of the ministers still hesitated to address racism, the great unmentionable subject even in this setting. The sermon was just generic Thanksgiving fare.

Reverend David Schramm, however, began the service by asking us to be thankful for the progress we'd made in discovering that we are brothers and sisters, with hope that this could be a new beginning, and that no group could come into the community to divide us. In the audience I heard some fervent "amens." Then at the very end we came together in the middle of the sanctuary, joining hands for the benediction. These moments moved me.

What I had noticed the minute I walked in was that I had come to my grandparents' church. They'd left First Presbyterian for a new church sometime in the 1950s. I had not remembered the exterior but knew the sanctuary. First United Methodist. I'd been here many times as a girl, but I had never been to an integrated church service before—anywhere. I choked back embarrassed tears as we sang "We Gather Together."

THE MINISTER AT MARION'S largest black church saw that, for his older parishioners, the impending rally led straight back to August 7, 1930.

Reverend Frederick Greene didn't participate in the unity service; nor had other African Methodist Episcopal preachers. I had not expected even to discuss the lynching with him, but I wanted his perspective on race relations as both an insider (spiritual leader) and an outsider (new in town).

Greene admitted he'd come to Marion "kicking and screaming" when his bishop appointed him—shortly before the Klan rally—to take the pulpit at Allen Temple A.M.E. After growing up in Fort Wayne, serving with the marines in San Diego and Korea, and pastoring in nearby Peru and then Hammond, a short drive from Chicago, Greene just didn't want to live in a small town again. But at the time of our conversation, he'd been in Marion for about a year and found that he liked it: the sense of community, the friendliness, the quiet that allowed him to sit outside at night and think. He hadn't known anything about the lynching when he moved in. He'd seen the photo but never knew where it was taken.

Arriving so close to the Klan rally, however—"that's when I found out," he said. "Everyone came to me and showed me that picture." Greene then saw the picture more than he cared to, as older people in his congregation kept bringing it in, telling him "Here comes the Klan and they're going to march right where it happened." The minister recalled: "I got really inundated with all this information. You know—'that was the jail cell, that's where the tree was,' the fact that they cut the tree down, the old mayor in such-and-such nursing home, all of that. That's when I really made a lot of observations. I thought, 'Wow.' "

Greene was in his early thirties, working on his master's in both divinity and social work and employed part time by Marion's Drug and Alcohol Resource Team on top of his ministerial duties. He referred to his older parishioners as survivors. I'd never looked at it that way, but of course he was right. I thought, for example, of Sadie Pate, who never wanted to discuss the lynching but told me several times, *"I'll never forget that day."* She had a milder form of Cameron's obsession and, like Cameron, made an automatic connection between the lynching and the Ku Klux Klan.

Greene said he'd noticed a generational difference in people's reactions. Those in their fifties and older still seemed traumatized in 1995 by the events of 1930. "The thing that struck me the hardest is that it's almost like an anniversary for them," said Greene. "They really hold on to that [memory]. It's very ritualistic. Every year around that time, here comes all that pain and all that emotion. Then they let it go and pick it up again next year, and I think that's really limited the amount of healing." They couldn't read Cameron's book, he said. It overwhelmed them.

"That's in the black community," Greene continued. "I think in the white community, it's just the opposite. They are trying so hard to forget. They're really expressing a wish to leave it alone. But you can hear the pain in their voice when they're talking, too. You can hear a lot of regrets." That was the yearly cycle, as he saw it: black people brought their feelings about it to the forefront while white people suppressed theirs, but both sides were suffering.

"We haven't purged it. I worried initially that the young people would be socialized to do the same thing, but I don't see it happening with them." Once more time had passed, he said, "the level of emotion associated with it will go down." But he thought both black and white people still needed "some sort of catharsis . . . I'm just scared we're going to get a primal scream."

He knew firsthand the difficulty of dealing, emotionally, with a lynching. His own uncle had been lynched in Florida back in the 1950s for looking at a white woman. "So when I speak it's not from sitting in an ivory tower," Greene said. His father had moved north after this happened, "and a lot of that was about trying to bury the hurt."

What he saw in Marion was an inability to grieve. "We're still in the denial stage. And that's the first stage."

▲ ▲ ▲

EARLY THANKSGIVING MORNING Tom Wise called and asked me to phone Cameron in Milwaukee. Cameron wanted whatever information I had on the rally, and this was when he told me about his conversation with Mowery, how the mayor complained that he was tired of Cameron showing up in Marion with a camera crew. So Cameron reminded Mowery again about Adolf Hitler and told him that the Klan "has to be shouted down" and he would not be bringing a camera crew. He may have neglected to mention that the *Milwaukee Journal-Sentinel* was sending a reporter and a photographer, but it hardly mattered. No doubt the mayor knew that the presence of the lynching survivor, protesting the Klan just a stone's throw from where the tree once stood, was certain to draw media, publicize the rally, and resurrect the embarrassing specter of August 7, 1930.

That same week a couple of black leaders close to the mayor phoned Tom Wise and asked him to somehow persuade Cameron not to come.

"People don't understand James," Wise told me. "It isn't just a thing in passing for him."

Cameron was the proverbial prophet-without-honor in his own town, regarded skeptically in both black and white Marion, though not by all. I often found myself defending him to African Americans of his own generation with a line like "He's not really making any money on that museum."

I knew he could be a broken record, endlessly repeating the points he wanted to get across. And I'd seen that his book's account of the lynching didn't completely stand up under scrutiny. But I also felt that his actions were guided by principle. He would not waver from what he felt was correct, in his story or his deeds. The local attitude toward this living reminder of August 7, 1930, seemed to be part of the town's pathology about the lynching.

"I HOPE IT SNOWS so we won't have to see them." That was one of the little jokes I heard about the upcoming rally. But the Saturday after Thanksgiving dawned snowless, if quite cold, and it was going to be a long one. The Klansmen intended to do a rally in Elwood right after Marion's, and I thought I should see that, too. At eight forty-five A.M. I ducked into the post office just west of the square to do an errand and saw that the police had already blocked off the entire downtown. The rally wouldn't start until one.

Ignoring the Klan was going to be one big headache. And costly. The few businesses still on the square would be closed on one of the busiest shopping days of the year, the authorities shut down the state highway running past the courthouse, and they were going to have to pay for all the extra law enforcement they'd brought in from surrounding counties.

With so many streets blocked off, I decided to walk to the Holiday Inn east of the square, where I had agreed to meet the reporter from Milwaukee for breakfast. Orange snow fencing surrounded the courthouse and ran through the intersections on a diagonal. There was already a police car on the west side of the square at nine A.M. I smiled at the officer, who watched me suspiciously. I left the square to make a wide circle, cutting through parking lots, passing more suspicious officials at the county building. I smiled or said "Good morning" to everyone. They all glared.

I found Crocker Stephenson from the *Milwaukee Journal-Sentinel* in the motel's restaurant, where we sat watching the troop movements through the window. All those extra cops. For me, there was already something eerie about the day, what with everyone's attention focused on the east side of the square, the wait for James Cameron, the old jail visible from the Holiday Inn parking lot. The motel had been built on the site of Marion Machine, and I remembered one of my eyewitnesses telling me how *some men had broken into Marion Machine and were walking out with sledgehammers and crowbars.*

Stephenson had been assigned to trail Cameron around during his encounter with the KKK, but the reporter had arrived the day before while the lynching survivor was driving from Milwaukee that morning, a trip of at least five hours. We didn't catch up with Cameron until twelve-thirty. He was about to go through the security checkpoint at the rally site.

Police had set up a pair of metal detectors on the drive-in teller lanes at an Adams Street bank. Pro-Klan spectators went in through one and anti-Klan through the other, sluiceways into widely separated pro and anti stockades. Cameron was in the middle of being searched. He gave me a big smile as the police confiscated some medicine he was carrying. No one could take anything inside but money, keys, and their placards. Even so, the reporter from Milwaukee decided he better stick with Cameron. He surrendered everything, even his pen, while a state trooper walked me around to the press area. Right past the lynching site.

Thanks to Cameron's presence, media from Indianapolis to Fort Wayne had turned out. One woman reporter got aggressive and walked into the big neutral zone between the pro and anti demonstrators, making a beeline for Cameron. Naturally the rest of us followed. "You aren't under our protection when you're out of the press area," shouted one of the eight sheriff's deputies posted between the press and the pro-Klan people. Protection from what? I wondered. Choppers hovered overhead.

Over at the orange snow fence around the anti-Klans, Cameron was holding forth, barely audible through the helicopter din. I heard the words "We are one single and sacred nationality." A group of militant-looking young black men surrounded him. I learned later that they were locals who had assigned themselves to act as Cameron's bodyguards for the day.

He was holding a homemade sign that read STOP THE KLAN. LET DECENT AND FREEDOM-LOVING WHITE PEOPLE BREATHE SOME FRESH AIR. I thought it extraordinary that Cameron's first thought here would be for white people. He told me later it was because white people found it harder to speak up.

A reporter asked him where the lynching had happened, and he pointed to it. And how did it feel to be back? "I feel the same here as anywhere else."

A deputy ordered us back to the press area. Shortly after one o'clock a young unhooded Klansman—chunky, blond, in a black robe with orange-striped sleeves—emerged from the east door of the Grant County court-house to set up some speakers. As more robed and hooded figures emerged from the door, the speakers blasted ZZ Top: *"Gimme all your loving, all your hugs and kisses too. . . ."*

The blonde stood testing the mike: "Welfare CHECK! Welfare CHECK! AIDS testing 1-2! AIDS testing 1-2! F-A-G! F-A-G! AIDS testing F-A-G!"

A new ZZ Top song pumped out its infectious rhythms: *"Every girl crazy 'bout a sharp-dressed man. . . ."* It had to be a joke, right? Somehow kickass rock and the KKK fit together about as well as—well, sharp-dressed and a bedsheet. But they did seem to be sharp-pressed bedsheets, and color-ful. Blue, purple, green, black with orange, black with red, along with the usual white. I counted thirty all together, both men and women, some of them unmasked. No Larry Hitler that I could see. The only ones without robes wore the black of Aryan Nations. At the back a couple of Kluxers dis-played a large banner identifying themselves as the American Knights of the Ku Klux Klan, complete with phone number.

Next on the Klan soundtrack a deep devilish voice intoned the Twenty-third Psalm over a wailing guitar riff, then thundered out a warning about a coming apocalypse: "At the flick of God's switch, all the lights in the world are out . . . and if we don't change quick, it's coming."

The techno beat behind this had barely died before a voice notably less strong and distinctive called out from the group of Kluxers, "White race is great, white brothers and sisters!" Those were the simple first words, packed with resonance, I thought. Like: if you have nothing else to feel good about,

up our streets? Is the memory of
Washington street and the holes forgotten?

"We want a low tax rate," said Mr.
Bedell, "but we want to be unselfish
and fair enough to admit that we owe
a duty to the other fellow, and a greater duty to our city."

COUPLE IS HELD

A man and woman, giving their
names as Floyd Rankin and Joseph-
ine Rose, were arrested last night on
the public square on charges of adultery, by Patrolmen Patterson and
Treuex. Cash bonds in the sum of $100
each were provided by Rankin and
they were released. They were arrested on information supplied by the alleged husband of the woman, who denied she was married. The man claiming to be her husband resides in Kentucky.

Conkey, president; Thomas McConkey, vice president; Harvey McConkey, secretary and treasurer. The reunion was largely attended. The meeting next year will be held on the third
Sunday in August. The McConkey reunion, always is largely attended.

Sypolt Funeral

The funeral service for William
Sypolt, 73 years old, who died at his
home two miles east of the Soldiers'
Home corner early Tuesday morning,

Klan news and ads like this one from the *Marion Leader-
Tribune,* August 30, 1923, ran in many Indiana newspapers
during the Ku Klux Klan heyday of the 1920s. "The Old Man"
was Indiana's legendary Grand Dragon, D. C. Stephenson.

COURTESY OF THE AUTHOR

In November 1922, after a spectacular parade around the Grant County courthouse, the Klan initiated some 1,700 new members in a public ceremony at Goldthwait Park. Thousands of spectators witnessed the event since, as both Marion papers reported, there was "nothing to conceal." COURTESY OF W. A. SWIFT COLLECTION, ARCHIVES AND SPECIAL COLLECTIONS, BALL STATE UNIVERSITY LIBRARIES

By all accounts, this wooden door at the old Grant County jail was the same one that was there in 1930. Mobsters eventually broke the stone holding the lock. On the paintless area in the middle, indentations left by the sledgehammers were still visible in the late 1990s. CYNTHIA CARR

Mary Ball in a family photo from the 1930s. COURTESY OF JOHN LLOYD

Mary Ball and her husband, Clyde McNaul, in San Clemente, California, 1958. COURTESY OF CLYDE MCNAUL, JR.

James Dean in downtown Fairmount during his last trip home in 1955. The actor was born ten miles away in Marion in 1931, a couple of blocks from the Grant County courthouse, in a house the city tore down during the 1970s. DENNIS STOCK/MAGNUM PHOTOS

Jack Edwards became mayor of Marion in 1929, at age 28. He left for Indianapolis on the afternoon of August 7, 1930, maintaining until his death in 1998 that he didn't know a lynching was in the works. JEFF MOREHEAD, *Marion Chronicle-Tribune*

Sadie Weaver Pate holding her wedding picture, taken at Weaver, the African American farming community named for her father, John Henry Weaver. CYNTHIA CARR

John Taylor, a grandson of John Henry Weaver, purchased this corner of land at the heart of what was once the Weaver settlement and commissioned an artist to paint what used to stand there: the Weaver store and the Pettiford blacksmith shop. CYNTHIA CARR

James Cameron in his office at America's Black Holocaust Museum on the day we met in August 1993. CYNTHIA CARR

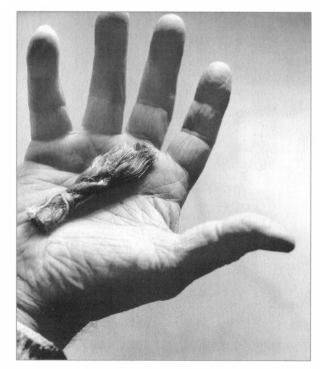

Cameron holds a piece of one of the lynching ropes, sent to him by a white man in Marion who got it from his father. Such artifacts were routinely distributed among spectators after a lynching. KERI PICKETT

The American Knights during their Fort Wayne rally in January 1996. Imperial Wizard Jeff Berry is the bearded man in the dark robe and hood. Larry Hitler is in the black baseball cap.
CYNTHIA CARR

The American Knights rallying at the Grant County courthouse in November 1995.
CYNTHIA CARR

Oatess Archey, Indiana's first African American sheriff, in front of the old Grant County jail. In 1930, one of the lynching victims was hanged from a window on this side of the jail before being dragged to the square. JEFF MOREHEAD, *Marion Chronicle-Tribune*

Cameron in Marion after protesting another Klan rally in July 1999. The sign says: STOP THE KLAN! LET DECENT AND FREEDOM LOVING WHITE PEOPLE BREATHE SOME FRESH AIR. CYNTHIA CARR

The author with her grandfather in Marion, 1950. COURTESY OF THE AUTHOR

you have your whiteness. Or, don't feel bad about what the white race has done. Or, white supremacy's eroded some, but here we are to restore it. All of this and more, I suppose.

We were asked to bow our heads by Klan chaplain Jeanette Stubbs, who was hooded but not masked, young and sharp-faced. The anti-Klans responded with boos and catcalls. I estimated there were about seventy of them, both black and white, with maybe sixty whites on the pro-Klan side. "Lord, I'd like to thank you," said Mrs. Stubbs, "for a chance to give our message to people up here who don't really know any better. Maybe today they can open their hearts and learn a little bit what we're about and stop judging us before they even know what they're doing."

And so the Klansmen would prop up their narrow world with the Bible and the Constitution, incorporating every good symbol into their system and acting as if their job was to enlighten the rest of us. It was maddening, and I would come to see that as another part of their self-appointed job. They loved enraging those who didn't agree with them.

They began their first round of White Power saluting: someone would call a question like "What's the solution?" as the Kluxers chanted "White Power" behind the Nazi salute. "Save our land! Join the Klan! America is being destroyed!" shouted the Kluxer master of ceremonies.

The rhetoric went on for about fifty minutes. I'll just mention some of the lowlights.

The chunky young guy who had set up the speakers, who identified himself as "Mark Fuhrman," told us about a big problem in America today— the "so-called Bloods, so-called wannabe Crips." I'd never noticed Bloods and Crips to be a problem in, for example, Marion. But why expect the Kluxer pronouncements to make sense?

"Fuhrman" unrolled an argument that was a chain of nonsequiturs, leading somehow from gang warfare to people who burn the flag. "People died for the American flag, but no—they want to discriminate against it. They need their ass kicked!"

This glorious idea prompted another round of White Power salutes. "Fuhrman" added one last attack against "faggots that spread the AIDS virus to innocent people. Who accept Negroes. You guys are filth." More White Power salutes.

The Kluxer MC followed up by thanking God for "the wonderful disease of AIDS . . . the greatest thing to come along since sickle cell anemia."

Grand Titan Joe came to the mike in green robe and hood, one of the few to appear masked. He wanted to talk about the First Amendment and the Constitution, "disappearing before your very eyes." The Titan said we were already living under "admiralty law," code words meaningless to anyone unfamiliar with the wacky ideologies of the militia movement. One key belief on the paramilitary lunatic fringe is that the Constitution and Bill of Rights are "God's Law" while the amendments that followed—the ones that freed the slaves, gave women the vote, established a federal income tax, and so on—are part of a Jewish conspiracy to bring down the white race. In other words, the Constitution was written for white men, who have inalienable rights and are bound only by common law. Everyone else has only their bogus "civil rights" and lives under "admiralty or equity jurisdiction." The Titan didn't go into all this but said the Klan would send a copy of the Constitution to anyone calling the number posted on the banner.

The black-robed Imperial Nighthawk Al Ferris read a statement about an appalling discovery he'd made while watching cable TV at a Motel 6: the Black Entertainment Network, clear evidence of prejudice against white people. Another issue currently bothering him was government, "or should I say communism. That's what it's coming to, folks. The Brady Bill took away nineteen assault weapons from honest hard-working Americans."

The rally amounted to one big gripe session, where people who would otherwise spend their lives unnoticed had a chance to stand in the spotlight and air their nonsensical or at least ill-founded opinions.

The next speaker, Imperial Wizard Rodney Stubbs, informed us that if we could just get rid of minorities, we'd have no crime. Stubbs, a heavyset middle-aged guy with sideburns, warned us that the government was taking us down the path to socialism. Just like Adolf Hitler had in Germany. As proof, Stubbs cited the government "trying to take our guns away." Just as Hitler took guns away. The other big issue for Stubbs was race-mixing. Constantly promoted by Jews who control the media, he said. "Watch your child's TV shows. They're promoting race-mixing pre-kindygarten. You gotta be warned! It's a sin!"

Then the MC introduced the purple-robed, unmasked National Imperial Wizard Jeff Berry, who immediately began baiting the anti-Klan demonstrators. "I want to say hi to all you niggers over there. I'm gonna say the n-word because you idiots don't even know what it means. The only reason you're here today is because your crack cocaine daddy busted your damn television and you can't watch the basketball games. You people are like flies. You show up when you're not wanted. This is white America. It's idiots like you that think you're going to take it over. You're not going to. This is America."

Berry's complaints were all couched as insults. "You must be ashamed of your race because you're trying to mix it with ours." And "You guys are the hate group. We don't hate ya. We pity ya. It's a bunch of thugs." And "The only thing you know how to do is riot" and on and on. Then he taunted them for not rushing the stage. "That plastic fence wouldn't hold *me* back."

"Fuhrman" then returned to tell us, "You got the right to bear arms. Why? Because of pathetic thug Negroes like them. I can't say the n-word? All right, we'll just call 'em booty-scratchers. African booty-scratchers. You get five or six black men together, that's okay. That's not a gang. But try to get white men to stand together. It's a crying shame. The damn niggers can get a Million Man March, but try to get one million white people out there. You're all chickenshit. You need to stand up for your rights!"

"Now there's a working man," Berry said approvingly as he returned for the final word, more on gun control. "Within a few years, they're going to have everybody's guns. The government wants to know where you're at. They don't care about the black man. They control the black man. Every one of 'em's on welfare. They got a file on 'em, and they are too stupid to notice." He invited everyone to join the American Knights at the Elwood rally in another hour, and at a Fort Wayne rally on Martin Luther King's birthday or, as he put it, "James Earl Ray Day."

As the rally broke up, a black man at the front of the anti-Klan crowd began calling, "We love you! Don't come back now, hear?"

I hadn't seen Cameron heckle or even open his mouth during the various diatribes from the Kluxers. I could see him walking to the back of the anti-Klan pen, people approaching him to shake his hand, people clumped around him, following him out.

BY THE TIME I CAUGHT UP WITH Cameron, he was standing in front of the Holiday Inn, surrounded by reporters. I couldn't get near enough to hear him or even stick my microphone in, but I did catch the phrase "single and sacred nationality."

I went inside with him and his six self-appointed security guards. They were led by Gary Stokes of the local Urban League. I thought the Urban League wasn't coming, I said to Stokes. There had been a difference of opinion, he told me. One of the security team was a young woman in a Supersonics jacket. They all seemed thrilled to be in Cameron's presence.

Crocker Stephenson of the *Journal-Sentinel* wanted to do an interview with the lynching survivor up in his room and said I could eavesdrop. We were a crowd, what with the bodyguards and a few of their friends and family. Once we got to Stephenson's room, Cameron removed his blue overcoat, and I saw that he was wearing a bulletproof vest. He took it off to sit down with Stephenson, but he had worn it all the way down in the car and would wear it all the way back. On the lapel of his suit was a pink button, I EXPERIENCED A MIRACLE, and in the breast pocket his ever-present felt patch labeled AMERICA'S BLACK HOLOCAUST MUSEUM.

Stephenson asked him why he'd worn the bulletproof vest. "Maybe because the mayor asked me not to come down," Cameron replied. "You can think all kinds of things lately."

He had not participated in shouting at the Klan, he said, because, "my sign was sufficient for what I had to say." Stephenson asked him to elaborate on what it meant.

"Wherever you find black and white people living in a town, you always find decent and freedom-loving white people. They're the ones that put the sheriff on alert," said Cameron, and I wondered if everyone present knew that he was suddenly talking about August 7, 1930. "It was the decent and freedom-loving white people in Marion who called up Dr. Bailey, the black doctor in town, as early as five o'clock in the morning and told him that some white people were planning on breaking into the jail, that we got to do something to get those boys out of there so they have a fair trial. And they bombarded the sheriff's office, the decent and freedom-loving white and black people, and begging to get us out of there. He wouldn't do it. He said everything was under control. It was. It was under Ku Klux Klan control."

Stephenson asked how it felt to hear those diatribes. "You've been the victim of that. How do you respond?"

"I'm above it. I wouldn't let myself sink that low, into the cesspool of ignorance and poverty as to think that about people in this country."

"Once you got the keys to the city here. Now the mayor is telling you, 'Don't come.'"

"He didn't demand it. He just requested. I want that understood."

"Why did you decide to come anyway?"

"To fight un-Americanism. Not only in Marion but everywhere else."

I HAD A DROP IN ADRENALINE after the Marion event and drove to Elwood, thinking the next rally would be a letdown. I had zero emotional connection to Elwood. Nor would Cameron be there. I just wanted to see what kind of welcome mat would be rolled out in the legendary Klan town.

Here too the authorities had blocked off the main road, but the police seemed much less uptight. I noticed sharpshooters on rooftops, yet cops let me pass into both the pro- and anti-Klan stockades in full regalia, from pen to camera. Everything was a little smaller, and the opposing demonstrators were only ten or twelve feet apart.

The rally was under way by the time I arrived. The American Knights stood in front of Elwood's municipal building, looking a little stunned at the reception, much more emotional and vociferous on both sides than it had been in Marion. Every time the Klan yelled "White Power," their supporters saluted and the anti's yelled "Fuck you!" For the most part, I could not have told the pro and anti folks apart if I'd met them on the street. Most had that small-town Hoosier look—mullet haircuts, T-shirts, baseball caps. The Klan guys seemed taken aback to encounter any resistance at all in Elwood. They got into abortion and Randy Weaver and black helicopters—issues never touched on at the Marion rally. They were giving it everything they had. Finally National Imperial Wizard Jeff Berry said, "If you don't have niggers in this town, how the hell you get so many nigger-lovers? What the hell is going on?!"

The people on the anti-Klan side kept chanting, "Leave our town! Leave our town!" I picked out the most vocal protester and asked him why he was there. He said he was a native of Elwood, and now he was in college but he'd come back for the rally because of the town's reputation. He wanted to speak against the Klan. As he told me how the rally had shocked him, he seemed to be on the verge of tears. I did not see any black people anywhere.

THEY WERE MAINSTREAM in the 1920s and terrorists in the 1960s, but now the Klan was marginal, and it served a more insidious function in perpetuating racism.

I'd thought a lot about the Klan—its terrible usefulness. It represented the white id. That's why the masking was so necessary; a Kluxer could be *any* white person. So it was tempting to go shout at them. It seems that it is now a major Klan function to act as the bad white people, so the rest of us can think we're the good ones. That peaked hat is a sort of lightning rod allowing us to discharge our guilt. We're not like them! And it feels good to look at their racism instead of our own. They tempt us into feeling self-righteous, when very few of us have earned the right to feel more than humble, considering our history and the damage yet to undo.

I mean, how hard is it for most white people, really, to say they disagree with the Ku Klux Klan?

A couple of weeks after the Marion rally, I called the number displayed on the American Knights banner, expecting to get voicemail, leave a message, and see what happened. But someone actually picked up the phone and said, "White Power!" A young-sounding male. I told him I was writing a book and asked for an interview. He wanted to know if I was anti-Klan: "It's better if you're honest."

I told him that while I couldn't say I agreed with him, I would try to represent him accurately and really wanted to hear what he had to say. I asked who he was, and he said, "Anthony Berry. You probably want to speak to my father, Jeffrey." I'd dialed right into the Wizard's kitchen.

I asked Anthony if he happened to know a Klansman named Larry Hitler. The kid said he knew where Larry was but could not divulge that information. Jeffrey would be busy for about an hour. I should call back. I said okay and good-bye. Within minutes the phone rang. It was Jeff Berry, the National Imperial Wizard. I had not left my phone number.

The Wizard agreed to an interview time several days hence. I hoped that by making this contact, I would gain access to current Kluxers living in Grant County. But just as I had with Jim Ferguson, I hoped I could also learn something about racism. What were they getting out of it? What nourished their hatred, and what in turn did the hatred nourish? What was the impact of racism on those who perpetuated it?

"White people are going through now what blacks went through in the sixties," Berry was telling me. I didn't know how to respond to this stunning announcement.

"As for your reference to that brother Klansman," he said.

Larry Hitler.

"He is sitting right here, and he has been reprimanded for speaking to you." Only officers could speak to the press, the Wizard explained, and Larry was no officer. "He is my Imperial Bodyguard."

SIXTEEN

"THE WHITE HAS FELL"

One day at the Marion library, I asked for the clipping file on the Ku Klux Klan. The white librarian blanched, then handed it over as if with tongs. There I found a series of articles from the 1979 *Chronicle-Tribune* called "Unmasking the Klan." In the first piece, two Kluxers named Jim and Bill drove a local reporter to the klavern, after blindfolding him and driving in circles. Once there the reporter couldn't tell if he was in the city or the country, but he got a look at the "inner den" with its seven desks for the county officers, an altar, and a bookcase with a set of *The Americanist Writings* and the transcripts of the House Un-American Activities investigations into the Ku Klux Klan in the mid-1960s. Jim Ferguson had admitted to me that yes, he was the Jim named in the article, but no, he wouldn't take me to see the Grant County klavern. They'd packed it up after the demise of United Klans of America.

Two things stayed in my mind about that article, though: Bill's comment about how much he loved cleaning the klavern—"It's like a church"—and that reporter's ride with the blindfold.

I had some apprehension about meeting the Wizard. He had directed me to phone from a certain shopping mall in Auburn, a town north of Fort

Wayne, and someone would come pick me up. I didn't like the idea of being miles from my car with various unknown Klansmen. Still, as I drove to the rendezvous through the freezing rain, I couldn't get that silly "Off to See the Wizard" tune out of my head. It was actually prescient. In time I would come to see Jeff Berry as something like the great and powerful Oz, controlling things from behind his curtain and not really all that he seemed.

But that day I didn't know what to expect, and when I called him from the mall, Berry simply gave me directions to his place in the little town of Newville some twelve miles farther east. I would know his house by its two flags, American and Confederate.

In the front yard stood a barking guard dog. It was a small ranch-style home, partly unpainted. Berry came to a side door that opened several feet off the ground, too high to be usable. He told me to go to the back, over the new sun deck. They were remodeling. There'd been a fire.

Berry was a burly guy in his early forties with a reddish-brown beard, moustache, and thinning shoulder-length hair, dressed in a plaid shirt with jeans. He introduced his son, Anthony, the rosy-cheeked blond kid who had identified himself as "Mark Fuhrman" at the rally. Anthony, or Tony, twenty-one, wore a Bears sweatshirt and black baseball cap with the logo NEVER LEGAL. He was the Exalted Cyclops of DeKalb County. We sat down at a kitchen table set with four Christmas placemats featuring happy cats in red tam o'shanters.

Jeff Berry was fashioning a new KKK for the twenty-first century. No easy task, since everything about the organization—from its now-marginalized ideology to its goofy outfits—seemed anachronistic. One of the first things he told me was that Nathan Bedford Forrest was a traitor. Sure, the ex-Confederate general had founded the Klan, but then he'd disbanded it, too. So Berry definitely had his own spin on Klan traditions. Then unlike the 1960s Klan, this new incarnation of the Hooded Order encouraged whole families to join, which helped sell it as another "traditional values" outfit. (There had been separate organizations for women and children in the 1920s.) Some of the new Kluxers did not bother concealing their identities. The Wizard described himself as proud and outspoken: "I don't care who knows I'm in it." The American Knights did rallies constantly to recruit members, something an old-school Klansman like Ferguson did not believe in. And Berry ridiculed Klancraft, the supposedly secret words like AKIA ("A Klansman I Am") and some of the old-fashioned rituals. At one point he got up to demonstrate, saluting and hopping on one leg, which he said was what you had to do in the old days if you wanted to speak at a meeting. "Klancraft. It's stupid stuff."

They had not abandoned their old ritual of intimidation, however—the bundle of switches laid on a porch. "Switches" was the old word, the Wizard informed me. "We call them clubs." He assured me that this warning worked. Last year they had used it three times, and "only one guy did we have to go beat." They couldn't burn crosses in people's yards anymore. Now it was a hate crime, and "you automatically get five years." But they still used them in their ceremonies, when it was called a cross-*lighting*. "It's the light that shines upon darkness. Of the world," said Tony the Cyclops. "Back in the old days, they used to stick it in a nigger's yard or an interracial-marriage couple. Then if that light lit up, the Lord looked down on why it was lit up at that particular location."

"To let everybody see what's going on," the Wizard added.

I told them I had talked with a Klansman in Grant County (Ferguson) who was part Indian. The Wizard was adamant that no one with Indian blood could be a Klansman. The guy must be a fake. The Wizard advised me to stop talking to him immediately.

So much for the updates into modernity.

The American Knights, born in 1994, was already growing fast when I met the Berrys in 1995. I wondered what still attracted people to this throwback group, given the new popularity of militias on the paramilitary right. According to Berry, only in the Klan did you have to be "a white native-born American Christian. The militias take all colors. Some do." Meanwhile the American Knights had incorporated the militia rhetoric about the corrupted Constitution and the dreaded New World Order into their list of grievances. Berry didn't seem to quite have the ideology down, but as he explained, "Anything after the original amendments of the Constitution—it's not right. It's not a law. And that's what the common law is." He said that common law citizens did not have to pay taxes or get a driver's license but could carry a firearm "no matter what."

He wondered if I'd seen all those cops in black uniforms at the Marion rally. I did not particularly recall seeing black uniforms. Well, he said, those were the New World Order police. "Anytime you see them in the black, that is part of their training. They are training right now to kick in the doors and take all of our guns away because they want control of us." The government had already set up concentration camps in Michigan and Kansas, he informed me. "See, we have people in high places. You don't know who the

Klan is." He assured me that while he was the highest officer, he was not the smartest, that there were people in his organization with six and even eight years of college. "We're just trying to wake up the white American people's eyes to what the government is doing to them."

Of course, the realities they wanted to share were almost laughably wrong. The Wizard described the Urban League, for example, as "a bunch of money-hungry preachers." According to him, the NAACP was government-funded. And so on. The Wizard's world was unrecognizable to me and had its own unrecognizable history. He began explaining the reason laws against interracial marriage had been repealed in the 1960s: "Our preachers got together and said, 'Wait a minute. A lot of these people aren't going to church. Our money is going down. What are we going to do?' So they lobbied and everything, and they got the bill passed where it's okay for a nigger to marry a white. And that brought their church population up and that brought their money up." I hardly knew what to say. I mean, where would one begin?

Given that "basically your church is money-hungry grabbing people," the Wizard planned to create his own. He and the Cyclops were both studying by correspondence school with Universal Life Ministries. Both would become reverends. Unlike a Klansman of old, the Wizard didn't seem to care one way or the other about Catholics. "Our basic thing is we are against child molesting, interracial marriage, faggots, homosexuals, abortion. Our main goal is an organization for white people's rights, the Constitution."

He pulled out a recent newspaper clipping about the United Way. This had really riled the Berrys, this account of where the $6.6 million raised in the Fort Wayne area would go. Money for the American Red Cross, the Boy Scouts, Goodwill, Big Brothers—that was okay. But, the Wizard continued, "here's a good one. Fort Wayne Jewish Federation got $29,000. Fort Wayne Urban League got $151,000. Now these are your church groups. They're getting this money just because they are saying it's okay for blacks and whites to mix. You don't see one thing in there that says Ku Klux Klan or the Organization for White People's Rights. We don't get *any* of this money." Tony had been filling out some forms. As if maybe next year the KKK had a shot at some funding from the United Way.

This all sounded so bizarre, I had to wonder if it could even be sincere. Apparently it could be. Neither the Wizard nor the Cyclops exhibited a flair for irony. Yet something was off.

When I asked Jeff Berry why he'd joined the Klan, he said cryptically, "The Bible." Because the Bible says stay with your own tribe. Because the

Bible says put homosexuals to death. Because in Revelation it says that men in white robes will save the earth.

I wasn't buying it. *The Bible?* It didn't ring true as Jeff Berry's reason for joining the Klan, and not because of his antichurch sentiment. There was a veneer to the Wizard, and I wasn't getting through it. He was not letting me see him. This was something I usually experienced only in interviews with movie stars or other public figures, people who do not want a journalist to see their core. Interviewing Klansmen usually presented a very different problem. With them I entered a parallel universe, where the rules had changed, history had been rewritten, and I often felt disoriented. But even with someone like Larry Hitler, where the world was almost completely fictional, I could still feel his visceral connection with being a Klansman, and I didn't feel it here.

What I didn't know at the time was that Jeff Berry was a convicted felon and former drug informant for the DeKalb County prosecutor's office. His work as a snitch began in 1989, the year he was charged with three counts of felony theft and one of home improvement fraud. A sixty-two-year-old woman had paid him $1,600 for work he never did on her car, $1,050 for a roof repair he never made, and $400 for a water heater she'd already paid him for. It seemed that the Wizard was something of a con artist.

And he'd been a productive snitch. Information provided by Jeff Berry led to seventy arrests and 160 drug buys. In May 1994 the DeKalb County prosecutor dropped all but one of the charges against him, and for that he received a three-year suspended sentence and three years' probation.

At the time of our first meeting, however, I just saw that he was focused on spin control, and that I'd have to figure it out later. Another area that seemed murky was how the Wizard made a living. Berry told me that he did "a lot of building."

"Are you a contractor?" I asked

"I'm a subcontractor. Because I am a leader of the Klan, I cannot be a contractor. Because they will not hire no racist, okay? The government will not hire a racist. But I am a subcontractor."

"What do you contract to do?" I asked

"We do houses. We do buildings. Barns. Just general contracting," said Jeff.

And no one but the government builds houses and barns? I didn't ask. I left it, figuring that what mattered here was his sense of grievance, his complaint that he couldn't get work because of his racism, and it was all part of presenting himself as oppressed and downtrodden.

Besides, Berry had gone on to tell me that, for example, he'd rebuilt his entire kitchen himself after the fire. The arson. "How many Black Muslims, how many NAACP people do you know—civil rights leaders, because I am a civil rights leader—had their house shot up three times, had their house burned, had four bombs throwed at their house? How many do you know of?" Berry asked. "None. You're looking at one right now. We just built this back. They burnt it down July second."

Someone had thrown a Molotov cocktail into the kitchen, he said, and the police didn't seem to care. He claimed they found a second Molotov cocktail sitting outside, and the cops just picked it up instead of bagging it and checking for fingerprints. "They don't *want* to know who done it. *We* know who done it." So said the Wizard.

"December third last year [1994] was the night we will never forget," he continued. "They shot twelve-gauge deer slugs through here. The chair that I was in had a bullet hole in it, through the wall. They missed my daughter's head by an inch. If there wouldn't have been a screen behind the couch, she'd a been dead."

Of course, once I learned of his career as an informant, I thought it likely that people were taking pot-shots at a "narc," not a "civil rights leader." In fact, the day the Wizard got his suspended sentence, the DeKalb County prosecutor told the court that Berry had "provided a great service to the county at some risk to himself and his family, and his house was shot at."

What the Wizard wanted me to see, however, was a long article from the *Fort Wayne Journal-Gazette* describing some of these tribulations.

"Martin Luther King got assassinated, but Martin Luther King did not go through the stuff that my family has gone through because of what we believe in," he asserted. "Martin Luther King's daughter almost didn't get killed. Martin Luther King didn't get his house shot up. Martin Luther King's house did not burn. His house did not get so many bombs. You know, that just makes us more stronger. Just makes us pray more that God is watching out that none of us have really gotten hurt. And we have to be doing something right because it can be the shittiest weather in the world, knocking on wood—every time we have a Klan function, the sky parts."

Later, when I read the *Journal-Gazette* article about the Berry family troubles, I found no mention of the Ku Klux Klan, "civil rights," or drugs. The story, DUELING NEIGHBORS' BITTERNESS BREEDS HATRED IN SLEEPY TOWN, described a Hatfield-McCoy-style feud that started in 1988, the minute the Berrys moved in. Back then they were living in a mobile home.

The hauler carrying their trailer drove across a neighbor's lawn, creating tire ruts, then sinking and leaving part of the trailer on the neighbor's property. Then the Berrys, with no running water, rented a portable toilet. It took Berry two weeks to move the mobile home onto his own land, and then he filled in the tire ruts. But it took him months to get a septic system installed. And then some time after that to get a house built. The hostilities just continued to escalate. Annoyances from Berry, all denied. Violence from the neighbors, never proved. The Wizard complained to me that both his wife and his son had been arrested without cause for violating their restraining orders. The local prosecutor had even tried to revoke his wife's gun permit.

And all these injustices had intensified once the neighbors found out they were Klan. The neighbors, of course, were white. "I'm not moving," Berry announced. "This is America. I built this with my own hands."

Berry claimed that he'd been a Klansman for twenty-two years, naturalized under David Duke. But he didn't go public till March 1994, when Tony "got cut up by a bunch of niggers at a dance club in Hicksville, Ohio." He showed me a photo of Tony with a gash across his face. "This is what they done to him. Plastic surgery."

"But what do you mean by going public?" I asked.

"We threw a rally over there. A march," said the Wizard. The Berrys lived just two miles from Ohio, four from Hicksville.

They said that of all the rallies they'd done since, Elwood was the best. "People cheered when we pulled in," said the Wizard.

I said I thought there'd been a lot of protest there.

No, the Wizard insisted. The only people against the Klan there were "two loud-mouthed broads in the front. Three of them and a half-breed and two other white guys." The American Knights had enrolled a lot of old UKA members down there. That group had disbanded, but "you would not believe the robes and hoods that's in closets down there," the Wizard assured me. "If it comes down to a racial war, you'll see 'em all come out. That's what all of 'em has told us."

As for Marion, they had had no cooperation there. The chief of police had even said, according to the Wizard, "no fucking way any Klan organization is gonna have a rally on *my* courthouse steps." Then the authorities had driven them to the Grant County courthouse in the back of a Ryder truck "like a bunch of animals." Marion even had an assistant chief of police in the NAACP, "and he don't get no hassle over that. Well, let one of 'em become a Klan member and see how fast he gets fired."

Their next rally—Fort Wayne, "on the Coon's birthday"—was shaping up to be even worse. No one was supposed to be allowed to counter-demonstrate, according to the Wizard, and here the city had agreed to let the NAACP or the Urban League or maybe the Zulu Nation have a counter-rally at the same time as theirs. As the Cyclops put it, incredulous: "They even had it on the news where the commissioners support the NAACP, but they don't support the Ku Klux Klan. It said right on the news. On air. But yet we're considered a hate group, and they're not."

"And print in your book," the Wizard directed, "they claim that when the Klan has a rally it pisses off taxpayers because we're spending their money," when in truth Klan rallies were practically free, according to the Wizard. An article in the Marion paper reported that the rally there cost the city nearly $9,900 in overtime pay. Not true, said Jeff Berry. Police did not *get* overtime; they were on duty twenty-four hours a day. "Every policeman at that rally was on their shift except the ones that volunteered because they wanted to take pictures," he declared. And then there were all those New World Order police who worked for free—because they used Klan rallies for "training." No, the Wizard figured, Marion probably spent about $100 for that snow fencing and that was it.

He invited me to join them at the Fort Wayne rally. I could even stand right among them on the courthouse steps, and then I could see for myself what they had to put up with.

They could also give me facts about Klansmen who had been shot, tortured, stabbed, and framed. They could tell me much more about their own tribulations. The Wizard asked if I would consider collaborating with him on a book called *The Life and Times of a Klan Family*. Of course, they would have to get some royalties.

"Want some pictures for *your* book?" he asked, getting out his personal photo album and telling me to take anything I wanted. I selected two to take with me. One was a classic: Kluxers outside with a yet-unlit cross, rifles, Confederate flag, and myoak shields. The other was a snapshot of grinning Klansmen in robes waving at the camera in someone's wood-paneled bar. The Wizard asked what I was going to call my book and suggested I might borrow the "catchy title" they'd just given their new newsletter: *Thoughts Under the Hood*.

One of their current concerns was a new steel plant moving to DeKalb County. Because the government was forcing this plant to hire minorities. "We know how many niggers live in this county, and we know how many's moved in this county since they started [hiring]. We've got it all documented," the Wizard declared. He complained that the number of blacks in the county had now risen to thirty-two.

"And the crime rate has went up," added the Cyclops. "Believe it or not." He went on to say that he'd applied for a job at the new plant on the same day as a friend, a Mexican.

"He's not a friend," the Wizard interjected. "He's an acquaintance."

"Yeah, an acquaintance," the Cyclops continued. "And they called *him* for a job there—and he'll tell you—because he's Mexican."

I asked them what their goal was, ultimately.

"Equal opportunity," said the Cyclops.

"Equal opportunity rights," said the Wizard. "To let us have our constitutional rights. Give us the same rights that the blacks, the Mexicans, the Puerto Ricans have. Let anybody get a job through their qualifications."

There was a knock on the back door. Larry Hitler walked in.

I said, "How ya doing, Larry."

He didn't speak or look at me, just sat down at the kitchen counter looking dazed. He'd grown a long squared-off beard that made him look like a Civil War soldier. Larry had been the man in the blue robe and mask at the Marion rally. The Imperial Bodyguard. He was wearing a black holster.

As I packed up to leave, the Wizard mentioned that he and the Cyclops had put their own guns away because I was coming over. And now they would get them back out.

A FEW DAYS AFTER THIS interview with the Berrys, Tony and his sister, Tonia, were arrested for allegedly beating a black man at a Fort Wayne shopping mall.

According to the police, the two Berrys and a white male friend walked past a black man who was talking to a white woman. One of the three said, "Jungle fever," then "used a racial slur." When the black man confronted them, Tony showed them his KKK T-shirt and declared, "Do you want to mess with me? I am KKK." Then the four began fighting. Tony allegedly hit the black man in the face, cutting his cheek. Witnesses also told police that Tony kicked the man in the back after he fell.

This story about the "Klan kids" did not make the Marion paper till January 20. I knew nothing about it on the day of the Fort Wayne rally.

▲ ▲ ▲

I HAD DECLINED THE WIZARD'S invitation to stand on the courthouse steps in Fort Wayne with the Ku Klux Klan. Standing in the audience was hard enough. But I did want to observe while the police searched them before the rally.

So on January 13, the Saturday before Martin Luther King Day, I drove to the appointed truck-stop rendezvous site north of Fort Wayne. There wasn't a cop in sight, but out chatting near their rusted vehicles were two guys who looked like outlaws from central casting—one the husky hairy Hell's Angel type, the other one lean with snake eyes, sharp cheekbones, and Fu Manchu moustache. I'd found the Kluxers.

I recognized Tony Berry immediately despite the black ski mask covering his face. We shook hands. He indicated that they were just waiting for his father. A smug Fort Wayne TV reporter told me he was getting special information from Jeff Berry because his reports had been so fair. Indeed, he was the only other media person there. I followed Tony Berry. Three other men sat in his car. One pulled down the red, white, and blue bandanna covering his nose and suggested that if I was writing a book, I might want to know about Klansmen's personal lives. Like the fact that he had a two-week-old baby. Later I would learn that this young guy was the Grand Dragon of Indiana.

Suddenly the Wizard's car pulled in. The rendezvous coordinates had changed to Johnny Appleseed Park in town, and a long Kluxer caravan pulled out onto the interstate.

At the park I watched as a Fort Wayne policeman photographed everyone who arrived, and two other officers, one of them black, searched each Klan member. They were going to drive the American Knights to the courthouse in a big Greyhound-style bus, but packed the robes into a separate vehicle. "Don't put them on that dirty floor," the Wizard asked several times, as the cops proceeded to lay them on a dirty floor. Wizard Berry wore a bulletproof vest under his fatigue jacket. The police were in full riot gear, helmets and black jumpsuits. Some held rifles. "They should put this stuff in Bosnia with the UN troops," Berry complained to me. "Why are they doing this? We're a nonviolent organization."

Downtown at the rally site a bit later, I heard a huge cheer go up while I was at the Mobile Command Unit getting press credentials. Police had cordoned off one block in front of the courthouse and divided it into two holding pens marked SUPPORTERS and NONSUPPORTERS, with the media in the center. When I got to the press area, I saw one white-robed Kluxer standing alone on the courthouse steps with his arms crossed. Jeff Berry definitely had a gift for the dramatic.

This time the new rock 'n' roll Klan made an entrance to some heavy metal, switching, after a round of "White Power" salutes, to a cover of "Knockin' on Heaven's Door." A Dylan song? When I played the tape later, I realized I hadn't even made a note about this. Just a couple brief encounters with the KKK, and I'd already filled my irony quotient.

What the Klan said in Fort Wayne that day was even uglier than what I remembered from Marion and Elwood, beginning with Tony Berry, who declared that like Martin Luther King he had a dream: that Negroes would be shipped back to Africa where they belonged, that AIDS-infected homos would die in quarantine, that this would be a white-only nation.

I began to think of the rally as a contest in which Klansmen competed for the title of Most Offensive. Their targets this time included everyone from "mud people" (anyone who is not pure Aryan) to Barney the Dinosaur, whose television show was said to promote race-mixing and alternative lifestyles. One speaker declared that we ought to be celebrating Martin Luther King's assassin with a James Earl Ray Day. Another criticized Hitler because he couldn't even kill Jews properly. As always, they shoveled out a great deal of misinformation, announcing, for example, that United Nations troops were already in America because President Clinton had made amendments to the Constitution allowing them to be here.

The only speaker who didn't just dish out toxic invective was Joe the Titan, the green-robed officer who always kept his face covered. (He was running for sheriff somewhere, according to Wizard Berry.) Joe had more militia-style constitutional concerns, advising us not to sign our driver's licenses, for example, because if we did, we'd be entering into a contract with the government.

Jeff Berry kept taunting the protesters, "a bunch of chimpanzees," while giving out directions to that night's cross-lighting. New recruits welcome.

The rally was not without its moments of unintentional drollery, as Mike McQueeny, the Grand Dragon of Wisconsin and Illinois, advised all white men to "take your white women home to bed and breed breed breed." But the major point McQueeny wanted to make was that Jews controlled everything— government, schools, Hollywood—while the White House supported "every evil Jew program" and the Negro was "the greatest problem in civilization."

It was all I could do just to keep myself there. It was hard to listen to hate labeled as love, lies labeled as truth. It was also bitterly cold, and I couldn't feel my feet.

After more than an hour of this, the rally seemed to be drawing to a close, so I decided I could leave. Exiting, I passed a block-long line inching toward the Nonsupporters' pen, waiting to be searched by the very slow cops. Many of these people wore red and white buttons that said STOP RACISM. Later, I would hear the Klan folks discussing this line, saying that all of them were Klan supporters who had not been allowed to enter.

I WAS ONE OF THE FIRST to arrive at the cross-lighting site, a rural trailer park near the Michigan border and home to the Grand Dragon of Indiana. No one had plowed the snow from the gravel roads here, watchdogs bounced in the yards, and the nearest grocery store also sold bait. It was a nicer trailer park than many I'd seen, however. The Dragon even had a garage. Around five I pulled up there while the Dragon, Larry Hitler, and a guy in a Bulls jacket unloaded wood from somebody's vehicle.

I asked Larry when he thought the ceremony might start. He said it would be after dark, but he wasn't authorized to speak to me. He looked warily down the road as if he were afraid the Wizard had seen him say even that much. But Jeff Berry had not yet arrived.

Tony Berry, the Cyclops, was there, however. So polite. Always calling me "ma'am."

Tony invited me into the garage. The wall farthest from the door displayed many neatly arranged tools. Back in the corner across from the tool wall were a couple of easy chairs and an antique wood-burning stove. A long table was set up there, and I bought the first edition of the American Knights' newsletter, *Thoughts Under the Hood*—nine stapled pages. Someone brought in piles of hot dogs and a pot of corn. Larry and others wrapped twine around the tops of inch-square yard-long sticks. The torches. Larry was wearing all black, with military patches and buttons. I ventured a couple of questions. He'd left Marion "because of the niggers," he said. Then he'd had a falling out with his mother because of something she'd done, "but I'm not going into it." She was now living in Fort Wayne, or as he called it, "Fort Coon."

The Dragon, Rick Dietrich, suggested that I might be happier sitting in the house with the other women. I declined. Despite its women members, the Klan was clearly a male enterprise. I stood near the garage door till both the Wizards arrived. The American Knights had to be the only Klan group in history with two of them. The Wizard was the national leader, the Dragon a state leader. Jeff Berry had invented the odd title of State Imperial Wizard for Rodney Stubbs, because Stubbs had been a Kluxer since 1971, and Jeff thought he ought to have a fancy title. But Jeff was the Wizard who mattered here. He ran it all.

Stubbs approached and said, "Want to ask me anything?" He was another one who claimed he'd joined the Hooded Order because of his strong Christianity. "Klan laws are Bible laws," as he put it. While his parents were not members, he'd grown up "with Klan morals and beliefs. The way America's went, it confirmed we were right." I had estimated his age at early fifties. He was forty-three. His wife of three years—the chaplain—used to be anti-Klan out of ignorance, he said. Thanks to the media, she once thought Klansmen were monsters.

The garage was suddenly very noisy and chaotic as more people, including children, arrived. Rick the Dragon wanted to tell me something about himself—that he had once owned a pet store and then a garage, but now he was trying for disability. He had a bad back. He wished he could get out of heavy work and learn law instead, "or something where I could sit down and type." His great-great-grandfather had been a Klan member in Hazard, Kentucky, but he described himself as "not prejudiced." Half his family was Mexican, though he himself would never breed with another race. Stubbs piped in to assure me that "Ricky's bloodline is pure."

Jeff Berry asked what I thought of the rally. When I hesitated, he jumped in with his own assessment: "Too many issues thrown out there at once. But like I said, no white people started no fights." He complained that the police had done a "crappy job and pulled a lot of violations of people's civil rights today." When I asked how, he told me they took cigarettes away from various Klansmen and wouldn't give them back. Rodney Stubbs added that they'd dirtied the robes.

"Got footprints on 'em and stuff," Jeff agreed. Meanwhile, had the police searched everyone who went to the counterrally? The one with speakers from the NAACP and the Urban League? No! "I mean, if you're *for* Martin Luther King, you can get away with stuff," he groused. According to Jeff, the cops also let the anti-Klan spectators in faster than pro-Klan. "Because we had more *for* us than against us, and that don't look good on the news media."

I went back to chatting with Stubbs. About the KKK stronghold in Elwood. About various changes in the Klan: allowing Catholic members— yes; "hanging niggers from trees"—no. He even had black neighbors. They moved in, and he told 'em the rules: leave me alone, I'll leave you alone. "I'm not saying we don't believe in violence. We believe in self-protection."

Four children chased each other around the pile of torches.

A bearded man in overalls approached along with a woman, saying Jeff Berry had asked them to speak to me. They were from Marion, both new members. This had been one of my goals for the day—finding people from Grant County. I wanted to know how much of a presence the Klan was there.

When I asked the new members why they'd joined, they began to bicker over who would get to tell me first. They couldn't wait to unburden themselves. The woman said she was tired of getting stepped on, tired of not getting anything. "It's all for the black. We have been here longer. We gave them their rights, and they're abusing them, and I would like to live as well as they do through the government. They say they're from Africa. Fine. Let 'em go back. If that's what they're going to yell. In America, they have no right to be here. Ship 'em back. And they're gonna be cocky and arrogant toward every white man, cause trouble, hurt people. We don't need 'em. I believe in the Ten Commandments, and they ain't showed me nothing that they prove toward the Ten Commandments or anything else. And you can quote me on that."

The man said the same went for him. "I'm tired of society's way with the nigger," he announced. "Tired of having to keep my goddamn mouth shut about color. Tired of it. Every time a white turns around to a nigger, he's in trouble. I want the white people to understand. The son of bitches come over here and take every goddamn thing they can from us, the government steps in, knocks down the KKK, and you can thank your goddamn President John Kennedy for giving 'em their goddamn civil rights, which was stupid. Hell, now we're the minority. Bullshit, okay? But to educate the white people today, I don't know what the hell to do."

"Yeah, they got all these laws. NAACP," said the woman, who asked to be called Kathleen.

And, cried the man, who asked to be called Dusty, "You got goddamn people out here look at the Ku Klux Klan like we're a bunch of goddamn racists."

"Thugs or something," Kathleen concurred.

"We're not only against the goddamn nigger," Dusty pointed out. "We're against whites that don't do right. We're against any nationality that doesn't do right by the Bible."

"Ten Commandments," said Kathleen.

"Hell, they still look at ya. They don't come to goddamn rallies," declared Dusty. "I wanted to get with a white organization, where it's solidly white."

"We stand up for our own rights," said Kathleen.

"Divided we fall," said the anguished Dusty. "And goddamn it. The white has fell. We have fell underneath. So the reason I am joining is to help promote unity within the whites. I'm sure you was up there at the rally. That ain't to antagonize those damn niggers out there and the queers and everything else. Hell no! We're trying to get white people to understand what the hell's going on." And now his voice was rising: "Son of a bitches ain't going to show up, what the hell are you going to do? Unity! That's what I'm after. With white people!"

"Like the niggers have," said Kathleen. "Unity between themselves and the government."

More so than Kathleen, Dusty just radiated rage. *The white has fell.* He had such an urgency to lay out his grievances that things came blurting out all disjointed and out of order. Like—he was tired of turning on ball games and seeing all those black athletes. School—they took the prayer out! And now the government was trying to take the guns right out of your home. No-knock warrants! And man was *not* created equal. All those shows on TV putting black and white together? Interracial marriage? "Jesus Christ! Twenty, thirty years ago, Marion would have hung the son of a bitches for it!! Both of 'em!" And their kids come out speckled!

"And you know something that *really* pisses me off?" Dusty continued. "The nigger has been given everything by the whites for what—thirty years? Let's face it. Thirty years! Well goddamn, now we're in the minority. We're under! We're not going to be for long. I know that. And I just want to be one of the white supreme-ists."

I NEVER EXPECTED TO SPEND six hours at the Grand Dragon's home. Wizard Berry told me originally that they would do a cross-lighting and then one of their top-secret naturalization ceremonies—the initiation for new members—and I couldn't be there for that. But at some point Berry had changed his mind. They'd light the cross last.

I talked for a while with the leader of Fort Wayne's skinheads, Gypsy. He had a high-pitched giggle and some sixty-five to seventy tattoos, including the words MADE IN USA etched just above his hairline. While his real work was organizing and recruiting skinheads, he had a day job making cake pans. He'd lived in California and Georgia but thought he'd settle in Fort Wayne. He felt safe there.

The Wizard entered the garage holding the Dragon's two-week-old baby girl wrapped in a Mickey Mouse blanket. "Listen up!" he shouted, holding the baby up in the air. "This is the newest member of the Klan! This is my godchild!" Around me young men were filling out applications.

Gypsy was explaining to me that people were wrong to always talk about "hate groups." He simply loved his heritage. "And I love it enough to kill."

The American Knights probably hoped to recruit these skins, whom they regarded as less evolved because of their admiration for Hitler. I eavesdropped on an argument between a young skinhead who declared that "Hitler to me was like George Washington," and a young Kluxer who argued that—no, Hitler took people's guns away. Then they argued about when it would be appropriate to go out and start "wasting queers." The skinhead thought you had to build an army first, and he "couldn't relate to the violence." But the Kluxer announced that they were sinning "right now tonight" because they weren't out killing gay people. "It says in the Bible, shoot 'em," so, he concluded, "if you shoot queers and race-mixers, you got His blessing. You earn Brownie points." The conversation then moved to the less fraught topic of saluting, whether to use the right hand or the left. *Ah,* I thought, *the endless search for common ground.*

I really really really wanted to leave.

Not that everyone wasn't polite. Dragon Rick came over to talk about the Marion lynching, to tell me that he thought the Klan didn't do it. Wasn't their style. They'd never do a lynching in public like that. They'd do it in secret, "out in the woods somewhere." He moved on to collect twenty-dollar donations from applicants. To cover the dinner and the cost of the cross, he explained. They'd spent sixty bucks on the lumber and twine.

I peered outside where I could see the cross all ready, lying in the snow. The Wizard had just left to buy some kerosene. Somehow I was determined to be the dogged reporter and see the thing lit. I didn't know if I'd ever get another chance to observe this notorious Kluxer ritual firsthand.

I decided to snap out of it. At least part of my discomfort just came from the atmosphere of latent violence always generated by a mixture of alcohol and firearms. And I *did* want to know what they thought—hard as it was to then cope with the fact that they thought it. Their beliefs got me down.

My grandfather wouldn't have fit with this crowd, either. Far from it. He would have despised their drinking and profanity. He would have equated them with the "hillbillies" who bragged about having "board floors." While the 1920s Klan attracted middle- and working-class people, most of the new Kluxers I'd met so far didn't even have jobs. The Klan was now far from "an upgoing thing." In fact, so many members were on disability that the group seemed, quite literally, to be a refuge for broken white people.

Some of them also radiated such menace that I never approached them. Eventually I stopped berating myself over this and concluded that it was okay to follow my instincts in angry-white-guy country. So I never interviewed Al Ferris, the Nighthawk, the one who looked like a western outlaw and stood watching everything like a coiled rattlesnake deciding what to bite. In 1999 Ferris would be shot dead by his wife in what was ruled a justifiable homicide. Then there was Mike McQueeny, the Grand Dragon of Wisconsin and Illinois who, unknown to me at the time, had already served six years in prison for trying to kill his wife. What I noticed about him that day was his white silk jacket, emblazoned across the back with the words KNIGHTS OF THE KU KLUX KLAN. I kept wondering, *Just where do you wear that thing?* But I didn't feel like asking.

Once the Wizard returned with kerosene, he instructed everyone who wasn't a Klansman or a wannabe to stay in the garage. The naturalization was about to begin in the yard and, said Berry, "You know what happens to people that see things they ain't s'posed to." Rodney Stubbs and a few others remained inside as well.

Since the porcine and jowly Stubbs was always ranting about "mud people" at rallies, I asked him if he was part of the Christian Identity movement, the quasi-religion propping up lots of far-right racism. Christian Identity teaches that white Anglo-Saxons are the true descendants of the lost tribes of Israel: God's chosen people. Everyone else is literally a "spawn of Satan" and not really human: mud people. Stubbs concurred with at least that much. As he explained it, the U.S. government was promoting a mud race in order to facilitate the New World Order. The idea seemed to be that a mud race would not identify with any particular race or be loyal to any particular nation.

Stubbs, well lubricated with beer at this point, then launched into a diatribe about religion. He'd been raised Methodist, but at some point in his Klan membership he found that his own pastor was protesting him. His own pastor! Protesting the Klan! This led him to discover that the Methodist Church promoted homosexuality and race-mixing. Now, if he went against his beliefs by attending a Methodist church, he would burn in hell. As for Christian Identity, he did have a few differences with them. They didn't eat pork, and he loved pork. They didn't vaccinate their children, while he would kill anyone who kept him from vaccinating his. Certainly he agreed with them about white people being the true Israelites. But if he said he was Christian Identity and then ate pork and vaccinated his children, he would burn in hell.

So he didn't know what religion he was. According to Stubbs, a sort of creeping Judaism had spread through all Christianity. The printed material that came to a church now—the sermons, a monthly devotional guide called *The Upper Room*—it was all written by Jews, to "gradually promote their Jewish ways into our religion." And Jews would burn in hell.

Stubbs was more confrontational than the others I talked to. He brought his big face up a couple of inches from mine and shouted, "Prove to me Jesus Christ was a Jew! Prove it!" Thus did I learn that God the Father is Caucasian. Stubbs offered proof: the Book of Revelation says that God has white hair and "eyes of water." Blue, right? I decided not to point out that, actually, water is colorless.

This was just the beginning of his revisionist Bible. He reminded me that Cain went to the land of Nod after killing Abel. But who could have lived there? No one even existed except Adam and Eve and Cain. Well, as Stubbs saw it, the land of Nod was where God sent Lucifer and the fallen angels (who were Satanic, he said, therefore black). According to the Bible, Cain "multiplied" with them. Now Stubbs's tortured theology, which had to support both his racism and a literal interpretation of the Bible, took on the problem of the Flood. How did black people come through the Flood, when God saved only Noah's family? Well, Noah took the beast of the field. "It's the colored race. The nigger as we know it today. Prove that I'm wrong." He said he felt "so strong" on this point that if I could prove him wrong, he would quit the Klan, and the Klan was his life.

"Doesn't 'beast of the field' mean animals?" I asked. But there's just no arguing with irrationality. Stubbs said I better read the Bible again.

THE TOP-SECRET CEREMONY moved into the garage, so Dragon Rick escorted me to his mobile home about thirty feet away. I could see that he was proud of it. Just a little over a year ago he and his wife and kids had been living in a camper. Rick was twenty-seven with short hair, goatee, and moustache, and he was suited up for the naturalization in his Dragon robe and hood. I asked about the green cross sewn to the front of his white mask. It was a look he'd come up with on his own. "I'm strong into the Bible," he said. "You know, there's four pages in there on segregation."

Rick introduced me to the room full of women, who stood around the wood-paneled kitchen-living room talking quietly. I listened for a moment to a serious conversation about what the Klan vows meant. Rick pointed out to me several times how neat everything was in the trailer. His wife—well, they weren't really married quite yet—did such a great job, he thought.

The Dragon was the one who'd suggested earlier that day that I should know about Klansmen's personal lives. He really wanted to show me things, beginning with what he called the most important book anyone could possibly own: *Black's Law Dictionary*. Then he pulled out the first book in a series he was ordering called *Mysteries of Mind Space and Time: The Unexplained*. The mysteries concerned UFOs, angels, lost civilizations, that sort of thing. He'd ordered another complete set of books—*Combat and Survival*—that explained, for example, how surveillance airplanes could pick up your footprints in your front yard. But he liked the *Mysteries* more and gave me a spare coupon in case I wanted to order a set.

The Klan too existed to explain mysteries: how downtrodden white people got that way and how they could rise. I knew they really believed the wild claims they'd been making all day. Dragon Rick told me, for example, that Clinton and Gore had posed together for a gay magazine. I'd seen that picture myself and thought it amazing that someone—apparently large groups of someones—could not tell it was Photoshopped, a collage. The Klan dealt in the most deadly kind of misinformation, the kind put forward as secret knowledge, the only truth. How appropriate that their titles and costumes made them seem like characters in a fairy tale. How unfortunate that their weapons were real.

Dragon Rick next wanted to show me his collection of salt and pepper shakers. He took out a set done as tombstones: *Here lies Salt; Here lies Pepper*. His people were hillbillies, he told me, and some of them had committed suicide. From stress, he thought. His not-quite-wife wore a black T-shirt with a hooded Klansman on it, labeled BOYS IN THE HOOD. She sat on the couch nursing the baby, covering herself and baby modestly with a light blanket. Rick said she divorced her first husband because "he wasn't a family values man." I noticed a wall plaque with the Ten Commandments, a pencil drawing of Rick's brother, dead in a car wreck, and next to the front door three rifles and a belt full of shells.

Talk slid easily from the apocalyptic ("every thousand years the world turns over") to the mundane ("you go to any members' houses—they're clean"). He showed me a pewter castle with wizards his wife bought him for

Christmas. Three hundred dollars at the Finger Hut, Rick said with some awe. Outside I heard what sounded like a gunshot. The Dragon thought he better rejoin the ceremony.

I just wished they would light the darn cross so I could leave. Feeling stir-crazy in the trailer, I wandered out onto the porch. I could hear the Kluxers shouting in the garage, while two stood outside guarding the door. Joe the Titan, who wore the green robe, nodded hello uncertainly. He seemed to be holding a mike in his hand. Al Ferris, the Nighthawk, was there too. Suddenly they shouted for every unnaturalized person to get back in the house quick. As I turned, I saw Jeff Berry leading someone out of the garage, someone who had his face covered with what appeared to be white bandages, like the Invisible Man.

Back inside the trailer, I began talking to Brad Thompson, the Catholic—or so he'd been introduced earlier in the evening when they wanted to prove to me that they had Catholic members. He had longish hair, a moustache, and a mild manner. Unaware, no doubt, that the Wizard had bragged to me about alleged members with six and eight years of university education, Brad Thompson let me know that he was their "only college grad." He'd done two years at a junior college. He worked at a foundry pouring iron. The Klan was willing to send him on through law school, Thompson said, if he would then become a civil attorney, just for the Klan. He stood there in his white robe and hood, ignoring the little kid who kept coming up to say, "Hi, Conehead."

Occasionally I glanced out a window and saw various robed and hooded figures running awkwardly through the snow.

"I was raised in a white town, in a white county," said Thompson. "I started waking up to how things are when I was fifteen. Either you're a factory worker or a farmer. I started reading." He indicated that books had inspired him in his racism. Then there was his trip to Tiger Stadium for a ball game in the late 1960s. Black people, he said, had destroyed that neighborhood. "That was the legacy of Martin Luther King."

The kids had settled in front of the television to watch *Casper the Friendly Ghost.*

"A little bitty group like ours," Thompson continued, "a little twelve-hundred-plus—strike that." Membership numbers were top secret, of course. "An unknown number of individuals tried to have a rally to gain membership and preach the word of Jesus Christ, tried to wake up individuals to their constitutional rights, moral values, equal rights. And we're shunned by our own race."

He said his foundry had just hired twelve "coloreds" when his own wife couldn't get a job there. Because she was white, he was certain.

By this time I'd moved to a couch next to a woman in a Washington Redskins sweatshirt. She turned out to be Edna Berry, the Wizard's wife. Like everyone else I'd met that night, she had a lot of complaints. And I was getting too exhausted to take them in. Finally, near eleven P.M., the naturalization festivities out in the yard came to an end, though Dragon Rick told me that a few people would have to go through it again. Somehow this had to do with it going too fast. He could not give me any top-secret details except that, as a rule, naturalization took all night.

So everyone gathered in the yard where a cross, wrapped in twine and about nine feet tall, stood between the garage and the road. The Klansmen and Klanswomen, all in their robes now, picked up their torches and formed a circle around it, while I watched from the back with the skinheads, the only other nonparticipants. The Cyclops, Tony Berry, began this most sacred of Kluxer ceremonies with his torch lit, saying, "America, these are dark times right now. We have niggers running rampant in the street. They have taken over our major cities. We have spics, Jews, and everybody else running crazy in the United States of America, but we the white people are here to take it back. We are in dark times, but where there is total darkness, there must come a light." Passing the flame to an officer next to him, he said, "Will you take the desire and the concern for your race, your nation, your country and keep it to yourself, or will you pass it to a brother Klansman?"

The officer said the ritual words, "I will pass it to my brother Klansman," and turned to pass it on, saying, "Do you accept the light?" They repeated this till a few officers had lit torches, then the flame was passed on more quickly around the circle, amid warnings to "watch your robe." Once everyone had a flame, the cross was lit, and they all raised their torches, chanting, "White Power! White Power!"

Jeff Berry stood at the center shouting, "We had another victory in Fort Wayne today! We got new members." Kluxers applauded.

"We also made a nigger police officer cry!" Berry roared, and the group laughed. "I was talking about Martin Luther King, tears were running down his eyes." The Wizard dedicated this beautiful moment to his new godchild.

The skins and I seemed to be the only people leaving. As I took a few last pictures, the Wizard came up and asked, "So which Klan group is the nuttiest?" Whew. Another question I didn't know how to answer. I said I didn't know, but that his group was by far the most open.

"The other ones don't know what they're doing," Berry declared. "They're in it for the money."

Scattered cries of "White Power!" still echoed around the yard, as the Wizard told me he'd gone home for fifteen minutes after the rally, and there were already fifty-two messages from new recruits on his machine.

The next day I read through *Thoughts Under the Hood.* Racist cartoons. Another screed directed at the United Way for discriminating against whites. Bible passages supporting the notion that "the only good fag is a dead fag." And most interesting to me, an editorial written by Dragon Rick called "What Do We Gain from Public Displays?" The editorial described a Klan with lowered expectations, a Klan that was not going to produce social change, and he suggested that it was time to refocus on personal goals. "Outward displays like public demonstrations help to affirm your beliefs," the editorial said. "We join together and demonstrate, not to change the world, but to keep the world from changing us."

TEN DAYS AFTER THE CROSS-LIGHTING, I went to court in Fort Wayne with the "Klan kids" for the alleged beating at the mall. At nine A.M. Wizard Berry stood waiting in the hall all stone-faced, dressed in a leather motorcycle jacket, while Tony Berry talked to his public defender in the courtroom about a plea bargain. When Tony emerged, he huddled briefly with Jeff, who then told me that for a guilty plea Tony would get a $25 fine and counseling. Only they didn't say how much counseling or what it would cost.

Tony was pacing, a big scared kid. His sister, Tonia, a blond mallrat in a Notre Dame jacket, didn't seem scared or even very engaged by the proceedings. But Tony had noticed a TV camera outside, and the anxiety was popping off him. His KKK activities were not known to his coworkers. Eventually the Berrys would become too notorious for any of them to remain anonymous, but at this point Tony always hid behind a hood or a mask at Klan functions in the Fort Wayne area.

The Wizard went outside to talk to the reporter from Channel 15, giving him the Berry spin on what had happened at the mall: Some "white chick" who knew Tony from high school told her black boyfriend that Tony was a Klansman. So the black guy and his buddies followed Tony and Tonia around the mall and attacked them "because of their religious beliefs," as the Wizard put it. "Stand around and get your ass beat because you're white— that ain't gonna go," he scowled with outrage.

I noticed that the Berrys had brought their Imperial Bodyguard. I asked Larry if he was still using the name Hitler.

"No," said Larry. "Cuz he was a Nazi." He said he'd changed his pseudonym to Larry Hitt, adding a second t because *hit* might make people think of *hitman,* and "I don't want people to get the wrong impression."

We went into the courtroom around 9:20, and it took nearly two hours to get to the Berrys. After the court cleared a bit, Jeff walked to the row in front of me and sat down. Talking quietly over his shoulder, he said the justice system was a joke. Had I noticed how the black guy got a $25 fine for marijuana possession, while the white guy just after him got $250 for mere paraphernalia? "Watch the color," he murmured. Funny. I'd actually been thinking how even-handed it all was, how like a conveyor belt—with the great majority getting $100 fines and fifty days of community service as they came forward to answer for their Class A misdemeanors.

So had I missed some huge disparity between a black guy and a white guy? I didn't think so. Jeff just wanted it to be there. He needed it to be there. In the Klan mind, this country—despite all evidence to the contrary—was now in the business of giving black people every break, everything they wanted.

Jeff then predicted that his kids would go last, that the authorities wanted to cover this up. But the Berrys were called soon afterward and simply given another date.

Outside on the plaza I saw that the Wizard and the Cyclops were in disagreement about the possible plea bargain. Tony the Cyclops seemed convinced that he'd end up in jail if he pleaded innocent and went to trial, while Jeff Berry did not want his children pleading guilty.

"If a person can't stick up for his rights because he's white, then this country's not shit!" fumed the Wizard before storming off.

"Sure," Tony told me after his father walked away. "I want to fight the system. But I might go to jail for a year."

As he rushed off to join his father, I wished I could talk to Tony away from the Wizard who so tried to control everyone's behavior. When I'd first met the Berrys, I'd actually been impressed by the front they put up as a family. *They're so tight,* I thought. Now I was beginning to see it as Jeff and his team, patriarchy in action.

As it turned out, this case was not resolved for another three months, when the "Klan kids" did plead guilty after all and were ordered into non-violence counseling and fined. By then I'd stopped going to court appearances with the Berrys. There were just too many of them.

SEVENTEEN

"NOWHERE ELSE TO TURN"

The angry new members from Marion lived in a little white chicken coop of a house near the bypass. Dusty was alone when I arrived, kneeling in front of the fridge as he unpacked a case of Bud Light. He scowled up at me. Kathleen was at the store, he said. Back in a minute. And did I realize that the Ku Klux Klan was a secret organization, and they were serious about enforcing it and the penalty could be death and he knew it for a fact? He was only talking to me now because I'd been at the cross-lighting and the Wizard had asked him to.

Dusty's barely controlled fury would set the tone for the whole afternoon. "Let me ask *you* some questions," he demanded as we sat down at a small round kitchen table, and he opened his first beer. He'd put the Pekingese out in the side yard on a leash and propped a child's mattress in front of the hole in the storm door. The house was tidy but felt frail, about as secure as a large cardboard box. He wanted to know if I'd written other books about the Klan and how long I'd been a journalist. He kept offering me beer, RC, coffee, beer.

If I'd ever had any delusions that people like Dusty and Kathleen could be educated out of their racism, my encounter with them that day pointed out the futility—and the arrogance—of that thought. From their point of view, it was someone like me who had to be educated. Dusty in particular seemed genuinely amazed that certain white people did not agree with the Klan.

Dusty began by speaking bitterly of these "hypocrites," the local "high rollers who go to church to outdress the Joneses, sister-better-than-you-Bertha sitting front row center," and if they'd ever admit to their heritage, they too had Klan in their families. "I mean all the whites around here." And now, if they had the guts to come to a rally at all, you'd find them lined up with the anti-Klans. "They've got an eyeful coming before long if they think the Klan is dead."

Dusty often seemed to be talking through clenched teeth: "The older I get, the madder I get at situations in this country that I know can be controlled. You understand? I want to be part of the white movement that controls this!"

He'd grown up in Converse, ten miles west of Marion. "A white community. They clan together. That's what helps that little town to keep niggers from coming in and taking it over, and I appreciate that so much. My hometown. I love it." I had never heard Converse discussed as a Klan stronghold, but Dusty assured me that he had grown up there believing all whites were Klansmen. He wouldn't tell me whether "all" included his own parents, since they were still alive. But he did tell me this: he'd been taken along in the car once in the early 1960s when the Klan delivered a bundle of switches. He was five years old, and he never forgot the sticks tied together with a white rag labeled KKK and dropped on a farmhouse porch north of Converse. The white man living there "laid out drunk" and beat his family. Apparently he ignored the Klan's warning, because the next time they went to see him, young Dusty had to stay home. No doubt they administered the standard beating. All Dusty knows for sure is that this man "hasn't drank since." Dusty had been born in 1953 and said this stuck with him his whole life—that the Klan had its ways of correcting a situation.

And situations needed correcting right now. Things had gotten so bad that you couldn't even trust a white man anymore. But you could trust a Klansman. Now, sick to death of "how the white are being treated by the nigger," he believed in his heart that before the year 2000 the white race would wake up and unite as one. He just wished every white person would take the initiative to join the Klan. "I mean the ones that can qualify."

Kathleen arrived with groceries and a new coffeemaker. The two had been a couple for ten years but were not married. They were living on Dusty's disability checks.

Once the three of us sat down together, the lynching was almost the first thing that came up, though I did not ask about it. Dusty had told me at the cross-lighting that he knew of other Klansmen in Marion, but all they did was sit in the bars complaining.

So I began by saying, "You said you'd encountered other Klansmen around Marion, but they didn't seem to do much."

"You can hear anything in a tavern," said Dusty. "But I don't think there's anything been done since the niggers were hung back in the twenties or thirties."

"Just a lotta blow and no go," Kathleen agreed.

I asked if he thought the Klan did the lynching. "There was Klan there," said Dusty. "I've heard it ever since I was ten years old. As far as the Klan actually doing the lynching, I can't say that. I think it was a congregation of all types of white people."

He'd seen snapshots of the lynching as a kid—four different pictures showing the mob. They belonged to his cousin, who never said how he got them, and Dusty never knew if the cousin was Klan. But a neighbor, now dead, was a Klansman, and he used to tell Dusty stories about being down there in the jail that night. "He swore to be damned if he ever knew how he got in that jailhouse." The Klan neighbor had been out front, and the crowd pushed like a bulldozer. Whole cars were overturned. So the neighbor had been pushed right into the jail, where, he claimed, the bars came open without being unlocked.

"The nigger that did not get hung—he made national media," Dusty seethed. "This goddamn town give that nigger son-of-a-bitch the key to the city. By the mayor. Then told all the goddamn people to stay away from the Klan rally. See what I'm saying? It's not right! It's bullshit! It needs to be taken care of! That son of a bitch was down here and even held up a sign against the Klan!"

Apart from enraging him, incidents like this sent Dusty into despair. He just didn't know what to do. He wasn't sure if overthrowing the government was the answer. But he was so glad he'd joined an organization that was going to do *something*.

"Whatever it takes, I'm one of 'em," he declared. "I served in Vietnam, and my God, I come home to what? The Vietnamese were already here. You think that don't hurt?"

"Spitting on him, too," Kathleen added.

"Slant-eyed son-of-a-bitchin' gooks that you was paid a few bucks to kill and the son-of-a-bitches beat you back *home!*" he fumed.

Dusty had been a Navy SEAL. As he opened a second beer, he said,

"I come home to sadness, I come home to disappointment, I come home to depression." He had had five nervous breakdowns, beginning, he thought, in 1988. But he wouldn't blame that on the war.

Before the breakdowns began, he'd worked as a professional musician, a drummer with country-western bands. He'd even toured with Garth Brooks and Travis Tritt.

He felt that he'd just recently recovered from the last breakdown, which had happened during a show almost a year before we met. He'd been playing music with some people just for fun. "God is my witness," he said, "I stepped off that stage, and I collapsed. I went into—they said a frenzy, a-crying and shaking and blurred vision. I couldn't see. It hit me just that fast."

But no, he said, "I am not blaming 'Nam."

"I lived a war here in the states," Kathleen said enigmatically. I tried to get her more involved in the conversation. What war? She managed to indicate that she had had a hard life, offering some fragments. Had her first job at age six, taking care of a baby. Her dad rambled. She'd been to twenty-nine different schools by the time she reached high school at age sixteen. That was the year her mother died and her father abandoned the family, so she quit school to take care of a younger sister and brother. She'd grown up with the Klan and seen more than she was supposed to see. Her sister was a drug dealer and prostitute. Her brother had spent most of his life in prison. Her first husband had tried to kill her. She'd been "beat up, shot up, everything else." She changed the subject.

"The blacks are getting all the rights," she said, "and the white man is the minority now and no one is acknowledging it. Except the ones that feel it. That can get no help."

Dusty apologized for interrupting but was burning to reiterate his central point: Too many white people didn't care. And were afraid to stand up. And would not believe in "real truth and reality."

Kathleen added that while blacks had the NAACP and many other organizations, white people had nothing. Only the Klan. While foreigners came in and got welfare and small business loans—"without no questions asked. It's guaranteed to 'em"—white people were denied or made to wait for ten years.

"White people's toes are being stepped on, and if you don't know it, I don't know what kind of sheltered life you're leading," said Dusty.

They told me about a "colored man" from the neighborhood who'd been harassing Kathleen. He'd sit outside the bedroom window and drink. He'd bring four buddies with him. He'd ask other whites for money, and whites gave it to him. "That's how the whites are!" Dusty cried. "See what I'm saying?" He and Kathleen filed police reports. They got their landlord to talk to the man. Nothing worked. In the old days the Klan would have fixed it. But apparently there weren't many American Knights in the county. "Hell, by the time they'd get down here, we'd be laying here dead. Full of blood. I told Berry that. It's not his fault." Dusty had a gun "loaded and ready to go" but couldn't shoot the guy just for hanging around. They couldn't shoot him unless he actually broke in. They didn't know what to do.

They remembered times not long ago when a white person could be protected. Dusty was working on his fourth beer when he got to the story of the cross-burning in Gas City in the late 1980s. He'd been drumming with a band in a bar there, and some blacks started patronizing the place. "A nigger couple," he said. "Older couple."

"Sweet as a button," Kathleen added.

"They were," Dusty agreed. "But you got to understand, it's an all-white town. All-white bar. You have to understand. They come in two, three weeks, and pretty soon here come more niggers. These goddamn nigger bucks come in, and they was gonna overthrow everything."

So one night while Dusty was standing at the bar, he looked outside and saw fire. Rushing outside, he saw a burning cross stuck in a bucket of sand and three robed Klansmen down the street. The newspapers all claimed it was done by children. Kathleen said she knew it was going to happen, because she waitressed there and twenty-five Klan guys came in three nights in a row to check out the scene.

"How did you know they were Klansmen?" I asked.

"I don't know how to describe it," said Kathleen. "How they moved their eyes and watched, watched."

"You have your ways of knowing. As a white person," declared Dusty.

At least that was the Klan mystique. So after the cross-burning, the blacks never came back, but neither did the whites. The bar closed.

Kathleen brought me a tiny photo album. On the first page was a dog-eared photo of Dusty with Garth Brooks and Travis Tritt. They'd done twenty-six shows together.

Then Dusty began to talk about Charley Pride, the only African American star on the country music scene. Dusty had drummed for him. "People have asked me, knowing how I feel about niggers—he is a nigger. All right. But Charley. Charley is a white guy inside. You have to know him."

"He's a decent—" Kathleen began.

"Nigger," Dusty concluded.

"Person," she corrected him.

"Person," he said. "Black. I'll tell you how this guy was to me. And I'd love to have this in your book about Charley Pride."

Back in 1988 Dusty had played seventeen shows in five days with Charley Pride. Then one day the lead guitar player found Dusty between two beds upside down foaming at the mouth, and he ran to get Charley, who called Dusty's parents and got him to a hospital. This was Dusty's first nervous breakdown.

"He was with me at the hospital," said Dusty. "I was out completely. He canceled seven shows in Florida to be with me. Now hear me out. He flew with me. Paid everything. Paid the flight. Met Mom and Dad down here at the airport at Indianapolis. Got in their van. And went with me. Took me to the hospital in Fort Wayne. I was still unconscious. They couldn't get me to come out of it. Couldn't get me to come to myself. He waited. He exhausted his seven days, and he cried and he couldn't wait no longer. He had to go on back because of his tour. Which is understandable. That man waited. He paid. He paid for my mom and dad. All expenses. Turned around, and he had a line open with my mom and dad at their house. Paid for it. Him and them. My mom will tell you. That man called. I'm telling you. This is how much. For a black man. You hear me speaking."

"He's a black man," said Kathleen.

"Right there is a fine example," said Dusty.

"He's a good man," said Kathleen.

"And that man has called and called when I didn't even know it," said Dusty. "Asked about me and wanted me to come back and play."

"Or just ask about you," said Kathleen.

"So maybe that will give you a little insight," Dusty concluded. "Yeah, we're racist. Right. Wrong. Wrong. We're not. We're not." He got up from the table and walked into the tiny hallway for a minute or two. He looked like he was about to cry.

Then he returned to the kitchen table, sat down, gathered himself, and gritted his teeth as he declared: "We're tired of their shit. That are niggers. Against us whites."

As he opened his fifth beer, he told me about the rage he felt seeing his nephew wear a T-shirt featuring "that goddamn no-good-for-nothing nigger that plays basketball. Name's Jordan." Sadly he concluded that "the kids of today are patronizing the nigger," and his nephew "actually thinks the nigger's better than the white."

Dusty had a fantasy of sending everyone back. "The niggers and blacks to Africa. The Catholics to Rome. The Jews to Jerusalem."

"We could be more sympathetic if they were in their own land," Kathleen agreed.

They both firmly believed in a future apocalyptic war between blacks and whites. As Kathleen, put it, "There's a day coming that you're gonna wish you were white or hope you were white. Or are white."

"A revolution?" I asked.

"Oh, yeah," she said. "Just like the North and the South."

"I don't know what it's gonna be called," Dusty said. "It'll be a sad bloody situation." It would be nationwide. And the government would go down. But the whites, of course, would win this war, and the blacks would be annihilated.

"What about Charley Pride?" I asked. "What will happen to people like Charley Pride when this war happens?"

Dusty seemed momentarily taken aback. "I'm not educated enough to know that yet," he finally said. He suggested that I ask "Mr. Berry or Mr. Stubbs," because they would know what to do. He had great confidence in the two Wizards. "What they tell you, you can take it to the bank." But he was pretty sure that if Charley Pride "sticks up for the nigger people, he'll go down with the nigger people. I hate to say that about him, but that's the way I see it."

ALL THROUGH THE INTERVIEW Dusty confronted me with pointed questions: "Do you agree with the Klan ways?" "Are you tired of being the minority as a white?" "Are you sad when you walk down the street? Are you sad about nigger and white together?" "Do you support our cause?"

I managed to sidestep, but I probably managed only because he was drinking. And it was easy to turn him back to his own concerns. He had so many.

I thought the interview was over, but as Dusty opened beer number six, we were just getting to the good part. Dusty confessed that he had spent last summer in jail for back child support. Kathleen said her ex was trying to get $75 a week in child support from her, and she didn't even clear that in wages. So she'd done some jail time, too, and she hadn't seen her kids in three years. She was the one who'd filed for divorce after her husband put a nine-millimeter to her forehead and threatened to kill her. "I left my house running. My kids didn't even have shoes.

"The judicial system ain't worth a fuck," she concluded.

"It's true," said Dusty. "Sorry about the language, but I'm telling you. We've lived it. We know. I know damn good and well that we're trying to get supported through the Klan. I guarantee you I will take up arms with the Klan in a goddamn minute. In just a minute. And will die a Klansman." He let out a sigh. "I just don't have nowhere else to turn."

Again I thought the interview was over, and I put the tape recorder into my bag. They both wrote down their post office box numbers in my notebook, as Kathleen began to talk about her father. Suddenly she was spilling everything she'd been holding back. I got the tape back out and asked her to start over.

Her dad was high up in the Elwood Klan, she told me. One night she saw him nearly burned at the stake by his klavern. The dad had been horribly abusive to the family and was turned in by his own brother, Kathleen's uncle, also a Klansman. The uncle wanted her to witness the dad's punishment, so he instructed her to hide in the car, in the backseat on the floor. Her father never knew she was there, and he thought they were headed for a regular meeting when her uncle took the wheel. Instead he drove them to a wooded area in the country, and there the klavern confronted him.

"He was told that night when my uncle delivered him that he was not to hurt his family any longer. That he had went against the Ten Commandments. That he had went against anything the Klan believed in. But because of what he had done for the Klan, upholding these Ten Commandments for—fifteen years that I know of—he was gonna get off easy. They were just gonna whup him. But they had pinned him to a cross that they was going to burn. But they told him that they would just whup him and he better never ever do it again. Or he would get burned."

Crouching in the backseat of the car, Kathleen had watched as thirty-five to forty robed and hooded Klansmen beat her father with sticks.

"He blamed my mother for it," said Kathleen. "He thought she turned him in." According to Kathleen, he then killed her mother, though the doctor called it "heart failure."

"How did you know he killed her?" I asked.

"I was in the closet, and I heard the nightmare. I held her as she died." Tears welled up in Kathleen's eyes. "He wanted her dead." The father refused to call an ambulance for forty-five minutes. Kathleen finally made the call.

She did not know her father's Klan title, just that he was second in command. The "rambling man" had rambled for the Klan all over the country. "A mobile hurt man," Kathleen said.

"A hitman," Dusty corrected her.

A horror. One of the crimes his klavern confronted him with was his attempt to sell Kathleen. She said that when she was ten years old, her dad needed $10,000 to pay somebody off. He found a childless couple who wanted her. He started taking her to their house every day, to get her used to the idea, and they gave her dolls and pretty dresses and "food like I never had before." Finally he signed the contract, which gave him three days to renege on the deal. On the third day he came to say good-bye. "I wouldn't let him go," Kathleen recalled. "And I was still in my raggy old dress and stuff. My mama tried to do best, but Daddy always stole her money and got drunk, so I had tears rolling down my cheeks and I told him bye. I made him feel so damn guilty, he took me with him. And for a month after that my mother screamed my name every time I was out of her sight. She screamed bloody murder. She thought I was actually kidnapped and I never told her. Till the day she died, I never told her that Daddy tried to sell me."

Kathleen saved the most sordid story for last. When she was six, her father gave her to a man who used her sexually. In fact, the father handed her over repeatedly for a period of two years. "Me and my sister. He had sold my mother to the same guy. Because he wanted his business. So he blackmailed this guy, and he knew he had a weakness for kids. And women." Kathleen laughed. "But see, the Klan never knew all this." She was sure they would have stopped it if they'd known.

The father had just been so charismatic and charming. Big Bob, people called him. Few outside the family ever knew what a monster he was.

Dusty opened his seventh beer. He'd even known Big Bob, back when Bob gave parties that went on for days, and Dusty was a teenager who came to play drums till his hands blistered. Bob had authority, Dusty recalled. "There was a lamb there, but also a lion in his eyes. Whatever he said, it went."

"Through the whole county," Kathleen added. "The police or anything else never bothered him because they knew better."

"That's right," Dusty concurred. "And hell, they come to his door, and he'd run 'em off. I seen that happen."

Obviously neither Kathleen nor Dusty saw any contradiction in following in the dad's footsteps by becoming Klan members.

"You don't think of him as an example of a Klansman?" I asked.

"No way, shape, or form," Dusty asserted. "You can ask Mr. Berry or Mr. Stubbs, either one. You don't lay a hand on your people!"

They were almost giddy by the time I left, as might be expected from people who've perhaps unexpectedly bared their souls and want to feel good about it. Kathleen revealed that she had never told her story before to anyone but Dusty. I thanked her for telling it to me. The pseudonym, Kathleen, was her mother's name.

As I drove away, Dusty stood in the front door, waving good-bye. I was in my usual post-Kluxer state of complete disorientation, induced by hours spent with the irrational. These were people, for example, insulted by the label "racist," yet—Charley Pride aside—they expressed deep revulsion for black people. Racism gave them scapegoats and a way to understand their lives. They were the most anguished Kluxers I would meet, and among the most downtrodden. I had looked at their meager possessions, the rusted husk they drove, the house a big bad wolf could blow down, and wondered how they would ever afford to buy robes and hoods. They had little to hold on to but their whiteness. These were failed, damaged people, and joining the Klan was how they made themselves feel better, and it was deeply sad.

EIGHTEEN

GOD FORGIVES/
THE BROTHERHOOD DOESN'T

Wizard Jeff Berry invited me to a Klan social, scheduled for Saturday, February 17, 1996, at his house. I would have to show up sometime between the top-secret officers' meeting in the afternoon and the top-secret naturalization ceremony in the evening.

The Wizard's place was an hour and a half from Marion on a good day, and the weather that weekend was terrible. I passed wrecks all over the interstate yet drove doggedly on. I couldn't take "access" for granted, and getting to know Klansmen was the only way I had to determine the group's popularity in Grant County. Then, hard as it was for me to feel comfortable schmoozing with Kluxers, curiosity got the better of me every time. And as it turned out, this day did mark the beginning of a certain unlikely narrative.

As I pulled into Jeff's driveway, two carloads of young white men piled out right next to me. New recruits, I figured. Skinhead types, late teens or early twenties, they stared at me wordlessly before striding into the noisy crowded garage, party central.

I found the Wizard in his kitchen, gathering up chips and salad to take outside. In the garage, Dusty and Kathleen, the new members from Marion, greeted me with great warmth. Across the room Brad Thompson—"the Catholic," as he'd been introduced last time—was shouting something about the Grand Dragon over a pounding Stones track. I noticed that Dragon Rick was not present. Nor was young Hitler.

Rodney Stubbs, the other Wizard, wanted me to meet his wife, Jeanette. Stubbs was the big guy who had said to me so memorably at the cross-lighting, "Prove to me Jesus was a Jew!" I remembered Jeanette from the Marion rally: the chaplain who'd prayed that God would open our hearts to the Klan's message. She had since become Grand Dragon of the women's group. She told me she'd been anti-Klan herself once, and she'd married Rodney without knowing his long history with the Hooded Order.

Rodney piped in: "She said, 'If you ever do join the Klan, I'll tell you one thing. There won't be no Klan meetings in our garage.'"

I figured her conversion had become one of the amusing stories they now told as a couple. Jeanette picked up the thread: "He said, 'Well, meet the people,' and it just changed my mind totally. I thought it was going to be a bunch of hoods and thugs, but they were nice decent people. Good Christian morals and values." Women joined after every rally, she said. Sometimes they joined first and their husbands afterward.

"We don't believe in the husbands beating up their wives, or going to the bar and drinking up the paycheck," Jeanette explained. "We protect our Klanswomen so they don't get abused." It was striking how close this was to what Kathleen had told me. As if women mainly joined the Klan for protection. From their white husbands.

I asked Jeanette if she hadn't also joined to get behind white supremacy. Surely she must agree with it.

"I believe in equal rights, not special rights," she replied, but race seemed an issue with which she was less viscerally connected. Instead, Jeanette talked about her earlier relationships with men who beat her. She herself had proposed marriage to Rodney, who was as big and round as she was petite and angular, and he'd always been good to her.

When I said hello to "the Catholic," Brad Thompson, he asked, "Did you hear what happened? I'm the Grand Dragon of Indiana!" He'd been promoted that very day, at the officers' meeting. When I asked what had happened to Dragon Rick, he motioned the Wizard over.

"Rick wasn't doing his job," Jeff explained. "He don't have time to do his duties."

As I began a conversation with Jeff, he then delivered a stunning piece of news. Larry Hitler was out of the Klan. "Put this in your book," the Wizard directed. "Larry is banished from any Klan organization in the United States." I'd last seen Larry on January 23, at court, when he told me he was changing his pseudonym to Hitt. He'd been banished on February 7. For the true Kluxer—and Larry appeared to be one—this was the worst punishment imaginable. What crime, what betrayal, what ideological dust-up could have provoked such a thing?

Larry had stolen the beer money.

That's what the Wizard said, explaining that they passed the hat one night, and Larry pocketed the cash. Also took some money off the Berrys' kitchen table. And "he broke the oath of secrecy and told other Klans our stuff," said Jeff, "like how we're getting so many members."

Larry was back with his mother, living in a Fort Wayne housing project. "She used to be in the Klan," I told him.

"No, she wasn't," said the Wizard. "His mother is a habituous liar just like Larry. That's all she is. Says she used to be in the army. Used to be a police officer. Used to be this, be that. She is a bigger liar than he is, and I don't say nothing about nobody unless I check it out."

The Wizard told me that Larry even got out the picture of John Howard one day and claimed to his fellow Klansmen that this was his grandfather. Of course, a couple of the Kluxers immediately recognized who it really was.

"He lies so much he believes his own lies," said Jeff.

I was still thinking about Larry as I drifted back to the elated new Dragon. After his election that afternoon, he'd driven the ten miles home to Auburn, whooping and shooting his pistol out the window. He'd told his wife that now he was "really somebody." Brad Thompson was the first Catholic Dragon, so far as he knew. He'd read a lot of Klan history and felt that now he was on a par with his idol, D. C. Stephenson, the 1920s Grand Dragon who used to declare, "I am the law in Indiana," before the authorities carted him off to prison for the murder of Madge Oberholzer. Brad believed that the murder rap was a setup.

"I guess I was born a racist," he shrugged. He came from a small town in Ohio and had no Klan in his family, but when he encountered the KKK in books during high school, he remembered thinking, *That's for me.* Now he was thirty-six years old. In his euphoria Brad rushed from one topic to the next, segueing from the evils of Reconstruction to the gall displayed by the Fort Wayne officials who actually wanted to bill the American Knights for rally expenses. "We could have furnished our own security. I got mine right here," he said, opening his denim jacket to show me a nine-millimeter handgun in a shoulder holster. "When they made me give up my gun, it became their responsibility to protect me."

"Why do you carry a gun?" I asked him.

"It's just my constitutional right." He wore a tiny gold pistol as an earring.

The young Kluxer who'd talked about "wasting queers" at the last gathering kept hovering, wanting to talk. He turned out to be Rodney Stubbs, Jr., much like his dad in both his bulk and his beliefs.

"I love people like this," the new Dragon said, clapping young Stubbs on the shoulder. "My main thing is, I want to educate people. About how white people are losing their rights in America. Affirmative action. HUD subsidy housing. Gun control."

Young Rodney told me he was running one klavern so secret that the members didn't even know one another's identities. They all wore robes and hoods to meetings and went by fake names. He said it was public knowledge that 40 percent of the police officers in his county were Kluxers. He'd joined at fifteen and now he was a twenty-one-year-old Exalted Cyclops.

So both Wizards had a Cyclops for a son. I began to wonder if I was truly just seeing a tip of some iceberg, as they liked to suggest. Or if the group was really incredibly small, given that all the state and national officers seemed to live within a county or two of Fort Wayne.

For the first time I noticed a skeleton painted black, hanging from a rafter by a noose. On the two parts of the pelvis someone had written in silver, "KKK was here." On its forehead were the words "I love the Klan." Squealing children chased each other around the garage.

Dragon Brad had moved to the corner, where he was holding forth in front of the young skinheads. I tried to eavesdrop, but they were so close to the stereo—the Stones, "You Can't Always Get What You Want"—that I caught just a couple of lines: "to guard against what happened back in the sixties with Martin Luther King" and "we need to be under one flag." I made note of a paddle on a bench, with the words "God Forgives/The Brotherhood Doesn't." Near it was a paper I tried very hard to read. I got down the words "Look to the Heavens and Rejoice/Wash Your Flesh with the Blood of Christ/Praise YWHY . . ." when a husky Kluxer named Grizzly Smith saw me and snatched the paper away. In the part I hadn't gotten to, there was something about "Our Race Is Revived."

When Brad finished with the young guys, I asked him who they were.

"These are Aryan Nation, these gentlemen. My job is to try to sway them our way."

"What's the difference between Aryan Nations and the Klan?"

"Hitler is their savior and our savior is Jesus Christ," he said. "You won't find no swastika on *my* members. If there is, it's because they had it tattooed from a previous membership, and there's nothing they can do about it. One time we had a naturalization out here, and we made several members throw their swastika emblems away. Rip 'em off their coats and throw them in. And that was my idea. The paddle over here was my idea, too. See that paddle? Back in the old days they flogged 'em. That's for our own membership. If a white woman's living with a black man two miles from here, we're not gonna flog him or flog her. That's not what we're gonna do. But if one of our members is a dissident or an infiltrator or if he goofs up, he's gonna get paddled."

Suddenly the music shut off, and Jeff Berry told everyone planning to get naturalized to raise their hands. I counted nine or ten. One of the children volunteered, too.

"I have a little two-and-a-half-year-old that knows 'White Power,'" Brad told me proudly. Then he left the garage to put on his robe. I didn't know it yet, but his was the story I would be following over the next couple of years.

AT THE TIME, THOUGH, I was focused on Larry Hitler. I had to find him, if only to fill in all the things I failed to find out during that first interview, on the day that he'd chased his brother around the backyard with an ax. I didn't even know how old he was. By the time I tracked him down later that week in Fort Wayne, he was at war with the Berrys.

The newest Hitler residence was in a low-rise housing project—two-story townhouses painted a drab brown, with no trees, no decor, no difference from one courtyard to the next or one dwelling to the next. Each courtyard surrounded a big parking lot.

Though I hadn't called to say I was coming, Larry did not look surprised to see me. He was shirtless and wearing red swimming trunks. I'd interrupted a conversation he was having at the kitchen table with a man who turned out to be a state police investigator. Within minutes the investigator left, and Larry informed me that he'd *quit* the Klan. He had *not* been banished. "Why am I going to remain in an organization that's going to constantly stress me out, assault me, the whole nine yards."

"They assaulted you?"

"Choked me. Jeff did," said Larry. "I've got it in the paper." He showed me a story in the previous day's *Fort Wayne Journal-Gazette:* ARMS REPORTED SEIZED AT KLAN LEADER'S HOME.

Larry was pressing charges against both the Wizard and the Cyclops. Three days after the party I attended in their garage, Jeff Berry had been arrested for misdemeanor battery and Tony Berry for criminal recklessness, a felony. According to the *Journal-Gazette* piece, Jeff hit Larry while Tony threatened him with a rifle. Authorities also searched the Berry home for automatic weapons and explosives.

So Larry had opened the door for the state to get the Wizard, an amusing development for sure and a surprising one. Larry seemed so invested in his Klan membership, his identity completely entwined or propped up by his notions of white supremacy. Being in a group helped hold it all together, so surely he would try to join another, banishment or not.

But Larry assured me, "I'm going to be out of the Klan, period. I'm just tired of it." Of course, he also claimed that he'd talked to his uncles in Alabama, that they happened to be the Wizard, the Dragon, and the Imperial Nighthawk for the Royal Knights of the Ku Klux Klan, and that they were, in addition, an ex–Green Beret, an ex–Navy SEAL, and an ex–Army Ranger. And they were "very very pissed off."

I was back in familiar terrain with Larry. Fantasyland. One of the first things he wanted me to know was that he'd called David Duke, and they'd had a long conversation about Jeff Berry. That sounded even less plausible than those uncles with their impeccable macho credentials. So I had little reason to believe Larry's claim that the Wizard himself had been banished. Eventually, however, I learned that this was true. (The Liberty Knights had banished Berry "for being a snitch" in 1994, just before he started the American Knights. But Larry must have been spinning his wheels here. At this point, his own officers did not know Berry had been banished.)

Larry was telling me about his own prison term for "serious bodily harm injury to the Marion police department" when a young black woman walked in from outside, disappearing into the living room. She clearly felt at home, and Larry ignored her. He went on talking about his arrest in Marion, how he broke his handcuffs and used them as a weapon, then started "using my martial arts. I put six police officers into the hospital."

I wondered what kind of witness Larry would make for the state.

Larry's mother appeared in the kitchen and declared, "Jeff treated my son dirty. That's not like the Klan."

"She's from the old school," Larry commented.

He was obviously tense. He got up and looked out the window every time a car drove into the courtyard. Kluxers had been nightriding through the projects for days, usually showing up around midnight or one in the morning in four or five cars. Apparently they just drove around yelling and never got out of their vehicles. "Called me every fucking name in the book,"

Larry said. The new Dragon, Brad Thompson, later confirmed that the nightriding occurred, but he didn't say who participated.

To further complicate matters, Larry and family had again lost their phone service. When the nightriders came now, he had to "fly out the front door" and run to a neighbor's house to call the police. I thought it possible that Larry and family were the only white people living in this particular court. At least they were the only ones I saw. On Sunday Larry had actually gone from door to door, telling his neighbors that the Klan was after him. As he put it, "I done told all these colored people around here about the situation, and they are well armed. Every last one of 'em." I rather relished the idea that the Ku Klux Klan was riding into this courtyard at night to terrorize the one white family.

"Kind of ironic," I said. "You getting protection from black people."

"My protection is coming from the militia," Larry bristled. Soon he would be moving to "another location," and the militia would do surveillance on his house. Specifically the Wolverines, the Renegades, and the Warriors, the toughest of the tough. Of course, they didn't seem to be around now when he needed them. I noticed that police cars were driving by every half hour.

"Jeff told me you took some money."

"No, that's a lie. I didn't steal nothing. All I had on me was *my* money. Which was four dollars."

He launched into a long detailed story about what, supposedly, had happened. I won't repeat what seems unlikely to be true, but what stood out was his claim that he went to the DeKalb County prosecutor only because the Berrys threatened his brother. Larry was a walking contradiction: a hardcore racist who put his brother above the Klan. His brother who associated mostly with black people.

The young black woman came back into the kitchen and stood right behind Larry's chair as he complained about having to give his robe back. Again Larry ignored her. The American Knights charged $85 and up for a robe and hadn't even reimbursed him.

Suddenly his brother Bobby burst in through the kitchen door, waving that day's *Journal-Gazette,* announcing breathlessly, "They found dope in Jeff's house! Dope! Marijuana!"

"I told y'all," said Larry's mother.

"Oh my fucking god!" Larry yelled. He took the paper and painstakingly began to read the article out loud. It seemed that while searching the

Berry place the day the Wizard and the Cyclops were arrested, police found a marijuana pipe with possible drug residue, and a rifle they thought might have been modified into an automatic weapon. Converting a rifle to fully automatic was illegal. As a convicted felon, Jeff Berry could not legally own or carry a firearm. No doubt that gun and the others—two twelve-gauge shotguns, the handguns of .357 and .22 calibers, and a second rifle—were registered with the other Berrys. The Wizard denied that the marijuana pipe was his, and no new charges had been filed.

But Larry announced, "His ass is history."

"I guess I still got the narcotic pop in me," the mother boasted, turning to me to ask, "Did you know I was a detective?"

I didn't. So she informed me that she'd once been part of the Dade County (Florida) sheriff's department, and that she had the ability to walk into a room and sense the presence of drugs. This seemed about as likely as Larry's claim that day that he'd been contacted by Paramount Pictures and offered a job as a consultant on a Klan movie.

The mother made her way back into the living room, where she sat watching two different shows on two televisions. I stayed in the kitchen with Larry as he wondered again and again how Jeff could banish him when Jeff had been banished himself. "He has no authority to operate an organization. Don't quote me wrong. I do like Jeff. Don't quote me wrong." On he went, laying out all his contradictory feelings about the Wizard. For example, Jeff was "doing a fine job," but "he only uses seven ranks."

"What happened to the Klexter, the Klargo, the Klabee, and the Klagripp? The Kleagle? The Imperial Kleever?" groused the ex-member. "What happened to all those? If you don't have a Klexter and Klargo, you don't have an organization. If you don't have a Kleagle, you definitely don't have an organization. And if you don't have a Klagraff, you're shit out of luck."

Larry said he still supported the Klan 110 percent. "But the thing is, I can't find no organization that I can feel at home."

As for that big question I had about Larry's age (later corroborated by court documents): the day we met in Marion I'd judged him to be pushing thirty. In fact, he'd been twenty-one. By the time we spoke in Fort Wayne, he was twenty-two.

TEN DAYS LATER, on March 4, Larry Hitler reported to Jeff Berry's lawyer and signed an affidavit stating that the police had coerced him into providing false information against the Berrys. He was dropping all charges. Certain Kluxers hinted later that some coercion *had* taken place, but it came from the Klan, not the police. I could never confirm this, but what an irony if Larry had actually been telling the truth about the Berrys. Meanwhile the Wizard and the Cyclops had been arrested again on March 18—Jeff Berry pleading not guilty to receiving stolen property and false informing, Tony Berry pleading not guilty to criminal mischief. All the new charges were part of the Larry mess, the Wizard informed me in a terse telephone conversation. The motions for dismissal were already filed.

I'd left Indiana for the month of March, and by the time I got back, Larry was unreachable again. Originally I'd found him at the housing project by going to his old Marion neighborhood and looking for friends of the Hitler family. I got lucky, but now the friends were gone, too. Poor people lead unstable lives.

Then one day in June I again encountered those friends near the old Hitler residence in Marion. They would not give me a phone number for Larry but invited me into a living room decorated with a large Confederate flag, dialed the phone, and handed it to me. On the other end was Larry, telling me that now he talked to the Wizard almost every day. They were buddies again. He'd dropped his charges because "a lot of the shit that was said was false. I'm not going to testify on something that's false."

What could I do? Roll my eyes. Larry announced that he and the Wizard were both going to file lawsuits against the state now. "It's lawsuit city." And that was my last contact with Larry Hitler.

Eventually I found his records at the Grant County courthouse. Larry had been arrested for stealing to stoke his fantasy life. He had managed to lie his way inside the Marion Martial Arts Academy on January 28, 1991, shortly after his seventeenth birthday. He convinced the owner of the building that he was part owner of the academy and borrowed tools from him to pry open the lock. Among the items stolen: a black belt, many lesser belts, gi's, and a Japanese sword.

Larry pleaded guilty to burglary, receiving a four-year suspended sentence. He went on probation. That was revoked in 1992, after he was picked up for disorderly conduct, resisting arrest, and battery—the latter directed at one Marion police officer, not six. He went to jail.

Another court document stated that there had been both "numerous domestic disputes" and four suicide attempts in which the Marion police got involved. "Following one of the suicide attempts, the defendant had to be removed from the emergency room after a disturbance with the attending doctor." After the last suicide attempt, he went to a mental health facility for evaluation. A doctor there concluded that Larry "can distinguish the difference between right and wrong, reality and fantasy—he just does not choose to do so."

PART IV

"Truth Does Not Bring Back the Dead but Releases Them from Silence"

NINETEEN

THE RECONCILERS

During the year I lived in Marion I read a lot of James Baldwin, and I thought about that vision of racial reconciliation at the end of *The Fire Next Time:* "If we—and now I mean the relatively conscious whites and the relatively conscious blacks, who must, like lovers, insist on, or create, the consciousness of the others—do not falter in our duty now, we may be able, handful that we are, to end the racial nightmare, and achieve our country, and change the history of the world."

I even thought it could come to pass in Marion, Indiana, where something so terrible had happened. Those who fall farthest from the right course get a chance to take the biggest step. Of course, no one in Marion or anywhere else knew how to make that leap.

So it seemed that the work of reconciliation was always beginning.

In Marion the first attempt came with Breaking Barriers, the short-lived group set up in the 1960s to get blacks and whites talking. MARION BLACK, WHITE DIALOGUE SUCCESSFUL, announced the *Chronicle-Tribune* on November 8, 1968—after the groups had been meeting for six weeks. Always the hope that it would be easy. Exactly one week later came the "riot" at the high school.

Apparently the discussions tailed off during that time of great tension,

299

since the newspaper carried a notice in February 1969 that Breaking Barriers was about to resume. (The firebombings started four months later.) None of the participants I spoke to remembered these discussions lasting for more than a year all together. At the most.

Shirley Barbour, an African American who'd served several terms on the Marion City Council, recalled one white woman coming to her house for a Barriers meeting, a woman who was not racist but who seemed shocked that Barbour lived in a nice place, in a nice neighborhood. Barbour didn't want to mention the woman's name and cause her embarrassment. No doubt it was just one of many awkward moments. As Barbour summarized it, "Some of the white individuals were uncomfortable in our homes. And they felt uncomfortable having us in theirs."

Reece Baird, a white woman, told me that before she got into Breaking Barriers, she had simply not been aware of the hardships black people faced. She had not been aware of the cultural differences. Raised a Mormon in Utah ("both my grandfathers had three wives"), Baird had never even seen a black person, except for one porter on a train, till high school, where there was one African American in a student body of eighteen hundred. Yet Baird emerged from this background with an open mind, curious about difference, not threatened by it. She'd long ago left Mormonism for Unitarianism. Her late husband, Verne Baird, served as president of the Marion Urban League at some point in the 1970s.

It seemed to me that these first meetings of the town's relatively conscious whites and relatively conscious blacks *had* done some good, though the work barely began before Breaking Barriers collapsed. Maybe things were just too hot in the 1960s. Maybe white ignorance and black rage made for too volatile a mix. Ex-Panther Marcus Cannon mentioned that he had also participated in "that Breaking Barriers mess." He chuckled as he recalled the atmosphere in his particular group: "It was just so hostile. It was a time for these young blacks to take out all their anger on these white people: 'You did this and you did that.' You had to be strong to hang in there."

Several decades of silence followed. Then during the 1990s an impulse began growing in fits and starts to try exorcising what haunted the town.

I INCLUDED MYSELF among the "relatively conscious," the white people who at least meant well, who did not want to be racist. But I often just felt inadequate. What exactly could one do? I thought of how the James Baldwin quote continued: "If we do not now dare everything, the fulfillment of that prophecy, re-created from the Bible in song by a slave is upon us: *God gave Noah the rainbow sign, No more water, the fire next time!*" Of course, that prophecy had already been fulfilled in Marion and other cities. The fire had come. It could again. We hadn't yet dared everything. We didn't know how.

A couple of weeks before the Marion Klan rally, a white woman named Linda Mui invited me to attend what she called a healing racism institute at the local Y, stipulating that I had to come as myself, not as a journalist, and could not write about what occurred. So I can only say that when I got to that first meeting, in a bare room just big enough for a long table surrounded by folding chairs, I saw that Linda had Xeroxed a pile of material for us and had written out an agenda neatly labeled "Institute for the Healing of Racism, Grant County, Indiana," and that there were three of us in attendance—me, Linda, and one other white woman. It was a start. Again.

These meetings of what came to be called the Race Healing Circle went on for about a year, always organized by Mui, most often attended by her, myself, and one or two other black or white women. (Mui had never intended it to be a women's group, but that's who showed up. I suspected that it had to do with the word *healing*.) During the fourteen months that I lived in Marion, Linda Mui did as much as anyone I encountered to address the race issue. When we first met in August 1995, she told me about working with members of the Black History Council to plan a Race Unity Day at the library earlier that summer. She mentioned in passing that she'd had enough threatening phone calls from other white people then to unlist her phone number.

Mui came from Washington County in the southern part of the state, a county singled out by *The Negro in Indiana Before 1900* for its particularly virulent racism after the Civil War. Washington County's white population made it clear back then that blacks were not just unwelcome but in danger. For example, one old black man was murdered when he persisted in attending a white church. Eventually such ugliness drove out every black resident, and a 1916 Washington County history "boasted that no colored man or woman lived within her borders." So Linda Mui grew up on a farm in a part of the state that still had just a handful of African Americans at the end of the twentieth century.

I already knew that family, geography, local history, and the lack of exposure to people who were different *could* influence someone's racial politics. Or not. Nothing about racism was easy or predictable. The white sheriff in Anderson so revered by James Cameron—he'd come from Elwood.

Linda Mui found that encountering other cultures opened her mind.

When she went off to college for an education degree, she deliberately chose an integrated school, then interned in Indianapolis with the Urban Student Teaching Project to prepare herself to teach in one. There she also became aware of "the need for white people to educate themselves." The Marion schools recruited her right out of college. Eventually she married the owner of a local Chinese restaurant, Ming Mui, and they had three children. She also converted to the Bahai faith, which extols racial equality as a core belief.

We didn't get around to an official interview till nearly a year after that first meeting at the Y, at a point when the "healing circle" was in transition to a "study circle." Mui had called in the Indiana Interreligious Commission on Human Equality for help setting it up. She thought community leaders would have to get involved at this point or it would never work, "and I don't know if that will ever happen. It discourages me that it looks like race is a political issue. It just shouldn't be."

It was practically the first thing she said when she arrived for our talk, that she was discouraged about this topic. "I call it bummed out. Like you can't have an effect, so why try?" But then she speculated that maybe it wasn't important to deal with racial issues directly. Maybe indirectly was okay. Maybe it just had to be done on a personal level, through friendship.

When I asked her how she felt about the low attendance at the healing circles, she insisted that she had never had expectations. She had wanted to do the group for herself, to learn to talk openly about race and "now I can do it in a nonconfrontational way. If you can't talk, how can it get better? It was helpful to me."

I observed that there didn't seem to be that many white people in Marion who were as committed as she was, but she said maybe others were working in subtler ways. "We talk about celebrating our diversity, and I guess I appreciate the diverse ways people look at racism. Any way people want to work on it is okay." Mui just couldn't speak ill. She also seemed worried that I would emphasize the negative and put Marion in a bad light.

"I think Marion's like a little microcosm of the United States," she declared. "But I think because we had that specific history of the lynching, we also have a specific opportunity to make a statement that could have nationwide impact. You know, race issues are so hard to talk about because they're so nebulous and—boy, that wasn't nebulous at all. That happened. It's part of our history here. So I think just facing that history, not denying it and not glorifying it or overdramatizing it and making it bigger than it was—I mean, it *was* very big. But it's not the only thing that shaped this town." Mui had no idea how the town should address it but said wistfully, "It would be so neat if Marion could be an example of a small town that came together."

MUCH OF THE RACIAL RECONCILIATION work was going on in the churches. That seemed right in a county that had one multiplex and about ninety churches by the beginning of the twenty-first century. It seemed appropriate for an activity that might require confessing and forgiving. And as a number of people pointed out to me, the hour of worship on Sunday morning was still the most segregated of the week. I also felt that hating and fearing and, in other ways, objectifying black people for so many years had created, for white people, a serious spiritual problem. And this was true no matter what religion one practiced or whether one had a religion at all.

The two ministers who got the most press in Marion for working on racial harmony were Reverend J. D. Williams and Reverend Tim Helm. Williams pastored at the all-black Greater Second Baptist right in the heart of town, across the street from the high school. Helm's all-white Hanfield United Methodist lay about five miles north of Marion. While they may have been the first in the area to come up with the idea of joint church services, I figured what also made the effort so newsworthy was Williams's history.

Born in Georgia, Williams came to Marion in 1963 after twenty years in the air force, and he immediately became an activist. "Up until 1994, I had assumed the role of the civil rights leader in the city of Marion," he told me one afternoon at the church office. "I was the advocate for blacks whenever there was injustice." Twice during the 1960s he ran for city councilman at large, mostly because no African American had ever won a major political office in the county. (He lost.) A *Chronicle-Tribune* article from 1973 described his nightly drives through the volatile neighborhood around 18th and Meridian, where he tried to calm racial tensions. He criticized the police for their brutality, but he also criticized the young blacks who threw firebombs. "One of the problems in Marion," he told the newspaper back then, "is that we're unable to get a united front of black adults. We never have been able to. The older blacks in Marion still remember August of 1930. We're not going to get black people together until they forget about that tree on the square."

When I spoke to him some twenty-three years later, Williams observed that the lynching had affected *all* the old families in the town, both black and white. The Marion-ites, he called them. The blacks among them became passive after the lynching and adapted to whatever was going on, while the whites accepted the status quo, never trying to improve it. "Anyone that interfered with that was called an outsider," he concluded. He felt that when he moved in and almost immediately ran for the city council, the insiders would not support him. "You look at the things being done to improve the city of Marion, and I think you'll find in most cases, they come from the outside."

He thought the whole town needed to accept the fact that the lynching did take place.

And what do we do to move on? I asked.

"Listen to the story. Whites never fully understand what blacks are going through." And he meant the story beginning way before August 1930, "the climate that led to it."

Williams said his own attitude about race relations changed in 1994 after attending Marion's yearly evangelism crusade. According to Williams, the white evangelist Steve Wingfield had preached for nine straight nights that if Grant County was ever going to be won to Christ, the believers would have to come together. Across racial lines. Across denominational lines. Williams decided that he had been "alienating folk rather than pulling them together." He resolved then and there to change his style. "My ministry was directed to blacks, meeting their needs. Now I had to come up with a ministry that would meet the needs of people regardless of their race, color, or creed." Williams met Tim Helm during that crusade, Encounter 94, and suggested to him, "We need to do something to keep this spirit going."

What the two churches were trying was revolutionary and unprecedented in the county's history, but it also seemed a very small wave against history's tide. In 1995 these churches had two joint services. Period. Still, it was a start, and in the late 1990s this effort reached more people than any other program set up to combat racism in Grant County. Hundreds attended the services. That year Greater Second Baptist also sponsored a week of revival meetings around the theme of "unity." Reverend Williams invited other churches and ended up enlisting eight—six of them white. That signified. Older citizens might remember that Greater Second Baptist was the church where disgruntled black students from Marion High School came for some kind of comfort after the "riot," and now it had a sign out front that said EXPE-RIENCE THE DIFFERENCE, with a picture of a black hand shaking a white hand.

It was not unusual, however, for black people to extend a hand. As the minority, it behooved them to try, at least, while whites didn't have to. But I could see that that was beginning to change. Other white and black churches in Grant County started partnerships in the 1990s, and this was all to the good. It just seemed to me that they were still "breaking barriers." And many residents of the county did not go to church at all.

THAT WINTER IN MARION I was sick a lot. Just colds, really, but I often had the sensation that my throat was closing, that I couldn't speak. I was choking up. Maybe it was all the inexplicable emotion I'd stirred up in myself. Sometimes I would drive away from an interview in tears, and I wouldn't know why. Of course, the truth is I *wanted* to feel things. It seemed the only way to get at the problem. Then came the day that I took it to another level and actually cried *during* an interview, quite an embarrassing moment, and it came with the Reverend Tim Helm out at Hanfield United Methodist.

Helm turned out to be one of those Christians who just exude joy and peace. Born in Kokomo, he grew up in Virginia and saw God's hand in all the coincidences that led him back to Indiana in 1982. "I see that even fourteen years ago God had a plan for me to be involved in some of this reconciliation that God's doing. There's no doubt in my mind that that's one reason I'm here." Helm told me that before the Encounter 94 crusade, he'd been profoundly affected by two things: a book on evangelism pointing out how racial conflict blocks God's work; and his Promise Keepers meetings, where reconciliation had become a central theme. Both led him right to the lynching: "I thought, boy, Marion has this wound from the 1930 lynching. I'm not from here, but it's obvious to me. I can see it. And I don't even know that many black people, but I can just tell that there's still that bitterness—maybe 'hurt' more than anything. 'Rift.' I thought, boy, I'd sure like to see that wound healed."

He told me about meeting J. D. Williams during Encounter 94 when both were interviewed for a local cable television station. When they left the station together, "J. D. stopped and said, 'Maybe we could have a joint worship service.' And here I'd been wondering how in the world to begin. So I just said, 'Let's do it. I can see God's hand in this.'"

I told Reverend Helm that the lynching survivor, James Cameron, believed he'd been saved by God.

"Oh, I didn't know that," he said.

Of course, hardly anybody in Marion knew what had actually happened on August 7, 1930, apart from the general fact that two men were hung. If they'd heard a family story, they simply had one piece of the big puzzle that no one wanted to put together. Few had read Cameron's book.

Helm said that at the first of the joint services at Greater Second Baptist, he felt the shadow of the lynching. "I knew that was in their minds. I felt that it was. Like here we are sixty-five years later, and there's still a rift, but it's beginning to heal." Marion could wring something positive out of that terrible event yet, Helm thought. He compared it to the cross, a symbol of death that became a symbol of resurrection.

So I decided to tell him about that moment I thought of as Cameron's "vision," about that moment he had near death—and I began to choke up. That moment when the noose was around his neck—I stopped, apologized.

"It's okay," said Helm. "It's affecting me, too."

I described it with my voice shaking: how at that moment near death when the noose was around his neck, Cameron thought that everything around him froze, and it looked like a film negative, and he couldn't tell anymore if the people were black or white.

Cameron's perception at the moment, written in his book and told over and over to whomever would listen to him ever since—I saw that as his gift to the people of Marion, but no one in the town seemed able to look at it. Except for a few people like Tim Helm. So I shared it with him and had my unprofessional moment. But again—I hadn't come to Grant County as an impartial news gatherer. I wasn't above it all. I was part of it, and I actively wanted black and white Marion to reconcile.

Helm told me that the mayor wanted to erect a statue on the courthouse square where the lynching tree once stood: "With two lifesize figures, a white person and a black person shaking hands over a tree stump. With an inscription describing the unity and the peace that we want to bring about."

I was surprised that city leaders were suddenly considering such a public gesture and wondered if it could possibly really happen.

I ATTENDED ANTIRACISM MEETINGS or interracial church services in Marion at least once a month, and I'd found a general pattern. For white people, it was often a big step just to show up, a really big frightening step, while the black people approached it with a sigh of "here we go again."

One Saturday I went to an all-day workshop on institutionalized racism at the Holiday Inn. Seventy people attended, but fifty-five of them were black, and I doubted that these African Americans really needed to learn more about this problem. Where were the white people?

We counted off like schoolkids and divided up to analyze seven areas of city life—like "government," the topic my group addressed. Nothing happened until after lunch, when each group made a presentation, and a debate erupted over education. A black woman spoke strongly for more black teachers, suggesting that white teachers couldn't be role models for black kids and wouldn't encourage them. Then during a discussion of the justice system, a black man told a long story about a white man he'd seen arrested but not charged, when any black man would have gone to jail. The arresting officer happened to be one of the fifteen white people in the room, and he was incensed. According to him, this story had no relationship to reality.

So here was a bit of leakage, two punctures into feelings usually kept sealed away: black cynicism over white intentions (often well earned); white failure to understand that blacks may see something as racist when it isn't, because that's the default position when racism is in your life every day. Such outbursts don't get resolved in one-day workshops. We just continue to move forward over the fragile veneer covering black bitterness, white insensitivity, black despair, white guilt, everyone's fear.

During a break I crossed the room to say hello to Marcus Cannon, the ex–Black Panther. "Same old same old, isn't it?" he said. "I heard it all ten years ago." I was surprised he hadn't said twenty or thirty. I left this event thinking, how *will* things ever change?

I THOUGHT THERE WAS a lesson for Marion, with its very specific problem of the lynching, in the controversial work of "truth and reconciliation."

Journalist Antjie Krog begins her account of South Africa's commission, *Country of My Skull,* by acknowledging skepticism over its worth, then relating what led to her quick conversion. She had been exposed to the thinking of Chilean legal philosopher and activist José Zalaquett, a member of the truth commission that investigated atrocities committed during the Pinochet regime.

If you have to choose between truth and justice, said Zalaquett, choose truth. "Truth does not bring back the dead but releases them from silence."

Despite the great differences in circumstance and degree, certain principles behind the truth commissions applied to Marion because they're really about repression. Zalaquett insisted, for example: "A community should not wipe out a part of its past, because it leaves a vacuum that will be filled by lies and contradictory, confusing accounts of what happened."

And: "Perpetrators need to acknowledge the wrong they did. Why? It creates a communal starting point. To make a clean break from the past, a moral beacon needs to be established between the past and the future."

Another thinker Krog cites is Jürgen Habermas—for the crucial observation that there is no such thing as collective guilt. "Whoever is guilty will have to answer individually," Habermas says. "At the same time there is such a thing as collective responsibility for a mental and cultural context that makes possible crimes against humanity."

Given that the guilty were probably dead, this was what Marion struggled with still. Collective responsibility.

Given that the guilty were probably dead, justice could never be done. Truth was the only thing left to hope for. But there might be a small measure of justice in having the guilty parties known. That's what drove me obsessively on. I'd begun to think that maybe I could set something right.

THE MORE FACTS THE BETTER. For example, I speculated that the wound inflicted by the lynching might have healed a bit more if people had known the story told in the Deeter family.

Claude Deeter was the white man mortally wounded on Lover's Lane the night of August 6, 1930. I had already found the newspaper story (never printed in Marion) stating that his parents disapproved of the lynching and that, in fact, they did not believe in capital punishment. But there was more.

Claude's nephew, Carl Deeter, acted as spokesman for the family. He told me that after Claude died around midday on August 7, Claude's mother went to see the mothers of both Abe Smith and Tommy Shipp to say that her son had forgiven their sons. That so as far as the Deeters were concerned, it was now over. Unfortunately, someone for whom it was *not* over had already set the lynching plan in motion.

Still, I found the Deeter story astonishing. To think that it had been settled among the mothers. Immediately. And no one ever knew. If this story had been publicized back in 1930, reconciliation between black and white Marion might have begun then—between the relatively conscious whites and the relatively conscious blacks. It wasn't to be, and one ironic consequence of repressing the facts was that Deeter's murder had almost disappeared from the story, while the obvious injustice done to Tommy Shipp and Abe Smith had been highlighted for decades.

Carl Deeter had made a decision to get his family's version out there. Besides, his uncle Claude was probably the one person among the principals who was innocent of any crime except, perhaps, soliciting a prostitute. The night I went to interview Carl, he talked for three and a half hours. He was like a fountain. I didn't have to ask a single question on my list. He just started spouting.

Born in 1935, Carl Deeter had never even known of his uncle Claude's existence until he was fifteen. He found out one day when he went home with his best friend, Dick Treber, son of the man who was then sheriff, Vaughn Treber. As they sat doing homework in the sheriff's house—the same house attached to the jail where Jake Campbell had once lived—Vaughn Treber came in and said, "Deeter. You any relation to Claude Deeter that was murdered out here at the river? When they lynched the two blacks?"

Young Carl had no idea what he was talking about.

So the sheriff told him, "There was a Deeter murdered by two blacks and the crowd tore them out of the jail." The sheriff then took him out to the jail and, Carl remembered, "he showed me where the crowd had torn the bars out and gave me his personal thumbnail history of it, and he showed me the famous photograph. He brought that out. The big eight-and-a-half-by-eleven." Carl had never seen it before.

He went home, and when his father came in that night, he asked him, "Dad, are we any relation to Claude Deeter that got murdered, and there was some lynching here in Marion?"

His father, Carl Senior, told him, "Yeah, that was my older brother."

Carl Senior then related the family story: How his mother, Grace Deeter, stayed at the hospital with Claude, praying and begging him to forgive his attackers. How, at first, Claude refused to forgive, but the mother broke him down. How she and her sister, Gertrude Whybrew, took turns going outside to the spirea bushes to kneel and pray, coming back in to "work over Claude to get his soul saved." The family story is very dramatic, culminating with Claude finally raising his arms and saying, "I forgive them," and then dying. According to Carl, Grace Deeter went immediately to the homes of the accused and told their mothers: "I have forgiven your boys and I got my son on his deathbed to forgive 'em and he will be with Christ."

Carl gulped as he told me this, fighting back tears, saying, "Excuse me. I get a little choked up about that."

His grandmother Grace Deeter then got her family together and told them, in Carl's words: " 'This is the official family ruling. By golly, we have gone through a terrible terrible ordeal. We'll all miss Claude forever. But we have forgiven them. It's the Christian ethic, and as a family we will forgive them, and this subject will never be discussed again.' Until I was fifteen and asked my dad, it never was."

I gave Carl a copy of a letter I'd found in the NAACP archive, because it mentioned his family. Writing on August 9, 1930, local NAACP leader Flossie Bailey told national leader Walter White about Claude Deeter's dying statement to his aunt, Gertrude Whybrew, "that the girl [Mary Ball] was not attacked by either of the boys, but that [Claude] recognized the Smith boy and called him by name, which was the reason he thought that he was shot. She [Whybrew] and the rest of the family tried to get the newspaper here to publish her statement, but they refused. I shall try to get a signed statement from her. She, of course, is white."

There was no signed statement that I could find, but based on Flossie Bailey's reputation, I was ready to believe this information reliable if she did—that there had been no rape, and that Deeter had been shot because he recognized Abe Smith. To me, it was also important to learn that Whybrew and the Deeter family had tried to make these facts public and that the local newspapers had repressed it.

But none of this seemed to make a big impression on Carl Deeter. He had his own version of what Claude had said on his deathbed. "Uncle Claude's story to the family was that they had put him in the river to drown him," said Carl. "After they shot him, the gun jammed. Three shots and it jammed. Now, to drown him, they couldn't get him under control, and while one was grappling with him, another one took a great big stick from the ground and they hit him as hard as they could on the side of the head, and his skull concussion—that's what killed him. The doctors told my Grandmother Deeter that he had to die because there was nothing they could do. The brain would swell and in those days they had no medicine, no way to stop the swelling. It was just a question of time."

Carl intended to write his own book about his family someday. For now he was too busy. He had had a series of jobs in "fiberglass, plastics-related businesses," in both management and marketing. He was often on the road or helping his mother out at her trailer park. But he'd done a great deal of research, tracing the Deeter line back to the early eighteenth century. The lynching would be just one chapter. Over the years he had interviewed everyone in the family about it.

In fact, when he first learned about his uncle Claude, he wondered immediately if his own father and uncles had been involved in the hanging. Wouldn't they have wanted to avenge their brother? He'd investigated all of his family, he said, wondering if "aha!—I'm going to find a skeleton in the closet. I was driven." Carl knew that some of them had been spectators, but he came away convinced that no one in the family had participated.

In 1930 Claude had been the oldest sibling at twenty-four. Next in line came Ralph at twenty-three, who went to the square that night with his wife and baby. The next younger brother, Otis, twenty-one, had a job as a baker up in South Bend, while Carl's father, Carl Senior, nineteen, was working in Lawrenceburg, Tennessee. Neither made it back to Marion before Claude died, but Carl Senior did drive to the square during the lynching, where, he told his son, he "couldn't get close." The rest of Claude's siblings still lived at home in 1930: Howard, seventeen; Morton, sixteen; Willie, fourteen, and Faith, who had just turned ten.

One of them, Claude's youngest brother Willie, was still living in Marion.

"There was people well connected, high up, that wanted this to happen," Carl said. "I'm convinced of that. And I'll go to my grave not knowing who it was or what it was. I've put in no small amount of effort, and I've had my aunts and my uncles helping me."

I too figured that if anyone could get access to the "inside" stuff, it would be a Deeter.

He told me, for example: "Uncle Willie knows a Ku Klux Klan member who was there at the lynching. Who gave my uncle William word for word who did what, where, and when. And Uncle Willie's relayed that to me, and that's pretty good information." (The Kluxer in question was the ninety-one-year-old I'd tracked down, the man suffering from Alzheimer's.) Apparently this Klansman had seen it all but was only a spectator. Carl dismissed the idea that Ku Kluxers had organized the lynching. He added that that was no Klan robe on Tommy Shipp (as Cameron claimed), just a sheet from J.C. Penney's near the square, draped around Shipp to hide his nakedness.

Carl would not tell me anything the old Klansman had related to Willie. Those were among the "pearls" he was preserving for his own book. But he did share his Mary Ball stories. Mary had had the audacity to come to the Deeter house for the wake, where she announced to the family that she and Claude were almost engaged. No one in the family had ever heard of her.

Youngest brother Willie, in fact, had witnessed Claude's last moments in the Fairmount farmhouse's kitchen, and they did not seem to be the prelude to visiting a fiancée. On August 6, 1930, Claude Deeter had been laid off at Superior Body. He was upset because he had car payments to make on a new 1929 Chevy. So he announced that he was going to take his last paycheck—for $5.06—and go have a good time.

"He was depressed," said Carl. "And Grandmother stood in the doorway of the farmhouse. She'd had this premonition. 'If you leave tonight, something terrible is going to happen.' And she locked her arms across the doorway and said, 'You're not going to leave. I want you to stay here tonight.' But he was strong as a bull, Uncle Claude was. And he just said, 'Mom,' and grabbed her and picked her up, turned her sideways, and set her back down. He says, 'Don't you worry.' And away he walked."

Carl's uncles had no doubt that Claude went to downtown Marion to find a streetwalker. "You'd drive around the square and whistle and get somebody's attention. He picked her up."

Nevertheless, the Deeter parents never questioned Mary Ball. Grace Deeter gave her Claude's bloody tie as a keepsake.

THERE WAS ALSO A DISTRESSING element to the Deeter family story. Carl believed firmly and sincerely that James Cameron shot his uncle Claude. This too had come from what Claude reportedly said on his deathbed—and I quickly realized that nothing was going to budge Carl Deeter from this conviction. I pointed to Mrs. Bailey's letter, for example, reading the line aloud where Claude's aunt Gertrude relates what she heard him say while he was dying: *"He recognized the Smith boy and called him by name, which was the reason he thought that he was shot."*

"Not the Smith boy," Carl insisted. "Cameron." Carl simply had total faith in his family's integrity, so the account he'd heard at home had to be true.

I'd heard many a rumor and allegation. But Cameron pulling the trigger? This was a first. Carl felt he had a story incriminating Cameron, however. This account originated with Roy Cox, described by Carl as "the cop that arrested Cameron." Cox was now dead. He'd been friends with Uncle Willie and told the Deeters that when Cameron was picked up, his trousers were wet to the knee. Claude had supposedly been thrown in the river, so Carl Deeter felt certain that Cameron had been part of that scenario. Pants wet to the knee proved it.

Roy Cox happened to be one of the people Tom Wise interviewed in the late 1970s. Wise gave me a copy of the tape. Cox, then the last living member of the 1930 police force, had asserted that he was not on duty the night of the hanging. And, he added, he was not on duty the night before, when

Shipp, Smith, and Cameron were arrested. The "night men" did the arrest, he told Wise, but he was present at police headquarters when they brought Cameron there for questioning. Cox did appear as a witness at Cameron's trial. What he told Wise about that was "I testified on what I had heard at police headquarters."

More hearsay against Cameron came from the old mayor, Jack Edwards. In 1992 Carl Deeter and his aunt Faith, Claude's sister, went to videotape an interview with Edwards, who announced almost immediately (but off camera) that Cameron not only pulled the trigger but owned the gun. To me, this was startling news, since Edwards had never told me any such thing during the course of our seven interviews. To me, the old mayor had said that Cameron deserved a medal, that he was "a pretty good guy," and during our last interview: "I think they should give him the jail." Maybe Edwards, a consummate politician, just excelled at telling people what they wanted to hear.

I was back in the muck of August 6 and 7, 1930, with its conflicting narratives and endless unknowables. And everyone was sticking to his story.

ASSISTANT CHIEF OF POLICE Roy Collins went to the River Road in an ambulance to pick up Deeter the night of August 6, 1930, and testified on Deeter's condition at the court of inquiry a week later.

According to Collins, Deeter talked on the way to the hospital. He said he knew the men who shot him "but I don't know their names." Then he added, "They bought their car in Fairmount." Deeter described the actual shooting "in a meager way," said Collins. "He talked out of his head part of the time. I couldn't get it straight. I had to come down and straighten up his story from the girl. He couldn't tell me the straight of it. He said something about a corn field, and I couldn't imagine what he was doing in a corn field. The way he told the story, he was standing in a corn field."

Collins then described Deeter's injuries—gunshot in the left hand, gunshot in the left side, gunshot just below the right pocket. "The only thing he did say about the shooting," Collins related, "was, he started to run to get away from him and they hit him over the head with a blackjack. He said, 'I then turned and started to fight and they shot me.' That is all he said."

I took a copy of this deposition to Carl Deeter. He, in turn, dubbed me a copy of his videotaped interview with Walter Fansler. Walter was the brother to Rex Fansler, the man who owned the old jail. After the attack happened right down the hill from the Fansler farmhouse, Walter went down with his mother to give Deeter first aid. Obviously, he had valuable testimony to offer. While he'd refused all entreaties from the media, the Deeter name got Carl through the door. Walter had since died.

On the videotape made by Carl Deeter in 1994, Walter Fansler sits in his Gas City home, an old geezer in overalls. He tells Carl that on the night of August 6, 1930, he was seventeen years old, sitting out on his front porch. He saw the car carrying Claude Deeter and Mary Ball drive in from the north and park. The car was visible down there until Deeter turned off the headlights.

"The colored fellas came from the south," says Walter on the tape, launching into a story about Deeter fighting, someone whacking him with a club, Cameron running away. But I couldn't determine whether Fansler had actually witnessed this with his own eyes or pieced it together later. Eventually I got access to an interview Fansler gave in 1977 and realized that he had heard "a racket," gunshots, but had not seen what happened down the hill in the darkness.

One thing he seemed sure of in both interviews, though, was that Claude's assailants had dragged him to the riverbank and dumped him over. As he told Carl Deeter, "These boys evidently drug [Claude] across through the weeds and there was a dewlike—we had a lot of dew on our grass, weeds, and their pants legs was all wet." At the spot where they dumped Claude over the bank, there was a sandbar and no water. Fansler knew this because he checked it out the next day. He also found the bloody club.

Walter thought the first shot was fired after they got Claude to the river. His father, Dave Fansler, then grabbed his rifle and walked out into the front yard. Someone fired again. "Dad hollered at 'em if they didn't quit, he'd come down there and help 'em."

Walter heard a car start, then a third shot. His father got into his Model T to give chase but soon lost the shooters. He drove to the jail to report the crime to Jake Campbell.

Meanwhile Walter's mother had come outside, and she said, "There's a woman coming up the hill." Mary Ball.

"Crying," added Walter in the earlier interview.

Mary Ball asked them "to come down to help her boyfriend who'd been shot," Walter recalled. "I said, yeah. So we got a gasoline lantern and a bucket of water and a washpan and some towels and washrags before we went down there."

Carl told Walter Fansler that this corroborated the family story, that Uncle Claude told them he crawled the thirty yards back to the road from the river and found Mary Ball lying there and said to her, "Go get some help. I'm dying."

Carl asked Walter if Mary Ball appeared to be injured.

"It didn't look like it," said Walter. "She had her dress on. It didn't look like it had been torn or nothing."

When they got to him, Claude was not able to talk. "He was just groaning. His head was busted wide open. I could see his brains." As Walter described this, he began to cry. He said he washed the blood off Claude's face and out of his mouth. "I don't know where the girl was at that time, while I was down there wiping his face off. She was back at the car or something."

Walter Fansler was one of so many I wished I could have spoken to in person. What an enigma. Though he'd refused to speak to the press, Walter seemed completely caught up in this event in which he'd played a small part. At one point on the tape he pulled out an old copy of *Ebony* magazine with a feature on Cameron. He had also read Cameron's book.

Of course, Carl's purpose in talking to Walter was to get support for the family story. He asked if his uncle Claude's clothes were all wet—from being in the river, since, in the family story, the assailants try to drown him. Walter, who had already told him about heavy dew and the sandbar, replied that Claude's clothes were wet "because of the dew on the grass. He hadn't been in the river."

Carl remained focused on getting evidence of Cameron's participation. So for him, the crucial question was how many people took off in Tommy Shipp's car—two? Or three? Walter did not remember seeing them leave. But if he had any issues with the scenario laid out in Cameron's book, he did not mention them.

Still, Carl Deeter remained confident that Cameron had helped to kill his uncle Claude. "They threw him in the river, and here's Cameron with his pants wet above the knees. So Cameron, how did your pants get wet above the knees if you were two or three blocks away running home when the shots went off?"

"Cameron was there. In my heart—he was there, and I forgive him anyhow. But a fifteen-year-old boy—he's gonna cut from his eighteen- and nineteen-year-old buddies? He's gonna cut the scene and leave it? Before the shots? Not likely."

However, Carl added, he liked Cameron personally. "I think the guy's got a lot of charm, and he gets out there with his historical museum, striving to do good with his life and—after all, Jesus said, forgive him."

▲ ▲ ▲

OF ALL THE FILM CREWS that came to Marion, the one that stayed longest and dug deepest was from the BBC. I knew from my own experience how tenacious they could be. They had called me periodically for a whole year after my *Voice* article appeared, wondering if they could just follow me around with a camera crew as I began my research.

"When the Brits were here, they drove me nuts," Carl Deeter recalled. "They were going to get every ounce of every detail of everything I knew, and then they wanted a confrontation between Uncle Willie and Cameron."

This demand horrified the older generation of Deeters. Carl explained that everyone who'd lived through August 1930—his mothers, aunts, uncles—were all still afraid. Some people had blamed the Deeters for the lynching, and Claude's brothers had lived with death threats. Now the family consensus was, don't rehash it. Let it be.

And since the Deeters also believed Cameron to be the triggerman who killed Claude, they worried over what Willie would say to him. "Uncle Willie—he's got that mercury-quick temper, and he's fiery," Carl said. "He's the old walrus bombastic German. Crazy, strong-willed, uncontrollable, unpredictable. And here's the British Broadcasting Company, and they are just begging, pleading, cajoling, offering money. They're doing everything. The family says, 'Absolutely not. Your uncle William could explode and call the guy a murderer. We could have race riots in Marion again.' "

But the BBC crew "just wouldn't let it go," said Carl. They informed him that they would not leave Marion until the confrontation happened.

Finally Carl agreed to set it up—if the meeting could take place at their church, with the minister present. As Carl put it, "I thought, by the grace of God, we're gonna take their evil intentions and turn it into good."

The subsequent encounter between Willie Deeter and James Cameron is actually quite moving, but I think it surprised everyone. The finished BBC documentary, *Unforgiven: Legacy of a Lynching*, even suggests in its voice-over narration that the meeting was Uncle Willie's idea, no doubt to give what ensued some emotional logic. "He still grieves over Claude," the narrator explains. "He believes it might ease his pain were he to reach out to another survivor, James Cameron. The two have never met. Cameron has agreed to come to Deeter's church, where the minister has offered pastoral mediation."

In what was captured for posterity, there's no hint that Willie Deeter thinks he's meeting the man who killed his brother.

Willie sits in a pew chatting with his minister. Cameron enters the sanctuary through a door behind them. "There we go," says the minister.

"Is he here?" asks Willie, not turning to look. He is a white-haired old man about Cameron's age, dressed in his Sunday suit, as is Cameron.

The tension is palpable. Cameron's walking down the aisle as the minister says, "Yeah. Yeah, stand up there and greet him."

"Howdy," says Cameron as he gets to the pew, and Willie gets up.

"James Camerman?" Willie mispronounces the name, but from here on the stage is his, filled with the sheer force of his emotion. With one hand he takes Cameron's hand, with the other he grips Cameron's shoulder, and his voice rises as he introduces himself: "William Deeter, Jr., youngest brother of Claude Deeter."

"Yes, I knew Claude," says Cameron.

"You knew Claude, yes," says Willie. "You told me by phone that Claude was your friend."

"Yes, he was," Cameron says.

"And I'm here to welcome you . . ."

"Thank you."

"To this church, to this group . . ."

"Thank you."

"And I'm gonna ask you to the depths of my heart to forgive me," Willie quavers, as he puts an arm around Cameron's neck, hugging him. "I love you."

"Thank you."

"There's no discrimination ever in my heart toward you." Willie is again gripping Cameron's hand and shoulder.

"I knew that," Cameron assures him.

"My father, mother, Claude, all the eight boys. Never a word written, spoke, said, published about . . ." Willie pauses. "The situation."

"I understand."

"It's great to be here," says Willie.

"Thank you."

"Wonderful to be here."

"Thank you."

Willie wants them to go to the altar to kneel.

Later Carl Deeter chuckled over this, because the cameramen were unprepared and had to jump over the pews. But they caught a few moments of it: Willie Deeter saying to James Cameron as they kneel at the front of the sanctuary: "God has brought us together. God has brought us together."

Cameron seems overwhelmed throughout the encounter, unsure how to respond to this rush of emotion from Willie with anything but good manners.

They sit back in one of the pews with the minister, as Willie says to Cameron, "I'm so thankful for your attitude and spirit. I'm so thankful," reaching over to hug Cameron around the neck.

"Thank you," says Cameron. "Thank you."

Willie is close to tears as he says, "It's just great to be here."

"Beautiful," Cameron says. "Thank you."

"Great to be here. Great to be here."

"Thank you."

"Just wonderful. You're just wonderful."

The minister suggests that they pray for reconciliation among all people. They are all holding hands. The minister begins, and in the style of evangelical churches, Willie begins to pray out loud as well, his eyes shut tight.

"Thank you, Lord, for the spirit," begins the minister.

"Thank you for the spirit that's here," Willie's prayer overlaps. He again seems near tears. "Thank you for what you've done."

"Thank you, Lord, for the spirit between these two precious men," the minister is saying as Willie chimes in: "Thank you for Mr. Camerman."

"They both went through a lot in their lives," says the minister, as Willie adds, "Thank you for our attitude. Thank you for causing fellowship and love."

Minister: "We ask you, God, to bring reconciliation like these two men have had . . ."

Willie: "Thank you, Jesus."

Minister: ". . . to our whole nation . . ."

Willie: "Thank you, God."

Minister: ". . . and our whole world. Amen."

"Amen," says Cameron. "Amen."

THIS ENCOUNTER RESONATED DEEPLY with someone who hadn't even seen it. Harold Vermilion was a white minister organizing integrated prayer meetings. Concerts of Prayer, he called them. I went to see him about his reconciliation work and expected a short meeting, but as soon as I sat down with him in his home office, he began to talk about the meeting between Willie Deeter and James Cameron. He'd been so inspired and wished that he'd been there. He'd heard all about it from the minister who was present.

Once again I found myself doing an interview in which the events of August 7, 1930, bubbled to the surface unbidden. As it turned out, Harold Vermilion had seen the lynching when he was five years old. His father drove him downtown that night. Or maybe early the next morning. He kept thinking it was daylight. What he remembered clearly was the bumper-to-bumper traffic around the square and so many people "we'd like to have never got through there." He'd been so frightened that he got down on the floor of the car. He did not really understand what was happening, but he knew it was wrong. It had made him feel sick to his stomach. Still did, whenever he relived it.

"It was so indelible on my mind," he declared. "I saw the two guys hanging there on the tree, and that followed me all through my life."

He organized his first Concert of Prayer for Halloween night 1993 on the courthouse steps. "It was within sight of the spot where the men were hung, and I told the people that night, 'I saw that. I've never forgotten it.'" Vermilion's voice began to shake. "'And my prayer is that before I die, I will see this come to an end. I want to see this thing done.'

"I just want to see it written off our conscience and our book, our city. I don't know what it is—kind of a stigma. And it just is not gone, and I guess I'm of the opinion that after all these years, it's going to take the power of God to remove it."

Vermilion, now retired, wanted to use his Concerts of Prayer to create unity: "I just want to see a real friendship take place between black and white people, which we've never had. I'd like to see it be better here than anyplace else in the country." The unity he wanted would be not just interracial but interdenominational. He was trying to get all the pastors in the county together, and he kept the prayer meetings moving from church to church. The next would be at Allen Temple A.M.E. with two black and several white ministers officiating. "We're still going to be individually who we are, but together we're going to amount to something," Vermilion declared. "I get so hungry to see it sometimes, I can't hardly wait."

But he thought something specific had to be done to address the lynching. The statue, he thought. He was passionate about the idea of placing a statue on the site. He said that the mayor wanted it to show the two ministers who'd begun the reconciliation work—J. D. Williams and Tim Helm. But Harold Vermilion thought otherwise; it just had to be a statue of Willie Deeter embracing James Cameron. "I want to see them two with their arms around each other, driving a stake, saying, 'This is done. This is the finish.'"

▲ ▲ ▲

APART FROM HAROLD VERMILION, few people in Marion ever knew about the encounter the BBC had organized between Willie Deeter and James Cameron.

In February 1996, however, the *Marion Chronicle-Tribune* invited the head of the Urban League, a white minister, the president of Marion's NAACP, and a few others to watch the BBC show in the publisher's office, then discuss it. They were the only residents of Marion ever to see the tape.

One of the black participants told me later that the things they then discussed were the same things he'd heard discussed thirty years ago.

SOMETHING KEPT DISSOLVING the effort toward reconciliation. The people making good-faith efforts just never reached critical mass. It reminded me of what had happened with the abolitionists, how their legacy had evaporated, their deeds not even passed on to their children's children.

So during the weeks of Community in Unity church services, I nearly skipped the evening at Weaver, since what, after all, would be accomplished? Fortunately I decided I *had* to go because the service would be held at Hills Chapel A.M.E., the church built by black pioneers in the 1840s.

Though the original structure had burned down, the current church sat on the same spot, with rectangular leaded windows, a wood-burning stove, ceiling fans, and four thrones up front for the preachers, along with a small organ and a small choir area. John Taylor, the man who had driven me around Weaver, noticed me and nodded as I sat down by myself in a pew labeled "Beck." I looked again at the brass nameplates at the end of each pew, each with the name of an old Weaver family. Beck: the blacksmith who managed to buy his own family out of slavery. Smith was the very first on the left, I noticed. Abe Smith's family. I counted maybe fifty people in attendance, roughly thirty black and twenty white.

I noticed immediately that this service seemed much more comfortable with its black-and-whiteness than the service I attended before the Klan rally. But I didn't know why. A white minister gave the opening prayer for the community, using that coded spiritual language onto which one can project: "Lift the heaviness around us in Grant County . . . the spirit of heaviness has ravaged the people." He came back to sit in the pew right in front of me with a black friend. Then during the testimony time, he got up again and said, "I think about the theme 'Community in Unity.'" And he went on, trying to talk about race, maybe even saying something about how we all have the same God, but nothing specific enough that I made notes. Nothing that made any difference.

Reverend Fred Greene from Allen Temple A.M.E., the young minister who'd talked to me about the impact of the lynching on his older members, then delivered a sermon about communication. What you *meant* to say versus what someone *heard* you say versus what you *did* say.

I noticed Harold Vermilion sitting across the room. At the very end of the service he went up to the pulpit and began by talking about race in the usual way, with the usual generalizations like "We all have the same God."

But suddenly he began to talk about the lynching. So right there a great taboo was broken. I was witnessing something that had never happened in Grant County before.

Vermilion said publicly for the first time what he had told me privately: "I live to see that which caused a great rift in our community healed. I was five years old when I saw them hanging on the tree, and I didn't know what it meant, but it hurt me inside. I live to see the day when that thing is eradicated from Grant County. I want to publicly ask my brothers [the other white ministers] in the audience to stand here before you to say we're sorry."

Now the white preacher who'd talked about Community in Unity got up, red in the face, and embraced the black friend who'd been sitting next to him. He was crying. Emotion fluttered through the little church. Four white ministers stood in the front, saying they were sorry, and I almost felt that I should go up there, too, but I knew it would be inappropriate.

"It will be more than a revival; it will be a renewal of spirit," said Vermilion. He explained his idea that there be a statue of James Cameron and Willie Deeter and a plaque that said, "It is finished." Right on the lynching site. He said that if the city officials didn't agree, the churches would do it. "We need to stand here as a promise that this thing will happen." There was a murmur of agreement from the congregation. That they would drive a stake in it. That they would say, It is finished.

To end the service then, we all joined hands and sang a song. As people were putting on coats, the Hills Chapel preacher called out, "There is a relative here tonight of one of the men who was hung! She just told me that this is the first time any white person ever apologized! Praise the Lord!"

I thought this astounding. I pushed my way up toward Vermilion. He motioned me over and introduced me to the niece of Thomas Shipp, Ruth Anne Nash.

I told her my own story—my grandfather in the Klan—and finally managed to say that I too wished to apologize. Why couldn't I come right out with it? I was halting and ungraceful, but Nash put her arms around me and then said that she couldn't talk anymore and had to leave because she was feeling too emotional. I wasn't doing too well with my journalistic mission. I didn't record this, didn't ask her for an interview. I had to let this be a human encounter. I watched her flee out the back door of Hills Chapel in tears.

Then I drove home thinking about how awkward I'd been when it was so clear what this woman wanted to hear from me. And how much that event of sixty-six years ago was still present for her, though she had not even been alive when it happened. I thought about all the theoretical political essays I'd read on whether white people should apologize. I'd never advocated this. It was truly the placing of a Band-Aid on a broken body. But I had just met someone to whom it clearly made a difference.

THE NEXT DAY TOM WISE stopped by to pick up a book I had on the Klan. I told him all about the service at Weaver, and about Harold Vermilion's wish to bring an "end" to the lynching.

"How does he think he's going to end it by putting up a statue?" asked Wise.

TWENTY

BROTHERS AND SISTERS

It wasn't just Claude Deeter who still had family in Grant County. All the principals involved in the tragedies of August 6 and 7, 1930, had relatives there. But I waited before approaching any of them. After my article in *The Village Voice* triggered its little media blitz in 1994, every crusading reporter who charged into town went directly to the families, creating exactly the bull-in-china-shop scenario I had feared, and I was going to have to live with the wreckage.

Mary Ball had the most family still in the area, a brother and three sisters living in or near Grant County. They were also the least cooperative. I knew that none of the television crews got very far with the Balls, so I began by calling her most approachable relative, a nephew Tom Wise happened to know.

John Lloyd lived in Iowa. He told me that his family was difficult and paranoid: "I really don't get along with any of them. That's why I'm out here." But he *had* liked his aunt Mary, "just a nice person," and he'd even gone to visit her in California. Mary Ball had died in 1987 in San Bernardino.

Lloyd told me that while growing up in Marion, he'd always been curious about the lynching, but his family shut down every time he asked about it.

I wondered if he thought his aunt had been raped. "My mom says yes," he told me. "My grandmother said yes. My aunt said yes. Because they remember pulling the thorns and everything out of her legs. That's what they told me. And my mom—she'll vouch for it. Because they can remember when they brought her home that night. And they've been paranoid about it ever since. That's the reason they don't want to say anything. They're afraid."

"Afraid of what?" I asked.

"Black people."

Already I didn't understand the Balls. I spent days thinking about how to approach, writing out the exact words I would say, and then finally calling Mary's sister (and John Lloyd's mother) Nancy. I didn't get far. As soon as I said the words "the hanging," the sister spat: "I don't want nothing to do with it! There's enough niggers already!" Click.

There's enough niggers already? I spent the rest of the day mulling that one over. I was also thinking, *Poor Mary Ball. Who would defend her if not her own flesh and blood?*

So I called her younger brother, Chet, who'd been fourteen at the time of the lynching. He did not hang up on me. In fact, he assured me that "if I knowed anything, I'd tell ya," but he didn't happen to know a damn thing. Then he informed me that Mary had moved to Texas after the hanging, that he never knew her married name, and that he didn't know where his older sister Margarite lived exactly. Somewhere near Huntington, but "I never could find her."

Mary Ball had one last sister, Mildred, living in a trailer park in Bucktown. I decided that this time I would not call. I'd knock on the door.

So I did, countless times. No answer.

I began to drive by in the evening. No lights.

Chet told me that Mildred "works someplace, takes care of some old man." Naturally he didn't know where.

If only I knew why Chet Ball wanted to mislead me, I might know everything. When I called the nephew, John Lloyd, again, he told me that Mary had never lived in Texas, that Chet used to visit her in San Bernardino, and that Chet definitely knew the husband's name: Clyde McNaul. The nephew remembered that Mary lived "right at the bottom of Big Bear Mountain" and worked at Norton Air Force base along with McNaul, her second husband. The first husband "wasn't that nice," according to John Lloyd. He recalled that his aunt Mary's nickname was Pitty, and she used to come back to Marion every year to visit the family.

That was it. And none of it put me any closer to solving the central mystery about Mary Ball: ravished innocent or bad girl? Somehow it seemed too neat the way every story made her one or the other. No doubt the truth was more complicated. And sometimes I would remember with a start that in August 1930 Mary Ball was just seventeen years old.

If she *had* lied about the rape, if she *had* been in cahoots—then she'd set this whole thing in motion. Certain people in Marion believed that.

Clearly she'd done some lying to try to salvage her reputation, playacting the fiancée role to the hilt. I remembered the newspaper's description of her at Claude Deeter's funeral, "her face a twisted mask of grief." As the pastor declared that Deeter died "defending one who was helpless," she responded with "a cry of grief which stirred the congregation into a sea of movement." But was she crying over a lost sweetheart? Or because she felt guilty?

Mary Ball got to tell her own version of events during Cameron's trial in Anderson the next summer, though apparently what she most wanted was to avoid testifying at all. The prosecutor took the precaution of placing her in custody about a week beforehand though he released her on her own recognizance after three days in jail. Since transcripts of Cameron's trial disappeared long ago, the most detailed account that remains is in the Anderson newspapers. Certainly Mary Ball presented herself as a good girl on the stand, telling the court that she was to marry Deeter in September 1930 and that they'd stopped on the River Road so he could change a tire. But true to the course of everything I seemed to encounter, the two Anderson newspapers did not quite agree on what she said next. According to the *Anderson Daily Bulletin,* she testified that Tommy Shipp marched Deeter down the road at the point of a gun, while the other two assaulted her. According to the *Anderson Herald,* "she said she became frightened and ran when one of the negroes marched Deeter through a field at the point of a gun, the other negroes pursuing and capturing her. She was assaulted by one of the colored youths, supposedly Abe Smith."

Both the Anderson and the Indianapolis newspapers reported that Mary Ball could *not* identify Cameron as one of her assailants. Both the Marion newspapers reported that she *did* identify him. But then the Marion authorities had an investment in both Cameron's guilt and Mary Ball's innocence.

I took another look at what Walter White had had to say about Mary Ball. His source for this could only have been the police. I regarded much of his information as good, but he clearly had a few things wrong as well, like the date of the holdup on the River Road: August 7, he said, when it happened August 6.

"Mary Ball, according to popular rumor, was criminally assaulted,"

White wrote in his article for the *New York World.* "Investigation, however, cast grave doubts upon this story. When taken to the police station and questioned, she stated that she did not know whether she had been assaulted or not and in another statement is reported to have said that she was not assaulted by Abe Smith as a passing motor car had frightened him away."

LYNCHING VICTIM TOMMY SHIPP had a number of nephews and nieces in Marion, like the woman I'd met at Hills Chapel, but no one from his family had ever talked.

Abe Smith still had two brothers in town, and they'd both appeared briefly in a Dutch documentary called *De Dederman* (The Third Man). Verlin Smith indicated one reason for the family's silence during that interview: "That's a serious crime. When it comes down to your own flesh and blood, you don't talk about that."

"The crime [Abe] committed?" the interviewer clarified.

"Yes," Smith replied.

There was another thing in *De Dederman* I couldn't help but note. The Dutch crew interviewed the Smith brothers separately. Asked to pick Abe out in the famous photograph, Walter Smith pointed to the body farthest from the tree (and according to Cameron, this is correct). But Verlin Smith pointed to the body nearest the tree. No one in the film is identified, so spectators will never know that the Smiths don't agree on which victim is their brother.

I found the sloppiness of the filmmakers all the more irritating since they'd made my job harder once again. By the time I got to Marion, a number of older black people had decided that they would no longer speak to the media. One of them was Walter Smith, the older of the two surviving brothers. Actually I wasn't sure Walter knew that much. In the Dutch film he just tells a story about Abe stealing ivory rings from his grandfather's prize horses and getting a whipping for it. (Abe's grandfather, Alfred Smith, ran the racetrack at Weaver.)

When I went to see Verlin Smith, I understood immediately how he might have misidentified his brother in the photograph. In August 1930 he was still several months shy of his fifth birthday. He told me that he had no memories of his brother Abe at all. "If I do, I just blocked it out somewhere along the line. Forgot about it."

The lynching was never spoken of in the family—"you daren't ask." What Verlin did remember was that on the day after, August 8, 1930, his dad hitched up the horses, and the whole family rode out to Weaver. They stayed out there with relatives for four days.

Verlin had never even seen the infamous photo till a few years ago. "That must have been a shock," I suggested.

"I don't pay that stuff any attention," he replied. He hadn't known any details about the lynching till he read a book on it—Cameron's, no doubt, but he couldn't remember—and he never finished it. He had never heard of Claude Deeter or Mary Ball. He had never known Tommy Shipp.

Abe was just a half-brother. He and Verlin had different mothers. Verlin told me that one day he heard his dad talking about his first wife, Abe's mother, explaining that once he came home from work early and found her drinking and gambling. That, apparently, was the end of the marriage. Verlin's mother, the second wife, was a Pettiford, and he had fourteen brothers "counting half-brothers."

"Do you remember Abe's funeral?"

"Nobody went to it."

"Nobody went?"

"Not to my knowledge, they didn't."

Verlin seemed certain, in fact, that there had been no funeral at all and that Abe was buried somewhere in Muncie. When I told him that I was sure both Abe and Tommy were buried at Weaver, he looked at me incredulously but simply said, "I don't know."

I began to think that Verlin had let me come to his house only out of a compulsion to be polite. Clearly he didn't want to talk about any of this. Whenever possible, he changed the subject, discussing his work life at the VA Hospital and at Sears.

He volunteered some examples of how well he got along with white people. Stories like that always made me sad; I saw them as evidence of trauma. But I didn't interrupt, either. So Verlin told me about the woman who bought a range at Sears, where he drove a delivery truck. How she announced to the salesman, "I don't want no black man in my house," but Verlin delivered the range and installed it and "she didn't say a word." Of course, he admitted, he often passed for white. He was very light-skinned. He used to deliver for Sears down in Elwood. He'd drive right past the infamous Elwood warning sign: NIGGER, DON'T LET THE SUN GO DOWN ON YOU HERE. "And not once did I ever have a problem," he declared. "Not one time."

His philosophy was "As long as you treat people right, they'll treat you right."

I asked him about Klan activity, a question I asked everyone. Verlin told me that, while delivering for Sears in the 1950s, he saw a few daytime Klan gatherings out east of Marion. He would see the cross, and the men in robes and hoods milling around on some farm. "I kept right on going," he laughed. "I never had no problems with 'em.

"I try my best to stay away from racial trouble," he added.

Verlin had a fenced-in yard with three guard dogs. He had to come outside and hold them off as I entered and exited. The house itself was cozy and very neat with lots of knickknacks—chiefs, eagles, elephants, angels. I noticed a Jimmy Swaggart book, *Revelation,* and two *Last Suppers* there in the living room. All the family pictures showed white people. Fine, I thought, but there was something disconnected here.

THE DEETERS WERE RELUCTANT to let Uncle Willie talk to another journalist, but after I'd been acquainted with Carl Deeter for several months, he agreed to set it up. Willie Deeter, Claude's last surviving brother, was eighty years old when I met him one night at Carl's house. He had the rough-hewn look of an old farmer, which he was. He'd also driven a truck for eighteen years.

I saw immediately what had so worried the family about his meeting with James Cameron. Willie was still filled with bitterness about "Camerman" and all the "lies" in his book, and this more than a year after that moving encounter filmed by the BBC. Clearly the meeting at the church had healed nothing for Willie, who announced that he was going to write his own book to get the truth out.

More proof that moments of public reconciliation were really just moments of hope.

"I'm the only living one that knows what Camerman knows," said Willie. "All my brothers is deceased. Camerman played it smart in what he did. It will all be straightened up after he's gone. I won't fight him while he's living."

Carl explained that they wouldn't put Willie's book out until Cameron was dead. If Uncle Willie died first, Carl would incorporate Willie's manuscript—the deathbed conversations with Claude—into his own book on the Deeter family history.

"What mistakes did Cameron make in his story?" I asked Willie.

"The whole thing," he declared. "The whole story. Everything. Word for word."

Willie was vociferous, emotional sometimes verging on irrational, and uncensored by any concept of political correctness. He said of my own project: "If you're going to write a book, you're just beating your head against the wall, because you'll write it without the truth." Pointing out that I could write the truth if he'd tell it to me was quite useless.

I began by reading the list of the seven men indicted for the lynching. He had never heard of a single one.

He talked about Shipp, Smith, and Cameron leaving his brother for dead in the Mississinewa. "My brother, we used to swim a lot, and we'd play like we was drowning, and we'd play like we was dead. All kinds of acts. So they thought he was drowned. Cameron said, 'Now I got my chance.' The fourth one involved here is Mary Ball. It wasn't just the three. It was also Mary Ball."

"You met her, didn't you?" I asked.

"Oh definitely," said Willie. "Yes. I talked to her."

"What about?"

"Well, that's in *my* book," he replied.

Carl asked his uncle if Mary Ball had any wounds.

"She showed me her body where she was throwed in a side ditch while she was being raped," said Willie. "And if you know anything about a spike nail, there was holes in her body as big as a quarter inch. Mammoth big thorns had pierced her body. This was the second day after this happened, and there was a black and blue spot around each hole that you just about stuck your little finger around, they was so big."

She could have fallen, I suggested.

"She said they put her on the ground," Willie told me. He saw wounds on her arms, shoulders, and back. He remembered thinking that she would have scars for the rest of her life.

"You think she was in cahoots with the three men."

"Sure. Sure. Sure."

"So it *wasn't* a rape," I said.

"But she wouldn't admit that at the trial," said Willie. "N-o-o-o. N-o-o-o." He wasn't quite making sense. All this detail about her injuries, then resentment that she'd presented herself as an injured party who played no role in Claude's death.

Without prompting from me, Willie then began to relate what happened the night his brother was shot. He'd been fourteen, but he remembered it like it was yesterday—how hot the weather was, how he went upstairs to bed with two brothers and his sister, how they couldn't sleep because they had no electricity, no fan. So they took the bedclothes outside to sleep on the ground. "And we was laying on them bedclothes when the phone rung."

Willie returned again and again to how his brother Claude had suffered, while "Camerman knew he was safe in telling anything he wanted to tell."

Willie invoked "the pants legs soaked to the knee"—proof to him that Cameron had been in the river trying to drown his brother. That moisture could not have come from dew, he said, because "on a real hot night, no dew sets in till midnight."

Willie said that he could also give me evidence of Mary Ball's involvement. When Claude got out of the car, according to Willie, "he said to the holdup men, 'Here's the keys to my car, here's my money, and I'll never tell nobody I know you boys.' You know what they said? 'We have to kill you.' Why didn't they say, 'We have to kill you *and* Mary Ball?' "

Yet Willie believed Mary Ball's story that one of the three stayed with her, while the other two took Claude to the river.

Then Willie told me why he was still so angry at Cameron after meeting him at the church. Because Cameron told him his own version of the story. "He said he throwed the pistol down and run because he couldn't do it. I made my confession to him about forgiving. You know what he said? 'Claude was my friend.' You don't throw a pistol down to your buddies that you know is going to kill your friend."

Claude, said Willie, was "the most kindest person I ever knew." The two used to sleep in the same bed, and Claude called him "Curt." He'd take him along in his car and let Willie pull the exceedingly loud air horn, though their father had forbidden it. He'd take Willie to the train station when he went there to hang out with his pals, and "I knew right then there'd be an ice cream, a piece of candy, or a pop."

"Claude was the most well known of all the boys in our community," said Willie. "For his strength and hard work." Claude could pick up one end of a Model T. He could carry a pile of 125-pound cement bags when other men carried one. He could break a pitchfork in two with his bare hands. "And he was more kind to me than my mother and father," Willie remembered. "He hugged me."

Willie did not go to Marion to see the lynching. "I didn't even know it was going on." But he remembered the astonishing sight he saw the next morning. He took the cow to the woods down near the highway and saw that State Road 9 was jammed with cars heading south. "Some looked like they had twelve and fourteen people in them. Them open cars in that day. Just full of colored leaving Marion. Just rows of cars of colored leaving Marion."

Willie still saw the lynching as he must have seen it then, a community's impulsive response to the loss of his wonderful brother. "It was such a shock to people that something that hideous could be done to somebody as kind as Claude," he said. "They just was overwhelmed with it. Good Quakers, hundreds and hundreds and hundreds, sanctioned that. And the one leader was a Quaker. Quaker raised. And even the Ku Klux Klan wasn't needed. He told [the Klan] that himself. 'We're going to do it.' Yeah. It was that desperate. Yeah."

"So," Carl interjected, "you're saying the Klan didn't organize that."

"N-o-o-o-o-o-o-o," said Willie. "Heavens, no. See, Camerman brings it on as the Ku Klux Klan definitely. And they were there and all that kind of stuff."

Here he digressed into a story about trying to get to the courthouse during the recent Klan rally to talk to the Kluxers. But the police wouldn't let him through.

"What did you want to talk to them about?" I asked.

"I would have told them the true story," Willie announced. "Because we owe it to the world for this mark against us to be erased."

An image flashed through my mind—Willie Deeter telling all to Jeff Berry. Not that Willie even knew the Wizard's name, but I had seen that the Klan was still alive and powerful to people of Willie's generation, both black and white. And for him they filled the role of last recourse for aggrieved white people. I didn't quite know what to say. I imagined Jeff Berry commiserating, then handing him a membership application.

Clearly Willie was torn between the forgiveness he'd been taught to extend and the rage and pain he still felt about losing his brother. Apparently those bad feelings ruled him much of the time. To him Cameron was a murderer who'd done just a couple of years in prison to pay for it. Willie went on to tell me that he tried to protest to the governor when Cameron got his pardon. And he tried to protest to the mayor when Cameron got the keys to the city.

It was all just political, said Willie. He felt that the story had been rewritten to make Cameron the biggest victim. "You know what I've been called by the blacks?" Willie demanded. " 'There's the son of a bitch.' 'There's the son of a bitch.' 'There's the son of a bitch.' "

"That don't do anybody any good to bring that up, Willie," Carl told him. Willie just chuckled.

"You know your mom and dad forgave them, and you know you have, too," Carl continued. "And to bring up the dissent—"

"It kind of gets to you," Willie interrupted. "The tombstone. Reading the dates."

Carl said he wondered if his grandparents had been right to tell the family not to ever talk about Claude.

"We took it as a loss and it was over with," said Willie.

I told Willie that I thought his parents had tried to stop the cycle of revenge.

"They never approved of the lynching," he said. "N-o-o-o-o-o. N-o-o-o-o-o. No. No. No. No. No."

Carl thought it was awful that there had been a backlash against his family "after my grandparents' Christian charity, after the family's noble gift to Cameron." The Deeters, he said, had appeared before Cameron's parole board (something I couldn't confirm) to say that he was forgiven, that the family felt no malice, and that's how Cameron got out of prison. Yet Willie had heard about a plot back in the 1960s that "the colored was going to kill two Deeter boys in retaliation." Carl's father had been threatened, too. Then Willie told me a long story about finding some women stealing turnips from his field one day, telling them to leave, and fifteen minutes later "four colored men drove up in a car." One of them hit Willie in the throat, rupturing his thyroid, and he lay in his field for an hour playing dead in case they were still watching him. The next night a black man with a gun came to the factory where he worked as a truck driver, but Willie had a black friend there who warned him: "Bill, leave now."

"I'm marked by the colored," Willie declared. "I'd be afraid to go out on the porch and set." Fear—that's why Claude's death was never investigated, Willie told me. Because "the law was scared to death."

Scared of what?

Race riots.

I wanted to get back to what Willie knew about the lynching. "You said before that there was a Quaker who planned the lynching," I said. "Was he from Fairmount?"

"No, he wasn't in Fairmount."

"Was he from Marion?"

"It didn't have to be him," Willie declared. "There was plenty of support right behind his shoulders. Plenty of support."

"Some people have told me that the lynching was organized in Fairmount," I said. "Do you think that's true?"

"No. No. No. No," Willie replied. "It didn't have to be organized.

N-o-o-o-o-o. The whole thing I'm trying to get you to see was the respect for Claude. What they did to him. 'In face of such brutality, we'll give brutality.' That they realized, such a loss—he'd never been arrested, he was honorable, he didn't steal, he was a worker, he was honest, everybody knew his reputation."

"What was your impression of Mary Ball?" I asked.

"She was immoral," said Willie. "I was just a kid—and she was cast as 'There goes the whore,' 'Here's the whore,' 'Here's the whore.' She went out with anything. Mary Ball was classified as the lowest down that there were. Yeah."

"Wow." Carl laughed. "What was your brother doing with her?"

Willie said nothing.

"I have to tell this story," said Carl, and he related how Claude swore to his mother on his deathbed, "Mom, I never touched her."

"Had you ever heard of Mary Ball before that night?" I asked Willie.

"No no no no no no. N-o-o-o-o-o-o. N-o-o-o-o-o-o."

"But she came over to your house."

Willie said he was standing in the living room, looking into his brother's casket, when Mary Ball walked up in a black silk dress and pointed to Claude's skull, saying, "That's why he had to die. The brains seeped out of his skull." Then she told Willie how she'd tried to help, climbing to where she saw a light up on the hill. It was only after the lynching, said Willie, that she became "the talk of the young. 'There's the whore.'"

"Did you ever hear about your mother going to see the Shipp and Smith families?" I asked Willie.

"She went to the families," declared Willie. "Yes, she did. And apologized to them."

Willie's story did not quite match with Carl's in regard to the Deeter parents. Carl presented his grandmother as a sort of saint, going to the Shipp and Smith families as soon as her son was dead to say, "We forgive you." But in Willie's version, she went to see them the day after the lynching to apologize. As Willie put it: "She just did it to say, 'I want to let you mothers know that we had nothing to do with it, and we didn't approve of it.' That's all it was. She had sympathies for the mothers because they lost their boys just like she had."

Carl said he would defer to Willie's version of events. Willie's was a bit less dramatic than Carl's, but still. That was the first apology for the lynching right there. And no one ever knew.

I kept circling back to these stories, because Willie went off on tangents, often about Cameron, who "got sixty-five more years of life" but was still complaining, while Claude got "nonexistence."

Carl began explaining Cameron to his uncle Willie. "It's an extremely noble thing he's doing," said Carl, "trying to eradicate prejudice"—all by focusing attention on the lynching. "The fact that he was with people and committed murder is irrelevant. It's irrelevant to his bottom line. His bottom line is to teach the world that the Ku Klux Klan is evil, racial prejudice toward blacks is evil, and it should be wiped out."

Willie began to tell the story of Claude leaving the farmhouse that night, after his mother told him not to. "And the phone rung an hour and a half later. Dad and Mom said, 'Well, we've got a peace of mind that he was disobedient. He didn't have to be there.' And it come to my mind—Claude, you'd have better minded Mom." That sounded harsh, yet his story rang truer than Carl's sentimental version. In Willie's recollections, his parents were stern people who decided that Claude had been punished for disobeying his mother. Or maybe that was the message they wanted to convey to a fourteen-year-old. "They knew he shouldn't have carried that kind of life out," Willie explained. "Whether he ever touched her or he was just immoral for even being there. That's the reason I'm saying, Dad and Mom didn't blame the colored. They blamed him for not minding."

A more tender recollection came from Faith Deeter Copeland, the sister who had just turned ten when her brother died. On the night either just before or just after Claude's funeral, the Deeter parents got into bed with her and talked. "It was just coming daylight," Faith remembered, "and I couldn't tell you the exact conversation at all, beyond the fact that they were just so terribly, terribly saddened by the whole thing." Claude's death. But also the lynching.

I HAD ALWAYS BELIEVED that if anybody in the county had been let in on the secret of who organized the lynching, it would have been Claude Deeter's brothers.

Indeed, when I told Willie I'd found a sledgehammer used on the jail door, he said that someone had offered to get that for him. But he didn't really want it.

So I asked him, "When you write your book, will you be able to say who organized the lynching?"

"Sure. Sure," he said. "Yeah."

Carl seemed more surprised than I was. "Willie," he said, "are you sure you can do that?"

The old man nodded yes.

"So someone told you?" I queried, while Carl marveled, "You can name who organized the lynching?"

"Yes," said Willie. "It *was* no organization or meeting place. They was there. And someone said, 'Let's do it.' There didn't have to be no organization at all. No group had to go down like the Klan and say, 'We're going to take over.' N-o-o-o-o-o."

"So it was spontaneous," said Carl. "You know who the leader was of the spontaneous crowd."

"Yes. Yes. Yes. Yes. Yes, I do," Willie declared. "He was raised a Quaker, but he didn't go to Quaker church, and he didn't live like a Quaker."

The lynching had happened, Willie insisted, with no organization, no plans, no meeting, no nothing. But if there was one thing I knew for a fact about the lynching, it was that it was *not* spontaneous. So I had discovered something important: Willie Deeter did not have a clue about who really put it together. Still, the "Quaker" could have been part of the mob.

"Can you tell me his name?" I asked.

"I won't say his name," said Willie. "No. That's for *my* book. I'll just say this—it needs to be straightened up."

"Hold it," said Carl.

"We owe it to our people of this country and other countries," Willie began.

"Hold it," said Carl.

"The way we're misrepresented by one man!" cried Willie.

"Hold it. Sometimes it's best *not* to tell the truth," said Carl. "If this truth creates hard feelings among both blacks and whites and creates more riots and more bloodshed, what good would it do to have the truth come out?"

"If I would publish the truth, I wouldn't live an hour," Willie declared, "and Cameron wouldn't live an hour."

"Why would you want to create more death, destruction, and race relation problems?" Carl asked him. "Why would anyone want to do that? The truth can be as ugly as the lie. And if it focuses on the fact that Cameron has been living a lie, then it destroys his goal of race harmony through eradication of prejudice. It only inflames *more* prejudice. That's not worth publishing. Let's have the races get along."

"At his pardon," said Willie, "I was surprised there wasn't a riot then. Yes, I was."

"How did you feel about actually meeting him?" I asked Willie.

"As far as I was concerned," he said, "ever since the phone rang and said Claude was shot, and then when I was at the hospital and they said he was dead, it satisfied my mind—why not forgive it and forget about it? Because I knew what Mama told him the night before. 'If you just minded, Mom, Claude—I wouldn't even have to forgive what they done to you.' It don't make any difference to me if it was colored or white. I'm not that way. No. That don't have nothing to do with it. They're a human being. They can make mistakes just as well as I can."

"So you *do* forgive," Carl said to him. Then turning to me, he added, "He does forgive, but he can't stand the other guy fomenting a lie and getting mileage out of it."

"No, you're not looking at it right, sonny," Willie declared. "What he has done to some *millions* of people. He hasn't done it to myself. He done it to millions by false accusation in the whole thing. If he had told the truth all the way through—he doesn't say let's build a memorial out there at the river and let's tell the truth and everything we done [to Claude] is going to be in there, too."

Later it was Carl who brought up the statue idea, Cameron and Uncle Willie in bronze. Carl was all for it—"as the BBC showed them, shaking hands or embracing. It would show the harmony of the races, and I don't think the city and the county and the whole world could do a better thing to put a final cap on this thing."

"So how would you feel about that?" I asked Willie. "If there was a statue of you on the square?"

Willie began talking about the meeting at the church again, how he wanted to go to the altar to pray with Cameron, and before they even got there Cameron lied. Told him, "Claude was my friend." A lie, because you don't leave a friend like he did. Then someone had telephoned Willie to tell him about a magazine article on Cameron, "that he was talking about how terrible the Ku Klux Klan was. That isn't forgiving."

"So what about the statue?" I asked.

"I don't agree with that," said Willie. "No. Not at all. Not till he comes clean."

"You don't think that leaving a harmonious end to this whole thing would bring peace with the races?" Carl asked him. "You don't think that would be a noble thing to do?"

"It's all under false pretenses," said Willie.

I asked Willie if he'd heard the story that Cameron was the triggerman directly from Claude. Or did he hear it from another family member?

"I'm not making no mental blocks about that!" Willie said fiercely, mysteriously. "I was right there when Claude died. Ask Cameron if *he* spent fourteen hours a-dying!" Willie did *not* actually speak to Claude in the hospital, however.

The phone rang, and as Carl took the call, Willie confided that he might be willing to meet with me and Cameron. "It can endanger my life, but I'd be willing to sacrifice that. I offered CBS to do it for fifty thousand dollars, and I said, whoooo, I wouldn't live an hour. Because retaliation would get me." He meant by black people. "And then the Ku Klux Klan would get Cameron. The Ku Klux Klan would come alive again. Because the Ku Klux Klan don't know about this. N-o-o-o-o. N-o-o-o-o."

"What don't they know?" I wondered.

"The truth!" he said, as Carl rejoined us. "The truth! The Klan doesn't know the truth, or Cameron wouldn't live an hour."

"You tried to go tell the Klan the true story," I said.

"Sure did," said Willie. "Sure did."

"What would have happened if you'd have told them that, Willie?" Carl asked him.

"It's not right for Cameron to—" Willie began.

But Carl persisted: "What would have happened if you'd told the Klan the story?"

"I'd have been bumped off," Willie declared.

Carl just chuckled at that.

"And they'd have bumped *him* off," Willie continued.

"Cameron?" I said.

"Sure," said Willie. "S-u-u-u-u-u-re."

"Then why would you have done that?" asked Carl.

Willie did not reply.

"That's not a very Christian thing to do," Carl told him.

Willie sat in silence for a moment, and then declared, "Something needs to be straightened up."

AFTER THIS ENCOUNTER I wondered what the minister at Bethel Worship Center could have possibly said to Willie Deeter on the day he met Cameron.

Reverend Michael Henson told me that he and Uncle Willie simply prayed together and then Willie talked about his mother going to see the mothers of the lynching victims. Henson said he told Willie, "You have an opportunity to be used by God to demonstrate forgiveness and Christian love." Willie said he had prayed about it, and he knew what to do. The minister recalled that what Willie seemed focused on was kneeling at the altar with Cameron.

I also discovered another of this story's many contradictions: Bethel Worship Center had the most racially integrated congregation in Marion. I already knew from Carl Deeter that his father had been instrumental in founding this church. The move to integrate began when Henson arrived in 1991. At that point Bethel was a congregation in trouble, its membership down to under a hundred people, but Carl's father, Carl Deeter, Sr., "kept the little band going," said Henson.

The minister knew nothing of the town's racial history then and made achieving an interracial congregation part of Bethel's mission statement. They would build their congregation back up with that theme in mind.

One family left after Henson's first sermon, when he declared, "If you don't want to be part of an integrated congregation, you don't want to be here." Henson preached reconciliation. He preached openness. He preached that racism is sin. Of course, integrating in a world of white churches and black churches is easier said than done. So, Henson said, they prayed that God would send a strong African American couple to pioneer the way. And the Lord did that. Thanks to all the preaching he'd done on the subject, that first black couple felt welcome. Then more began to come.

He estimated that the congregation was still 60 percent white as they approached the year 2000, with the other 40 percent split between black and Latino. But the church did not keep records of who was what. They didn't count. There was no quota.

The minister said that in recent years—since I published my article, basically—Cameron's new visibility had continually opened old wounds for the Deeters. But as Henson observed, the intention of the lynching was never to get justice for Claude Deeter. "That mob wanted to send a message. And they did."

That was how I saw it. In a county that once had the potential, at least, for good race relations, a lynch mob decided to reassert white supremacy.

So, I asked Henson, what should Marion do to heal this? He wasn't sure. The lynching had been "a defining moment in the community," he said, and now Marion needed another defining moment—one that would identify the town with racial harmony. But what?

▲ ▲ ▲

IT WASN'T UNTIL 2005 that I heard something fairly definitive about Claude Deeter's dying words. I got access to an old interview with his cousin, Mildred Whybrew, who'd been twenty-two in 1930. Her mother, Gertrude Whybrew, was the woman mentioned in the NAACP correspondence as witness to Claude's statement that "he recognized the Smith boy." Gertrude and Claude's mother, Grace Deeter, were sisters. According to Mildred Whybrew, "He realized he was going to die because Aunt Grace told him, my mother told him, and I never will forget, they said he said, 'Well, I forgive 'em. I don't know who did it, but I forgive 'em.' "

Mildred clarified: "I think he knew maybe one of the gang or something, but he didn't know who shot him."

Back in 1996, however, I decided I better visit Cameron in Milwaukee to get his response in person to the charge that he was the triggerman who killed Claude Deeter. I also hoped he could tell me something about Mary Ball. If she *had* been involved with either Smith or Shipp, wouldn't he have known?

I called him at America's Black Holocaust Museum to make an appointment, without telling him exactly what I wanted to discuss.

We settled on a date a week or so away, and then Cameron told me that no one had come to the museum all that day. But he still had an hour and a half before closing. Someone still might come.

I WENT TO SEE OPAL LARKIN after hearing that she'd witnessed the lynching. She had, but only from a distance. What she *did* know something about was Mary Ball.

Opal was twenty years old in August 1930. She and "a bunch of we kids," maybe three or four couples, wanted to go joyriding around Fairmount that night. When they stopped at a Marion service station for gas, the attendant looked up at the sky and said, "Good night for a lynching." Opal didn't know what he was talking about, but an hour later when they came back into town, traffic was terrible. They made their way to the square. Their boyfriends went off together, probably to get a good look. The women stayed on Washington Street, taking refuge in the dollar store where Opal worked.

So Opal hadn't seen much. But years later she worked at RCA with Mary's sister—probably Nancy, the woman who'd hung up on me. The sister told her that the events of August 1930 had ruined the Balls, and that

Mary "wasn't allowed back in Marion. She'd slip in at night to see her mother. But she died a wealthy woman."

Opal also knew Carl Deeter, Sr.—and Chet Ball, who came out to do something or other with the horses Opal's husband kept. When Chet came over, she said, "I had to keep Mr. Deeter in the house," because Carl Deeter, Sr., was so convinced that Mary Ball was implicated in his brother's death. "I had to sit here and talk to him," Opal recalled, "and I'd tell him, 'Mr. Deeter, Chet had nothing to do with it. He couldn't help what happened.'"

"I've heard that Mary Ball did not have a good reputation," I said.

"She didn't," said Opal. "And she was on the street the next morning. She came into the store where I worked."

"Did you speak to her?"

"Had to wait on her," Opal declared.

I asked if Mary Ball appeared to be injured.

"No-o-o-o," replied Opal.

"No cuts or anything?"

"No," said Opal, hesitating. Then she blurted out, "She wasn't a very nice person." In fact, Opal thought that Mary Ball was definitely a prostitute and definitely involved with Shipp and Smith.

"Do you think her sister knew that Mary was a prostitute?" I asked.

"Oh, she did," said Opal. "She talked to me one day and said, 'I know you know what happened.' And she said, 'I know you know it was my sister.' She said, 'Do you think less of me?' And I said, 'Honey, we can't help what the rest of our family does.'"

Finally I understood something about the rudeness and the lying: the Balls were ashamed. But I didn't know why. Because Mary had been raped? Or because she'd been Abe Smith's lover and accomplice?

I told Opal I had called both Nancy and Chet, thinking they might want to defend her.

"Uh-uh," Opal told me. "Her sister never defended her. And Chet never did, either."

THERE'S ONE FINAL TWIST to the mystery of Mary Ball.

I did manage to find her stepchildren in California in 1997, and they'd never heard a thing about the Marion lynching. That wasn't exactly a surprise. But Clyde McNaul, Jr., the stepson who was closest to her, told me that the one thing he never understood about her was her passionate hatred for black people. She went out of her way to avoid them, he said. Just hated their guts. "She was very vocal about it." It was so pronounced that Clyde Junior finally went to his father to ask what the problem was. "Is she part of the KKK?"

His father said no. "He made a couple remarks about her having problems at a younger age," Clyde Junior said, "and some of these were amplified by the fact that she wasn't what was considered a normal, proper young lady for the times. She was kind of like Rosie the Riveter. I guess she rode motorcycles and did things that upset some people's ideas of what a young woman should be doing. And he said that there was a big problem, and some people turned against her, and some believed her, and there was quite a big to-do, and that's all he ever told me."

Mary got into real estate in San Bernardino, buying foreclosures cheap and reselling them. At one point, she also owned eight or nine rental properties. Then, early in the 1960s, she had an automobile accident. "That made her afraid to drive," said McNaul. "That's when the whole thing started to unwind. She lost her zeal for life." He described her as "very extremely sensitive to other people, not really in a normal fashion, but in a very frightened, almost reactive fashion."

Years after this conversation I spoke with Clyde's ex-wife, Madeline Patterson, who knew Mary Ball for about eighteen years and described her as shut down, guarded. "One time I asked her what her maiden name was," Madeline remembered. "Before she answered, she studied me. Then she said 'Ball' and kept studying me to see my reaction. I'm sure she was wondering if I was on to the story." Madeline found it hard to believe that Mary Ball could have been a prostitute. The Mary she knew had never been flirtatious and was so averse to physical contact that she stiffened if you hugged her. Mary and her husband slept in separate rooms. Madeline recalled Mary's shirtwaist dresses, her doll collection, her "girly girl" bedroom decorated in lace eyelet. "Fear shrouded that woman," said Madeline. "She was just so rigid. So not trusting."

Madeline too recalled Mary Ball's "very deep aversion" to black people. But the "aversion" applied *only* to blacks. "I am of Mexican background," Madeline said. "I am olive-skinned with dark hair, dark eyes. But Mary never showed any prejudice toward me."

I ARRIVED AT AMERICA'S Black Holocaust Museum in Milwaukee to find James Cameron in his cluttered office, happy to see me but not feeling well. A powerfully built black man in head scarf and pink T-shirt, a gun and badge at his waist, stood in the corner behind Cameron's desk telling someone on the telephone that Mr. Cameron had been experiencing shortness of breath.

Cameron picked up some papers. "I was just scratching this out while I was at the print shop five minutes ago," he said, launching into the draft of a new letter to the Indiana Historical Society. The topic: turning Marion's old jail into a museum for the prevention of lynching.

"Now is the opportunity for the state of Indiana and the city of Marion to erect a national memorial much like the Vietnam Wall in Washington, D.C." he began.

The young man got off the phone. He was a Milwaukee cop who volunteered at the museum, and he told Cameron that his doctor would be calling him back.

Cameron went back to his letter. He had the whole Marion museum worked out in his mind. There would be a large wall inscribed with the names of all lynching victims throughout American history; the jail itself would become a National Historic Landmark, thus leveraging federal money for 80 percent of the rehab costs; the building across the alley would be razed and replaced with a pavilion; he would move his national headquarters there from Milwaukee (he hoped to open branches of the museum in several states); and as he put it in his letter, "Marion, Indiana, could become the most tourist-attractive city in the United States of America."

It was a pipe dream, both naïve and grandiose, but it could only have been hatched by a true idealist. Actually Cameron was well aware of the obstacles he faced. He wouldn't go in without approval from the citizens of Marion, so there would have to be a referendum, a city council vote, the mayor signing off on it. Then he'd have to get landmark status for the jail. And he didn't know how he'd manage to buy the jail from Rex Fansler, who was now asking him for $200,000. That was why he hoped to get the Indiana Historical Society involved. "It might tip the scales," he said.

I told Cameron that Fansler had apparently sold the jail to the city for $25,000 but they hadn't yet paid him a dime, and he wasn't even sure the contract was legal. "Maybe you could offer him twenty-five thousand dollars," I suggested.

"I don't have any money," he said.

The phone rang. It was his doctor, telling him to come to the hospital for tests.

"Should we stop?" I asked. "I can drive you."

He said I could drive him but that first we should have our conversation.

So I got right to my points. Mary Ball. Was she part of the robbery plan? Was she Abe Smith's girlfriend?

"I don't think that's true," said Cameron, with some outrage.

It appeared that I had at last found someone from Marion who would defend the honor of Mary Ball. "The Klan always does that," he continued, "when a decent white woman is caught in a web like that, they always try to make out like she was a whore. Aw, I wish they wouldn't do that. That was just a decent white girl out there at the wrong place at the wrong time. Every time there's a white woman involved, they do that in order to justify lynchings of black people. No, I never did believe that."

"So you heard stories that she was involved?"

"Yeah. Involved with him, and she'd set it up and all that stuff. That's awful. That's just Ku Klux Klan propaganda."

"How well did you know Abe Smith?"

"I didn't hardly know him at all."

"Supposedly he and Tommy had committed some robberies before this."

"That was my first time with them. If they'd done anything before that, I don't know anything about it."

"How did you feel about your meeting with Willie Deeter for the BBC show?"

"I felt emotional. Yes. Yes."

"You're glad it happened?"

"Yes, I am. I think it did a lot to heal the family wounds, and also it did a lot to heal my wounds. In a spiritual way."

"The Deeters say that Claude's mother went to visit your mother—and Abe's and Tommy's."

"I don't remember anything about that," said Cameron, "but I wouldn't put it past his mother to do that, because she was a Christian woman. And she lived her life as she thought God wanted her to."

I got to my big question, the "truth" that Willie Deeter thought would kill him and which even Carl regarded as a bombshell.

"Did you know that the Deeters believe you were the triggerman? Carl told me."

"He never gave me that impression," said Cameron.

"Apparently that's what Claude said on his deathbed."

"Isn't that awful?" said Cameron. "You know what, when the police found Claude out there at the scene of the crime, they said he was unconscious. Now how did he become conscious in the hospital and tell all these things? That doesn't make sense. There's some fabrication going on there somewhere. Evidently one of my two buddies shot the man. There's no doubt about that. Yeah. But which one, they don't know."

"The Deeters say Claude was hit in the head with a club."

"Yeah. Hit in the head with a club. That doesn't make sense. Of course, I wasn't there so I don't know. It doesn't make sense to me."

"They say that when you were arrested, your pants were wet from the knee down."

At this Cameron laughed.

"So they figure you were in the river," I added.

"I know one thing," Cameron declared. "When I got home I was wringing wet with sweat. 'Cause I had run all the way, about six miles, from there to my home. That was perspiration. That's all that was." He went on to talk about hearing the shots fired once he'd run the equivalent of three or four blocks. He sat in silence for a moment before saying, "I met Carl a number of times, and he never mentioned anything to me like that."

I told Cameron that the thing Carl, in particular, wanted to emphasize about his family was their effort to forgive, but he did believe that Cameron had killed Claude.

"Isn't that something?" said Cameron. "He has a wrong belief, I can tell you that."

I asked him if he remembered driving to the River Road with Shipp and Smith. He described their route, corroborating what Walter Fansler had said, then talked about how foolish he was to be there, how ashamed he felt. "That's why I gave the gun over," he said. "Told them I didn't want to have nothing to do with them and left them out there. And then people, these Monday quarterbacks, say, 'Why didn't you take the gun and run away and not give it back to 'em?' Well, you don't think about things like that on the spur of the moment."

We talked maybe half an hour. I went over some details with him—like what exactly he could see from the jail window the night of the lynching. I confirmed that he thought the Virgin Mary saved him that night. But Cameron was clearly not feeling well, so I didn't want to draw it out.

He sent home the assistant/receptionist—she was the only other person there—and locked the museum up, then drove home with me following. After he put his car in the garage and said a few words to his wife, he got into my car and we drove to the hospital. I offered to wait with him.

"No," he said. "It's all right. I have carfare."

Tom Wise told me later that Cameron had been admitted to the hospital and stayed for six days—which upset him because he had to keep the museum closed the whole time.

Back on the job Cameron sent me a copy of his finished letter to the Indiana Historical Society, proposing that the Marion jail be converted "into a shrine of sorrow and forgiveness for all the world to visit and admire. The site would, indeed," he wrote, and the caps are his, "be one of THE WONDERS OF THE WORLD."

A COUPLE OF WEEKS AFTER my visit with Cameron in Milwaukee, I ran into Barbara Stevenson from the Grant County Black History Council. I mentioned that James Cameron really wanted to come back to Marion to open his museum in the old jail.

"Do you think people around here might go for that?" I asked.

Stevenson said that people might go for the museum but not for James Cameron. "A lot of people think his book is a lie." There were black people of Cameron's generation, she told me, who believed that he was in jail only for stealing chickens the night of August 7, 1930, that he was never lynched, and that he was never even present at the crime scene on the River Road.

TWENTY-ONE

WHAT AUNT RUTH SAID

"This town with its rednecks and crackers and trash." That's what Aunt Ruth said of Marion, probably more than once when I was a girl. But near the end of her life, she developed a great nostalgia for the place she would never see again. Whenever I visited, she would tell me that she was homesick for Marion.

Aunt Ruth knew that I was writing a book about Grant County, but she had no idea I'd be focusing on race, the lynching, and my grandfather's Klan membership. My parents warned me never to tell her about the *Village Voice* article I'd already written. They were certain she would hate it and never speak to me again.

Still, she was the best family source I had on the two taboos—the Klan, the tribe. Ruth was not only more interested than my father in the family history. She'd been born in 1918, while he was just a baby during the Ku Klux heyday. I thought she might remember the Klan parades. No, she said, but she remembered a cross-lighting. She recalled that clearly, and that it happened at Goldthwait Park, up on a hill after dark. (Goldthwait was the park east of Marion, where, for example, seventeen hundred men were initiated into the KKK one night in 1922.) Aunt Ruth couldn't remember anything else about the night of the burning cross, including who she was with. She added that "everybody who was anybody" was in the Klan, and she didn't know that Grandpa was all that active. After his death, though, she found what she described as "Klan stuff—clippings and things." She didn't want them in her house and passed them on to my father. He did not recall getting them but said Grandpa had once organized a Klan parade down Nebraska Street that was praised in the newspaper. I could speculate that that was a clipping he'd saved.

The thing I most dreaded asking Ruth was whether my grandmother had also belonged to the Hooded Order. Hundreds of thousands of Hoosier women joined the Klan in the 1920s, many coming in through the temperance movement, a cause my grandmother strongly supported. I never had to ask, though. Ruth brought it up herself during the cross-lighting story when she observed, "Mother was less than enthused about the Klan."

Less than enthused. I felt great relief.

My aunt volunteered another story about my grandmother. One year when Ruth was four or five, she made valentines for everyone. "I colored one brown and said, 'This is for Sid.'" That was their mailman, who was black. Grandma told her, "Don't you know, everyone's the same underneath? You mustn't treat them differently than anyone else." So Aunt Ruth made another red valentine for Sid.

Ruth also told me that my grandparents had had a black cleaning lady, probably during the 1920s. News to me, but according to Ruth, this was something all white people in Marion tried to do back then, no matter how poor they were. She remembered going to see some relative or family friend so poor they had their mattress sitting on orange crates—and they had a maid. This ended during the Depression, however. The family never had "help" again.

I asked Aunt Ruth if she had any idea who those black women were I occasionally saw at my grandparents' house. She didn't know but guessed, as I did, that it had something to do with church work. She remembered Grandma talking about a church conference she was to attend with a light-skinned black woman, and how worried Grandma was that this woman would not be allowed to stay at the hotel. Aunt Ruth remembered my grandparents discussing it, indicating that Grandpa probably wasn't too sympathetic to the problem. But things worked out when the woman was able to "pass."

BACK IN MARION, I decided to attend the Easter Pageant I'd seen so often as a child, and it would have to be the sunrise service preferred by my grandmother. That way, she always said, we would get there in the darkness and leave in the light.

To my kid eyes, the pageant had never been a spectacle of particular interest. I most remembered the aggravation of getting up early enough to reach Marion Coliseum by five or five-thirty A.M. for a good seat on one of the hard, backless bleachers. What interested me now was the fact that the pageant had started in 1937, with the stated goal of bringing all races and creeds together, and apparently my grandparents had been part of it from the start.

So said Ruth Thomas, who'd been the pageant's drama director for thirty-five years. She was the woman who'd reported seeing the streetcars offline the night of the lynching. She'd known both my grandparents and my aunt.

The pageant was the brainchild of a large interdenominational youth group started during the Depression. (No church in Marion could afford to run its own youth group then.) My grandparents, Thomas told me, had been among the group's sponsors. And it wasn't just the usual white Protestants but blacks and Catholics, too. "All together for the first time in the history of the community," said Thomas. "And that wasn't too many years after that terrible lynching."

During one of my visits with Aunt Ruth, she told me that she was in the first pageant. She played the Angel at the tomb. Grandpa was in it, too, role unknown. "He wore burlap." So many people used to attend that there would be a line from the Coliseum stretching a good couple of blocks.

There was no line in 1996, but nothing else had changed. Here was an early-twentieth-century artistic sensibility preserved in amber, complete with Isadora Duncan–ish choreography. After a long processional into "Jerusalem," the local talent acted out the story of Christ's death and resurrection in a series of tableaux vivants, including a re-creation of Da Vinci's *Last Supper,* which my grandmother had always found especially impressive. The show was so quaint, so sincere, yet somehow self-righteous.

I tried to imagine the pageant emerging from postlynching guilt. Had the town really been motivated by some hope for redemption? If so, they hadn't exactly worked at it. I noted two black children in the cast of hundreds and maybe seven black women in the audience.

FOR ALL THE STORIES my grandmother used to tell about her family, I knew surprisingly little. I had the family tree that allowed her to join the

Daughters of the American Revolution, traced back through her father. The alleged Indian was apparently her mother's mother's mother. All those women—at a time when the census didn't record much information about mere women.

Near La Fontaine, in a small cemetery which I'd never visited with family, I found my great-great-great-grandparents, Charles and Sarah Scarlett Newell. Charles's nickname, "Judge," hinted at a colorful personality but not a single story had come down to us. I knew only his nickname and his profession (shoemaker) from an old manuscript about the vanished town of America, where the Newells had lived. Sarah Scarlett Newell had long outlived her husband and moved into La Fontaine, where according to my father, "she kept a loaded shotgun by the door." In the only other family lore that touched on her, my young grandmother tried to saddle a calf one day to go visit "Grandma Newell." (It's what even her obituary called her.) The Newells had lost a son, Myron, in the Civil War, and Sarah Scarlett Newell also outlived her daughter, Emily Nixon, my great-great grandmother, who was buried in a corner of that same little cemetery.

Emily wasn't even on the cemetery record, but I could feel her name on a toppled headstone coated with moss and grime. In a newspaper almost too fragile to bear page-turning, I found an account of how she'd keeled over dead at the dinner table in 1886 while her second husband laughed heartily.

I didn't think even my grandmother knew these things, so I thought I was having many triumphs. But nowhere in these glimpses of lost lives was there anything about Native Americans.

I had only my grandmother's story about what happened after Emily's death, how Emily's daughter Elizabeth, my great-grandmother, had been treated like a servant and locked in an upstairs bedroom whenever her stepfather and his new family went out. "Then one day she just crawled out the window." I remember my grandmother telling me that.

What Aunt Ruth said, though, was that Elizabeth crawled *in*. Yes, she ran away, but she came back one Sunday while the family was at church, put a ladder up, and crawled in the window, collecting everything of her mother's that she could carry away in an apron. Like a Lily of the Valley Staffordshire vase that my grandmother later inherited. Aunt Ruth had seen it before someone stole it from my grandparents' house on Fifth Street.

MY SISTER JOANNE DROVE DOWN from Michigan. Just as she had been disturbed by the lynching picture when we found it and was keenly interested in the mystery of my grandfather's parentage, she wanted to understand what I was learning in Marion.

We set out to visit some of the ancestors in the ground, first my grandmother's side. I showed Joanne the cemetery just north of La Fontaine and the Newell graves. At the fallen headstone where Emily Nixon lay, we applied shaving cream to make the name readable. To me she would always be Emily Nixon, but as Emily Hittle she lay snug against the second husband, John Hittle—one of those who drove our great-grandmother to climb either in or out of a window. Emily's first husband, our great-great-grandfather George Nixon, lay all by himself in a graveyard west of La Fontaine underneath a white headstone accorded to Civil War soldiers. It identified his regiment but gave no birth date. He remained our most mysterious ancestor. I had conflicting data on where he'd been born.

My sister and I then decided to search for the ruins of Barley Mill. A few years after her birth in the village called America, my grandmother and her family moved a few miles south into Grant County to live in the mill. I sensed that those years were important to her. In fact, when the mill was demolished, Grandma somehow acquired the key. I remembered her showing it to me, and her girlhood recollection about opening a trap door near the water wheel—seeing *hundreds of black snakes in their glistening home.* The site lay in what was now an outer subdivision of Marion. We followed a path dotted with beer cans down to the Mississinewa. Joanne first spotted what was left of the mill's foundation and walked the flooded square that the beams made in the shallows.

Much of my grandfather's family was buried in Gas City. We drove to the old graveyard there, Riverside, and fooled around with our shaving cream and chalk on the Carr grave, trying to read the inscribed poem or Bible verse chiseled down one side of the obelisk. No luck. We suspected that Grandpa's mother, Josie, lay there, unmarked, with her sister and brother whose names were legible on the stone. Nearby, unexpectedly, we found the grave of Ode Roush—my grandpa's father. I felt so disconnected from him.

We stopped after visiting our grandparents, though we had more ancestors in other cemeteries. Really we were visiting the mysteries, as if the graves could tell us something.

I SPENT DAYS AT THE LIBRARY in Wabash, looking for Newells and Nixons. There in the 1860 census I discovered that Emily Newell Nixon had been born in Ohio, while her parents, Charles Newell and Sarah Scarlett Newell, had been born in New York State and Vermont respectively.

That proved rather conclusively that they were *not* Miami Indians.

Still, someone could have been part of another tribe. I had now found all their obituaries and all their graves. No mention anywhere of Indians, but I had ample evidence by now that people had hidden such information.

Soon afterward I visited my parents and Aunt Ruth on the occasion of my mother's birthday. The day before the party I drove over to my aunt's house with all the genealogical material I'd been able to gather so far. I knew that lately she'd been occupied with painting and repainting her front door to get just the right shade of yellow-green. On a tiny house on a dead-end street in a working-class neighborhood. The door was a wonder, really, like a color I'd never seen. Lemon chartreuse? Aunt Ruth greeted me wearing a turban and an ankle-length shift.

She didn't turn off CNN and didn't look at much of what I'd collected, but she was interested in the Nixon-Newell material. This time she pulled out the pen-and-ink drawings of George Nixon and Emily Newell Nixon for me. I was thrilled to see these mysterious objects of so much speculation. My great-great-grandparents, sketched on what appeared to be shirt cardboard. George looked nothing like the description I found in his Civil War records, which call him dark-complected with black hair. The anonymous artist gave him blue eyes, with brown hair and a moustache. I thought Emily very appealing, pensive. She had a pink scarf tied around her collar, dangling earrings, and a Spanish comb holding her hair up. And a line under each eye. "Kidney problems," said Aunt Ruth. Of course, I was looking for clues to Indianness, but the drawing seemed inconclusive.

Aunt Ruth pulled a white envelope off her bookshelf. Inside was a sheet she'd copied from the fragile old Nixon Bible, showing that George and Emily had married in the disappeared town of America, near La Fontaine, where five of their six children were then born. Another was born in the Grant County town of New Cumberland, now called Matthews. I opened the brown paper around the Bible itself and found the letter my grandmother had received from a cousin about the Scarletts and the ancestor on the doorstep. It seems that not just a scarlet shawl was involved but a basket. Supposedly the foundling inside was Sarah Scarlett's great-grandfather. Nothing here about Indians. I decided I would just have to give it up. No Indian ancestor.

Ruth tantalized me by mentioning that somewhere among her boxes she had a picture of "the daughter of the last Miami chief," a friend of my grandmother's. But Ruth wasn't going to look for that picture.

Next day at the birthday dinner, with my brother and his family present, too, I asked my father and Aunt Ruth again: "Why do we kids remember Grandma saying that she was part Indian?"

"Oh, that was on the Nixon side," said Aunt Ruth. I was floored. After all that denial. Then she declared that it may have been Sarah Scarlett Newell. In the one tintype we have of her, Sarah "looks like an Indian. Or else," my aunt quickly added, "Portuguese."

I spent the rest of my visit trying to persuade her to look for the tintype. No, she said. She wouldn't know where to begin.

TWENTY-TWO

A FEW BAD APPLES

I had not been in touch with Imperial Wizard Jeff Berry since the Larry Hitler adventure, but I'd been monitoring the dubious progress of his American Knights in the newspapers. They were now the fastest-growing Klan in the country, staging a rally almost every other weekend.

They went from Bryan, Ohio, hometown of the new Grand Dragon Brad Thompson, to LaGrange, Indiana, where they railed against the local Amish population, who, according to the Klan, get special rights. Then they rallied in Portage, Indiana. In Dobson, North Carolina. In Seymour, Indiana. And in New Castle, where the Wizard and six others were arrested for disorderly conduct, resisting arrest, rioting, and obstructing traffic. They moved on to Ann Arbor, where the Wizard's wife, Edna Berry, was hit in the head with a rock, one anti-Klan demonstrator broke a leg, and eleven others were arrested. Next stop Kokomo, where a certain equilibrium returned: no arrests or injuries, but as the local newspaper reported it, the Klan belittled "everybody but themselves."

When I called Imperial Wizard Jeff Berry, he asked, "Where you been? On vacation?"

The Wizard gave me the usual positive spin on all current activities. They'd picked up a whole klavern in Kokomo—sixty guys who'd once been part of United Klans of America. And they now had eighty-five hundred members in Indiana alone. I didn't think I could believe him. Klansmen usually don't give out numbers except to inflate them.

As for the New Castle arrests, "we did not do nothing." I knew from newspaper reports that the American Knights had not followed standard procedure there, which was: rendezvous with police, get searched for weapons, get driven to the rally site. They arrived late so they went right downtown and started marching around the barricades set up for the rally. A widely published photo showed two helmeted officers wrestling the Wizard to the ground. Eventually he and his State Nighthawk, Grizzly Smith, would plead guilty to obstructing traffic and disorderly conduct, but in those first weeks following the arrest, Berry was harping on his injuries and promising, "We're going to get a heck of a lawsuit out of that."

They had also filed a lawsuit against the city of Marion, alleging that big Rodney Stubbs had been "jostled" and hurt his back when city personnel drove the Kluxers to the Marion rally in the back of a Ryder truck.

Berry was sure that the Marion lawsuit would go his way. And he was in the middle of preparing another one against the city of Ann Arbor, speculating that "maybe we'll get enough to build our church." His wife had needed three or four stitches after being hit with the rock. The Wizard told me with pride: "She got stoned and some people said to her, 'Now that you got stoned, you gonna quit?' Outta the clear blue sky, she says, 'Jesus Christ got stoned and that didn't stop *Him*, did it?'"

So often, they rendered me speechless.

ONE MORNING TOM WISE called to tell me there were Klansmen on *The Jerry Springer Show*. I tuned in to see some glum-looking Kluxers, among them a Wizard, facing an audience of howling banshees. Okay, no one deserved it more. But kangaroo courts don't exactly advance the discourse.

Then in late September, about a month before I was scheduled to leave Marion, Imperial Wizard Jeff Berry invited me to attend another rally and cross-lighting. "*Jerry Springer* is doing a thing on us," he added. "They're sending a camera crew."

Berry was well aware of how Klansmen were treated on the show, but he'd made a deal with the producers. *Jerry Springer* would run the American Knights' phone number. As a recruiting tool, this promised to be worth more than a full year of rallies. Members going to the show had been meeting together to prepare. The Wizard declared, "Springer pops a question, he's gonna get answered very educated."

THE RALLY WAS SET FOR Knox, Indiana, about a hundred miles northwest of Marion. The Klan came into these little places like a blight, a pestilence. Arriving a bit late, I parked a block from the courthouse and walked past white people who stood frozen, looking tense and disturbed as they listened to what was coming over loudspeakers from the heart of their town. At the square the scene was eerie. Apart from the police, the streets were almost deserted, like the aftermath to a bombing or a war. Up before the old Victorian court building stood the robed and the hooded. As I got into the press area, one of them was crowing, "We're getting bigger, nigger."

No African Americans were present. The pro and con spectators, all of them white, were nearly a block apart. Each group numbered about thirty, making for quite a tiny rally, no doubt at great taxpayer expense. The American Knights swaggered around, playing to Jerry Springer's camera crew. As Grand Dragon Brad Thompson told me later, they had made a point, for example, of attacking Jews this time, "because Springer's a Jew. It was a special little deal for Jerry Springer." The diatribes came larded with obscenity. More than usual. The televised result would be all bleeps. When they weren't shouting profanity, they were proclaiming what good Christians they were, that you had to believe in Jesus to join the Klan and family came first. The rally was also more locally specific in its complaints than any I'd attended. Knox was described as "a small communist community."

The Wizard asserted that anyone opposed to the Klan was just ignorant. "They was taught in the school that the Klan was bad. Well, you check your history book. The Klan is not that bad!"

"Take off your white sheets!" yelled a protester.

"These aren't sheets, buddy," the Wizard declared. "These are religious outfits. You're just mad because you can't fit in one cuz you're so fucking fat."

On and on went the schoolyard name-calling, all very tedious. This degrading exercise in First Amendment rights finally ended with Rodney Stubbs giving directions to his house in the country, announcing, "Come to the cross-lighting, you faggots and nigger-lovers. We got some trees you can hang around in."

Then they cranked up the music, exiting around the side of the courthouse to the tune of "Free Bird." ("And this bird you cannot chaaaaa-ange.

Lord knows, I can't change.") I suppose schmaltz *was* the perfect capper to all the crudeness.

Over at the holding pen for anti-Klan demonstrators, a few of them were talking with reporters. What I sensed in the protesters was outrage, hurt, shame. I spoke to one tweedy man with a moustache who talked about how much Knox had changed since his childhood, mostly because of immigrants who'd brought in new businesses and energy. He said there were a couple of black families in the town. "My wife's from Turkey. This freaks her out. I've been in twenty-nine countries, and I've never been treated this way anywhere."

Knox had suffered through three Klan rallies in three years. Desperate to keep them out, the town had even tried passing a mask law. That sort of thing drew the Wizard like a magnet. Just try to stop him—he'd come back harder. He was already planning a return to Ann Arbor.

RODNEY STUBBS LIVED SOUTH of Knox near Culver, a little town on a lake that was home to a military academy. I sat by that lake for a while, reluctant to actually get to the Stubbs home.

By the time I arrived, at least twenty cars were parked along the front of Rodney's property. As I backed into a spot, two rifle-toting Nighthawks approached, one male, one female, both wearing black. The woman came up to me as I got out of the car and patted me down. "Why the extra security?" I asked.

She announced that they were looking for someone "wearing a wire."

"I'm a journalist," I told her, "and I do have a tape recorder." The man piped up that he had seen me before. It was okay.

Rodney and Jeanette Stubbs lived in a trailer set on a couple of acres. They had a detached garage where food was being served and Nirvana pumped out of the sound system. A cross wrapped with twine, maybe ten feet tall, stood ready in the yard.

Tony Berry, the Cyclops, was sitting on the back flap of a pickup truck, yakking with his buddies about college football scores. He had on a new baseball hat with an orange insignia: KKK LIFETIME MEMBER. Just up the driveway stood his mother, Edna, and I asked her about the Springer show.

"We said no at first," she explained. "We said, 'You're not going to make idiots out of us.' And I think we converted 'em." Now Springer was planning "a family show," and the Kluxers would all take their kids.

The Wizard had such faith in his ability to spin people, he too seemed to believe the we-converted-them line. "This isn't his regular crew," Jeff Berry informed me. "It's a different producer. They kind of believe a lot of stuff that we're talking about."

Edna added: "They're letting us pick out the audience. We can give passes to our friends."

"Oh, we made *big* demands," Jeff bragged. "You're going to see our phone number right across the screen. That's going to be in writing or there ain't gonna be no show. I done told them that. I said, I don't care how much time, how much money you spend out here, we're going to get our rights."

I asked the Wizard about the security, those Nighthawks guarding the perimeter. "It's just that we're beefing up," he said. "We're getting too popular. Basically what it is—I think we're getting too big for our own britches as the government wants to put it, and he's going to send whoever the heck he wants out here to mess with us."

"You mean infiltrators?"

"Drive-bys. We got kids here." The Wizard pointed at five preschoolers playing in the fenced area in front of Rodney's trailer. "That's our future." Every once in a while over the course of the evening, I would hear some four-year-old scream out, "White power!"

The Wizard now went by the name of the Reverend Jeff Berry, and he'd changed the name of his organization to the Church of the American Knights of the Ku Klux Klan. The Klan mask was a "religious veil," the Wizard asserted.

"We're more close with God than any religion. Okay, you say some of us so-called swear. Well, *swear* is a word. The only vulgar word, like the Bible says—Thou shalt not use the Lord's name in vain. These words that we use now that people say is cuss words, that's just because people say it is. If nobody said it was, they'd just be normal words like me and you talking."

Just outside the open garage, Tony Berry stood at a microphone, announcing that he would now read a paper on interracial marriage. He'd put on a white robe and hood. I suspected that all this seriousness was for the further benefit of the *Jerry Springer* crew, there to film the cross-lighting. Tony read just a paragraph or two—about how race mixing used to be condemned, but then "in 1972 a professor from left-wing Harvard University coined a new smear word called 'racism'" and all the scientific studies of racial difference were suppressed, only to be replaced with "unscientific racial equality screeds written by Marcus [*sic*] Jews like Ashley Montagu" ("man-tongue," as Tony pronounced it).

Suddenly someone tossed a black baby doll at Tony's feet, where

Jeanette Stubbs kicked at it viciously. "Keep it away from me!" yelled some in the crowd, and Tony called, "Smear the queer!" as the doll was tossed to a guy in a BOYS IN THE HOOD T-shirt, and someone else called out, "Pass the nigger!" A gaggle of Kluxers kicked it around, while one of the Nighthawks in black robe and hood approached with a thick rope. He made a noose.

"Now, now," said Rodney Stubbs, stepping into the circle of people kicking at the doll. "We're white separatists, not white supremacists." Then Rodney stepped aside, stuffing a chaw of Red Man into his mouth, while the Nighthawk hung the doll. Another unnerving moment of Klan "fun." That lynching impulse never went away.

Stubbs told me his comment about being a separatist was "just a joke." As speeches continued outside, he'd taken a seat in his garage where he'd made himself a kind of den: a bar with three or four stools, a wood-burning stove, flags both Confederate and American, a Klan figurine, an illustration of Clint Eastwood.

I never went into the Stubbs's trailer, but it looked shabbier than Dragon Rick's, site of the January cross-lighting. "It's not the best, but it's paid for," Rodney commented. He'd driven a truck for eighteen years, and now he was on disability—a househusband. He cooked, cleaned, and watched the kids, while Jeanette worked a factory job.

Outside at the microphone Grand Dragon Brad Thompson went through the whole list of the year's rallies, briefly assessing each. The ups, like Kokomo: "my best, because of the history, because in the twenties, Kokomo was the Klan hotbed of the nation." And the downs, like New Castle: "a worst-case scenario of a rally going bad because of law enforcement." In conclusion, the Dragon estimated that they had cost the government something like a million and a half dollars by exercising their First Amendment rights. But that was "a bargain when you consider the billions and billions of dollars this country wastes on rinky-dink countries, like that Jewish country, Israel."

In the fast-fading twilight I could see two guys over at the cross, standing in the bed of a pickup, spraying the top with kerosene.

Then, with the darkness, came another chilling moment of that day, an earnest impassioned speech by a young officer I hadn't met before—the Hydra. Illuminated by the harsh lights of the television cameras, he stood unrobed, blond, and almost sweet-looking, like the young Nazi at the end of *Cabaret* who sings "Tomorrow Belongs to Me." The Hydra was a true believer, not a buffoon or a know-nothing or someone with low self-esteem looking to become one of the ultrahigh muckety-mucks. Nor was his anti-Semitism just "a special little deal for Jerry Springer." It was right out of the pages of *The Turner Diaries* and utterly heartfelt. He spoke with a kind of breathless intensity: "You *got* to realize who the real enemy is. Not the niggers. Not the Mexicans. They're all stupid. They're thugs. It's the Jews!"

"It's niggers," someone called from the crowd.

"The JEWS!!" shouted the Hydra. *"They're* the ones that fucking got the power, man. *They're* the ones that got all the control of the money, the publicity. You watch when we go on *Jerry Springer*. You watch how much of it's going to be true, and how much of it they're going to cut out. Okay? And make us look like fucking *in*breds. The Jews control everything! I got sixty TV stations with niggers on forty-nine of 'em. The Jews are trying to get us to breed interracially! Wake up, people!! We're not going to have no real white people left! Get your Bibles out. Start reading, man! God has given us our right to be white and to carry on His word. People, you HAVE to be educated. You HAVE to multiply!"

At this point Jeff walked up in his Wizard robe, carrying the Hydra's baby—just a few months old and wearing white shorts with K K K printed across the back about belt high. "Greetings white brothers and sisters," said the Wizard. "It's great to look out over the countryside and not see no niggers. Or no Jews."

Tony Berry ordered everyone to get robed up, face masks down, no cigarettes. As they prepared, individual Kluxers occasionally let out a lone call of "White Power!!"

About forty robed Klansmen formed a line in front of the garage and marched solemnly into a circle around the cross, where they stood with unlit torches, evenly spaced. I felt certain they'd rehearsed.

The notable thing this time was the political tirade from Rodney Stubbs, who paced near the cross, declaring loudly that many Americans "don't have enough white Aryan blood in 'em to stand up. And that's why the rest of us boils with anger, discontent, and even hatred." Was God a racist? Yes! It was in the Bible: the chosen race. Did Jesus believe in violence at the proper time? Yes! He drove out the moneychangers, and "if He had lived today, He would have carried an AK-47."

So torches were lit. Raised. White Power. The cross began to burn.

That night a few other journalists had been invited along with the *Springer* crew, and the ceremony ended with one last photo op—a Klan wedding. Both the bride and the groom wore hoods, as "Reverend" Berry spoke the familiar words. It came off as oddly perfunctory. Brad Thompson and his wife, Brenda, had decided to renew their vows. At the words "You may now kiss the bride," both raised their masks.

I could leave. I said good-bye to the Wizard, and he replied, "Be careful now, okay? We look at you as one of us."

"Great," I said in shock.

One of us? It was mortifying to be seen as a benign witness to their horrible cause. But the Wizard's claim of connection went further. Earlier that day he'd said to me, "You're like family." That one stuck in the craw. Of course, he meant it as a compliment. And all I could manage in the end was "Great," instead of something that would have distanced me.

The fact was, I was afraid and disturbed about the ways in which I might be "one of them." I wasn't just there as a journalist, after all, but as someone with a certain inheritance to confront. A grandfather I loved in the Klan. A town I loved responsible for the lynching. It didn't matter that my grandfather was so different from the Wizard. That I was, too. I would be "one of them" unless I worked on it. I couldn't just anoint myself their opposite— the "good white person." Racism survives on such complacency.

Even when I was horrified by what these Klansmen did and said, I didn't think it appropriate to assume some sort of moral superiority. I'd begun to think that this threw us off—and by *us* I mean the "relatively conscious" white people. Very few of us deserved to be anything but humble.

Moral indignation was the motor driving Jerry Springer, for example, when he used his shows to mock and browbeat Kluxers—a spectacle that only added fuel to their fire. Acting as the scapegoat for all of white racism is a Klansman's job, part of his function as the "bad white." He is the decoy who leads us away from looking at ourselves.

So somehow they had to be resisted, not scapegoated. But it was hard to know what to do. Empathy didn't exactly work, either. They seemed to be too far inside their alternate universe to ever be reached.

As THE WIZARD AND OTHERS drifted off to the garage for their party, I settled in for another half hour near the still-burning cross with a reporter from South Bend, listening to the Dragon, Brad Thompson, and the Exalted Cyclops of Allen County (Fort Wayne), one David.

The Dragon informed us that all major Klan organizations in the country had just met together in South Carolina at an Imperial Council. Cyclops David read the list of goals and demands they'd come up with: begin drug-testing for welfare recipients, end affirmative action, protect America's jobs, close all borders to illegal aliens, outlaw homosexuality. At the end of the twentieth century such an agenda almost passed for normal. It was just the right wing of normal. I could think of people in Congress who might agree with every point.

David explained that they weren't really anti-Semitic. "We're not talking about a friend of a friend that's a Jew. We're just opposed to the international banking system controlling our destiny." International banking mythology is quintessential anti-Semitism, however. Dragon Brad mentioned that he'd just read *The Protocols of the Elders of Zion.* Purported to be a secret Jewish plan for world domination, *The Protocols* were fabricated in Russia near the beginning of the twentieth century, fueling the hatred behind the pogroms. But the Dragon clearly had no idea that *The Protocols* was fiction, and he wouldn't have believed me if I'd told him. I hadn't even read them. He had, and he and the Cyclops were there to educate me.

My education continued as they explained that we were destined to have microchips planted in our hands so the government could keep track of us, that UN troops from places like Bosnia and Chechnya would soon come into our homes to take our guns away as part of the imminent "world hand-gun ban," and that the things happening now were the same things that had happened under English rule before the Revolutionary War. Just replace "king of England" with "federal government."

"If we're pressed enough, we'll uprise," the Dragon sighed.

Behind them the cross smoldered and threw sparks. They explained that freedom of religion did not include, say, Hindus. That wasn't what Thomas Jefferson had in mind. "Granted, we have to put up with them."

"We don't really have that much exposure to Jews around here," the Dragon admitted. "But we feel the shock wave from their—all their culture and the big banking deal. Chemical Bank, Chase Manhattan, the Rocke-fellers. David Rockefeller, he's the head of the trilateralist group. You know what a trilateralist is? It's a small group of Jews that controls a large sum of money." *The Protocols of the Elders of Zion* had really opened his eyes. "That's what we do. We read, we educate ourselves, and then we educate other people. Just like we're doing right now. We're Ku-Kluxing you guys."

"Of course, you've got a lot of people that just refuse," the Dragon con-tinued. "They're closed-minded. They're misguided white people. They hate the Klan for what the Klan used to stand for. Unfortunately we had a few bad apples—back in the twenties, and the thirties, and the forties, and the fifties, and the sixties."

▲ ▲ ▲

A COUPLE OF WEEKS LATER I called Grand Dragon Brad Thompson to arrange our interview. That same afternoon he and the American Knights were heading to Chicago to tape *The Jerry Springer Show*. He was clearly impressed that a fleet of stretch limos would pick them all up. *Springer* would also put them up somewhere and hand out $100 apiece in food money. State Nighthawk Grizzly Smith had already left to check everything out—"and if he doesn't like how it looks, it's off." The American Knights were proud of how they were controlling this whole *Springer* thing. According to Thompson, they had "final cut."

They had also just applied for a permit to display a cross on the courthouse lawn in Auburn during the twelve days of Christmas. And they had a rally set for Peru. Thompson sounded tired, but he was so eager to talk, he then launched into the story of how he came to join the Klan. In 1975 he found some Klan business cards on a Greyhound bus during a trip to Mexico. But mostly he'd become a Klansman by reading. An unlikely path. "I can go anywhere in a book. I experienced racism in my readings."

When I asked for directions to his house, he said, "I guess I fit two stereotypes of a Klansman. I chew tobacco and I live in a trailer." I would know his trailer by the three vehicles parked there with Klan bumper stickers. He talked about how intimidated his neighbors were. "A lot of people are plain scared silly of us."

THE DRAGON LIVED IN AUBURN, about an hour and a half north of Marion. A young blond guy was standing on the parking slab in front of the yellow trailer. "Brad's not here," he announced. Thompson had left for Kokomo at eight that morning. I sat parked in front of the narrow strip of yard with its swingset and tossed toys, watching teenage boys come and go, one of them Thompson's son. Then I drove out of the bleak trailer park into a dismal shopping area. Next to this, Marion was an oasis of splendor. Checking back every so often, I managed to kill three hours. Always a different car on the slab. I noted the window stickers in one: Nirvana. Pantera. AKIA ("A Klansman I Am"). Back home I found a message from the Dragon on my answering machine. Car trouble. "I feel bad. I apologize."

Two days later I was back in Auburn. This time the complication was that Thompson had to go parlay with the city planning commission over the cross the Klan wanted to place at the DeKalb County courthouse. When I arrived at two-thirty, he was in full pacing mode, anxious about the meeting. He'd assembled a big pile of clippings on the American Knights plus all of his speeches and suggested that maybe I could go make copies while he talked to the commissioners.

He pulled out a cloth about a foot square with a Klansman in a black robe painted on it, along with the words IMPERIAL NIGHTHAWK. One of the Dragon's many jobs was to correspond with members in prison, and some incarcerated brother had sent this to him. Thompson then gave me directions to the copy shop and left me alone in the trailer, saying he totally trusted me, and I should make myself at home.

The copying took well over an hour, so Thompson got back to the trailer before I did. Now he was a bit freaked because the Fort Wayne TV stations had turned up to cover the meeting, and he was going to be on the news. For the first time everybody in town would see his face labeled "Klansman." He hoped he had made good statements. Thompson's wife Brenda was home from the factory where she worked as an assembler (packing boxes), and she turned on the television.

There was something genuine about the Dragon, despite those moments of grandiosity when he supposed himself the heir to D. C. Stephenson, legendary Grand Dragon of the 1920s. We sat down at the kitchen table, which did not look big enough to accommodate the household. Thompson still had four children at home. As he began to answer my questions, he sounded exhausted. The Dragon was almost constantly sleep-deprived. One of the few Klansmen I'd met with an actual job, he commonly worked twelve-hour shifts at a local foundry where he poured iron, usually from six P.M. to six A.M., six days a week. He always wanted the overtime. Then he'd spend the day Ku-Kluxing. He averaged about three hours of sleep. That day he'd had two.

The *Springer* taping sounded like exactly the sort of debacle that made the program so notorious. Thompson wasn't sure when it would be televised. He described how the American Knights had taken their children along for this "family show," and Jerry Springer then accused them of abusing the kids by teaching them Klan ways. Brenda got so mad she lunged at the host, and the show devolved into a shouting match. Then they were kicked off. Apart from that, "we got treated real good," Thompson reported. Again he mentioned the stretch limos. One had come right to his door.

The Dragon was wearing an "Irish" baseball cap, T-shirt, and jeans. He began to talk about his meeting with the planning commission, how they told him they were going to start landscaping the courthouse lawn in the middle of December and that would take precedence over erecting a Klan cross. He was getting a runaround, he complained, and on top of that he figured he'd get hate mail and hate calls.

Why do you even want to do this? I asked. "Religious significance for our organization," said the Dragon. That sounded like something cooked in the Wizard's brain. I thought it rather ironic that Berry's in-your-face style kept forcing white people to say no to white supremacy in these little all-white towns. DeKalb County had a few hundred Mexicans, a few dozen blacks, and according to Thompson, two Jews.

The day he missed our interview the Dragon had been in Kokomo protesting at the state NAACP meeting. "Because the free ride's got to stop," he said, laying out the standard Klan line—that people of color now had more rights than white people, and if the NAACP wanted to raise a cross at the courthouse, the commission would approve it immediately. He began to worry again about the repercussions he might face because of going public today. But he admitted, as Kluxers rarely did, that some Klansmen were violent. Not the American Knights, but others. "I've met some of 'em," he said. "They scare the hell out of me."

I wanted to get a sense of where Grant County stood in Klan membership compared to the rest of the state. The Dragon said it was about average, while Allen County (Fort Wayne) had the most members. "In Grant County," he said, "there's right around—a big round number. There's right around—three hundred. And that's just the applications I know of." But he had thought about that number before saying it, and I could see the lie.

Thompson knew of two other Klans active in Indiana—the National Knights out of South Bend, and a group near Bloomington that called itself Klan but was really skinhead. "Now don't get me wrong," he said. "There's always someone breaking off with about ten or fifteen guys and calling themselves a Klan and getting a thousand cards printed and saying 'I'm Imperial Wizard.' I could do the same thing."

Rodney Stubbs had assured me that there were five or six active Klans in Grant County alone, and Stubbs had been a Klansman longer. Yet somehow the Dragon was more credible. He said people from other groups kept coming to join the American Knights "because we're so popular."

After encountering so many people who still feared the Klan, I was interested to discover that it barely existed in Indiana apart from Jeff Berry's group. Maybe the guys who were still hanging out in Elwood at the "Klan bar" all belonged to the American Knights now, but the very idea of them had been scaring people for years. Obviously busting up United Klans of

America had never diminished the myth, and myth was what made the Klan strong.

Brenda interrupted us as the Klan story began to air. The Dragon and I got up to move closer to the set as the TV reporter announced, "Klan members are depending on freedom of speech and freedom of religion to get the commissioners' approval. But some DeKalb residents we talked to today are depending on those same commissioners to keep the Klan out of town." Then came the soundbites from random citizenry, whose sentiments were summarized well enough by the last of them: "Flatly, no. I don't think there's any place for the Klan in DeKalb County."

The Dragon groused, "They didn't even talk to the ones that are *for* it."

As if in answer, the announcer then said that they *had* found one person who defended the Klan's right to freedom of expression, though that person didn't agree with their views.

Brenda said, "They didn't even show you, Brad."

He said, "Good."

As we sat down again at the kitchen table, the news reader declared that an interview with the Grand Dragon would run at ten.

"This TV thing I hate," anguished the Grand Dragon of Indiana. "I hate every bit of it. But I have to, because it's what I believe in. I'll catch all kinds of hell. Maybe. I don't know. I've been on TV before. My name's been in the paper and I haven't had any repercussions, but this is going to be a good five-minute spot. Prime time."

"Is this the first time your face will be on TV?" I asked.

"Pretty much," he said. "I've been on before, but I've always had my mask on." He wasn't worried about his job at the foundry, he said, but now he wondered if his family was going to have some trouble. And what if the owners of the trailer park saw it? "See, I risked quite a bit."

We got back to the interview. I wanted to know more about the reading he'd done that had so influenced him to join the Klan.

He'd begun as a teenager with a book from his high school library, *Circle of Fire*, which he described as "a colored child's view of what it was like to have the Klan around." Then he read *Hooded Americanism*, "a long hard book," but he'd struggled through the whole thing. Both these books are anti-Klan—and they only made him more interested. What attracted him was "the secrecy, the white part. That there's still a group out there for the white man."

As for the Klan business cards on the bus, he'd been on his way to Mexico with his high school Spanish class when he found them. They had an address for the Christian Knights in East Texas. He wrote them and joined up. "I was a mail-order Klansman." But he dropped out after four or five years, frustrated that he couldn't participate in their functions. "It was nice to get the literature, but it was pointless." He joined the American Knights soon after the group began in March 1994. He'd heard about the Hicksville event via CB radio and went to see it. "The Hicksville parade is what did it for me."

The Dragon gave me the first straightforward account I'd heard of the birth of the American Knights. Jeff Berry created the group, proclaiming himself Imperial Wizard, after Tony Berry was beaten up in Hicksville. The Wizard had told me that that was merely when they "went public," implying that they'd been around much longer. But according to Thompson, the American Knights had four members at that point, and the parade through Hicksville was the first thing they ever did, and "it's just growed and growed." He listed all the states where they now had members, from New Jersey to West Virginia to Arizona.

I wondered if his parents had come to the Klan rally in Bryan, Ohio, his hometown.

"Nope."

"They don't support your Klan membership?"

"No, they sure don't." He and his parents were estranged. Even so, they had endured crank phone calls at all hours of the night for nearly a month. "And my sister was fired because of my rally."

While the Dragon had not learned racism at home, he hadn't learned antiracism, either. He and his parents had never been close. His dad worked two jobs, both were strict, and Thompson spent most of his time in his room, reading. By the time he was out of high school, he'd read "everything" written about Nazis, including *Mein Kampf* and Goebbels's diaries. His parents never tried to discourage his Klan membership when he first joined through the mail. They thought it was "a fad," while Thompson described his racist feelings as "a natural instinct." He had never liked seeing Mexican farm workers with white girls around his hometown. There weren't any blacks. His reactions to them were based on what little he saw of them during trips to Toledo and Fort Wayne. "I'd watch them and see how they acted. Then I'd watch TV and see all the trouble they got into. Who was doing the murders, the raping, the robbery?" He said that, even as a little boy, "I knew there was something not right about the black race."

Thompson's wife, Brenda, was Women's State Nighthawk, and unlike the Dragon, she had grown up around the Klan. But she didn't join with him because they were divorced at the time. The Dragon had married Brenda twice, once in 1978—and that lasted thirteen years—then again in 1995. They had four children and a grandchild. During the four-year interval, he'd married someone else, the mother of his three-year-old. The other child born of this in-between marriage choked to death in November 1994. He mentioned this a couple of times. He showed me a picture of the boy. He was still grieving. The second wife hadn't known about his Klan membership until after the divorce, "but she suspected it because of my views."

He said it had meant a lot to him and Brenda to renew their vows at the cross-lighting. They'd done their second marriage at the courthouse, then gone to Subway for a sub, and then Thompson had to go to work. "That wasn't very romantic."

Brenda called over to us. Another Klan cross story. We again went over to the television, where another reporter was outlining the conflict: Klan freedom of speech versus Klan-not-welcome. Here they cut to Thompson, wearing round blue-tinted shades: "We're unified that we're celebrating this, our celebration, and we're in the community. It's part of our contribution to the courthouse because everybody else does it. Other churches, other religions." The segment ended with the promise of more Grand Dragon at eleven.

"They wanted me to take my glasses off real bad," said the Dragon as we sat back down. "Well, we'll see what happens. What kind of retribution."

He started talking about that afternoon's meeting again, how one of the commissioners came up and said, I'm glad you didn't bring any of those Berrys. Thompson said he had no idea why the Berrys were unpopular. "Jeff told me, after seeing how much we've grown, that he could give me the reins and go somewhere else and start it all over again. That's how confident he is."

But Thompson didn't seem to have any aspirations to become a Wizard, the national leader. He liked being Dragon, the state leader. He described himself as "Jeff's personal secretary, Jeff's gofer, Jeff's bodyguard, Jeff's best friend." Jeff Berry showed him how to be Grand Dragon, "and I've changed the organization. I've put my mark on it." The Dragon was going to rewrite the old Kloran from the 1920s. He was going to update the oaths. He and the Wizard were having a disagreement about Klancraft, however. The Dragon thought they needed it, but modernized, while the Wizard had no use for it at all.

I remembered how, at the cross-lighting, the Dragon had told me he sometimes wished he could have lived back in the 1920s. In Kokomo. "Of course, then I'd be dead right now." Now as the interview wound down, he showed me his two most recent tattoos, a myoak inside his left arm and a robed Klansman on horseback inside his right arm—the latter a gift from a new member. "I don't hide."

He got up and looked at the television again. "Well, my phone ain't rang." As he sat back down, he said, "The worst that could happen is people start driving by, figuring out that I live here. Worst that could happen is that my tires would get flattened, my windshields would get broke out. They'll throw stuff at the trailer. That's the worst. But maybe people have fear of a trailer park. Maybe they're saying, 'I don't want to drive down there. I don't know who else is Klan.' "

THAT NOVEMBER 1996 *Jerry Springer* aired the "family show" featuring the American Knights. Or as one newspaper ad put it: "Klan Families . . . Babies in White Hoods! Innocent children taken to cross-burnings by their KKK parents! HATE—The Next Generation."

The Wizard, the Dragon, the Hydra, and State Nighthawk Grizzly Smith all appeared with their families, entertaining the masses with the usual screaming match. The real story was what came after, because Springer, as agreed, ran the American Knights' phone number. The Dragon and the Wizard spent two weeks answering calls at the Berry home, ultimately logging in more than 6,200 queries from people who wanted to join. "We had so many envelopes to mail out that the post office in Auburn complained," the Dragon reported later.

Springer's producers ran a phone number for the antiracist Southern Poverty Law Center along with Berry's. But "many of those calling the Center seemed confused," said the SPLC's *Intelligence Report.* "They, too, were looking to join up."

Early in December the DeKalb County commissioners announced that the American Knights of the Ku Klux Klan would be erecting a six-foot cross on the courthouse lawn. The commissioners felt they had little choice, since they would face a lawsuit if they did not grant what one of them termed "an awkward, very unpopular request." The American Knights told the press that they were merely trying to bring religion back to Christmas.

TWENTY-THREE

THE SNAKE UNDER
THE TABLE

By the time I reached my last months in Marion, I'd seen that every topic related to race was radioactive, and there were limits to how close I would ever get to certain facts. It wasn't just the shame-induced secrecy around the old Invisible Empire, populated by many grandfathers apart from my own. Or the silence of the Miami, bullied for a generation or two into burying their own culture. Even the noble history of the underground railroad had been hidden to some extent. But the lynching was subtly different. What had happened on August 7, 1930, was a living secret—undead—still pulsing just under the surface. People had never stopped talking about it, at least in private, because they had never stopped having feelings about it.

"This snake is still under the table," observed Bill Munn, a teacher at Marion High and director of the Community History Project. "What happens when you never find out the truth—it gets wormy."

From the start I'd simply dismissed what I knew to be "wormy." Like the story that Cameron was only in jail for stealing chickens. Or the one about Sheriff Jake Campbell throwing keys out to the mob. I was looking for facts, so it took me a long time to understand the power of these narratives and to realize how many people believed them. Eventually I began to make a distinction between the stories that were plain wrong and those that were mythic.

Folklore served its classic function in Marion as a return of the repressed, a way to acknowledge indirectly what couldn't be acknowledged directly. But it also provided a license to distort the facts to the point of obliterating them.

THE STORIES TOLD IN black and white Marion were sometimes different. For example, only in the black community did people say that Cameron was in jail for stealing chickens. At least, I never heard a white person make such a claim. I had assumed that just a tiny percentage of the county's African Americans believed this, until I heard more and more people talk about it. In the end I concluded that the majority probably didn't accept this story, but those who did were absolutely adamant. That Cameron was already in jail on August 6, 1930, and that he was never lynched on August 7. As one black woman told me, with some pique, he invented his story later "to get the glory."

This really puzzled me. Cameron's trial was a matter of public record. He had actually faced the electric chair for his part in the River Road crimes, indicted for murder in the first degree while perpetrating a robbery; murder in the first degree, accessory before the fact; rape in the first degree; and rape in the first degree, accessory before the fact. He'd signed a confession. The NAACP thought him such a lost cause they didn't want to use the organization's scarce resources to defend him. But once again Cameron proved to be extraordinarily lucky. For some reason, the NAACP's Flossie Bailey and Walter White changed their minds. Thus Cameron ended up in court with two distinguished African American attorneys, Robert L. Bailey and Robert L. Brokenburr. (Bailey—no relation to Flossie—became Indiana's assistant attorney general in 1931; Brokenburr went on to serve a couple of decades in the state senate.) These lawyers got Cameron his crucial change of venue, from Marion to Anderson, one county south. There they managed to quash the confession, which Cameron said he had never read. Finally, in the summer of 1931, he was found guilty as an accessory to voluntary manslaughter in the death of Claude Deeter and sentenced to two to twenty-one years.

Cameron's trial was typically underreported in the Marion papers. But that doesn't explain the chicken story, or the suspicion and resentment of Cameron I'd encountered in so many African Americans of his generation. "We older people know the reason why he didn't get hung," Reverend William Perkins declared in an oral history interview, explaining that it was "chickens or something" that put Cameron in jail. "Of course, [Cameron] doesn't talk to us, because we know him, see."

I sought out Reverend Perkins, who was eighty-one years old in 1996 and still barbering full time at his one-man shop. On Sundays he preached at the House of Worship for All People.

Perkins had been friends with both Shipp and Smith. The night before the murder on the River Road, Perkins and a friend set up a tent in the backyard, and Abe Smith slept in the tent with them. Perkins had lived near the Shipp house and learned about the lynching when carloads of white people began driving by, yelling, "We just got your boy!"

Perkins had also known Cameron. "I played with him." When I asked about his belief that Cameron was in jail for stealing chickens, he said he couldn't prove it. It was just what he heard. "People said he couldn't have been out there [on the River Road] because he was already in jail. Of course, history—I don't know. If you're going to write a book, you probably add a lot to make the book."

Add a lot? I mentioned that Cameron had gone to trial and to prison for what happened on the River Road. Perkins's reply was terse. I couldn't quite hear it. He didn't say it again.

Maybe a few people were jealous of Cameron—his notoriety, the supposed money he was making. But I thought the chicken story also related to how much people *didn't* want to remember. What had happened to Cameron touched everyone in Marion's black community in 1930. Not only did he embody that trauma, he insisted on keeping it alive—and did so from a distance. (He hadn't lived in Marion since 1930.) The chicken story transformed Cameron's terror into something inane, trifling. In jail over a chicken. It diminished him.

Reverend Perkins's tone was laconic as he recounted the lynching of his friends. He recalled that, the morning after, he drove down to the square in a Model T. "Quiet. Wasn't nothing." Within a week, however, his family had packed him off to Chicago, where he stayed with an aunt for six months.

"You must have been shocked when it happened, though," I said.

"Oh yeah," he replied. "Of course, if you're doing things that are bad, bad things happen to you."

Years after talking to Perkins, I discovered inadvertently where the story about Cameron originated. I had called Roger Smith on another matter. Smith was the former NAACP president whose daughter had not been allowed to skate. Smith told me his father heard the story from Charles Truex, a white man and police captain in 1930. "Truex said he arrested [Cameron] for something else," Smith remembered.

Now it made sense to me. Truex was the one who apparently saved

Cameron at the tree. I'd already heard from Mayor Bill Henry (whose father, a fireman, was present on August 7 and knew Truex), *"Truex told* [the mob], *'Yes. This is a guy I caught getting off the freight.' Lied through his teeth. And that's why they didn't hang Cameron."* I speculated that when Truex stood there lying, he named one of the offenses young men were most often jailed for during the Depression: riding freights, stealing chickens. Of course, I would never know if he'd been misunderstood when he talked later to people like Smith's father, or if he'd simply lied again.

THE POINTING MAN in the famous photo, I was told, died in a terrible accident when the ghosts of Shipp and Smith appeared on the hood of his car. I've already mentioned a couple of other stories about these avenging ghosts. That's one way to exact a punishment when the courts won't do it.

Another "injustice story" was even more literal. I heard it from Lillie Roebuck, director of Marion's Human Relations Commission. An African American who'd spent most of her life in Marion, Roebuck wondered if I had ever spoken to anyone involved in the lynching. I could tell her only about those who'd witnessed it. And what were *their* feelings? she wondered. This led me to talk eventually about Harold Vermilion and his hope to place a statue at the spot where the hanging occurred.

Roebuck then related a statue story, which may have been told exclusively in the black community. At least I never heard a white person tell it. "There *was* a statue there—on the spot where the hanging occurred," said Roebuck. "But it fell." She couldn't remember the details.

"There are some unresolved feelings here about the lynching," she continued, "but the next generation . . ." She addressed her assistant, a young black woman named Dawn: "What do *you* think about the lynching?"

"I never think about it," said Dawn. But she too had heard the statue story. "It was a scale," she said.

"The scale of justice," Roebuck then remembered. "It was always toppling over. There was a rumor that it was cursed because of the hanging."

Here was another story that was true at the level of metaphor: the scale of justice had fallen down at the lynching site. In fact, there was a sculpture known locally as Lady Justice at the courthouse, placed atop the dome in 1881, and still there to witness the events of August 7, 1930. One of her hands held the proverbial scale; the other hand, either a book or a sword. Accounts vary. Her head had been modeled on the Statue of Liberty. But she never fell over. In 1943 the dome was declared unsafe and was removed.

The courthouse has been domeless, a building beheaded, ever since. Lady Justice went to Matter Park, where people apparently used her for target practice. By the time the city hauled the bullet-riddled sculpture off to a junkyard in 1980, the body was damaged beyond repair, but a Marion man rescued the head and donated it to the library.

When I was a girl in the 1950s and 1960s, the courthouse was still the center of town. I recall old farmers on benches, a cannon (I think), and definitely the trees. County officials had them all cut down in 1987, after trying everything else to cope with the thousands of birds who'd settled in and left so many droppings that "it looked like snow." As the *Chronicle-Tribune* reported on one attempt to drive the birds away in the early 1970s: "Officials have had someone retained to rid the courthouse of its own special 'curse.'"

I had also heard from Roger Smith that his uncle poisoned the lynching tree. But a white man assured me that the city cut it down because of pressure from the black community. That they'd used the plague of birds as an excuse. I wondered if this was more folklore, a guilt story from the white community: that they cut down every single tree to get the one.

I HAD HEARD THAT Sheriff Jake Campbell threw keys out to the mob within my first twenty-four hours in Marion. It was a story with some currency in both the black and white communities.

All the evidence, however, indicated that the mob had battered the doors with sledgehammers and that only a couple of those inside the jail were actually locked. In the depositions, the police talked repeatedly about this hammering, and while I certainly considered their testimony dubious, I found photographs of the jail's broken locks in the August 9 *Indianapolis Star*. If the mob didn't hammer the locks, the police must have done it themselves, which seems unlikely. The sledging of the locks is corroborated by Ogden's investigator and various reporters, all of whom visited the jail soon after it happened.

I also felt that the sheriff had no reason to risk handing the keys over. He couldn't know who exactly was milling around in that crowd. What if there'd been just one righteous witness, just one out-of-town newspaperman, who saw him do it? Even if Campbell was "in it with 'em," he had to make a show of trying to stop the mob. Yet it also seems noteworthy that the two most detailed stories I heard about the mob having the keys came from men connected to the sheriff's department—after the Campbell era, so they were not present themselves during the break-in. Still, I had to wonder what it could mean that such stories were circulating, decades later, among Grant County sheriffs and deputies.

Tom Wise had taped an interview with Vaughn Treber, who served two terms as Grant County sheriff, 1937 to 1940 and 1948 to 1950. At the time of the lynching Treber was a special deputy, mostly because he had a car. "Grant County didn't even own a spark plug, let alone an automobile," he told Wise. The night of August 7 he was at a garage fixing up a Model T for his brother, when some men came by to tell him to report to the jail. He went immediately, but the lynching was over. "I was told, I didn't see it," said Treber, "that when the mob gathered on the outside, there was one of them had a sledgehammer and he was trying to knock the hinges off the door and they said—now this is hearsay—that Campbell came out on the porch and threw the jail keys out in the yard."

The other story I'd heard about the keys came from the Ex-Deputy, who'd been part of the Grant County sheriff's department in the 1950s. According to the Ex-Deputy, the mob had used an acetylene torch to get through the front door. "Jake was setting inside there, and he wouldn't let them in, so they took the torch and cut [the lock]. And he said, 'Boys, the keys are laying on that desk. I won't hand 'em to ya.' They got the keys and went up. Being deputy sheriff there, I've heard all that many times."

Again there was a kind of metaphoric truth to the story of the keys. But apparently the mob didn't need them.

I WONDERED HOW THERE could still be so much speculation and innuendo about the relationships among Deeter, Ball, Shipp, Smith, and Cameron. This should have been knowable.

As it turned out, the story I heard my first day in Marion—that Shipp, Smith, and Ball did robberies together—was just one variation on a theme. In that one she'd pick up a white guy downtown and bring him to Lover's Lane, where the other two would roll him.

There was also a story that Deeter and Smith had been partners in holding up filling stations and had argued over money.

Then there was a story that Deeter, Smith, Shipp, Ball, and Cameron were all part of a gang that committed stick-ups together, and they'd argued.

I also heard it said that Deeter and Smith were both dating Mary Ball, that Smith became enraged when he found her with Deeter on Lover's Lane. And the cops found her wearing Smith's watch.

In another account just like the above, the cops found her wearing

Smith's diamond ring. (The *Leader-Tribune* reported that the robbers tried to take Ball's watch and high school ring.)

The ugliest of these tales had Deeter taking Mary Ball out on a bet—because he knew that she was dating Abe Smith. As one of my informants put it, "They said [Deeter] couldn't do anything with her after she had a black man, and he was going to prove to her he could." Another put it more bluntly: "Once you've had black, you never go back." This version of events shocked me with its unthinking endorsement of racist myths about black sexuality—and both my sources were African Americans. In their story, Shipp and Smith came along to save Mary Ball.

While I don't think this account was widely believed, any heat that remained had collected around the Deeters, not the Balls. I remembered Willie Deeter's complaint: "I'm marked by the colored." Most of the alternate takes on the River Road robbery found fault with Deeter, while much of the folklore said that Mary Ball had a black sweetheart. Such stories serve as rebuttals to the rape claim, but I doubt their veracity.

All of these accounts are about shifting blame away from Shipp and Smith or, at least, giving everyone a share. Making Cameron part of the robberies. Making Ball part of the robberies. Making Deeter part of the robberies. The only evidence I ever found to support any of this was that Cameron was initially charged for both the River Road holdup and one at a filling station. The charges were dropped. As Cameron began his two-to-twenty-one-year prison sentence, prosecutor Harley Hardin "saw no reason to spend more money in carrying on an unnecessary prosecution," according to the *Leader-Tribune.* Cameron has always maintained that he never participated in any stickup before the River Road.

Another story circulating in the black community (at least a small part of it) asserted that a Deeter was present at the lynching tree, and there one of the victims slapped him in the face. Ever since then—so the story goes—Deeters have been born with purple handprints on their faces. "I've seen some of them growing up," one black woman told me. Another assured me: "I've seen one of the girls. It's a full handprint."

One day I heard that a black woman named Laverna Jones had a picture of the Marion lynching that showed three victims. I immediately called Jones, then went to her house to have a look. She pulled out a 1975 *Ebony,* and—sure enough—there was a lynching picture with three victims labeled "Marion, Indiana." It was a misidentification. I knew from my research that this particular lynching had taken place in Duluth, Minnesota.

Mrs. Jones told me she had known Joe Deeter, one of Claude's nephews.

According to Carl Deeter, the family spokesman, Joe was "an outlaw, a lot of trouble, a family outcast." And he had certainly done his family no favors, fingering one of the white men in the Duluth photo and telling Mrs. Jones: "That's a Deeter."

THE SOUVENIRS OR MYTHIC objects that were distributed—the rope, the clothing, even body parts—were like relics collected from saints or martyrs, charged with that luminosity conferred by suffering. Back in 1930 certain white people must have taken pleasure in that.

Cameron owned a rope piece passed to him by Dick Treber, son of Sheriff Vaughn Treber, who may have gotten it from Jake Campbell himself. Cameron treasured this as an artifact for his museum. No doubt there were other relics still squirreled away in Marion attics. They were like the snapshots taken that night that had since disappeared from so many family albums. Those who weren't ashamed to have them knew that they were supposed to be. I encountered a teenager one day who told me that his grandpa had lynching pictures he kept somewhere in his bedroom, that occasionally the old man would go in there and shut the door to look at them. As if they were porn.

Maybe for some people, any evidence of what really happened acquired an aura of the forbidden. One Marion man told me that when he first saw the famous lynching photo, he was fourteen, and the friend who showed it to him announced, "It's against the law to have this."

Phyllis Farmer, a white woman active in the NAACP, recalled one outrageous incident from the 1950s, a period when the lynching was still "quite dominant here," as she put it. One night she and her mother visited a man her mother knew, and they all got to talking about the hanging. The man then brought out a jar and announced proudly, "Here's one of their toes." Farmer got up and left in a huff. Later the man apologized, explaining, "I didn't cut it off. Somebody else give it to me."

She would not tell me the man's name, only that he was now dead. Farmer doubted that the toe had really come from one of the victims. But I didn't.

Farmer had another story that illustrated the workings of the snake under the table. As long as the lynching was so much legend and lie, the story could be shaped and used. As long as no one knew who was in that mob, they could come back at any moment.

Farmer had moved to Marion early in the 1950s, from the mostly white town of Frankfort, Indiana. She was about eighteen then and got a job at RCA, where she became friends with a black woman. One day some of her white coworkers took her aside, told her about the lynching, and warned that if Farmer didn't break off the friendship, "this could happen again."

She didn't strike me as someone easily intimidated. Retired after nearly twenty-five years as a forklift operator at General Tire, Farmer was active not just in the NAACP but in the United Way, the Harry S. Truman Democratic Club, and most of all—her union. To Farmer, a true union person treated everyone else in the shop "as a sister or a brother." She took the no-nonsense approach to racism: it was not fair. Period.

So Farmer did not end her friendship with the black woman, but she was laid off soon after her coworkers threatened her. Then she moved to Cleveland, got married, and didn't return to Marion until the early 1960s. By then her black friend had died of cancer.

BILL MUNN MOVED TO Marion in 1969, a year of peak civil rights unrest complete with firebombings. As he began teaching seventh grade in North Marion, he asked his all-white class to tell him something about the town, and one student immediately announced: "We hung the niggers." Munn also recalled white people offering to show him the lynching picture, saying, "I've got it in the trunk of my car."

Decades later maybe a few white people still gloated over their grisly artifacts or photos, but they probably didn't devote much time to thinking about what they meant or why the lynching had happened. For the black community, though, those were crucial questions—survival questions—that the authorities were never going to address. Stories spread to explain it. I know that's why I heard more of them from black people than from white. As time passed, however, the generation that had lived through the events of August 7, 1930, wanted it all to disappear.

Early on I'd had a frustrating encounter with an elderly black man whose wife was Abe Smith's cousin. I was certain he knew something. He hinted that the River Road incident just detonated something that had been building for a while. My guess was that it had to do with miscegenation, but he wouldn't say more. "There is a story behind the story that should stay behind and never be told," the man declared. People still living would be embarrassed, he explained. "It doesn't pay to dig up a dead cat."

IN THE YEAR 2000 Marion's most infamous photo appeared in an exhibit called "Witness" and its accompanying catalog, *Without Sanctuary: Lynching*

Photography in America. White people all over the country had documented these atrocities without shame, often posing as nonchalantly as the Marion crowd, often printing the picture as a postcard and sending it through the mail with a breezy message. The antiques dealer who'd collected them all, James Allen, found them at flea markets and garage sales. In the early to mid-1990s, at a postcard show in central Florida, he purchased a copy of the Marion photo that someone had crudely matted with locks of hair—apparently from one of the victims—and inscribed: "Bo pointn to his niga. Klan 4th, Joplin, Mo. 33."

Had some Missouri klavern really been involved? I thought the caption was more likely an example of Klan "humor." But the pointing man remained the person in the picture most speculated about. The photo's composition made him the focal point, and he had that moustache. "Like Hitler," as more than one person helpfully observed. And what did it mean that he was pointing? I was told first that he was the photographer's assistant. Someone else was sure that he'd worked at Bell Fibre. Larry Hitler tried to claim him as a grandfather.

Then one day I got a plausible-sounding tip that he'd been a barber at a Marion shop still in business. I went to see the current owner. He stood there cutting someone's hair, telling me—no, the pointing man wasn't familiar to him and no barber in 1930 would have had a tattoo. But he had a regular customer who knew something about the hanging.

Later I would learn from this regular, Sonny, that the day after the lynching, his neighbor's wife was trying to wash blood from a shirt. Sonny's family had always speculated that this neighbor was involved in the hanging, but as Sonny put it, "You wouldn't dare ask somebody if they was there. No one would even hardly discuss it." Sonny claimed to have no memory of the neighbor's name.

Did everyone with roots in the county have a story? During the minute it took the barber to get me Sonny's phone number, the customer in the chair piped up and said that *his* uncle had one of the original photographs sold on the square the day after the lynching.

So what was *not* discussed? The names. Whodunnit. Meanwhile I had only to scratch the surface, and some hideous detail came leaking out: Blood on a shirt. *Here's one of their toes.* Again, it astonished and appalled—the way the ripples from this event seemed to have touched nearly everyone in town.

TWENTY-FOUR

TELLTALE

Sometimes I wondered if James Cameron wasn't offering the town a way out of its dilemma about how to address the lynching.

With America's Black Holocaust Museum ensconced in the old jail, Marion would be facing the past big-time and making a show of turning things around. Of course, that would also force many white residents to confront what a father or grandfather had done (or failed to do) on August 7, 1930. I didn't really see support for the idea in the black community, either. Reverend Perkins, for example, suggested, "There should be forgiveness and going ahead. Shouldn't have something to stir that up all the time. If you keep stirring stuff up, it makes hatred." Even some of the locals dedicated to racial reconciliation couldn't get behind the idea. As one of them told me, such a museum would "dominate the town," and "people wouldn't want it to be the focus."

Cameron had already made it clear that he wouldn't move his museum to Marion if he wasn't wanted. And he didn't have the money. Even so I always suspected that the specter of America's Black Holocaust Museum was one more reason the city wanted to get the old jail away from Rex Fansler. Cited as one of Indiana's ten most endangered landmarks, the deteriorating eyesore was also an embarrassment passed by every visitor driving in from the interstate.

Fansler's income came to less than $1,000 a month, and he had never paid taxes on the place. He'd signed the Option to Purchase in October 1995, and a sale to the city had seemed imminent in April 1996, when the Marion Redevelopment Commission discussed the details in a meeting: Fansler would be out by June 1, taxes forgiven, and he would get $25,000.

But when June 1 rolled around, Fansler was still living in the old sheriff's quarters. He didn't seem to know why. He told me that on the day he was supposed to pick up his check, someone had called from city hall to tell him not to come.

The hapless Rex. About three weeks later he was arrested. The startling front-page headline read: MAN FACES CRUELTY CHARGES. Fansler kept seventeen horses on someone else's property just outside Marion. According to the Humane Society and the sheriff's department, the animals didn't have enough food, water, exercise, or medical treatment. Fansler spent the night in a real jail before posting bond. He'd been booked on nine counts of cruelty to animals by neglect.

When I went to see him, he denied everything. But a state livestock investigator had been out to assess the situation, and the horses were described as "spindly" with ribs showing. Fansler had been convicted on the same charge in 1990 in LaGrange County.

THE INDIANA HISTORICAL SOCIETY replied to James Cameron's letter about the old jail, and he immediately sent me a copy.

Locating a museum for the prevention of lynching at the jail seemed "historically appropriate" and "quite exciting," wrote Wilma Gibbs, the IHS archivist for African-American History, but she pointed out that this was really a preservation issue. She suggested that Cameron contact the Historic Landmarks Foundation of Indiana, among other things, and offered to bring up the issue as a member of the foundation's African-American Landmarks Committee.

Early in August I stopped by the old jail to show Rex Fansler the letter. He turned off his soap opera and sat on the couch, snorting at the contents. Someone from the Historic Landmarks Foundation had been there years ago. "He wanted me to *give* him the jail," Fansler complained. "When I refused, he said he'd like me to allow him and two men with him to be agents to sell it." Given all current predicaments, that sounded like a lost opportunity.

The highest appraisal Fansler ever got on the place was $20,000 to $30,000—from the Historic Landmarks Foundation. Another came in at $10,000. Meanwhile he still wanted to charge Cameron $160,000 or more.

Fansler had decided by this time that the cruelty case was political, that he'd really been arrested because the city wanted the jail. He showed me videotape of the horses. To my admittedly untrained eye, they did look terribly thin.

That November a Grant County jury would find him guilty.

ONE AFTERNOON IN OCTOBER, I went to see *The Chamber*, a standard Hollywood approach to racism in America: black victim, white hero, an evil racist we will never be asked to identify with. In this case a vapid young lawyer-hero tries to save his KKK grandfather from the gas chamber.

Near the end the lawyer-hero hears his aunt's explanation about what turned the grandfather into such a racist monster. The aunt pulls a book out from under her mattress and opens it to a picture: the Marion lynching! But Hollywood had altered the photo. There next to the pointing man with the tattoo on his arm, the movie people had inserted a little boy, supposedly the KKK grandfather as a ten-year-old, circled in red and labeled "Daddy." In other words—see something racist; become racist. If only racism were that easy to explain.

I thought about all the white people I'd spoken to who really *had* seen the hanging as children. They'd all found it so upsetting. None became monsters.

The photo in the movie also had a caption identifying it as a Mississippi lynching. As if, of course, it had to happen in the South. I'd gone to a sparsely attended matinee, but around me in the theater I could sense tension, people shifting in their seats. I heard whispering. *Our* lynching. Witnessing this bizarre alteration of history in the town where it really happened felt insulting. As if what had happened on August 7, 1930, were trivial and could just be rewritten. Even those trying so hard not to face it there in Marion knew it wasn't trivial. Getting it so dramatically wrong made it worse.

WHEN I SPOKE ONCE AGAIN to Harold Vermilion, the pastor who wanted to erect the statue on the lynching site, he told me that his relationship with

Mayor Ron Mowery was now "a little estranged." But Vermilion wasn't giving up. He had the whole ceremony worked out in his head: James Cameron and then Willie Deeter would each drive a stake partway. Then they would hug. They would ask each other's forgiveness.

"What would be better than to have the thing settled?" asked Vermilion. "Show the world we can do it. Get national TV in here and watch them drive that stake."

By now I'd begun to understand that the statue fantasy was Vermilion's way of healing what he himself had experienced on August 7, 1930. I decided not to ruin his dream by telling him that Willie Deeter would never cooperate.

I WAS DOWN TO MY last weeks in Marion when I found the man with the Klan safe. Andy, as I'll call him, talked to me for an hour before consenting to tell me his real name.

The safe, about four feet tall, sat in his backyard. He'd bought it twenty years ago at an estate sale held in a garage that used to be the headquarters of the Grant County Social Club. A Klan front, he informed me. Andy still had nearly everything that had been in the safe, including six to eight ledger books: Ku Klux Klan membership lists for all of central Indiana up to the 1930s. He'd placed everything in a safe deposit box in Indianapolis.

He'd also found seven or eight pictures of the lynching in the safe. Not the famous photo. Different ones. I began stopping by almost every day, standing on his porch until he consented to come outside. Andy would not divulge his phone number and never let me enter the house. On one of these later visits, he decided that maybe he got the lynching pictures from his grandfather. Whatever the case, he was sure they'd been taken from the third floor of the Resnick Building on the southeast corner of Third and Adams.

Meeting this eccentric threw me into a frenzy of possibility, but it did seem too good to be true. What if he'd made it all up?

I drove to the area where Andy said he bought the safe and looked around for a likely garage. Then, at the library, I made a list of everyone who'd lived on that block twenty years ago, thinking Andy might remember the name if he saw it. He refused to look at the list.

I called Jim Ferguson, the man from the local klavern, and asked, "What was the Grant County Social Club?" expecting him to say he'd never heard of it.

Instead, Ferguson chuckled and said, "Oh, that was kind of a tongue-in-cheek thing. They pulled pranks, made fun of politicians, wrote letters to the editor, that sort of thing." He said some Klansmen had dreamed it up, but lots of Klan sympathizers were part of it as well. It had started in 1968 and lasted five years.

So it was real.

Then, in the city directory for 1930, I looked to see what was on the third floor of the Resnick Building, the office Andy's lynching photos had been taken from. Third floor: the Junior Order of United American Mechanics.

Amazing.

JOUAM was a nativist anti-Catholic fraternity known to be a close ally of the Klan. In Georgia the two groups even put out a newspaper together back in the 1920s. I felt certain that Andy couldn't have known any of this when he specified where the pictures had been taken.

He had to be telling the truth. I tried to imagine what those photographs must have captured. The Resnick Building was directly across from the hanging tree.

THEN, SOMETIME DURING my last week in Marion, I heard the most amazing account yet of the lynching. My witness had seen a white man try to stop it.

One white man. One.

Elliot (as I'm calling him) was outside doing yard work when I arrived for our interview. He didn't want his name included "being that I have a lot of black friends," and his wife hadn't wanted him to talk to me at all. So we headed to the back of the property, down a slope carpeted with periwinkle and fallen yellow leaves. Elliot lived near Jonesboro. He was a lynching witness I'd known about for almost a year. It had taken that long to get a phone number.

I told him I'd once been nearby, searching for Telltale, the African American settlement founded about the same time as Weaver, in the 1840s. I didn't have my recorder on yet, so I don't remember how he put it. Something like "Oh, it's right down the hill." But this was how, inadvertently, I found Telltale. Just walked right down into it. I was stunned to see that the foundations of a building or two were still there, somewhat camouflaged by vegetation. Once this Eureka moment was over, however, I took a closer look and saw that the foundations were poured concrete. And if the settlement had a name, Elliot never knew it. But I still think I found Telltale. Elliot told me older structures had been there before, in the bottomland, but the state dug up everything and piled landfill on top of it when they put in the highway. Later at the recorder's office, I discovered that in the 1840s the property in question had belonged to ardent abolitionist Obadiah Jones, more likely than most to turn a patch of his land over to runaway slaves and freedmen. Finally, the site was exactly where the county historian had said it would be—behind the Frog College. Elliot had pointed out to me where that schoolhouse used to stand. Also, I'd been told that Telltale was an integrated community, and the settlement he knew of had seven households, five black and two white. His wife's great-grandmother had lived there.

So we stood in the ruins of Telltale, and Elliot began to talk about the night of August 7, 1930. He and his friend Bill had gone downtown with Elliot's uncle, unaware that anything was afoot. Elliot and Bill, who were both eight, would go to the movies, while the uncle played euchre in a basement place on the north side of the square. But they arrived to find a huge crowd congregating there and the uncle started asking questions. Then he told the boys to climb a tree and look down at the jail to see what was happening. Elliot and Bill were up there on a limb when some men came up with ropes, and said, "Here, catch. Throw 'em over a limb."

Elliot said he asked the men what they were going to do, "and when he told us, down we come."

"You were in the hanging tree?"

"Yeah, yeah. Right out on the limb," said Elliot. "They said, 'We're gonna hang us a couple of'—of course, they didn't call them 'blacks.' My kids will tell you, I don't allow that other word on my property."

"Did they try to throw you two ropes? Or three?"

"Three."

Elliot said he heard a boom coming from the direction of the jail. "Blowed out the back wall," he assured me. Of course, that didn't happen, so there's no telling what the noise really was. Elliot never went down to the jail. After he and Bill jumped out of the tree, they ran up onto the north steps of the courthouse and stood on the stone banister. "We wanted to see it and we didn't," said Elliot. "Curiosity said 'look,' but your heart told you not to."

There they witnessed the one heroic gesture made by a white person on that horrific night, the exception proving the rule. Elliot's uncle ran up to Abe Smith and threw his arms around him, trying to pull him away from the mobsters. Then someone smacked the uncle across the nose with a crowbar.

Elliot was guessing that it was Smith his uncle tried to save. He knew that Smith had worked for his uncle at some point. And it probably *was* him, since most observers agreed that Tommy Shipp was the first one out, that he

was killed in the jail yard and initially hung from a window, that Smith came
out second and was still alive when he got to the tree.

"Your uncle put his arms around the guy?"

"He tried, yeah."

Then Elliot's friend Bill saw his father. The two boys were still standing
on the banister when the mobsters took the bodies down and tied them to
the back of Bill's father's car. Bill's father was KKK, but Elliot had no idea if
he actually drove the car or just let the mob take it. The father never knew
that Bill was there—Bill never told him—but "his dad wondered why Bill
was so very distant with him later."

The car started down Third, then turned onto Washington, dragging the
bodies. "We couldn't take it," Elliot said of the sight. The uncle had located
them by this time, and they left. Cameron had not yet been brought out.

Elliot remembered sitting in the car somewhere with Bill while a doctor
packed gauze up in his uncle's nose. "Me and Bill was half-sick for days."

"Did you recognize anyone in that mob?" I asked.

"I didn't," he said. "My uncle did. He knew they was Klan. See, they
tried to get him to join for years." By now I knew some Kluxers had participated, but even Elliot wouldn't say that they were Marion Kluxers. He said,
"Half of Elwood was there."

"So you didn't recognize anybody?"

"I probably did, but I couldn't say for sure. Bill—he knew some of the
people. His neighbors." Unfortunately Bill was dead. "Lot of 'em were
drinking," Elliot volunteered.

"How do you know that?"

"Oh, I could smell it."

"Did you see any police come up to that tree?"

"I never saw one."

Asked if he'd seen anyone in Klan robes, Elliot said no. He saw his first
robes a couple of years later at Matter Park, where the Klan guys were having a picnic. "Probably seen some blacks out there and wanted to scare
'em." He remembered asking his grandmother about the KKK. "I was probably ten or twelve years old then. I got interested in knowing what the Klan
was about. I remember I come out of the service, they tried to get me to
join, along about 1946 or 1947."

Elliot was of the opinion that at least one of the lynching victims deserved the death penalty, "but not that way." And to think that it was all over
a white woman "that they did not rape."

He began to talk about Mary Ball: "She would take these guys, take a married man, go in a tavern, flirt around a little bit, look at one who looked like he might have a pretty ring, a watch. Well, she'd make eyes at him, he'd make eyes at her and follow her outside, and she'd say, 'I know a nice place out here on the river.' "

"How did you hear this about Mary Ball?" I wondered.

"My uncle." Once Elliot was grown up, his uncle had told him. "He used to go out with her himself. See, he wasn't a married man, so he didn't care."

"She was a prostitute?"

"A whore."

Bill came to see Elliot after they were both out of the service in the 1940s. "He come to see me and he said, 'Remember that down there on the courthouse square?' I said, 'You better believe I do.' " They also confessed to each other that they had hated killing the enemy, Bill from his submarine, Elliot from his B-17. Thirty-five missions over Germany. "I hated it that I was blowing people up."

The lynching was such a bad memory that he knew he couldn't go to Cameron's museum.

"You've seen the famous picture of it," I assumed.

But he hadn't. By choice. "Guy tried to sell me one," he explained. "I said, 'Man, you couldn't *give* me that picture.' If I was President of the United States who knowed about it, I'd order 'em all burnt. I wouldn't even look at it."

He said he didn't understand why, if a black man raped a white woman, it was thought to be worse than if a white man did it. "Why bring race or color into it? It's just as bad one way or the other."

By this time Elliot and I had walked back to where I'd parked. I told him that I would love to tell the Grant County Black History Council about the Telltale site.

A look of fear came up in his eyes. No, he wouldn't want the site revealed. He wouldn't want the family name mentioned to anyone. He was worried about the Klan. "I think I got one living close to me."

SOMEONE ALWAYS KEPT the fear alive. One of the white people working on racial reconciliation told me, "Everybody working on race gets phone calls. Black people tell me, 'Don't take it lightly.' " I had indeed heard reports about harassment from many of those, both black and white, working toward better race relations in the county. Nails in tires, eggs thrown at carports, threatening letters, anonymous calls.

One of the white reconcilers phoned me a couple of days after our interview to say that talking to me brought up "old fears that if you talk about race" et cetera and "I've been warned" et cetera. The reconciler hoped I'd get someone to speak to this at length. Someone else.

Elliot too told me a story that convinced me he had something to worry about. I can't even repeat it since the details might give him away. But in his case and in the others, I wondered if those who were calling, vandalizing, and otherwise patrolling the boundaries of whiteness were actual Kluxers. Probably some were, but unfortunately one can't put it all off on them. Once something like a Ku Klux Klan exists, all of white racism can shelter behind it.

Terror had always been a Klan tool. While I'd seen fear in a couple of black women who were old enough to remember both the Kluxer heyday and the lynching, the rest of the frightened ones I spoke to were white. From what I'd seen of the Klan, their focus now was on policing other whites, to keep them anxious, to keep them from dealing with race at all, to give them a reason for maintaining the status quo.

Fear was key. Even a thousand miles from the nearest klavern, we whites who did not want to be racist might choose not to deal with black people because of a whole different fear: Will I say the wrong thing? Are they angry? Do they hate me? This is irrational stuff, rooted in the segregated lives so many of us still lead. But the anxiety is real and could easily lead us to keep our distance.

Talk about a cycle. Fear breeds separation. Separation breeds fear.

ON MY LAST NIGHT IN MARION I went to Andy's house one last time. I knew he was in there. A woman came to the door, nodded at me, and slammed the door shut again. About five minutes later Andy emerged, saying that he was just about to call me. He wondered if we could meet somewhere like the library or my apartment so he could show me the newspapers he'd found in the Klan safe. Some dated from the 1880s, he announced.

I was only half packed, so this was about the last thing I needed. But I couldn't say no. He hinted that he had other things to tell me as well.

A couple of hours later he showed up at my door carrying a large suitcase. This he put down in the midst of my boxes and piles, saying that before he showed me what was inside, he had to tell me something about Marion. He stood there in the middle of the room, glancing occasionally at an index card where he'd scribbled some words. What he wanted to tell me

was that Jews controlled Marion. He talked about how they started as ped-
dlers going down alleys and now they were among the richest people in
town and pulled everyone's strings.

Once he had that out of the way, he laid the big suitcase on the table and
opened it. All the papers inside were moldy and fragile and had nothing to
do with the Klan. I didn't even see a paper from Marion. One was from Peru.
They were too fragile to open. Then there were drawings of some 1930s film
star I couldn't name, a few movie posters, and a drawing of a kitten. Apparently a Ku Klux kitten. Andy claimed that this was an original Currier &
Ives, but I had the impression that he'd never even looked at this stuff before. I began to understand him as someone who wanted to acquire things
yet didn't much care about them after he had them. And that's who can end
up controlling the information.

In the years to come, as I made return visits to Marion, I showed up at
Andy's door many many times, offering money for Grant County's Klan
membership list, trying to cajole him into looking for the lynching photos.
But the suitcase he showed me that night was the most I ever got to see.

LEAVING MARION THE NEXT DAY felt anticlimactic. Between the shipping
and the errands, it was dark by the time I was ready, but I had to make one
last stop. My grandparents' house. I sat there in the car for a while, almost
too numb with exhaustion to feel anything but a sort of inchoate yearning.
So much had eluded me here, or else seemed to crumble in my hands.

PART V

The Return of Oatess Archey

TWENTY-FIVE

HISTORY-MAKER

The Primary / Spring 1998

An election brought me back to Marion in May 1998. Oatess Archey was running for sheriff, a development so unexpected, so potentially "historic," it seemed to send a little tremor through the county. A win would make him the first African American sheriff in the history of Indiana. Putting a black man in the Grant County sheriff's office would serve as a rebuke, at last, to the (in)actions of Jake Campbell. Here was a shot at redemption.

But given that Archey was not only black but a Democrat, in a county that was over 90 percent white and very Republican, I didn't expect him to win. In fact, I wasn't sure he'd make it through the Democratic primary.

Archey had been the town's first black teacher back in the 1960s, though the storyline most often associated with him was "first they made him a janitor." With his Marion career constantly on hold because the town "wasn't ready," Archey allowed himself to be recruited away to Ball State, then to the FBI. During the fourteen months I lived in Marion he was one of the nonresidents I heard most about, and no one expected him to move back. Then in 1997, retired from the Bureau, he did—just in time to fulfill his residency requirement.

Arriving the day before primary voting, I headed immediately for Archey headquarters but couldn't resist a brief stop at the old jail when I saw the new fence—and an open gate. The place looked more gothic and gloomy than ever, its yard wildly overgrown. Rex Fansler no longer lived in the old sheriff's residence, and I jotted down the phone number he'd left on the porch. It would take me a couple of days to find him.

After his conviction on animal cruelty charges, Fansler had been incarcerated for forty-five days early in 1997 and watched from the window of the real jail as workers changed the locks on his doors and put up a chain-link fence around the property. Fansler was definitely a delinquent taxpayer, but nearly a year after the lockout he still hadn't been able to collect his belongings. Peeking through a window, I saw white tufts all over the floor, as if an animal had pulled stuffing out of the furniture. County commissioners had given the building's deed to an Indianapolis-based company—as allowed under state law once a property had been through two consecutive tax sales without a buyer. The new owners planned to convert the old jail into low-income housing: Castle Apartments.

So much for James Cameron's improbable dream of moving America's Black Holocaust Museum to Marion.

In the year and a half since I'd last been there, many more who'd somehow experienced the events of August 1930 had died. Like Willie Deeter, who would never get a chance now to change his mind and consent to a statue of himself embracing Cameron. Deeter had been buried in Fairmount near his beloved brother, Claude. Then there was Blaine Scott, the fireman who'd seen a woman at the lynching tree pulling a rope, swinging one of the bodies while she held a baby in her other arm. Also Walter Gunyon, who was seven years old when his father drove him downtown the afternoon of August 7, 1930, and parked his family there in front of the tree till it was over. *A horrible thing to see.* And the elderly Boy Mayor, Jack Edwards, who'd told me so much, though I was certain he had taken even more to the grave.

Here was the thing that interested me: the eyewitnesses died, the facts disappeared, and somehow the pain lingered on.

I ARRIVED AT OATESS ARCHEY'S campaign headquarters just as the candidate got there to meet with his poll watchers. Inside the tiny South Marion storefront, fifteen teens and a handful of adults were seated along the wall and around a table. Archey gave the assembled volunteers a pep talk about his qualifications, because, as he put it, "We want you to believe in what you're doing."

Archey projected a quiet authority. Gray-haired with gold-rimmed glasses, he was an ex-athlete who still looked fit and seemed younger than his sixty years. What he selected from his résumé that afternoon was probably intended to get the attention of the young people there, everything from "I was the agent who took the call when Ronald Reagan was shot" to his mention of a postretirement job as Ralph Sampson's bodyguard.

Archey would stress again and again that he wanted to be judged on his qualifications. "If you live in America, anything is possible," he told the kids. And he said it with conviction, despite the barriers laid down in front of his own possibilities years ago. "If I win, Grant County wins."

No African American had ever even run for Grant County sheriff, "the most powerful elected position in the county and definitely one of the highest paid," in the words of the *Chronicle-Tribune*. Archey faced one rival in the Democratic primary, Bill Norton, while three men were battling for the Republican slot. Often the sheriff's job went to someone who'd put his time in as a deputy, as Norton had. And Norton appeared to be better funded. He had billboards. The big strike against Archey, of course, was that he'd left town, and Norton's ads were careful to praise their man as a "lifetime resident of Grant County."

But once I saw the Archey campaign in action, I decided that my pessimism about his chances was unfounded. Clearly he had the enthusiastic support of many people, all races. The excitement around Archey was palpable. As one white woman said to me, "We hardly ever have someone this qualified to vote for." And while Archey had been gone for decades, he had never been forgotten—this former star athlete, teacher, coach, neighbor. An elderly white woman named Mildred Thompson needed a walker to get around, but she too was working on the campaign and told me she'd known Archey since he was a little boy who'd gone to school with her son.

The storefront was a Norman Rockwell painting come to life, between the idealism on parade and the red, white, and blue decor. I couldn't help but notice one other thing. After all the workshops, church services, and support groups I'd attended, where racial harmony was talked about, wished for, and prayed over, here at Archey headquarters it was just happening, and no one discussed it.

After the meeting I stood out on the stoop with him, and he talked about how he'd gone off to college after getting six scholarship offers and then came back to Marion only to be turned into a janitor. Then, after retiring from the FBI, he worked as director of security for World Cup Soccer and escorted Pele and Whitney Houston to the center of the field one night,

thinking, "I've come from the toilet bowl to the Rose Bowl." This had become one of his catchphrases.

"The first time I came back to Marion, I wasn't good enough. Now my
opponents are saying I'm overqualified. So I say to my hometown, 'What do
I have to do to be accepted?' "

He thought that some of his rivals were trying to make it "a racial race,"
when really, he said, pointing to a campaign poster with PEOPLE FIRST in the
center of a five-pointed sheriff's star, "this is what it's about."

Archey could say repeatedly—and did—that race was not an issue, but
there was no escaping how freighted this was. People working for Archey
wondered if he could win out in the county, in the little all-white towns and
farmlands. He would never make it if he won just in Marion. But Archey had
a strategy. Wherever possible he found one or two well-respected people in a
community who could introduce him around the town. In Gas City, for example, he had Gene Linn, their popular mayor, and Larry Leach, their former police chief.

The candidate had also named two campaign managers, one white and
one black—Richard "Pete" Beck, a former state representative, and Tom
Wise, who was of course a longtime politico.

"Wouldn't it be ironic," Archey said to me, "with those black guys taken
from the jail"—Shipp, Smith, Cameron—"if Grant County ended up with a
black sheriff?"

THE NEXT DAY OATESS ARCHEY won the Democratic primary in a landslide, getting 68 percent of the vote. In November he would face Mike Back,
a twenty-five-year veteran of the sheriff's department, who'd won the Republican primary with his own landslide—67 percent.

The mood at Archey headquarters was ebullient when I got there
shortly after seven, thinking the tally wouldn't be done yet, only to have
people laugh at me: "This isn't New York!"

They'd taken the tables down to give people room, and I walked around
soaking up the euphoria:

"A lot of people were saying they never voted Democrat in their life!
People in their fifties and sixties saying, 'I'm voting Democrat.' "

"And in the fall, we'll have a bigger crossover."

"Like one guy, he's passing out Republican literature and he tells me,
'This fall I'll be voting for Archey!' "

A white man in a baseball cap was declaring to Tom Wise, "They said it couldn't be done!"

And Tom was telling him, "People were still begging for Archey signs yesterday!"

The candidate himself was one of the calmer people there. He got up on a chair to do a thank-you speech, and I noted that at least half the supporters present were white. He told them they were a grassroots movement, that they hadn't won it with money, and that he would continue to emphasize qualifications. "We're not going to sling mud. The people of Grant County are tired of it. People *do* want someone with qualifications."

Afterward I spoke to one white man, a Marion policeman, who said, "He's the best hope this county's had in I don't know how long. I was sold on him the first time I met him. I said, 'You wait and see. You hear him speak one time, and if you're not sold, you wasn't there.' "

Other Democratic candidates began drifting in, and a man named Herb Wilson got up to announce that the campaign had started "in the home of Betty Wilson"—and himself. Oatess Archey had the look of a winner, even a history-maker, the kind of candidacy people wanted to be part of and wanted credit for.

I HAD CALLED IMPERIAL WIZARD Jeff Berry before I left for Indiana to see what was current in Klanland. His daughter, Tonia Berry, answered the phone and told me that she was running for DeKalb County Council, while her mother Edna was running for township trustee.

Then when the Wizard took the phone, he gave me the most unexpected news of all: "Brad Thompson is no longer with us. He became a idiot. He's claiming he's not in the Klan."

The Dragon dropped out?

"Well, we threw him out," said the Wizard.

I was surprised, to say the least. "He seemed so dedicated."

"He's a good con artist," said the Wizard. "He's nothing but an alcoholic and womanizer."

"Was there some specific thing he did?" I asked.

"We have rules in here. Moral rules," the Wizard declared before itemizing a number of drunken or violent acts supposedly perpetrated by the Dragon, concluding with: "He went on some TV show saying he was no longer a Klansman. Winded up apologizing to the minorities. So he kind of lost it, but we're getting stronger than ever. The History Channel done a thing on us. German TV done a thing on us. French TV . . ."

The Wizard continued with his progress report on the upward surging American Knights, which now had klaverns in thirty-eight states. On election night the Kluxers would carry out "a massive lit drive" all over America. Meaning that wherever Klansmen lived, they would be slipping Ku Klux flyers into the local free newspapers and shopping guides. Then the next weekend they would rally at Ann Arbor. "You can come with us," the Wizard offered.

What I really wanted to do was talk to the former Dragon.

THE DAY AFTER THE ELECTION I bought a Fort Wayne newspaper to see how the various Ku Klux candidates had done up in DeKalb County.

Women's Imperial Wizard Edna Berry: five votes.

Women's Imperial Nighthawk Tonia Berry: sixty-four votes.

The former Dragon Brad Thompson had also run for county council (in a different district) and beat both Berrys with seventy-five, but—like them— he got the fewest votes in his category.

Thompson had a new phone number, unlisted. I would have to drive all the way to Auburn and knock on his door.

I MET OATESS ARCHEY at his storefront campaign headquarters a few days after the primary. In a couple of hours he would head off to his substitute teaching job at McCulloch Middle School. ("I'm trying to finance my own campaign.") We sat down at one of the tables he'd put back up in the middle of the room. They all had plastic tablecloths decorated with little liberty bells and phrases like "Oh say can you see" and "My country 'tis of thee."

He was curious about the Klan connections I'd made. I told him that, in general, the Kluxers were uneducated, angry, and poor. "That's a dangerous combination for any race," Archey observed. He'd heard a rumor that some local Klansmen were actually thinking about voting for him. "We thought that was a compliment," he said. "We welcome all people. Our campaign is 'People First.'"

He began to lay out his life story like someone who'd reflected on what he'd been through and knew how he wanted to present it. For me, Archey's story was a culmination. It summarized so much of what I'd found in Marion about how racism deforms a life.

He'd been born in 1937 in a house his great-grandfather built near 17th and Meridian. He estimates that he was three or four when the family moved to North Marion. His father was hauling coal at that time, and one day his partner, a white man, offered him a chance to buy a home there. North Marion was all white. As Archey put it, his father said, " 'Yeah, I'll buy it,' not really realizing . . ." So the Archeys became the first African Americans ever to live in North Marion, and the parents worried about their two sons. The father installed a basketball hoop and a horseshoe goal, "and we stayed in our own yard." But then the white kids came over and asked, "Can we play, too?" Soon the Archey house became the neighborhood hangout. From kindergarten through ninth grade Oatess and his brother were the only blacks in their school classes. They never had any trouble, he said. So his story wasn't all bad, just as Marion wasn't all bad.

Some of the same white people he'd grown up with were still in town. One of them, the mother of a friend who'd been "like a brother," came to a Democratic rally, and, said Archey, "I told her that as long as she lives, I still have a mother. She almost cried when I told her that. She just said how proud she was of my accomplishments. That family—when it wasn't politically or socially correct to have a little black kid with them—they used to take me everywhere."

Archey's parents were very strict, and one thing he learned from them was the lesson of the lynching. "It was talked behind closed doors. Interracial dating was just taboo because of that lynching. 'You stay in your place. Or you could end up like those boys that were hung.' That was pounded into young black males." For most of his boyhood, however, Archey had no black friends at all. The only time he ever saw other black kids was at Allen Temple on Sunday. But once his older brother Thomas started driving, they'd go to East or South Marion to try to meet girls.

In other ways he experienced what the black kids growing up in South Marion or Johnstown did. He remembered going to the Matter Park pool with his brother, "putting our fingers through the fence and watching the white kids in the pretty blue water." He had to swim in the gravel pit with the poor white kids.

Sometimes it had been a strain being the only black kid in his circle. His friends from North Marion would say things like "Uh-oh, here come some niggers." Then Archey would say, "Hey, don't forget who I am," and they'd say, "You're not like them."

His white friends didn't seem to understand that he couldn't sit downstairs with them at the movies, and he never mentioned it. Instead he always talked them into sitting upstairs with him. "I was very persuasive. They never knew that I couldn't go down." He still remembered a night at the movies when a white man grabbed him by the nape of the neck and jerked him out of a line waiting for the bathroom, ordering, "Nigger, you go to the end of the line."

Apart from that experience, he always felt that he could go anyplace and do anything. Except date white girls. The lynching was "always in the back of your mind." He told me a story I'd heard before about a star athlete at Marion High School in the 1950s—an African American who got his white girlfriend pregnant. This at a time when interracial dating was absolutely unacceptable and interracial marriage illegal. They'd kept the relationship a secret, of course. Then—so the story goes—their baby was found east of town, dead. "It affected those of us in sports for years to come," said Archey, "because they said, 'See, let 'em play sports, and the girls start chasing these guys.'" So blacks got less playing time. And fewer were picked for the teams. "The community wanted to win but did not want us to be the stars." Still, when Archey graduated in 1955, he was All-State in football, a starter on the basketball team, and state champion in the 120-yard high hurdles. He set a state record in that event that stood until 1962.

With six scholarship offers to choose from, he picked Grambling, then an all-black school: "I wanted to find myself. For once in my life, I could let down. I didn't have to worry about ropes and lynching." When he entered this all-black environment, however, he learned that blacks too were suspicious of anyone different. "I could hear the hatred on both sides, and it was really because neither side knew the other side," said Archey. "Both were scared."

Archey's brother Thomas had arrived at Grambling two years earlier, so Thomas was the first to return to Marion and apply for a job teaching at the high school. Marion "wasn't ready," and Thomas Archey moved to Louisiana. I wondered why Oatess had even tried to teach in Marion.

"Because I was twenty-one years old, and I was naïve," said Archey. "Everybody loved me in high school. I was a Marion Giant, and everybody was screaming and yelling for me. I thought everybody loved Oatess Archey. So I came back, and they slammed the door in my face, which was just devastating to me. Like—hey, don't you remember me? It was just four years ago. The coaches voted me Most Outstanding Athlete in three sports. Football, basketball, and track. Then I come back and—boom. I'd done everything my parents, minister, coaches, and teachers said to do. Be good. Study hard. It was just a crushing blow.

"What I didn't realize is that in high school I was looked upon as an entertainer, not a serious candidate to be a teacher."

He did not even get a job interview. It was 1959.

Archey was newly married to Barbara, part of the Casey family from Weaver. A number of Caseys worked at RCA and got Oatess a job there on second shift. After three weeks he was laid off in the summer shutdown. He went to Fisher Body and worked for two weeks before getting laid off in a steel strike.

Then one day he happened to walk past the Marion Community School Maintenance Department and went inside. The man who was superintendent there, Merle Rife, had been the starter at track meets. He gave Archey a job. "I hauled ashes, cut weeds, plastered, mixed cement, tiled floors, you name it."

Then one day Rife called him in and said, "What are you doing out here? Don't you have a degree?" Rife set up an appointment for him with the superintendent. Archey was then given the official word on his teaching possibilities: "Marion isn't ready yet."

Archey told Rife, who replied, "You gotta be kidding." A few days later Rife promoted him to "night foreman," giving him a raise from $1.56 to $1.60 an hour. During the winter he would stoke the furnaces and get the schools warmed up before the children arrived. In the spring and fall he would be janitor at the football field, liming the field and cleaning the restrooms.

One Friday in October as Archey was putting down the yardage lines on the field, Rife came out to him, asking, "Do you still want to teach?" He was to report to the administration building first thing Monday.

Excited, he called everyone in his family that weekend, telling them, "I'm going to be the first black teacher."

On Monday he signed his first teacher's contract for $4,200, then met with the superintendent, who informed him that he wasn't exactly going to teach. It seemed that one of the fifth-grade teachers had lost control of her class. "All we want you to do is just sit in the back of the room and keep 'em quiet."

Archey was stunned. He still remembered sitting there and saying to himself, "A bachelor's degree."

Still, it beat picking up trash. He went to the unruly class and quickly had them under control, because the children (he later learned) thought he was Archie Moore, the professional boxer. He sat there stewing that day. "I'm outta here." He'd worked so hard, made the honor roll, excelled on every team, and now, he thought, "they're gonna do me like this?" That night, though, when he told his wife, she encouraged him to develop his own job. "So I started reading to the kids, taking them out at recess, grading papers." Soon, as winter set in, all the other teachers had him taking their classes out too, so they could stay inside.

Thus he got a foot in the door. The next school year, 1960–61, he became an elementary school gym teacher in the morning and taught health and history at a junior high in the afternoons. So he was in. The first black teacher.

Then he asked if he could coach.

No. No, he couldn't.

But the year after that they let him assist the math teacher (who had never played sports) with the junior high football team. Over a period of four years he worked his way up to head coach of the ninth-grade basketball team, compiling the best record in the Marion schools: 64–7. When the high school basketball coach was fired, Archey applied for the job. Again, he didn't even get an interview. Then when he applied for the reserve job, they did interview him, but the first question they asked was, "If you don't get the job, how is that going to make you feel?" The next day he read in the newspaper that the job had gone to a white man who'd compiled a record of 15–15. Archey was told that he could do better "in the feeder system, bringing the young boys along."

He decided then to leave Marion. It was 1965. Soon he had a job offer from Crispus Attucks High School in Indianapolis—assistant basketball coach. This was an all-black school with an all-black faculty. Oscar Robertson's alma mater, Attucks had been a basketball powerhouse all through the 1950s.

Marion's new school superintendent then called Archey in and pleaded with him not to leave. "The next time a coaching job opens up, you'll get it," he promised. Archey didn't believe anyone anymore, but that summer he was offered the job of head coach for Marion High School's track and cross-country teams, and he took it. Of course, he didn't realize what bad shape the teams were in. At the first meet they lost badly, and he thought, "Maybe people are right. Maybe I don't know what I'm doing." His wife counseled, Give it time, you can do it. "Within four years I had taken fifteen boys to the state, and in 1969, my last year in Marion, I was nominated for Indiana High School Track Coach of the Year. I didn't get it, of course. I was the first black coach in the North-Central Conference."

At this point Ball State University in Muncie recruited him to become its assistant track coach. Within four years he was assistant department head in physical education and had coached one boy all the way to the Olympics in the steeplechase. He'd earned his master's degree in counseling, a black belt in tae kwon do, and had one year of work in toward a Ph.D.

Then the FBI came along in 1973, "looking for qualified blacks." He'd never imagined a career in law enforcement but clearly loved the work. He felt that, during his FBI years, he'd been evaluated according to what he could do.

ARCHEY INTERRUPTED HIS narrative when a few people working for other Democratic candidates came in to drop off some campaign signs. They planted themselves in chairs along the wall, wanting to shoot the breeze. It seemed to me that people liked hanging around with Archey.

When he got back to telling me his life story, he talked in some detail about his FBI career, but I'll just summarize the résumé:

He started at the Detroit field office in the 1970s, working the Patty Hearst kidnapping and some housing discrimination cases. The FBI moved him around a lot and often took advantage of his teaching skills. From Detroit he went to the FBI Academy at Quantico, where he taught police officers from around the country, then went to the physical training unit as a defensive tactics and physical fitness instructor. He also traveled the country as a certified police instructor, then worked with the violent crimes unit on a case in the Virgin Islands. Back in Washington, he took the call when Reagan was shot and helped organize the subsequent investigation. He became the Washington-based supervisor for the Midwest and West Coast offices as they worked the Tylenol poisonings, the D. B. Cooper case, and a couple of skyjackings. Then he joined the FBI tour unit as chief firearms instructor, demonstrating weapons to a quarter of a million people a year. Detailed to the Drug Enforcement Administration, he traveled the country with Nancy Reagan, guarding the celebrities involved in her "Just Say No" campaign. He then headed up a new FBI police force in charge of guarding all FBI facilities in the D.C. area. Finally, the Bureau posted him to Los Angeles as its bank robbery supervisor. This was the busiest squad of its kind in the world. That year, for example, they had 2,355 bank robberies. "Once we had five in an hour, twenty-six in a day. That was such a stressful job. I was even out on New Year's with my supervisor in a hostage situation at a bank. So I asked to be relieved of that duty." They moved him to the domestic terrorism squad, where he set up a sting operation to catch some skinheads who planned to bomb L.A.'s largest black church "to restart the riots." Eventually the squad arrested ten of the leaders and also foiled a completely separate skinhead plot that stretched from California to Germany.

Archey retired from the FBI in 1993, while he was still based in Los Angeles, and soon became director of security for the World Cup Soccer finals in Pasadena. At the last big game, escorting the celebrities to the center of the field, he had his toilet-bowl-to-Rose-Bowl moment. "That's when it dawned on me where I'd come from. It was the most sobering moment of my life."

The United States Olympic Committee sent three people to observe him in Pasadena, then offered him a job running security at the 1996 Games in Atlanta. He turned it down because his mother was ill and staying with him. But his wife reminded him that he'd always wanted to be part of the Olympics and convinced him to go for the last six weeks. He ended up working as assistant security manager at the welcome center where all the athletes were checking in, though he left early when his mother took a turn for the worse. After that he set up a business in Los Angeles that provided security for celebrities and corporate executives.

That completed the list—his qualifications to run for sheriff of Grant County.

Sheriff was not a post he'd ever expected to seek. Nor had he expected to move back to Indiana. But in May 1997 Marion's Exchange Club invited him to speak at the Law Enforcement Officer of the Year banquet and gave him a plaque in appreciation for his dedication to law enforcement. When the NAACP found out he was coming back for the Exchange Club banquet, they invited him to speak at a luncheon a few days later. There he was presented with the Sagamore of the Wabash, Indiana's highest civilian award. But Grant County was not finished heaping honors on a man whose greatness had been overlooked when he actually lived there. The same community school system that so often thwarted him in the 1960s honored him this time with a plaque, citing him as an outstanding educator and law enforcement officer. The NAACP and some local businessmen announced that they were setting up a scholarship in his name. The Black Teacher's Alliance gave him an award for being their trailblazer. And to cap it all off, Mayor Ron Mowery presented him with the key to the city.

It cost him forty dollars to ship all the hardware back to California. "I took it into my office and mounted it on the wall while I talked to my wife," Archey recalled. "I was saying, 'Maybe it's time to go home. Maybe people want me to come home and get involved.'"

He knew that the sheriff's job (which has term limits) was opening up. While in Marion, he'd discussed the possibility with Tom Wise, who was an old friend. Back in California, Archey called Wise to ask him to take the temperature locally. Would people be interested if he ran for office?

A week later Wise called back, laughing. "He said, 'You aren't going to believe this.' He said, 'The outpouring of support is overwhelming.' And I said maybe we better go another week, because I thought he'd get a different reaction. But he called me back a few days later and said, 'You need to make a decision, because this rumor is running rampant in the city.' So right then I said, 'I'm gonna do it.'" That was September 1997.

He hadn't expected the landslide victory in the primary. "But Tom kept telling me, people like what you stand for. You're not one of the Good Old Boys. People see you as an FBI agent and Mr. Clean. You went to school with them, or taught their kids, and they're proud of you."

"I'm trying to tell people that I'm like Larry Bird," said Archey, referring to the Hoosier basketball superstar who'd recently returned to coach the Pacers. "Larry Bird could not play for the Boston Celtics in French Lick, Indiana. To fulfill my dream, I had to leave home."

It seemed fair to say, in fact, that thirty years ago Marion almost forced him to leave home. But that was not the sort of assertion Archey would ever make himself. What he did say was: "A lot of people are ashamed that I had to start as a janitor. Some of them want to make up for it."

AFTER OATESS ARCHEY WENT off to teach, I headed up to Auburn to find Brad Thompson. I decided to visit the Wizard first, curious as always about the latest activity at Klan central. Jeff Berry told me on the phone that I could stop by for an hour or so while they got ready for the rally in Ann Arbor.

At this point the American Knights were probably at the height of their notoriety, and the Wizard at the peak of his hubris. He was still crowing over the debacle they'd created months earlier on Martin Luther King, Jr.'s, birthday—in Memphis, where King was assassinated in 1968. Some twelve to eighteen hundred anti-Klan demonstrators showed up, threw tomatoes, and broke store windows. Police responded with tear gas and arrested twenty-five people. The story even made *The New York Times*.

I asked Berry why he now wanted to go back to Ann Arbor after what happened last time—the near-riot, his wife Edna getting hit in the head with a rock. He replied that he was going to do "all things necessary" to get his rights.

Edna joined us at the kitchen table, and they described the court battle they'd had when Cicero, just outside Chicago, tried to deny them the right to rally. This was another recent coup. Desperate to keep the Kluxers out, Cicero officials ultimately made a disgraceful deal with the Wizard. They would pay the American Knights $10,000 to print and distribute Klan literature to everyone in town, in exchange for a canceled rally. Klan watchers at the Southern Poverty Law Center denounced Cicero's decision as "a dangerous precedent."

We moved to smaller matters, like Rodney Stubbs's lawsuit against the city of Marion. "Brad Thompson messed that up," Berry groused. "He got drunk and told them to drop it." The Wizard kept badmouthing his former Dragon, telling me, for example, that they had had a couple of hundred members in Indiana when Thompson was in charge, and now they had seven hundred. Of course, back when Thompson really *was* running things, the Wizard had told me they had eighty-five hundred members in the state. Either number could be true. Or both could be lies. I would never know. But the Wizard seemed determined to furnish me with ammunition against Brad Thompson.

Apart from that, and the account of recent triumphs, the Wizard didn't really want to be interviewed. When a loud television program suddenly boomed from the living room, he suggested: "That's that German show. You want to watch that real quick?"

Standing near the television in the wood-paneled living room, I had time to take in the changes in the Berry home. They'd completed much of the rehab started after the alleged firebombing. By Klan standards, of course, the Wizard was rich: he had a house. But now he also had a big television, two sofas, and what looked like new carpeting. The home improvements didn't end there. They'd stocked a new "computer room" with both a desktop and a laptop, a fax machine, and a color copier. On the new American Knights website, browsers could download an application and buy Klan merchandise.

Nine Kluxers I'd never seen before sat in the living room watching the tape, along with Tonia Berry. Most appeared to be in their twenties. The German documentary couldn't have lasted more than ten minutes, and someone replaced it with the tape of a recent rally in North Carolina. This would be the last time I ever laid eyes on the Berrys, but what stayed with me from this visit was that room full of young Kluxers watching tapes of their own events with rapt attention.

The Wizard sat at the kitchen table on the phone, obviously talking to a reporter since he was blathering on about his First Amendment rights. So I listened to the rally, much of it focused on just who would or wouldn't be going to heaven. "We all go to church," declared one speaker on the tape. "We smell good, we look good. Y'all are ignorant. If you don't join the Ku Klux Klan, you'll be in hell with the niggers and the Jews." As protesters yelled, "Racists! Losers!" a Klan officer named Reverend Jimmy Ray Shelton reinforced the message in his southern drawl, "Y'all are going to hell. I came to help you. . . ." In 1999 Shelton would be sentenced to ninety-nine years in a Texas prison for trying to kill two policemen during a car chase and gun battle.

I decided to make one more attempt at conversation with the Wizard before leaving. As I turned away from the television, I caught a last priceless phrase from one of the speeches: "faggots mixing together making mud babies."

I asked the Wizard again how he made a living.

"Well, as we're talking right now, I'm making a living," Berry declared. "Because I own two tow trucks and a car hauler. So I have drivers, and anytime they make money, I make money, and they don't cheat me."

"You talked before about being a contractor."

"Right now what we're doing is buying up houses and property. And you're going to start seeing churches. American Knights churches."

Tomorrow in Ann Arbor they would challenge the mask law by keeping their faces covered. "We already won in Pennsylvania," said Jeff. He bragged that he now had piles of legal briefs. *American Knights vs. the State of . . .* or *American Knights vs. the United States.* He, one man, kept taking on the government and winning.

"They're starting to nickname us the Nike Klan." The Wizard beamed. "A lot of reporters and stuff. You know why, don't ya? Their motto is—'Just do it.' "

Berry said that before I left I really had to see the History Channel show on the KKK. "It starts from clear back at Nathan Bedford Forrest," he declared, "and ends up with Jeff Berry and the American Knights."

He followed me into the living room and got down on the floor to advance the tape to the "beautiful cross-lighting" they'd done, featured at the end of the program.

The young Kluxers sat there discussing the ceremony. Biggest crosses ever. Two forty-footers and two twenty-footers. No one in the room seemed to notice or care that the show was very anti-Klan. Apparently what mattered was that a few moments of their marginal lives had been preserved in an important documentary. Berry took another phone call. While the video explained that the KKK has always cloaked itself in religion, a Klansman on the sofa pointed, "That's us right there."

I heard the Wizard ask his caller, "Since when is freedom of speech a hate crime?"

I LEFT THE BERRY HOME with some relief and drove to Brad Thompson's trailer park. It was dark, but I managed to find his lot. A daughter well into her teens answered the door, and then Brad's wife Brenda appeared. Brad was at work till ten, she said. Since I was leaving Indiana early the next day and had a long drive back to Marion, I couldn't wait for him. I asked if I could step inside out of the rain for a minute. A computer now covered the one small round table in the kitchen.

"So Brad quit the Klan?" I asked.

"It was quit or get a divorce," said Brenda. "It was too much on me and the kids."

It sounded like it was too much on Brad as well. He'd gained a hundred pounds. He'd joined AA. He was writing a book about it.

TWENTY-SIX

UNITY DAY

The Election / Fall 1998

On November 3, 1998, Grant County voters would elect everyone from a coroner to a U.S. senator, but as one *Chronicle-Tribune* headline put it: SHERIFF'S RACE HOTTEST IN COUNTY. The matter of Democrat Oatess Archey versus Republican Mike Back was looking too close to call.

Meanwhile, in the week leading up to the election, Marion would celebrate a Week of Unity, culminating on October 31 with a ceremony dedicating the bypass as "Martin Luther King Jr. Memorial Way."

When I arrived in Marion on October 26, I found certain Archey supporters—and not just campaign workers—nearly apoplectic over the timing of this symbolic gesture. "It's political." "It's a ploy." "Republicans are running scared." As I talked to more people, I saw that skepticism about Unity Week abounded, especially in the black community. The event had been planned, however, by Marion's Ethnic Diversity Task Force, which reported ultimately to the Chamber of Commerce and had no affiliation with a political party.

Tom Wise had been invited to sit on the stage among the local dignitaries during the dedication ceremony, and he hadn't decided yet if he would. He said he'd been part of the original committee that tried for six years to get the city interested in naming a street after King, only to see the mayor relegate it to a back burner. Now, Wise complained, they'd cooked up a plan to "dedicate" the bypass but not rename it. Officially it would still be Baldwin Avenue. Everyone would still call it "the bypass."

The story put out to justify this was that Baldwin Avenue had been named for the family once active in the underground railroad. This handy assumption was probably untrue. I dug up the original plat description at the recorder's office and found it signed by a Frank Baldwin, civil engineer. The street was probably named for him. That was in 1888, when no one could have envisioned a "bypass" or imagined Baldwin Avenue becoming an important thoroughfare.

During the year I lived in Marion the Race Relations Task Force had been a nonforce, unfunded and leaderless. In 1997 new cochairs took over: a black woman, Yvonne Washington, and a white man, Jerry Whitton. Whitton's one condition for taking the job, he told me, was that the group change its name to the Ethnic Diversity Task Force, "because 'race relations' sounds like a black-white negative thing." And, he pointed out, Marion now included people from more than eighty different cultures.

The reinvigorated task force finally gave a home to the study circles Linda Mui had been pushing for so long—a program they renamed "Harmony 2000." When I called Mui, she joked that the name gave them a deadline.

The Unity Week schedule looked a little thin and not particularly festive. It would begin with an evening of study circles on Wednesday, and a barrel watch on Thursday. (This was a local custom. Neighborhood associations set up barrels with fires in them outside crack houses, hoping to get the druggies to leave.) For Friday they'd set up an interfaith church service. On Saturday, Unity Day, people would gather in Matter Park, then march down the bypass to the dedication site. Martin Luther King III would speak at the ceremony. That was it.

Mui told me there hadn't been many RSVPs for the study circle so she didn't know if that would even take place. "You can't force stuff to happen," she said—not for the first time.

Thanks to Jack Edwards, I knew that Charles Lennon, one of the two men tried and acquitted for the lynching, eventually went to prison for killing a man named Red Whitton in 1941. Lennon fought Whitton outside a downtown tavern, striking and killing him when Whitton hit his head on the curb, according to the *Marion Chronicle*. The same judge who'd presided over the lynching trials gave Lennon one to ten years for involuntary manslaughter. That was a shorter sentence than Cameron's, but still—it was something.

So when I went to see the cochair of the Ethnic Diversity Task Force, Jerry Whitton, I asked him first if he'd had anybody in his family named Red. Jerry Whitton was the director of a technical school, Tucker Vocational, and president of the local chapter of Habitat for Humanity. Any connection to this old story seemed like a long shot, but as we sat down in a conference room at Tucker, he told me that yes, he'd had an uncle named Red. His dad's brother.

"He was in a fight and hit his head on a curb is what I always heard," said Whitton. He had never heard a thing about any Charles Lennon. When I told Whitton that his uncle had been killed by someone who probably participated in the lynching, Whitton said, "Really? Good grief."

He'd grown up in South Marion, hearing as a boy that the black men who were lynched had raped a girl and gotten what they deserved. Exactly what I'd learned in my own family. Like so many of the rest of us white people, Whitton grew up oblivious to racism. "I walked through life not knowing that people were being hurt. I hadn't paid that much attention." His family wasn't hateful or hurtful to black people but wouldn't associate with them, didn't trust them. Again, this was typical.

When the topic of racism came up in some college classes, however, he woke up. More than that, he eventually committed to doing something about it but couldn't say how or why, just "through being educated about the whole thing and through my faith." (Lutheran.) Still, he said he'd told people in his study circles that he was probably a "closet racist." He thought all white people were. "Most of us aren't hatemongers," he explained. "We just live in an atmosphere of accepting certain kinds of racism."

The effort to get a Marion street named after King began years before he and Yvonne Washington took over as cochairs of the task force. What finally got the project rolling was Mayor Ron Mowery's new willingness to get behind it. That had happened "just this year," said Whitton.

I could see why certain Democrats had reacted so cynically to this event, why they suspected that the whole thing was just a reaction to Oatess Archey's run for sheriff, announced in the fall of 1997. But Whitton maintained, "It's not a political thing."

He described Mowery as "very, very supportive." What kept the mayor from supporting it sooner, Whitton speculated, was "I think probably his fear of what it might do to the community. I don't sense that he was ever not wanting it because he was racist. I don't know what changed his mind."

"Fear of what it might do to the community?" I asked.

"That it might divide the community," Whitton explained. "If we were to name the bypass, would it run businesses away? Would people be reluctant to build on a Martin Luther King Highway? Or if we were to name Nebraska Street and people had to change their addresses, would it cause friction among those who lived north of the line where it turned white? Would it cause people to protest?"

So city officials looked for a "short street" to name after King. They found one in South Marion a block long. Nice and safe. There was nothing on it. Of course, Whitton pointed out with a laugh, renaming such a street would be meaningless. Then the mayor started to get behind black leaders who wanted the bypass selected. In January 1998 the city council passed a unanimous resolution to dedicate part of the road to King. Since they were dedicating, not renaming, no one would even have to change a letterhead.

The odd dedication date of October 31—not just close to election day but Halloween—had been dictated by Martin Luther King III's itinerary. They had really wanted him to speak, and that was when he was available.

Whitton had big hopes for Unity Day as a portrait of black and white coming together, but he seemed a little worried that white people wouldn't hold up their end, that the event had already been perceived as a day for black people. They'd advertised a poster contest in the Marion schools. Frances Slocum Elementary, with its majority black student body and a black principal, turned in seventy entries. Other elementary and middle schools turned in a few, and the high school submitted two entries from one student. The Marion High School Band was originally supposed to lead the march from Matter Park to the dedication site, then backed out, citing "fall break." Then some of the white singing groups dropped out, but none of the black groups did, so it looked increasingly like a black celebration.

"Some people see this as part of the healing process," said Whitton. "Because of the cloud that hangs over us from the hanging." I knew that the night the city council passed its resolution on this, the president of Marion's NAACP told them that dedicating the bypass "would help change the negative perception of the city that resulted from the lynchings."

This did not mean that anyone would actually *say* anything about the lynching on Unity Day. "Black people more than anyone want that to be kept low key," said Whitton. "They don't want to talk about the hanging in public. I think they're afraid that if they make that an issue, it brings out all the hatred, brings out the Klan—all those things we don't want to come out."

I MET THE FORMER GRAND DRAGON of Indiana at a Bob Evans restaurant in Auburn, north of Fort Wayne. Two years had passed since the day Brad Thompson had petitioned the city planning commission to place a Klan cross at the courthouse, then came home worried about his appearance on the local news. Thompson had a new self-possession, a new gravitas. While not exactly a repentant bigot, he now said that he wasn't one, and that seemed like a big step, coming from the man who'd once told me, "I guess I was just born a racist." True to the inscription printed on his black T-shirt— SILENCE IS NOT F#$&* GOLDEN—Thompson had decided to spill the beans on Wizard Jeff Berry.

We ordered coffee. "When did your doubts begin?" I asked.

"There was a chain of events, small minute things that started getting my mind turned around," said Thompson.

The first of these occurred in 1996, when he and the Wizard drove to Ann Arbor to set up the first rally there. As Thompson recalled, "Jeff made the comment, 'Wouldn't it be great if these towns would just pay us cash not to come.' "

This was exactly what Berry had pulled off in Cicero early in 1998, when town officials agreed to pay the American Knights $10,000 to produce and distribute Klan literature—in lieu of a rally. The literature was never distributed, however. The Wizard never sent any. "Never saw or heard from them again," said Cicero city attorney Paul Karkula, who confirmed that the money was sent to Berry. According to Thompson, the Wizard pocketed the cash. Berry denied this, however. "There was no money given to us by Town Hall," he said. It came from "an anonymous donor" to cover printing costs, and "some pamphlets did get passed out."

I asked Thompson what he thought when Berry first broached the cash-for-no-rally scheme. "First thing that crossed my mind," recalled the former Dragon, "was, 'That's extortion.' But Jeff said, 'Look we're costing these towns seventy to a hundred thousand dollars for an hour and a half of rally time. We'd be doing them a favor. Plus we'd be making money for the cause.' "

From that point on Thompson's disillusionment with the Klan kept pace with his growing conviction that the cause was "Jeff Berry's back pocket." Then part of Thompson's job as Grand Dragon turned out to be absorbing various Klan expenses, for which he was never reimbursed. Berry directed him to get "a phone for a hotline" and a post office box. Thompson paid for both, then made all the long-distance phone calls for the American Knights, at a cost of $400 to $500 a month. "Never got a dime back. Never got an offer. Or a thank you."

Meanwhile, said Thompson, the Wizard kept all the dues. The ex-Dragon gave me a couple of examples and invited me to do the math. There was one klavern in North Carolina, he said, with "people struggling to survive, struggling to live, and they'd be the only ones that paid their dues on time." Three or four hundred members at $100 a family. Then there was the windfall that came in courtesy of that first *Jerry Springer* appearance. After he and Berry mailed out the 6,200-plus applications, they got back all but eight with $20 each. (That bought the new mail-order Klansman a membership card and a certificate.) There was no telling how much money had come in after five or six subsequent *Springer* appearances by the American Knights, plus the reruns. Thompson reported that the Wizard kept cash and money orders but ripped up personal checks.

Then, said the ex-Dragon, the Wizard was making good money if even 10 percent of the people who looked at the American Knights website bought the "Klan merchandise" Berry sold there, from T-shirts to belt buckles. "He makes a heck of a markup on that stuff," said Thompson. "That's where the money's at."

According to Thompson, the Wizard never let anyone look at the books, even though he always said, "All you gotta do is ask." If someone did ask, the former Dragon recalled, "He'd get very irate and say, 'It's none of your damn business.' And here this guy is not working. The man hasn't punched a time clock since 1994."

As for Berry's claim to be a tow truck driver, Thompson insisted that the Wizard hadn't owned a tow truck in a year and a half. "Somehow he got ahold of a brand-new one when he was on *48 Hours* last week, but that's not his tow truck.

"Then, here *I* am, working seventy, eighty hours a week plus setting up the rallies plus going on the weekends to North Carolina, Pennsylvania, Illinois, Michigan, all over Indiana. And I'm starting to see there's no reward in it. I'm starting to get burned out. I'm starting to see the true face of Jeff Berry."

The Wizard did not return my repeated calls to his home, and a letter sent him via Federal Express came back to me unopened. However, shortly after Thompson began making these charges publicly, Berry told the *Goshen News*: "The Klan does not make any money. How can it? You got to put out letters, you got to put out a newspaper, there's stamps, telephone calls . . . If we were getting so much money, why do I have to take it out of my pocket to run the organization?" He continued to maintain that he'd thrown Thompson out of the American Knights, that his Dragon had simply joined another Klan.

"Was there some specific thing that pushed you over the edge?" I asked Thompson. "Some trigger?"

"Oh, a big trigger," said the ex-Dragon. "Big trigger. April fifth, 1997. The Pittsburgh rally. That did it for me." As Thompson told this story, he also indicated what had kept him in the group for nearly a year after his misgivings began. He had argued about this particular rally on the phone with the mayor of Pittsburgh, and "that made me feel like big shit," said Thompson ruefully. "Because I was able to talk to the mayor of Pittsburgh. That gave me a power trip."

But once the American Knights got to Pittsburgh, he continued, "My power trip was deflated bigtime. There was twelve thousand protesters there that wanted to slit our throats. The only thing separating us from them was those cement dividers they use on the highways plus a four-foot fence, and they were rocking that back and forth, throwing things at us. It sounded like a roar from hell: all these people shouting about the Klan. What was the point of it? We got three members out of that deal. Cost the city of Pittsburgh a hundred and some thousand dollars. For three members. I'm like— it's madness. What are we trying to do? Meanwhile Jeff was in his prime, strutting around like a peacock. Afterward we drank until morning, me and a couple other hardcore drinkers. But I kept saying, 'This ain't right.' And I kept thinking on the way home, 'This ain't right.' "

By that time Thompson was also having serious marital problems, "which was generated by Jeff. Because he seen my wife trying to talk sense into me." The Dragon's wife, Brenda, wanted him to quit the Klan. The Wizard told Thompson he should find "someone more dedicated" and set him up with various women in the organization. "Yeah, there was womanizing," said Thompson. "Yeah, I was a drunk." And behind the Dragon's back, the Wizard was going to Brenda, telling her about it. One day he even played her tapes of Thompson with another woman. Brenda decided at that point that she wanted a divorce and filed for possession of the trailer. The police showed up a few days after the Pittsburgh rally and escorted Thompson out of his home.

On April 12, 1997, Thompson sent his letter of resignation to Berry. It read:

Because of our differences of opinion on the direction that this organization is going, and for the fact that I cannot, nor will I allow it to control my personal life, work life or family life.

Must respectfully resign my membership from this organization. It is not in my best interest to participate, communicate or associate myself any further with this organization or its membership. Unless said members have resigned themselves and have become members of the Empire Visible.

Nothing personal, Mr. Berry. I intended on joining a religious civil rights fraternity—not a cult! You have a gray notebook that belongs to me. I trust that it will be returned. As for my robes, although I paid money for them, you can have them as a going away present.

Thompson didn't move back in with his wife until July. They'd begun divorce proceedings and had two or three court appearances behind them before they finally compared notes and understood the role Berry had played in trying to break them up. Berry had told Brenda before the first hearing, for example, that Thompson intended to shoot her.

"I decided it was time for me to pay back Mr. Berry," said Thompson. "So I went around to every town that we ever had a rally at, went to the newspaper and apologized and told them basically what I've just told you. Denounced him and exposed him. I made Mr. Berry very, very mad. His defense was, 'Thompson joined another Klan' or 'I kicked Thompson out.' And that's when he started retaliating bigtime."

The Wizard never personally harassed him, but the ex-Dragon still held him responsible. Someone painted "KKK" on the side of Thompson's car, bashed out his windshield, and slashed his tires. I couldn't help but remember my first interview with Thompson—after he first showed his face on local television as the Dragon—and how he'd speculated that anti-Klan zealots might get his windshield or his tires but "that's the worst" that would happen. When the Klan came after him, it was far from the worst. He was harassed at his job. Several times someone distributed flyers through the foundry parking lot saying that Thompson was a member of the Man-Boy Love Association, or that he was now in another Klan, or that he'd killed his own son. (And whoever wrote the flyer must have known how painful that would be for Thompson.) People began calling the foundry to ask for Klan information in an attempt to get the ex-Dragon fired. He had to go to everyone he worked with and explain what was going on. Then a couple of people with guns showed up at his home. Both were chased off by the fierce Brenda. The first guy came to the trailer door and threatened to kill everybody. "My wife jumped out the front door, tried to grab him by the throat, and chased him around the corner into the back of a pickup." Jeff Berry happened to be sitting in the driver's seat. The other frightener was Al Ferris, who *was* a person to be feared. The former Imperial Nighthawk, a gunslinger type with a Fu Manchu moustache and tattoos, Ferris was the man who would eventually be shot dead by his own wife. ("Justifiable homicide.") But the day he came to Thompson's trailer, Ferris got almost up to the door when Brenda ran out with a nine-millimeter and told him to get in his car and never come back. The ex-Dragon told me that everyone in the American Knights knew Brenda as a crack shot and "no one to mess with." She'd always won all the shooting contests.

"How long did this harassment go on?" I asked.

"It's still going on," he said. "I got my truck tires slashed in late July."

He expected the book he'd just completed with journalist Worth Weller to be a big success. "It's going to rock old Jeff." He figured that once he started making money from the book, he'd get his KKK tattoos removed.

Thompson had lost sixty-five of the hundred pounds he'd gained during his Dragonhood, but he hadn't quit drinking for a year after leaving the Klan. Why so long?

"I went on a pity trip."

The striking thing about this Ku Klux soap opera was that none of it had to do with race, but I couldn't really tell if Thompson had sworn off the Klan ideology. He just seemed ambivalent. When I asked him directly, he said, "I was never really that hateful. I was more into the fraternity part of it, the secret stuff, the fellowship of men getting together."

"But you aren't anti-Klan now?"

"I feel anti anything that's going to get me out of the house, get me into trouble, and have money pulled out of my pocket for stupid reasons," said Thompson. "But I'm not going to lie and say that I'm totally against the Klan. I respect the real Klan and their beliefs just as well as I respect the NAACP and their beliefs. I'm against Jeff Berry and his ways. But I don't view that as Klan." Thompson had decided, in fact, that Jeff Berry started the American Knights solely for protection, fearing revenge after all the narking he'd done.

Geography had placed him in the orbit of the American Knights, but if he'd lived near the Keystone Knights, "it might be a different story right now," said Thompson. He said he'd "rubbed elbows" with a number of other Wizards and knew that the "real Klan" regarded Jeff Berry as a Patriot for Profit and a joke.

"Am I a racist?" he said. "I don't know. I never had any dealings with blacks. I never had any racial problems." While he still had a hard time with things like interracial marriage, he now declared, "It doesn't affect me. I don't care."

Clearly he was still figuring it out. The ex-Dragon thought there were good people in all the Klan groups. "So I'm not going to say I'm against them. But the racism part. Yeah, I'm against the racism part. I don't see the necessity of it."

"How do you feel about Jeff's line that white people are oppressed?"

"Ahhhhhh," he replied with great disdain. "That's just a sales pitch."

Finally, I realized, I had a chance to find out how many people in Grant County belonged to the American Knights, the biggest, most active Klan in the country.

"At the time that I was in—fifteen," said Thompson.

I TORE BACK DOWN the interstate to Marion for my first Unity Week event. Thirteen people had convened for the study circle, which met under the usual stipulation of confidentiality. What I *can* report is that I sensed a change from the meetings I'd participated in two years earlier—a bit more openness and trust. Here was one tiny increment of progress. On the other hand, the participants numbered only thirteen: four black and nine white. Maybe there had always been thirteen people in Marion who could carry on such a dialogue, and if Thompson could now be believed, they were still outnumbered by active Kluxers.

The story of those working on "race relations" always seemed to be the story of diminishing expectations. When Harmony 2000 began in 1997, for example, Linda Mui told the *Chronicle-Tribune* that she hoped the study circles would eventually involve five hundred people. When I talked to her at primary time, spring 1998, Mui told me, "By the year 2000, we might have two hundred. At the most." As of Unity Week, in fall 1998, eighty people had been through the program.

THE NEXT NIGHT, FRIDAY—four nights before votes would be counted— more than two hundred people gathered for the interfaith service. These reconciliation events always seemed to end up back in church. Even when that wasn't literally true, they were certainly about preaching to the converted. I arrived at Bethel Worship Center during the first number from the Interfaith Choir, "Dreaming of a Colorblind World," a maudlin song, but at least it addressed racism head-on. That was still a rarity in these "mixed" services.

I felt the usual cognitive dissonance that goes with overlooking what's right under your nose. We were sitting in the Deeters' church. In this very sanctuary Willie Deeter and James Cameron had met for *their* reconciliation, filmed by the BBC. I was certain that hardly anyone there knew that such a thing had ever happened. Despite what Willie Deeter said about it later, that little piece of film captured a true moment of catharsis, the kind that emerges only from risk. I knew exactly why Harold Vermilion wanted to cast it in bronze. And now it couldn't even be talked about. In a week devoted to racial healing, no one was supposed to discuss the worst moment in the town's racial history.

At the time of this service Bethel had the only really integrated congregation in town. Reverend Michael Henson, Bethel's white minister, announced, "I can't wait to walk with my brothers and sisters from this community to honor Dr. King." He did indeed sound joyful, though I had expected the service to be better attended. Divided pretty evenly between black and white, there was nowhere near a full house. They responded with a smattering of applause, of calling out, when Reverend Henson said that Dr. King's dream was "at least in a little part becoming a reality" in Marion, and while there was much work to do, we had to start somewhere.

WHEN I GOT TO MATTER PARK the next afternoon, I could hear the purple strains of "Colorblind World" wafting from the bandshell. The entertainment had started at ten that morning. Again I'd expected a bigger crowd, though there must have been four to five hundred there, ready to march, with more joining in later at the dedication site. And I found myself feeling very disappointed that Unity Day wasn't illustrating more unity. The majority of the people at the park—listening to music, chatting, lining up for hot dogs and chili—were black.

I spoke to some people I'd met the night before at the interfaith service. When I told them what my book was about, one young white man immediately provided a lynching anecdote. Growing up in Fairmount, he'd always heard stories about men sitting on rooftops with rifles the day after the lynching, ready to guard the town from blacks.

The march began to organize itself, people grouping together at the lip of the park. Someone I couldn't quite hear seemed to be leading a prayer. Then we set off up a hill, a force six to eight people wide, some carrying homemade signs with messages like "Dedication Saturday, We Shall Overcome." As we got out onto the bypass itself, a couple of black men on a golf cart drove back and forth along the line of marchers. One had a bullhorn; he was reciting King's "I Have a Dream" speech.

We marched about a mile to Five Points, a major intersection where the bypass split into two state highways, bisected by a local thoroughfare, Kem Road. Here on a triangle-shaped safety island, a covered stage had been set up in front of the new green highway sign, still veiled. It would mark one end of the dedicated portion of the bypass. I noticed Tom Wise onstage. He'd waited till the last minute to tell them he'd sit up there.

On that day I shared his cynicism. Several introductions and one song into the ceremony, the assembled dignitaries went back to the new sign and pulled off what looked like a white sheet, revealing the words "Martin Luther King Jr. Memorial Way." When one of the local black leaders came back to his seat onstage—hands held high in triumph—I thought, *That's gratitude for small favors.* I wondered if drivers on the bypass would even see the sign, since it actually faced Kem Road on one side and a dogleg on the other. Maybe visibility would improve once they added a bust of Dr. King, as planned. Still, that night I would write in my journal: "The Way is a very short street."

But ultimately I decided that I was wrong to take this attitude. I never doubted the sincerity of the task force, and I sensed genuine excitement in the crowd. Maybe symbolic gestures against racism were important, no matter what motivated them. The lynching itself had been a symbolic gesture meant to reinforce racism, not just a fatal act for two men but a message aimed at every African American in Marion.

King III's speech was gracious. "Marion has been burdened with a reputation of having the last community lynching in the north," King declared to calls from the crowd of "That's right."

"My father would be pleased to know that Grant County has come a mighty long way," he continued to more applause. "That Grant County has nominated for the office of sheriff on the Democratic side an African American candidate." This pronouncement evoked the first cheers of the day. "A man with many qualifications," King went on. "It shows that Grant County has adopted the process of judging a person not by the color of his skin but by the content of his character."

The next day's *Chronicle-Tribune* would report that King had endorsed Oatess Archey from the stage "without saying his name." That was a bit of a stretch, and the Archey camp worried that it would make people mad. Especially since, as the article explained, "Task Force organizers tried to discourage campaigning during the dedication."

There was more to the ceremony, of course. More speeches. More prayers. Many of the ministers I'd interviewed, both black and white, participated in some way. It was a day intended to build some hope. Reverend Henson did the closing prayer, asking everyone in the audience to join hands. "Father, it is such an honor for us to stand here. We've come today for a healing, a healing in our land, a healing in our city. Forgive us for racism so there may come a healing today."

Afterward I ran into Marcus Cannon, the former Black Panther, who'd been videotaping the whole thing. He gave me a hug and said, "I hope it's real."

ON ELECTION DAY OATESS ARCHEY moved his base of operations to Democratic headquarters, a storefront a couple of blocks from the square. When I stopped by that morning, a campaign manager for another Democratic candidate mentioned that complaints were coming in from voters: a Republican judge at the downtown polling place was pushing buttons for people by way of showing them how to work the new voting machines. Another campaign worker reported that there was such a long line at one South Marion polling place (and only one machine working) that voters were giving up and going home. As far as I knew, though, these were isolated problems.

I walked over to the downtown polling place. The Republican judge who'd allegedly been "instructing" voters by pushing buttons for them appeared to be about ninety. The new push-button voting machines resembled big blue suitcases laid open. There was one voter there, and he was told he was "done" after he'd voted only for school board. By mistake, he'd hit the red button to record his vote, instead of the green button to turn the page. The voter looked stunned, then said he should have read the instructions and walked out.

Later I chided myself for not casing the polling places all day long. Because when I got back to Democratic headquarters at six P.M., the campaign manager I'd spoken to earlier laid out a list of the day's appalling problems from precincts all over the county. Most related to machines breaking, voters being denied paper ballots, and people having to wait in line for hours. Tom Wise said he'd never seen anything like it before in a Grant County election.

Don Penrod, a Democratic city council member, reported that at one polling place some people had waited for two hours, then had to leave for work without voting. Since they'd already signed in, they were not allowed to come back and vote later. "They're trying to steal it," declared Penrod, "and they're in the driver's seat." Everyone from the county clerk to the current sheriff was Republican.

Oatess Archey walked in to the Dems' sparsely furnished storefront to a round of applause, but the ambience was tense and a bit gloomy.

At the back of the room stood a homemade stage, where Archey sat down to talk with a *Chronicle-Tribune* reporter. He was very distressed about the voting problems. People were being denied the right to vote, he said. It was a disaster. "Four backup machines for sixty-two precincts. I just feel like crying."

NO RETURNS HAD COME IN yet on the sheriff's race at seven P.M., but Archey decided to begin his thank-yous to everyone who'd helped. The leader of the local Young Democrats sat monitoring a radio at a long table to the side of the stage. The storefront was crowded. Democrats who'd been active in the county for years told me that usually half as many showed up on election night. "Oatess has energized this party," said one.

Archey said nothing about the difficulties of that day beyond "we've had some problems with machines breaking." The first tallies came in at seven-fifteen. With 29 of 62 precincts reporting, Archey had 54 percent, Back 46 percent. A huge cheer went up. That was the biggest lead Archey would have, however, and the gap kept closing as the speeches went on.

The final numbers didn't come through until nine forty-five P.M. No one had left, but the speeches were over, and Archey sat at a front desk, talking on the phone. Suddenly the radio boomed: ". . . this is just minus a few absentees. Let's take a look at this latest report." The room went completely silent. "For county sheriff right now. Oatess Archey has 10,778 votes, fifty-one percent. Mike Back with 10,198 votes . . ." Cheers and applause drowned out the rest.

Archey made his way to the stage. Taking the mike, he announced, "I told my wife and a few others, if I won I was going to dedicate this race to Millie Thompson. Where's Paul?" Millie Thompson was the elderly white campaign worker who'd been hobbling around with a walker the night of the primary. She had since died.

Her son, Paul Thompson, a Democratic city councilman about Archey's age, made his way to the stage, where he and the sheriff-elect embraced. Then both began to cry. They turned their backs to the audience and stood at the back of the stage—a black man and a white man blowing their noses. Archey's wife, Barbara, took the microphone and said, "Well, it looks like I'm going to have to take over here." The crowd roared.

Once Archey had composed himself, the speeches began again, people coming forward to praise him, to revel in the victory. It was one big lovefest. But no one that night mentioned the history they'd just made. Grant County had just elected the first African American sheriff in the history of Indiana.

Tom Wise told me that he didn't think people had really taken in what had just happened. I was standing behind the stage with Wise and other Archey staffers. Larry Leach, the ex–Gas City police chief and the campaign's treasurer, a white man, said to me, "Grant County's a winner tonight." Leach was a little choked up. "This is kind of emotional for me." He recalled meeting Archey for the first time when their fathers were both hospitalized in the same room years ago. "It's just a pleasure to even be associated with him," said Leach. "He's just a great man. Comes from a great family. The only thing I regret is that I would have liked to stand side by side with him in uniform and worked with him as a law enforcement officer." Leach had been injured in a freak accident in 1996 and forced into retirement.

I said something to Leach about the historical significance of Archey's win, and he replied, "My mother witnessed the lynching. And today she voted for Oatess."

THE NEXT DAY'S *Chronicle-Tribune* reported that, despite all the heat around the sheriff's race, voter turnout had actually been lower than usual. I wondered just how many had been disenfranchised because of the voting problems. No Democrat but Archey won a county-wide office.

Three Indianapolis television stations sent reporters to Marion that morning to interview the sheriff-elect. Down at his headquarters some major campaign supporters gathered outside on the sidewalk to wait for him: Larry Leach; Gene Linn, the mayor of Gas City; Shirley Barbour, former Marion city council member; Marcus Cannon, the ex-Panther; and Jim

Lugar, the campaign's media coordinator and a Republican, second cousin to Senator Richard Lugar. We watched as Archey walked toward us down Washington Street, two cameramen walking backward in front of him filming the approach to headquarters. Archey looked a bit bemused by it all.

The crews from two stations were there. No doubt they'd been assigned to cover the race angle—"first black sheriff in Indiana." But Archey seemed determined to play that down. When they asked him about the significance of his victory, he said simply, "It was a team effort."

One reporter asked about the town's "infamous past." Had that motivated him to get into law enforcement? "Regardless of whether you're black or white," said Archey, "you can't dwell on the past. We're trying to move into the future."

The other reporter asked if anything had happened on the campaign trail "to make you think this wasn't a good idea"—fishing, I assumed, for some racist incident. Archey said that everyone had predicted he could never win, but he'd been warmly received all over the county. He recounted marching in parades in various communities, where he could hear people saying, "There he is," and they'd run out to shake his hand. "I think Grant County got a bad rap way back when," said Archey, "when a few bad people took over and caused a cloud to form over this county."

Then Archey went briefly through the tropes of his life story. From the toilet bowl to the Rose Bowl. Interviews complete, the crews filmed outside as the new sheriff crossed 31st Street and headed toward his car. Drivers, both black and white, honked and waved when they spotted him.

He had really inspired passionate support, even if he didn't get the most votes (compared with some of the other winners). The people who'd been for Oatess Archey had been for him 200 percent. The feeling was palpable, a happiness hanging in the air. Blacks and whites had united as equals to elect a good man. Now the whites were proud and the blacks were encouraged. Some kind of bridge had been made.

"His trouble hasn't started yet," said Tom Wise, who stood watching all this in front of headquarters.

Just then a third camera crew arrived. Archey walked back into headquarters with the new reporter, who asked the same basic questions. Being "the first"? It meant nothing to him.

LATER, AT A NORTH MARION RESTAURANT with Archey and a few others who'd been part of the campaign, people came by the table to congratulate the new sheriff. Then, as lunch ended, Archey told me he'd been very up-beat about the racial stuff with the television reporters, but in fact there *had* been some incidents.

We moved over to a corner table, and he told me first what had happened at Clara Jeffries's funeral. She was his father's first cousin, and she'd been a classmate of both James Cameron and Thomas Shipp.

Archey and Tom Wise had both gone to the interment at Estates of Serenity, where my grandparents were buried. As Marion's oldest cemetery, it dated to the days when black and white couldn't lie in the same ground together, and Jeffries's grave was in "the so-called black section," as Archey put it. He and Wise were walking back to their cars through that section when they passed a cement slab, the base for someone's tombstone, maybe thirty inches by eighteen. There in the cement someone had drawn a Confederate flag and written in the four corners: "KKK" and "RIP" and "White Power" and "Kill All Niggers." Archey and Wise went to the cemetery director, who told them yes, he knew about it, and that's why he had people park where he did. So they wouldn't walk by and be offended.

The symbols would be covered once the tombstone arrived. They would also stay there permanently. "I think somebody wanted to have some fun," said Archey. "So Tom and I told him, you better get that out of here."

Archey went back the next day with Jim Lugar, a former cop, his campaign's media director, a white man. They found that someone had gouged the slab up and flipped it over. And that took some doing. It was about a foot thick. Nevertheless Archey and Lugar turned it back over to photograph it and saw that whoever flipped it had tried to deface it first. Archey went back to the cemetery director and told him, "This is a hate crime." Then he called the police so there'd be a report.

He was substitute-teaching at the high school now and found himself making an assessment of what exactly had changed in the town since 1969, the year he left for Ball State. "Marion used to be 'The City on the Move'" said Archey, "but we were moving in the wrong direction." The population then was 39,000 and now it was 29,000. In 1969 the high school had 3,000 students, and now it had 1,600. Even the "three R's" had changed—to racing, 'restling, and recess. Grant County had among the highest pregnancy rates in the state, among the lowest number of high school graduates, and the average salary was $17,000.

"The fact of the tombstone—is that because of our educational level?" asked the new sheriff. "Is that what makes us still hang on to this mentality of hatred?"

TWENTY-SEVEN

POOR MARION

The Rally / July 1999

During Oatess Archey's first summer in office, three Klans scuttled back into Marion for a joint rally. The black sheriff concerned them.

Not that they said that at first. Apparently the Kluxers didn't think of the "first black sheriff" angle until journalists started asking. When they made their initial request for a permit in April 1999, they told the *Chronicle-Tribune* that certain unnamed politicians and police in Grant County were harassing their members in unspecified ways. And they wanted to talk about the Columbine High School massacre in Colorado.

Poor Marion.

The three Klans represented more of Jeff Berry's disgruntled ex-members. Grizzly Smith, Al Ferris, and the Grand Dragons of both Wisconsin and Pennsylvania had followed Brad Thompson out of the American Knights. But unlike Thompson, they hadn't rejected the Klan. I had an e-mail from Thompson telling me: "They are going around now trying to grab the glitter of Jeff's rallies. They long for the good ole days."

Grizzly Smith and Al Ferris had declared themselves part of the Invisible Empire, Indiana Ku Klux Klan. Their group would have no Wizard, no national leader, no one higher than a Dragon. This, I guess, was their idea of reform. So Al Ferris served as Indiana Dragon, and Grizzly was the state religious leader, or Kludd.

Grizzly the Kludd. I relished this name. Downright medieval.

I called the Kludd every few weeks for an update. In May he told me they were rallying because Marion police had harassed certain citizens for flying Confederate flags. Not the sheriff, the police. In a later phone call he told me they were coming to Grant County because of something said on *The Jerry Springer Show*. According to Grizzly, the black man who'd been James Cameron's self-appointed bodyguard during the 1995 Marion rally appeared on some *Springer Show* and said, in substance, I'll make sure the Klan never comes back to Grant County. It didn't matter that this particular man no longer lived in Marion. "You don't tell us we're never coming back," declared the Kludd.

In June, a denial from the Grant County commissioners in hand, Grizzly announced that because the Invisible Empire was getting "jerked around," two more Kluxer groups would join them in Marion for a unity rally: the National Knights and the Knights of the White Kamelia. He speculated that the police and the sheriff had had something to do with rejecting them. "Because the sheriff down there is black."

The Klan finally enlisted the Indiana Civil Liberties Union and threatened to sue. The date was set for July 24. The disparate worlds I'd been navigating would come together for one last woeful afternoon of Ku Kluxing at the Grant County courthouse. The new sheriff, the lynching survivor, and the former Dragon would all be there to face the anti-Jeffs.

ON JULY 8 EX-DRAGON Brad Thompson sent me a news article by e-mail about the death of Al Ferris, shot down by his wife with his own nine-millimeter pistol. Thompson had given reporters his assessment of Ferris: "It's like he wanted to be a biker and he didn't have a Harley. There's a large part of the membership that's like that."

The former Dragon was now a Ku Klux authority, more notorious than he'd ever been as a Klansman, thanks to his book, *Under the Hood: Unmasking the Modern Ku Klux Klan*, written with journalist Worth Weller.

"I still don't understand why I supported an organization with all my effort for almost three years, that has committed so many crimes against humanity," Thompson confessed in his book. "Being in the Klan is like watching a fire in an old dry field. You burn fast, tall, and hot. And when the fire passes, nothing is left inside you but gray dusty ashes."

Both Jeff Berry and Grizzly the Kludd assured me that Thompson had never left the Klan at all, that he was playing both sides, that he'd simply switched to the Keystone Knights where he went by the name of D. C. Stephenson II. I thought it possible that he'd briefly taken that name, though Thompson denied it. What I knew for sure was that leaving the American Knights had been easy. Leaving racism behind took longer.

When I wrote to thank him for sending the Ferris news, I mentioned that I'd be going to the Marion rally. Thompson replied: "I wouldn't waste my time with any more rallies they are all alike. I should know. LOL. [e-mail shorthand for "laugh out loud"] Brad."

About a week later Thompson e-mailed again: "I guess I am going to this big farce. My co-author invited me. . . . I did not plan on attending this, but it may be interesting to see how they all behave after the shooting death of there [sic] enforcer. LOL. Brad."

ON JULY 22 GRIZZLY THE KLUDD phoned me early at my Marion hotel to say he'd be in town that day around noon. We could meet at the rally site. He promised to introduce me to a Grant County Klansman if I would give the Kluxer anonymity. Then he chose to describe himself, though I'd been around him at American Knights events: "I'm a big boy. Five-ten, two hundred seventy-five pounds. I'll be wearing a leather vest and a white shirt with a bolo." I should look for a golden van.

I spent the rest of that morning talking on the phone with Opha Betts, the retired nurse who was writing a history of the African American settlement at Weaver. One thing I told her about was the trouble I'd had finding descendants of abolitionists who knew anything about what their ancestors had done.

"It's like everybody wanted to forget it," she observed. "Both sides. Like they don't want that to get in the way of what they're trying to do with their lives."

She could be talking about the lynching, I thought. Of course, when it came to race, good history could be as taboo as the bad.

I also told Betts about finding the Telltale site and said I hoped I could show it to her someday. I almost didn't tell her because I felt so guilty. She may have even had ancestors there. Yet I could know where it was, and she couldn't.

On that note I went off to meet the Kludd.

▲ ▲ ▲

GRIZZLY WAS STANDING NEAR the east entrance to the Grant County court-house. His bolo tie's clasp had a Klansman in the middle with an American flag and a cross. We walked to the golden van, and I saw that there were two other big tattooed guys in there. The older bald and bearded man behind the wheel was introduced as Duane the Nighthawk. I was asked to climb in back next to the younger man, who looked like a skinhead in his gray fatigue pants, combat boots, and skull-dragon-White Power tattoos. This turned out to be Jack, the Exalted Cyclops of Grant County.

I suggested heading to the bypass. None of them had heard of it, which stunned me. Not even Jack, leader of the Grant County klavern. How could anyone live in the county and not know the bypass? I would learn later that Jack had been a resident for just five months and lived on a farm. Still. Five months certainly seemed long enough. I saw it as part of a bigger problem, a serious inability to be curious, to look around, get the lay of the land—and I don't mean merely geography. So I named the various franchises out on the bypass, and they perked right up. Steak 'n Shake. I gave directions.

Once seated at the restaurant, the Cyclops and the Kludd ordered buck-ets of Surge (high sugar, high caffeine), and Duane had an iced tea. Before I could even ask a question, they began dishing the dirt on Jeff Berry. By this time I also had a whole newsletter on the Wizard's alleged misdeeds from the Kentucky-based Imperial Klans of America. So I knew that among cer-tain Kluxers it was now a priority: this trash-talking about Berry to anyone who would listen, especially if that person was "the media."

What interested me was the energy these "brothers" expended in de-nouncing him. The attacks on Berry were more passionate than anything I'd heard them directing at, say, black people. For these guys, black people were an abstraction. Hating them was a theory.

To change the subject, I asked once more, Why a rally in Marion?

Jack answered: "Since the sheriff got elected, people have been harassed for flying rebel flags." And so it had evolved. "The sheriff" was now the first thing out of their mouths. Jack himself had been one of those pulled over for flying the stars and bars in Marion—by a policeman, not a sheriff's deputy. They still held the sheriff responsible. After all, he was black.

They had, of course, other complaints. The usual complaints: Martin Luther King Day. The state of Arizona forced to observe it. Black History Month. Mexican History Month. (Unknown to me.) All the history months. (Unknown to me.) Loss of the white heritage. Welfare queens in Lincoln

Town cars. Schools forced to change their name from Jefferson, because the man had owned slaves.

Their list was long. These were people who took the time to brood over things like "Chinese restaurants don't have to hire white waiters."

"Marion's only one stop for us," Grizzly said. "True, it's the first county in the state to have a black sheriff. It's just coincident that he was just elected here." But then all this harassment started, he said. "If he wants to be sheriff, fine. As long as he takes and upholds that law like he's supposed to. Myself, I can't see how a black man can have the same type of beliefs when it comes to our Constitution as a white man does. Because they believe we owe them something."

I kept trying to get the silent Duane into the conversation. He was fifty-two and finally told me that he'd been part of the American Nazi Party in the 1960s. But he'd "run around with the Klan" since he was eighteen, in Mississippi, in Kansas. "Like a bad penny always comes back," he said. Without irony.

Back to the standard litany of woe: the white race still "having to pay for slavery," the history books rewritten, homosexuality taking over, businesses forced to hire unqualified blacks.

I kept being aware of how loud they were talking. When the Kludd mused that at the rally people would finally have to listen to them, Jack observed: "We are only a vehicle for self-thinking."

Grizzly complimented him on this observation, while I thought, "Huh?"

I'd reached that point I got to in every Klan interview, where I could barely react to the wacky ideas anymore. My eyes were glazing over.

But I suppose I knew what he meant. I could imagine Jack in school being labeled one of the dull kids—plain, paunchy, dead enough in the eyes that he appeared none too bright. But he actually had a lot to say. The Klan had given him a voice.

Jack worked on a farm. Duane lived on disability. Grizzly said he was self-employed: "I build shelves."

They ordered plates full of French fries smothered in chili and cheese. Grizzly confided that he was going through a lot of "turmoil" these days, as he tried to determine whether black people had souls. "I haven't quite figured that one out. I mean, because the Bible's incomplete." This was news to me, but I let it pass.

"Look at certain skulls," the Kludd continued. He mentioned a well-known anatomy program on CD-ROM that, according to him, proved that racial differences don't end with skin color. I looked up the CD-ROM later, and of course he'd misread it. No doubt he'd seen what he wanted to: "Our brains and skulls are different. Our muscle structure is different."

"Ours weave. Their muscles weave and twist," said Jack.

"Weave and twist," Grizzly repeated.

"A black man's skull is thicker," said Jack, "with a smaller"—Grizzly chimed in on the word—"brain."

But then he corrected himself: "Not actually smaller. Mushier." I stifled a laugh. They didn't notice. "It weighs less than ours does," Grizzly was saying. "It doesn't have the same density."

Outside it felt hot enough to pop corn, with no break predicted before rally day. "And I've got that heavy robe," sighed the Kludd.

AT THE LIBRARY THE NEXT DAY I learned that three men identifying themselves as Kluxers had come in the week before and asked for information on the lynching. Grizzly had mentioned that they wanted to bring it up at the rally. One Klansman even signed the guestbook with name, address, and "KKK," but I couldn't find him in the phone book. I thought about driving to the address and tracking him down. But somehow, after years of hunting for any Grant County Klansman I heard about, I felt that I'd had my fill. I was losing my patience.

I headed over to the sheriff's office, where I had an appointment with Oatess Archey. Half a year into his first term the new Grant County sheriff still seemed to be reliving his victory. The county was 91 percent white, he marveled. "They said it couldn't be done."

Archey had a big office, with a conference table at one end. On the walls he displayed his awards and copies of a couple of the articles written about him, like INDIANA TOWN WITH TAINTED PAST ELECTS FIRST BLACK SHERIFF. I saw nothing personal on his desk except for one little plaque with a Bible passage: "I can do all things through Christ which strengtheneth me. Phillipians 4:13."

I told him about the Klan complaints that people were being harassed for flying Confederate flags. Archey kept calling staff members into the office to hear the story. Then he explained that Eastbrook High School, serving the northeastern part of the county, had called on the sheriff's department for help after banning Confederate flags from the premises. Certain Eastbrook students—the self-styled Good Old Boys, or Goobies—flew huge rebel flags from the backs of their pickups. "By the time we got out there, though, they'd already taken them down," Archey told me. "And the two boys who didn't take them down had already been suspended from school. So we've never had a confrontation with any group about Confederate flags."

There'd been another incident at Taylor University in Upland, where two black women students were followed home by a couple of guys flying Confederate flags from pickups. They then sat outside the women's residence shining lights on the top of their trucks into the windows, terrorizing them. The women were not American and had no idea what the flag even meant. By the time campus police arrived, however, the trucks were gone.

"A year away from the millennium," Archey said with a wry chuckle, "and we're still dealing with grown men in hoods and sheets." He hoped that people would ignore the rally and avoid the downtown completely.

"The people of Grant County resent this," he declared. "It's a step backward, back into the twilight zone. Especially in this community that had the big cloud over it from the 1930 incident. People just don't want anything that resembles hate coming back here. And the good black and white people of Grant County resent what happened in 1930, too—the ones that didn't have anything to do with it, that were blamed and looked upon in a negative way for what a few hooligans did. So the mood of this city right now is very somber."

RALLY DAY PROVED TO BE another one of hammering heat. I kept calling Tom Wise's house, since Cameron planned to stop there beforehand. He hadn't made it by the time I left for the twelve-thirty press briefing.

As I joined the rest of the media in the city council chamber, someone called hello from a few rows behind me—Brad Thompson, the former Grand Dragon of Indiana, wearing a black T-shirt that said HATEWATCH.ORG.

Police officer Vern Owensby went through the rules with us. How we had to stay in our corral and so on. Owensby was the highest-ranking black officer on the force, and someone asked him how he felt about the rally. He said that at one point black people would have been up in arms, but now— "What are you gonna do?" The Klansmen were a bunch of idiots, and he was missing his family reunion in order to watch over them.

There would be even more of a police presence this time than last: a SWAT team (maybe two), the bomb squad, "tactical intervention," K9 including bomb dogs, helicopters, EMS, the fire department, and the state police.

We waited in the lobby until Owensby was ready to lead us to our holding pen. One reporter began interviewing Thompson about why he'd joined the Klan. "I joined because I needed something," he told her. "I lost a son, went through a divorce, and was an alcoholic. The Klan filled a void." I noticed that his past kept changing as he rethought it. Certainly that would feed people's doubts about him. But it would also be the sign of a changing consciousness.

I asked Thompson what he was doing with Hatewatch, a website that tracked the racist right. Evaluating "hate" websites, he said, to help decide what to post. The inscription on the back of his shirt read: HOW IT INFURIATES A BIGOT WHEN HE IS FORCED TO DRAG OUT HIS DARK CONVICTIONS. LOGAN PEARSALL SMITH.

I said, "Grizzly tells me you're now the Grand Dragon of the Keystone Knights."

He seemed to blush and said, "Still trying to float that, are they? That's crazy."

We began moving off to the checkpoint behind Vern Owensby and a state trooper. There sitting in the gazebo in front of the municipal building was James Cameron with his Milwaukee entourage. The same white man who'd driven with him last time stood there berating us: we *could* be stopping to interview the lynching survivor; instead we were getting ready to pay all our attention to the stupid Klan. True enough. But on that supercontrolled afternoon, we had one chance to get into the media corral, and this was it. Cameron himself had not tried to get our attention.

Once we got to the courthouse, we had nearly an hour to wait. Already I was distracted and too hot. But the former Dragon had some news for me. Jeff and Edna Berry had divorced. Edna moved east somewhere, after Jeff took up with another Klanswoman. So much for the Imperial Family.

Seated on a bench, completely at ease, the former Dragon offered some opinions on the upcoming rally: "They're trying to follow in the footsteps of Jeff and the American Knights. Every rally's an experiment with membership. Sometimes you get a hundred fifty people, sometimes four. The one thing they are banking on is media coverage. When they see media packing up and leaving, that angers 'em. *I'm* gonna aggravate 'em just standing here."

To think that during all those tedious afternoons with Jeff Berry and the American Knights, I'd been experiencing the gold standard among Klan rallies. Who knew?

I walked out to the sidewalk. They were giving us limits this time. No walking within fifteen feet of the anti-Klan demonstrators, for one thing. But after Cameron got into the anti-Klan pen, he called out to me and extended his hand. I went up to him and grabbed it. A state trooper came flying out of nowhere to order me back. Someone might grab my camera, he said. The cops were so tense. They had German shepherds dotted along the front of the courthouse lawn, some straining at their leashes.

I told Cameron I would see him later and went back to the press area. The media had the only spot with shade. I heard Thompson telling another reporter that the Klan recruited women because once you had them, you had the whole family. He explained that Jeff Berry had done his anti-Amish rally in LaGrange after a young girl got killed in a farming accident near there, and the American Knights decided to denounce them for child abuse. The Klan always looked for an excuse to come into a community. Farming accident. Black sheriff. Whatever.

The former Dragon had definitely changed in the nine months since I'd last seen him. I didn't think I would hear any more from him about his respect for "the real Klan." Thompson told me that with his foundry on strike, he'd begun work at another factory that was 70 percent black. And many had recognized the former Grand Dragon of Indiana. One interview about his book ran on a Fort Wayne channel, which kept recycling clips in an ad to promote the news program. He figured he was on TV now ten or twelve times a day. So he'd said to his black colleagues, "Anything you want to know, I'll tell ya." He'd never had any trouble with them. A few of these coworkers had become friends, had come to his house.

Of course, he had told me before that he knew black people at the foundry. "Not like this," he said. "Not where there's seventy-five or eighty on one shift, out of a hundred ten people. I respect them. Most of 'em work two jobs. Then these guys"—he gestured toward the area where the Kluxers would soon stand—"they don't work."

I thought he was making a real attempt to be self-aware, though the post-Klan career also appealed to his ego. "I try to be ordinary as much as I can, considering," he told me. "I don't really put too much into the fame. I do the radio interviews, and I try to do the best I can to educate. I don't really let it go to my head like I did when I was Grand Dragon. I let that go to my head. I really thought I was something important in my mind's eye. Then I got brought down to reality when I resigned and sent copies of my resignation to the local media, and they told me it wasn't newsworthy."

Suddenly the Kluxers were outside the courthouse door, setting up their speaker. I stood up on one of the benches to get a better view. The Marion authorities had cleverly constructed the event so that between the bushes and the war memorials on the courthouse lawn, the Klansmen and the spectators might not even be able to see each other. I could hear Brad telling someone, "I hadn't realized what I was putting my kids through. My kids hated that I was in it, and I didn't care."

I walked over to a spot on the sidewalk where all the TV crews had set up their cameras, right in front of the KKK gang. The Kluxers began by playing a recording of "Amazing Grace" on bagpipes. Certainly I was inured to them by now—the way they appropriated everything sacred and all-American in their efforts to make the world worse—but hearing this old hymn made me so sad I felt like crying. *"I once was lost but now am found, was blind but now I see."* How dare they?

Grizzly the Kludd had solved the problem of his heavy robe by not wearing it. Instead he'd dressed in black with a square black mask over his face. He, the religious leader, kicked off the rally with a prayer "for guidance and understanding . . . that what we do will be pleasing in Thy sight." Already the event was a bad joke.

Throughout the prayer anti-Klan protesters chanted, "We don't want you here!" They kept it up as the Kluxers played another song, "Proud to Be an American." I estimated the anti-Klan crowd at seventy people, most of them white, some holding small placards that read STOP THE KLAN. Cameron held his usual sign: STOP THE KLAN! LET DECENT AND FREEDOM-LOVING WHITE PEOPLE BREATHE SOME FRESH AIR. It looked a bit battered now. He'd been dragging it to Klan rallies all over the Midwest.

Grizzly announced that they were dedicating their rally to Al Ferris and launched into the first diatribe: be a good role model for children.

Back in the shade, I stood on the bench and counted seventeen people on the pro-Klan side. No one over there was yelling "White Power" or responding in any way at all. They all looked like young men. Thompson speculated that they might already be Klansmen, imported from Fort Wayne. He talked about a rally he'd been to where no one came to stand on the pro-Klan side, so the leader ordered a few Kluxers to take their robes off and go stand there. I counted sixteen people "on stage." The city had been expecting about fifty.

Ray Larsen, Imperial Wizard of the National Knights, came forward, wearing black with a black baseball cap. "Hello, Marion. It's so good to be here in the home of the last lynching in the state of Indiana. 1930." I thought about Cameron out among the spectators, hearing the worst moment of his life turned into a pep talk rallying cry for the bad old days.

Larsen then moved to the usual gripes—most of them blessedly inaudible because he was holding the microphone wrong. I caught a few phrases like "leeches on society" and "trying to revert back to the ways of the savage," then the promise that the Klan would take over "right after RaHoWa," the long-anticipated racial holy war.

The next speaker, Charles Edward Foster, had been the Grand Dragon of Pennsylvania while a member of the American Knights, but now he was part of the Invisible Empire and called himself a "Grand Wizard." A former motorcycle gang member with a BORN TO LOSE tattoo, Foster was notorious for his aggression. He did two years in prison for leading a gang rape in 1969. Afterward he had torched the woman's car and run a pool cue through her dog.

His was the most vile speech I'd ever heard at a rally—and that was saying something—beginning with the line "We hate niggers and we hate Jews!" He was bouncing off some invisible wall, screaming sexualized racial slurs, ripping his hood off after about two minutes because it was getting in his way. He began singling out protesters to insult with as much obscenity as he could muster. Of course, like the rest of Jeff Berry's Grand Dragons, Foster had become a "reverend." His spiritual advice was probably his least crude bit: "If you kill a nigger, it don't matter because it has no soul. It is not of the Christian race. If you're not a born-again Christian, washed in the blood of the Lamb, then you're a piece of shit!"

His was the longest speech of the day, and I could barely stand listening. Instead I eavesdropped as Brad Thompson explained to yet another reporter why he'd joined the Klan: "I had a character defect. Now I see the monster I created. It almost sickens me."

Foster announced that everyone could come meet the Klan later, naming the exit and a truck stop off the interstate. Thompson pointed out that this meant they did not have anywhere to go locally for the cross-lighting. "That tells me they have no supporters in this area. Otherwise they would have some property already lined up."

I reminded Thompson, "You told me that about fifteen people joined after the last Marion rally."

"And they didn't last very long," he said. "Maybe six months." I recalled those passionate Marion members, Dusty and Kathleen. Dusty had died early in 1999.

I began to tell the former Dragon about the lynching, where the tree had been, where the old jail still stood. And over there in the anti-Klan pen was the man who'd survived it.

"He has the same sign he used back then," said Thompson. "It would be a pleasure to meet the gentleman."

A new Klan speaker was talking about gun control. Jack the Cyclops, I realized.

"See, this guy talking about gun rights is what fascinated me at my first rally," said Thompson. "It made sense. There wasn't much racial talk at my first rally. Constitutional stuff. Militia stuff. I'm still a big believer in gun rights and militia. They try to say that militias are hate groups, but it don't hold much water with me. For the most part, the militia tries to stay clear of the Klan."

Thompson decided to leave with his coauthor, Weller. It was about three. The rally was going on, but I could no longer concentrate on the tirades. I was sick of paying attention to their pathetic beliefs. I followed Thompson and Weller. The former Dragon had decided he wanted to meet the survivor of the Marion lynching.

Cameron had moved to the back of the anti-Klan pen, where he was sitting down. Thompson and Weller both got in with all their equipment, but I was stopped because I had a camera. I hovered and eavesdropped on the other side of the fence, as Weller asked Cameron why he'd come all this way to protest the Klan.

"Silence equals consent," Cameron replied.

Weller introduced the former Grand Dragon of Indiana. Thompson told Cameron that he'd participated in the last Marion rally and that he remembered his sign. "It's a pleasure to meet you on this side of the fence," said the former Dragon. Then he and Weller got up and left.

Cameron himself emerged a few moments later, and we hugged. I walked back toward the municipal building with him. "You just met a reformed Klansman," I said to him.

"That's beautiful," said Cameron. "He gave me a copy of his book."

The rally was still bleating over the loudspeakers.

"I felt that I'd had enough," I said.

"Me, too."

Cameron looked slighter, balder, shorter. He was now eighty-five, and he'd left Milwaukee at six that morning with six other people, two black and four white. They'd come in two cars and been delayed by a blowout. I invited Cameron to the Holiday Inn for a cool drink, but he told me he had to do some interviews, then head to Anderson to see his brother, then drive all the way back to Milwaukee that night.

The police wouldn't let us into the gazebo in front of the municipal building, so we sat under a tree. I asked him to talk again about his sign. What did that slogan mean to him?

"It means that a lot of decent and freedom-loving white people don't want to speak out," said Cameron. "There's a certain reticence on their part. They don't want to get in Dutch with the white people among whom they live, because they'll be known as a nigger lover."

He added, "I don't think things are getting any better, Cynthia. I think they're getting worse. With what's going on on the Internet. It's pitiful. And they call that free speech. I was talking to Mayor Mowery just before I went in there [the anti-Klan pen]. He said, 'We shouldn't be publicizing this.' And I said, 'Why shouldn't we?' I said, 'You're never going to live it down. Why don't you take that jail and make a museum out of it?' "

Then Cameron went through the rest of the fantasy I'd heard so many times: the giant wall with the names of the thousands who'd fought for racial equality, people coming from all over the world, Marion doubling in population.

"You know they're turning the old jail into apartments?" I asked.

Said the lynching survivor: "Can you imagine?"

So ended the last Klan rally of the twentieth century in Marion, Indiana. In fact, Klan activity across the state fell off precipitously after Wizard Jeff Berry went to prison in December 2001. His charisma had built the American Knights, and groups like Grizzly's boomeranged off their hatred of him. He was the linchpin.

But he had made a big mistake. The man who'd built his notoriety and, to some extent, his whole organization on accessibility to the press actually took two reporters hostage in November 1999.

George Sells IV and Heidi Thiels of WHAS-TV, Louisville, Kentucky, interviewed Berry at his home and admitted that they also planned to speak with ex-Dragon Brad Thompson. The Wizard then said he didn't want to be part of the story and demanded that the journalists turn over their tapes. They refused. According to the complaint filed by the journalists, Berry and a second Klansman then locked and blocked the door, while a third Klansman blocked their vehicle out in the driveway. A fourth hooded Klansman entered the room and pumped a shotgun. Twenty to thirty minutes later the journalists gave up the tapes and left. They filed a complaint with the DeKalb County sheriff.

In January 2000 the Southern Poverty Law Center filed a civil suit against Berry on behalf of the reporters. The Wizard alleged in turn that the SPLC, the TV crew, and the ex-Dragon had conspired to deprive him of his freedom of religion. Eventually a federal judge in Fort Wayne ordered Berry to pay each journalist $60,000.

Roughly a year after the original incident, in November 2000, DeKalb County authorities finally arrested the Wizard on criminal charges that he termed "fictitious." Then the day before his trial was to begin in October 2001, Berry copped a plea.

Not that pleading guilty meant he was admitting to anything. At his sentencing in December 2001, Berry took the stand and declared that he was being persecuted for his political beliefs. Like Dr. Martin Luther King, Jr.

The Wizard's attorney, an African American he'd hired in Fort Wayne, pleaded with the judge to keep "Reverend" Berry out of the state prison system, where his KKK activity would make him "a marked man." But the judge was having none of it. He sentenced the Wizard to seven years for conspiracy to commit criminal confinement with a deadly weapon.

By the year 2005 the Klan appeared to be almost dormant in Indiana—and not just the American Knights. Just a rally or two a year was making its way to the Klanwatch lists. But I didn't doubt that racist hatred was still there, waiting for a leader to give it direction.

PART VI

Truth and Reconciliation

TWENTY-EIGHT

FOUR DAYS IN AUGUST

I finished the book. I wrote an ending I've now discarded after a "last trip" to Marion in 2002. What I most recall about those twelve days is gloom. My second night there I had dinner with some friends, lifelong residents, who reported that unemployment had just hit 10.4 percent, and that didn't count people who'd gone off the rolls without finding work. Over a year had passed since the *Chronicle-Tribune* ended its "Moment of Truth" series filled with those terrible statistics on job loss, illiteracy, and other indicators of the county's decline. Since then more factories had closed while others began layoffs, among them Marion's biggest employer, Thomson Electronics. My friends began to speculate about how long it would take before Thomson shut down completely. (The answer: two years, with a total loss of nearly three thousand jobs since the 1990s at that factory alone.)

I remembered how the town's poverty had startled me on my first visit back in 1994, an impression based on the grim condition of the courthouse square. In 2002, however, I immediately noticed the cosmetic changes downtown—brick laid in the intersections, more buildings spruced up and occupied. It was all part of the town's struggle to pull itself back from a precipice. Billboards declaring, WE BELIEVE IN MARION had been put up in every part of the city.

The other physical change that immediately caught my eye was the place now called Castle Apartments, though no one was likely to mistake it for anything but an ex-jail. The renovation had left most of the bars in place on the windows, though in some of them a large rectangle had been cut out of the center. One day I stopped by and found the front door open. I wondered if it could even be the same door. Now whitewashed, it had a new window, and I couldn't see the dents made by the sledgehammers anymore.

I stepped inside. Everything was pristine, though of course I couldn't help but think of the mob that had surged through here. At the bottom of the corridor leading into the former cell blocks stood one barred door, open, of course, and now merely picturesque. I think it was unlocked on August 7, 1930. Each cell block had become two apartments. They'd put in elevators, but I went up the same stairway that was there before, the one where certain officers reportedly stood watching the lynch mob break into the west cell block. Upstairs was the passageway into what had once been the sheriff's house, and there on the wall were some portraits of old sheriffs—though no Jake Campbell. Was it only me for whom the events of August 7, 1930, still echoed so loudly here?

When I went to see Sheriff Oatess Archey at the current jail, our talk turned immediately to the local economy. Archey had been to a recent meeting about what could be done, and he'd asked the facilitator, an out-of-town consultant who'd traveled the whole state, "How are we perceived by the other ninety-one counties in Indiana?"

The man told him: you're very blue collar; your political leaders can't work together; and you have racial problems.

Archey, the only African American present, objected to that third characterization. He named all the political positions blacks had held in Marion since the late 1980s. Police chief, assistant chief, president of the school board, president of the city council, superintendent of schools, county councilman, and now sheriff. First in the history of Indiana. Elected in a county that was 8.8 percent black. "How could I have won if this was such a racist place?

"We're making more strides than some of our fellow counties," Archey declared. "Maybe the rest of the state doesn't see this. They're still looking back to 1930, and maybe that's our fault here in Marion. We're not selling ourselves." In his opinion, what Grant County had was a perception problem. It needed a publicist, someone to market it.

In "that fiasco back in 1930," he said, "if someone among the business leaders or the good citizens of Grant County had just said, 'We're not going to tolerate this,' and those mobsters had been brought to justice, I think Marion and Grant County would be further along than where we are today."

Archey also thought that both blacks and whites were ashamed of the crimes committed on August 6 and 7, 1930. "We have suppressed it. 'Just let that die and let it go away.' That's what we've all been taught, those of us that grew up in Grant County. After being away from home for twenty-nine years, I came back and heard the same thing as when I left: 'Shhh, we don't talk about this.' My mother-in-law—she's James Cameron's age, grew up with him—she was taught that if everybody, black and white, stops talking, it'll go away. But it hasn't."

Sheriff Archey was about to run for reelection unopposed in the Democratic primary. He was now so popular in Grant County that the Republican Party had not actively pursued anyone to run against him in the fall.

I'd started to wonder what I could learn anymore in Marion. One day I drove to the disappeared village of Old Somerset, usually covered by the Mississinewa Reservoir, but in 2002 the water was so low, I could walk the old streets and see the old foundations. The submerged town felt like a metaphor for the whole trip. Things were buried, and then they came to light, but not really. I decided that I'd gotten all the information I would ever get.

But there was more. There always would be.

August 4, 2003

After several strokes Aunt Ruth entered a nursing home, where she remained completely bedridden until the end of her life. When I visited in the spring of 2003, she was gossiping and fretting about various relatives who'd been dead for decades. Her failing mind had not only taken her back in time; it had taken her to Marion. I felt happy for her, that she could at least live in that fantasy. She hated the town where she'd moved years ago to be near my parents.

In August, when I returned for my mother's birthday, Ruth could barely speak and wasn't conscious most of the time. I wasn't sure she recognized me.

My parents had taken the boxes of family pictures to their house. We found them in some disarray. As it turned out, we had one possession other than a locket that had belonged to Grandpa's mother, Josie: a photo album embossed with her name. And it was empty.

Aunt Ruth had removed all the pictures, then numbered them on the back. I couldn't tell if we had them all. None of the people were identified, and my father had no idea who they were. Aunt Ruth had always said that she would get to them someday.

I recalled looking at pictures of the Carr family with her when I was a girl—maybe even these—and she'd been guessing at most of them. So I wasn't sure we could blame her for our ignorance. Really, it was Grandpa's doing for leaving his history a blank. During my genealogical research, I'd been surprised to discover that he too had ancestors in the Revolutionary War; for example, a great-great-great-grandfather present at the surrender of Cornwallis. Maybe he hadn't known or hadn't cared, but it also seemed quite possible that he simply refused to claim it, since any mention would have drawn unwanted attention to his family tree.

In contrast, most of the pictures from my grandmother's side of the family had been labeled, either by her or by my aunt. One I'd never seen before was Grandma's friend, "the daughter of the last Miami chief," as Aunt Ruth always described her. The photo shows two Miami women seated in a photographer's studio and posed with their heads together. Based on their attire and the photo process (it's a cabinet card), my guess is that the picture dates to the 1890s or very early 1900s. On the back my aunt had identified one of the women as "Eliza Newman, last full-blooded member of the Miami Indian tribe," while the other was unknown.

Most important, however, I found the tintype of our alleged Indian ancestor, my great-great-great-grandmother Sarah Scarlett Newell. She had strong features, the lined and weather-beaten face of a pioneer. Or an Indian? I couldn't tell.

Through the Internet I'd found a distant Scarlett cousin who traced the family back to a Newman Scarlett in Massachusetts, born about 1740. Where we had a story about an ancestor on a doorstep, wrapped in a scarlet shawl, the cousin had a story about an ancestor washed ashore from a shipwreck, wrapped in a red blanket or else wearing a red suit, but in either case too young to know his own name. Thus *new, man,* and *scarlet.* My newfound cousin *had* heard something about a Native American in the family, however. He thought it was on the Newell side. Or, I thought, maybe it was on that mysterious Nixon side. Or maybe it was just not there.

My grandmother wouldn't lie. Clearly this information about being part Indian had been passed to her, but it could still be wrong.

I only knew for sure that the ancestors could surprise you. They could wash ashore from shipwrecks, be found on someone's doorstep, or end up in an unmarked grave. They could be like Frances Slocum, "The White

Rose of the Miami," claiming and living an identity she wasn't born with. And they could come from anywhere. You almost had to be royalty to know who, exactly, was back there on the family tree. This seemed a good thing to remember when regarding someone from another race or culture: you had to stop and tell yourself, maybe I'm one, too.

August 5, 2003

I drove to Marion, intending to spend a day and a half clearing up some details at the library.

As soon as I got to the history/genealogy section—where most of the librarians knew me—I learned that Ruth Anne Nash had just been in, looking for information about Mary Ball.

Ruth Anne Nash was the niece of Tommy Shipp. He was the only one among both the lynching victims—Shipp and Smith—and the River Road victims—Deeter and Ball—who had no living siblings when I began my research. In fact, no one from the Shipp family had ever granted an interview, but I'd come close with Ruth Anne Nash. She and I first met at the Weaver church in 1996 during that astonishing reconciliation service—when Harold Vermilion, the white minister who wanted to erect a statue at the lynching site, got up and apologized for August 7, 1930, on behalf of white Marion.

During my last trip in 2002 my failure to finally get an interview with Nash had been my biggest disappointment. She had remembered meeting me at Weaver. She'd been wanting to unburden herself for years and thought maybe I was the one to hear her. We even arranged a meeting time, but she said she had to clear it first with the rest of the family. And that was the end of that. The family said no.

Nash's interest in Mary Ball was a puzzle. I left the library immediately and called her. Again, she remembered me but still seemed a bit hesitant to talk. Then I promised, "I'll tell you everything I know about Mary Ball." She agreed to meet me back at the library.

As we sat down, I noticed that Nash had with her a homemade book with a plastic binder and clear plastic cover labeled "Shipp Family Tree Memory Book." It contained, among other things, photocopies of the lynching picture, Shipp's death certificate, and a photo of him as a boy posed formally with his family. I'd been told that the Shipps kept a scrapbook about the lynching, but apparently it was more a scrapbook of their whole family history.

Nash said that she didn't care anymore what the rest of her family thought: "I need closure." She then proceeded to tell me an amazing story. She'd gotten a phone call from someone claiming to be the grandson of Thomas Shipp and Mary Ball. The caller wouldn't give his name or say where he lived, only that he and Nash had a mutual acquaintance. Ultimately he'd hung up on her, but his story happened to jibe with a bit of Shipp family lore about Tommy. Growing up, Nash had learned that one day back in 1930 Tommy Shipp had come home and told his mother, "She's pregnant." It was understood in the family that "she" meant Mary Ball. He never said the baby was his, however. Just "she's pregnant." Nash had been going through marriage records at the library, trying to figure out who Ball married and what had become of her.

Of course, the story I'd been hearing since my first trip to Marion was that Ball had been involved with Abe Smith. If she'd been involved with anyone.

"Abe took the blame," said Ruth Anne Nash.

"But why would he do such a thing?" I wondered. This she could not answer.

I allowed myself some time to hallucinate over a Shipp-Ball grandson and what that person might know, but this fantastic story imploded rather quickly. Over the next month or so Nash would talk to senior citizens in the African American community who convinced her that Abe Smith was Ball's boyfriend—while I still doubted that either Shipp *or* Smith was her boyfriend. Eventually Nash concluded that whoever had called her claiming to be the grandson was playing a cruel joke, though she still believed the story about Tommy Shipp's declaration—"she's pregnant"—because she'd heard it from her grandmother, and "my grandmother wouldn't lie."

The person she did regard as a liar was James Cameron.

She believed he'd been in jail for stealing chickens, though she didn't appear to believe it fervently, saying, "I appreciate the fact that, *if* he was there [at the lynching], he got out." She'd heard the chicken story only recently, but it fit her other feelings about Cameron—that he was in it for the money, that much of what he'd written wasn't true.

When Cameron self-published his book back in the 1980s, Nash bought a copy and her mother burned it. Her mother, Alberta, had been about fourteen when her brother Tommy was lynched. Alberta didn't read Cameron's book. She just didn't want to be reminded. And she discussed the lynching with Nash only once. "She said she wasn't going to tell me anything and I didn't need to know." Tommy, or Joe Thomas as he was known in the family, had also had two younger brothers. Nash was one of five surviving nieces and a nephew.

It seems unbelievable, but Tommy Shipp's mother went to work for ex-sheriff Jake Campbell in the 1940s, as his housekeeper. One day Ruth Anne went along with her grandma to help wash dishes. She was six or seven. After finishing her chores, she went to Campbell's library to look for a book. There she spotted two notebooks she was nosy enough to pull from the shelf. They happened to contain a personal account of the lynching—written by Campbell himself, Nash speculates. She had time to read only one ("a coil-bound secretary's book") before her grandmother caught her and ordered her out of the library.

Naturally, she couldn't remember much of what she'd read, except that "it told a lot about the mob. Not who was there, but how many he thought was there. They were some of them common people, some of them dressed in suits, but they were all raising sand. He said he tried to hold them off. And Jack Edwards wasn't no help because he had gone out of town. At the time," Nash concluded, "it didn't mean too much to me." But she had seen the name Shipp in this notebook. When she got home, her grandmother and father explained what they thought she should know.

That was the only time Ruth Anne ever accompanied her grandmother to the Campbell home. "After they found me reading them books, I couldn't come back." So the sheriff, or someone in his family, had written a journal account. The lynching victim's niece had found it. But now this was just another story of lost evidence.

Then that same day, suddenly and unexpectedly, in the course of one phone call, I found out who planned the lynching.

I'D HAD SUSPICIONS FOR YEARS. My first two days in Marion I heard anecdotes about 18th Street. The message sent to the sheriff from 18th and Adams. The barbershop at 18th and Meridian said to be "the hotbed of that group." And right between them the factory where Claude Deeter had worked: Superior Metal Products, commonly known as Superior Body. This information was suggestive, but that's all. Then in 1999 I got a real lead.

On the morning of August 7, 1930, Superior Body's plant manager John Sisson came in at 9 A.M. to find that the shop was empty. Everyone had clocked in at the usual starting time (6 or 7), then clocked back out. Also missing were a sledgehammer and a rope. I learned this from Sisson's grandson, John Milford, a Marion attorney.

Milford said that he thought the time cards from August 7, 1930, had been turned over to a researcher named Larry Conrad back in the 1970s. Conrad was a former Indiana secretary of state who intended to write a book about the lynching. Stories I'd heard about him indicated that he really wanted to solve this crime. Ruth Thomas, the woman who'd told me about seeing streetcars offline the night of the lynching, met Conrad while she was working as the librarian at the Marion newspaper. Conrad told her something she didn't quite remember about an umbrella, that he'd been able to identify someone thanks to this umbrella. Odd, but he was clearly moving on some detective track. He died, however, before he could write his book, and his widow passed on the material he'd gathered in Marion to Indiana University history professor James H. Madison.

After Madison published his book on the lynching, I called to ask him about the time cards Conrad had supposedly collected from Superior Body. There weren't any, Madison said, but he did find and send me payroll sheets for Claude Deeter. Attached were two typewritten lists of names. A search of city directories confirmed that all of them—eighty-five names altogether— had worked for Superior Body in 1930, except for two men I couldn't find in any directory. Certain names on the longer list had checkmarks next to them.

I'd brought the two lists with me to Marion. After showing them to a couple of people, I had a name to call. The man I phoned was related to someone on those lists. As it turned out, he'd grown up around men from that factory, and they were often at his house when he was a boy.

"Ever hear anyone talk about Claude Deeter?" I asked him. "Ever hear any talk about the hanging?"

"I heard a lot," the man said. "I've got stuff pertaining to the lynching. Personal stuff. I could write a book." He wondered, therefore, why he should talk to me, since I would then make money by telling the story, and "that would be silly."

Yet the big secret was finally cracking open. The flashpoint on August 7, 1930: Superior Body. (And what horrible irony in that name.) I just hoped to keep the man talking.

"The sheriff backed up and the police backed up," my informant continued. "It was all planned, the whole thing, and the way they slid it under the table, law enforcement and everybody else—it's quite a story really."

Could he tell me that story?

"What kind of cut would I get?" he asked, but he kept going. He'd read Cameron's book. Some of that account was like he heard. Some of it not.

The guys who did the lynching always said they didn't hang Cameron because he was too young, just a boy. Apparently the mobsters discussed it freely. "I heard this at the kitchen table while they was playing pinochle."

I told him the other stories and rumors I'd heard about who participated, but every path led back to Superior Body. For example, people had seen men walking toward the jail from the Malleable. From Marion Machine.

Superior Body did work for all the other factories around Marion, said my informant, and those workers would have gotten the word.

I told him the story about men showing up at Midwest Paper and Envelope to recruit lynchers.

That was just five or six blocks from Superior Body, he said.

The old mayor had identified Charles Lennon and Phil Boyd as ringleaders.

"Lennon? Did he work at Superior Body?" the man asked.

"No."

"He wasn't one of the leaders. Bystander participation—that's where I'd put him. He may have participated, but he wasn't organizing it. Also Phil Boyd. He didn't work down at Superior, but he was a roughneck, and he was known for his fighting, known for being mean."

"Was there any one leader?" I wondered.

No. It was a group decision. There was no one person. "Not in the stories I heard."

He speculated that maybe men working at Superior Body were related to men in law enforcement. "Somebody had to have pull in order to get this done."

He was way off base about the events of August 6, but even this was telling. He'd been told a grotesque tale of savage blacks, a warrior white man, and ravished white womanhood, and I feel safe in speculating that many in the lynch mob believed this story. That Mary Ball had been mutilated. Her nipples were chewed off, the man told me. This was, in fact, very close to the Madge Oberholzer story, which had no doubt lodged in many a Hoosier consciousness. Just five years before the lynching, in 1925, Oberholzer had been mutilated—bitten—by Grand Dragon D. C. Stephenson. She died soon after. This sex scandal was usually credited with bringing down the 1920s Klan. My informant had been told that Mary Ball died soon after the encounter on Lover's Lane. And that Deeter was a mean character, "the type of guy that wouldn't take it from nobody. If he seen a conflict coming, he started fighting. That's why they shot him. He come out of that car fighting."

During the course of this conversation, the man made it clear that he didn't agree with what had happened in 1930. "Our city government, our state government, and everybody else backed out of that situation knowing they was wrong. I mean, that's completely wrong."

But he seemed to savor having this secret—something, he pointed out, that even other people in Marion didn't know. Referring to his relative on my list, he chuckled. "I still got his gas mask."

A gas mask?

"They threw tear gas," he said. This I knew. The shocking thing was the implication that the mob had prepared for it, that they knew in advance what the sheriff was going to do.

"I could tell you more than that, but I won't do it," and he chuckled again. "I heard the complete story. How it was done. How it was planned. I heard the whole deal, and I know my mother, she wouldn't lie about it. There was a group that took it under their arms."

Then he would not say more until he met me. I arranged to meet him first thing in the morning, before I left town. I expected a case of amnesia to set in by then.

August 6, 2003

I got to the man's house at nine A.M., and just as I feared, he had now decided that he didn't know a thing. I began by taking out the two lists of names that came from Conrad's material. The workers at Superior Body. Had Conrad made one list of men who participated and a second of those who didn't? Or had he simply gathered some names first, some later? There was no way to know.

My informant didn't appear to recognize many names on the list. He said he thought there had been some Klansmen at Superior Body. My first thought—they're convenient scapegoats. But of course, I'd heard from others that some of them *were* involved. Once the spark was lit, it must have spread beyond the Superior Body workforce. Beyond the other factories. But that was the part my informant was withholding. How word got to every hill and dale in the county and beyond. How everything from the streetcar shutdown to the cover-up had been planned.

All the man would volunteer now was: "The sheriff knew. The mayor knew. Everybody knew."

We sat on the couch, while his wife was in a chair to my left. "So," I said, "Superior Body was definitely involved?" His wife sat there nodding her head yes, as the man said, "I can't say yes." That stopped her nodding, and she remained silent.

Then the man said to her: "Get out the time cards."

The wife went to another room and came back with an envelope of old manila cards dating from the early 1920s. That was the curious thing. They had nothing at all to do with August 7, 1930. Yet they'd been kept at Superior in the office safe for over thirty years. The man said he got them from the plant manager sometime in the 1960s. Then, when Larry Conrad came looking for them in the 1970s, someone from the plant called my informant and asked if he still had them. He laughed when he told me this. He'd said no.

I wrote down the eleven names.

I kept asking how the lynching was planned. The man kept replying that I knew as much as he did. I decided that maybe he'd needed to meet me first, needed to decide he could trust me. I would come back to him.

I did not remark on the words scrawled in red ballpoint across the envelope that now lay on his coffee table: "TIME CARDS. SUPERIOR BODY. Some of the men involved in the hanging of 1930."

As I soon discovered at the library, the top card belonged to someone who was dead before 1930. Three other names on the time cards did not appear in any city or county directory. That left seven potential mobsters—all of them long dead, and there was certainly no way to know for sure if all seven had participated.

I never did learn more from the man with the time cards. When I went back to him, he said, "I think we'll just leave it where it's at."

Still, I felt confident that the lynching had started at Superior Body, 18th and Branson.

When the rest of Larry Conrad's material went to an Indianapolis library in 2005, I listened to all the interviews he'd taped back in 1977 and a few more puzzle pieces clicked into place.

I learned, for example, a new fact about Dave Fansler, the farmer who'd lived up the hill from the crime scene on the River Road, who'd chased Shipp's car away and then driven into town to get the sheriff. Dave Fansler's son-in-law worked at Superior Body. The son-in-law's last name was on one of the time cards.

I also learned that, as Claude Deeter reached the hospital, a friend of his from Superior Body ran to tell Claude's aunt and cousin about the shooting as they sat out on their front porch at 19th and Meridian. The cousin,

Mildred Whybrew, then called Deeter's parents in Fairmount, and all of them went to the hospital. In other words, men at the factory knew about the shooting even before Deeter's family did.

Meanwhile, the sheriff had come into town with Dave Fansler in tow—so the farmer could identify the weeds stuck under Shipp's car as growth from the River Road area.

Then, either late that night or early the next morning, someone went out to the River Road and asked Fansler to go to the sheriff "and get his answer about lynching 'em." The farmer was directed to take the sheriff's answer to the corner of 18th and Adams, where someone would meet him. That corner was one block from Superior. Fansler told the men who approached him there that the sheriff had said, "We have to abide by the law."

This story came from Conrad's interview with Walter Fansler, who had been seventeen in 1930. (When Carl Deeter interviewed Walter many years later, they did not discuss this.) Rex Fansler, who had just turned six at the time, always said his father took a message *to* the sheriff from 18th and Adams. Maybe. Walter only said that a message came there *from* the sheriff, and that the unidentified men his father spoke to then got into a car and drove away.

Mildred Whybrew, Deeter's cousin, declared during her 1977 interview that she'd heard someone named Byrd was a ringleader. Finn Byrd had already been identified to me as "definitely involved," and he appeared on Walter White's list (as "Thin Beard" or "Bird"). Now I also knew that he worked at Superior Body. He was on one of the typewritten lists. Like Claude Deeter, he was a riveter.

Of course, Mildred Whybrew had also heard that the mob came from the ketchup factory on 22nd Street. Those people, she pointed out, were mostly southerners. But I never found a thing to support that contention. All the anecdotal evidence points to a four-block stretch of 18th Street, from Adams to Branson (Superior Body) to Meridian (Bailey's barbershop, "the hotbed of that group"). And these are short blocks.

Today 18th Street is the hotbed of nothing. Superior is gone, replaced by another factory. The city is trying to bring back Adams Street between 18th and 19th with some Habitat for Humanity houses. And down at Meridian there's a vacant lot where Bailey's barbershop used to be. Studying 18th Street through old city directories, I noted that Bailey's barbershop eventually became a tavern called Little Harlem in the 1970s.

I had once talked to Marcus Cannon, the former Black Panther, about the street. I told him my suspicions about what had happened there in 1930, and I knew for sure that during the civil rights era 18th Street became the "geographic and political center of black unrest."

First the place where the lynching originated, then a place where white people were afraid to go.

"And now," said Cannon, "it's dead."

August 7, 2003

I had volunteered to read at Cameron's museum in Milwaukee on the seventy-third anniversary of the lynching. I knew it to be almost ten years to the day since I'd first met him, but looking back through my notes and journals, I couldn't determine the exact date in 1993 beyond "early August." I thought this a sign of how frightening it had been for me to begin this process, that is, to begin acknowledging the wages of racism in some personal way.

As I drove into Milwaukee, I saw that official green highway signs now marked the turnoff to America's Black Holocaust Museum, an indication of the institution's new status. Cameron had accomplished his life's work, the task he thought God intended for him when he was spared on August 7, 1930—the opening of a place in which "to educate the public about the violent injustices suffered by people of African American heritage," as the new mission statement put it, "and to provide visitors with an opportunity to rethink their assumptions about race and racism."

It was almost startling to remember how I found Cameron there in 1993, ensconced alone in one room stuffed with books and papers, while most of the space was just a big gym—all hoops, lockers, and ancient weightlifting equipment. That building was unrecognizable now. Glass doors opened into a lobby—administrative offices to the right, gift shop to the left. A small permanent exhibit on the Middle Passage led to the galleries.

I'd last visited in February 2001, soon after Cameron was diagnosed with multiple myeloma—cancer of the bone marrow. The museum had wanted to honor him at a Founder's Day celebration on his eighty-seventh birthday and invited me to be the keynote speaker. After his cancer went into remission in 2001, he had a heart attack and doctors came close to installing a pacemaker. To hear Cameron tell it, he'd then experienced another miracle. He got all the way to the operating room, when doctors decided not to proceed. They had determined that, in Cameron's words, "my two hearts beat as one."

"It's wonderful having these near-death experiences," he told me. "It does something to the soul. It makes you realize that all is vanity." But he'd never really recovered his strength. He arrived in a wheelchair for the seventy-third anniversary of the lynching, billed as the First Annual Commemorative Fundraiser Reception.

One of the other presenters on the program was a young man named Reggie Jackson, who'd gone to Marion on a fact-finding mission. He'd taken slides. He showed us the "COL" (for "colored") still designating black veterans on Grant County's World War I memorial and left the audience incredulous with pictures of the old jail turned into Castle Apartments. I read some of my eyewitness accounts of what had happened on August 7, 1930. But I think we were all waiting to hear from Cameron himself.

His son Virgil wheeled him to the front, and he read his short speech, a restatement, really, of his basic theme: we are one single and sacred nationality.

TWENTY-NINE

IN THE PICTURE

Cameron and I didn't have a chance to talk privately in the midst of that event. I phoned him later with the news: I had learned where the lynching was organized. In his seventy-odd years of keeping that event in everyone's face, Cameron himself had never focused on the whodunnit question, and I wondered if he even wanted new information about something he seemed to revisit in his head every day. So I asked: "Does it matter to you to know?"

"Yes!" he said.

So I told him. He said nothing beyond "uh-huh" and "I'm glad to know that," but he was breathing so heavily—panting, really—that I worried about his heart.

In the autumn of 2003 twenty Marion ministers—ten white, ten black—organized the first-ever attempt at a public atonement for the lynching. After seventy-three long years, this event came together very suddenly: announced in September, carried out in October, and for that whole month, steeped in controversy. Many in Marion, both black and white, did not want it to happen.

455

The inadvertent provocateurs, Reverend Larry Batchelor and Reverend Mike Henson, said they decided they had to do *something* after that year's Martin Luther King Day observance at Taylor University, east of Gas City. The speaker, Dr. Gardner C. Taylor, pastor emeritus at Concord Baptist Church of Christ in Brooklyn, began with a little joke. He said he'd told Vernon Jordan that he was going to a school near Marion, Indiana, and Jordan advised, "Be careful. They hang people of your color out there."

Henson was a white minister from Bethel Worship Center, the Deeters' church, the man who sat with Willie Deeter during the dramatic meeting with James Cameron filmed by the BBC. Batchelor was a black minister from New Light Baptist, and his brother had married into the Shipp family. They were as acquainted as almost anyone in Grant County with the human cost of August 6 and 7, 1930, but they sat together on Martin Luther King Day feeling, as Henson put it, "upset that this is the legacy of our community."

Batchelor and Henson met in 1998 during the last big reconciliation event: Unity Day, the dedication of the bypass as "Martin Luther King Jr. Memorial Way." Henson, onstage to offer a prayer that day, began with the confession he always made when speaking at black churches: "People that look like me have offended you, have done wrong, have been unjust, and I ask you to forgive us." Batchelor approached afterward, introduced himself, and asked if they could talk. "Just seemed like our spirits kind of mixed," said Batchelor.

Months after the King Day celebration, Batchelor and Henson settled on planning "a day of forgiveness" and recruited ten white and ten black ministers to join them. In one harmonious meeting these pastors mapped it all out. The white community would apologize for the deaths of Abe Smith and Tommy Shipp. The black community would apologize for the death of Claude Deeter and the assault on Mary Ball. (As Henson pointed out, she was violated in some manner, even if only emotionally.) Since the lynching was not just murder but a symbolic assault on the entire African American community, officials from both city and county governments would apologize to that community—for the first time. Then, they'd all dedicate a monument to the idea of reconciliation, right at the spot on the courthouse lawn where the lynching occurred, replacing the stigma of August 7 with the new hope of *their* day, October 19.

When this news hit the front page the next day, the town seemed to gasp. The ministers just hadn't anticipated the reaction. Said Batchelor, "I got calls from white folk and black folk wailing, 'Leave it alone. It'll go away.'" One female caller even claimed to be Deeter's sister, and not only did *she* want no one to touch this issue, but so did Mary Ball (dead since 1987). Besides, the alleged sister went on, "you wasn't born here." True enough. Batchelor had moved to Marion in 1973.

At a couple of black churches, the uproar was so intense their ministers immediately dropped off the planning committee. I found all the negativity hard to parse. The reasons people gave me were contradictory.

In the black community, reactions ranged literally from "there's too much racism" to "there's [relatively speaking] so little." Roger Smith, the former NAACP president who'd been active in the 1950s and 1960s (and was no relation to Abe), assured me, "I know the majority of people wish they'd let it die. *All* the people I know, including me. Marion is far better than all the rest of the counties in the state of Indiana. We've had a black superintendent of schools, a black postmaster, black principals in the school system, and now the sheriff. We had a chief of police and assistant chief of police at the same time, and we got a school named after Thurgood Marshall." Smith blamed Cameron—whose story he did not believe—for keeping the issue alive, and he had called one of the county commissioners to weigh in against the monument. "You don't put up a monument where somebody's committed a murder," said Smith. "That's the bottom line with me."

The county commissioners, however, quickly approved both the service and the monument. I was not in Marion while the details were hashed out and argued, but based on the news coverage, African Americans became the most publicly vocal opponents of the monument—soon reduced to a plaque, then reduced to a plaque hanging inside the courthouse instead of at the lynching site and worded to make no reference to what had happened in 1930. "As citizens of Marion, Grant County, Indiana," it would say, "we acknowledge that hatred, violence, and bigotry have scarred this community. We confess that this legacy touches all of us. We both seek and offer forgiveness. We commit ourselves to the pursuit of healing, unity, and peace."

Many still saw that lynching hidden between the lines. Xen Stewart, age seventy-three, an African American descended from one of the original Weaver families, spoke passionately against the plaque at an October 6 commissioners' meeting: "This is sick, as far as I'm concerned. The generation of my father believed that this community will never prosper until those who were involved in that lynching are dead and gone off the face of this earth. You don't heal from a plaque."

A seventy-six-year-old black woman named Joan Bowman told the commissioners in a trembling voice, "Why wait till now to do something? It should have started long ago. Every time we go in the courthouse and see that plaque, we're going to remember all the injustice we've had over the years."

But no one did more to forestall such a marker than Tommy Shipp's niece, Ruth Anne Nash. She sat up one night till three in the morning typing out a "no plaque" petition, collected 529 signatures on it, and read a statement at the next commissioners' meeting: "We resent the implications that this act will bring closure to us, the Smiths, the Deeters and this town, being that the town is still very prejudiced towards blacks of any age, past or present." Besides, she told me later, she didn't want a plaque around, reminding her of August 7, 1930. And it *would* remind her. Even if it was inside the courthouse. Even if it said nothing about the lynching.

There was probably even less support in the white community for some permanent reminder of Marion's racial history. In an unscientific telephone poll conducted among all races on October 10, the *Chronicle-Tribune* found that only 35 out of 427 people (8 percent) favored a plaque. One white woman told a reporter she owed no one an apology, since the lynching happened "years before I was even born." I suspect that this feeling was widespread among white people. Perhaps just as common was the belief expressed by someone I encountered as I trolled for more information about Superior Body. As this particular white man put it, "We're sitting on a bubble right here in Marion." Meaning, one false move, and they'd have a race riot.

Then there were the avowed racists. Someone claiming to be a Klansman called Nash and threatened to show up on Reconciliation Day with the rest of the Hooded Order to rip that plaque off the wall or maybe tear down the whole courthouse. Nash says she told him, "You go right ahead 'cause we on the same page."

On October 13 the commissioners met to rescind their earlier vote. The service would proceed but would leave no marker, either inside or outside the courthouse. "The Marion community isn't ready to put up a racial reconciliation plaque," read the beginning of the *Chronicle-Tribune* coverage. "Not ready." There was that heartbreaking phrase again, evocative of a not-so-distant past when white people were "not ready" for a black teacher or an integrated pool.

But something amazing happened that day at the commissioners' meeting as well. In the middle of the arguments, the nieces, nephews, and others related to Tommy Shipp and Abe Smith suddenly got up and apologized to Carl Deeter for what had happened to his uncle Claude in 1930. Deeter then told them the family story of his grandmother speaking with their grand-mothers, and that they'd always been forgiven.

It could be settled among the families. Actually, that was the easy part. The fateful choices made by Shipp, Smith, Deeter, and Ball had never been about race but about human frailty in all its endless originality. For the rest of the community, though, what happened in August 1930 was *only* about race. I thought about the rage on display the night of the lynching—the mob virtually chopping through solid stone to get into the jail, going through tear gas unfazed, then killing both Shipp and Smith many times over. At some point the lynching had stopped being about them as individuals and tapped into feelings that were much more primitive and ugly. And it was hard to know how to apologize for that.

I think that's what Linda Mui was saying when she declared herself uninterested in the October 19 reconciliation. And few white people had done more work in Marion to confront racism. She pointed out first that the service would be Christian, and she was Bahai. But beyond that—

"Why do I feel so blah?" Linda mused. "Because it's not enough."

IT WOULD BE ONE MORE symbolic gesture. But these did matter to some people and even seemed to help them. Those who convened on Reconcilia-tion Day numbered about four hundred by the *Chronicle-Tribune*'s count. The ministers would insist that there were more. I know there were more white than black, but I didn't count. I felt overwhelmed by emotion in a way I hadn't expected and kept slipping out of my journalist mode. The portents began immediately. We had gathered at the same entrance to the courthouse where all the Klan rallies were held.

I'd attended many reconciliation events in Grant County, but the one held October 19, 2003, certainly outdid them all in its fervor. At one point everyone dropped to their knees right there on the sidewalk, on the lawn, and on the makeshift stage. "We've sinned Lord, forgive us" remained the focus of the day, while the subtext was a lamentation over the plight of the town.

Marion had begun to face certain facts about itself, and that could only be good. I was moved to see the lynching addressed, finally, without euphe-mism right where it happened and found myself wishing that more people could have been there. Like Cameron, whose health did not permit him to make the trip from Milwaukee. He'd favored the plaque. He thought it should be erected right at the lynching site.

Much of what was said that day was just basic truth, never before uttered in public—at least not by government officials. The county prosecutor, James Luttrull, pointed out that the dome, and its crowning statue of Lady Justice, had once made a statement. In August 1930 that statement had been mocked, and now both dome and statue were gone. A shameful assault on the community and on the rule of law had been permitted on the most symbolic part of Marion. "Residual effects still linger," Luttrull continued. "Do those in the mob have any idea who or what was hanged? They were putting a community's faith in the justice system at risk."

The ministers had hoped to get all the families there. In the end they had Carl Deeter, Tom Wise representing his cousin James Cameron, and Minnie Thompson Batchelor, whose mother had been Tommy Shipp's cousin. No one even distantly related to the Smith family appeared, and the only one who considered coming for Mary Ball was her stepson's ex-wife, Madeline Patterson, who decided in the end not to make the trip from California.

Even so, apologies were offered. Speaking to Carl Deeter on behalf of the black community was Reverend J. D. Williams, the man who'd once described himself to me as Marion's civil rights leader from the early 1960s into the early 1990s. Talk about symbolism. This was the man who used to drive down 18th Street every night trying to calm the racial tensions. This was the preacher who'd conducted Robert Johnson's funeral. And now he was apologizing for the death of Claude Deeter.

"He had tears in his eyes," Carl Deeter told me later. "I was humbled by that."

Grant County commissioner Jeremy Diller offered the mea culpa for local authorities. "We the elected officials of Grant County did little to prevent the wrongs that took place in August of 1930." He listed the wrongs, from not protecting the inmates to not bringing the mob to justice. "We as a group of elected officials were wrong. I ask you, the African American community, to forgive us for the wrongs committed against you."

A white minister picked up that thread and asked the black community for forgiveness on behalf of white Christians. This was the real beginning of the wailing and gnashing of teeth, prayers wafting up like heat, people kneeling on Adams Street. "We have sin-n-n-ed." The crowd generated a sort of energy as only the many united in attention can do.

Then Reverend Batchelor came forward to accept the apology of the white community. "We forgive those who failed to stand up," he said. "From this day forward, we will rise up out of the ashes of disgrace. They can say what a beautiful spirit we have in the city of Marion."

There were limits to how many people would ever apologize, and there were limits to the good an apology could do, just as there were limits to forgiveness. I had come to Reconciliation Day feeling that it couldn't heal the wounds. But I left the service feeling that that was the wrong standard to hold it to. Certain scars would just be there. We couldn't make up for what the ancestors had done. We could only acknowledge the pain it had caused.

When the ceremony ended, I spotted Harold Vermilion, the white minister who'd witnessed the lynching at age five and had wanted to place a statue of James Cameron and Willie Deeter on the site. For days before the ceremony he'd had a knot in his stomach, he told me, "wanting it to be everything we wanted it to be." Now he seemed the picture of relief. Any disappointment about the plaque was more than counterbalanced by all those apologies—a first, he said. And getting all these black and white ministers together—another first. He'd had a stroke a few years ago. Wasn't as sharp as he used to be. Couldn't pray like he used to pray. And he'd forgotten things. Important things. "Still, with all that, I remember them guys hanging on the tree."

FOR MYSELF, I DIDN'T WANT "CLOSURE," if that meant forgetting. I wanted to remember what had happened in my Marion.

That was one of the tasks I'd set for myself. Dig it up. Face the facts. I felt I needed to know the truth to face what it meant to be a descendant of that place—which was my second, harder task.

Of course, this question of truth is not simple. I mean, to what layer do you uncover it? No doubt I could keep digging in Marion for the rest of my life.

Which brings me back to the famous photograph, where this project began. Though I heard the family story of the lynching as a child, though I found it troubling and confusing, I'm not sure I would ever have sought out James Cameron and begun this work if it weren't for that picture and what it revealed about white people in the town that I'd loved. So self-righteous. So clueless about their own hatred. So willfully unaware of what they'd wrought. It's more than heartbreaking. Of course, I too could say: I wasn't there. I've made different choices. Yet there was a chain of implication, and I'm linked because of my feelings for my grandparents and the town.

I remembered my childhood disquiet with that Bible verse about "visiting the iniquities of the fathers upon the children unto the third and fourth generation." It was so unfair, yet I worried that it might be true. I no longer think of this as the curse of a wrathful God, but as the curse we bring on ourselves by refusing to look at our histories. We white people don't want to feel guilty, of course. Who does? But too often we compensate by feeling nothing.

The paradox at the heart of my project, always, was that I felt protective of my grandfather, even as I began telling, then writing, that he'd once been a Klansman. Since so few white people are willing to admit to anything racist, I worried that I would turn him into a scapegoat. I've said this before: I felt terrible for him, for the narrowness of his world, for the private shames and fears he must have hidden behind that impassive face. I also loved him. I couldn't have searched so long and hard otherwise.

So I puzzled over my final revelation, which concerns the picture. In 2002, I picked up Philip Dray's lynching history, *At the Hands of Persons Unknown,* which used a fragment of the infamous photo taken in Marion on its cover, much enlarged. There, right in the center, I saw my grandfather. This after years of looking at that image almost daily, admittedly in bad prints or photocopies. But let me be precise. I *think* it's him, and I will never know for sure. He's way in the back. He's blurry, but I think that's his hat and his nose and the plane of his face. I'm relieved that he does not appear to be celebrating.

I knew he'd gone down to the square, of course. So in a way he was always "in the picture." Getting caught on camera didn't really make that better or worse. What did it matter? Well, somehow it mattered enough to me that I actually called Cameron—called him up specifically with this news, as if that were the logical and obvious thing to do.

"By his silence, he gave approval," said Cameron.

I knew that. I knew that.

Thinking about it later, I had to ask myself, *Why'd you call him? What was that? A confession?* In a way, yes. I think it was. The fact that I'd spent years searching for "truth," years staring at the photo without seeing my grandfather, was embarrassing. Though I'd talked to two other people who admitted to having a relative in that photo and seemed untroubled by it, I personally found it painful. That's the problem with "truth." So often there's no comfort in it. Yet there was a kind of poetic justice in finding my grandfather's face. I thought of our family story, about the man who phoned Grandpa the night of August 7, 1930, and joked that if he walked to the square, *You might see something you don't want to see.* We white people can always go on thinking we're not connected to anything terrible. That's the white illusion, and it's so tough to drop. That's what I had really called to tell Cameron.

I had opened my eyes.

NOTES

One. My Marion

3 FROM A QUARTER TO A HALF MILLION MEMBERS   John Bartlow Martin, *Indiana: An Interpretation* (New York: Alfred A. Knopf, 1947), p. 192. For a further parsing of Klan membership numbers, see first note in Chapter Two.

Two. The Survivor's Story

14 FROM ROUGHLY A QUARTER TO A HALF MILLION   In 1920 Indiana had 1,358,645 native-born white males (http://fisher.lib.virginia.edu/cgi-local/censusbin/census/cen.p1). The lowest membership estimate for the Indiana KKK in the 1920s is 240,000 in Kenneth T. Jackson's *The Ku Klux Klan in the City, 1915–1930* (Chicago: Ivan R. Dee, 1967), p. 237. Wyn Craig Wade sets the number at 350,000 in *The Fiery Cross: The Ku Klux Klan in America* (New York: Touchstone, 1988), p. 245. John Bartlow Martin says it was "nearly half a million" (p. 184) and "a quarter to a half million" (p. 192) in *Indiana: An Interpretation*. James H. Madison reports that the Klan claimed 400,000 Hoosier members in 1923, while Klan opponents set the figure at less than 300,000, according to *Indiana Through Tradition and Change: A History of the Hoosier State and Its People, 1920–1945* (Indianapolis: Indiana Historical Society, 1982), p. 45. Kathleen M. Blee, whose study of women Kluxers focused on Indiana, says total membership in the state numbered "almost half a million" in *Women of the Klan: Racism and Gender in the 1920s* (Berkeley: University of California Press, 1991), p. 96.

14 BETWEEN ONE-QUARTER AND ONE-THIRD OF ALL NATIVE-BORN WHITE MEN IN THE STATE   Leonard J. Moore, *Citizen Klansmen: The Ku Klux Klan in Indiana, 1921–1928* (Chapel Hill and London: University of North Carolina Press, 1991), p. 7.

16 THIS IS CAMERON'S STORY OF THE LYNCHING   James Cameron, *A Time of Terror: A Survivor's Story* (Baltimore, Md.: Black Classic Press, 1994).

16 BOTH NINETEEN   According to their death certificates, Joe Thomas Shipp was born on March 1, 1911, and Abraham L. Smith on October 14, 1910.

16 HE HANDED THE GUN BACK TO SMITH AND RAN   Cameron says in his book that he handed the gun to Smith (*Time of Terror,* p. 30), but certain news accounts assert that he said he handed the gun to Shipp. See, for example, "Trial of Two Youths Is Set," *Marion Leader-Tribune,* October 23, 1930.

21 "IN A PRUDENT MANNER"   "Sheriff Lauded by Jury," *Marion Chronicle,* October 9, 1930.

22 AN ACCESSORY TO VOLUNTARY MANSLAUGHTER IN THE DEATH OF CLAUDE DEETER   That is the court's language. *State of Indiana v. Herbert Cameron,* Madison Circuit Court Order Book No. 115 [July 11, 1931], Clerk of Madison County Courts, Anderson, Indiana. Cameron has always insisted, however, that he was "an accessory before the fact."

26 LET MARION SET A BEACON LIGHT   *Marion Chronicle-Tribune,* February 14, 1993.

Three. "We Never Recovered"

29 "FEEDING FRENZY"   "Tale of Lynch Survivor Draws Big Notice for Small Press Title," *Publishers Weekly,* February 21, 1994.

30 THAT HE COULD SEE HOODS FROM THE JAIL WINDOW   Cameron discusses the Klan presence in several places, but see, for example, *Time of Terror,* p. 55.

31 "[MY FATHER] WAS SITTING ON THE FRONT PORCH"   Ed Breen, "August 7 1930 Returns to Haunt Us," *Marion Chronicle-Tribune,* April 3, 1988.

37 HE SAID THAT MARION HAD A BLACK POPULATION OF 1,081   Not bad for a ninety-three-year-old: the 1931 Marion city directory puts the "colored" population at 1,087.

Four. Things I Didn't Learn in School

49 ESTIMATES OF THE DEAD GO AS HIGH AS TWENTY THOUSAND   Philip Dray, *At the Hands of Persons Unknown: The Lynching of Black America* (New York: Random House, 2002), p. 49.

49 "IT HAD INITIATED THE PROCESS"   Ibid., p. 47.

50 "WE TOOK THE GOVERNMENT"   Ibid., p. 112.

51 THE TUSKEGEE ARCHIVE CITES 162 LYNCHINGS OF BLACKS, WHILE THE *CHICAGO TRIBUNE* PUT THE NUMBER AT 241   The Tuskegee archive is cited in ibid., p. viii, while the *Tribune* number appears in Ida B. Wells-Barnett, *On Lynching* (reprint, Amherst, N.Y.: Humanity Books, 2002), p. 71.

51 WHITE LYNCHING VICTIMS OUTNUMBERED BLACKS UNTIL 1886   Dray, *Persons Unknown,* p. viii.

51 "I LED THE MOB WHICH LYNCHED NELSE PATTON"   Leon F. Litwack, "Hellhounds," in James Allen et al., *Without Sanctuary: Lynching Photography in America* (Santa Fe, N.M.: Twin Palms Publishers, 2000), p. 20.

51 DETERMINED MOB AFTER HOSE   Grace Elizabeth Hale, *Making Whiteness: The Culture of Segregation in the South, 1890–1940* (New York: Pantheon Books, 1998), p. 210.

52 HOSE PROBABLY DID NOT ASSAULT THE WIFE   Dray, *Persons Unknown,* p. 16.

52 "BEGAN TO TURN ASIDE FROM MY WORK"   David Levering Lewis, *W.E.B. Du Bois: Biography of a Race, 1868–1919* (New York: Henry Holt & Co., 1993), p. 226.

52 "CIVIL RIGHTS ROLE MODEL TO AN ENTIRE RACE" Lewis, *Du Bois*, p. 4.

52 LYNCHED DURING THE SIXTY-TWO YEARS BEGINNING IN 1882 Dray, *Persons Unknown*, p. viii.

52 IT HAD FOUND 2,522 BLACK AND 702 WHITE VICTIMS *Thirty Years of Lynching in the United States, 1889–1918* (New York: National Association for the Advancement of Colored People, 1919), p. 29.

52 "THE ANXIETY OVER INTERRACIAL SEX WAS SO GREAT" Dray, *Persons Unknown*, pp. 60–61.

53 "TO GET RID OF NEGROES" Ibid., p. 63.

53 "AN UNCOMFORTABLY LARGE PERCENTAGE" Walter White, *Rope and Faggot: A Biography of Judge Lynch* (reprint, Notre Dame, Ind.: University of Notre Dame Press, 2001), p. viii.

53 AT LEAST TWENTY AFRICAN AMERICANS Emma Lou Thornbrough, *The Negro in Indiana Before 1900: A Study of a Minority* (Bloomington: Indiana University Press, 1993), p. 276.

54 "HE WAS FEARED BY EVERY WHITE WOMAN IN TOWN" "The Acquittal," *Marion Weekly Chronicle*, September 18, 1885.

54 DIDN'T WAKE UP UNTIL THE NEXT AFTERNOON "The Vigilants: Attempt to Hang a Negro But Are Resisted by the Sheriff and Marshall," *Marion Chronicle*, July 17, 1885.

54 "ASSAULT AND BATTERY WITH INTENT TO COMMIT RAPE" "The Trial of Wallace," *Marion Weekly Chronicle*, September 18, 1885.

54 "WHISPERED CONVERSATIONS" "Vigilants: Attempt to Hang a Negro."

54 "BROKE UP THE LYNCHING PARTY FOR THE EVENING" Ibid.

54 "IT WAS SETTLED THAT THE HANGING" "Trial of Wallace."

54 HORSE THIEF DETECTIVES Emma Lou Thornbrough, *Indiana in the Civil War Era, 1850–1880* (Indianapolis: Indiana Historical Society, 1965), p. 6.

54 GRANT COUNTY'S FOUNDING MEMBERS "Fernist [sic] the Horse Thieves," *Marion Chronicle*, January 21, 1887.

55 I FOUND NEWS STORIES THAT MENTIONED THEM. "The Monroe White Caps," *Marion Chronicle*, August 9, 1889, and "Marion Man Gets White Cap Notice," *Marion Daily Leader*, June 3, 1902.

55 A MUSIC TEACHER . . . WHO ALLEGEDLY RAPED A THIRTEEN-YEAR-OLD GIRL " 'Lynch Him!' Cried a Frenzied Mother," *Marion News-Tribune*, July 8, 1903.

55 A MOB HUNTS A MAN "A Mob at Farrville: Fifty Men Turn Out to Avenge the Betrayal and Death of a Young Girl," *Marion Chronicle*, July 19, 1889.

55 A GANG WHIPS TWO WOMEN FOR GOSSIPING "An Outrage That Must Be Punished," *Marion Chronicle*, August 2, 1889.

55 A MOB IN GAS CITY "Tramp About to Stretch Hemp," *Marion Chronicle*, March 9, 1890.

55 A MOB IN VAN BUREN "Mob Tries to Lynch Frank Stecher, Van Buren Lawyer," *Marion Chronicle*, September 26, 1902.

55 A YOUNG MAN IS NEARLY HANGED "Attempt Made to Lynch Young Negro," *Marion Chronicle*, May 26, 1902.

55 "THE INSOLENCE OF THE NEGROES" Wade, *Fiery Cross*, p. 106.

55 "BECAME THE KEY DOCUMENT" Ibid., p. 107.

56 "MORE PEOPLE SAW *THE BIRTH OF A NATION*" J. Hoberman, "Our Troubling Birth Rite: The Library of Congress Moves to Suppress American Movie History," *Village Voice*, November 30, 1993.

56 IN COMPARISON, *TITANIC* MADE See www.boxofficemojo.com/movies/?id=titanic.htm.

56 "WHERE NO MOVIE THEATER EXISTED" Dray, *Persons Unknown,* pp. 204–205.

57 "IT IS LIKE WRITING HISTORY WITH LIGHTNING" Wade, *Fiery Cross,* p. 126.

57 "FILTHY PERVERTED JEW" Ibid., p. 144.

57 "THE WORLD'S GREATEST SECRET, SOCIAL, PATRIOTIC" David M. Chalmers, *Hooded Americanism: The History of the Ku Klux Klan* (reprint, New York and London: New Viewpoints, 1981), p. 30.

58 "REMEMBER, EVERY CRIMINAL, EVERY GAMBLER" Wade, *Fiery Cross,* p. 232.

58 "TO FIND OUT WHAT LIFE IN A SEGREGATED CULTURE HAD DONE" Lillian Smith, *Killers of the Dream* (reprint, New York and London: W.W. Norton & Co., 1978), p. 13.

Five. Marion's Hooded Order

60 AT THE TIME MOST HOOSIERS WERE NATIVE-BORN (95 PERCENT) James H. Madison, *The Indiana Way: A State History* (Bloomington: Indiana University Press, Indiana Historical Society, 1986), p. 168.

60 JEWS NUMBERED FEWER THAN 25,000 Madison, *Indiana Through Tradition and Change,* p. 47.

61 "BY 1920, THE WORD *HOOSIER*" Wade, *Fiery Cross,* p. 221.

61 INDIANA'S GOVERNOR WENT TO FEDERAL PRISON Madison, *Indiana Through Tradition and Change,* p. 51.

61 "THAT CONCERNED ITSELF PRIMARILY" Moore, *Citizen Klansmen,* p. 11.

61 "THE KU KLUX KLAN WAS LIKE THE LEAGUE" Madison, *Indiana Way,* pp. 290–91.

61 "A NARROW AND ANXIOUS PATRIOTISM" Madison, *Indiana Through Tradition and Change,* p. 46.

61 "TYPICAL OF THOSE HELD BY INDIANA KLANSMEN" Moore, *Citizen Klansmen,* p. 61.

61 MUNCIE, KOKOMO, AND ANDERSON Ibid., p. 58.

62 IN MAY 1923 THE HOODED ORDER WENT TO FEDERAL COURT "Klan, In Panic, Seeks Injunction!" *Tolerance,* May 20, 1923.

62 "IN THE INDIANA OF THE 1920S" Blee, *Women of the Klan,* p. 171.

63 THE STORY OF A KKK LEADER IN WABASH COUNTY Ibid., p. 149, and Chalmers, *Hooded Americanism,* p. 162. The former says he was a carpet salesman, the latter a corset salesman.

64 "YOUR HONOR, YEARS AGO I RECOGNIZED" Marguerite Young, *Harp Song for a Radical: The Life and Times of Eugene Victor Debs* (New York: Alfred A. Knopf, 1999), p. xx.

68 MANY OTHERWISE RELIABLE TEXTS STILL REPEAT THE TALE, PROBABLY APOCRYPHAL See, for example, Martin, *Indiana: An Interpretation,* p. 193.

68 STEVE'S OWN ESTIMATE OF TWO HUNDRED THOUSAND M. William Lutholtz, *Grand Dragon: D. C. Stephenson and the Ku Klux Klan in Indiana* (West Lafayette, Ind.: Purdue University Press, 1993), pp. 86–87.

69 BACK IN 1852 WHEN THE INDIANA LEGISLATURE AUTHORIZED Thornbrough, *Indiana in the Civil War Era,* p. 6.

70 "HE DISLIKED NARROWLY DEFINED SCAPEGOATS" Wade, *Fiery Cross,* p. 228.

70 HE GOT $2.50 OUT OF EVERY TEN-DOLLAR MEMBERSHIP FEE Moore, *Citizen Klansmen,* p. 212n40.

70 "WELL DOES HE KNOW THAT" "Klansmen of Indiana," *Fiery Cross,* May 16, 1924.

72 "READ THIS TO YOUR PEOPLE" "Ku Klux Pays Visit During Band Concert," *Marion*

Leader-Tribune, September 10, 1922, and "Trio of Ku Klux Attend Concert," *Marion Chronicle,* September 11, 1922.

73 "COMMENDING HIM ON HIS HIGH MORAL CHARACTER" "Van Buren Sees Odd Procession," *Marion Chronicle,* September 18, 1922, and "Ku Klux Klan Gives Money to Rev. E. E. Lutes," *Marion Leader-Tribune,* September 19, 1922.

73 (THAT SUM WAS ABOUT A WEEK'S SALARY FOR A MALE FACTORY WORKER) See Robert S. Lynd and Helen Merrell Lynd, *Middletown: A Study in Modern American Culture* (reprint, New York and London: Harvest/HBJ, 1956), pp. 86–87.

73 "SPOONING PARTY" "Klansmen Give a Clear Order to Auto Party," *Marion Chronicle,* September 28, 1922.

73 THE TWO COUPLES IN THE CAR HAD JUST GOTTEN OUT "Ku Klux Again," *Marion Leader-Tribune,* September 28, 1922.

73 ON SUNDAY, OCTOBER 1, REVEREND E. F. RIPPEY "Says Method of the Klan Is Not Correct," *Marion Leader-Tribune,* October 3, 1922. A shorter piece appeared in the *Chronicle:* "Rippey Attacks Ku Klux Action in Sunday Talk," *Marion Chronicle,* October 2, 1922.

74 "A LARGE CROWD" "Gives Talk on Ku Klux Klan," *Marion Leader-Tribune,* October 17, 1922.

74 IT RATED THREE SHORT PARAGRAPHS ON OCTOBER 25 "Not Ku Klux Klan," *Marion Leader-Tribune,* October 25, 1922.

74 IN EARLY NOVEMBER A REVEREND W. R. HOWARD "Ku Klux Klan Denies Threat Against Pastor," *Marion Leader-Tribune,* November 4, 1922.

74 "SPOKE IN THE HIGHEST TERMS" "Klansmen Visit Baptist Church at Fairmount," *Marion Leader-Tribune,* November 14, 1922.

74 "THE EYES OF THE KU KLUX KLAN ARE UPON" "Another Thrill Given Fairmount by Ku Klux Klan," *Marion Leader-Tribune,* November 15, 1922.

75 I FOUND SEVERAL MORE REPORTS OF EITHER "Old Church Gets Ku Klux Gift," *Marion Leader-Tribune,* November 18, 1922; "Pastor Talks on Ku Klux," *Marion Leader-Tribune,* November 22, 1922; "Talks on Ku Klux," *Marion Leader-Tribune,* November 24, 1922; "Speaks to K.K.K.," *Marion Leader-Tribune,* November 25, 1922.

75 "NOTHING TO CONCEAL" "Ku Klux Klan Gives Parade in this City," *Marion Leader-Tribune,* November 26, 1922; "Spectacular Parade Given by Klansmen," *Marion Chronicle,* November 27, 1922.

75 "STATING THAT THE KLAN WAS NOT ANTI-JEW, ANTI-NEGRO" "Spectacular Parade."

75 "I BELIEVE THAT IF JESUS WAS ON EARTH TODAY" "Claims Christ Would Belong," *Hartford City News,* September 2, 1923.

75 A NICKNAME, NO DOUBT BORROWED Steve Bunish, *The Golden Age of Marion* (self-published booklet, 1989), p. 89.

76 "I AM THE SPIRIT OF RIGHTEOUSNESS" Dwight W. Hoover, "Daisy Douglas Barr: From Quaker to Klan 'Kluckeress,'" *Indiana Magazine of History* 87, no. 2 (June 1991).

76 "THE OPEN SUPPORT OF THE KLAN" See the November 4, 1925, editions of both the *Marion Leader-Tribune* and the *Marion Chronicle.*

76 BUT THEY DIDN'T DISBAND The tribunals's exhibits and statements were among the Klan documents compiled during the 1920s by Indianapolis-based journalist Harold C. Feightner, now located at the Indiana Historical Society. The list of Klan officers and membership figures was presented to Feightner by Alf Hogston himself. Apparently the

Evans/Bossert faction put this list together after the break with Stephenson—to name officers faithful to the Wizard and to assess the damage done, or not done, to membership figures. Grant County reports a membership of 2,329. Jack Edwards told me that the local klavern had "over five thousand" in its heyday before the scandal.

Six. The Three P's

79 IN 1949 *NEWSWEEK* REPORTED THAT AT LEAST A DOZEN DIFFERENT KLANS Wade, *The Fiery Cross,* p. 289.

80 UKA LEFT A BLOODY TRAIL Bill Stanton, *Klanwatch: Bringing the Ku Klux Klan to Justice* (New York: Grove Weidenfeld, 1991), p. 201.

81 ONE GOT DEATH; ONE GOT TEN YEARS TO LIFE Ibid., pp. 195–99.

Seven. "They Were Strangers to Me"

102 FIVE THOUSAND PEOPLE POURED INTO DOWNTOWN MARION "Human Fly Climbs Bank Building; Thousands Watch Breathlessly," *Marion Leader-Tribune,* August 7, 1930.

102 THE DAY OF THE LYNCHING, TEMPERATURES HIT ONE HUNDRED DEGREES "Mercury Hits Century Mark Again Friday," *Hartford News,* August 8, 1930, and "Wednesday Heat Due to Humidity," *Marion Leader-Tribune,* August 7, 1930.

105 SHERIFF JAKE CAMPBELL TOLD THE COURT OF INQUIRY THAT HE HADN'T HAD A CLUE All quotes from the court of inquiry come from Testimony of Thirty Witnesses, Grant County Court of Inquiry, August 13, 14, 15, 1930, Lynching Depositions, Box 20, James M. Ogden Papers, Indiana State Archives, Indianapolis.

108 "GUILTY OF FAILURE OF OFFICIAL DUTY" "Sheriff to Face Charges," *Marion Chronicle,* October 15, 1930.

109 "WE WANT THEM NOW!" "Two Negroes Held for Attack on Girl Are Lynched at Marion," *Wabash Plain-Dealer,* August 8, 1930.

118 "THAT CHANT OF THE KU KLUX KLAN" Cameron, *Time of Terror,* p. 67.

125 "IN THIS DEBATE MUCH STRESS WAS LAID" "Peace and Order Prevail in Marion," *Indianapolis News,* August 9, 1930.

126 A SEVENTEEN-YEAR-OLD GIRL STANDING ON A TRUCK WITH THE FIRST PRISONER The *Indianapolis Star* identifies this woman as "Helen Ball, sister of the attacked girl." Mary Ball did not have a sister named Helen.

126 "SHE FLEW AT THE PROSTRATE AND UNCONSCIOUS NEGRO" "Two Negroes Held," *Wabash Plain-Dealer.*

126 "A MAN MOUNTED THE SIDE OF THE BUILDING" "Local People Tell of Scene at Lynchings," *Hartford City News,* August 8, 1930.

126 "WHO KNOTTED ROPES AROUND NEGROES' NECKS" William E. Hallberg, "Graphic Story of Lynching Is Told by Writer, Eye-witness of Hangings," *Indianapolis Times,* August 8, 1930.

126 "A GROUP OF YOUTHS PILED UP RUBBISH" "Two Negroes Held."

127 "A SIGN WAS POSTED NEARBY" "Local People Tell."

127 THE MORE THAN 23,000 WHITES Population figures are based on the 1931 city directory.

Eight. "No Likelihood of Conviction"

128 "THEY GOT WHAT THEY DESERVED"   "Governor Is Called Upon to Protect Negroes," *Hartford City News,* August 8, 1930.

130 "REPUTED TO BE ONE OF THE LEADERS OF THE KU KLUX KLAN"   Walter White, "Sheriff's Fears Permitted Indiana Lynching," *New York World,* August 24, 1930.

131 JUST FIVE THIRTY-SECONDS BLACK   Dray, *Persons Unknown,* p. 237.

135 ANOTHER WHO REMEMBERED THE POSTLYNCHING TRAUMA   Don Stewart, interview by Larry Conrad (1977), Larry Allyn Conrad Papers, Ruth Lilly Special Collections and Archives, University Library, Indiana University Purdue University, Indianapolis.

138 MARY BALL'S UNCLE DECLARED HIMSELF "SATISFIED" WITH TWO   See for example William E. Hallberg, "Eye-Witness Tells Story of Marion Riot," *Huntington Herald Press,* August 8, 1930.

141 IN 1929, FOR EXAMPLE, INDIANA'S AVERAGE FOR DISMISSALS   Howard C. Smith, "Grant County Leniency Held Cause of Marion Lynching," *Indianapolis Star,* November 9, 1930.

141 "WOULD EXPLAIN THAT COLD, DOGGED, AFTER-THE-EVENT"   Howard C. Smith, "Dismissals in Grant Courts Exceed State's Percentage," *Indianapolis Star,* November 10, 1930.

141 "AS THE RESULT OF A LOVE AFFAIR"   "Laxity of Courts Is Given as Spur to Lynching Mob," *Indianapolis Star,* August 10, 1930.

142 HIS STATEMENT WAS CORROBORATED BY BLOTZ'S WIFE   See "Blotz Denies Knowledge of Hammer Blow," *Marion Leader-Tribune,* May 29, 1930, and "Making Wide Search for Head of Torso," *Marion Leader-Tribune,* June 7, 1930.

142 A SENTENCE OF TWO TO TWENTY-ONE YEARS   "Blotz Begins 2 to 21 Year Prison Term," *Marion Leader-Tribune,* June 27, 1931.

143 "THE EARLY INVESTIGATION OF THE LYNCHING HAD"   "Lynching Writs Denied by Judge," *Indianapolis Star,* August 19, 1930.

144 "THE CITY WAS IN THE CONTROL"   "That Mob Again," *Marion Leader-Tribune,* November 13, 1930.

145 "IT WAS ASTONISHING TO SEE AND FEEL THE MOB ATMOSPHERE"   William Pickens, "Aftermath of a Lynching," *Nation,* April 15, 1931.

Nine. The Ironies

153 A BLACK POPULATION IN SINGLE DIGITS   See www.census.gov/population/estimates/county/crh/.

154 EVEN SO THE 1820 CENSUS FOUND 190 SLAVES   Thornbrough, *Negro in Indiana,* p. 25.

154 FROM THE NONSLAVEHOLDING CLASS   Thornbrough, *Indiana in the Civil War Era,* p. 14.

154 THEY MANIFESTED THE PREDICTABLE BIGOTRIES   Thornbrough, *Negro in Indiana,* p. xi.

154 THERE MAY HAVE BEEN MORE RACISM IN INDIANA   Thornbrough, *Indiana in the Civil War Era,* p. 19.

154 "ANTI-NEGRO"   Ibid., p. 13.

154 THOUGH IT NEVER AMOUNTED IN FACT TO MORE THAN ONE PERCENT   Thornbrough, *Negro in Indiana,* p. xi.

154 BANNED AFRICAN AMERICANS FROM MOVING INTO THE STATE   Ibid., p. 31.

154 A WHITE QUAKER NAMED AARON BETTS   Mrs. Asenath Peters Artis, "The Negro in Grant County," in Rolland Lewis Whitson, ed., *Centennial History of Grant County, 1812–1912* (Chicago: Lewis Publishing Co., 1914), p. 349.

154 BOOTS MADE IT A CONDITION FOR GIVING HIS LAND   Statement of Anna Fox in Leslie Neher, *Hoosier Founders of Grant County, Indiana in Celebration of 175 Years of Indiana Statehood,* unpublished manuscript, April 30, 1992, Indiana Room, Marion Public Library.

154 ESTABLISHED THE COUNTY'S FIRST CHURCH   Ellwood O. Ellis, "Society of Friends in Grant County," in Whitson, *Centennial History,* p. 639.

154 HIS ABOLITIONIST *HERALD OF FREEDOM*   John Miller, ed., *Indiana Newspaper Bibliography* (Indianapolis: Indiana Historical Society, 1982), p. 132.

154 IN 1843 FREDERICK DOUGLASS VISITED JONESBORO   William S. McFeely, *Frederick Douglass* (New York and London: W. W. Norton & Co., 1991), p. 112.

154 GRANT COUNTY HAD ONE OF THE LARGEST QUAKER POPULATIONS IN THE STATE   The largest Quaker populations were in Wayne and Henry counties. Thornbrough, *Negro in Indiana,* p. 48.

155 PETITIONS ARRIVED FROM JUST THREE COUNTIES   Randolph and Union counties were the other two; ibid., p. 66.

155 HE'D BEEN ABLE TO GET MONEY TO OPEN   W. H. McGrew, *Interesting Episodes in the Early History of Marion and Grant County, Indiana* (Marion: Grant County Historical Society, 1966), p. 21, speaks of Ratliff's involvement, as does June R. McKown, *Marion: A Pictorial History* (St. Louis: G. Bradley Publishing, 1989), p. 22; see also *Journal of the House of Representatives of the State of Indiana during the Forty-sixth Regular Session of the General Assembly Commencing Thursday January 7, 1869,* pp. 273–74 and 513–14, Indiana State Library, Indianapolis.

155 SOME COMMUNITIES WERE SO HOSTILE   Thornbrough, *Negro in Indiana,* p. 224.

155 EARTHWORKS NOW KNOWN TO BE A COUPLE OF MILLENNIA OLD   At one site still intact near Anderson, the largest mound dates to about 160 B.C. See Donald R. Cochran, "Adena and Hopewell Cosmology: New Evidence from East Central Indiana," in Ronald Hicks, ed., *Native American Cultures in Indiana: Proceedings of the First Minnetrista Council for Great Lakes Native American Studies* (Muncie, Ind.: Minnetrista Cultural Center and Ball State University, 1992), pp. 30–34.

155 "ON THE SLIGHTEST TOUCH"   *Combination Atlas Map of Grant County, Indiana, 1877* (Kingman Brothers; reprint Knightstown, Ind.: Back Creek Monthly Meeting of Friends, 1987), p. 21.

155 THE MIAMI, WHO ONCE CLAIMED THE ENTIRE STATE   Stewart Rafert, *The Miami Indians of Indiana: A Persistent People, 1654–1994* (Indianapolis: Indiana Historical Society, 1996), p. 60.

156 FRANCES SLOCUM *BECAME* MIAMI   Details of the Slocum story vary from one account to the next. My version is based on "Frances Slocum, the Indian Captive," Miami File, Indiana Room, Marion Public Library; a transcription of Indian trader George Ewing's letter; Slocum family letters; and an original article from the *Peru Forester,* September 26, 1837.

157 "CIVIL INDIFFERENCE"   George S. Cottman, "Sketch of Frances Slocum," *Indiana Quarterly Magazine of History* 1, no. 3 (1905), p. 121.

157 "IN ACCORDANCE WITH FORMAL INDIAN ETIQUETTE"   Ibid.

157 JONESBORO SUPPORTED AN ANTISLAVERY STORE   "Stories of the Long Ago: The Omnibus Chapter," in Whitson, *Centennial History,* p. 500.

157 BUT MRS. ASENATH PETERS ARTIS Artis, "Negro in Grant County," in Whitson, *Centennial History*, p. 348. Artis had been Marion's first black high school graduate in 1888. See Thornbrough, *Negro in Indiana*, p. 341.

158 WEAVER HAD BEEN NAMED FOR HER FATHER Ronald L. Baker, *From Needmore to Prosperity: Hoosier Place Names in Folklore and History* (Bloomington: Indiana University Press, 1995), p. 341.

158 "WAS LOOKED FORWARD TO WITH GREAT ANTICIPATION" Artis, "Negro in Grant County," in Whitson, *Centennial History*, p. 352.

158 "OLD TIME COUNTY FAIR" "Many Thrills Occur at the Weaver Track," *Marion Leader-Tribune*, September 5, 1922.

159 HER GREAT-GRANDFATHER, THE EXTREMELY According to his obituary (see next note), Becks earned $600 to buy his way out of bondage. The family says he was given his freedom in his master's will. Becks's emancipation record, confirming the family's version, appears in Wilma L. Gibbs, ed., *Indiana's African-American Heritage: Essays from "Black History News and Notes"* (Indianapolis: Indiana Historical Society, 1993), p. 205.

159 AFTER TELLING HIS STORY AT CHURCHES "Death of Matthew Becks," *Marion Weekly Chronicle*, July 4, 1884.

159 "WERE COMPOSED TO A LARGE DEGREE" Xenia E. Cord, "Black Rural Settlements in Indiana Before 1860," in Gibbs, *Indiana's African-American Heritage*, pp. 106–107.

162 ONE NIGHT IN FEBRUARY 1887 McGrew, *Interesting Episodes;* p. 88.

162 THREE YEARS LATER TWENTY-FIVE NEW FACTORIES Bunish, *Golden Age*, p. 5.

162 THE POPULATION MORE THAN DOUBLED TO ABOUT 8,800 McGrew, *Interesting Episodes*, p. 95.

162 MARION ENTREPRENEURS HAD TAPPED INTO Martin, *Indiana: An Interpretation*, p. 76.

162 WITH MUNCIE AT ITS HUB Clifton Philips, *Indiana in Transition: The Emergence of an Industrial Commonwealth 1880–1920* (Indianapolis: Indiana Historical Bureau, 1968), p. 193.

163 WHEN THE TOWN FINALLY BUILT A POOL AT MATTER PARK "New Pool at Matter Park to be Ready," *Marion Leader-Tribune*, April 6, 1924.

163 "AS REPRESENTATIVE AS POSSIBLE OF CONTEMPORARY AMERICAN LIFE" Lynd and Lynd, *Middletown*, p. 7.

163 "NEGRO CHILDREN MUST PLAY IN" Ibid., p. 479.

163 "MIDDLETOWN SHUDDERED AND FELT CONFIRMED" Robert S. Lynd and Helen Merrell Lynd, *Middletown in Transition: A Study in Cultural Conflicts* (reprint, New York: Harvest/Harcourt, Brace & World, 1965), p. 464.

164 A BLACK HIGH SCHOOL GRADUATE (IN 1888) Emma Lou Thornbrough, *Since Emancipation: A Short History of Indiana Negroes, 1863–1963* (Indianapolis: Indiana Division, American Negro Emancipation Centennial Authority, 1963), p. 53.

164 TWO AFRICAN AMERICAN CONTRACTORS McKown, *Marion: A Pictorial History*, p. 131.

164 ON THE FIRST DAY OF FREE MAIL DELIVERY "Noah Burden," *Marion Daily Leader*, March 7, 1904.

164 HE WAS DEFENDED, THOUGH A BIT TEPIDLY, IN THE REPUBLICAN *CHRONICLE* See, for example, the front-page political cartoon in the *Marion Daily Leader*, February 24, 1904, and several times a week thereafter until the end of March. For a defense of Robinson's candidacy, see the unsigned editorial in the *Marion Daily Chronicle*, April 13, 1904.

164 "COLORED PEOPLE ARE HOME OWNERS!" "A Glimpse on the Progress of the Citizens of Marion, Indiana," *Freeman,* August 9, 1913.

164 MARION HAD TWO BLACK DOCTORS Jerry Miller, "People of Color: Grant County's Black Heritage," *Marion Chronicle-Tribune Magazine,* July 9, 1978.

165 THE NEOCLASSICAL HOME PLATO BUILT Katherine M. Jourdan, "The Architecture of Samuel Plato," in Gibbs, *Indiana's African-American Heritage,* p. 182.

165 THE MARION BRANCH HAD ONLY THIRTY-FOUR DUES-PAYING MEMBERS James H. Madison, *A Lynching in the Heartland: Race and Memory in America* (New York: Palgrave, 2001), p. 60.

165 "WHICH VANQUISHED THE SUPREMACY OF THE RED MAN" "No Monument Marks Place Where Brave Heroes Fell," *Marion Leader-Tribune,* December 19, 1924.

165 METOCINA, WHO STILL HAD DESCENDANTS None of the soldiers did. The soldiers were from Kentucky, Ohio, Pennsylvania, and Michigan. Murray Holliday, *The Battle of the Mississinewa 1812* (Marion, Ind: Grant County Historical Society, 1964), p. 14.

167 "MY TOWN THRIVES ON DANGEROUS BIGOTRY" David Dalton, *James Dean: The Mutant King* (San Francisco: Straight Arrow Books, 1974), p. 85.

168 A CIVIC GROUP TRYING TO REVITALIZE "Dean's Birthplace to Be Miniaturized," *Marion Chronicle-Tribune,* February 27, 2001.

168 MARCUS AND ORTENSE WINSLOW, DIED IN 1976 AND 1991, RESPECTIVELY See Donald Spoto, *Rebel: The Life and Legend of James Dean* (New York: HarperCollins, 1996), footnote, p. 247.

Ten. The Ancestors

173 AND SHE DID MEAN SARAH SCARLETT NEWELL, WHOM SHE'D CALLED "GRANDMA" My grandmother never knew Emily Newell Nixon, her real grandmother, and always addressed her great-grandmother Sarah Scarlett Newell as "Grandma."

173 INDIANS WEREN'T EVEN OFFICIALLY INCLUDED IN THE CENSUS UNTIL 1890 Russell Thornton, "What the Census Doesn't Count," *New York Times,* March 23, 2001.

175 "AS A RACE, THEY ARE NOW ALMOST A THING OF THE PAST" Claude Stitt, "Meshingomesia's Band," in Clarkson W. Weesner, ed., *History of Wabash County, Indiana* (Chicago and New York: Lewis Publishing Co., 1914), p. 65.

175 IN 1838 THE TRIBAL COUNCIL DECIDED THAT ONLY MIAMI INDIANS Rafert, *Miami Indians,* p. 97.

176 THEN, OVER A PERIOD OF TWELVE YEARS, MIAMI DESCENDANTS GOT Ibid., pp. 240, 255, 258.

Eleven. Underground

178 ONE OF THE FEW STORIES RELATED IN THE COUNTY HISTORIES Mrs. Angelina Pearson in Edgar M. Baldwin, *The Making of a Township: Being an Account of the Early Settlement and Subsequent Development of Fairmount Township, Grant County, Indiana, 1829–1917* (Fairmount, Ind.: Edgar Baldwin Printing Co., 1917), p. 149.

179 TWO MORE STORIES IN THE OLD HISTORIES Ibid., pp. 149–51.

179 WHEN TWO ABOLITIONISTS, ONE BLACK AND ONE WHITE The white abolitionist was Arnold Buffum; the black man was never identified.

179 "SLOWLY DID PUBLIC OPINION CHANGE" Grant County Indiana, Old Records, compiled and typed by Agnes L. Kendall, Grant County Indiana D.A.R (N.P), Marion Public Library, Indiana Room.

179 HISTORIANS ESTIMATE THAT OF 25,000 QUAKERS IN THE STATE   Thornbrough, *Negro in Indiana*, p. 78.

179 ALL THESE SECEDERS WERE THEN DISOWNED   Ellis, "Society of Friends," in Whitson, *Centennial History*, pp. 654–55.

180 "THERE WAS MORE UNITY"   Ibid., p. 656.

180 THE RENEGADE CONGREGATION OF DEER CREEK   "John V. Shugart," in Whitson, *Centennial History*, p. 1099.

181 I FOUND ANOTHER STORY OF PURSUIT AND ESCAPE   Larry Wills, "Underground Railway Gave Safe Journey to Runaway Slaves," *Marion Chronicle-Tribune*, June 9, 1969.

181 "TOOK THE TIME TO SEE THE PROFICIENCY"   Donald Spoto, *Rebel: The Life and Legend of James Dean* (New York: HarperCollins, 1996), p. 36.

183 SEVERAL MEN TRIED TO SHUT HIM UP   "Moses Bradford: Recollections of his Early Days," *Marion Weekly Chronicle*, July 31, 1885.

183 "RECEIVED FROM HIS KIND MASTER"   Ibid.

183 IN 1858 THE BLACK ABOLITIONIST   "Moses Bradford: Recollections of his Early Days," *Marion Weekly Chronicle*, August 7, 1885.

184 THE MOST SERIOUS DRAFT RIOT IN THE STATE   W.H.H. Terrell, *Indiana in the War of the Rebellion: A Report of the Adjutant General* (reprint, Indianapolis: Indiana Historical Bureau, 1960), p. 359, and Thornbrough, *Indiana in the Civil War Era*, p. 132.

184 THERE WAS PLENTY OF OPPOSITION TO THE LINCOLN ADMINISTRATION   G. R. Tredway, *Democratic Opposition to the Lincoln Administration in Indiana* (Indianapolis: Indiana Historical Bureau, 1973), p. xiii. Much of the opposition came from Democrats apoplectic at the thought of "negro equality" and alarmed by signs of burgeoning federal power. Actual fomenters of treason were few, however, and Indiana furnished volunteer soldiers "on a scale scarcely matched by any other state." (See Thornbrough, *Indiana in the Civil War Era*, p. 124.) Some twelve thousand Hoosiers volunteered to fight, though the state's quota was 4,683 (ibid., p. 104). But it was all about saving the Union. The legislature passed a resolution that Hoosier men and money must not be used to abolish slavery "or any other constitutional right belonging to any of the states" (ibid., p. 111).

184 THE LEADERS OF THE SONS OF LIBERTY   Thornbrough, *Indiana in the Civil War Era*, pp. 216–17.

184 THE GROUP'S GRAND COMMANDER   Terrell, *War of the Rebellion*, p. 385.

184 ENROLLMENT RECORDS REVEAL   Benn Pitman, ed., *The Trials for Treason at Indianapolis* (Cincinnati: Moore, Wilstach, & Baldwin, 1865), p. 320.

185 BRADFORD PURCHASED NINE YARDS OF RED   "Moses Bradford: Recollections of His Early Days," *Marion Weekly Chronicle*, September 11, 1885.

185 "THEIR POLITICS: 27 DEMOCRATIC"   "Moses Bradford: Recollections of His Early Days," *Marion Weekly Chronicle*, September 18, 1885.

185 "TRUE, VAN BUREN TOWNSHIP PRODUCED"   "Moses Bradford: Recollections of His Early Days," *Marion Weekly Chronicle*, September 25, 1885.

186 "A LARGE FORCE"   Ibid.

Twelve. Weaver

190 HOWARD WEAVER LEFT GRANT COUNTY FOR A DISTINGUISHED CAREER   Obituary for Reverend William Howard Weaver, *Marion Chronicle-Tribune*, June 11, 1975.

190 THAT'S WHEN THE BAILEYS' DAUGHTER DIED "Funeral Services for Bailey Child," *Marion Chronicle,* March 20, 1923.

190 SO SHE WOULD HAVE BEEN EIGHTEEN Sadie Weaver Pate was born on May 6, 1904.

195 THE QUESTION OF WHETHER TO "MIX" Thornbrough, *Negro in Indiana,* p. 329.

Thirteen. A Riot Goin' On

199 "WHAT DO YOU NEGROES WANT" "Crackpot Threatens Marion Rights Leader," *Indianapolis Recorder,* August 7, 1954.

200 "NEGROES WILL NEVER SET FOOT" "Marion Officials Resign in Huff in Rights Fight," *Indianapolis Recorder,* July 24, 1954.

200 "THEY WERE GOING TO DESTROY PROPERTY AND THE SWIMMING POOL" "Armed Officers Bar Negroes' Use of Public Pool," *Indianapolis Recorder,* June 26, 1954.

200 "WE THINK THAT ON THIS BASIS" "Marion Officials Resign in Huff."

201 NORMAL ATTENDANCE WAS SEVEN HUNDRED "Attendance Is Down at Pool," *Marion Sunday Chronicle-Tribune,* July 25, 1954.

204 "A VARIETY OF INTERRUPTIONS" "Marion Teacher to End Unique Career," *Marion Chronicle-Tribune,* June 3, 1973.

206 HE SAID A WHITE TRUANT OFFICER WAS RIGHT IN THE MIDDLE OF IT "Civil Rights Commission Probing Marion Unrest," *Marion Chronicle-Tribune,* November 23, 1968.

206 THE GLOVED ONES HAD DRAFTED A LIST OF DEMANDS "Racial Unrest Jolts Marion High School," *Marion Chronicle-Tribune,* November 16, 1968.

207 "NO POLICIES BE ADOPTED IN RESPONSE TO OVERT OR THREATENED ACTS OF VIOLENCE" "School Board Gets Discipline Petitions," *Marion Chronicle-Tribune,* November 27, 1968.

207 (MARION WOULD NOT HAVE AN AFRICAN AMERICAN ON THE CITY COUNCIL UNTIL 1982) Walter Peak became Marion's first black city councilman in 1982. See "Walter Peak Dies," *Marion Chronicle-Tribune,* February 12, 1992.

208 IT HAD A RACIAL COVENANT Such covenants, forbidding the sale of property to minorities, were outlawed by the Fair Housing Act in 1968.

210 "GEOGRAPHIC AND POLITICAL CENTER OF BLACK UNREST" William R. Wood, "The Corner," *Marion Chronicle-Tribune,* October 12, 1988.

210 A RASH OF FIREBOMBINGS HIT MARION "13 Law Officers Shot at Kokomo During Disorder," *Marion Chronicle-Tribune,* June 27, 1969; "Sniper Fire in Kokomo Plagues Police Patrols," *Marion Chronicle-Tribune,* June 28, 1969.

210 WITH MONDAY'S PAPER CAME THE NEWS "3 Charged for Possession of Arson Tools, Materials," *Marion Chronicle-Tribune,* June 30, 1969.

211 THE SHERIFF'S DEPARTMENT REPORTED A BLACK MAN "Arsonist Blamed for Lumberyard Fire at Swayzee," *Marion Chronicle-Tribune,* June 30, 1969.

211 THREE MEN FACE WEAPONS CHARGE "Three Men Face Weapons Charge," *Marion Chronicle-Tribune,* June 30, 1969.

211 "WE HAVE NEITHER HEARD NOR RECEIVED ANY REQUESTS OR PROTESTS" "Mayor Appeals for Calmness," *Marion Chronicle-Tribune,* June 30, 1969.

211 "'NEGRO FRUSTRATION PROBLEM' BROUGHT ON BY MANY THINGS" "'Program of Action' Outlined for City," *Marion Chronicle-Tribune,* July 1, 1969.

211 TUESDAY AFTERNOON, JULY 1, A FIRE "Two More Marion Firms Hit by Fire," *Marion Chronicle-Tribune,* July 2, 1969.

211 "OF CONTINUED POLICE BRUTALITY, ABUSE" "NAACP Asks State, Federal Help in Marion," *Marion Chronicle-Tribune,* July 2, 1969.

211 THAT NIGHT MARION'S ALL-WHITE CITY COUNCIL "Marion Council Okays Purchasing Police Dogs," *Marion Chronicle-Tribune,* July 2, 1969.

211 "A STEP THAT SHOULD HAVE BEEN TAKEN TWENTY YEARS AGO" "Negro and White Leaders Focus on Marion Tensions," *Marion Chronicle-Tribune,* July 8, 1969.

212 "THE SITUATION AT FISHER" "Talks Held on Racial Turmoil," *Marion Chronicle-Tribune,* July 9, 1969.

212 "A SHOT OF ADRENALINE TO THE MORALE" "3626 Sign Pro-police Petition," *Marion Chronicle-Tribune,* July 17, 1969.

212 THE SAME DAY THE NAACP ANNOUNCED PLANS "NAACP Announces Plans for Parade Here Sunday," *Marion Chronicle-Tribune,* July 17, 1969.

212 "I WANT TO SERVE NOTICE RIGHT HERE AND NOW" " 'March on Marion' Rally Peaceful," *Marion Chronicle-Tribune,* July 21, 1969.

212 "MOST OF THE THINGS IN THIS 'MANIFESTO' " "Mayor Denies Charges," *Marion Chronicle-Tribune,* July 23, 1969.

216 "A WASTE OF TIME, BECAUSE THE PEOPLE" I was able to corroborate Cannon's story about being shot at in the parking lot but not the incident inside the plant.

218 BY 2000 INHABITANTS NUMBERED 31,320 Cathy Kightlinger, "County's Population Shrinking," *Marion Chronicle-Tribune,* March 13, 2001.

220 "DID NOT COME FROM A POLICE WEAPON" "Marion Mayor in Bid to End Racial Disturbance," *Marion Chronicle-Tribune,* September 22, 1970.

220 "WE CHECKED THE WEAPONS" "Talks Held After Policeman Is Shot: Mayor, Negroes Meet," *Marion Chronicle-Tribune,* September 21, 1970.

220 "THE POLICE SHOT THAT PLACE UP" Jim Perkins, interview by Lucas White, April 24, 2001, in William Munn, ed., *Community History Project: Collected by Students in Advanced Placement U.S. History at Marion High School, Marion, Indiana 2001.* Indiana Room, Marion Public Library.

221 SIX DAYS AFTER HER ARREST AT THE FOOTBALL GAME "Police Aided During Search," *Marion Chronicle-Tribune,* September 25, 1970.

221 "WHEN I'VE BEEN LIED TO ALL DAY" "Dispute Police Account of Shooting," *Marion Chronicle-Tribune,* September 23, 1970.

222 ON THE NIGHT OF MAY 14, 1973 "Shots from Auto Kill Marion Boy," *Marion Chronicle-Tribune,* May 15, 1973.

223 FIREBOMBINGS HIT A COUPLE OF LUMBER YARDS AND A WAREHOUSE "4 Charged with Arson," *Marion Chronicle-Tribune,* May 16, 1973.

223 "THREE INSTANCES OF WOODEN CROSSES BURNING" "Police Doubt Racial Factor in Boy's Death," *Marion Chronicle-Tribune,* May 17, 1973.

Fifteen. In His Bulletproof Vest

241 "THE PEOPLE OF MARION WOULD HAVE TO" "Cameron Eyes Jail as Black Museum," *Marion Chronicle-Tribune,* August 21, 1994.

248 "ADMIRALTY OR EQUITY JURISDICTION" James Ridgeway, "Freemen's Law: A Far Right Guide to the Constitution," *Village Voice,* April 16, 1996.

Sixteen. "The White Has Fell"

253 HE GOT A LOOK AT THE "INNER DEN" "Getting Introduced to the Klan," *Marion Chronicle-Tribune,* June 17, 1979.

257 IN MAY 1994 THE DEKALB COUNTY PROSECUTOR Sarah True, "Man Who Helped Klan Organize Rally Served as Drug Informer for Police," *Fort Wayne Journal-Gazette,* May 7, 1994.

258 "PROVIDED A GREAT SERVICE TO THE COUNTY" Ibid.

258 DUELING NEIGHBORS' BITTERNESS BREEDS HATRED IN SLEEPY TOWN Meghan Erica Irons, *Fort Wayne Journal-Gazette,* February 6, 1994.

260 THE RALLY THERE COST THE CITY NEARLY $9,900 IN OVERTIME PAY "Children of Klan Leader Arrested," *Marion Chronicle-Tribune,* January 20, 1996.

261 "USED A RACIAL SLUR" Ibid.

269 THEN THERE WAS MIKE MCQUEENY "Knights of Thuggery: Klan Group Builds Record of Aggressive Action," *Intelligence Report* (published by the Southern Poverty Law Center), Issue 93, Winter 1999.

269 "MUD PEOPLE" James Ridgeway, *Blood in the Face: The Ku Klux Klan, Aryan Nations, Nazi Skinheads, and the Rise of a New White Culture,* 2nd ed. (New York: Thunder's Mouth, 1995), p. 71–72.

Eighteen. God Forgives/The Brotherhood Doesn't

288 "REALLY SOMEBODY" Worth H. Weller with Brad Thompson, *Under the Hood: Unmasking the Modern Ku Klux Klan* (North Manchester, Ind.: DeWitt Books, 1998), p. 76.

290 THREE DAYS AFTER THE PARTY I ATTENDED "Arms Reported Seized at Klan Leader's Home," *Fort Wayne Journal-Gazette,* February 21, 1996.

291 LARRY'S CLAIM THAT THE WIZARD HIMSELF HAD BEEN BANISHED The Kentucky-based Imperial Klans of America devoted two editions of their newsletter (issue 11, January–February 1999, and issue 12, March–April 1999) to denouncing Berry. A message they included from Berry's former State Nighthawk, Grizzly Smith, says Berry was banished for "being a snitch," but the Liberty Knights' banishment papers (reprinted in issue 12) indicate that there was more to it than that.

292 IT SEEMED THAT WHILE SEARCHING THE BERRY PLACE "6 Guns, Marijuana Found in KKK Leader's Home," *Fort Wayne Journal-Gazette,* February 22, 1996.

293 NO NEW CHARGES HAD BEEN FILED. "Police Confiscate Weapons During Search of Klan Head Berry's Home," *Fort Wayne News-Sentinel,* February 22, 1996.

293 TEN DAYS LATER, ON MARCH 4, LARRY HITLER "Witness Coercion Alleged in Berry's Arrest," *Fort Wayne Journal-Gazette,* March 6, 1996.

Nineteen. The Reconcilers

301 ITS PARTICULARLY VIRULENT RACISM AFTER THE CIVIL WAR Thornbrough, *Negro in Indiana,* pp. 224–25.

303 A *CHRONICLE-TRIBUNE* ARTICLE FROM 1973 Ed Breen, "A View of Black Marion," *Marion Chronicle-Tribune,* May 20, 1973.

307 JOURNALIST ANTJIE KROG BEGINS HER ACCOUNT   All quotes are from Antjie Krog, *Country of My Skull: Guilt, Sorrow, and the Limits of Forgiveness in the New South Africa* (New York: Three Rivers Press, 1999), p. 32. Krog has smoothed out Zalaquett's language but not changed the sense. For his original, see *Hastings Law Journal,* University of California, Hastings College of Law, August 1992. For Habermas, see Jürgen Habermas and Adam Michnik, "Overcoming the Past," *New Left Review* 203 (January–February 1994).

313 ASSISTANT CHIEF OF POLICE ROY COLLINS   Lynching Depositions, Box 20, James M. Ogden Papers, Indiana State Archives, Indianapolis, pp. 19–21.

314 AN INTERVIEW FANSLER GAVE IN 1977   Interview with Walter Fansler, 1977. Larry Allyn Conrad Papers, Ruth Lilly Special Collections and Archives, University Library, Indiana University Purdue University, Indianapolis.

Twenty. Brothers and Sisters

325 "HER FACE A TWISTED MASK OF GRIEF"   "He Died Defending Helpless One, Deeter Funeral Pastor Intones," *Indianapolis Star,* August 10, 1930.

325 THE PROSECUTOR TOOK THE PRECAUTION   "Special Venire of Jurymen to Report Friday," *Anderson Herald,* June 23, 1931.

325 HE RELEASED HER ON HER OWN RECOGNIZANCE   "Cameron Trial Opens Today in Madison Court," *Marion Leader-Tribune,* June 26, 1931.

325 ACCORDING TO THE *ANDERSON DAILY BULLETIN*   "Testimony in Cameron Case Nears Close," *Anderson Daily Bulletin,* July 2, 1931.

325 "SHE SAID SHE BECAME FRIGHTENED"   "Murder Trial Recessed in Circuit Court," *Anderson Herald,* July 3, 1931.

325 MARY BALL COULD *NOT* IDENTIFY CAMERON   "Testimony in Cameron Case Nears Close," *Anderson Daily Bulletin,* July 2, 1931, and "Jury Will Get Marion Murder Trial Monday," *Indianapolis News,* July 2, 1931.

325 REPORTED THAT SHE *DID* IDENTIFY HIM   "State Rests in Death Case," *Marion Chronicle,* July 2, 1931, and "State, Defense Rest in Trial of Marion Boy," *Marion Leader-Tribune,* July 3, 1931.

325 "MARY BALL, ACCORDING TO POPULAR RUMOR"   Walter White, "Sheriff's Fears Permitted Indiana Lynching," *New York World,* August 24, 1930.

334 "SO TERRIBLY, TERRIBLY SADDENED BY THE WHOLE THING"   Interview with Faith Deeter Copeland, 1977, Larry Allyn Conrad Papers, Ruth Lilly Special Collections and Archives, University Library, Indiana University Purdue University, Indianapolis.

337 DID *NOT* ACTUALLY SPEAK TO CLAUDE IN THE HOSPITAL   Willie's sister Faith recalled that the Deeter youngsters were all sitting down to a meal when someone called from the hospital to say "come quick." They left the farm immediately, and "we had just gotten on the floor just as he had passed away." Interview with Faith Deeter Copeland, 1977, Larry Allyn Conrad Papers, Ruth Lilly Special Collections and Archives, University Library, Indiana University Purdue University, Indianapolis.

339 "HE DIDN'T KNOW WHO SHOT HIM"   Interview with Mildred Whybrew Dailey, 1977, Larry Allyn Conrad Papers, Ruth Lilly Special Collections and Archives, University Library, Indiana University Purdue University, Indianapolis.

Twenty-one. What Aunt Ruth Said

347 HUNDREDS OF THOUSANDS OF HOOSIER WOMEN   Blee, *Women of the Klan*, p. 101.

349 THE VANISHED TOWN OF AMERICA   Frank C. Stewart, "Yesterdays," *Lafontaine Herald*, February 25, 1938.

Twenty-two. A Few Bad Apples

353 AND IN NEW CASTLE, WHERE THE WIZARD   Niki Kelly, "Arrest Clouds Klan Leader's Probation," *Fort Wayne Journal-Gazette*, June 12, 1996.

353 "EVERYBODY BUT THEMSELVES"   Mike Fletcher, "Local Officers Reflect on Rally," *Kokomo Tribune*, July 14, 1996.

354 EVENTUALLY HE AND HIS STATE NIGHTHAWK   "Klan Leaders Plead Guilty," *New Castle Courier-Times*, October 6, 1997.

354 THEY ALSO FILED A LAWSUIT AGAINST THE CITY   "Klan Wants Restitution for Injuries," *Marion Chronicle-Tribune*, April 17, 1996.

357 A PAPER ON INTERRACIAL MARRIAGE   The paper was by E. R. Fields, of the neofascist National States Rights Party.

368 "WE HAD SO MANY ENVELOPES TO MAIL OUT"   Weller, *Under the Hood*, p. 112.

368 "MANY OF THOSE CALLING THE CENTER"   "Knights of Thuggery: Klan Group Builds Record of Aggressive Action," *Intelligence Report* [published by the Southern Poverty Law Center], no. 93 (Winter 1999).

368 "AN AWKWARD, VERY UNPOPULAR REQUEST"   Associated Press, "Klan to Erect Cross in Downtown Auburn," *Marion Chronicle-Tribune*, December 4, 1996.

Twenty-three. The Snake Under the Table

370 FINALLY, IN THE SUMMER OF 1931, HE WAS FOUND GUILTY   "Negro Youth Sentenced to Reformatory," *Anderson Herald*, July 12, 1931.

370 "WE OLDER PEOPLE KNOW THE REASON"   "Remarks on the 1930 Lynching," in Barbara J. Stevenson, ed., *An Oral History of African Americans in Grant County* (Charleston, S.C.: Arcadia Publishing, 2000), p. 98.

372 I'VE ALREADY MENTIONED A COUPLE OF OTHER STORIES   See Chapter Eight, page 140.

372 THE OTHER HAND, EITHER A BOOK OR A SWORD. ACCOUNTS VARY   A sword in John White, "They Built a Place to House the Court," *Marion Chronicle-Tribune*, March 9, 1980; a book in Roger RyDell Daniels, "Justice Returns with Stony Glare," *Marion Chronicle-Tribune*, June 8, 1996.

373 COUNTY OFFICIALS HAD THEM ALL CUT DOWN IN 1987   "Courthouse Square to Lose Its Trees," *Marion Chronicle-Tribune*, January 21, 1987.

373 "OFFICIALS HAVE HAD SOMEONE RETAINED"   "Strictly for the birds . . .", *Marion Chronicle-Tribune*, January 17, 1973.

375 THE *LEADER-TRIBUNE* REPORTED THAT THE ROBBERS   "SHOOT MAN, ASSAULT SWEETHEART," *Marion Leader-Tribune*, August 7, 1930.

375 CAMERON WAS INITIALLY CHARGED FOR BOTH THE RIVER ROAD HOLDUP AND ONE AT A FILLING STATION   "Plan Cameron Robbery Trial," *Marion Chronicle*, July 8, 1931.

375 "SAW NO REASON TO SPEND MORE MONEY" "Drop Second Cameron Trial," *Marion Leader-Tribune,* July 9, 1931.

375 CAMERON HAS ALWAYS MAINTAINED THAT HE NEVER Robert Sullivan, the alleged partner of Shipp and Smith arrested the night of August 6, was convicted of the gas station robbery. See "Plan Cameron Robbery Trial," *Marion Chronicle,* July 8, 1931.

Twenty-four. Telltale

380 MAN FACES CRUELTY CHARGES Brian Stearman, "Man Faces Cruelty Charges," *Marion Chronicle-Tribune,* June 25, 1996.

381 THAT NOVEMBER A GRANT COUNTY JURY Caryn Shinske, "Fansler Guilty of Cruelty," *Marion Chronicle-Tribune,* November 21, 1996.

383 JOUAM WAS A NATIVIST ANTI-CATHOLIC FRATERNITY Nancy MacLean, *Behind the Mask of Chivalry: The Making of the Second Ku Klux Klan* (New York and Oxford: Oxford University Press, 1994), p. 7.

Twenty-five. History-Maker

393 "THE MOST POWERFUL ELECTED POSITION" Cathy Kightlinger, "Sheriff Race Close Call," *Marion Chronicle-Tribune,* May 3, 1998. (The outgoing sheriff had served the maximum two terms, earning $98,000 a year.)

396 TO SEE HOW THE VARIOUS KU KLUX CANDIDATES "Election '98," *Fort Wayne Journal-Gazette,* May 6, 1998.

403 HE WAS STILL CROWING OVER THE DEBACLE THEY'D CREATED Emily Yellin, "A City Strives to Balance Its Role in King Legacy," *New York Times,* January 19, 1998.

404 "A DANGEROUS PRECEDENT" See www.splcenter.org/klanwatch/kw-21.html.

405 IN 1999 SHELTON WOULD BE SENTENCED Associated Press, "Klan Figure Is Sentenced to 99 Years in Shooting," *New York Times,* September 19, 1999.

Twenty-six. Unity Day

407 SHERIFF'S RACE HOTTEST IN COUNTY Cathy Kightlinger, "Sheriff's Race Hottest in County," *Marion Chronicle-Tribune,* October 25, 1998.

408 THE STORY PUT OUT TO JUSTIFY THIS WAS Cathy Kightlinger, "City May Honor MLK," *Marion Chronicle-Tribune,* January 15, 1998.

408 LENNON FOUGHT WHITTON OUTSIDE A DOWNTOWN TAVERN "Fight Stories Show Conflict," *Marion Chronicle,* January 14, 1941.

409 THE SAME JUDGE WHO'D PRESIDED "Lennon's Term Is Sustained," *Marion Chronicle,* March 18, 1941.

410 "WOULD HELP CHANGE THE NEGATIVE PERCEPTION" Cathy Kightlinger, "Council Backs King Proposal," *Marion Chronicle-Tribune,* January 21, 1998.

411 "NEVER SAW OR HEARD FROM THEM AGAIN" Worth H. Weller with Brad Thompson, *Under the Hood: Unmasking the Modern Ku Klux Klan* (North Manchester, Ind.: DeWitt Books, 1998), 63.

411 "THERE WAS NO MONEY GIVEN TO US BY TOWN HALL" www.liberator.net/articles/KKKJeffBerry.html.

412 "THE KLAN DOES NOT MAKE ANY MONEY"   Amy Rogers Rensberger, "Ku Klux Klan Leader Quits Group, Apologizes for Rally," *The Goshen News*, August 29, 1997.

419 "WITHOUT SAYING HIS NAME"   Lauren Waggoner, "King's Son Welcomes Dedication of Bypass," *Marion Chronicle-Tribune*, November 1, 1998.

421 VOTER TURNOUT HAD ACTUALLY BEEN LOWER   Avon Waters and Stacey Lane Grosh, "Broken Voting Machines Send Voters Home," *Marion Chronicle-Tribune*, November 4, 1998.

Twenty-seven. Poor Marion

424 WHEN THEY MADE THEIR INITIAL REQUEST   Cathy Kightlinger, "Klan Plans Marion Rally for May 22," *Marion Chronicle-Tribune*, April 24, 1999.

425 "I STILL DON'T UNDERSTAND WHY I SUPPORTED AN ORGANIZATION"   Weller, *Under the Hood*, p. 96.

426 I THOUGHT IT POSSIBLE THAT HE'D BRIEFLY TAKEN THAT NAME   Among the anti-Berry screeds I received from the Kentucky-based Imperial Knights of the Ku Klux Klan was an e-mail sent by one D. C. Stephenson II advising all Klansmen to buy Thompson's book, with a link to the website where they could order it.

436 IN JANUARY 2000 THE SOUTHERN POVERTY LAW CENTER   See www.splcenter.org/legalaction/la-13.html.

437 EVENTUALLY A FEDERAL JUDGE IN FORT WAYNE   Laura Emerson, "Intimidation Costs Klansman $120,000," *Fort Wayne Journal-Gazette*, January 4, 2001.

437 BUT THE JUDGE WAS HAVING NONE OF IT   Josh Kinman, "KKK Leader Gets 7 Years," *Auburn News-Sun & Evening Star*, December 4, 2001.

Twenty-eight. Four Days in August

441 UNEMPLOYMENT HAD JUST HIT 10.4 PERCENT   Kristin Harty, "Jobless Rate Hike Called Temporary," *Marion Chronicle-Tribune*, February 7, 2002.

441 (THE ANSWER: TWO YEARS)   Kristin Harty, "Thomson Pulls Plug," *Marion Chronicle-Tribune*, March 17, 2004.

448 PAYROLL SHEETS FOR CLAUDE DEETER   Conrad had also collected payroll sheets for Claude's brother, Ralph Deeter (who worked at Superior for three months early in 1929) and a third man, Guy Spahr (who'd worked there in 1928 and 1929). Ralph Deeter went to see the lynching with his wife and baby, according to his brother, Willie. Guy Spahr was not listed in any city directory of that era except for 1925. Also, it should be noted that by the late 1990s, the Marion library's one copy of the 1930 city directory had disappeared. I looked up all names in both the 1929 and 1931 directories, but relied mostly on the latter since the directories seemed to be about a year behind. For example, Claude Deeter is still listed as living in rural Fairmount in the 1931 directory.

448 CERTAIN NAMES ON THE LONGER LIST HAD CHECKMARKS   When I looked through Conrad's material in 2005, I found a third list of 52 names. All but eleven of them already appeared on the other two lists. Most of these eleven names did not have an employer listed in the city directory. Larry Allyn Conrad Papers, Ruth Lilly Special Collections and Archives, University Library, Indiana University Purdue University, Indianapolis.

452 SOMEONE WENT OUT TO THE RIVER ROAD   Walter Fansler did not witness this encounter and thought it possible his father had been approached in town, though it

seemed more likely to him that someone came to the house. (The Fanslers did not have a phone.) His exact words to Larry Conrad: "Somebody come to Dad—I don't remember whether they come out to the house or whether he was in town. It might have been that night that they came to him, but couldn't hardly been because—hell, they was up there to the police station and things. But they asked him to get the sheriff's answer, said they were coming in the next night to lynch 'em. And they said that they asked Dad to go get the sheriff's answer. So they must have come out to the house the next day. Because they asked Dad to go to the sheriff and get his answer about lynching 'em. Because they was coming in to lynch 'em." Interview with Walter Fansler, 1977, Larry Allyn Conrad Papers, Ruth Lilly Special Collections and Archives, University Library, Indiana University Purdue University Indianapolis.

453 THE "GEOGRAPHIC AND POLITICAL CENTER OF BLACK UNREST" William R. Wood, "The Corner," *Marion Chronicle-Tribune,* October 12, 1988.

Twenty-nine. In the Picture

457 "THIS IS SICK, AS FAR AS I'M CONCERNED" Kristin Harty, "Monument, Service Get Go-ahead," *Marion Chronicle-Tribune,* October 7, 2003.

458 "WHY WAIT TILL NOW TO DO SOMETHING?" Kristin Harty, "Revote: No Plaque," *Marion Chronicle-Tribune,* October 14, 2003.

458 "WE RESENT THE IMPLICATIONS" Kristin Harty, "Family Protests Plaque," *Marion Chronicle-Tribune,* October 10, 2003.

458 IN AN UNSCIENTIFIC TELEPHONE POLL Harty, "Revote: No Plaque."

458 "YEARS BEFORE I WAS EVEN BORN" Tim Evans, "Marion Event Seeks Healing for Lynching," *Indianapolis Star,* October 19, 2003.

458 "THE MARION COMMUNITY ISN'T READY TO PUT UP A RACIAL RECONCILIATION PLAQUE" Harty, "Revote: No Plaque."

BIBLIOGRAPHY

Archives

Larry Allyn Conrad Papers, Ruth Lilly Special Collections and Archives, University Library, Indiana University Purdue University, Indianapolis.

Harold C. Feightner Papers, Indiana Historical Society, Indianapolis.

Harry Leslie Papers, Indiana State Archives, Indianapolis.

National Association for the Advancement of Colored People Papers. Manuscript Division, Library of Congress, Washington, D.C.

James M. Ogden Papers, Indiana State Archives, Indianapolis

Books

A Century of Development: Grant County, Indiana. Marion, Ind.: Grant County Junior Historical Society, 1937.

Allen, James, Hilton Als, John Lewis, and Leon F. Litwack. *Without Sanctuary: Lynching Photography in America.* Santa Fe, N.M.: Twin Palms Publishers, 2000.

Baker, Ronald L. *From Needmore to Prosperity: Hoosier Place Names in Folklore and History.* Bloomington: Indiana University Press, 1995.

Baldwin, Edgar M. *The Making of a Township: Being an Account of the Early Settlement and Subsequent Development of Fairmount Township, Grant County, Indiana, 1829–1917.* Fairmount, Ind.: Edgar Baldwin Printing Co., 1917.

Baldwin, James. *The Fire Next Time.* New York: Vintage, 1993.

———. *Nobody Knows My Name.* New York: Vintage, 1993.

———. *Notes of a Native Son.* Boston: Beacon Press, 1957.

Barnhart, John D., and Dorothy L. Riker. *Indiana to 1816: The Colonial Period.* Indianapolis: Indiana Historical Bureau & Indiana Historical Society, 1971.

Biographical Memoirs of Grant County, Indiana. Chicago: Bowen, 1901.

Blee, Kathleen M. *Women of the Klan: Racism and Gender in the 1920s.* Berkeley: University of California Press, 1991.

Bunish, Steve. *The Golden Age of Marion.* Self-published booklet, Stephanie Bunish Fuller, ed., 1989.

Cameron, James. *A Time of Terror: A Survivor's Story.* Reprint. Baltimore: Black Classic Press, 1994.

Cayton, Andrew R. L. *Frontier Indiana.* Bloomington: Indiana University Press, 1996.

Chalmers, David M. *Hooded Americanism: The History of the Ku Klux Klan.* Reprint. New York and London: New Viewpoints, 1981.

Combination Atlas Map of Grant County, Indiana, 1877. Reprint, Knightstown, Ind.: Back Creek Monthly Meeting of Friends, 1987.

Dalton, David. *James Dean: The Mutant King.* San Francisco: Straight Arrow Books, 1974.

Dray, Philip. *At the Hands of Persons Unknown: The Lynching of Black America.* New York: Random House, 2002.

Gibbs, Wilma L., ed. *Indiana's African-American Heritage: Essays from "Black History News and Notes."* Indianapolis: Indiana Historical Society, 1993.

Ginzburg, Ralph. *100 Years of Lynchings.* Reprint. Baltimore, Md.: Black Classic Press, 1988.

Hale, Grace Elizabeth. *Making Whiteness: The Culture of Segregation in the South, 1890–1940.* New York: Pantheon Books, 1998.

Hicks, Ronald, ed. *Native American Cultures in Indiana: Proceedings of the First Minnetrista Council for Great Lakes Native American Studies.* Muncie, Ind.: Minnetrista Cultural Center and Ball State University, 1992.

History of Grant County, Indiana. Chicago: Brant & Fuller, 1886.

Holliday, Murray. *The Battle of the Mississinewa 1812.* Marion, Ind: Grant County Historical Society, 1964.

Jackson, Kenneth T. *The Ku Klux Klan in the City, 1915–1930.* Chicago: Ivan R. Dee, 1967.

Krog, Antjie. *Country of My Skull: Guilt, Sorrow, and the Limits of Forgiveness in the New South Africa.* New York: Three Rivers Press, 1999.

"Lest We Forget": Reminiscences of Pioneers of Grant County, Indiana. Marion, Ind.: Marion High School, 1921.

Lewis, David Levering. *W.E.B. Du Bois: Biography of a Race, 1868–1919.* New York: Henry Holt & Co., 1993.

Lutholtz, M. William. *Grand Dragon: D. C. Stephenson and the Ku Klux Klan in Indiana.* West Lafayette, Ind.: Purdue University Press, 1993.

Lynd, Robert S., and Helen Merrell Lynd. *Middletown: A Study in Modern American Culture.* Reprint. New York, London: Harvest/HBJ, 1956.

———. *Middletown in Transition: A Study in Cultural Conflicts.* Reprint. New York: Harvest/Harcourt, Brace & World, 1965.

MacLean, Nancy. *Behind the Mask of Chivalry: The Making of the Second Ku Klux Klan.* New York and Oxford: Oxford University Press, 1994.

Madison, James H. *Indiana Through Tradition and Change: A History of the Hoosier State and Its People, 1920–1945* (Indianapolis: Indiana Historical Society, 1982).

———. *The Indiana Way: A State History.* Bloomington: Indiana University Press, Indiana Historical Society, 1986.

———. *A Lynching in the Heartland: Race and Memory in America.* New York: Palgrave, 2001.

Martin, John Bartlow. *Indiana: An Interpretation.* New York: Alfred A. Knopf, 1947.

McFeely, William S. *Frederick Douglass.* New York and London: W. W. Norton & Co., 1991.

McGrew, W. H. *Interesting Episodes in the Early History of Marion and Grant County, Indiana*. Marion: Grant County Historical Society, 1966.

McKown, June R. *Marion: A Pictorial History*. St. Louis: G. Bradley Publishing, 1989.

Miller, John, ed. *Indiana Newspaper Bibliography*. Indianapolis: Indiana Historical Society, 1982.

Moore, Leonard J. *Citizen Klansmen: The Ku Klux Klan in Indiana, 1921-1928*. Chapel Hill and London: University of North Carolina Press, 1991.

Munn, William, ed. *Community History Project: Collected by Students in Advanced Placement U.S. History at Marion High School, Marion, Indiana 2001*. Indiana Room, Marion Public Library.

Neher, Leslie. *Hoosier Founders of Grant County, Indiana in Celebration of 175 Years of Indiana Statehood*. Unpublished manuscript, April 30, 1992. Indiana Room, Marion Public Library.

Philips, Clifton. *Indiana in Transition: The Emergence of an Industrial Commonwealth 1880-1920*. Indianapolis: Indiana Historical Bureau, 1968.

Pitman, Benn, ed. *The Trials for Treason at Indianapolis*. Cincinnati: Moore, Wilstach, & Baldwin, 1865.

Rafert, Stewart. *The Miami Indians of Indiana: A Persistent People, 1654-1994*. Indianapolis: Indiana Historical Society, 1996.

Raper, Arthur F. *The Tragedy of Lynching*. Reprint. Mineola, N.Y.: Dover, 2003.

Ridgeway, James. *Blood in the Face: The Ku Klux Klan, Aryan Nations, Nazi Skinheads, and the Rise of a New White Culture*. 2nd ed. New York: Thunder's Mouth, 1995.

Sims, Patsy. *The Klan*. Briarcliff Manor, N.Y.: Stein & Day, 1978.

Smith, Lillian. *Killers of the Dream*. Reprint. New York and London: W.W. Norton & Co., 1978.

———. *The Winner Names the Age*. New York and London: W.W. Norton & Co., 1982.

Spoto, Donald. *Rebel: The Life and Legend of James Dean*. New York: HarperCollins, 1996.

Stanton, Bill. *Klanwatch: Bringing the Ku Klux Klan to Justice*. New York: Grove Weidenfeld, 1991.

Stevenson, Barbara J., ed. *An Oral History of African Americans in Grant County*. Charleston, S.C.: Arcadia Publishing, 2000.

Terrell, W. H. H. *Indiana in the War of the Rebellion: A Report of the Adjutant General*. Reprint. Indianapolis: Indiana Historical Bureau, 1960.

Thirty Years of Lynching in the United States, 1889-1918. New York: National Association for the Advancement of Colored People, 1919.

Thornbrough, Emma Lou. *Indiana in the Civil War Era, 1850-1880*. Indianapolis: Indiana Historical Society, 1965.

———. *The Negro in Indiana Before 1900: A Study of a Minority*. Reprint. Bloomington: Indiana University Press, 1993.

———. *Since Emancipation: A Short History of Indiana Negroes, 1863-1963*. Indianapolis: Indiana Division, American Negro Emancipation Centennial Authority, 1963.

Tredway, G. R. *Democratic Opposition to the Lincoln Administration in Indiana*. Indianapolis: Indiana Historical Bureau, 1973.

Trelease, Allen W. *White Terror: The Ku Klux Klan Conspiracy and Southern Reconstruction*. Reprint. Baton Rouge: Louisiana State University Press, 1995.

Wade, Wyn Craig. *The Fiery Cross: The Ku Klux Klan in America*. New York: Touchstone, 1988.

Weesner, Clarkson W., ed. *History of Wabash County, Indiana.* Chicago and New York: Lewis Publishing Co., 1914.

Weller, Worth H., with Brad Thompson. *Under the Hood: Unmasking the Modern Ku Klux Klan.* North Manchester, Ind.: DeWitt Books, 1998.

Wells-Barnett, Ida B. *On Lynching.* Reprint. Amherst, N.Y.: Humanity Books, 2002.

White, Walter. *Rope and Faggot: A Biography of Judge Lynch.* Reprint. Notre Dame, Ind.: University of Notre Dame Press, 2001.

Whitson, Rolland Lewis, ed. *Centennial History of Grant County, 1812–1912.* Chicago: Lewis Publishing Co., 1914.

Young, Marguerite. *Harp Song for a Radical: The Life and Times of Eugene Victor Debs.* New York: Alfred A. Knopf, 1999.

ACKNOWLEDGMENTS

This project would never have begun without the particular wisdom and encouragement of two people: James Cameron, whose generosity of spirit gave me the courage to take the first steps, and Robbie McCauley, whose insight and honesty inspired me to try addressing a white person's part in the racial conundrum.

I have many people to thank in Indiana.

First and foremost, the aptly named Tom Wise, who generously shared his own research into the lynching along with his knowledge of the town's politics and people. He literally showed me where to begin and was always ready with a suggestion or a phone number.

Many others shared their own expertise and passion for all or part of Grant County's past. Bill Munn of the Community History Project answered many a question and alerted me to things (like the racial element in the 1904 election) that he'd discovered in his own research. Barbara Stevenson of the Grant County Black History Council shared some crucial interviews before they were published in her *Oral History of African Americans in Grant County*. John Taylor gave me a thorough tour of the Weaver area, and Marita Fields drove me to all the underground railroad sites. Thanks also to Gerald E. Rhoades, Louis Ebert, and Richard Simons. And to Jack Miller in Wabash County.

The Marion Public Library was my home away from home during the fourteen months that I lived in Grant County. I am especially grateful to everyone in the Indiana Room: Kay Clemons, Jacqulin Mauk, Rhonda Stoffer, Barbara Love, and Betty Reynolds, who deserves particular thanks for alerting me when people came to the library with relevant stories and helping me to track down many details.

I used to fantasize about inviting the many great people I met in Grant

County to a party, just to make sure they all knew each other. I won't attempt a list for fear of forgetting someone, but this somewhat impoverished county does have many treasures. One I must single out for special thanks is John Milford. I will always be grateful to everyone who spoke to me on the uncomfortable subject of race and the county's worst moment.

I benefited from James H. Madison's earlier work on the lynching and appreciate his willingness to send me a key piece of material collected by Larry Conrad in the 1970s.

Wilma Gibbs at the Indiana Historical Society went out of her way to be helpful. Stephen Towne at IUPUI's Ruth Lilly Special Collections and Archives gave me access to Larry Conrad's important material almost immediately after acquiring it. And thanks to Tim Durbin for his hospitality in Indianapolis.

I have many people to thank in New York.

It was my great good fortune to have Ann Snitow as first reader of every chapter, first reader of the completed manuscript, and one-woman focus group for my ideas. She acted as shepherd to this project and was supportive in every way. I can never thank her enough.

I was also fortunate to have Karen Durbin as my other one-woman focus group. I benefited greatly from her close reading of the manuscript and her feedback on problems I encountered. I can never thank her enough, either.

I very much appreciate everyone who took the time to read and comment on all or parts of this manuscript: Shelagh Doyle, Richard Goldstein, Su Friedrich, Dave King, Robbie McCauley, Amy Sillman, and especially Donna Mandel, who read it in two different incarnations. I'm most grateful to those who supported me in other crucial ways: Susan Edwards, Tom Rauffenbart, Alix Kates Shulman, and Frank Tartaglione.

I owe particular thanks to my acquiring editor at Crown, Karen Rinaldi, whose leap of faith enabled me to embark on this quest. Emily Loose was a supportive editor at a crucial point in the process. My ultimate editor, Chris Jackson, helped me to give the book a narrative and emotional spine and to get an unwieldy manuscript to wield. I also want to thank my agent, Joy Harris, for her guidance and her enthusiasm for this project from the get-go.

Meanwhile, back in Marion, I was delighted to find some wonderful long-lost family members, John and Sedonna Roush. As a boy, John actually met my great-grandfather, Odos Roush, and had a picture showing Odos at about the time he would have met my great-grandmother Josie. I can say for sure that he was not the man in her locket, and that, despite the best efforts of us all, certain things will remain unknowable.

INDEX

M

About the Author

CYNTHIA CARR was for many years a columnist and arts writer at *The Village Voice*, with the byline C.Carr. She lives in New York.